Michigan Railroads and Railroad Companies

Grand Trunk Western #6326 at Durand Station, 1949

Michigan Railroads and Railroad Companies

Graydon M. Meints

Michigan State University Press
East Lansing
1992

All Michigan State University Press books are produced on paper which meets the requirements of American National Standard of Information Sciences—Permanence of paper for printed materials
ANSI Z39.48-1984

Michigan State University Press
East Lansing, MI 48823-5202

Printed in the United States of America

Library of Congress Cataloging-in-Publication Data

Meints, Graydon M.
Michigan railroads and railroad companies / Graydon M.Meints.
p. cm.
Includes bibliological references.
ISBN 0-87013-318-7 (alk. paper)
1. Railroads—Michigan—History I. Title.
TF24..M5M45 1992
385' .09774—dc20

92-32966
CIP

Front cover and frontispiece photo by Cleland Wylie (from a private collection).
Back cover photo by Cleland Wylie (from C.T. Stoner collection).
All other photos in this book from a private collection.

With thanks for the direction, the encouragement, and the unfailing support, I dedicate this book to LeRoy Barnett.

CONTENTS

MAPS AND PHOTOGRAPHS

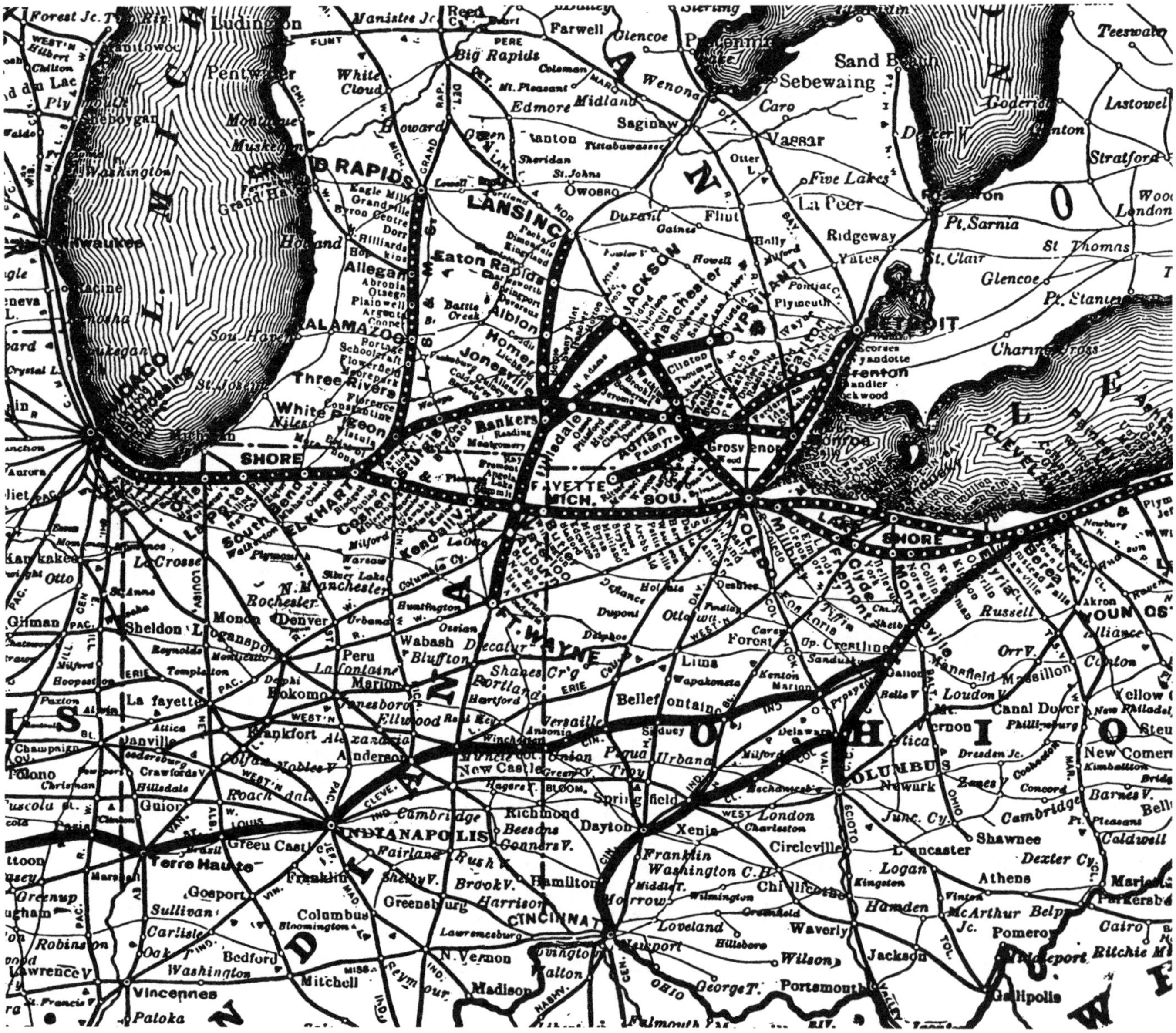

Map of the Lake Shore and Michigan Southern Railway, April 1890

PREFACE

This book began in 1978 as a set of 3 x 5 cards. They were to be a handy reference of some of the important details about Michigan's railroad corporate organizations. The amount of detail soon outgrew the capacity of the cards.

When the idea of this book first developed, the plan was to include only corporate data about those railroads that actually operated in Michigan. Research, not the researcher, made this evolve into a more inclusive work. Electric lines were added first. Then logging and mining railroads. It was obvious then that the work should be truly comprehensive and that it was necessary to include projected or "paper" companies that were never built.

What you hold in your hand attempts to identify all of the companies that did actually operate, or that were formed to operate, a railroad in Michigan. Giving as broad a definition to the word "railroad" as possible, the work now includes common-carrier "steam" and "electric" companies, incorporated logging and mining railroads, privately owned industrial and logging roads, and as many other enterprises that operated on rails, both primitive and contemporary, as could be found. Amusement park railroads are the only enterprise specifically not included.

Chapter 2 of this work is an alphabetical listing of the companies that actually did operate a railroad within the state of Michigan or that were formed for that purpose. Included are the date and purpose of organization, subsequent events in its corporate life, and the final disposition of the company. Chapter 3 contains a number of "family trees" showing the corporate antecedents of some of the more important companies.

Chapter 4 is a chronology of selected corporate events detailed in Part 1. Included in this section is a finding aid for the source of the data. Chapter 5 offers year-by-year totals of those events.

Chapter 6 is a county-by-county listing of the railroads that operated and that were proposed in each county of Michigan.

No undertaking of this scope could ever be done without the patience, the knowledge, and the considerable assistance of many people. Well deserved thanks must go to Judith Caldwell of the Michigan Department of Commerce for opening the records of the Corporation and Securities Bureau, Art Teusink and Don Riel of the Michigan Department of Transportation, Don Kline and Rich Santana of the State Records Center for their indulgence and assistance, and especially to LeRoy Barnett of the State Archives for direction and encouragement when they were needed. Each of them has made a more important contribution than they realize.

My thanks also go to David Hager and Sam Breck for their willingness to read parts of the manuscript and for their helpful suggestions, to Sam again for his remarkable photographic talents on the company heralds as well as for finding them, and to Tom Bodett for leaving the light on.

Most of all, I must thank my wife Gerlinde and my two children Cynthia and Rick. They tolerated, without complaint, all those days away from home and all those hours in my office typing and revising.

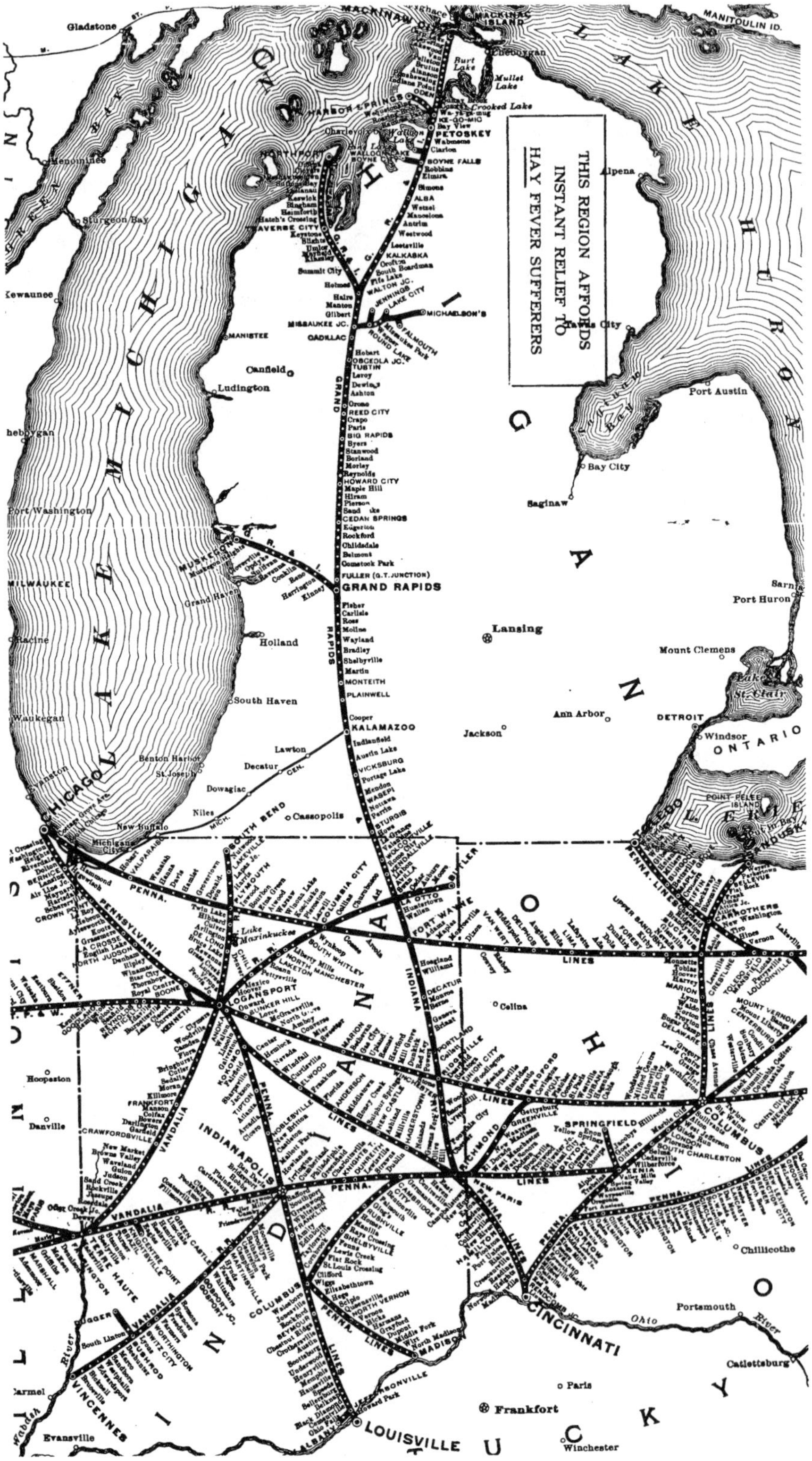

Map of the Grand Rapids and Indiana Railway, September 24, 1916

INTRODUCTION TO MICHIGAN RAILROADS

A railroad is a business. And the purpose of any business is to make a profit for its owners. A railroad employs land, people, technology, and money to accomplish its purpose. Of all of these tools, money is the most critical. Without the ability to raise capital the railroad enterprise cannot be started. Without the ability to arrange additional financing the company will fail to grow or remain competitive. Without a continuing flow of profits the railroad company will ultimately fail. The history of railroading, and of each of its constituent companies, can be viewed from many perspectives. But underlying each of them is the need to consider it in terms of its first and most fundamental basis—money.

FROM THE BEGINNING TO THE SALE OF THE STATE'S RAILROADS

Late in July 1830 Lewis Cass, Governor of the Territory of Michigan, was busy wrapping up his affairs in Michigan and preparing to move to Washington to take the office of Secretary of War in President Jackson's cabinet. On July 31, he signed legislation granting a charter for "the President, Directors, and Company of the Pontiac and Detroit Railway Company." This charter, the first in Michigan and one of the first in the Northwest Territory, came at a time when the railroad was a novel and untried means of transport. The Baltimore & Ohio had begun operations in May 1830 with a horse pulling carriages on its thirteen-mile line. Construction had begun on the Mohawk & Schenectady and on the South Carolina, but there was not much else except the charters that several states and territories had granted. The Pontiac & Detroit was planned by five Pontiac businessmen—several of them also involved with the Pontiac Company, the townsite company promoting Pontiac—to link Pontiac with Detroit. Capital was authorized at $100,000, or about $5,000 per mile of road to be built. The charter allowed the company use of twenty feet of the Saginaw Road. In exchange, the company was to be "constructed as to admit of the easy and safe passage of wagons, carts, sleds, and trams, at the points where public and private roads intersect said Saginaw Road, and when new highways or private roads shall be built."[1]

Nearly two years later, on June 29, 1832, Michigan's second railroad charter was granted to the Detroit & St. Joseph Railroad. This far more ambitious undertaking was projected to cross the state from Detroit to the mouth of the St. Joseph River, serving as a rail equivalent to the Erie Canal. Expected to be about two hundred miles long, the capital authorized was $1,500,000—$7,500 a mile.[2] Such a sum was well above the means of any of the organizers individually or even all of them joined as a partnership. The list of commissioners to sell the stock was impressive—John R. Williams, Charles Larned, Eurotas P. Hastings, John Allen of Ann Arbor, Samuel W. Dexter, Isaac E. Crary, Caleb Eldred, and Calvin Brittain were among them—and probably many were picked for their name recognition. But subscriptions to the stock sold slowly and, despite minimal down payment requirements, little cash was raised. The promoters took to petitioning the federal government for assistance of any sort. With Lewis Cass in Washington they must have had hopes of a supportive voice, but help was scanty, and none of it in cash. The War Department finally did authorize Col. John M. Berrien to go out in 1834 and make harbor surveys and, while in Michigan, to make a survey for the D&SJ line.[3]

By the end of Michigan's territorial status in 1837, the Legislative Council and the newly formed state legislature had granted charters for nineteen more railroads. A number of these were very local projects, such as the Monroe & Ann Arbor, the Clinton & Adrian, the St. Clair & Romeo, the Romeo & Mt. Clemens, and the Kalamazoo & Lake Michigan. Others were to connect a town with a port. The Constantine & Niles was to be a shortcut for the circuitous St. Joseph River and could build either a railroad or a canal. Others were more ambitious. The River Raisin & Grand River was proposed to build across the state. The Erie & Kalamazoo line was to be built from Port Lawrence (now downtown Toledo and then considered to be in Michigan) to the Kalamazoo River.

Of the twenty-one charters granted before 1837, only five ever built any rail line: the Erie & Kalamazoo from Toledo to Adrian, the Detroit & Pontiac from Detroit to Pontiac, the Shelby & Detroit from Shelby (now Utica) to Detroit, the Palmyra & Jacksonburgh from Palmyra to Tecumseh, and the River Raisin & Lake Erie in Monroe. The Detroit & St. Joseph did grade some of its line between Detroit and Ypsilanti. A few others did little spots of grading. Most made no progress. Each one experienced difficulty in raising capital. There simply were not investment funds in the territory adequate to undertake projects of this size.

In 1830, the population of Michigan was 32,538. By 1834, it was almost tripled at 87,278. The number doubled again by the 1837 census to 174,619.[4] Many of the newcomers were affluent. Their money went first to buying land and building a homestead. The remainder, for many, went into land speculation; government land was offered at $1.25 an acre and bought for resale at a profit. The best that many railroad companies could do was to raise enough to pay for a survey of the line and with that go out and beat the drum to raise start-up capital. It took the Detroit & St. Joseph, which had some of the strongest and most prestigious backing, nearly four years to get together enough money to begin grading a line on land that was most often donated.

The territorial legislature was able to extend one bit of assistance to a few of the fledgling companies. In March 1835, it amended the charters of the Detroit & Pontiac and the Erie & Kalamazoo to permit them to establish banks at Pontiac and Adrian, respectively.[5] It was hoped that this activity would provide financing for railroad construction and at the same time provide needed banking services. In August 1835 the charter of the Detroit & St. Joseph was amended to allow it to begin a bank in Ypsilanti.[6] The charters granted at the same time to the Macomb & Saginaw and the River Raisin & Grand River included permission to establish banks. For the Macomb & Saginaw, it never provided any help. The River Raisin & Grand River banking operation took on a completely undesireable character and did nothing to further the railroad.

Some grading began in 1835 on the Detroit & St. Joseph and the Erie & Kalamazoo. Of these, the E&K was the first to complete a part of its line. It began operations between Toledo and Adrian on November 2, 1836.[7] The first train was several stagecoach-like carriages pulled by horses. It was not until June 1837 that the E&K received its first steam locomotive.[8] The Erie & Kalamazoo proudly claimed itself as the first railroad operating west of the Allegheny Mountains, the first in the states of Michigan and Ohio, and the first to operate a steam locomotive west of the Alleghenies.

The Detroit & Pontiac had a harder time of it than did the E&K. It began grading in 1836, and took until July 31, 1838, to build its line between Gratiot Avenue and Royal Oak. A year later it was opened to Birmingham. Four more years were needed to complete the road from Birmingham to Pontiac.[9] It took the operations of its bank in Pontiac and a state loan of $100,000 to get this done.[10] If construction was slow, so too was the service, if the accounts of some are to be believed [11]

In October 1835, the voters of Michigan ratified a constitution forming a state and on November 3, Stevens T. Mason was sworn in as Michigan's first state governor.[12] Up to this time Michiganians had been frequent and persistent petitioners of the federal government for assistance—of any sort—for transportation projects. Before 1830 they had started asking for help in surveying and building a canal across the state. This was supplemented by requests for new roads. After 1830, requests began for help to build, or at least survey, a railroad across the state. Much of the impetus came from New York state's Erie Canal. This was a familiar route of travel and was used by many who came to Michigan. Washington had given small amounts of money or grants of land to support a few transportation projects in the Northwest Territory, mostly for roads and canals. In 1832, President Jackson vetoed the Maysville Road Bill but continued to support appropriations for the National Road. Michiganians continued their petitioning, citing national importance rather than local "internal" improvement in their reasoning.[13]

Then a small windfall appeared. As a state, Michigan would be entitled to share in the distribution of the national surplus—payments of which were to begin in 1837. Although there were many motivations behind the impetus for statehood, the prospect of money coupled with the additional pressure that could be exerted by elected congressional representatives, gave support to the movement. While the push for statehood was growing, another idea took hold of the popular imagination. "Internal improvements"—an early day name for a transportation infrastructure—came to the forefront in Ohio, Indiana, and Illinois. Seaboard states had been funding canal projects since about 1825. Ohio had been building a canal system over the preceding ten years. With the anticipated federal surplus, internal improvements programs took on renewed vigor. Indiana had passed a $10,000,000 program in January 1836. A similar program had become law in Illinois in January 1837. Both Indiana and Illinois had approved substantial bond issues to finance their projects. Governor Mason touted such a program for Michigan. In his 1836 message to the Legislature, he supported the entire concept and encouraged the lawmakers to follow the guidance of the 1835 state constitution, which directed that "Internal Improvements shall be encouraged by the government of the state."[14] He encouraged the Legislature to decide which works were to be done and to arrange funding for them. Also, he proposed that a loan be negotiated so the state could invest in desirable works to assist their completion.[15]

By January 1837, several years of debate on the subject of internal improvements had been held. In his 1837 message to the Legislature, Governor Mason urged measures to authorize a $5,000,000 loan and legislation for the state itself to undertake a program of internal improvements.[16] In March the legislature finished its work: authorization for a $5,000,000 loan, and a laundry list of internal improvement projects.[17] Governor Mason named Justus Burdick of Kalamazoo, David C. McKinstry of Detroit, Hart L. Stewart of Mottville, John M. Barbour of Bertrand, Gardner D. Williams of Saginaw, Levi S. Humphrey of Monroe, and James B. Hunt of Pontiac (who replaced Daniel LeRoy of Pontiac, who was defeated in the confirmation voting) as commissioners in charge of the work.[18]

Engraving of Michigan's first operating railroad, the Erie and Kalamazoo, circa 1838.

The results had something for everyone. Three railroads were authorized: a Southern line from near Monroe to New Buffalo, a Central line from Detroit to the mouth of the St. Joseph River, and a Northern line from either Palmer (now St. Clair) or the mouth of the Black River (Port Huron) to either the Grand River in Kent County or Lake Michigan in Ottawa County. A canal or canal-railroad combination from Mt. Clemens on the Clinton River to the mouth of the Kalamazoo River, and a canal connecting the Saginaw River with either the Maple or the Grand River were stipulated. Improvements to navigation on the St. Joseph, Kalamazoo, and Grand Rivers were included. The board was authorized to purchase the work done by the Detroit & St. Joseph Railroad and the charter of the Havre Branch Railroad—which was authorized to build from Havre on Lake Erie at the Ohio border to a connection with any other railroad. Preliminary funding for surveys was provided.[19] Two additional acts authorized the purchase of the Detroit & Pontiac Railroad and a survey for a canal around the falls at Sault Ste. Marie.[20]

With the federal surplus distribution as start-up money for the public works, Governor Mason sailed for New York, and into trouble. His efforts to negotiate the sale of the state's bonds went badly. The Panic of 1837 was beginning to move over eastern banking; it was not possible to sell the bonds in the United States. After several trips to New York, and several changes in the enabling legislation, Mason was able to sell a fraction of the bonds in Detroit and in New York. But it was not until June 1838 that the Morris Canal & Banking Company agreed to handle the entire issue. The bank began paying the promised installments and kept up through the January 1, 1840 installment, and then it stopped paying. The state received a little over $2,000,000 in cash for its $5,000,000 issue.[21] Although funds were slow in arriving, the commissioners pressed ahead with work on the different projects. On April 22, 1837, the franchise and property of the Detroit & St. Joseph was purchased for $139,802.[22] The next, and much more difficult, step was to decide the specific routes for the three railroad lines. Work was pushed to Ann Arbor on the route which the D&SJ had chosen. A survey of the Southern route was made, hearings were held at Jonesville, more surveys were made to satisfy the complainers, and more hearings were held.[23] Construction began at Monroe, but progress was slow and the continuing dissatisfaction over the route made the commissioners cautious. Of the several routes possible for the Northern line, the board finally chose Port Huron over St. Clair as the eastern terminus.[24]

Regular service on the Central road began on February 3, 1838, between Detroit and Ypsilanti.[25] By the end of November 1838, the board had spent nearly

$1,000,000 on all of its works. The $5,000,000 loan did not generate funds quickly enough to provide payments to contractors. The excitement that launched the internal improvements program soon changed to disgust. Allegations of fraud and mismanagement were heard. Citizens were unhappy if the railroad bypassed their community. To top it all the economic problems of the Panic of 1837 now extended to Michigan. Hard money became scarce, government land sales dropped, and Michigan's system of "free banking"—the "wild cat" banks—proved disastrous. The internal improvements programs in Indiana and Illinois were in no better shape, and possibly in worse. But the state kept working at it. The Central line was finished to Ann Arbor on October 17, 1839, and to Jackson on December 29, 1841.[26] The Southern route was completed as far as Adrian on November 23, 1840.[27]

In 1840, the installments on the internal improvement bonds stopped. The state resorted to notes payable from future installments to keep the work going. Script was issued as a temporary measure. Finally, the state issued warrants based on the sale of a five hundred thousand acre land grant received in 1841.[28] Construction took all the money that could be raised. The state was no longer able to pay the interest as it came due. With no other means of raising money, the state finally admitted it could go no farther and stopped contracting for new work. In 1843, the Legislature stipulated that the Central line was to be built only to Kalamazoo and the Southern was to end at Hillsdale.[29]

The Southern line was completed to Hillsdale on September 25, 1843.[30] In June 1844, the state purchased the Palmyra & Jacksonburgh and made it into the Tecumseh branch of the Southern.[31] The Central was finished to Marshall on August 12, 1844, to Battle Creek on November 25, 1845, and to Kalamazoo on February 1, 1846.[32] A grade between Port Huron and Lapeer was all that was ever done on the Northern line. In 1841, the Legislature ordered that project converted into a wagon road.[33] By the end of 1845 the state had expended just over $4,000,000 for all of its internal improvements works.[34] This amount did not include the five hundred thousand acre land grant from the federal government. Governor Alpheus Felch reported the cost of the Central as $2,238,289 and the Southern as $1,125,591.[35] These amounts are subject to dispute, given the quality of the recordkeeping and the varying accounting methods employed by the board itself, but they are a fair indication that substantial sums were spent on the two railroads actually built.

After some years of mumbling about it, the Legislature of 1844 began openly discussing the possible sale of the Central and Southern railroads. The whole affair had become an embarassment to the state as well as a financial debt that the state could not repay. In his message to the legislature on January 6, 1846, Governor Felch discussed the matter at great length. He admitted that a completed Central could become a very profitable road. But the upshot of it was that the state did not have the money to extend the road, keep it in repair, and at the same time pay the interest on the outstanding debt. The roads would have to be sold.[36] The state simply abandoned the canal projects. In 1847, the Legislature authorized the transfer of the Northern route to the Port Huron & Lake Michigan Railroad as part of that road's charter.[37]

The Central road was the best of the projects. John W. Brooks, superintendent of the Rochester & Syracuse Railroad, came to Michigan to inspect the road. His response was enthusiastic. Brooks enlisted the help of Detroit attorney James F. Joy, and together they began lining up capital to buy the road. The final group was headed by John Murray Forbes of Boston, Erastus Corning of Albany, Joy, Brooks, and a number of other New England financiers. The Legislature issued a charter for the Michigan Central Railroad on March 28, 1846.[38] The founders were given six months to agree to buy the Central for $2,000,000, subject to a down payment of $500,000, with the remainder due one year later. They were given two years to rebuild the first fifty miles west of Detroit. And they had to complete the line to Lake Michigan within three years. Payments could be made in state bonds, which were widely available at depreciated prices. Just under the wire the incorporaters raised the down payment and bought the line on September 24, 1846.[39]

There were two bidders for the Southern. A group of New York residents offered $600,000.[40] A group of Michiganians, headed by Detroit attorney Elisha Litchfield and accompanied by a number of Monroe and Detroit residents, bid $550,000.[41] The Legislature preferred to have Michigan owners and, on May 9, 1846, granted them a charter for the Michigan Southern Railroad. The agreed sale price was $500,000, to be paid in installments of $25,000 semiannually after a $50,000 down payment. Deadlines were established for completing the line to Lake Michigan and the branch to Jackson.[42] On December 23, 1846, the state sold the Southern and the Tecumseh Branch to the Michigan Southern.[43]

Even though the state had taken a commanding role in railroad construction in 1837, Governor Mason had not excluded private enterprise. Four railroad charters were granted in 1837 and four more in 1838. The Port Sheldon & Grand Rapids was formed to promote a new Lake Michigan port—but it came to nothing after the promoters built a hotel, railroad depot, and several homes at Port Sheldon. The Ypsilanti & Tecumseh did some grading with a state loan of $100,000, and then became defunct. The first known railroad in the Upper Peninsula was built about 1839 by John Jacob Astor's American Fur Company. Horses pulled cars of freight around the rapids of the St. Marys River at Sault Ste. Marie. It continued to operate until about 1855.[44]

1846 TO THE PANIC OF 1857

Chicago was becoming the golden city—the gateway to the West. It had four thousand residents in 1840 and would have thirty thousand in 1850. Stagecoaches had been running from Detroit down the Chicago Road to Chicago since the early 1830s. Each time the state extended its Central railroad, it made the trip to Chicago just that much faster. The owners of the Michigan Central had realized that Chicago had to be the eventual goal of the line, and the charter specified the road had to be built to Lake Michigan, not specifically to St. Joseph. In 1847, they began planning the route west from Kalamazoo. Early in 1848, the Legislature allowed the MC to assist other companies building between the Michigan state line and Chicago.[45] By October 1848, the MC line was completed to Niles and on April 23, 1849, the road was in operation to New Buffalo.[46] From its Lake Michigan piers the MC hired Captain Eber Brock Ward to operate steamships to Chicago.[47] That same year the MC also began operating the steamship *Mayflower* between Buffalo and Detroit.[48] The next year the MC took another step toward completing a rail line to Chicago. On October 29, 1850, it completed its line to Michigan City, Indiana.[49]

The Michigan Southern had a harder time getting started. In 1857, the three Litchfield brothers persuaded their brothers-in-law Teunis B. VanBrunt and Jacob Ten Eyck to invest in the company.[50] By 1849, they were back in Lansing asking for more time. The Legislature obliged the company with relaxed time limits for making payments and for building extensions of the railroad.[51] More money came into the picture when, in 1848, Washington Hunt and George Bliss, Jr. bought the Erie & Kalamazoo.[52] In August 1849, Hunt and Bliss talked the Michigan Southern into a perpetual lease of the E&K, and Bliss, who had a strong railroad background in Massachusetts, became president of the MS.[53] In 1850, the company was back in Lansing asking for still more time to comply with the charter requirements, and once again the Legislature obliged.[54] This latest legislation had one sticky point in it—a requirement that the company must build a line to the St. Joseph River before it could build into Indiana.

In 1850, construction finally started in a serious way. By the end of 1850, the MS was operating as far as Coldwater. White Pigeon was reached the following July.[55] Now the requirement to build to the river became a problem. About 1850, Bliss and the Litchfields had bought into an Indiana company named the Northern Indiana, a road which had a colorful past and little else except the rights to build east and west across northern Indiana. Late in 1850, the same men incorporated the Northern Indiana & Chicago in Illinois.[56] All that remained was to close the gap between White Pigeon and the Indiana state line. Judge Thomas S. Stanfield of South Bend offered to build a private line on behalf of the Michigan Southern and Bliss accepted the offer.[57] On October 4, 1851, MS trains began operating into South Bend.[58] The next year the Southern did build a branch from White Pigeon to the St. Joseph River at Constantine, and so legitimized the whole project. The Northern Indiana line was completed into Chicago, to a station in the vicinity of 63rd Street, on February 20, 1852, and from there made use of Rock Island tracks to a station on 22nd Street. It was not until October that trains began running into a downtown Chicago station, and then it was on tracks jointly owned with the Chicago, Rock Island & Pacific.[59] On April 25, 1855, the organizational structure was simplified by a merger of the Northern Indiana, which had already combined a number of Indiana, Illinois, and Ohio companies, and the Michigan Southern into the Michigan Southern & Northern Indiana Railroad.[60]

The Michigan Central had not been idly watching all of this. By helping out the New Albany & Salem Rail Road, which had rights to build in Indiana toward Chicago, construction began west from Michigan City. The Northern Indiana went to court to try to stop them, but the MC won out.[61] The MC then agreed to help out the Illinois Central Railroad financially through an arrangement made by David A. Neal, an incorporator of the MC and a director of the IC. On May 21, 1852, the IC completed a line between 13th Street and Kensington, where it connected with the MC, and the MC began operating trains into Chicago.[62]

As the Michigan Central built toward Chicago, it was well aware that it could not continue to rely on Lake Erie steamships as the road's tie with the East. A railroad connection was more desireable. The MC knew about the recently chartered Great Western Railway that was planned across Ontario, running between the Niagara and Detroit rivers. James F. Joy enlisted Henry N. Walker, who was then Michigan's attorney general, to help. Walker and Joy visited Toronto and Niagara Falls with Great Western and New York Central officers to line up assistance to build the road. Construction started, officially, on October 23, 1849, at London. Initial financing appears to have come from England. A meeting in May 1851 brought forth a resolution that "the Great Western Railroad will be a necessary link in the Great Trunk Railway from the Atlantic to the Mississippi" and that statement resulted in American stock subscriptions in the amount of $1,000,000.[63] This was enough to ensure completion of the road. Brooks and Erastus Corning joined the Great Western board of directors. The road was finished between Niagara Falls and Windsor by Christmas 1853 and regular service began on January 17, 1854.[64] Detroit celebrated the completion as much as any community in Ontario.[65] Ferry service began immediately across the Detroit River. In March 1855, the suspension bridge over the Niagara River was completed. The MC now had its outlet to the East and had established a cordial relationship with the Great Western that was to last into the 1870s.

Alfred Williams had been operating the Detroit & Pontiac since 1841. In 1848, he, Horace C. Thurber, and some others obtained a charter for the Oakland & Ottawa to build a line from Pontiac to Lake Michigan.[66] They got permission from the Legislature to connect their Detroit & Pontiac to it,[67] then set about raising money for the road. But money was hard to come by, and the company had to have its charter amended to allow it to issue mortgage bonds.[68] Henry N. Walker went out to try to raise funds. In 1852, he made a trip to England and another in 1855. On February 13, 1855, the Legislature granted a charter for the Detroit & Milwaukee Railway, which was to be formed out of a merger of the Detroit & Pontiac and the Oakland & Ottawa.[69] Walker became the new road's president.

Construction began immediately. Fenton was reached in 1855, Owosso on July 1, 1856, and the line was in Ionia by August 1857.[70] Once again the money ran out. Walker went to see a friend, C. J. Brydges, who had built the Great Western and was its managing director. On November 7, the Great Western loaned the D&M enough money to complete its road and in exchange obtained a mortgage on the road and control of its capital stock.[71] Brydges' Great Western now controlled a line that would extend from Niagara Falls to the eastern shore of Lake Michigan. One source says Brydges was also involved with the Lacrosse & Milwaukee road that was to build across Wisconsin to the Mississippi River.[72] Construction resumed; the line reached Grand Rapids on July 4, 1858, and Grand Haven later that same year.[73] Despite its ownership of the D&M, the Great Western continued to have a friendly relationship with the Michigan Central—an arrangement that produced far more traffic for the Great Western than its ownership of the D&M ever did.

The Michigan Southern & Northern Indiana knew exactly what effect the alliance of the Michigan Central with Great Western would have, and it had started taking steps to protect itself. Its line of steamships on Lake Erie was a temporary measure. About 1850, a number of small railroad companies strung along the south shore of Lake Erie were formed. Two were between Toledo and Cleveland, another east of Cleveland, one at Erie, and another west from Buffalo. The Cleveland, Painesville & Ashtabula soon acquired the designation "the Lake Shore Road." As construction progressed, the companies began to work together more closely, and the name was applied more broadly. On January 24, 1853, the four lines were finished and one could ride by rail between Buffalo and Toledo.[74] It was necessary to change trains several times, but it was possible to get through. From Toledo, the Michigan Southern made the run through to Chicago.

Having extricated themselves from their venture into railroading, Michigan's legislators made certain it would not happen again. When the new state constitution was adopted in 1850, the door was shut firmly. The state was forbidden to be a party to any internal improvements work. Further, the state was prohibited from buying stock in any private corporation, or extending the state's credit to assist it. One other provision affected railroads; no corporation (of any sort) could be created by a special act of the Legislature. Up to this time, all railroads had been chartered by acts of the Legislature. It was felt, and there may have been justification, that abuses might creep in and monopolies be established that would not benefit the state as a whole. It was not until 1855 that the Legislature was finally able to pass a general incorporation law for railroads. The Legislature did grant two more charters in 1855, after the new constitution was adopted. That of the Port Huron & Lake Michigan appears to be justified as an extension of its earlier 1847 charter, and that of the Detroit & Milwaukee was permission to merge two chartered companies under a new name.[75]

The 1850 constitution removed the right of the Legislature to pass acts to incorporate companies. Incorporation laws for iron and copper mines, plank roads, toll bridges, and for general manufacturing corporations already had been in place. One was passed for railroads in 1853 by the House, but it lost in the Senate. The influence of the Michigan Central was thought to be the cause of the defeat.[76] In 1855, an incorporation bill finally became law. It provided that a company could be incorporated by twenty-five or more stockholders who had subscribed to stock at the rate of $1,000 or higher per mile, on which they had paid at least a five percent deposit. The act specified the amount of capital that had to be paid in before construction could begin, the duties of officers, and called for a variety of safety regulations. The permitted methods of acquiring right-of-way were stipulated. The Legislature was given some power to lower the rates charged. The act also set an annual railroad tax at a rate of one percent of the capital stock and exempted the company from all other state and local taxes.[77]

With the enactment of the general incorporation law for railroads a new burst of activity followed. Twelve new companies were incorporated in 1855, and eight more in each of the two years following. The very first was the Iron Mountain Railroad, projected by Heman B. Ely to connect Marquette with the iron mines to the west.[78] This short line was completed in August 1857, and later became part of the Duluth, South Shore & Atlantic.[79] The second company incorporated was the Detroit, Monroe & Toledo, a Detroit-sponsored undertaking to link that city with the developing Lake Shore route at Toledo.[80] It immediately got financial assistance from the Michigan Southern & Northern Indiana, and was leased to that road when the line was completed in

July 1856.[81] Many of the remainder were local projects, but a few of them were quite ambitious—and a gift from the federal government was the reason for that.

Although the states had been petitioning for years for aid of any sort for railroad, highway, harbor, and canal projects, the federal government had usually kept the purse strings tight. In 1850, Senator Stephen Douglas of Illinois was able to persuade enough congressmen of the value of his own pet project, and obtained a grant of federal land to help in building the Illinois Central Railroad. To get the needed support he had to throw in similar grants for projects in Mississippi and Alabama. This was followed in 1852 by legislation giving any railroad a hundred-foot-wide right-of-way over public land. In 1853, land grants were awarded in Missouri and Arkansas. Douglas' idea had worked. By the end of 1854, construction was well under way on the Illinois Central. Washington then let down the barriers. In 1856 and 1857, grants were made of nearly twenty million acres to eight western states to promote forty-five different rail lines.[82]

Michigan's grant was made on June 3, 1856, and consisted of nearly forty-million acres—more than six thousand square miles—an area roughly equal to all of the land between Detroit and Kalamazoo extending south to the state line. Washington set all the provisions that had to be met, and then gave the land to the state of Michigan to distribute.[83] A railroad company had to build twenty miles of line to be eligible to receive any land. Then it would be awarded those odd-numbered sections of land lying within six miles on either side of the completed line that had not already been sold. If there was not sufficient land in the twelve-mile wide strip, the railroads could select farther away, but not more than fifteen miles from the rail line. As subsequent twenty-mile sections were put in operation, additional sections of the grant were awarded. The federal government stipulated what routes were to be entitled to receive grants; the state had the dubious privilege of selecting which companies were to receive the grants. In Michigan, nine rail routes were designated; five in the Lower Peninsula and four in the Upper Peninsula: Amboy (in southern Hillsdale County), via Lansing to Little Traverse Bay; Grand Rapids to Little Traverse Bay; Port Huron to Flint; Flint to Grand Haven; Flint to Ludington; Marquette to Little Bay de Noquet; Marquette to Ontonagon; Marquette to the Wisconsin state line; and Ontonagon to the Wisconsin state line.[84] There were other requirements, and of course a deadline to complete the rail lines.

There was a feeding frenzy in Lansing. Two companies were formed for the Amboy-Little Traverse Bay grant, three competed for the Grand Rapids-Little Traverse Bay. The other routes drew less interest. By February, 1857 after all of the competing suitors had sufficiently romanced the Legislature, the grants were awarded to the most favored. The Amboy, Lansing & Traverse Bay received the grant covering the longest distance; the Grand Rapids & Indiana received the other going to Little Traverse Bay. The Port Huron & Lake Michigan got the Port Huron-Flint, the Detroit & Milwaukee the grant to Grand Haven, and the Flint & Pere Marquette the Flint-Ludington (then named Pere Marquette). In the Upper Peninsula, the grants went to the Bay De Noquet & Marquette, the Marquette & Ontonagon, the Marquette & State Line, and the Ontonagon & State Line. All of these companies were organized between June 1856 and January 1857, except the Grand Rapids & Indiana, the Detroit & Milwaukee, and the Port Huron & Lake Michigan, which were organized in 1855.[85]

THE PANIC OF 1857 TO THE CIVIL WAR

The frothy times of 1856 obscured a gradual financial tightening that had been foreshadowed in 1854. Capital became harder to raise. The Detroit & Milwaukee's experience in raising construction funds was representative. In August, the Panic of 1857 moved in. Cochrane and Miller, in *The Age of Enterprise*, attribute much of the cause of the panic to the capital absorbed by the railroads in the first half of the decade, capital which did not produce the expected profits when the lines were completed. The whole railroad structure had been built on borrowed funds, and these funds had been diverted from other enterprises to the railroads. Some railroads were not able to pay interest on bonds as it came due.[86]

The Michigan Southern & Northern Indiana and Michigan Central together had built more than two hundred miles of line in 1855-1857, and both had bought steamships for use on Lake Erie. The two had been in furious competition for five years for traffic out of Chicago. The effort drained both companies to the extent that, in 1857, they signed an agreement to divide the business by formula.[87] That same year the MS&NI had to go to the bond market and float a $2,700,000 second mortgage bond issue. The company's stock dropped from 115 in 1856 to 6 in 1859.[88] Earnings also dropped by almost forty percent.[89] In the summer of 1859, Henry Keep, a Wall Street speculator, began buying into the Michigan Southern and soon had control of it at bargain prices.[90] To make matters even worse, a new railroad, the Pittsburgh, Fort Wayne & Chicago, was completed in 1858 and supplied a new through route to the East Coast. The Michigan Central itself had not built as much as its competitor, and it came through the panic in better shape.

Of the companies that received land grants, the Amboy, Lansing & Traverse Bay was the first to be able to construct some of its line. Its Owosso-based promoters were able to pull together enough money to build southwest from Owosso toward Lansing, and by 1859 had finished it as far as Bath—about nineteen miles. By the end of 1860, a few more miles were built, enough to qualify for the first section of grant land.[91] The other roads had a much more difficult time getting started.

Railroad trackage in the state increased from 353 miles at the beginning of 1850 to a total of 770 miles at the end of 1860.[92]

The Civil War prolonged the railroads' slow development in Michigan. Capital moved to those war-supporting industries that yielded the greatest profits. The Flint-based owners of one company, the Flint & Pere Marquette, were able to start construction in 1859, apparently with local capital. That wasn't enough money and, in 1860, two Detroiters and a New Yorker appeared on the Board of Directors. Captain Eber Brock Ward became president. By September 1860, the company had built twenty miles of line from Saginaw toward Flint and received the first installment of its land grant. By December 8, 1862, the road had been built thirty-three miles toward Flint.[93]

In the Upper Peninsula, a group of Chicago men, including president William B. Ogden of the Chicago & North Western and Charles T. Harvey of Soo Canal fame, incorporated the Peninsula Railroad to build a line between Escanaba and Marquette County. Soon after its incorporation in 1862 the company obtained the Marquette-Wisconsin state line land grant from the Marquette & State Line, probably through Harvey's efforts. In September 1864, the railroad was finished between Escanaba and Negaunee and began hauling ore from the Marquette Range to its ore docks on Lake Michigan. Ogden and his partners also appear to have owned some of the iron mines themselves. After the road was completed it was sold to the Chicago & North Western.[94]

With the end of the Civil War, American railroads were ready for a new era. In his survey, *American Railroads,* John Stover writes:

> The Civil War strengthened American railroads. [It] brought new efficiency in both track and bridge construction, and the bulk of the wartime traffic brought prosperity to most northern lines. Finally, the stimulation of wartime demands resulted in an enforced and healthy co-operation among railroads, created new methods of handling mail on trains, and forced the beginnings of a change from iron to steel rails and a comparable shift in fuel from wood to coal. American railroads achieved a measure of maturity in the expansion of the fifties and the challenges of war which followed. In 1865 they stood on the threshold of their golden age.[95]

The war brought prosperity and cash to the major northern railroads. More importantly, the Civil War put new money in the hands of New England entrepreneurs who would have to find a use for it when the war was ended. The average man was also introduced to the railroad. As a soldier he rode to training camp and moved from theater to theater by train. His supplies, almost his life, depended on the railroad. This lesson was not lost on the manufacturers and farmers, who became more heavily dependent on the rails.

During the war, important events began to shape the future of the American railroad network. On July 1, 1862, on the day of the battle at Malvern Hill, President Abraham Lincoln signed the Pacific Railway Bill. Construction began before the end of the war.

THE CIVIL WAR TO THE PANIC OF 1873

Michigan's railroad construction during the Civil War lagged behind that of other states in the Northwest Territory. In 1865, Ohio, Indiana, Illinois, and Wisconsin all had more miles of road than did Michigan.[96] Part of the impetus had been the drive by eastern lines to reach Chicago. The development of roads west and northwest of Chicago also benefited both Illinois and Wisconsin. Michigan was out of the path of both of these movements, and its roads continued to be built to reach purely local destinations.

The end of the Civil War changed this. Between 1864 and the end of 1873, Michigan's railroad mileage grew wildly. More than twenty-three hundred miles of road were built, increasing the total by more than two and one-half times. Land grants, established before the Civil War, played an important part in this construction. Capital from outside the state became an important source of funds. Finally, Michigan municipalities started pledging direct support to railroad construction by issuing their own municipal obligations.

The land grant played an important part in the development of the Flint & Pere Marquette. Construction began at Saginaw toward Lake Michigan and by the end of 1867 tracks were into Midland. Each year saw more construction, until Reed City was reached in 1871. Each twenty-mile segment made the company eligible for another share of its land grant. In 1868, the F&PM leased the Bay City & East Saginaw, which had been built the year before by a group of Bay City men. The price was a guarantee of the interest on BC&ES bonds and on those issued to the road by Bay County. Also in 1868, it absorbed the Flint & Holly that Henry H. Crapo had built in 1864. In 1865, local residents incorporated the Holly, Wayne & Monroe. It was not until 1871 that the first part of this road was opened for business, and in 1872 it was completed to Monroe. The F&PM consolidated this company in 1872. At that same time it also merged the Bay City road, and two other small companies, one of which had built a line between Flint and Otter Lake.[97] By the end of 1873, the F&PM reported total road and equipment investment of about $11,000,000, of which more than $7,000,000 was in secured and unsecured debt. Interest expense now exceeded net income.[98] As fast as money was received from any source it was used for construction.

New England money remained in firm control of the Michigan Central. In 1867, Detroit attorney James F. Joy became president of the road. Joy was also heavily involved with John Murray Forbes and John W. Brooks in several companies that made up the Chicago, Burlington & Quincy and Joy served as that company's president as well. The MC undertook a different approach to expansion. As connecting companies were built, Joy arranged construction funds for them. When they were completed Joy leased them, usually for a guarantee on the bond interest.[99] Five different lines were obtained this way in 1871 and 1872: the Kalamazoo & South Haven, the Joliet & Northern Indiana, the Grand River Valley between Jackson and Grand Rapids, the Michigan Air Line between Jackson and South Bend, and the Jackson, Lansing & Saginaw. The latter three lines were the product of a group of men in Jackson who also promoted a line to Fort Wayne as well as a city horse car line. The JL&S had been started in 1863 as the Lansing & Jackson. In 1865, the name was changed and in 1866 the road had bought the franchise and land grant rights of the Amboy, Lansing & Traverse Bay from Lansing northerly. By the end of 1867, its line extended from Jackson to Bay City. At the end of 1871, the road was pushed as far as Alger, and in July 1873, to Gaylord.[100]

Joy was the pre-eminent figure in Michigan railroading for ten years after the Civil War. In addition to what he accomplished for the MC as shown above, he also tried to gather in other companies as well. At the request of its promoter, Daniel L. Quirk of Ypsilanti (with whom Joy had worked on the CB&Q),[101] Joy helped in financing the Detroit, Hillsdale & Indiana, which built a line between Ypsilanti and Hillsdale in 1871-72.[102] It appears that he lost out to the road's president, Detroiter Christian H. Buhl, in an attempt to bring the line into the MC flock. Joy became president of the Detroit & Bay City after its line between Detroit and Bay City was completed in 1873. The MC operated the company from its beginning and eventually leased it.[103] Joy also made a try for the Kalamazoo, Allegan & Grand Rapids, but was not successful in getting it.[104]

Joy was also involved with several other projects. One was the Chicago & Michigan Lake Shore, a little company that Alexander H. Morrison of St. Joseph had formed to connect St. Joseph with the MC at New Buffalo.[105] To get financing, Morrison turned to Joy, and soon a number of MC financiers were in control of the company. The line was extended rapidly north along the Lake Michigan shore. By the end of 1872, it was built to Pentwater and had a branch to Grand Rapids.[106] Another of Joy's financial involvements was the Detroit, Lansing & Lake Michigan. This road had been assembled from several parts. In 1864 the Detroit & Howell had been incorporated, followed in 1868 by the Howell & Lansing. These two were merged in 1868 as the Detroit, Howell & Lansing. The Ionia & Lansing was built in 1869 between its namesake cities and connected with the Jackson, Lansing & Saginaw. The I&L was absorbed in 1871, and the new company named the DL&LM. By the end of 1871 its line was completed between Detroit and Howard City.[107] In 1873, Joy became president of the company and brought several of his friends and their money to its board.[108]

The Michigan Southern remained the Michigan Central's arch rival. Both fought for Chicago traffic. The roads made pooling agreements that were quickly broken. When the Pittsburgh line was built to Chicago in 1858, the situation was further complicated. Much of the turmoil can probably be attributed to the Michigan Southern's owners, Henry Keep and Legrand Lockwood—a pair of New York plungers who had taken control in 1859. Keep and Lockwood were also able to get a voice in the management of the companies that loosely comprised a route between Toledo and Buffalo. Now they needed an outlet at Buffalo to the East and there were two possibilities—the New York Central & Hudson River and the Erie. Lockwood and Keep flirted with both roads. One chance was with Jay Gould, who was at the head of the Erie, but Gould could be a most uncertain friend. They decided to make a move on the New York Central & Hudson River. Commodore Vanderbilt had acquired some stock in the Central in 1863 and two of his representatives had seats on the Central's board. In December 1866, Keep and Lockwood moved in and took control. Vanderbilt reacted by cutting off the Central's Albany connection to New York City. Freight shippers screamed and passengers complained loudly. Within a year the other major stockholders of the Central asked the Commodore to return and take over the management of the line.[109] Vanderbilt obliged and Keep retired to become president of the Chicago & North Western. Eventually the majority of stock, including Keep's, passed into the Vanderbilt family's hands.

Lockwood was able somehow to stay on good terms with the Vanderbilts and was able to maintain a reasonably amicable relationship to move traffic between the Central and the lines west of Buffalo. Apparently the Commodore was persuaded about this same time by his son William to begin buying stock in Lockwood's roads—no doubt to assure a peaceable connection to Chicago. To hold off the Vanderbilts, Lockwood executed several consolidations east of Toledo, eventually renaming one of them as the Lake Shore Railway. Finally, on April 6, 1869, Lockwood brought all the parts together in one giant consolidation, and the new company was named the Lake Shore & Michigan Southern.[110] Vanderbilt continued to buy stock and bided his time while Lockwood continued his efforts to keep his line independent. Lockwood continued his flirtation with the Erie. Vanderbilt started buying stock in both the Michigan Central and the Great Western in order to have an alternate route to Chicago. The Commodore also invested west of Chicago in the Chicago & North Western.[111]

In early September 1869, Commodore Vanderbilt pounced on Legrand Lockwood. Lake Shore stock began to drop in price. Vanderbilt sold and it dropped some more. At the same time Lockwood's brokerage firm was involved in a gold corner that collapsed on September 24th—"Black Friday." When the debris settled, the Commodore owned Lockwood's Lake Shore stock and Lockwood resigned from the railroad. Vanderbilt promoted Horace F. Clark, his son-in-law, to the LS&MS presidency. The Commodore owned his own railroad all the way from New York City to Chicago.[112]

In the last months of his ownership of the LS&MS, Lockwood was able to make some small additions to the system in Michigan. In 1868 and 1869, a Kalamazoo railroad contractor, Ransom Gardner, built a line between Kalamazoo and Grand Rapids—the Kalamazoo, Allegan & Grand Rapids. He leased that road to Lockwood in September 1869.[113] Gardner also assembled a line between Kalamazoo and White Pigeon by building part and buying part from another company. Lockwood formed a wholly-owned subsidiary, the Kalamazoo & White Pigeon, and bought Gardner's line in August 1869.[114] During 1870, Gardner was contracted to build a railroad between Allegan and Muskegon, but LS&MS president Clark did not pick up that line.[115] In 1871 and 1872, Gardner built a line between Jonesville and Lansing for the Northern Central Michigan. In 1867, this company had obtained part of the land grant of the Amboy, Lansing & Traverse, but had done nothing with it. Apparently Clark felt it had some possibilities and in about 1871 agreed to buy out its owners' stock. It may be that Clark had hopes of extending the road north from Lansing, but nothing ever developed.[116]

Clark also bought some of the bonds of the Grand Rapids, Newaygo & Lake Shore and of the Michigan Lake Shore, but never became actively involved in either company. On July 19, 1873, Clark passed away. The Commodore had been quite lenient with his son-in-law's activities, but now stepped in. He made himself president of the LS&MS and named Amasa Stone, Jr., as managing director.[117]

The Grand Rapids & Indiana was founded in Hartford City, Indiana in 1854. It was one of two companies that together proposed to link Grand Rapids with the Ohio River near Louisville. Joseph Lomax, the company's president, moved to Sturgis in 1855 and began lobbying Washington, and then the state legislators, for a land grant for the road. In 1857, Governor Bingham signed the grant act awarding the Grand Rapids-Little Traverse Bay grant to the GR&I.[118] Even with the grant in hand, the company had little success in raising the capital needed to build. State legislators granted Lomax one extension after another. In 1866, he resigned the presidency, and it went eventually to Joseph K. Edgerton of Fort Wayne. Edgerton had close ties with predecessors of the Pittsburgh, Fort Wayne & Chicago, which was then being built. Also, he had contacts with the management of the Pennsylvania Railroad, which leased the PFW&C in 1869. Edgerton signed a construction contract in 1867 to have the GR&I line built from Grand Rapids north. The first section, between Grand Rapids and Cedar Springs, was finished that same year.[119] But this achievement used up all the funds the company could raise. The City of Grand Rapids refused to pay a $10,000 bonus it had promised; the GR&I had to sue in order to get the money. The company went into receivership.

Receiver Jesse L. Williams, also of Fort Wayne, had to still the demands in the Legislature that the company either build its line or forfeit the land grant. Williams went to George W. Cass, president of the Fort Wayne road, and interested him in the GR&I as a connecting line. Cass brought in Thomas A. Scott, a vice president of the Pennsylvania, and William Thaw, a railroad contractor. The three formed the Continental Improvement Company in 1869. Continental agreed to build the GR&I under the deadlines necessary to keep the land grant, but it demanded a high price. Continental took $8,000,000 in mortgage bonds, all of the common stock, and the land grant rights as its price for the contract. But build it did. Within eighteen months, the line was built between Fort Wayne and Grand Rapids and extended north from Cedar Springs to Paris. By the end of 1871, the road was complete to Cadillac. By May, 1874 it was finished to Petoskey.[120]

Continental turned the road over to the Fort Wayne company in 1869, which covered the risk its president and his friends had taken. The Fort Wayne then assigned its agreement upstairs to the Pennsylvania.[121] In 1872, as a side venture, Continental also built the Traverse City Railroad between Traverse City and Walton Jct. for Perry Hannah and, in the same kind of deal, took that company's stock and some bond proceeds in payment.[122]

The main line of the Grand Trunk Western began to take form in this period, but it began as several completely independent enterprises. During this same period two Canadian railroads played a role in the events that followed. The Great Western Railway's completion into Detroit in 1854 and its subsequent control of the Detroit & Milwaukee have been noted earlier. In 1853, the Great Western formed the London & Port Sarnia. The Panic of 1857 slowed the construction of that line a bit, but it was completed into Sarnia by the end of 1858.[123] At the same time the Grand Trunk Railway of Canada assembled a line beginning at

Chicago & West Michigan's locomotive 137, circa 1870

Portland, Maine, and completed it into Port Edward, opposite Port Huron, in 1859. A year earlier the Grand Trunk's owners made plans for a westerly extension by incorporating the Chicago, Detroit & Canada Grand Trunk Junction to build a road between Detroit and Fort Gratiot.[124] That line was completed in 1859.[125] With a ferry across the St. Clair River, and an agreement with the Michigan Central to handle traffic between Detroit and Chicago, the Grand Trunk had assembled an impressive railroad in a very short period of time. But both the Great Western and the Grand Trunk were looking covetously toward the American Midwest.

Two companies had been formed to build west from Port Huron—the Port Huron & Lake Michigan and the Port Huron & Milwaukee. In 1865, both companies came under the control of William L. Bancroft of Port Huron. He merged the two dormant companies, managed to raise enough money to begin construction in 1868, and had a line completed into Flint by December 1871.[126]

At the same time a group of Battle Creek businessmen were active. In the autumn of 1865, they incorporated the Peninsular Railway to build a line between Battle Creek and Lansing.[127] Construction began the next year and the line was put in service in June 1870.[128] The same group formed the Peninsular Railway Extension Company in January 1868 to build southwest from Battle Creek. They planned to get to Chicago eventually, since later they incorporated companies in Indiana and Illinois to complete that plan. The Peninsular was put in service from Battle Creek to South Bend in the fall of 1872, and by late summer 1873 was finished to Valparaiso, Indiana.[129]

Some failed projects also tried to enter this same field. In 1865, a group based in southwestern Michigan incorporated the Chicago & Michigan Grand Trunk. It was to build from Ridgeway on the Port Huron-Detroit line, via Lansing, to St. Joseph and then to Indiana. In January 1867, another group formed the Grand Trunk Railway of Michigan to build from Ridgeway, through Jackson and Niles, to Indiana. Lastly, in 1868, some Jackson men formed the Grand Trunk Rail Road of Michigan, which was planned to run from Ridgeway, via Lansing, to Indiana. Nothing came of any of these attempts. But, in July 1868, the second company renamed itself as the Michigan Air Line Railroad, absorbed two Indiana companies, and in 1869 constructed a line between Ridgeway and Romeo.[130] It appears that the Grand Trunk of Canada had no direct involvement with any of these Michigan efforts in the 1860s.

One other company's presence in Michigan must be noted. In February 1869, a predecessor company of the Canada Southern Railway was formed. Construction began at Niagara Falls in 1870 and headed in a beeline for Chicago. Half of the road's stock was owned by

Daniel Drew, who had just ended a career of plundering the Erie Railroad.[131] In the early 1870s several Canada Southern-sponsored lines were incorporated in Michigan to connect Grosse Ile and Chicago, Detroit and Toledo, and St. Clair and Lansing (but changed the next year to Lake Michigan). In 1873, before the CS reached Amherstburg, the Michigan lines were built. The Panic of 1873 brought everything to a stop. The line from St. Clair was built only to Ridgeway. The Chicago goal was never reached—it ran out at Fayette, Ohio. The Wabash Railroad later used the same projected route into Chicago.

In the Upper Peninsula, the Chicago & North Western hooked up its Escanaba-Negaunee line to its tracks in Wisconsin in 1872 and had a through line to Chicago.[132] The Marquette, Houghton & Ontonagon continued to extend west and north from Marquette and was in service to L'Anse by December 1872.[133]

THE PANIC OF 1873 TO THE PANIC OF 1879

The Panic of 1873 was triggered in September by the failure of the Philadelphia firm of Jay Cooke & Company. Cooke was deeply involved in the construction of the Northern Pacific Railroad and that railroad finally wound up in receivership. The Panic affected business throughout the nation and the railroads were especially hurt. The heavy absorption of capital to finance an unprecedented construction surge that began after the Civil War did not yield the profits anticipated. The Panic and its aftermath stopped railroad construction everywhere. Michigan's rail network had 3,253 miles of trackage at the end of 1873. Of this, 2,322 had been built since the Civil War. More than five hundred miles of line were built in Michigan in 1871, and at least four hundred miles in 1870, 1872, and 1873. Just two hundred miles were built in the years 1874-1877, and another two hundred in 1878-1879. The number of companies incorporated dropped from a high of twenty-nine in 1869 to eight in 1873, four in 1874, and to a low of three in 1875.

After the death of Horace F. Clark, Commodore Vanderbilt tightened where his son-in-law had been lax. He curtailed or cancelled outright construction projects on the Lake Shore & Michigan Southern. He put Amasa Stone, Jr. in charge of operations as general manager, while he kept the financial reins. He loaned the road his own money to replace its iron rails with steel ones. Out of retained earnings he paid off debt at such a rate that by the end of 1876 the floating debt was gone. When the Commodore died on January 4, 1877, the bulk of the estate went to his son, William Henry Vanderbilt. William stepped in as president of the LS&MS.

The Panic of 1873 humbled the proud Michigan Central. Business dropped sharply, forcing the company to omit dividends. The stock began to fall. President Joy was busy juggling his railroad presidencies. In 1873, he left the presidency of the Chicago & Michigan Lake Shore. In 1875, he had a falling out with John Murray Forbes, who felt Joy had mishandled some funds of the Chicago, Burlington & Quincy. Joy was forced out. The Vanderbilts stepped up their buying of the Michigan Central's stock, and by 1877 had enough influence to name Samuel Sloan as the MC's president. The next year William H. Vanderbilt installed himself as president and solidified his family control of the Michigan Central.

With the completion of the Canada Southern from Niagara Falls to Amherstburg, Ontario, the Grand Trunk, the Great Western, and the Vanderbilts all had to consider a changed equation. The CS had completed, in 1873, some of its line on the Michigan side of the Detroit and St. Clair rivers. A route to Chicago remained the goal, but more importantly the Detroit-Toledo line provided new access to both termini. The Panic of 1873 stopped the extension to Chicago and drove the Canada Southern into bankruptcy. In June 1876, Commodore Vanderbilt gained control of the company by guaranteeing the interest on its bonds.[134] The Great Western saw the threat. Although the Commodore was also an owner of the GW, it was no longer important to his plans now that he had the CS in his pocket. In 1878, the Great Western was able to strike a traffic agreement with the Canada Southern.[135] This gave the GW some improvement to its earnings. Despite Vanderbilt control, the Great Western's traffic relationship with the Michigan Central continued unimpaired.

In October 1876, Sir Henry Tyler became president of the Grand Trunk. The prospects of the company improved immeasurably with his genius at the tiller. Tyler felt, as he had said for nearly a dozen years, that the Grand Trunk should take over the Great Western. The Great Western, however, continued to resist. Tyler also continued to look ahead to his own route to Chicago—as a means of insuring the profitability of the GT. William Henry Vanderbilt forced Tyler into action. Vanderbilt took the presidency of the Michigan Central in June 1878. Tyler realized that his arrangement with the Michigan Central to reach Chicago would be continued only at Vanderbilt's sufferance. Earlier, in 1878, Vanderbilt had bought the bonds of the Chicago & Northeastern, which owned the line between Lansing and Flint. Some freight had been moving to the Grand Trunk over this line, which served as a connector between the two segments of the Chicago & Lake Huron. Vanderbilt closed the C&NE to through traffic headed for the Grand Trunk. This move forced the C&LH into receivership. In mid-1879, when the foreclosure sale was finally held, Tyler bought the entire C&LH at a bargain price. Then he announced that he would build his own line between Lansing and Flint and simply ignore Vanderbilt's line. Vanderbilt saw what had happened, cut his losses, and sold the C&NE

to Tyler at a loss. Tyler then had to finish building the line between Valparaiso and Chicago—which he did—and by early in 1880, had his own route into Chicago.[136]

Before these events, in 1875, Tyler had taken another step to reach Chicago. He formed the Michigan Air Line Railway to take over the rights of a company that planned to build a line between Ridgeway and Jackson. The MAL did not figure importantly in the eventual outcome, but did provide Tyler with an alternative.

During this period, some of Michigan's railroads began taking a serious interest in the state's newest growth industry—lumbering. Lumbering had been a strong element in the formation of the Flint & Pere Marquette and the Grand Rapids & Indiana. It shaped the growth of the Chicago & Michigan Lake Shore on the state's west coast and it bought several companies that tapped forest areas.

The Grand Rapids & Indiana was built as far as Petoskey in 1874, and the Jackson, Lansing & Saginaw to Gaylord in 1873. Among the bold projects brought forward for the same purpose were the Kalamazoo, Lowell & Northern Michigan; the Owosso & North Western; the Grand Rapids, Greenville & Alpena; the Coldwater, Marshall & Mackinaw; and the Cincinnati & Great Northern. All of these were early victims of the Panic of 1873.

In 1874, George and Hugh Campbell built a twelve-mile line west from Pinconning to haul their sawed lumber. They converted their road to the Glencoe, Pinconning & Lake Shore in 1875. Credit for the earliest successful joining of railroading and lumbering deservedly goes to Winfield Scott Gerrish who conceived the Lake George & Muskegon River and operated it from 1875 until 1882.

Gerrish combined the low cost of a narrow gauge line—thirty-six inches between the rails—with lightweight locomotives operating on tracks that were moved when needed to new cutting operations. He ran his railroad year-round, and in doing so revolutionized lumbering operations. No longer dependent on springtime river drives to move logs, he transformed lumbering into an immensely profitable operation.

As early as the 1850s, lumbermen had used horses to pull cars of logs on rails—from cutting areas to banking grounds or to saw mills. A few bought used steam locomotives. The Campbells and Gerrish found the right combination and the railroad became an integral and critical part of the lumbering industry. Their success led to the fomation of several dozen similar carriers in the next two decades—some of which survived into the twentieth century as full-service railroads.

Very little construction occurred on the components of the Pere Marquette system in the years 1873-1879. The costs of the extensive construction before 1879 affected them dramatically. James F. Joy's Detroit, Lansing & Lake Michigan went into receivership in June 1876 and emerged from a friendly foreclosure later that year as the Detroit, Lansing & Northern. Joy and the directors all kept their jobs, although Joy did leave the company in 1878. In western Michigan, with Joy's departure from the Chicago & Michigan Lake Shore in 1874, more Boston money moved in and the presidency went to Nathaniel Thayer of Boston. Still, the company went into receivership late in 1876. The Michigan Lake Shore, a competing line between Allegan and Muskegon and controlled by the Pennsylvania Railroad, slid into receivership in 1874. Apparently the Pennsylvania gave up trying to make something of the MLS, for it and the C&MLS were consolidated in 1878 into a new company named the Chicago & West Michigan—with the Bostonians in firm control. The Flint & Pere Marquette remained solvent until July 1879, when it too went into receivership. It emerged a year later but with more New York City money on its books.

THE PANIC OF 1879 TO THE PANIC OF 1893

As the new decade began, a new-found optimism imbued the railroad industry and new levels of profitability encouraged new growth. Lines were extended and new companies founded. Between the beginning of 1880 and the onset of the Panic of 1893, Michigan railroad mileage increased from 3,657 to 7,447—more than doubling in little more than a decade. In fourteen years, a total of 233 new companies were incorporated, nearly equal the 256 that had been founded between 1830 and 1880. They were heady times, but full of pitfalls. Fourteen foreclosure sales were held during the 1880s. Seventeen companies were merged into others, fifteen more leased, and nineteen sold outright during the decade.

At the opening of 1880, William Henry Vanderbilt was the leading figure in Michigan railroading. He owned the majority of stock of the Lake Shore & Michigan Southern, the Michigan Central, and controlled the Canada Southern. He had substantial interests in other companies, but all of them were outside of Michigan except the Chicago & North Western. In 1881, Vanderbilt had the Michigan Central obtain a lease of the Detroit & Bay City. That same year the MC was extended to Mackinaw City. Also in 1881, he leased the Detroit, Hillsdale & South Western to his Lake Shore & Michigan Southern, and the next year he obtained a lease of the Fort Wayne & Jackson. In 1882, his Canada Southern built a short branch from Essex to Windsor, Ontario, linking the CS main line to Detroit and his Michigan Central, and then he gave the MC operating control over the CS.

In little more than half a decade, from the death of the Commodore in 1877 to 1883, William Henry Vanderbilt had expanded and solidified his control of a railroad empire. He had both the means and the skill to suppress competition and to establish supremacy wherever he wished. In the southern two tiers of Michigan's counties—from Detroit west to Lake Michigan—the Vanderbilt railroads reached everywhere. No city above one thousand in population was missed in this territory of nearly eight thousand square miles. But the wealth he had created, the financial colossus he ruled, weighed on him heavily. Talented and amiable, he began experiencing feelings of guilt at the size of his fortune and its responsibilites. The continually growing pressures of managing events became a burden he wanted to give up. His health was being affected. In 1883, with the guidance of J. P. Morgan, William Henry began selling his stock. He resigned the presidencies of a myriad of companies, retaining only directorships. In less than a decade he had more than doubled the inheritance he had received from the Commodore from $75,000,000 to $200,000,000.[137] He groomed two of his sons, William K. and Cornelius, to follow in his place, and both became involved in active management of Vanderbilt lines. Another son, Frederick W., sat on boards of directors but never in a management seat. A fourth son, George, went to North Carolina and is better remembered than all the others because of the home he built—Biltmore. On December 8, 1885, William Henry Vanderbilt fell to the floor of his office and died.[138]

So also passed Thomas A. Scott, who had been one of the principals of the Continental Improvement Company, which built the Grand Rapids & Indiana. Scott moved to the presidency of the Pennsylvania Railroad in 1874, and by his hand came some of the great expansion of that road. Scott left the Pennsylvania in June 1880 and died on May 21, 1881, at age fifty-six.[139] Scott and Vanderbilt had gone head to head many times to further their ambitions and the fortunes of their companies. Within a year after Scott's death, the GR&I completed its line to Mackinaw City. In 1886, the GR&I built a branch line from Grand Rapids to Muskegon.[140]

The year 1880 brought two new names to Michigan railroading. James McMillan was one of the founders of the Michigan Car Company and the Detroit Car Wheel Company at the end of the Civil War. In 1879, Sir Henry Tyler asked his legal help in reorganizing the property that became the Chicago & Grand Trunk and McMillan became a director of the company. Also in 1879, McMillan and a group of Detroit businessmen formed the Detroit, Mackinac & Marquette to build a railroad from the Straits of Mackinac to Marquette. The idea had first taken form soon after the end of the Civil War and the Marquette, Sault Ste. Marie & Mackinac had been formed in 1872 to build it. Despite a substantial grant of state land, the Panic of 1873 did in the MSSM&M. McMillan and his friends obtained the state land grant and began construction in 1880. In 1880, they also formed a company to build a bridge over the St. Marys River at Sault Ste. Marie, and in 1881, a company called the Sault Ste. Marie & Marquette. The line between St. Ignace and Marquette was completed on December 19, 1881.[141] McMillan and his friends gained new wealth from the company until it went into bankruptcy in 1886.

Russell A. Alger made his money in lumbering. Along the Lake Huron shore he had built several small logging railroads to reach his timber lands. The most important of them was the Tawas & Bay County, which he bought in 1882 and sold to his Bay City & Alpena. In 1883, he extended it to connect with the Mackinaw Branch of the Michigan Central. On September 20, 1886, he completed the road into Alpena as the Detroit, Bay City & Alpena.[142]

In 1880, a familiar name returned to Michigan railroading—James F. Joy. That year Joy became a director of the Fort Wayne & Jackson, a position he retained until his death in 1896. In 1881, Joy persuaded McMillan, Alger, and Christian H. Buhl to join him in forming the Detroit, Butler & St. Louis. Jay Gould's Wabash, St. Louis & Pacific had been operating into Detroit by using other railroads from Toledo to Detroit. But relying on Vanderbilt goodwill did not appeal to Gould. He also owned the Detroit, Eel River & Illinois, which extended as far as Butler, Indiana, but had gotten no farther toward Detroit. Apparently Joy and Gould had a meeting of the minds, and Joy proceeded to build a line between Detroit and Butler. The road was completed on August 15, 1881, and before it was finished it was sold to the Wabash.[143] Gould made Joy a director. When the Wabash went into receivership in 1884, Gould resigned the presidency of the road. Joy took his place until 1887, when he dropped out of active management.

Once the Wabash was into Detroit, Gould tried to pressure the Great Western into allowing him to run trains over that road between Windsor and Niagara Falls. The Great Western was more concerned with preserving amicable relations with Vanderbilt and with fending off the merger proposed by the Grand Trunk. Gould received no special favor, but he did route freight over the Great Western rather than give it to Vanderbilt's Lake Shore line at Toledo.[144]

The Great Western was having no easy time of it. It depended on the favor of William H. Vanderbilt for traffic connections at both ends of its line. Also, it competed against Vanderbilt's Canada Southern over its entire route. Finally, there was Sir Henry Tyler, whose Grand Trunk's announced purpose was to acquire the Great Western. Tyler was concerned that the Canadian Pacific Railway, with government backing for a transcontinental line, was assembling a Quebec-Toronto route. Once into Toronto, the CP would be able to connect to the Great Western and become a formidable competitor, and Tyler had to prevent this.[145] Rather than continue negotiating with the GW's management, Tyler went directly to its stockholders. They had some more clarity of vision, and in 1882 leased the GW to the Grand Trunk.[146]

With the lease of the Great Western, Tyler also gained ownership of the Detroit & Milwaukee in Michigan. That company had gone through another receivership in 1875, and emerged from it as the Detroit, Grand Haven & Milwaukee. Tyler had some hope of extending his railroad into Toledo, since he could no longer use Vanderbilt rails between Detroit and Toledo. He began extending the Michigan Air Line, and it was completed to Pontiac in 1880. He then swung to South Lyon where he could connect with James Ashley's Ann Arbor Railroad to Toledo.[147] The MAL was pushed on to Jackson in 1884.[148] The Toledo connection through South Lyon never developed satisfactorily.

In 1887-88, a line named the Toledo, Saginaw & Muskegon was built from Ashley to Muskegon. Its route paralleled the Detroit, Grand Haven & Milwaukee line but the company appears to have been short of capital. Tyler bought up the company in 1888 to prevent any other road buying it.[149] Some of the same owners also formed the Toledo, Saginaw & Mackinaw, and between 1888 and 1890 built its line between Durand and Bay City.[150] In 1890, its owners renamed the road the Cincinnati, Saginaw & Mackinaw and offered it to the Grand Trunk. Tyler wasn't quite so sure about it and initially signed only a ten-year lease of the road.[151]

Probably the most flamboyant of all of Michigan's railroad personalities was James M. Ashley. Ashley had been a congressman and served as territorial governor of Montana. His home was Toledo, and he is reported to have said, "I got out of a job in politics, came back to Toledo, and, having no business to get back into and very little money, I decided to build a railroad."[152] In 1877, Ashley bought the grade and franchise of the Toledo, Ann Arbor & Northern and formed the Toledo & Ann Arbor to build the line. He was able to raise enough money in the Ann Arbor area to build, and completed the line in 1878. Ashley persuaded Thomas Scott of the Pennsylvania to sell him a short line to reach downtown Toledo. In 1878, Ashley formed another company to build a line from Ann Arbor to Pontiac. He probably figured that at South Lyon he could get the Toledo-bound traffic of the Detroit, Lansing & Northern, and at Pontiac similar traffic from the Grand Trunk-owned Michigan Air Line. In 1881 Ashley formed the Toledo & Saginaw Bay to build a line from Pontiac into the Thumb. After the September 1881 forest fire that devastated the Thumb area, Ashley changed his plans. He decided to build into northern Michigan lumber country. In 1882, he incorporated the Toledo, Ann Arbor & North Michigan and in 1883 bought a graded line that extended from Owosso to St. Louis.

Ashley was the contractor for building his own lines. He would form a construction company, sign an agreement to build a line, and when it was completed, would sell it to his own North Michigan company. Ashley's usual price was $20,000 per mile in capital stock and $20,000 in mortgage bonds. The bonds he would sell for what he could get to raise construction funds; the stock he kept for himself. Using this technique, he had been able to build the Toledo-South Lyon line, then from Owosso to St. Louis, and then to join the two disconnected sections. By 1884, it appears that Ashley had decided to build to Lake Michigan and to establish a railroad ferry service across the lake. By 1886, his road was completed into Mt. Pleasant and he incorporated a construction company to build to Cadillac. In 1889, he formed another company to build to Frankfort—a good harbor on Lake Michigan. Ashley toyed with the idea of building to the Straits of Mackinac, and in 1891 formed a company to do so, but then dropped the idea. In 1889 he connected up with the Frankfort & Southeastern, which had built a line southeast from Frankfort. In 1890, Ashley placed an order for two railroad car ferries to operate across Lake Michigan, and began a break-bulk freight service that lasted until the delivery of the ferries.

It was quite an accomplishment. James M. Ashley had been able to "push a railroad three hundred miles into new undeveloped territory with inadequate money, 'on wind' as Jim Ashley, Junior, put it."[153] Ashley used every tactic available to build his railroad. He built where he could get free land, or for the price of free passes. When he couldn't buy he simply built and let the landowner sue. He muscled his way across other railroads by building on Sundays when no court injunction could be issued to stop him. And he built the entire project with borrowed money.

As the Detroit, Lansing & Northern and the Chicago & West Michigan came out of their reorganizations after the Panic of 1873, they were operated as separate companies, but had identical owners from Boston. In 1879, these men bought the Saginaw Valley & St. Louis which lumberman Ammi W. Wright had built in 1873. In 1881, they bought, at foreclosure, the Chicago, Saginaw & Canada, which, despite its impressive name and the presidential talents of Civil War general Daniel Sickles, owned only a thirty-five-mile line west from Alma.[154]

The Detroit, Lansing & Northern had its capital restructured and its deficits capitalized as part of the reorganization of 1876. The cleanup allowed the road to show a profit every year until 1893. The same actions were taken with the Chicago & West Michigan when it was reorganized in 1879. In 1881, the C&WM bought the Grand Haven Railroad, the Grand Rapids, Newaygo & Lake Shore, and the Indiana & Michigan, which extended from New Buffalo to LaCrosse, Indiana. In 1884, the New England owners put the very capable John B. Mulliken, the DL&N's general manager, in charge of all of their roads. To further develop their railroads, a new company was formed in 1887 to link them together. By August 1888, a line between Grand Ledge and Grand Rapids was completed and an improved east-west route was established. In 1891, the

C&WM formed the Chicago & North Michigan to extend from Baldwin to the Straits of Mackinac. By June 1892, the line was completed as far as Bay View. The principal benefit was the entry to untapped lumber territory.The Flint & Pere Marquette came out of receivership in 1879 in a stronger position. The company had built a number of branches which fed traffic onto its main line headed for the lumber mills at Saginaw. Much of the timber from Clare County moved on F&PM rails. Traffic across Lake Michigan by ferry from Ludington added to revenues and continued to make a substantial contribution in the 1880s as the lumber traffic began to diminish. In 1889, the F&PM bought the Port Huron & North Western, which gave it entry to the Thumb area. The PH&NW had begun a decade earlier as a narrow-gauge railroad and when purchased extended from Port Huron north to Harbor Beach, Bad Axe and Port Austin and from Port Huron west to Saginaw. The Saginaw-Port Huron line proved the most valuable part of the deal, since it provided a good connection with the Grand Trunk Railway of Canada for eastbound shipments. The acquisition never proved especially profitable for the F&PM, but did eventually provide the connection to the Canadian Division when it was acquired after the turn of the century.

In the Upper Peninsula the Marquette, Houghton & Ontonagon continued its business of hauling iron ore from the mines to its dock in Marquette. Although it lost money during the Panic of 1873, it was able to avoid receivership. Its owners rode out the hard times, retired some of its bond debt by an issue of preferred stock, and by 1880 the company had a net surplus. In July 1883, the MH&O completed a line to Houghton.[155]

The Detroit, Mackinac & Marquette, as mentioned earlier, was completed between St. Ignace and Marquette in December 1881. To prop up the company, it announced in 1883 that it would build west from Marquette to Ishpeming and the iron mines in that vicinity. That same year the DM&M's owners incorporated the Marquette & Western for that purpose and completed the road within twelve months.[156] The MH&O did not need this competition, and in any event, the DM&M was probably not strong enough to force the issue on a sustained basis. The MH&O arranged a lease of the Marquette & Western and admitted James McMillan and his son, Hugh, to its board. One of McMillan's partners in the DM&M was George I. Seney, who was heavily involved in the construction of the New York, Chicago & St. Louis Railroad—the Nickel Plate Road. Seney, its president Columbus R. Cummings, and vice president Calvin S. Brice, sold the Nickel Plate to William Henry Vanderbilt in October 1882. More accurately, Vanderbilt bought it to suppress a road that might become an unwelcome competitor.[157]

Seney must have felt the MH&O was a good deal, for the group bought into it in 1886. McMillan became the MH&O's president, and Seney, Brice, and Cummings all joined the board. In September, McMillan organized the Wisconsin, Sault Ste. Marie & Mackinac to extend the MH&O west to the Wisconsin state line near Ironwood. In December 1886, they formed the Duluth, South Shore & Atlantic, which was to consolidate the MH&O, the WSSM&M, the Marquette & Western, and the DM&M when it emerged from its foreclosure sale. The new company issued $22,000,000 in common and preferred stock and $4,000,000 in bonds for its capital, equal to the $26,000,000 it showed for the cost of its road and equipment.[158] This amount is nearly equal to the combined amounts of its predecessors, even though the DM&M had been through foreclosure. It appears that the DM&M's owners came out of the foreclosure financially intact. In October 1887, the DSS&A completed its branch line to Sault Ste. Marie, and in September 1888, completed its line west to Duluth.[159] At Duluth the DSS&A made a connection with Henry Villard's Northern Pacific Railroad—a valuable traffic feeder.

There had been other lines projected to reach the Soo. Since about 1880, the idea of a road connecting Minneapolis with the Soo had been talked about. Several companies had been formed to build it, but nothing came of the idea. The motive behind all of this was the line that the Canadian Pacific announced it was going to build to Sault Ste. Marie, Ontario. In 1883, a group of Minneapolis businessmen, headed by John S. Pillsbury, formed the Minneapolis, Sault Ste. Marie & Atlantic, and began construction east from the Twin Cities. In 1885, they formed the Menominee & Sault Ste. Marie to build the road in Michigan. The road was opened to formal public service on January 1, 1888.[160] In June, the company added some other out-of-state companies and became the Minneapolis, St. Paul & Sault Ste. Marie—but was much better known as the Soo Line.

The contrast between the Soo Line and the DSS&A after Seney-McMillan took over is remarkable. The commissioner of railroads for Michigan reported in his 1888 *Annual Report* that the Soo Line's 787 miles were built at a cost of $39,000,000, and the company capitalized, both stock and bonds, at a total of $42,000,000. This works out at a cost of $49,000 per mile, and a capitalization of $54,500 per mile. The DSS&A showed a cost of $28,600,000, a per mile cost of $73,500 for its 390 miles, and had a capitalization of $83,500 per mile. The commissioner, as he commented on his inspection trips over the two roads, was complimentary of the Soo, but made a number of critical observations about the quality of the DSS&A.[161]

In 1888, the two companies and the Canadian Pacific joined together to build a bridge over the St. Marys River at the Soo.[162] To insure the friendliness of its Michigan connections, the CP began buying into both companies. In 1888, three Canadians were sitting on the board of the DSS&A, one of whom was William C. Van Horne, the genius behind the expansion of the

Canadian Pacific, and in 1890 he also took a seat on the Soo Line's board. Controlling interest of both companies moved into CP hands.[163]

The Copper Country saw its first railroad in 1867, when the Calumet & Hecla Company built a narrow-gauge line between its mines at Red Jacket and Calumet and its stamp mill at Lake Linden.[164] It was pretty much a company operation and didn't haul much except C&H freight. In 1872, the Mineral Range was formed to connect Hancock and Calumet and its line was finished before the end of the next year.[165] When a competing company, the Hancock & Calumet, was formed in 1885, its operations were taken over by the Mineral Range. In 1888, the MR went into receivership and was acquired the next year by new owners. They did not appear to want the company, and in 1892-93 a majority of MR stock was acquired by the DSS&A, which provided its only rail connection.

The Vulcan Mine, near Quinnesec, was opened in 1877, and the Chicago & North Western formed a subsidiary and built to the mine. As the Menominee Range developed, other subsidiaries extended further, first to Iron Mountain, then Crystal Falls, then to Caspian and Iron River, which it reached in 1882.[166] The ore was moved to the C&NW's massive ore docks at Escanaba. The western part of the Upper Peninsula and the Gogebic Range were reached by another company—the Milwaukee, Lake Shore & Western. This company's predecessors dated back to 1866, and by 1884 its rails had reached Ironwood. The next year the road was opened to the Lake Superior port at Ashland, Wisconsin, and Gogebic Range ore began moving there. The MLS&W competed with the C&NW between Milwaukee and Green Bay. Although the MLS&W appears to have been in no particular financial difficulty, the C&NW offer to buy was attractive enough to persuade its owners to sell. The C&NW completed purchase of the company in 1893.[167]

One last Upper Peninsula company made real progress before the Panic of 1893. The Milwaukee & Northern was incorporated in Wisconsin in the early 1870s, and began building a line due north from Milwaukee to Green Bay. In 1884, it completed a branch line into Menominee, and in 1887, completed its main line through Iron Mountain and Republic to Champion.[168] At Champion it connected with the DSS&A to Marquette and the Copper Country. In 1890, the M&N bought a rundown line called the Ontonagon & Brule River which had managed to build about forty-five miles of line between Ontonagon and Sidnaw.[169] It had to use DSS&A tracks to bridge the gap between Champion and Sidnaw. It was not until later that it built its own line between Channing and Sidnaw. The Chicago, Milwaukee & St. Paul bought control of the M&N in June 1893, and eventually merged the company.[170]

A new type of rail service gained prominence in the 1880s, but had its Michigan beginnings in the early 1860s. In 1863, the Detroit City Railway was formed with a modest $100,000 capitalization. The next year it began horse-drawn street car service on Jefferson Avenue between Third Street and Mt. Elliott. Lines soon appeared on Woodward, Michigan, and Gratiot Avenues. Within the next ten years other lines, owned by other companies, appeared in Detroit.

Saginaw appears to have had the first street railway, beginning in December 1863. By 1865, Bay City, Port Huron, and Grand Rapids had horse-car lines. These expanded quite slowly until the 1880s, when a new interest in this form of city transport developed. Between 1882 and 1886 Jackson, Battle Creek, Kalamazoo, Lansing, Muskegon, and Sault Ste. Marie all acquired horse-car lines. Most were modest ventures. Battle Creek's first company was capitalized at $25,000, as was Muskegon's, the Soo's for $25,300, and Jackson's for $50,000.

The use of horses or mules posed a serious limitation on the development of this form of transport. First was the cost of buying, feeding, and caring for the animals. Speed was slow. Hills were an insurmountable obstacle. Disease was always a factor. In the 1880s attempts were made to adapt electricity to this service. In 1888, Frank J. Sprague successfully installed an electric operation in Richmond, Virginia, and the barrier to expansion was eliminated.

Existing horse-drawn lines were converted to electric operation. New systems came into existence in Adrian, Ann Arbor, and Benton Harbor. By 1900, every major city in Michigan had electric street car service.

The urge to consolidate companies was equally strong. In 1883, the Street Railway Company of Grand Rapids increased its capital from $50,000 to $400,000 and bought three other companies. By 1890, all the lines in the city were owned by one company. In Detroit a similar process took longer. Between 1876 and 1882 the Detroit City Railway bought up four other companies. It was eventually acquired by the Detroit Citizens' Street Railway in 1891. Detroit Citizens' also bought the Grand River Railway and leased the Detroit Suburban (which was the owner of five earlier companies), and the Detroit, Fort Wayne & Belle Isle. Detroit Citizens' was capitalized at $4,000,000—a major investment in that day for a strictly local enterprise.

THE PANIC OF 1893 TO THE END OF THE CENTURY

By the beginning of 1893, the Michigan railroad network was substantially completed. There would be more construction during the next twenty-five years, but the major systems were in place much as they would exist for the next fifty years. The business Panic of 1893 was more an industrial depression—throwing laborers out of work, closing factories, forcing foreclosures, and liquidating businesses. The Panic of 1873 had been brought on by a shortage of capital induced by a lack of profitability. But this time railroad profits were affected dramatically, and before the Panic of 1893 had run its course, some 170 railroad companies in the U.S., with nearly thirty-eight thousand miles of track, had gone into receivership.[171]

In Michigan new construction nearly came to a stop. During the years 1894-1898, only 314 miles of new road were built, and half of that mileage was built in one year—1896. The larger Michigan roads came through the Panic with their profits unimpaired. But a number of roads had very real financial problems. The first road to go into receivership was James M. Ashley's Toledo, Ann Arbor & North Michigan on April 27, 1893. Through 1890, expanding revenues and new borrowings had kept the company solvent. In 1891, revenues dropped and expenses had to be cut sharply to keep profits high enough to cover interest payments on the debt. In 1892, net income barely covered interest payments. In 1893, the delivery of two car ferries and new locomotives and rolling stock added more than $1,000,000 to road and equipment assets and these were paid for with more borrowings. Net income that year was negligible and some $3,000,000 in new debt was put on the books. The company's earnings simply did not support the amount of interest that had to be paid on borrowed funds. In September 1895, the company was reorganized into a new company that was called the Ann Arbor Railroad.

The Detroit, Bay City & Alpena went into receivership in October 1893. Its staple traffic was lumber, and tonnage had dropped from 885,500 tons hauled in 1890 to 508,000 in 1893. The company was not able to pay all of its bond interest in 1891 and 1892. In 1894, lumber traffic was down to 154,000 tons, and the receiver was able to cut expenses by only about forty percent from 1893. President Alger and his friends also formed the Alpena & Northern in 1893 as a traffic connection. In December 1894, the DBC&A was reorganized by the bondholders as the Detroit & Mackinac and James D. Hawks, its new president, began his long career in Michigan railroading. The following spring the D&M bought the Alpena & Northern.

The Cincinnati, Jackson & Mackinaw Railroad had one of Michigan's more appealing corporate names—and it was as weak financially as its name was impressive. It was incorporated in 1886 and was in receivership by the end of 1889. In January 1892, it was reorganized as the CJ&M Railway. In December 1894, it was back in receivership. In 1895, the CJ&M's owners incorporated the Jackson & Cincinnati to finish the line by building an extension from Addison Junction to Jackson. The work was completed the next spring. In January 1897, the CJ&M's east-west line from Dundee to Allegan was sold to a company that became the Detroit, Toledo & Milwaukee, and soon came under the control of the Vanderbilts. Its line from Addison Junction through Ohio, nearly to Cincinnati, was sold to the Cincinnati Northern. In 1898, the CN bought the Jackson & Cincinnati and had a through line with good traffic outlets at Jackson.

The Grand Rapids & Indiana suffered from a loss of traffic in the early 1890s and its owners decided to put the company through a foreclosure in 1896. The road had not been able to cover its bond interest for some years, and the Pennsylvania Railroad had been advancing the money to pay it. The reorganization got rid of nearly $6,000,000 in debt, enabling net income to cover the bond interest. The Pennsylvania remained in firm control of the company.

In the summer of 1896, a small road named the Lima Northern was able to build a line from Lima, Ohio to Adrian.[172] As it was finishing this project, it went through a reorganization and became the Detroit & Lima Northern, now with the goal of building to Detroit. The next year the D&LN pushed north into Tecumseh. Then it acquired trackage rights to Dundee, bought a little used line to a place named Chandler, opposite Grosse Ile, and built a line from there into Detroit in 1898.[173] The combined costs of extending to Detroit and also extending its line south from Lima were too much, and the company went into receivership in September 1898. The receivership lasted until May 1901.[174]

On April 1, 1896, the Detroit, Lansing & Northern went into receivership. Net income had been dropping for ten years, much of it from a loss of lumber traffic, and the company was no longer able to pay its bond interest. A new line, the Detroit, Grand Rapids & Western, took over on January 1, 1897. Included in the new company were the Saginaw Valley & St. Louis and some other smaller subsidiaries. The Chicago & West Michigan was experiencing some of the same problems, but not as severely. By 1893 however, its earnings no longer covered its bond interest and the company had to dip into accumulated earnings. The Flint & Pere Marquette was the strongest of the three companies. In November 1896, it completed an extension from Monroe to Toledo which gave a number of very favorable connections.[175] President William W. Crapo felt there was an opportunity at hand and proposed a consolidation of his company with the other two. The Boston owners of the DGR&W and C&WM agreed to a merger and out of it came the Pere Marquette Railroad in November 1899.

The predecessor companies of the PM used the common, but pernicious practice of reorganizing a company by exchanging bonded debt for an issue of stock and by increasing the cost of the road itself by the amount of the accumulated deficit from operations. The result was a restructured company that began life with interest expense that could be covered by net income from operations, and with the profit and loss account set to zero because accumulated losses had been transferred to the book value of the road. To expand its operations, build a new line, or buy new cars or locomotives the company had to resort to the bond market for more money. As the interest costs increased, or if net income from operating the road decreased, the company again faced the identical problem that brought it to life. The outcome was often another reorganization and the cycle was set in motion again.

This was exactly the condition faced by the newly reorganized Pere Marquette. Its three predecessor companies had issued a total of $22,800,000 in common and preferred stock. The new PM replaced this with a total of $24,300,000—some of the excess necessary to persuade former owners to agree to the reorganization. In addition, the PM held another $3,700,000 in stock in its treasury to be used for some future purpose. The three roads had a total of $28,900,000 in debt, and this was exchanged dollar for dollar for the debt of the new company. To complete the situation, the road account was increased by $4,300,000, although the actual cost of the physical plant did not warrant such a change.[176]

The Chicago & Grand Trunk faced the same problem of having net income not able to cover the debt interest. Its owner, the Grand Trunk of Canada, was considering adding a second track to the Port Huron-Chicago main line to handle freight traffic more efficiently. The GT decided to let the C&GT go through a "friendly" foreclosure sale to restructure the debt burden. On November 20, 1900, only twenty days after the C&GT foreclosure sale, a new company emerged—the Grand Trunk Western Railway.

THE TURN OF THE CENTURY TO WORLD WAR I

At the opening of the new century the Michigan railroad network was pretty much in place. Every major main line in use today had been built by 1900. Total mileage at the beginning of 1900 was 7,929. This increased to a high point of 9,059 miles at the end of 1909, and then began a gradual downward trend. Although nearly every year saw new lines constructed, more and more this was offset by abandonments.

Many company names still familiar today had been established by this time: the Vanderbilt's Michigan Central, Lake Shore & Michigan Southern, and Big Four; the Pennsylvania; Grand Trunk Western; Ann Arbor; Detroit & Mackinac; Pere Marquette; Wabash; and Detroit & Toledo Shore Line. In the Upper Peninsula there were the Chicago & North Western; Duluth, South Shore & Atlantic; Minneapolis, St. Paul & Sault Ste. Marie (better known as the Soo Line); and the Chicago, Milwaukee & St. Paul (the Milwaukee Road to railroaders or "the St. Paul" for many residents of the U.P.). The Copper Range, the Mineral Range, and the Wisconsin & Michigan all were operating.

The newly-formed Pere Marquette's entry into the new century was not an auspicious one. President William W. Crapo, the son of Governor Henry H. Crapo, who had been involved in the early years of the Flint & Pere Marquette, had been president of the Flint & Pere Marquette since 1882. Charles M. Heald had served as president of both the Chicago & West Michigan and the Detroit, Grand Rapids & Western before the merger. These two capable railroaders moved the new PM on a cautious course. They bought several small feeder lines in 1900 to build up traffic. They spent what money they could to rehabilitate the tracks and buy new equipment. But their careful approach did not satisfy some of the directors.

By the end of 1902, F. H. Prince and a group of associates acquired working control of the PM by buying its common stock. Both Crapo and Heald resigned and the PM was left to Prince's ambitions. He envisioned the PM becoming an important east-west carrier and set out on a program to accomplish this. The first step, in late 1903, was to lease the Lake Erie & Detroit River from the Walker family. The LE&DR owned a line that extended from Walkerville, near Windsor, to St. Thomas, Ontario and a branch line extending from Sarnia southeast to Lake Erie at Erieau. East of St. Thomas he was able to negotiate running rights over the Canada Southern to the Niagara River at Suspension Bridge and at Black Rock. Later he obtained rights into Buffalo and East Buffalo and then had direct connections with all roads operating from Buffalo.

The next step was to incorporate a line to extend west from New Buffalo. By the end of the 1903, this extension was finished to Porter, Indiana and surveys had been made as far as Hammond. Prince was able to arrange running rights over the Lake Shore & Michigan Southern and several other roads and pieced together a route into Chicago more quickly than by building his own. In later years some changes were made in the companies used, but Prince did get the PM into Chicago.

The last phase was an attempt to shorten the PM's distance between Chicago and Detroit by building a cutoff. In 1903, the PM picked up three small lines in southwestern Michigan, although Prince most wanted the part of the South Haven & Eastern extending from Hartford to Paw Paw. Prince then went out to buy the Chicago, Kalamazoo & Saginaw—a line from Kalamazoo northeasterly to a junction with the PM at Woodbury. If he could buy the CK&S and build not quite twenty miles of line between Paw Paw and Kalamazoo, Prince could cut about thirty miles off his east-west main route, and have entry to Kalamazoo as a bonus. Just what happened in the negotiations is not a matter of record, but Prince's attempt to buy the CK&S failed; it went to the Michigan Central in 1906. The MC had no particular need of the straggling road, but the Vanderbilts must have felt they had helped Prince (and themselves) enough with the two ends of his line, and there was no need to make him into a major competitor by allowing him this added advantage.

Prince succeeded in making the PM into a more important midwestern carrier. The critical aspect of this rush to expand was that it was done entirely with borrowed funds. To dress up the company's appearance, and maintain the ability to borrow more money, dividends were paid. The funds to pay them came from reduced maintenance of the tracks and from short-term borrowings.

But Prince and his friends were not finished with the PM. There was money to be made. In 1904, the PM issued more bonds and bought a line from Hammond, Indiana to Cincinnati. It was owned by a member of the Prince syndicate and it was unloaded on the PM at an inflated price. Next, the syndicate bought Prince's PM stock at an astronomical $125 per share and turned it over the Cincinnati, Hamilton & Dayton Railway, which the syndicate also controlled, and which paid for the stock with its own bonds. Then the syndicate leased, and later sold, the Toledo Terminal & Railway to the PM to provide terminal facilities neither the PM nor the CH&D either needed or wanted.

Now, having squeezed out about all they could from both the PM and the CH&D, Prince and friends went to J. P. Morgan and asked his help to sell both the PM and the CH&D. There is some disagreement as to whether Morgan went to the Erie Railroad or the Erie came to Morgan but, in any event, the Erie bought the CH&D—and control of the PM—at $160 per share for the CH&D stock.

Almost within hours, the Erie found out how a bad bargain it had made. It went back to Morgan crying foul. Morgan played the innocent broker, claimed he would never knowingly mislead the Erie, and bought back the CH&D. Morgan had no use for it and could not sell it. He allowed both the PM and the CH&D to go into receivership in December 1905. William W. Crapo was brought back as receiver of the PM. Crapo did what he could to fix the PM's shabby financial structure. He disposed of the Hammond-Cincinnati line to the CH&D, which thought it could do something with it. He got the Toledo Terminal purchase cancelled and the PM received some damages for being misused. But that was about it. Crapo was unable to make any substantial change in the debt structure of the PM and its interest charges remained higher than could be covered by net earnings. The receivership ended in December 1907, just as the nation was sliding into the Panic of 1907.

In August 1909, the reorganized CH&D, which still retained controlling interest in the PM, was sold to the Baltimore & Ohio Railroad through the efforts of J. P. Morgan. The PM showed a profit in 1909 and 1910, but had a $1,800,000 deficit in 1911. Expenses for labor and materials increased sharply, and continued to rise over the next few years. The Baltimore & Ohio soon grew to feel that the PM was not a natural partner for it or for its CH&D. It put the CH&D's block of PM stock up for sale and in March 1911, J. P. Morgan bought it.

The PM was now in critical need of repair, of new equipment, and of refinancing on some of its maturing bonds. Morgan agreed to loan the PM $8,000,000, minus his five percent commission, upon the security of $16,000,000 in PM bonds. This was followed by other borrowings of smaller amounts, but all of the efforts only postponed the end. In April 1912, the PM went back into receivership. There it remained until April 1917, by which time $8,000,000 in capital stock and $36,000,000 in debt had been cut out of the financial structure of the company. These drastic measures brought the PM's interest charges down to a level that could be covered by reasonable earnings.

The growth of the electric street car system in Detroit provided modern transportation for all parts of the city. The owners of the companies had no end of difficulty with the city over franchises for the use of streets, and over fares to be charged. In 1890, Mayor Hazen S. Pingree led the call for city ownership of the street car lines. In 1894, Pingree's creation, the Detroit Railway, was formed. This company was to build some lines and would acquire the rest of the privately-owned companies. It never took place. Although it did build some lines, after Pingree became governor in 1896 the company was sold to the Detroit Electric Railway—and into private hands.

At the same time, some electric lines were being built from the city into its suburbs. A line to Wyandotte was built in 1893, and another to Mt. Clemens in 1895. The best known, the Ann Arbor & Ypsilanti Street Railway—the "Ypsi-Ann"—first ran in 1890 with horses pulling the cars. It was converted to electric operation in 1896.[177] Other entrepreneurs proposed a network that would spread in all directions from Detroit.

These ambitious schemes attracted the attention of two ambitious men from Cleveland, Henry A. Everett and Edward W. Moore. They already owned electric lines in Ohio as well some other utilities, and had plans to build more. At the end of December 1900, the Detroit United Railway was formed with a capital of $12,500,000. Its intent was to buy up all of the street car lines in the city of Detroit. Everett and Moore controlled the DUR and, on December 31, 1900, merged all of the city's street car companies.

This was just the beginning. The DUR acquired the Detroit & Port Huron Shore Line, which controlled all of the companies that made up the line from Detroit to Port Huron as well as the Port Huron city operation. Next, DUR bought the Detroit & Pontiac, the Detroit & Flint, and the Wyandotte & Detroit River. They incorporated the Detroit, Monroe & Toledo Short Line and built a high-speed heavy-duty line. At Toledo this connected with

Duluth, South Shore & Atlantic's freight locomotive 702, circa 1914

Everett and Moore's Lake Shore Electric to Cleveland, and some cars ran through from Detroit to Cleveland.

West of Detroit, they obtained control of the Detroit, Jackson & Chicago. That company had a line from Detroit to Jackson, branches to Saline, Plymouth and Northville, and a city operation in Ann Arbor.

Much of the interurban system—the intercity electric lines—were economically built as side-of-the-road opeations. The system concentrated on carrying passengers and left freight hauling to be an incidental byproduct. But the service did make money. Enough so that, until 1903, Detroit had more interurban lines radiating from it than any other city in the U.S.

Outstate there was just as much enthusiasm for interurbans. In 1894, a Saginaw-Bay City line began operating. In 1900, Michigan Traction built a line between Battle Creek and Kalamazoo, and then acquired the city street car lines in both cities. In 1905, its owners sold the company to a group headed by Myron W. Mills of Port Huron. Mills was building a traction empire of his own. In August 1903, he bought the Lansing City Electric Railway from J. D. Hawks and S. F. Angus, and followed this in 1904 with the Lansing & Suburban Traction, which had acquired the Lansing-St. Johns route. In 1905, he formed a construction company to build an interurban line between Jackson and Lansing, and also added the Jackson-Battle Creek line to his collection.

Hawks and Angus bought the "Ypsi-Ann" in 1898 and folded it into their Detroit, Ypsilanti & Ann Arbor Railway. In 1901, they formed the Detroit, Ypsilanti, Ann Arbor & Jackson Railway and began building from Ann Arbor to Jackson. At the same time, William A. Boland and William A. Foote of Jackson began building their own line from Jackson to Ann Arbor. They collided with each other near Michigan Center and Boland-Foote sold out to Hawks and Angus. In July 1907, all the lines were merged into a new company—the Detroit, Jackson & Chicago—and it was leased to the Detroit United Railway.

In December 1911, Boland and Foote formed the Michigan United Traction Company and bought heavily into Mills' Michigan United Railways. Boland and Foote had impressive sums from New York at their disposal. In 1911, Mills picked up a lease of the Kalamazoo, Lake Shore & Chicago, with an eye to electrifying the rundown steam railroad and incorporating its Kalamazoo-South Haven line into his system. Nothing came of this plan, and after years of losses, KLS&C went back to its owners in 1916. In April 1912, Mills agreed to lease all of his lines to Boland and Foote. With the help of his New York friends, Foote acquired all of the lines in the Saginaw-Bay City area and the Saginaw-Flint line. In 1915, he built the most modern interurban line in Michigan—a high-speed run between Kalamazoo and Grand Rapids. In

April 1916, he leased the Grand Rapids, Holland & Chicago, which operated from Grand Rapids through Holland to Saugatuck. As he acquired and leased properties, they were folded in the Michigan Railway, which was formed in March 1914 as a holding company. The Michigan Railway, in turn, was controlled by Commonwealth Power, Railway & Light, a holding companies that owned electric and gas utility company in outstate Michigan, principally Consumers Power Company.[178]

A number of smaller interurbans developed around the state. In 1902, the Grand Rapids, Grand Haven & Muskegon was built, and in 1912 it became the property of United Light & Railways Company. The Benton Harbor & St. Joseph Electric Railway & Light Company bought the lines in both cities in 1900, then built an interurban line to Eau Clair in 1906, extended it to Dowagiac in 1911, and built another line to Watervliet in 1910. In 1906, the Southern Michigan Railway began running cars from South Bend to St. Joseph. The Toledo & Western built a line between Toledo and Adrian by the end of 1901, and in 1902 and 1903 built a line from Allen Junction to Pioneer, Ohio, which had a curve through Morenci. In 1907, the T&W and the Toledo, Ottawa Beach & Northern came under the control of the Toledo Railway & Light Company. In the Upper Peninsula, the Houghton County Street Railway built from Houghton to Calumet in 1900. By 1908, it had extended its lines to Mohawk and also built a branch from Calumet to Lake Linden.

The Detroit & Lima Northern emerged from its reorganization, in May 1901 as the Detroit Southern. As part of the reorganization it absorbed the Ohio Southern, and in this way acquired a route that extended from Detroit to the Ohio River at Ironton, Ohio. The DS's traffic did not materialize as rapidly as it was able to spend money upgrading the property. The mild Panic of 1903 did the road in and it went back into receivership. In May 1905, it was reorganized as the Detroit, Toledo & Ironton Railway. In June, it bought controlling interest in the Ann Arbor Railroad. The AA proved to be no financial reward for its new owner, and in February 1908 the DT&I was back in receivership. In 1910, it sold off its Ann Arbor stock, but it was not until February 1914 that the DT&I came out of receivership as the DT&I Railroad. In 1916, it bought up a short line that provided a branch to Toledo. The DT&I had some thoughts about extending the Toledo branch to Ann Arbor, but nothing came of it.

The Vanderbilt family remained the predominant railroad owners in Michigan. The Vanderbilt's New York Central & Hudson River owned the majority of stock of the Lake Shore & Michigan Southern, the Michigan Central, and the Canada Southern, which had subsidiaries in Michigan. Both the LS&MS and the MC owned and leased other lines in Michigan as well as in other states. The Vanderbilts also controlled the Cleveland, Cincinnati, Chicago & St. Louis, better known as the Big Four, which came into Michigan through its lease of the Cincinnati, Wabash & Michigan which, in turn, owned a line extending from Louisville, Kentucky, through Elkhart and Niles, to Benton Harbor. In 1902 the Big Four leased the Cincinnati Northern which owned the line from Cincinnati to Jackson. The CN had already leased the Detroit, Toledo & Milwaukee's Dundee-Allegan line, but gave it up in 1902 and the DT&M stock was parcelled out, half to the MC and half to the LS&MS.

Commodore Vanderbilt, and William Henry after him, picked up all the railroads they could as they went along. Both Vanderbilts' main concern was that they reduce competition as much as possible, and the easiest way was to buy the competitor. If they didn't own the line outright, they were content with a long-term lease. The result was an impenetrable tangle of ownerships, leases, or stock ownership. Subsidiaries had subsidiaries that had other subsidiaries. Sometime after 1910, headquarters decided something should be done to simplify affairs. In April 1914, a consolidation agreement was finally signed that formed the New York Central Railroad. Into it disappeared the New York Central & Hudson River, the Dunkirk, Allegheny Valley & Pittsburg, the Chicago, Indiana & Southern, the Geneva, Corning & Southern, terminal railroads in Toledo and Buffalo, and in Michigan the Lake Shore & Michigan Southern, the Detroit, Monroe & Toledo, the Northern Central Michigan, the Kalamazoo & White Pigeon, and the Detroit & Chicago (which was a reorganized former subsidiary of the Canada Southern). It all became effective January 1, 1915. Six months later the NYC bought the Sturgis, Goshen & St. Louis. The NYC continued the leases of roads it did not own: the Kalamazoo, Allegan & Grand Rapids, the Fort Wayne & Jackson, and the Detroit, Hillsdale & Southwestern.

Getting this done was an ordeal and the NYC decided it had had enough. It contented itself thereafter with just owning a large majority of the stock of the Michigan Central, the Canada Southern, and the Big Four. It was not until 1930 that this arrangement was changed and those companies leased to the NYC. In September 1916, the Michigan Central consolidated nine companies, comprising almost all of its branchline network, that up to that time it had leased: the Grand River Valley, the Kalamazoo & South Haven, the Bay City & Battle Creek, the Michigan Air Line, the Detroit & Bay City, the Toledo, Canada Southern & Detroit, the Jackson, Lansing & Saginaw, the Detroit, Delray & Dearborn, and the Detroit & Charlevoix, recently acquired from lumberman David E. Ward's heirs.

Two late pieces of construction were completed as World War I neared. Bay City businessman Thomas L. Handy and some associates incorporated the Detroit, Bay City & Western in 1907. Gradually it extended a line east out of Bay City, through Caro, which finally ambled into Port Huron in 1916.[179] Once there, Handy bought the Port Huron Southern, a local line in Port Huron. Then he incorporated the Port Huron & Detroit and by 1918 that road built from Port Huron to Marine City.[180] Handy's project never got any nearer to Detroit, nor did the DBC&W ever build west of Bay City.

In 1905, the White family of Boyne City had depleted its timber in that vicinity and decided to extend their railroad east into Otsego County. Their Boyne City & South Eastern became the Boyne City, Gaylord & Alpena. About 1914, they began building east of Gaylord and their rails finally arrived in Alpena in August 1918.[181]

During the first two decades of the twentieth century, state and federal government regulation of the railroads assumed new force and began to have an effect on railroad earnings. Michigan had appointed its first railroad commissioner back in 1872. This came soon after similar moves in some eastern states and coincided with those forced by the Granger movement in other midwestern states. In his early years, the commissioner held largely an information gathering position. The Legislature gradually added other powers to his office. Governor Hazen S. Pingree, during his two terms from 1897 to 1901, badgered the Legislature continuously in an attempt to have higher tax rates imposed on the railroads. The Legislature, even when called into several special sessions, would not oblige. The Senate was particularly obstinate to spite the governor and defeated bills the House had approved. When Governor Aaron T. Bliss succeeded Pingree in 1902, he easily got the railroad tax increase through the Legislature. Within two years, tax revenues doubled; in 1906 they were five times the amount paid in 1896. The state's tax commission said that tax valuations were to be based on the cost for a railroad to replace its operating plant new. A valuation study, undertaken by Mortimer E. Cooley at the turn of the century, was a pioneering work in the field. On top of this, in 1907 the Legislature enacted the two-cent fare law which required most railroads to charge no more than two cents per mile for passenger fares. Exceptions were made for the less profitable Lower Peninsula and the Upper Peninsula lines which were allowed one cent a mile more than their downstate counterparts.

At the national level, a new regulatory body acquired more muscle. The Interstate Commerce Commission was created in 1887 and its first chairman was Thomas M. Cooley of Ann Arbor. The ICC was not much more than a fact-finding group; it had almost no enforcement powers except those it could acquire by taking its complaints to court. The courts were none too supportive. In 1906, President Theodore Roosevelt was able to get the Hepburn Act passed and it gave the ICC weapons it needed to enforce its decisions. It took over regulation of interstate freight rates and the courts later gave it power over intrastate rates that affected interstate commerce.

If all of this was not enough, the railroad labor brotherhoods had become strong and loud enough to be heard in the legislatures. In 1916, Congress passed the Adamson Law, which mandated an eight-hour working day for some railroad employees. They were able to bargain more effectively and won improvements in pay and changes in work rules. The outcome of all of this, from the states, from Washington, and from the brotherhoods, was to apply a heavier economic burden on the railroads. The Pere Marquette, along with its unique problems, was severly affected. The Grand Rapids & Indiana stopped paying dividends.

WORLD WAR I TO THE GREAT DEPRESSION

On January 1, 1918, the federal government took control of the railroads of the United States. The U.S. had declared war on Germany some ten months earlier. Washington felt that private management could not operate the railroads in a wartime emergency as well as the government could. Only a few Michigan short lines were not taken over. Control lasted until March 20, 1920, when the properties were returned to their owners, quite a bit the worse for wear and with equipment overused and run down.

Freight revenues had risen sharply up to 1920, but in 1921 they levelled off and remained little changed through 1930. Passenger revenues, nationally, dropped by one-third between 1920 and 1930. Net income, before interest, did improve throughout the decade, largely because operating expenses were kept under very tight control. For Michigan railroads the picture was no different. Lumber traffic all but disappeared in the Lower Peninsula. Manufacturing, particularly in the southern part of the state, did keep some lines profitable. Passenger traffic left the railroads. After 1900, the trains faced increased competition from the electric interurban railways. Then, thanks to Henry Ford and a good many others, the public discovered the automobile and abandoned the electric lines as well. In 1919, Michigan passed a $50,000,000 bond issue for a highway improvement program and passenger traffic in Michigan continued to ebb away.

The Pennsylvania Railroad had decided, back in 1917, that it was going to build a line to Detroit. The project appears to have had Henry Ford's support.[182] World War I postponed construction until 1922, and in 1923 some terminal lines in Detroit were built, one of which extended to Highland Park and the Ford factory.[183]

Henry Ford himself discovered a new fascination—the Detroit, Toledo & Ironton. In 1920, Ford planned to build a line from his River Rouge plant to Flat Rock to connect with the DT&I. In July 1920, Ford bought the DT&I itself for about $5,000,000. The branch to the Rouge was finished in 1922. In 1924 the DT&I built a shortcut line from near Dundee south-southwest into Ohio and eliminated its roundabout route through Tecumseh and Adrian. Ford cleaned and polished the DT&I, and spent his own money to modernize it. He proposed converting the road to electric power. Henry Ford eventually tired of the problems of dealing with connecting railroads and, in June 1929, sold the DT&I to the Pennsylvania Railroad's investment holding company, Pennroad Corporation. The sales price was about $36,000,000, giving Ford a $31,000,000 profit for his ten years of ownership.[184]

In 1925, the Wabash Railroad bought up a majority of the stock of the Ann Arbor Railroad. In 1928, the Wabash itself was bought by the Pennsylvania Railroad in a defensive maneuver. It appears that the Pennsylvania pretty much left the Wabash to operate on its own. Except for establishing a Detroit-Fort Wayne-Chicago passenger train service, the PRR did not try to integrate the Wabash into its operations.

The Pere Marquette acquired a new owner in this decade. That story starts in 1916 in Cleveland. Two brothers, Oris P. and Mantis J. Van Sweringen, were Cleveland developers and that year bought the New York, Chicago & St. Louis—better known as the Nickel Plate Road—from the New York Central. The NYC was forced into the sale by the Clayton Anti-trust Act. The Van Sweringens took to railroading very quickly. They added some other roads to the Nickel Plate. In 1922, they bought control of the Chesapeake & Ohio. This was followed by purchases of stock in the Erie and, in 1924, of a majority interest in the Pere Marquette. The Interstate Commerce Commission would not approve the brothers' plans to merge the four railroads, giving the financial arrangements as the reason. The eventual outcome was that the PM stock was sold to the Chesapeake & Ohio in 1929 and the Van Sweringens stayed in Cleveland and kept their Nickel Plate.[185]

There had been some track abandonments prior to World War I, but these were mostly lumbering lines—the Mason & Oceana, Michigan East & West (formerly the Manistee & Grand Rapids), and the Manistee & Luther. The Michigan Central and Grand Rapids & Indiana removed lumbering spurs from their northern branches. The same was happening to Upper Peninsula companies, and they also began to experience a reduction in the shipments of iron ore from the Gogebic and Menominee ranges. Probably the longest single abandonment in this period was that by the Manistee & Northeastern of its Kaleva-Grayling branch.

By World War I, the electric interurban had developed into a major transportation factor in Michigan. They succeeded by diverting local travelers away from the railroads and, more importantly, by developing an entirely new clientele of rural and suburban travelers. With Michigan United's completion of its high-speed Kalamazoo-Grand Rapids line in 1915, the electric network included nearly seven hundred intercity miles of lines. The spine was the Detroit-Kalamazoo service. Out of Detroit lines ran to Toledo, Pontiac-Flint-Saginaw-Bay City, Port Huron, a second line to Mt. Clemens, and branches to Northville and Trenton. From Jackson, a line extended to Lansing, then split into branches to Owosso and St. Johns. The Kalamazoo-Grand Rapids line made connections with two independent companies, one to Holland and Saugatuck and another to Grand Haven and Muskegon. At Montieth Junction it crossed its Battle Creek-Allegan line. Three other independents operated in the Lower Peninsula: the Toledo & Western from Toledo to Adrian and Morenci, the Southern Michigan between St. Joseph and South Bend, and another company from Benton Harbor to Dowagiac and Watervliet. In the Upper Peninsula, the largest operation was that of the Houghton County Traction Company, which extended from Houghton to Calumet, Lake Linden, and mining communities north of Calumet. There were modest operations between Ishpeming and Negaunee and between Ironwood and Bessemer.

This entire network had been built in the twenty years between 1895 and 1915. Its demise was complete within the next twenty years. By the early 1920s, profits almost completely disappeared. Companies were usually built quickly and cheaply, set up no depreciation accounts for the construction expense, and established no reserves for the future after they began service. When equipment needed to be replaced and tracks had to be upgraded, there was nothing to fall back on. Just at the time these demands became pressing the interurban companies came full-face against the automobile.

The popularity of this new type of vehicle, and the steadily improving roads on which it moved, swamped the interurbans. A service system that in 1915 had glowing prospects was by 1925 on its knees.

Detroit United Railway, after years of wrangling over franchises and fares with city officials, in 1922 sold its city streetcar lines to the City of Detroit. The remaining intercity operations could not provide an adequate profit, especially now that the DUR had to pay the city to operate its cars over city tracks. DUR went into bankruptcy in 1925. It abandoned some branch operations and, in September 1928, was reorganized as Eastern Michigan Railways. That month, EM let its interest in the Detroit, Jackson & Chicago go back to that road's bondholders. The DJ&C continued running for another year, until September 1929.

The Michigan Railway, the successor of the Michigan United Railways and several other outstate companies, was owned by Commonwealth Power, Railway & Light—a holding company which also owned Consumers Power Company. Commonwealth felt the immediate impact of the interurban company's poor

Grand Trunk Western high-speed passenger locomotive 6405, circa 1945

earnings. In 1907, the railways were in first place in its earnings; by 1921, they were a very weak last.[186] The railway's situation also affected the income of Consumers. In 1921, Commonwealth split the Michigan Railway apart, turned the Saginaw city runs over to a new company, abandoned Saginaw-Bay City service, gave the Jackson-Battle Creek-Kalamazoo and the Jackson-Lansing-St. Johns-Owosso part back to Michigan United Railways, and put the remainder into the new Michigan Railroad. The MUR and Michigan RR were still controlled by Commonwealth.

MUR ended Owosso city service in 1926, Kalamazoo-Jackson service in November 1928, and Jackson-Lansing-Owosso-St. Johns service in May 1929. It formed new companies to operate local service in Jackson, Lansing, Battle Creek, and Kalamazoo. The Michigan RR cancelled its lease of the Grand Rapids, Holland & Chicago at the beginning of 1924. It ended Saginaw-Bay City service in 1928, and Flint-Saginaw, Battle Creek-Allegan and Kalamazoo-Grand Rapids service in August 1928.[187]

The Grand Rapids, Holland & Chicago ended operations in November 1926, although a small section between Grand Rapids and Jenison was operated by another company until June 1932. The Grand Rapids, Grand Haven & Muskegon was abandoned in April 1928. The lines from Benton Harbor to Dowagiac and Watervliet were abandoned in August 1928.

THE GREAT DEPRESSION TO WORLD WAR II

The Great Depression was the critical time for Michigan railroads. Early on, two roads went into receivership: the Wabash, and the Boyne City, Gaylord & Alpena. Before the hard times ended, most Upper Peninsula roads were in receivership, with only the Soo Line escaping that fate. In the Lower Peninsula, companies reduced expenses as rapidly as revenues dropped. Freight tonnage in 1932 was half that of 1929 and revenues dropped a like amount. As traffic disappeared, companies decided that some branch lines were not worth keeping for any amount of traffic. When the Boyne City, Gaylord & Alpena was reorganized as the Boyne City in 1935, it also abandoned the eighty-five miles of road between Boyne Falls and Alpena that it had built less than twenty years earlier. The Michigan Central removed the last of its lumbering branches and also abandoned parts of a few other branches as well as a large part of the Chicago, Kalamazoo & Saginaw.

Michigan railroad mileage had dropped nearly 700 miles, from 8,770 in 1920 to 8,072 in 1930. In the ten years from 1930 to 1940, mileage was reduced to 7,303, a further loss of 770 miles. Despite the changes in mileage, there was little change in actual ownership.

Revenues did not improve substantially as the depression ended. Total revenues, nationally, were lower in 1940 than they had been in 1930. Net operating income was about seventy-five percent of the 1930 amount. Net income that was left after paying interest on debt was barely one-third the amount earned in 1930. Freight tonnage refused to increase, and was slightly lower in 1940 than in 1930. At the opening of World War II, the railroads were not in good financial health, nor had the operating plant or the equipment recovered from the devastation of the depression.

The Great Depression proved to be the final scene for Michigan's electric railways. The most important parts of the intercity system had already been abandoned. The economic hard times completed what the horseless carriage had begun. Michigan United Railways spun off its city streetcar lines in 1929. Between 1931 and 1936, operations ended in Saginaw, Battle Creek, Kalamazoo, Lansing, and Jackson last of all. The independent company in Muskegon made its last run in 1929. The final service in outstate Michigan was in Grand Rapids and Benton Harbor, and both ended in 1935. In the Upper Peninsula, cars ran in Sault Ste. Marie until 1931, and in Escanaba until 1932. The last in the Upper Peninsula was in Marquette in 1935, where since 1930 the employees had divided up each day's receipts for their pay.

In the eastern part of the state, Port Huron's cars stopped running in 1930, Saginaw's in 1931, Pontiac's in 1932, and Flint's in 1936. This left only Detroit with its city-owned system. It continued operating on Woodward Avenue until April 8, 1956.

The electric interurban's days were numbered. The Eastern Michigan Railways reorganization of the Detroit United Railways continued life for only a few years. Detroit-Port Huron service ended in 1929, although Detroit city cars ran as far as Mt. Clemens until 1931. Eastern Michigan abandoned the Detroit-Flint line in 1931. Last to go was the Detroit-Toledo service which stopped running on October 4, 1932.

Houghton County Traction ended the last Upper Peninsula interurban service in 1932. Only two Lower Peninsula companies remained after 1932. The first to go was the Toledo & Western, which continued operations between Toledo and Adrian until July 1, 1933. Then it sold some of its tracks to freight-only haulers. The Northern Indiana line between St. Joseph and South Bend lasted one more year until it finished on May 30, 1934.

CONCLUSION

The financial events that took place after the end of World War II have been documented extensively. In 1947, the Chesapeake & Ohio formally merged the Pere Marquette and that historic Michigan name continued for only a few more years as the Pere Marquette District of the C&O. In 1949, the Duluth, South Shore & Atlantic absorbed the Mineral Range which it had owned for many years. In 1955, the Manistee & Northeastern was bought by the Chesapeake & Ohio. In 1961, the Canadian Pacific combined the Soo Line, its controlled subsidiary, the Wisconsin Central, and the Duluth, South Shore & Atlantic, into a new company officially named the Soo Line Railroad. The Wabash was leased by the Norfolk & Western in 1964 and that company was renamed the Norfolk Southern in 1980.

The most spectacular financial move occurred in 1968, when those archrivals, the Pennsylvania and the New York Central, were merged after years of talking about it. Within a few years, Penn Central fell into bankruptcy. Conrail, the Consolidated Rail Corporation, took over some of Penn Central's lines and sold off or abandoned the rest of the two systems. The Ann Arbor and the Milwaukee Road also found themselves in bankruptcy courts. But aside from these three exceptions, Michigan railroad companies have been able to survive and prosper.

The lines in sparsely populated areas, and especially in the Upper Peninsula, continue to be a problem for their owners. The state has stepped in and provided some support to keep certain lines going. The Lake Michigan car ferry operations of the Grand Trunk Western were shut down. Those of the Ann Arbor were continued after the bankruptcy with the help of the state, but were finally abandoned in 1982. The Chesapeake & Ohio operations out of Ludington were sold to a private owner. The Straits of Mackinac ferry continued to sail until 1984. Major carriers have spun off branch lines to small locally-owned companies which have kept on providing needed service. The largest such sale was the Michigan property of the Soo Line which was transferred to the new Wisconsin Central Ltd.

NOTES

1. Michigan, *Territorial Laws,* (Lansing: W. S. George & Co., 1874) 3: 844-47
2. Michigan, *Territorial Laws* 3: 960-66.
3. Willis F. Dunbar, *All Aboard!* (Grand Rapids: Eerdmans, 1969), 32.
4. Willis F. Dunbar, *Michigan: A History of the Wolverine State* (Grand Rapids: Eerdmans, 1970), 151-52.
5. Michigan, *Territorial Laws* 3: 1387-97.
6. Michigan, *Territorial Laws* 4: 142-47.
7. R. I. Bonner and W. A. Whitney, *History and Biographical Record of Lenawee County* (Madison, WI: Western Historical Association, 1879-80) 1: 140; *Michigan Pioneer and Historical Collections* (1912) 38: 491. Dates from other sources range from the earliest, in October 1836, to various dates ranging throughout 1837.
8. Talcott E. Wing, *History of Monroe County* (New York: Munsell & Co., 1890), 217.
9. Silas Farmer, *History of Detroit and Wayne County* (Detroit: Gale Research, 1969) 1: 893.
10. Michigan, *Acts of the Legislature, 1838* (Detroit: John S. Bagg, 1838), 20, 66-69.
11. Farmer, 893; Dunbar, *All Aboard!,* 54-55.
12. George N. Fuller, *Michigan, A Centennial History of the State and Its People* (Chicago: Lewis Publishing Co., 1939) 1: 34.
13. R. Carlisle Buley, *The Old Northwest* (Bloomington: Indiana University Press, 1950), 1: 488n.
14. Michigan, *Constitution,* (1835), Article XII, section 3.
15. George N. Fuller, ed., *Messages of the Governors of Michigan* (Lansing: Michigan Historical Commission, 1925-1927) 1: 170.
16. Fuller, *Messages* 1: 170-71.
17. Michigan, *Acts of the Legislature, 1837* (Detroit: John S. Bagg, 1837), 130-33.
18. Michigan, *House Journal, 1837,* (Detroit: John S. Bagg, 1837), 408-14.
19. Michigan, *Acts of the Legislature, 1837,* 130-33.
20. Ibid., 282-84, 144-45.
21. The $5,000,000 bond sale negotialtion and its subsequent resolution have been the subject of extensive and intensive study. *See* Fuller, *Michigan* 1: 285-93; Henry M. Utley and Byron M. Cutcheon, *Michigan as a Province, Territory, and State* (New York: Publishing Society of Michigan, 1906) 3: 125-63; Kent Sagendorf, *Stevens Thompson Mason* (New York: E. P. Dutton, 1947); and Robert J. Parks, *Democracy's Railroads* (Port Washington, NY: Kennikat, 1972), 186-213 for a fuller discussion.
22. Michigan, *Senate Documents, 1838,* no. 11, 204.
23. Ibid., 156-70.
24. Ibid., 166.
25. Michigan, *House Documents, 1839,* no. 17, 289; Farmer, 896.
26. Farmer, 897.
27. Michigan, *Joint Documents, 1841,* no. 4, 157.
28. Fuller, *Michigan* 1: 280.
29. *Acts of the Legislature, 1843,* no. 25, 27-29.
30. Wing, 226.
31. Michigan, *Joint Documents, 1845,* no. 4, 4.
32. Farmer, 897.
33. Michigan, *Acts of the Legislature, 1841,* no. 42, 64.
34. Michigan, *House Documents, 1839,* no. 17, 289; Farmer, 896.
35. Fuller, *Messages* 1: 44.
36. Ibid., 44-47.
37. Michigan, *Acts of the Legislature, 1847,* no. 5, 5-19.
38. Michigan, *Acts of the Legislature, 1846,* no. 42, 37-64.
39. Farmer, 898.
40. Michigan, *House Documents, 1846,* no. 11, 1.
41. Ibid., 1-2.
42. Farmer, 902.
43. Ibid., 902.
44. Stanley Newton, *The Story of Sault Ste. Marie and Chippewa County* (Sault Ste. Marie: Sault News Printing Co., 1923), 151.
45. Michigan, *Acts of the Legislature, 1848,* no. 197, 276-77.
46. Farmer, 899.
47. Franklin Ellis, *History of Berrien and Van Buren Counties* (Philadelphia: D. W. Ensign & Co., 1880), 275.
48. Alvin F. Harlow, *The Road of the Century* (New York: Creative Age, 1947), 220.
49. Farmer, 899.
50. Harlow, 252.
51. Michigan, *Acts of the Legislature, 1849,* no. 128, 130-34, 214-61.
52. Wing, 217.
53. Ibid., 231.
54. Michigan, *Acts of the Legislature, 1850,* no. 195, 195-200.
55. Michigan, *Annual Report of the Commissioner of Railroads, 1875* (Lansing: W. S. George & Co., 1875), xxv.
56. Harlow, 254-55.
57. Timothy Edward Howard, *A History of St. Joseph County Indiana* (Chicago: Lewis Publishing Co., 1907) 1: 237.
58. Michigan, *Annual Report of the Commissioner of Railroads, 1875,* xxv.
59. Alfred T. Andreas, *History of Cook County Illinois* (Chicago: A. T. Andreas, 1884), 181. John B. Jervis was president of the CRI&P at the time, had been involved with Bliss and the Litchfields in the Northern Indiana earlier, and became president of the Northern Indiana in 1852 and later of the MS&NI.
60. Document filed with Michigan, Secretary of State, Department of Commerce, Corporation and Securities Division, Lot 756, folio 6, pp. 279-85, in State Records Center, Lansing.
61. Harlow, 225-26.
62. Andreas, 183; Carleton J. Corliss, *Main Line of Mid-America* (New York: Creative Age, 1950), 56.
63. G. R. Stevens, *Canadian National Railways* (Toronto: Clarke, Irwin, 1960) 1: 99.
64. Ibid., 106.
65. Farmer, 904.
66. Michigan, *Acts of the Legislature, 1848,* no. 234, 351-56.
67. Michigan, *Acts of the Legislature, 1850,* no. 96, 83-84.
68. Ibid.

69. Michigan, *Acts of the Legislature, 1855,* no. 140, 305-8.
70. Farmer, 895
71. Interstate Commerce Commission, *Valuation Document, 512,* (Washington, DC, 1928), 229; Stevens 1: 118.
72. Stevens 1: 118.
73. Farmer, 895.
74. Michigan, *Annual Report of the Commissioner of Railroads, 1876,* lxiv-lvx.
75. Michigan, *Acts of the Legislature, 1855,* no. 158, 368-91, no. 140, 305-8.
76. Ronald E. Seavoy, "Borrowed Laws to Speed Development: Michigan, 1835-1863," *Michigan History* 59 (Spring 1975): 62-64.
77. Michigan, *Acts of the Legislature, 1855,* no. 82, 153-79.
78. Michigan, Secretary of State, Corporation & Securities Division, Lot 756, 1: 1-2.
79. Michigan, Railroad Commission, *Aids, Gifts, Grants and Donations to Railroads. . .* (Lansing: Wynkoop, Hallenbeck, Crawford, 1919), 81.
80. Michigan, Secretary of State, Corporation & Securities Division, Lot 756, 1: 22-25.
81. Farmer, 902.
82. Dunbar, *All Aboard!,* 106.
83. U. S. Statutes at Large 11: 21.
84. Edmund A. Calkins, "Railroads of Michigan Since 1850," *Michigan History* 13 (Spring 1929): 9; A. N. Bliss "Federal Land Grants for Internal Improvements in the State of Michigan," Michigan Pioneer and Historical Collections (1886), 7: 66.
85. Dates of incorporations, mergers, leases, and sales are taken from the research published in this work, ant the citations are given in the Chronology section of this work.
86. Thomas C. Cochrane and William Miller, *The Age of Enterprise* (New York: Harper & Row, 1961), 81-86.
87. Dunbar, *All Aboard!,* 75.
88. Michigan, *Annual Report of the Railroad Commissioner, 1877,* xxviii.
89. Ibid., lxiv.
90. Harlow, 261-62.
91. Dunbar, *All Aboard!,* 110. Some fascinating tales about early operations are recounted in Mary E. Shout, "Reminisces of the First Settlement at Owosso," Michigan Pioneer and Historical Collections (1906) 30: 361-67.
92. Michigan, *Annual Report of the Commissioner of Railroads, 1875,* xxii.
93. Michigan, Railroad Commission, *Aids,* 40-41.
94. Michigan, *Annual Report of the Commissioner of Railroads, 1875,* xxii.
95. John F. Stover, *American Railroads* (Chicago: University of Chicago Press, 1961), 62-63.
96. John L. Ringwalt, *Development of Transportation Systems in the United States* (Philadelphia, 1888), 174.
97. Michigan, Railroad Commission, *Aids,* 40-41.
98. Michigan, *Annual Report of the Commissioner of Railroads, 1873,* 60-65.
99. *Michigan, Annual Report of the Commissioner of Railroads, 1879,* 382.
100. Michigan, Railroad Commission, *Aids,* 90-91.
101. Fuller, *Michigan,* 5: 528.
102. Michigan, Railroad Commission, *Aids,* 100-1.
103. Michigan, *Annual Report of the Commissioner oj Railroads, 1873,* 103.
104. Harlow, 231.
105. Michigan, Railroad Commission, *Aids,* 48-49.
106. Ibid., 48-49.
107. Ibid., 46-47.
108. Michigan, *Annual Report of the Commissioner oj Railroads, 1873,* 51
109. Wheaton J. Lane, *Commodore Vanderbilt* (New York: Alfred A. Knopf, 1942), 215-23.
110. Michigan, Railroad Commission, *Aids,* 100-1
111. Harlow, 278.
112. Lane, 260-70.
113. Michigan, Railroad Commission, *Aids,* 101.
114. Ibid., 100-1.
115. Ensign, *History of Allegan and Barry Counties Michigan* (Philadelphia: D. W. Ensign & Co., 1880), 78.
116. This possibility is discussed in some detail in Ford Stevens Ceasar, *The Lamp Road: A History of the Lansing, Alma, Mt. Pleasant & Northern Railroad* (Lansing: Rapid Printing, 1974).
117. Harlow, 290.
118. Michigan, *Acts of the Legislature, 1857,* 347ff.
119. Michigan, Railroad Commission, *Aids,* 115.
120. Ibid.
121. The difficulties of the early years of the GR&I are well described in Marie Johnston, "The Building of the Grand Rapids and Indiana Railroad, " *Indiana Magazine of History* 41 (1945): 152-66.
122. Interstate Commerce Commission, *Valuation Document* 351 (Washington, D. C.: Government Printing Office, 1929), 786.
123. Stevens 1: 104, 120.
124. Michigan, Railroad Commission, *Aids,* 34-35.
125. Ibid., 35.
126. Ibid., 39.
127. Ibid., 36.
128. Ibid., 39n.
129. Ibid., 37; A. B. Hopper, *Canadian National Railways: Synoptical History* (Montreal: C. N. R., 1962), 439.
130. Michigan, Railroad Commission, *Aids,* 39.
131. A. W. Currie, *The Grand Trunk Railway* (Toronto: University of Toronto Press, 1957), 200.
132. Michigan, Railroad Commission, *Aids,* 5.
133. Michigan, *Annual Report of the Commissioner of Railroads, 1875,* xii, xxxvi.
134. Harlow, 237.
135. Stevens 1: 141.
136. Dunbar, *All Aboard!,* 147.
137. Harlow, 336.
138. Ibid., 335.
139. George H. Burgess & Miles C. Kennedy, *Centennial History of the Pennsylvania Railroad* (Philadelphia: Pennsylvania Railroad, 1949), 341, 383.
140. Michigan, Railroad Commission, *Aids,* 115.
141. Ibid., 85.
142. Ibid., 111.
143. Ibid., 85.
144. Currie, 240.
145. Stevens 1: 142-43.
146. Ibid.,147.
147. Michigan, Railroad Commission, *Aids,* 39.

148. Ibid.
149. Ibid., 38-39.
150. Ibid., 34-35.
151. Ibid., 35.
152. Henry R. Riggs, *The Ann Arbor Railroad Fifty Years Ago* (Toledo, 1947), 5.
153. Ibid., 1.
154. Michigan, Railroad Commission, *Aids*, 47, 49.
155. Ibid., 83.
156. Ibid., 85.
157. Taylor Hampton, *The Nickel Plate Road* (Cleveland: World Publishing Co., 1947), 177, 192-93.
158. Michigan, *Annual Report of the Commissioner of Railroads, 1887,* 409.
159. Michigan, Railroad Commission, *Aids*, 85.
160. Ibid., 71.
161. Michigan, *Annual Report of the Commissioner of Railroads, 1875,* xivi, xiviii.
162. Michigan, Railroad Commission, *Aids*, 85.
163. Ibid., 73, 85.
164. Ringwalt, 174f.
165. Michigan, Railroad Commission, *Aids*, 87.
166. Ibid., 65.
167. Ibid.
168. Ibid., 61.
169. Ibid.
170. Ibid.
171. Fuller, *Michigan,* 1: 383.
172. Michigan, Railroad Commission, *Aids*, 69.
173. Ibid.
174. Ibid., 68.
175. Ibid., 43.
176. The financial details of the 1900 reorganization are discussed in detail in Paul Wesley Ivey, *The Pere Marquette Railroad: An Historical Study of the Growth and Development of One of Michigan's Most Important Railway Systems* (Lansing: Michigan Historical Commission, 1919). Ivey is extremely critical of the financial arrangements made at the time and also skeptical of the company's prospects improving as a result of the reorganization.
177. Junius E. Beal, "The Beginnings of Interurbans," *Michigan Pioneer and Historical Collections* 35 (1907): 260-63.
178. The career of William A Foote, his involvement with electric railways, and the life of Consumers Power Co. is found in George Bush, *Future Builders* (New York: McGraw-Hill, 1973). The endnotes have a wealth of detail.
179. Michigan, Railroad Commission, *Aids*, 67.
180. Ibid., 67.
181. Ibid., 61.
182. Burgess and Kennedy, 539.
183. Ibid., 539-40.
184. William C. Pletz, "The Railroad That Went No Place," *The Inside Track* 11, no. 1 (Jan. 1980): 3-5.
185. Hampton, 219-321.
186. Bush, 206.
187. Much of the data in this and preceding paragraphs is from George W. Hilton and John F. Due, *The Electric Interurban Railways in America* (Stanford: Stanford University Press, 1960), and from Central Electric Railfans' Association, *Electric Railways of Michigan* (Chicago: Central Electric Railfans' Association, 1959).

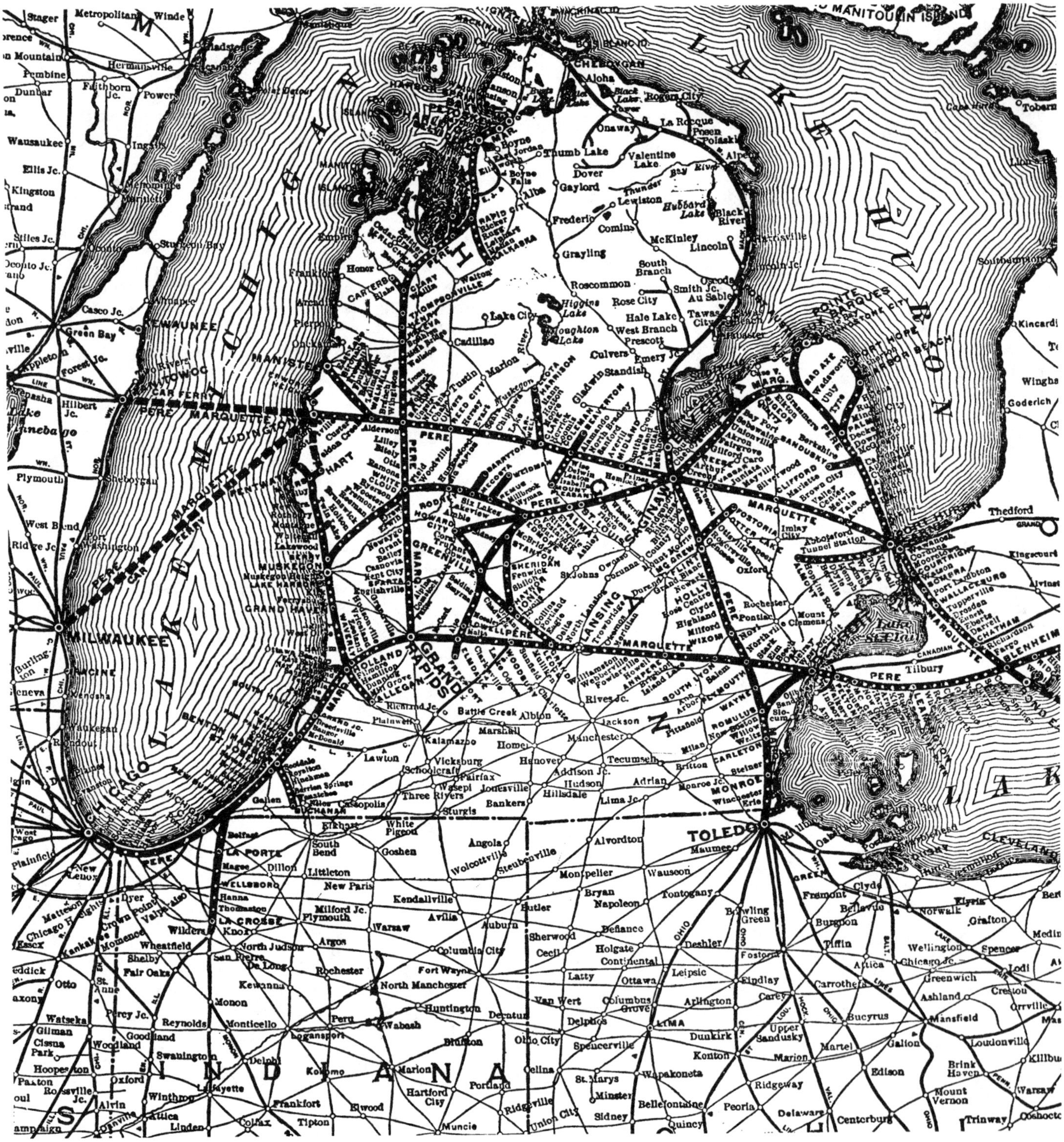

Pere Marquette Railway and Connections, September 25, 1921

LIST OF COMPANIES

This chapter is an alphabetical listing of all of the railroad companies that have operated in Michigan. It includes all the railroad companies that were formed to operate a railroad in Michigan which did not develop into an operating company and all of the individuals, partnerships, and other companies that operated some sort of rail line in Michigan.

After the name of each company is a description of the corporate structure and purpose of the company, followed by a listing of the changes to the corporate structure that occurred during the life of the subject company. To the greatest extent possible, a consistent arrangement of information and a standard terminology is used.

Some data is given about the completion and extent of the company's rail lines—its physical plant. This is given as incidental information to indicate the scope of the company's operations. It is not intended as a complete record of the acquisition, construction, and abandonment of the company's rail lines.

DATA SHOWN AND STANDARD TERMS USED FOR INCORPORATED RAILROADS

First line of each entry, if a chartered or incorporated railroad company, gives the correct legal name of the subject company. The use of "the," "and," or an ampersand (&), and the varying uses of "railroad" and "railway," and the word "company" are as given in the corporate articles. For example:

Battle Creek and Grand Rapids Railroad Company
Battle Creek & Sturgis Railway Company
The Bay View and Crooked Lake Rail Road Company
The Belding Street Railway and Improvement Company
City Street Railway Company of Saginaw

If variations of the corporate name have been used, the first line ends with a dash (—). For example:

Boyne City and Southeastern—

The first varying use appears in the third line of data that follows, and succeeding variations appear in the following lines.

Following the name on the first line, in parentheses, is the track gauge of the company if it did not use the standard gauge of 4 feet 8.5 inches. The letter "E" in parentheses indicates that the company did use or proposed to use electricity for motive power, the letter "H" that horses or mules were so used, the letter "C" that cars were moved by cable. For example:

The Allegan and Lake Shore Railroad Company (Gauge 3')
Ann Arbor and Ypsilanti Electric Railway Company (E),

Second line of each entry indicates by "O" each Michigan county in which the company operated rail lines, and by "P" each county in which it proposed to operate. An "O" entry followed by a "P" entry indicates each county actually operated in and each county proposed to be operated in. For example:

O: 004, 060, 071
P: 004, 005, 010, 028
O: 003, 008, 013 P: 038,

Each Michigan county is identified by a three-digit number.

001	Alcona	029	Gratiot	056	Midland
002	Alger	030	Hillsdale	057	Missaukee
003	Allegan	031	Houghton	058	Monroe
004	Alpena	032	Huron	059	Montcalm
005	Antrim	033	Ingham	060	Montmorency
006	Arenac	034	Ionia	061	Muskegon
007	Baraga	035	Iosco	062	Newaygo
008	Barry	036	Iron	063	Oakland
009	Bay	037	Isabella	064	Oceana
010	Benzie	038	Jackson	065	Ogemaw
011	Berrien	039	Kalamazoo	066	Ontonagon
012	Branch	040	Kalkaska	067	Osceola
013	Calhoun	041	Kent	068	Oscoda
014	Cass	042	Keweenaw	069	Otsego
015	Charlevoix	043	Lake	070	Ottawa
016	Cheboygan	044	Lapeer	071	Presque Isle
017	Chippewa	045	Leelanau	072	Roscommon
018	Clare	046	Lenawee	073	Saginaw
019	Clinton	047	Livingston	074	St. Clair
020	Crawford	048	Luce	075	St. Joseph
021	Delta	049	Mackinac	076	Sanilac
022	Dickinson	050	Macomb	077	Schoolcraft
023	Eaton	051	Manistee	078	Shiawassee
024	Emmet	052	Marquette	079	Tuscola
025	Genesee	053	Mason	080	Van Buren
026	Gladwin	054	Mecosta	081	Washtenaw
027	Gogebic	055	Menominee	082	Wayne
028	Grand Traverse			083	Wexford

Third line of each entry gives the organization date of the company. The actual date of the organizing articles is given whenever found. If "filed" precedes the date, it is the date the articles of organization were filed with the Michigan Secretary of State, and is used when the actual articles have not been found. If the company was chartered by the Michigan legislature, that is indicated by the word "chartered." In some cases an effective date is given and shown by "eff." "Inc." before the date indicates a company that is incorporated under one of Michigan's General Railroad Acts. "Inc.(T)" is an incorporation under one of the state's Train Railway Acts, "Inc.(S)" is an incorporation under one of the state's Street Railway Acts, and "Inc.(UD)" is an incorporation under one of the state's Union Depot Acts. "Inc.(Not RR)" indicates the company was organized under some other form of enabling legislation. When a company was organized under the laws of some other state, the name of the state follows the date of incorporation. Following the date of organization are the capitalization of the company and, when known, the headquarters office of the company. For example:

Chartered March 13, 1838; $50,000
Inc. Dec. 8, 1856; $5,000,000; Alpena
Inc.(S) July 31, 1896; $100,000; Ann Arbor
Inc.(not RR) Oct. 10, 1881
Inc. Sept. 24, 1888 (Ind. corp.)

If the first line of the entry indicates varying corporate names, the third line date is followed with "as" and the full legal name given on the document. The corporate name continues in this form until a new variant is used, which appears with a subsequent date. For example:

Inc. Jan. 7, 1881, as Manistee and Northeastern Rail Road Company; $600,000; Manistee

Fourth line gives the purpose of the company as stated in the articles of organization and begins with the word "to." Several forms of articles were used to form a railroad company: Articles of Association, Articles of Consolidation, Articles of Reorganization, and Articles of Incorporation. These different forms make legal distinctions that indicate rights and relationships of the new company to predecessor companies. These technical distinctions are identified more fully in the purpose stated in the articles and, therefore, the different forms of articles used are not shown herein.

The term "to own" is used in its broadest sense. It indicates that the company, usually under Articles of Association, has the privilege to build, purchase, own, operate, and maintain a railroad of the length and between the points named. Generally, the articles do not specify whether the company would build a line or would purchase an existing property. The term "to buy" indicates that the company intended to purchase and operate the line as shown. The term "to consolidate" usually indicates the use of Articles of Consolidation. "To reorganize" indicates that subject company was formed by Articles of Reorganization to acquire the assets of a predecessor, usually through purchase at foreclosure sale. Information on the fourth line inside brackets is clarifying material not given in the articles but supplied by the compiler.

Following lines, after the first four lines, give the events that followed incorporation in the life of the company. The term "filed" indicates the date the document was filed with the State of Michigan; filing dates in other states also include the name of the state in parentheses.

The meanings of the standard terms used are:

"Amend" indicates that subject company altered its organizational articles; the date of the amendment document and the alteration are given.

"Bankruptcy" is the date that subject company was so declared by a court.

"Bought" indicates that subject company purchased the company named. The date given is the date of sale shown on the deed.

"Consolidated" indicates that subject company acquired the other named company through a merger agreement. The document date is given; when pertinent, the document date is followed by "eff.," giving the effective date.

"Control" with "by" following the date indicates the named company acquired financial control of a majority of the common stock of the subject company. The date given is the date that control was obtained. "At inc." indicates that control was by ownership of all capital stock issued when the subject company was incorporated. If control was divided among several companies, each named company's percentage of ownership is shown.

"Control" with "of" following the date indicates the subject company acquired financial control of company named, usually through purchase of a majority of the capital stock. The date given is the date that control was obtained. "At inc." identifies that control was through ownership of all stock issued when the named company was incorporated. If control was divided among several companies, subject company's percentage of ownership is shown.

"Control ended" indicates that the named company ended financial control of the subject company.

"Control transferred" indicates that financial control of the subject company was conveyed from the first named company to the second named company.

"Conveyed" indicates subject company was transferred to the company named; the terms or means of conveyance cannot now be determined. The date given is the date the conveyance was made.

"Donated" indicates subject company was transferred to the company named; the terms of the donation are uncertain or cannot now be determined. The date given is the date the donation was made.

"Foreclosure" indicates the date of the sale at foreclosure.

"Lease" indicates that subject company obtained a lease of the company named. The date given is effective date; if two dates are given, the first is the date of the document followed by "eff.," giving the effective date of the lease. The term of lease is given when found.

"Lease cancelled" indicates that subject company terminated an earlier lease of the company named. The date given is the effective date.

"Leased" indicates that subject company was leased to the company named. The date given is the effective date.

"Line acquired" gives the date that the subject company acquired the line described. The acquisition most often was by purchase. "At inc." indicates that the line was acquired at the subject company's incorporation, and often was the result of a consolidation or a reorganization.

"Line completed" gives the date that a substantial part of the main line of the company, between the points named, was completed and opened to public service.

"Line opened" gives the date that the first section of the company's line, between the points named, was opened to public service.

"Operating agreement" with "of" following the date indicates that subject company operated the named company by an agreement. When "by" follows the date, it indicates that subject company was operated by the named company. The effective date of the agreement is given with "eff"; if there are two dates, they are the document date of the agreement followed by "eff.," giving the effective date.

"Owned" indicates that subject company or person(s) owned the property named.

"Owned by" indicates that subject company was wholly owned by the company or person(s) named. If the subject company is identified on the third line as a "Private . . . railroad," no attempt has been made to determine the form of ownership.

"Receivership" with "begun" or "ended" followed by the date of the event named. The name of the receiver is given whenever found.

"Reinc." indicates that subject company filed new organizational articles; the date of the reincorporation articles and the purpose are given.

"Sold" indicates that subject company was sold to the company named. The date given is the date of the deed; when pertinent, the deed date is followed by "eff.," giving the effective date of the sale. When a filing date is given, it usually is with the Register of Deeds in those counties in which the line sold was located.

"Stock Exch." indicates that on the date given, the stock of the subject company was exchanged for the stock of the named company. This event most often came about when the subject company created a holding company and then exchanged the subject company's shares in the hands of the public for the shares of the holding company. The holding company could then enter other business ventures that were barred to the railroad company.

"Transferred" indicates that subject company was transferred to the company named; the terms of transfer are uncertain or cannot be determined. The date given is the date the transfer was made.

Last line indicates the disposition of the subject company. The following terms are used:

"Abandoned", accompanied by the date, when known, that the rail line of the company was abandoned for use.

"Conveyed," "donated," "sold," and "transferred" have the meanings given above.

"Dissolved" indicates that the company formally terminated its corporate existence. The date shown is effective date. If there was a lapse of time between the document date and the effective date, the document date is given and followed by "eff." and the effective date.

"Lapsed" indicates that activity required by law or the legislative charter did not take place in time to continue the corporate life of the company. This length of time varied, depending on the enabling legislation, but usually was from four to seven years.

"Merged" indicates the that subject company was consolidated into the company named. The date given is the effective date of the consolidation; if two dates are given they are the document date followed by "eff.," giving the effective date. The filing date, when given, is shown with "filed" and is with the Register of Deeds in the various counties.

"Operations ended" indicates that subject company discontinued rail operations on the date shown. The company's corporate life may have continued after this date. Unless separately given, the date of the demise of the corporation is not known.

"Renamed" indicates that subject company was given a new name by its owners; the document date and the new name are given. Events continue under the new name.

DATA SHOWN AND STANDARD TERMS USED FOR NON-RAILROAD COMPANIES

A subject company that is not a railroad company, or is a railroad owned by a non-railroad company, has the third line showing "Private logging road," "Private mining road," or "Private industrial road." No attempt has been made to use or to determine the correct legal name of the company. If the name is one or more individuals, or is a partnership, that part of the personal names given in brackets is to identify more fully the individuals involved.

The third line gives the headquarters, when it could be learned. No attempt has been made to outline the corporate organization of the owning company. Such facts as have been found are shown only for the rail operation of the company and use the standard terms given above.

LISTINGS

A

Addis [William T.] & Creighton
O: unknown
Private logging road

Addis, William T.
O: 051
Private logging road
Manistee co.
Built 1878
———
Owned Bay Springs & Southeastern

The Adrian and Ann Arbor Electric Railway Company (E)
P: 046, 081
Inc. July 21, 1904; $300,000; Adrian
To own: 32 miles, Adrian via Tecumseh and Saline to Ann Arbor
Lapsed

Adrian & Blissfield Rail Road Company
O: 046
Inc. Jan. 14, 1991; $50,000; Britton
To: not stated
Agreement eff. Feb. 1, 1991, as Designated Operator for state of Michigan
Active corporation

The Adrian and Detroit Railroad Company
P: 046, 081
Inc. Sept. 15, 1870; $200,000
To own: 25 miles, Adrian to Saline
Lapsed

The Adrian & Jackson Traction Company (E)
P: 038, 046
Inc. Sept. 14, 1904; $320,000
To own: 40 miles, Adrian to Jackson with spur to Cement City
Lapsed

Adrian and State Line Railroad Company
P: 046
Inc. Oct. 7, 1871; $150,000
To own: 16 miles, Adrian to SE corner, Medina twp., Lenawee co.
Lapsed

Adrian City Electric Belt Railway Company (E)
O: 046
Inc.(T) Aug. 28, 1888; $50,000
To own: 5 miles in Adrian
Line opened 1889
Receivership 1891
Receivership 1897
Conveyed Feb. 12, 1900, to Adrian Street Ry

Adrian City Train and Street Railway Company
P: 046
Inc.(T) June 22, 1883; $6,000; Adrian
To own: 6 miles in Adrian
Lapsed

Adrian Clinton & Southern Railway Company
P: 046
Inc. June 21, 1976; $400,000; Grand Rapids
To own: line in Lenawee co.
Company not active

Adrian Street Railway Company (E)
O: 046
Inc.(S) Feb. 12, 1900; $40,000; Adrian
To own: in Adrian
Amend Feb. 22, 1905, to modify construction rights
Leased ca. 1907, to Toledo & Western RR
Dissolved May 16, 1927

Adventure Mining Co.
O: 066
Private mining tramway
Adventure Mine to stamp mill
Built 1855

The Air Line Railway Company of Michigan
P: 011, 013, 014, 023, 033, 038, 047, 050, 063, 074, 075, 081
Inc. April 6, 1869; $4,000,000
To own: 240 miles, Port Huron to Indiana state line (to Chicago)
Lapsed

Alabaster Railroad Company
O: Unknown
Private industrial road

The Alanson & Petoskey R.R. Company
O: 024
Inc. July 31, 1990; $500,000; not stated
To: operate railroad in Michigan
Began using Penn Central line between Alanson and Conway
Active corporation

Alaska Railway Company
P: 008, 019, 023, 033, 034, 041
Inc. Aug. 25, 1886; $600,000
To own: 65 miles, Grand Rapids to Lansing
Lapsed

Albion, Charlotte, Northern Railway Company (E)
P: 013, 023, 033
Inc.(S) Nov. 12, 1914; $100,000; Charlotte
To own: Albion, via Charlotte and Grand Ledge, to Lansing
Lapsed

Alcona Logging Railroad
See Platt & Miller

Alexander, Trueman
O: 066
Private logging road

Alger, R[ussell] A. & Co.
O: 001
Private logging tramway
3-4 miles, Harrisville northwesterly
Built ca. 1877

——

See also Alger, Smith & Co.

Alger [Russell A.], Smith [Martin S.] and Co. (Gauge 3' 6")
O: 001
Private logging road; Detroit
25 miles, mouth of Black River westerly
Also known as Black River RR
Built 1878
Conveyed May 17, 1886, to Tawas & Bay County Railroad Company (owned at the time by Detroit, Bay City & Alpena Railroad Company)

——

Owned Manistique Ry

Algonac Transit Company
O: 074
Inc.(Not RR) Nov. 4, 1930; $25,000; Algonac
To own: private railroad, Marine City to Algonac
Bought line July 1930
RR operations ended Oct. 15, 1957
Dissolved Jan. 20, 1958

Allegan and Holland Rail Road Company
P: 003, 070
Inc. July 18, 1868; $200,000
To own: 25 miles, Allegan to Holland
Merged Sept. 29, 1869, into Michigan Lake Shore

The Allegan and Lake Shore Railroad Company (Gauge 3')
O: 003
Inc. May 30, 1883; $100,000
To own: 22 miles, Allegan to Lake Michigan
Owned by W. G. Dewing & Sons
Line opened April 15, 1885, 5 miles Allegan westerly
Abandoned 1889

The Allegan and Marshall Rail-Road Company
P: 003, 013, 039
Chartered March 24, 1836; $400,000; Allegan
To own: 50 miles, Allegan to Marshall
Act April 6, 1838, authorized state to negotiate $100,000 loan to A&M
Act Feb. 11, 1842, authorized repayment to state by state bonds, stock, etc.
Conveyed 1842, rights to state of Michigan

Allegan and South Eastern Railroad Company
O: 003
Inc. Dec. 13, 1877; $1,500.000
To buy: Michigan property of Mansfield, Coldwater & Lake Michigan [probably controlled by MC&LM or by Pennsylvania RR which controlled MC&LM]
Line acquired at inc., Allegan to Montieth
Leased Jan. 1, 1879, to Grand Rapids & Indiana
Lease cancelled Oct. 19, 1882, eff. Dec. 31, 1882, by GR&I
Sold March 13, 1883, to Toledo & Milwaukee

The Allegan and State Line Railroad Company
P: Reorganizing company
Inc. March 5, 1887; $10,056,000
To buy Michigan & Ohio at foreclosure
[Articles were subsequently withdrawn and transfer to Cincinnati, Jackson & Mackinaw allowed]

Allen, William
O: 052
Private logging road
Built ca. 1888

Alley, J.
Owned Alleyton & Big Lake

Alleyton & Big Lake Railroad (Gauge 3')
O: 062
Private logging road
Owned by J. Alley
In T13N R12 & 13W
Built ca. 1878

Allouez Mining Co. (Gauge 4')
O: 042
Private mining road
2.25 miles, Allouez Mine to stamp mill
Built 1873

Alpena & Hubbard Lake (Gauge 3')
O: 004
Private logging road
18 miles, Alpena to Hubbard Lake (T29N R7E)
Built 1888; abandoned 1892

Alpena & Long Lake
O: 004
Private logging road

The Alpena and Michigan South-western Railroad Company
P: 001, 004, 018, 026, 037, 054, 059, 065, 068, 072
Inc. Dec. 15, 1874; $3,000,000
To own: 165 miles, Alpena to Greenville
Lapsed

Alpena and Northern Railroad Company
O: 004, 060. 071 P: 016
Inc. July 28, 1893; $700,000
To own: 85 miles, Alpena to Mackinaw City
Line opened Nov. 18, 1893, Alpena to LaRocque
Sold April 16, 1895, to Detroit & Mackinac

The Alpena and South Western Railway Company
P: 001, 004, 060, 065, 068, 072
Inc. Jan. 29, 1876; $1,050,000
To own: 70 miles, Alpena to point on Jackson, Lansing & Saginaw
Lapsed

Alpena & Western Railway Company
P: 004, 005, 060, 069
Inc. Oct. 8, 1900; $1,000,000
To own: 100 miles, Alpena to Bellaire
Amend May 2, 1901, to change number of directors
Lapsed

Alpena, Gaylord and Western Railroad Company
P: 004, 005, 010, 028, 040, 060, 069
Inc. March 15, 1901; $1,280,000; Alpena
To own: 160 miles, Alpena to Frankfort
Amend June 26, 1901, to increase number of directors
Amend May 7, 1902, to increase number of directors
Amend May 6, 1903, to reduce number of directors
Lapsed

Alpena Portland Cement Co.
O: 004
Private industrial road
Alpena

The Amboy and Traverse Bay Rail Road Company
P: 001, 004, 005, 006, 015, 016, 018, 019, 024, 026, 029, 030, 033, 035, 037, 038, 040, 056, 057, 060, 065, 068, 071, 073, 078
Inc. Dec. 8, 1856; $5,000,000; Alpena
To own: 350 miles, from Amboy, Hillsdale co., via Hillsdale, Jackson and Lansing, to a point on Traverse Bay
Lapsed

The Amboy, Lansing and Traverse Bay Railroad Company
O: 019, 033, 078 P: 001, 004, 005, 006, 013, 015, 016, 018, 020, 023, 024, 026, 028, 029, 030, 035, 037, 038, 040, 056, 057, 060, 065, 068, 069, 071, 072, 073
Inc. Jan. 23, 1857; $5,000,000
To own: 300 miles, Amboy, Hillsdale Co., via Hillsdale and Lansing to Traverse Bay
Line opened Nov. 1860, Owosso to Laingsburg
Act March 20, 1863, authorized to buy Grand River Valley
Line completed Aug. 25, 1863, Owosso to Lansing
Rights assigned Oct. 26, 1866, to Jackson, Lansing & Saginaw for property Lansing-north, and Jan. 12, 1867, to Northern Central Michigan for property Lansing-south
Foreclosure sale, Jan. 4, 1867, to Jackson, Lansing & Saginaw

Ambrose, George, & Son
O: 065
Private logging road
Ogemaw co.

American Fur Co.
O: 017
Private industrial tram road
In Sault Ste. Marie
Line opened 1839; sold about 1846 to McKnight Bros. & Tinker

American Shipbuilding Co.
O: 082
Private industrial road
In Wyandotte

American Traction and Lighting Co.
Non-Mich. holding corp.
Controlled Feb. 19, 1901, at inc., Muskegon Traction & Lighting

Amtrak
See National Railroad Passenger Corporation

Amygdaloid Mining Co.
O: 042
Private mining tramway
3000 ft., at Amygdaloid Mine

Anderson, A. F.
O: 083
Private logging road
Cadillac

Anderson, C. L.
O: 031
Private logging road
Planter

Anderson, R. E.
O: 066
Private logging road
Ontonagon

Ann Arbor and Ypsilanti Electric Railway Company (E)
O: 081, 082
Inc.(S) July 31, 1896; $100,000; Ann Arbor
To own: Ann Arbor, Ypsilanti, Pittsfield twp., and other points in Washtenaw and Wayne cos.
Acquired at inc. Ann Arbor Street and Ann Arbor & Ypsilanti Street
Conveyed Nov. 2, 1897, to Detroit, Ypsilanti & Ann Arbor

The Ann Arbor and Ypsilanti Street Railway Company (H, E)
O: 081
Inc.(T) Aug. 29, 1890; $50,000; Ypsilanti
To own: on streets of Ann Arbor and Ypsilanti and highways between
Line opened Jan. 9, 1891
Control Jan. 26, 1891, of Ann Arbor Street
Merged July 31, 1896, into Ann Arbor & Ypsilanti Electric

The Ann Arbor Interurban Railway Company (E)
P: 046, 058, 081
Inc. Oct. 13, 1904; $500,000; Deerfield
To own: 50 miles, Ann Arbor to Ohio state line in Lucas co., Ohio
Lapsed

The Ann Arbor Railroad Company
O: 010, 018, 019, 029, 037, 047, 051, 057, 058, 067, 078, 081, 083
Inc. Sept. 20, 1895; $7,250,000; Toledo
To acquire: Toledo, Ann Arbor & North Michigan at foreclosure
Line acquired Oct. 14, 1895, Toledo to Frankfort
Bought Oct. 15, 1895, Escanaba, Frankfort & Southeastern
Bought 1897, Ithaca & Alma
Control June 9, 1899, of Menominee & St. Paul
Control June 1, 1905, by Detroit, Toledo & Ironton
Control ended Nov. 25, 1910, by Detroit, Toledo & Ironton
Control April 1911, of Manistique & Lake Superior
Amend Sept. 19, 1914, to reduce number of directors
Control May 19, 1925, by Wabash
Amend May 19, 1926, to change term of directors
Amend May 17, 1927, to increase number of directors
Amend May 20, 1930, to increase number of directors
Control transferred Aug. 29, 1963, from Wabash to Detroit, Toledo & Ironton
Bankruptcy Oct. 15, 1973
Amend Oct. 15, 1973, to reduce number of directors
Sold April 1, 1976, part to state of Michigan and Grand Trunk Western
Sold July 1980, part to state of Michigan
Amend Aug. 31, 1982, to reduce number of directors
Sold Aug. 6, 1987, part to state of Michigan
Active corporation

Ann Arbor Railroad System
Operating name for properties operated by Michigan Interstate

Ann Arbor Street Railway Company (H)
P: 081
Inc.(S) Aug. 30, 1866; $25,000; Ann Arbor
To own: on streets of Ann Arbor
Lapsed

The Ann Arbor Street Railway Company (H, E)
O: 081
Inc.(S) Aug. 6, 1888; $75,000; Ann Arbor
To own: in Ann Arbor
Line opened Sept. 30, 1890
Amend June 25, 1890, to increase capital to $100,000
Control Jan. 31, 1891, by Ann Arbor & Ypsilanti Street
Amend Aug. 16, 1894, to change number of directors
Merged July 31, 1896, into Ann Arbor & Ypsilanti Electric

The Ann Arbor, Ypsilanti and Detroit Street Railway Company (E)
P: 081, 082
Inc.(S) Aug. 25, 1890; $50,000; Ypsilanti
To own: street railway
Lapsed

Antrim Iron Co.
O: 040
Private logging road
See also Cold Springs RR
Mancelona

Arcadia & Betsey River Railway Company
O: 051
Inc. Sept. 5, 1895: $165,000; Arcadia
To acquire: 20 miles, Arcadia to Copemish (Arcadia & Betsey River Train Ry)
Amend Sept. 22, 1928, to extend corporate life
Abandoned Dec. 4, 1936

Arcadia and Betsey River Train Railway Company
O: 051
Inc.(T) April 3, 1883; $25,000; Arcadia
To own: from Arcadia easterly 20 miles
Conveyed Sept. 5, 1895, to Arcadia & Betsey River Ry

Arms Lake Railroad Company (Gauge 3' 6")
P: 015
Inc. Nov. 11, 1885; $40,000
To own: 5 miles, Intermediate Lake in T32N, R7W, to South Arm
Lapsed

Arnold & Eagle Harbor Railroad
O: 042
Private mining road
Sec 15 T58N R31W to Sec 6 T58N R30W

Ash Brothers
O: Unknown
Private logging road

Atlantic & Lake Superior Railroad
O: 031
Private mining road
Owned by Atlantic Mining Co.; sold 1911 to Copper Range Co.
Sec 4 T54N R34W to Sec 21 T55N R35W
Built 1893

The Auburn and Lapeer Railroad Company
P: 044, 063
Chartered March 31, 1838; $300,000
To own: 30 miles, Lapeer to Auburn in Oakland co.
Lapsed

The Au Sable and Northwestern— (Gauge 3')
O: 001, 020, 035, 060, 065, 068, 069
Inc. July 15, 1891, filed July 17, 1891, as The Au Sable and Northwestern Railroad Company; $560,000; AuSable
To buy: Potts Logging Ry (140 miles, AuSable to Charlton twp., Otsego co. and Albert twp., Montmorency co. via Potts)
Sold Jan. 2, 1907, to Henry N., George A., and Edward F. Loud
Inc. Dec. 26, 1907, as Au Sable & Northwestern Railway Company; $216,000
To own: 54 miles, AuSable to Comins
Leased June 1, 1912, 5 years, to Detroit & Mackinac
Sold June 1, 1914, to Detroit & Mackinac

AuSable Lumber Co.
O: 035
Private lumbering tramway
AuSable, at mill
Owned by John C. Gram
Ran in 1880s

Ayers, A. D. (Gauge 3')
O:062
Private logging road
Newaygo co.

B

Backus, G. and J. (Gauge 3')
O: 035
Private logging road; office: Oscoda
At Oscoda

Baird, James, and Co.
O: 004
Private logging road; Alpena

Bangor & South Haven Division of the Toledo & South Haven Narrow
Guage Railroad Company, *see* Toledo & South Haven

The Baraga and Watersmeet Railroad Company (Gauge 3' 6")
P: 007, 027, 031, 066
Inc. Feb. 10, 1891; $1,000,000
To own: 40 miles, Baraga to Watersmeet
Lapsed

Baraga Lumber Co.
O: 007
Private logging road; Baraga

Barker City & Houghton Lake
See Roscommon Lumber Co.

Barnard [N. and A.]
O: unknown
Private logging road

Barnett Lumber Co.
O: 048
Private logging road
Luce co.

Bartlett Lumber Co.
O: 017
Private logging road
Eckerman

Battle Creek and Bay City Railway Company
P: 008, 009, 013, 019, 023, 029, 034, 037, 056, 059
Inc. Feb. 20, 1888; $2,500,000
To own: 130 miles, Battle Creek to Bay City
Foreclosure sale Sept. 11, 1889, to Bay City & Battle Creek

Battle Creek & Coldwater Electric Railroad Company (E)
P: 012, 013
Inc.(S) April 30, 1904; $25,000; Battle Creek
To own: Battle Creek to Coldwater
Lapsed

The Battle Creek and Grand Rapids Inland Lakes-Traction Company (E)
P: 008, 013, 039, 041
Inc. June 23, 1904; $520,000; Battle Creek
To own: 65 miles, Battle Creek, via Gull Lake, Hickory Corners, Prairieville, Orangeville, Gun Lake, Yankee Springs, Bowens Mills, Green Lake and Crosby post office, to Grand Rapids
Lapsed

Battle Creek and Grand Rapids Railroad Company
P: 008, 013, 039, 041
Chartered May 4, 1846; $600,000
To own: Battle Creek to Grand Rapids
Lapsed

Battle Creek and Marshall Traction Company (E)
P: 013
Inc.(S) Oct. 25, 1901; $200,000
To own: street railway in Calhoun Co. [construction company]
Control at inc. by Detroit & Chicago Traction
Conveyed no date, possibly to Jackson & Battle Creek Traction

Battle Creek and Southeastern Railway Company
P: 012, 013
Inc. Oct. 23, 1905; $500,000; Battle Creek
To own: 30 miles, Battle Creek to Coldwater
Lapsed

Battle Creek & Sturgis Railway Company
O: 012, 013, 075
Inc. Nov. 13, 1889; $1,000,000
To reorganize: St. Louis, Sturgis & Battle Creek bought at foreclosure
Line acquired at inc., Battle Creek to Sturgis
Control 1890, 83.5% by Michigan Central, 16.5% by Lake Shore & Mich. Southern
Leased Feb. 1, 1890, from Findley north to Michigan Central, from Findley south to Lake Shore & Michigan Southern
Merged July 1, 1969, into Penndel Co.

The Battle Creek, Coldwater and Southern Railway Company (E)
P: 012, 013
Inc. Dec. 11, 1908; $450,000; Coldwater
To own: 28 miles, Battle Creek to Coldwater (and buy rights of Grand Rapids Electric)
Amend Aug. 25, 1910, to change capital to $150,000
Lapsed

Battle Creek Electric Railway Company (E)
O: 013
Inc.(S) May 30, 1891; $100,000; Battle Creek
To own: in city and township of Battle Creek
Acquired at inc., Battle Creek Street Ry
Conveyed no date, to Citizens Street Ry of Battle Creek

Battle Creek Railway Company (H)
O: 013
Inc.(S) Aug. 21, 1882; $25,000; Battle Creek
To own: in Battle Creek
Line opened June 1883
Conveyed April 29, 1886, to Battle Creek Street Ry

The Battle Creek Street Railway Company (H, E)
O: 013
Inc.(S) April 29, 1886; $35,000; Battle Creek
To own: in city and township of Battle Creek
Acquired at inc. Battle Creek Ry
Amend May 3, 1887, to change number of directors
Conveyed May 30, 1891, to Battle Creek Electric

Battle Creek Transportation Company (E)
O: 013
Inc.(S) March 19, 1929; Capital not given; Battle Creek
To own: street railway in Battle Creek
Acquired at inc. line from Michigan Electric Ry
Operations ended Sept. 30, 1932

Bay Cities Consolidated Railway Company (E)
O: 009
Inc.(S) Feb. 14, 1898; $1,000,000; Bay City
To own: in Bay City and West Bay City and adjoining territory
Acquired no date, Bay City Street and West Bay City Street
Receivership begun July 1899
Control 1903, by Saginaw-Bay City Ry & Light
Foreclosure sale 1903, to United Traction Co.

Bay City and Alpena Railroad Company
O: 001, 004, 006, 009, 035
Inc. Jan. 17, 1881; $1,120,000
To own: 130 miles, Bay City to Alpena
Bought July 11, 1882, Tawas & Bay County
Renamed March 31, 1883, as Detroit, Bay City & Alpena

Bay City and Battle Creek Railway Company
O: 009, 056 P: 008, 013, 034, 037, 059
Inc. Nov. 11, 1889; $1,000,000
To reorganize: Battle Creek & Bay City
Line completed Dec. 1889, B.C.& B.C. Jct. to Midland
Leased Feb. 1, 1890, in perpetuity, to Michigan Central
Acquired Dec. 30, 1912, Hecla Belt Line
Merged Sept. 27, 1916, into Michigan Central

Bay City and Caro Railway Company
P: 009, 079
Inc.(T) Aug. 15, 1904; Capital not stated; Bay City
To: not stated
Lapsed

Bay City and East Saginaw Rail Road Company
O: 009, 073
Inc. April 8, 1864; $125,000
To own: 14 miles, Bay City to East Saginaw
Line completed Nov. 1, 1867, Saginaw to Bay City
Control Dec. 16, 1868, by Flint & Pere Marquette
Merged Feb. 1, 1872, into Flint & Pere Marquette

Bay City and Midland Railroad Company
P: 009, 056
Inc. April 26, 1882; $150,000
To own: 18 miles, Bay City to Midland
Lapsed

Bay City and Port Huron Railroad Company
P: 009, 074, 076, 079
Inc. May 31, 1904; $1,000,000
To own: 100 miles, Bay City to Port Huron
Lapsed

Bay City and Portsmouth Railway Company
O: 009
Inc.(T) Feb. 21, 1865; $24,000; Bay City
To own: 10 miles, Saginaw & 3rd Sts., Bay City, via Saginaw, 6th, and Water Sts., to Portsmouth and other points
Line opened 1865
Amend Nov. 10, 1868, to increase capital to $40,000
Renamed Sept. 30, 1874, as Bay City Street Railway

Bay City Belt Line Railroad Company
O: 009
Inc. May 29, 1889; $50,000; Saginaw
To own: 6 miles, Saginaw River in Bay City to Saginaw River, Hampton twp.
Amend June 29, 1889, to revise route, increase capital to $100,000
Bought Nov. 22, 1893, part of Detroit & Bay City
Leased Nov. 22, 1893, to Detroit & Bay City
Conveyed, no date, part to Detroit & Bay City
Sold May 6, 1903, to Pere Marquette

Bay City, Caro & Eastern Railway Company (E)
P: 009, 079
Inc. Feb. 19, 1910; $250,000; Bay City
To own: 30 miles, Bay City to Caro, and buy rights of Detroit Bay City Traction
Lapsed

Bay City, Caro & Port Huron Railroad Company
P: 009, 074, 076, 079
Inc. Feb. 6, 1886; $1,000,000
To own: 90 miles, Bay City via Caro to Port Huron
Lapsed

Bay City Street Railway Company (H)
O: 009
Inc.(T) Sept. 30, 1874; $60,000; Bay City
To own: in Bay City and into Portsmouth twp. and to rename Bay City & Portsmouth
Amend Jan. 2, 1875, articles not found
Leased 1879, to Detroit & Bay City
Amend Nov. 21, 1883, articles not found
Sold Jan. 1, 1886, some lines to Detroit & Bay City
Merged no date, into Bay Cities Consolidated

Bay City Terminal Railway Company
O: 009
Inc. Aug. 11, 1910; $15,000; Detroit
To own: 1.25 miles, Cincinnati, Saginaw & Mackinaw RR at Ionia and Chippewa Sts., Bay City, to east shore Saginaw River at 7th Street
Controlled at inc. by Grand Trunk Ry of Canada
Line completed Sept. 29, 1913
Merged Nov. 1, 1928, into Grand Trunk Western

Bay City Traction and Electric Company (E)
O: 009
Inc.(S) Dec. 1, 1903; $1,500,00; Bay City and Saginaw
To consolidate: United Traction Co. and Traction & Power Co.
Control at inc. by Saginaw-Bay City Ry & Light Co.
Renamed Dec. 30, 1909, as Saginaw-Bay City Ry

The Bay De Noquet and Marquette Rail Road Company
O: 052 P: 021
Inc. Nov. 21, 1856; $1,500,000
To own: 70 miles, Little Bay de Noquet to Marquette
Leased 1857, Marquette & Ontonagon Ry
Bought Dec. 31, 1858, filed April 5, 1859, Iron Mountain RR
Act Feb. 15, 1859, confirmed sale
Merged April 28, 1871, into Marquette & Ontonagon RR

Bay de Noquet Lumber Co.
Owned Nahma & Northern

Bay Springs & Southeastern
O: 015
Private logging road
Owned by William T. Addis
6 miles, sec 27 T33N R6W to sec 10 T32N R5W
Ran in 1882

Bay, Tuscola & Huron Railway Company
P: 009, 032, 079
Inc.(T) Dec. 7, 1897; $100,000; Bay City
To own: 30 miles, Bay City to Sebewaing
Lapsed

The Bay View and Crooked Lake Rail Road Company
P: 024
Inc. May 21, 1880; $50,000
To own: 6 miles, Bay View to Crooked Lake
Apparently conveyed to Grand Rapids & Indiana, date uncertain

Bay View Little Traverse and Mackinac Rail Road Company
O: 024
Inc. April 22, 1879; $50,000
To own: 6 miles, Bay View to Little Traverse
Line completed Feb. 1, 1882, Bay View to Harbor Springs
Foreclosure sale, Jan. 17, 1888, to Grand Rapids & Indiana

Beard [James R.] and Co. (Gauge 3' 6")
O: 001
Private logging road; Alcona
10 miles, Alcona westward
Built 1878

The Bear Lake and Eastern Rail Road Company (Gauge 3')
O: 051
Inc. Jan. 20, 1882; $250,000; Bear Lake
To own: 20 miles, Pierport via Bear Lake to Cleon twp.
Owned by Bear Lake Lumber Co. (Hopkins Manufacturing Co.)
Abandoned Sept. 1, 1902

Bear Lake Lumber Co.
Owned Bear Lake & Eastern and Bear Lake Train

The Bear Lake Train Railway Company (Gauge 3')
O: 051
Inc.(T) Nov. 27, 1875; $10,000; Bear Lake
To own: 5-3/8 miles, Bear Lake to Lake Michigan at Pierport
Owned by Bear Lake Lumber Co. (Hopkins Manufacturing Co.)
Apparently conveyed to Bear Lake and Eastern

Beidler Steam Logging Co.
See West Michigan Lumber Co.

The Belding Street Railway and Improvement Company (E)
P: 034
Inc.(T) April 28, 1892; $20,000; Belding
To own: 3 miles, Belding to Cooks Corners, Otisco twp.
Lapsed

Belle Isle Scenic Railway
O: 082
Inc.(Not RR) Feb. 28, 1902
To operate amusement park railway

Bellows, W. D.
O: 059
Private logging tram road
2.5 miles near Third Lake
Operated about 1880

Belt Copper Mines, Ltd.
O: 066
Private ore road
Belt (later Lake) Mine

Bennett and Brown Lumber Co.
O: 066
Private logging road
Bergland

Bennett and Ross
O: 026
Private logging road

Bennett Sewer Pipe Co.
O: 038
Private industrial road
Jackson

Benton Harbor & Eastman Springs— (E)
O: 011
Inc.(S) Aug. 21, 1897, as The Benton Harbor and Eastman Springs Street Railway Company; $25,000; Benton Harbor
To own: Benton Harbor to Eastman Springs
Amend April 1, 1899, as The Benton Harbor and Eastman Springs Electric Railway Company, to change rights: own in Benton Harbor and adjacent cities and twps.
Merged Oct. 10, 1900, into Benton Hbr. & St. Jos. El. Ry. & Light

Benton Harbor and St. Joseph Electric Railway and Light Company (E)
O: 011
Inc.(S) Oct. 10, 1900; $145,000; St. Joseph
To consolidate: Benton Harbor & Eastman Springs and a power company

Acquired at inc., Benton Harbor & Eastman Springs and St. Joseph & Benton Harbor Street
Conveyed June 27, 1906 to Benton Harbor-St. Joe Ry & Light
Dissolved March 18, 1924

Benton Harbor and South Eastern Railway Company
P: Indiana only
Inc. May 29, 1893 (Ind. corp.)
Merged April 6, 1897, into Milwaukee, Benton Harbor & Columbus

Benton Harbor Belt and Terminal Railway Company
P: 011
Inc. Feb. 4, 1890; $80,000
To own: 10 miles, Benton Harbor to Royalton twp.
Lapsed

The Benton Harbor, Coloma and Paw Paw Lake Train Railway Company (E)
O: 011
Inc.(T) Sept. 3, 1895; $25,000
To own: 11 miles, Benton Harbor to Paw Paw Lake
Line opened 1896
Sold May 7, 1903, to Pere Marquette

The Benton Harbor Electric Railway and Transit Company (E)
P: 003, 011, 080
Inc. Jan. 12, 1897; $650,000; Benton Harbor
To own: 80 miles, Benton Harbor via Spinks Corners and Sister Lakes to Dowagiac, and branch Sister Lakes via Decatur, Paw Paw and
Gobles to Allegan
Lapsed

Benton Harbor-St. Joe Railway & Light Company (E)
O: 011
Inc.(S) Jan. 23, 1906; $1,000,000; Benton Harbor
To consolidate: St Joe River Traction and a utility co.
Amend May 10, 1909, to increase capital to $2,000,000
Sold Aug. 21, 1928, to Twin City Ry
Dissolved Aug. 29, 1928

Benton Harbor Street Railway Company (H)
P: 011
Inc.(S) Jan. 5, 1888; $10,000; Benton Harbor
To own: in Benton Harbor
Lapsed

Benton Harbor Terminal Railway Company
P: 011
Inc.(UD) June 11, 1901; not given; Benton Harbor
To own: depot and line to Milwaukee, Benton Harbor & Columbus Ry
Lapsed

Bergland Lumber Co.
O: 066
Private logging road; Bergland

Berry, James
O: 018
Private logging tram road

Bessemer and Ironwood Interurban Railway Company (E)
P: 027
Inc.(S) May 31, 1904; $25,000; Ironwood
To own: in Ironwood and Bessemer
Lapsed

Bewicke [Charles], Comstock [A. W.] and Co.
O: 004
Private logging road
Hubbard Lake area

Bigelow Lumber Co.
O: 064
Private logging tram road
About 1884

The Big Rapids and Western Railroad Company
O: 054, 062
Inc. April 1, 1887; $100,000; Big Rapids
To own: 8 miles, Muskegon River sec 34 T16N R10W to sec 32 T16N R11W
Owned by Thomas D. Stimson
Abandoned

Bird and Holcomb
O: 055
Private logging tram road
Stephenson

Black River Railroad (Gauge 3')
O: 001
Private logging road
Owned by Alger, Smith & Co.
Sold May 17, 1886, to Detroit, Bay City & Alpena

Blake Logging Co.
O: 062
Private logging road
About 1880

Blaney and Southern Railway Company
O: 077
Inc.(T) Sept. 27, 1902; $10,000; Escanaba
To own: 7.5 miles, Mpls. St. Paul & Sault Ste. Marie at NE¼ NE¼ sec 22 T42N R13 to ¼ line sec 16 T43N R13W
Control Oct. 21, 1909, by Wisconsin Land & Lumber Co.
Sold July 1, 1925, to Wisconsin Land & Lumber Co.
Abandoned

Blendon Lumber Co.
O: 070
Private logging road
Line built ca. 1857, 7 miles, Blendon Landing (T7N R14W) to T6N R14W
Abandoned 1864?

Bliss, A. T.
O: unknown
Private logging tram road
Possibly in Clare co.

Blissfield Railroad Company
O: 046
Inc. not found, ca. 1935
Acquired ca.June 15, 1935, part of Toledo & Western RR in Blissfield
Operations ended Dec. 31, 1935
Sold ca. 1936 part to Ohio & Morenci, part to J. Schonthol Co.
Withdrawn as Michigan corporation Aug. 6, 1937

Blodgett, D. A. (and Byrne, ?) (Gauge 3')
See Portage Lake & Muskegon River and Clam River RRs

Bloomfield and Orchard Lake Railway Company (E)
P: 063
Inc.(S) Dec. 5, 1898; $25,000; Birmingham
To own: in city of Pontiac and adjoining villages and townships
Lapsed

Bond, Milton J. (Gauge 3')
O: 043, 059, 083
Private logging road
Montcalm co.
Bonds Mill, Wexford co.
Chase, Lake co.

Bonifas, William, Lumber Co.
O: 027
Private logging road
Watersmeet

Bourke, Henry P., Co.
O: 052
Private logging road; Marquette

Boyne City and Southeastern—
O: 005, 015, 069
Inc. April 26, 1893, as Boyne City and Southeastern Railroad Company; $56,000; Boyne City
To own: 7 miles Pine Lake, Boyne City to S¹/₄ post sec 21 T32N R5W
Line opened Aug. 28, 1893, Boyne City to Boyne Falls
Amend Aug. 8, 1894, as Boyne City and South Eastern Railroad Company; $256,000
To own: 32 miles South Arm Pine Lake east to Boyne Falls via Boyne City and Boyne Falls to railroad junction at Alba and industrial branches
Amend Oct. 26, 1897, as The Boyne City and Southeastern Railroad Company; $384,000
To own: 48 miles South Arm Pine Lake (in East Jordan) to Boyne Falls to Alba, as above; also from main line in NE¹/₄ SE¹/₄ sec 8 T32N R5W, to Vanderbilt
Sold March 17, 1905, to Boyne City, Gaylord and Alpena

Boyne City, Gaylord and Alpena Railroad Company
O: 004, 005, 015, 060, 069
Inc. March 17, 1905; $1,000,000; Boyne City
To own: 110 miles, Boyne City to Gaylord to Alpena (and to buy Boyne City and Southeastern)
Sold 1935, to Boyne City

Boyne City Railroad Company
O: 015
Inc. filed Jan. 15, 1935
To acquire: Boyne City, Gaylord & Alpena
Sold 1976, to Boyne Valley

Boyne Falls & Northeastern
O: 015, 024
Private logging railroad
Owned by Cobbs & Mitchell
8 miles, Boyne Falls to T34N R4W
Built about 1898

Boyne Valley Railroad Company
O: 015
Inc. May 22, 1976; $80,000; Boyne City
To own: 10 miles, Advance to Boyne City to Boyne Falls (to acquire Boyne City)
Operations ended ca. 1978
Abandoned 1982

Bradley and Kelly (Gauge 3')
O: Unknown
Private logging road
Possibly in Marquette co.

Briggs and Cooper
O: Unknown
Private logging road
Possibly in Roscommon co.

Broadwell, Hilliard
O: 004
Private logging tramway
In Alpena, woods to dock
Operated ca. 1860

Brown, Archie
O: 020
Private logging pole road

Brown, John C.
O: Unknown
Private logging road
Possibly in Cheboygan and Presque Isle cos.

Brunswick-Ewen Lumber Co.
O: 066
Private logging road; Ewen

The Buchanan & St. Joseph River Railroad Company
O: 011
Inc. Oct. 11, 1894; $20,000
To own: 1.75 miles, Buchanan to Buchanan Power & Electric Dam
Control at inc. by Michigan Central
Merged June 19, 1912, into Michigan Central

The Buckley and Douglas Rail Road Company (Gauge 3')
O: 051
Inc. Jan. 20, 1881; $40,000; Manistee
To own: 10 miles, Manistee River in T22N R13-14W to T23N R13-14W
Line opened June 20, 1881, 8 miles
Abandoned 1889

Burgess and Ladner
O: 062
Private logging tram road
6 miles, T14N R11W
About 1870

Burt [Wellington R.] and Gamble [Henry] (Lumber Co.) (Gauge 3')
O: 002
Private logging road
7 mi., built about 1882, Grand Marais southerly
Abandoned about 1890; some of grade used subsequently by Manistique

Burt Portland Cement Co.
O: 023
Private industrial road
Bellevue

Butters [Horace] and Peters [Richard G.] Co. (Gauge 3')
O: 053
Private logging road; Tallman
4 miles, near Tallman
Built 1882-1883

——
Also owned Mason & Oceana
——
O: 053, 064
Private logging road (also called South Branch RR)
7 miles, S. Br. River maybe in T16&17N R15W
Built 1883

Butters [Marshall] Lumber Co. (Gauge 3')
O: 007
Private logging road
L'Anse

C

Cable Street Railway Company of Grand Rapids
[Original articles have "Valley City" written before filed name and lined out before filing]
P: 041
Inc.(S) May 27, 1887; $500,000; Grand Rapids
To own: in city of Grand Rapids and adjoining townships
Lapsed

Cadillac and Evart Railroad Company
P: 057, 067, 083
Inc. Oct. 18, 1882; $360,000
To own: 44 miles, Crooked Lake, Missaukee co., via Cadillac to Evart
Lapsed

Cadillac & Lake City Railway Company
O: 057, 083
Inc. March 5, 1963 (Dela. corp.); $150,000; Lake City
To buy: part of Penndel Co. (Missaukee Jct. to Lake City and Falmouth)
Line acquired 1963, Missaukee Jct. to Lake City and Falmouth
Inc. revised Feb. 7, 1975, eff. Feb. 28, 1974 (Dela. corp.)
Service ended 1975
Line abandoned 1981
Active corporation outside of Michigan

Cadillac & Northeastern (Gauge 3')
O: 057, 083
Private logging road
Owned by Cummer Lumber Co.
Line opened 1884, 10 miles, Cadillac to NW corner Lake Missaukee
Extended 1885, 4 miles, to Lake City
Abandoned 1900

Cadillac Chemical Co.
O: 017, 083
Private logging road; Cadillac and Sault Ste. Marie

Cadillac Handle Co.
O: 024
Private logging road
Pellston

Cadillac, Manistee Valley and Lake Michigan Railway Company (Gauge 3')
P: 083
Inc. Dec. 18, 1884; $90,000; Sherman
To own: 21 miles, Cadillac to Manistee River at Sherman
Lapsed

Cadillac Sand and Gravel Co.
O: 081
Private industrial road
Geddes

Cadillac-Soo Lumber Co.
O: 017
Private logging road
Strongs

Cadillac Traction Company (E)
P: 083
Inc.(S) Sept. 17, 1903; $250,000; Cadillac
To own: street railway in Cadillac and adjacent townships
Lapsed

Calderwood Lumber Co.
O: 066
Private logging road
Calderwood

Calhoun County Railway Company (E)
P: 013
Inc.(S) Aug. 1, 1901; $100,000; Jackson
To own: in Calhoun Co. [construction company]
Control at inc. by Detroit & Chicago Traction
Conveyed no date, probably to Jackson & Battle Creek Traction

Calumet and Hecla Co.
O: 031, 042
Owned Hecla & Torch Lake and Trap Rock Valley

The Calumet & Lac La Belle Traction & Power Company (E)
P: 031, 042
Inc.(S) Dec. 14, 1907; $25,000; Red Jacket
To own: in Houghton and Keweenaw counties
Lapsed

Calumet Train Railway Company
P: 031
Inc.(T) Oct. 27, 1866; $200,000; Franklin twp.
To own: [Hecla Mine to Lake Linden]
Lapsed

Calumet Train Railway Company
P: 031
Inc.(T) Jan. 18, 1867; $200,000; Calumet twp.
To own: head of Torch Lake (sec 5 T55N R32W) to SW corner sec 23 T56N R33W
Lapsed

The Camden Southern Railroad Company
P: 012, 030
Inc. July 8, 1901; $256,000; Camden
To own: 32 miles, Coldwater to Ohio state line (sec 12 T9S R3W)
Lapsed

Campbell, E. P., and Co.
O: 004
Private lumbering tramway
In Alpena, 1 mile from mill to dock
Built 1868

Campbell, George, and Co.
Owned Glencoe, Pinconning & Lake Shore

The Canada and St. Louis Railway Company
O: 075
Inc. July 1, 1887; $2,500,000
To consolidate: Sturgis & State Line and Indiana & Southwestern (Ind. corp.)
Line opened about 1888, Sturgis to Goshen, Ind.
Foreclosure sale Aug. 17, 1889, to Sturgis, Goshen & St. Louis

Canada, LaCrosse & Southwestern—
P: 017, 021, 048, 049, 055, 077
Inc. Oct. 4, 1883, as The Canada, LaCrosse and Southwestern Railroad Company; $1,456,000
To own: 182 miles, Menominee River to St. Marys River
Inc. April 29, 1885, as Canada, LaCrosse and Southwestern Railway Company; $2,700,000
To consolidate CLC&SW RR and Sault Ste. Marie & Southwestern
Lapsed

Canada, Michigan and Chicago Railway Company
P: 025, 033, 050, 063, 074, 078
Inc. Dec. 6, 1871; $4,000,000
To own: 110 miles, Lansing to St. Clair
Lapsed

The Canada Southern Railway Company
O: Holding co.
Inc. Feb. 28, 1868 (Canadian corp.)
Control July 11, 1871, at inc., of Chicago & Canada Southern
Control May 29, 1872, at inc., of Toledo, Canada Southern and Detroit

Control Aug. 20, 1873, at inc., of Can. Southern Bridge Co.
Operating agreement, Dec. 12, 1882, by Michigan Central
Control 1882, of Michigan, Midland & Canada
Leased Jan. 1, 1904, for 999 years to Michigan Central
Control Sept. 25, 1906, of St. Clair & Western
Sold April 30, 1985, to Canadian National Rys and Canadian Pacific

Canada Southern and Chicago Railway Company
P: 030, 046, 050, 058, 082
Inc. Nov. 5, 1870; $800,000
To own: 80 miles, Detroit River to Hillsdale
Lapsed

Canada Southern Bridge Company
O: 082
Inc. Aug. 20, 1873; $1,500,000; Detroit
To consolidate: Detroit River Ry. Bridge & Tunnel (Canadian corp.) and Detroit River Railroad & Bridge
Control at inc. by Canada Southern Ry
Line completed Sept. 1873, Slocum Jct. to Stony Island
Operating agreement, Dec. 12, 1882, by Michigan Central
Line abandoned ca. 1925

Canadian National Railways
O: 074
Inc. Oct. 4, 1922 (Canadian corp.)
Acquired eff. Jan. 1, 1923, lines of Grand Trunk Ry of Canada
Control eff. Jan. 1, 1923, of Grand Trunk Western Ry
Consolidated March 31, 1958, St. Clair Tunnel Co.
Bought April 30, 1985, jointly with Canadian Pacific, Canada Southern Ry and Detroit River Tunnel Co.

Canadian Pacific Railway Company
Inc. Feb. 15, 1881 (Canadian corp.)
Control March 16, 1887, at inc., 50% of Sault Ste. Marie Bridge Co.
Control ca. 1888, of Duluth South Shore & Atlantic
Joint control Aug. 24, 1889, at inc., of Fort St. Union Depot
Joint lease Dec. 10, 1889, of Fort St. Union Depot
Control 1890, of Minneapolis, St. Paul & Sault Ste. Marie
Control Dec. 30, 1960, at inc., of Soo Line RR
Control 1984, at inc., of Soo Line Corp.
Bought April 30, 1985, jointly with Canadian National, Canada Southern Ry and Detroit River Tunnel Co.

Canfield, John
Owned Hobart & Manistee River

Capac and Northern Railway Company
P: 044, 074, 076
Inc. Nov. 23, 1879; $300,000
To own: 30 miles, Capac to Marlette
Lapsed

The Capitol Street Railway Company (E)
P: 033
Inc.(S) July 12, 1892; $25,000; Lansing
To own: street railway (no location stated)
Lapsed

Carey Hoop Co.
O: 024
Private logging road
Near Stutsmanville
Built 1900

Caro and Lake Huron Railroad Company
O: 032, 079
Inc. Feb. 5, 1901; $200,000
To own: 17 miles, Caro to Owendale
Line completed 1901, Caro to Owendale
Sold May 8, 1908, to Detroit & Bay City

Carson City and Palo Railroad Company
P: 059
Inc. Oct. 17, 1871; $250,000
To own: 20 miles, Carson City westerly, via Palo to line of Detroit, Lansing & Lake Michigan
Lapsed

The Cass Avenue Railway Company (H)
[Word "Street" written in original articles between "Avenue" and "Railway" lined out before filing]
O: 082
Inc.(S) Aug. 18, 1877; $100,000; Detroit
To reorganize: Central Market, Cass Avenue & Third St. Ry
Sold June 22, 1882, to Detroit City Ry

Cass City Branch of the Port Huron & Northwestern Ry
See Port Huron & Northwestern

The Cass River Railroad Company
P: 073, 079
Inc. Nov. 3, 1871; $500,000
To own: 35 miles, East Saginaw to Caro
Merged Feb. 1, 1872, into Flint & Pere Marquette

Cecil Bay Lumber Co. (Gauge 3')
O: 024
Private logging road
Owned by A. B. Klise
Carp Lake-Cecil Bay area
Built 1896

Centerville & Niles
See "Southern" line of state of Michigan

"Central" (line of state of Michigan)
O: 013, 038, 039, 081, 082 P: 011, 080
Enacted March 20, 1837
To build: Detroit to mouth of St. Joseph River
Line opened Feb. 5, 1838, Detroit to Ypsilanti
Line completed Feb. 2, 1846, Detroit to Kalamazoo
Sold Sept. 24, 1846, to Michigan Central

The Central Market, Cass Avenue and Third Street Railway Company (H)
O: 082
Inc.(S) May 30, 1873; $100,000; Detroit
To own: in Detroit
Line opened Oct. 16, 1873
Receivership began May 1877
Reorganized Aug. 18, 1877, as Cass Avenue Ry

Central Michigan—
P: 003, 008, 012, 013, 018, 020, 030, 034, 037, 041, 054, 059, 060, 068, 070, 071, 072
Inc. June 1, 1888, as Central Michigan Rail Road Company; $3,000,000; Grand Rapids
To own: 330 miles, Rogers City to Indiana state line in Branch co.
Amend Sept. 27, 1895, as Central Michigan Railroad Company; to change southern terminus to Ohio state line, Amboy twp., and to add branch: some point in Barry co. to Grand Haven, 365 miles
Sold Jan. 10, 1906, to Grand Rapids Electric

Central Michigan Railway Company
O: 009, 019, 034, 041, 056, 061, 070, 073, 078
Inc. July 15, 1987; $50,000; not stated
To: own a railroad
Bought Sept. 4, 1987, line (Durand-Midland, Durand-Muskegon) of Grand Trunk Western
Sold Dec. 14, 1989, part (Coopersville-Marne) to Coopersville & Marne
Sold Dec. 12, 1990, part (in Muskegon) to Michigan Shore
Active corporation

Central Michigan Railway Company
P: 059
Inc. Aug. 23, 1882; $30,000; Lansing
To own: 2 miles, Riverdale to Elm Hall
Lapsed

Champion and Heyward Lumber Co. (Gauge 3')
O: 062
Private logging road
Newaygo co.

Charcoal Iron Co. of America
O: 048
Private industrial road
Newberry northeasterly
Bought 1924 from Lake Superior Iron & Chemical
Sold 1929 to Newberry Lumber & Coal

Charlotteville Lumber Co.
O: 011
7 miles, in T6S R19W
Built 1856, abandoned ca. 1870

Char(r)on and Bougette (Lumber Co.) (Gauge 3')
O: 043, 053
Private logging road
4 miles, Lake and Mason cos.
Built 1881

The Cheboygan & East Michigan Railroad Company
P: 016, 024, 071
Inc. May 19, 1891; $450,000
To build: 55 miles, Rainy Lake (sec 6 T33N R3E) to Cheboygan to Brutus
Lapsed

The Cheboygan Southern Railway Company
P: 016, 024
Inc. Sept. 10, 1903 $200,000; Cheboygan
To own: 20 miles, Cheboygan to Pellston
Lapsed

The Chesapeake and Ohio Railway Company
O: 003, 005, 009, 010, 011, 015, 018, 019, 023, 024, 025, 028, 029, 032, 033, 034, 037, 040, 041, 043, 044, 045, 047, 051, 053, 054, 056, 058, 059, 061, 062, 063, 064, 067, 070, 073, 074, 076, 079, 080, 081, 082
Inc. July 1, 1878 (Va. corp.)
Control May 1929, of Pere Marquette
Consolidated June 6, 1947, Pere Marquette
Consolidated Nov. 30, 1955, Manistee & Northeastern and Flint Belt
Lease assigned Nov. 30, 1955, of Leelanau Transit from Manistee & Northeastern
Control June 15, 1973, by Chessie System
Control Nov. 1, 1980, by CSX Corp.
Bought Dec. 1984, Port Huron & Detroit

Control transferred July 1, 1986, by CSX Corp. to CSX Transp.
Consolidated April 30, 1987, Baltimore & Ohio (non-Mich. co.)
Merged Sept. 2, 1987, into CSX Transportation Co.

Chessie System

Chessie System, Inc.
O: Holding company
Inc. Feb. 26, 1973 (Va. corp.)
Control June 15, 1973, of Chesapeake & Ohio
Merged Nov. 1, 1980, into CSX Corp.

The Chicago and Canada Pacific Railway Company
P: 014, 039, 075
Inc. April 27, 1886; $300,000
To own: 30 miles, Vicksburg to Indiana state line, Porter twp., Cass co., via Three Rivers and Constantine
Reinc. Aug. 2, 1886, to reincorporate with same rights
Lapsed

Chicago and Canada Southern Railway Company
O: 046, 058, 082
Inc. July 11, 1871; $10,000,000; Grosse Ile
To consolidate: South Eastern Michigan and Chicago & Canada Southern (Ill., Ind. and Ohio corps.)
Control at inc. by Canada Southern
Line opened Nov. 13, 1873, Slocum Jct. to Fayette, Ohio
Control Nov. 1879, by Lake Shore & Michigan Southern
Leased Nov. 1879, to Lake Shore & Michigan Southern
Foreclosure sale Sept. 25, 1888, to Detroit & Chicago RR Co.

The Chicago and Grand Trunk Railway Company
O: 013, 014, 023, 025, 033, 039, 044, 074, 075, 078
Inc. Jan. 7, 1880; $6,600,000
To consolidate: Michigan Ry., Chicago & Northeastern, North Western Grand Trunk, Indiana Ry (Ind. corp.), Northwestern Grand Trunk Ry in Indiana & Illinois (Ind. and Ill. corp.)
Control at inc. by Grand Trunk Ry of Canada
Line acquired at cons., Port Huron to Chicago
Lease Dec. 22, 1880, of Grand Trunk Jct. (Ill. corp.)
Amend July 2, 1887, to reduce number of directors
Operating agreement Oct. 2, 1890, eff. Nov. 1, 1890, of Cincinnati, Saginaw & Mackinaw
Foreclosure sale Oct. 31, 1900, to Port Huron & Indiana (Mich. lines) and Indiana & Illinois (Ind. lines) and Chicago Lake County (Ill. lines)

The Chicago and Kalamazoo Terminal Railroad Company
O: 039
Inc. June 27, 1895; $100,000; Kalamazoo
To own: 7 miles, line in Kalamazoo
Control Feb. 28, 1907, by Grand Trunk Western
Amend July 21, 1909, to revise route: 7 miles, in Kalamazoo
Leased Aug. 1, 1910, line from Chicago, Kalamazoo & Saginaw (Pavilion to Pavilion Jct.)
Merged Nov. 1, 1928, to Grand Trunk Western

Chicago and Lake Huron Railroad Company
O: 013, 014, 023, 025, 033, 039, 044, 074, 075, 078
Inc. April 5, 1873; $10,000,000; Port Huron
To consolidate: Peninsular and Port Huron & Lake Michigan
Consolidated July 30, 1878, above named corps.
Line acquired at cons. Port Huron to Flint and Lansing to Valparaiso
Foreclosure sale Aug. 25, 1879, to Michigan Ry, Indiana Ry (Ind. corp.), and North Western Grand Trunk

The Chicago and Michigan Grand Trunk Railway Company
P: 003, 008, 011, 023, 033, 047, 050, 063, 074
Inc. Sept. 1, 1865; $2,000,000; St. Joseph
To own: 250 miles, Ridgeway via Lansing, Otsego, Paw Paw, Lawrence and St. Joseph to Indiana state line in Berrien co.
Lapsed

Chicago & Michigan Lake Shore—
O: 003, 011, 041, 061, 062, 064, 070, 080 P: 051, 053
Inc. April 23, 1869, as Chicago and Michigan Lake Shore Rail Road Company; $1,000,000; St. Joseph
To own: 30 miles, St. Joseph to Indiana state line
Amend July 12, 1869, as Chicago and Michigan Lake Shore Railroad Company
To consolidate: Lake Shore RR of Western Michigan
Line opened Feb. 2, 1870, New Buffalo to St. Joseph
Amend Aug. 15, 1870, to consolidate: Grand Rapids & Lake Shore
Amend Oct. 25, 1871, as The Chicago and Michigan Lake Shore Railroad Company, to consolidate: Grand Rapids & Holland and Montague Pentwater & Manistee
Line completed Jan. 1, 1872, New Buffalo to Pentwater
Amend July 27, 1872, as Chicago and Michigan Lake Shore Railroad Company; Muskegon (office in 1875), to consolidate: Muskegon & Big Rapids
Receivership begun Nov. 11, 1876, George C. Kimball, receiver
Foreclosure sale, Nov. 15, 1878, to Chicago & West Michigan

Chicago and Northeastern Railroad Company
O: 025, 033, 078
Inc. July 11, 1874; $1,000,000; Lansing
To own: 48 miles, Chicago & Lake Huron in Flint to C&LH in Lansing
Line completed Jan. 1, 1877, Lansing to Flint
Merged Jan. 7, 1880, to Chicago & Grand Trunk

Chicago and North Michigan Railroad Company
O: 005, 015, 024, 028 P: 045
Inc. Feb. 28, 1891; $1,500,000; Grand Rapids
To own: 135 miles, Leland to Straits of Mackinac
Control at inc. by Chicago & West Michigan
Leased June 1, 1891, for 999 years to Chicago & West Michigan
Line completed July 17, 1892, Traverse City to Bay View
Sold Nov. 3, 1899, to Chicago & West Michigan
Foreclosure sale March 26, 1917, to Pere Marquette

Chicago & North Western Railway Company
O: 021, 022, 027, 036, 052, 055, 066
Inc. June 7, 1859 (Ill. corp.)
Bought June 7, 1859, Chicago, St. Paul & Fond du Lac
Inc. Oct. 21, 1864; no capital limit; Chicago
To consolidate: Peninsula and Chicago & North Western (Ill. co.)
Line acquired at cons. Escanaba to Ishpeming
Amend June 21, 1870, not found
Control 1877, of Menominee River
Control ca. 1880, of Escanaba & Lake Superior Ry
Amend July 1, 1882, to consolidate Escanaba & Lake Superior and Menominee River
Control Oct. 11, 1886, at inc., of Iron River
Control Aug. 15, 1887, at inc., of Iron Range
Bought June 10, 1889, Iron River and Iron Range
Control June 14, 1890, at inc., of Paint River
Lease May 15, 1891, of Escanaba, Iron Mountain & Western
Bought June 4, 1891, Paint River
Bought Aug. 19, 1893, Milwaukee, Lake Shore & Western
Amend Feb. 10, 1903, to increase capital to $100,000,000
Amend Oct. 18, 1906, to increase capital to $200,000,000
Amend Nov. 18, 1929, to increase capital to $300,000,000
Consolidated Oct. 7, 1947, Escanaba, Iron Mountain & Western
Conveyed June 1, 1972, to Chicago & North Western Transpn. Co.

Chicago & North Western Transportation Co.
O: 021, 022, 027, 036, 052, 055, 066
Inc. May 1972; Chicago
To rename: North Western Employees Transportation Co.
Bought June 1, 1972, Chicago & North Western Railway
Control June 21, 1985, by CNW Corp.
Active corporation

Chicago & West Michigan—
O: 003, 005, 010, 011, 015, 024, 028, 040, 041, 043
Inc. Dec. 20, 1878, as Chicago and West Michigan Railroad Company; $6,151,000; Muskegon
To reorganize: Chicago & Michigan Lake Shore
Line acquired at inc. New Buffalo to Pentwater and branches
Control Nov. 14, 1879, at inc., of White River
Lease April 1, 1880, for 999 years, of White River
Amend April 20, 1881, to change northern terminus to Manistee
Amend July 16, 1881, as Chicago and West Michigan Railway Company; $6,796,833; Boston, Muskegon, Grand Rapids; to consolidate: Grand Haven; Grand Rapids, Newaygo & Lake Shore; and Indiana & Michigan (Ind. corp.)
Bought Feb. 7, 1884, White River
Control 1886, of Muskegon Lake
Verbal lease 1886, of Grand Rapids Transfer & Junction
Amend July 10, 1889; $6,800,000; to add branch: Baldwin to Mackinaw City
Control Feb. 28, 1891, at inc., of Chicago & North Michigan
Lease June 1, 1891, for 999 years, of Chicago & North Michigan
Amend Aug. 16, 1892, to increase capital to $7,525,000
Lease ca. 1898, for 10 years, of Grand Rapids, Kalkaska & Southern
Bought Nov. 3, 1899, Chicago & North Michigan
Sold Dec. 7, 1899, to Pere Marquette
Control 1903, of Grand Rapids, Kalkaska & Southeasern
Foreclosure sale March 28, 1917, to Pere Marquette

The Chicago, Detroit and Canada Grand Trunk Junction Rail Road Company
O: 050, 074, 082
Inc. March 18, 1858; $480,000; Detroit
To own: 60 miles, Detroit to St. Clair River at Port Huron
Leased July 1, 1859, for 999 years to Grand Trunk Ry of Canada
Line completed Nov. 21, 1859, West Detroit to Fort Gratiot
Merged Nov. 1, 1928, to Grand Trunk Western

Chicago, Detroit & Toledo Railroad Company
P: 058, 082
Inc.(T) April 21, 1898; $500,000
To own: 57 miles, Toledo to Detroit
Lapsed

Chicago, Indiana & Southern Railroad Company
O: not in Michigan
Inc. April 6, 1906 (Ind. corp.)
To consolidate: Indiana, Illinois & Iowa and non-Michigan companies
Control at inc. by Lake Shore & Michigan Southern
Merged Jan. 1, 1915, dated Dec. 23, 1914, into New York Central

Chicago, Kalamazoo and Eastern Railway Company
P: 014, 039, 080
Inc. Dec. 30, 1905; $250,000; Kalamazoo
To own: 30 miles, Kalamazoo to Paw Paw with branch from Texas Corners to Marcellus
Lapsed

Chicago, Kalamazoo and Saginaw Railway Company
O: 008, 023, 039 P: 014, 019, 029, 034, 073
Inc. June 7, 1883; $250,000; Kalamazoo
To own: 31 miles, Kalamazoo to Hastings
Acquired Dec. 31, 1884, part of right of way from Kalamazoo, Lowell & Northern Michigan
Amend Oct. 29, 1887; $2,000,000; to build: 141 miles, Chicago & Grand Trunk in NE corner Cass co., via Kalamazoo and Hastings, to city of Saginaw
Amend Dec. 9, 1887, to confirm amendment of Oct. 29, 1887
Line completed Sept. 1, 1889, Kalamazoo to Woodbury
Control 1906, by Michigan Central
Leased Aug. 1, 1910, for 99 years, part of line (Pavilion to Pavilion Jct.) to Chicago & Kalamazoo Terminal
Leased Feb. 1, 1930, to New York Central
Conveyed April 1, 1976, some rail properties to Consolidated Rail
Conveyed Oct. 24, 1978, rail properties to Penn Central Corp.
Merged Dec. 31, 1981, into United RR

The Chicago, Lake Michigan and Eastern Railway Company
P: 011, 014
Inc. Sept 4, 1891; $500,000
To own: 60 miles, St. Joseph River in St. Joseph twp. to Indiana state line at E line St. Joseph co.
Lapsed

Chicago, Michigan and Indiana Electric Railway Company (E)
P: 011
Inc.(S) June 15, 1903; $3,000,000; Benton Harbor
To own: from Indiana state line S of Cassopolis, via Cassopolis and Dowagiac, to St. Joseph and Benton Harbor, with branches to Kalamazoo and Allegan
Lapsed

Chicago, Milwaukee & St. Paul Railway Company
O: 007, 022, 031, 036, 052, 055, 066
Inc. Feb. 11, 1874 (Wisc. corp.); Chicago
Control Sept. 1890, of Milwaukee & Northern
Bought June 23, 1893, Milwaukee & Northern
Conveyed Jan. 13, 1928, to Chicago, Milwaukee, St. Paul & Pacific

Chicago Milwaukee Corporation
O: Holding company
Inc. June 24, 1971 (Dela. corp.); Chicago
Holding company of Chicago, Milwaukee, St. Paul & Pacific
Stock exchanged Jan. 14, 1972, for Chicago, Milwaukee, St. Paul & Pacific

Chicago, Milwaukee, St. Paul and Pacific Railroad Company
O: 007, 022, 031, 036, 052, 055, 066
Inc. March 31, 1927 (Wisc. corp.); $350,000,000; Chicago
To reorganize: Chicago, Milwaukee & St. Paul
Acquired Jan. 13, 1928, property of Chicago, Milwaukee & St. Paul (line Wisc. state line to Champion and Ontonagon)
Bankruptcy entered June 29, 1935
Reorganized Nov. 26, 1945, eff. Jan. 1, 1944
Stock exchanged Jan. 14, 1972, for Chicago Milwaukee Corp.
Bankruptcy entered Dec. 19, 1977
Operating agreement March 10, 1980, Mich. lines by Escanaba & Lake Superior
Sold Sept. 29, 1980, Mich. lines to Escanaba & Lake Superior

The Chicago, Saginaw and Canada Railroad Company
O: 029, 059 P: 025, 041, 044, 050, 061, 062, 070, 073, 074
Inc. Dec. 24, 1872; $4,200,000; St. Louis
To own: 210 miles, Grand Haven, via Fruitport, to St. Clair
Amend June 30, 1873, to own: 220 miles, Grand Haven, via Fruitport, to St. Clair
Line opened Aug. 15, 1875, St. Louis to Riverdale
Receivership begun Nov. 20, 1877, David D. Erwin, receiver
Foreclosure sale May 10, 1883, to Saginaw & Western

Chicago, St. Paul and Fond du Lac Rail Road Company
P: 022, 027, 052, 066
Inc. March 31, 1855 (Wisc. corp.)
Amend March 21, 1857, to consolidate: Marquette & State Line and Chicago, St. Paul & Fond du Lac (Ill. and Wisc. corp.)
Amend March 27, 1857, to consolidate Ontonagon & State Line
Foreclosure sale June 2, 1859, to Chicago & North Western

Chickering [C.] and Kysor [Frank] (Gauge 3')
O: 028
Private logging road; Grand Rapids
3 miles, Fife Lake
Built 1882

Chippewa Lake Logging Railroad (Gauge 3')
O: 054
Private logging road
Owned by Chippewa Lumber Co.
Line built 1883, 3 miles in T16N R8W; abandoned after 1883

Chippewa Lumber Co.
O: 017
Private logging road; Strongs

Owned Chippewa Lake Logging

Chippewa Portage Company
O: 017
Chartered March 17, 1847
To build road, plank road, or railroad around St. Marys River falls
Acquired about 1847 line from McKnight Brothers & Tinker
Abandoned about 1855

Chippewa Valley Railway Company
P: 037, 043, 051, 053, 054, 062
Inc. Sept. 25, 1888; $1,800,000
To own: 120 miles, Mt. Pleasant to Manistee
Lapsed

Chittendon Lumber Co.
O: 083
Private logging road
Cadillac
About 1892

Church Quarry Co.
O: 027
Private industrial road
Stickley

Cincinnati and Great Northern Railroad Company
P: 005, 009, 016, 018, 019, 020, 024, 026, 029, 030, 033, 037, 038, 040, 056, 057, 060, 065, 068, 069, 072, 073, 078
Inc. March 26, 1873; $2,200,000
To own: 275 miles, Amboy in Hillsdale co. to Straits of Mackinac
Merged June 7, 1873, into Cincinnati & Great Northern (Ohio corp.)

Cincinnati and Michigan Railroad Company
O: Reorganizing company
Inc. July 17, 1891 (Ohio corp.)
To acquire: Ohio division of Cincinnati, Jackson & Mackinaw RR
Merged July 17, 1891, into Cincinnati, Jackson & Mackinaw Ry

Cincinnati, Hamilton & Dayton Railway Company
Inc. Ohio corp.
Control Sept. 1907, of Pere Marquette RR
Control ended May 1912, of Pere Marquette RR

The Cincinnati, Jackson and Mackinaw Railroad Company
O: 003, 008, 013, 030, 038, 039, 046, 058
Inc. Jan. 20, 1886; $4,032,000
To consolidate: Jackson & Ohio and Cincinnati, Van Wert & Michigan (Ohio corp.)
Amend Feb. 10, 1887, to increase capital to $20,850,000
Bought March 25, 1887, Michigan & Ohio
Amend May 15, 1887, to adjust capital structure
Receivership begun Nov. 7, 1889, Walston H. Brown, receiver
Foreclosure sale Jan. 8, 1892; Michigan division to Michigan & Mackinaw, Ohio division to Cincinnati & Michigan (Ohio corp.)

Cincinnati, Jackson and Mackinaw Railway Company
O: 003, 008, 013, 030, 038, 039, 046, 058
Inc. July 17, 1891; $16,300,000
To consolidate: Michigan & Mackinaw and Cincinnati & Michigan (Ohio corp.)
Receivership Dec. 6, 1894, Frank B. Drake,receiver
Foreclosure sale Jan. 5, 1897; Michigan division to Toledo & Milwaukee RR, Ohio division to Cincinnati Northern

The Cincinnati Northern Railroad Company
O: 003, 008, 013, 030, 038, 039, 046, 058
Inc. Dec. 7, 1894 (Ohio corp.)
To acquire: Ohio division of Cincinnati, Jackson & Mackinaw Ry
Line acquired at inc. Addison Jct. to Carlisle, Ohio
Bought June 1, 1898, Jackson & Cincinnati
Lease Jan. 6, 1899, eff. Jan. 1, 1899, of Detroit, Toledo & Milwaukee
Lease cancelled Dec. 31, 1901, of Detroit, Toledo & Milwaukee
Control Jan. 1, 1902, by Cleveland, Cincinnati, Chicago & St. Louis
Leased Sept. 27, 1926, to Cleveland, Cincinnati, Chicago & St. Louis
Merged June 30, 1938, into Cleveland, Cincinnati, Chicago & St. Louis

Cincinnati, Saginaw and Mackinaw—
O: 009, 025, 073, 078 P: 046, 047, 081
Inc. Dec. 26, 1889, as Cincinnati, Saginaw and Mackinaw Rail Road Company; $5,000,000; Detroit
To own: 350 miles, Ohio state line in Seneca twp., Lenawee co. to Straits of Mackinac
Bought Dec. 31, 1889, Toledo, Saginaw & Mackinaw (Line acquired Durand to Bay City)
Operating agreement Oct. 2, 1890, eff. Nov. 1, 1890, by Chicago & Grand Trunk
Amend Dec. 8, 1890, as Cincinnati, Saginaw and Mackinaw Railroad Company, to change number of directors
Leased Jan. 1, 1901, for 99 years, to Grand Trunk Ry of Canada
Amend June 18, 1918, to reduce capital to $1,500,000
Lease assigned Nov. 15, 1928, eff. Jan. 1, 1928 to Grand Trunk Western
Merged Jan. 1, 1943, into Grand Trunk Western

The Cincinnati, Wabash and Michigan Railway Company
O: 011, 014
Inc. May 23, 1882; $4,000,000
To consolidate: Elkhart, Niles & Lake Michigan and Cincinnati, Wabash & Michigan (Ind. corp.)
Line completed Nov. 13, 1882, Benton Harbor to Goshen, Ind.
Control July 1, 1892, by Cleveland, Cincinnati, Chicago & St. Louis
Merged Dec. 17, 1913, into Cleveland, Cincinnati, Chicago & St. Louis

Citizens Street Railway Company (E)
O: 039
Inc.(S) March 21, 1893; $200,000; Kalamazoo
To own: in Kalamazoo and adjoining townships
Apparently acquired Kalamazoo Street Ry
Control Oct. 1, 1898, by Michigan Traction
Merged no date, into Michigan Traction

Citizens Street Railway Company of Battle Creek (E)
O: 013
Inc.(S) Oct. 1, 1894; $100,000; Battle Creek
To own: in Battle Creek and in Emmett, Penfield and Battle Creek townships
Acquired no date, Battle Creek Electric
Control Oct. 1, 1898, by Michigan Traction
Merged no date, into Michigan Traction

Citizens Traction Company
P: Holding company
Inc. ca. 1897
To: hold properties controlled by Detroit Citizens' Street Ry [Unclear if company did conduct any activity]

City and Suburban Traction Company (E)
P: 082
Inc.(S) March 10, 1894; $25,000; Detroit
To own: in Detroit, Dearborn, and adjacent villages and townships
Lapsed

City Contract Company
P: 082
Inc.(S) Aug. 25, 1928; capital not given; Highland Park
To own: in city of Detroit
Lapsed

The City Electric Railway Company of Port Huron (E)
O: 074
Inc.(S) May 19, 1892; $100,000
To own: in Port Huron and Fort Gratiot and adjoining named twps.
Acquired at inc. Port Huron Electric and Gratiot Electric
Amend Dec. 15, 1892, to increase number of directors
Control April 12, 1899, at inc., of Port Huron, St. Clair & Marine City
Control July 1900, by Detroit & Port Huron Shore Line

The City Electric Railway Company of Port Huron (E)
P: 074
Inc.(S) May 13, 1923; $100,000
To own: in Port Huron and Fort Gratiot
Lapsed

The City of Saginaw Street Rail Road
See Saginaw Street Ry (1886)

City Rail Road Company (H)
P: 074
Inc.(S) June 28, 1873; $50,000
To own: in city of Port Huron and Gratiot twp.
Merged April 5, 1877, into Port Huron Ry

City Street Railway Company of Grand Rapids
P: 041
Inc.(S) Oct. 10, 1887; $100,000; Grand Rapids
To own: in Grand Rapids and adjacent towns
Lapsed

Clam River Railroad (Gauge 3')
O: 057
Private logging road; office: Grand Rapids
Owned by D. A. Blodgett
5 miles
Built about 1881; abandoned about 1882

Clark, Snyder and Co.
O: 059
Private logging road; Coral
Line built about 1879, in T11N R9W

The Cleveland, Cincinnati, Chicago and St. Louis Railway Company
O: 011, 014, 030, 038, 046
Inc. June 7, 1889 (Ohio corp.)
Control July 1, 1892, of Cincinnati, Wabash & Michigan
Control Jan. 1, 1902, of Cincinnati Northern
Acquired Dec. 17, 1913, Cincinnati, Wabash & Michigan
Lease Sept. 27, 1926, of Cincinnati Northern
Leased Feb. 1, 1930, for 99 years to New York Central
Consolidated June 30, 1938, Cincinnati Northern
Conveyed April 1, 1976, some rail properties to Consolidated Rail
Conveyed Oct. 24, 1978, rail properties to Penn Central Corp.
Merged Dec. 31, 1981, into Penn Central Corp.

Cleveland Cliffs Iron Co.
O: 002
Private logging road .
ca. 60 miles, Vail southeasterly to T44N R19W
Built 1916; abandoned 1925

——

O: 052
Dixon northwesterly to T46N R21W
Built 1921; abandoned 1928

——

Controlled Lake Superior & Ishpeming; Marquette & Southeastern; Munising; and Munising, Marquette & Southeastern

The Clinton and Adrian Rail-road Company
P: 046
Chartered March 28, 1836; $50,000
To own: 15 miles, Clinton to Adrian
Lapsed

CNW Corporation
O: Holding company
Inc. March 27, 1985 (Dela. corp.)
Control June 21, 1985, dated April 19, of Chicago & North Western Transp.

Cobbs [Johnathan W.] and Mitchell [William W.] (Gauge 3')
O: 057, 083
Private logging road
5 miles, Wexford and Missaukee cos.
Built 1882

——

Owned Boyne Falls & Northeastern

Cody [Lorenzo J.] and Addis Lumber Co. (Gauge 3')
O: 062
Private logging road; office: Big Rapids

Cody [Lorenzo J.] and Moore
Owned Muskrat Lake & Clam River

Cody, L[orenzo] J., Lumber Co.
Private logging road; Muskegon

Coe Rail, Inc.
O: 063
Inc. Jan. 31, 1984; $50,000; Farmington Hills
To: not stated
Bought Aug. 1984, line (Wixom-Walled Lake) from Grand Trunk Western
Active corporation

Cold Springs Railroad
O: 005
Private logging road
Owned by Antrim Iron Co.

Coldwater and Central Michigan Railroad Company
P: 012, 013, 019, 023, 029, 034, 059
Inc. July 17, 1884; $1,500,000
To own: 100 miles, Coldwater to Riverdale
Lapsed

Coldwater, Marshall and Mackinaw Rail Road Company
P: 012, 013, 023, 034, 037, 059
Inc. Sept. 5, 1874
To rename: Marshall & Coldwater
Amend Nov. 14, 1876, to change northern terminus to Mt. Pleasant and change capital to $1,500,000
Sold Oct. 18, 1884, to Toledo, Marshall & Northern
Renamed Dec. 13, 1906, as Toledo Michigan & Lake Huron

The Coldwater Train Railway Company (E)
O: 012
Inc.(T) Sept. 21, 1905; $3,000; Coldwater
To own: 3 miles, clay beds (sec 32 T6S R6W) to LS&MS (sec 20 T6S R6W)
Amend Sept. 23, 1935, to extend corporate life
Abandoned

The Colfax and Big Rapids Railroad (Gauge 3')
O: 054
Inc. Jan. 17, 1887; $40,000
To own: 8 miles, E branch Muskegon River in S½ NE¼ sec 14 T15N R10W to Twin Lakes at N line sec 14 T15N R9W
Line opened March 1, 1887, 8 miles Big Rapids to T15N R9W
Abandoned 1889

The Columbus and Lake Michigan Railroad Company
P: 003, 008, 012, 013, 030, 039
Inc. Sept. 5, 1888; $1,000,000
To own: 125 miles, Indiana state line in Hillsdale co. to Saugatuck twp., Allegan co. on Lake Michigan
Merged Jan. 3, 1889, to Columbus, Lima & Milwaukee

The Columbus, Lima and Milwaukee Railway Company
P: 003, 008, 012, 013, 030
Inc. Jan. 3, 1889; $10,000,000; Lima, Ohio
To consolidate: Columbus & Lake Michigan and non-Michigan corps. (in Mich. and own line: Ohio state line to Saugatuck)
Lapsed

The Columbus, Marshall & Northeastern Railroad Company
P: 009, 013, 019, 023, 029, 034, 056, 059
Inc. Jan. 20, 1899; $1,200,000; Marshall
To own: 140 miles, Marshall to Bay City
Lapsed

Commonwealth Power Railway & Light Company
O: Holding company
Inc.(Not RR) March 8, 1910
Control at inc. by Commonwealth Power Co. and Michigan Light Co.
Controlled Saginaw & Flint and Michigan Ry (1914 corp.)

Comstock, C(harles) C. (Gauge 3')
O: 062, 067
Private logging road; Grand Rapids
Built 1882, 5 miles, T11N R12W
4 miles, T17-18N R9W

Conglomerate Mining Co.
O: 042
Private mining road
At Conglomerate Mine

The Congress and Baker Street Railway Company (H)
O: 082
Inc.(S) Sept. 15, 1875; $100,000
To reorganize: Detroit & Grand Trunk Junction Street Ry
Sold June 22, 1882, to Detroit City Ry

The Connecting Railway Company
O: Holding co.
Inc. July 22, 1901 (Penn. corp.)
Owned at inc., by Pennsylvania RR
Consolidated Dec. 9, 1956, dated Oct. 26, 1955, Pennsylvania, Ohio & Detroit
Owned Feb. 28, 1968, by Penn Central Co.
Owned Oct. 1, 1969, by Penn Central Transportation Co.
Conveyed April 1, 1976, some rail properties to Consolidated Rail
Conveyed Oct. 24, 1978, rail properties to Penn Central Corp.
Disposition uncertain

Connor Land and Lumber Co.
O: 027
Private logging road; office: Wakefield
Line, Connorville to T48N R46W and to T49N R45&46W

Connorville and Lake Superior Railway Company
O: 027
Inc. Dec. 30, 1927; $50,000
To own: 3 miles in Wakefield twp.
Uncertain if ever an active operating company

Conrail,
See Consolidated Rail Corp.

Consolidated Rail Corporation
O: 003, 011, 012, 013, 014, 033, 038, 039, 041, 058, 075, 081, 082
Inc. Feb. 10, 1976 (Penn. corp.)
(To acquire property of Penn Central in bankruptcy)
Line acquired April 1, 1976, part of Penn Central Transp. Co.
Operating agreement April 1, 1976, with state of Michigan
Owned Nov. 23, 1981, at inc., United Railroad Corp.
Consolidated May 31, 1984, dated May 7, Detroit Terminal
Sold April 30, 1985, Canada Southern Ry and Detroit River Tunnel Co. to Canadian National Rys and Canadian Pacific jointly
Active corporation

Consolidated Street Railway Company (E)
O: 041
Inc.(S) July 1, 1891; $2,000,000
To own: in Grand Rapids city and township and adjacent villages and to rename Valley City St. & Cable Ry
Amend Feb. 10, 1896, to increase capital to $3,000,000
Conveyed April 17, 1900, to Grand Rapids Ry

The Constantine and Niles Canal or rail-road Company
P: 011, 014, 075
Chartered March 26, 1836; $250,000
To own: 33 miles, Constantine to Niles, or to build canal
Lapsed

Consumers Power Co.
O: 062
Private industrial road
5 miles, Erwin to Croton Dam
Built 1906

Converse Lumber Co.
O: 062
Private logging road
Newaygo co.

Cook and Wilson (Gauge 3')
O: 017
Private logging road
Chippewa co.

Cook, Charles H.
O: 064
Private logging road; Montague
4 miles, near Montague
About 1878

Coopersville & Marne Railroad Company
O: 070
Inc. July 13, 1989
To: buy line, Marne to Coopersville
Bought Dec. 14, 1989, line from Central Michigan
Active corporation

Copley, E. J. (Gauge 3')
O: 043
Private logging road
Built 1884, 2.5 miles, in Lake co.

Copper Falls Mining Co.
O: 042
Private mining tramway
Copper Falls Mine to stamp mill

Copper Range Railroad Company
O: 031, 042, 066
Inc. Jan. 23, 1899; $5,000,000; Houghton
To rename: Northern Michigan RR and build 90 miles, Calumet via Greenland to Watersmeet
Line opened Dec. 7, 1899, Houghton to Winona
Line completed April 6, 1903, McKeever to Calumet
Lease 1917, of Mohawk Mining Co. RR
Amend June 16, 1937, to reduce capital to $3,280,000
Line abandoned March 2, 1973
Dissolved Dec. 28, 1979

The Corlies and Thunder Bay Train Railway Company
O: 004
Inc.(T) Jan. 21, 1864; $10,000
To own: 7 miles, N side Thunder Bay NWly to rapids in sec 1 T31N R7E
Owned by John Trowbridge and Brothers
Operated in mid-1860s

Covell [Andrew J. and Charles E.] Brothers (Gauge 3')
O: 064
Private logging road; Whitehall
Built 1883, 6 miles in T14-15N R15W

Crapo Lake & Northwestern
O: 069
Private logging road
Owned by Gratwick, Smith & Fryer Lumber Co.
8 miles, Crapo Lake northwesterly in T29N R1&2W
Built 1882

The Crawford and Manistee River Railway Company (Gauge 3')
O: 040
Inc. Sept. 16, 1885; $50,000; Manistee
To own: 10 miles, sec 13 T25N R5W, to sec 25 T26N R6W
Line opened Oct. 11, 1885, 10 miles
Abandoned 1904

Cross and Morrison
O: 053
Private logging tram road
Vicinity of Ludington

Croswell and Peck Railway Company (Gauge 3')
P: 076
Inc. Nov. 17, 1879; $50,000
To own: 10 miles, Lexington twp. to Peck
Lapsed

The Crystal Lake Railroad Company
P: 059
Inc. Nov. 10, 1891; $75,000
To own: 7 miles, line of Toledo, Saginaw & Muskegon in Bloomer twp. to Crystal Lake
Lapsed

Crystal Lake Railway Company
P: 019, 034, 059
Inc.(T) Sept. 25, 1900; $25,000; St. Johns
To own: 25 miles, Crystal, via Carson City and Hubbardston, to Maple Rapids
Merged no date, into Lansing, St. Johns & St. Louis

CSX Corporation
O: Holding company
Inc. Nov. 1, 1980 (Va. corp.)
Merged Nov. 1, 1980, Chessie System and Seaboard Coast Line Inds.
Control at inc., of Chesapeake & Ohio
Control transferred July 1, 1986, to CSX Transp., of Chesapeake & Ohio
Active corporation

CSX Transportation Company
O: *See* Chesapeake & Ohio
Inc. July 1, 1986
To: rename Seaboard System RR (non-Mich. corp.)
Control at inc., of Chesapeake & Ohio
Sold March 27, 1986, part (Kinde-Croswell) to Huron & Eastern
Consolidated Sept. 2, 1987, Chesapeake & Ohio
Sold Dec. 18, 1987, part to Mid-Michigan RR
Sold Dec. 22, 1988, part (Saginaw-Bad Axe) to Huron & Eastern
Active corporation

Culhane, Con
O: 017, 048
Private logging road
Luce co.
Operated 1893 to 1903

Cummer [Jacob] and Diggins (Gauge 3')
O: 083
Private logging road; Cadillac
Wexford co.

Cummer, J(acob), and Son (Gauge 3')
O: 083
Private logging road; Cadillac
Wexford co.

Cummer [Jacob] Lumber Co. (Gauge 3')
O: 083
Private logging road; Cadillac

Owned Cadillac & Northeastern

Curtis, W. A., Lumber Co.
O: unknown
Private logging road; State Line

Cutler [Dwight?] and Savidge [Hunter] Lumber Co. (Gauge 4')
O: 059
Private logging road; Grand Haven
Built 1882, 4.5-9 miles, Six Lakes to T12N R6W

D

Danaher and Melendy [Lumber Co.] (Gauge 3')
O: 043
Private logging road; Baldwin
4 miles, in Lake co.

O: 048
Private logging road
Danaher north
Built 1895; abandoned 1902

Owned North Branch & Sauble River

Darragh and Sellinger
O: 072
Private logging road
Roscommon co.
Built mid-1880s

Dead River Railroad Company
P: 052
Inc. Nov. 6, 1889; $25,000
To own: 3 miles, Duluth, South Shore & Atlantic in Marquette co. to near the mouth of the Dead River
Lapsed

Deer Creek and Marble Quarry Rail Road Company
P: 022, 055
Inc. Dec. 20, 1869; $1,000,000; Menominee
To own: 40 miles from Deer Creek in T36N R24W via Breen Mine to T39N R29W
Lapsed

DeHaas, N. N., and Co.
O; 007
Private logging road
L'Anse

DeLatrie and Anderson Lumber Co.
O: 066
Private logging road
Calderwood

Del-Par Railroad Corporation
P: not given
Inc. Oct. 19, 1981; $50,000; Saginaw
To operate RR in Michigan
Disposition uncertain

Delray Connecting Railroad Company
O: 082
Inc. March 24, 1904; $50,000
To own: 2 miles, Delray to Detroit Southern RR on Zug Island

Line completed June 29, 1904
Amend Dec. 24, 1915, to increase capital to $1,000,000
Amend April 18, 1918, to change number of directors
Amend June 20, 1919, to increase capital to $1,500,000
Amend March 15, 1922, to change number of directors
Amend Feb. 10, 1938, to change number of directors
Amend March 20, 1968, to reduce capital to $50,000
Active corporation

Delray Terminal Railroad Company
O: 082
Inc. Jan. 24, 1905; $50,000; Detroit
To own: 2 miles, Delray to Detroit Edison Co.
Line completed Feb. 1, 1905
Active corporation

Delta Chemical Co.
O: 021
Private logging road
Wells

Delta Lumber Co.
O: 077
Private logging road
Near Seney

Delta Traction Company (E)
P: 021
Inc.(T) June 15, 1909; $300,000; Escanaba
To own: 14 miles, Wells twp. to Gladstone, then to Rapid River
Dissolved Feb. 13, 1915

Dennis Brothers Salt and Lumber Co.
O: 067
Private logging road
Dighton

Denton and Rowe
O: 072
Private logging tram road
2.5 miles, Houghton Lake easterly

Department of Street Railways, City of Detroit (E)
O: 082
Acquired May 15, 1922, city lines of Detroit United Ry
Rail operations ended April 8, 1956

Detour & Western Railroad
O: 017
Private logging road

Detroit, city of
See Department of Street Railways, Detroit Transportation Corp.

The Detroit, Adrian, Logansport and St. Louis Railroad Company
P: 046, 058, 081, 082
Inc. April 9, 1869; $650,000
To own: 80 miles, Detroit through Adrian to Morenci
Lapsed

Detroit, Almont & Northern Railroad Company (E)
O: 044, 050, 063, 082
Inc. Oct. 6, 1913; $500,000
To own: 50 miles, Greenfield twp., Wayne co. to Almont twp.
Control at inc. by Detroit United Ry
Line opened July 8, 1914
Bought Feb. 5, 1917, Highland Park & Royal Oak
Operations ended July 5, 1927

Detroit and Adrian Traction Company (E)
P: 046, 082
Inc.(S) March 8, 1906; $25,000; Detroit
To own: Detroit to Adrian, via Tecumseh, Milan, Belleville and Woodmere
Lapsed

Detroit and Ann Arbor Railway Company
P: 081, 082
Inc.(S) Sept. 18, 1901; $100,000; Jackson
To own: in Washtenaw and Wayne counties [construction company]
Control at inc., by Detroit & Chicago Traction
Lapsed

Detroit & Bay City—
O: 009, 044, 050, 063, 073, 079, 082
Inc. May 16, 1871, as Detroit and Bay City Railway Company (Gauge 3'); $1,000,000; Rochester
To own: 100 miles, Detroit, via Utica, Rochester, Oxford and Lapeer to Bay City
Amend Oct. 21, 1871; $1,300,000; to own: 100 miles, Detroit, via Utica, Rochester, Oxford and Vassar to Saginaw River, and change to standard gauge
Control Oct. 18, 1872, at inc., of Lapeer & Northern
Line opened Oct. 31, 1872, Bay City Jct. to Oxford
Amend May 14, 1873; $1,500,000; to change northern terminus to Jackson, Lansing & Saginaw RR at Wenona
Line completed July 31, 1873, Bay City Jct. to Bay City
Lease 1879, of Bay City Street Ry
Foreclosure sale Feb. 12, 1881
Reinc. Feb. 21, 1881, as The Detroit and Bay City Railroad Company
To reorganize Detroit & Bay City Ry; $2,000,000
Leased March 10, 1881, for corp. life to Michigan Central
Bought Jan. 1, 1886, Bay City Street Ry
Sold Nov. 22, 1893, part of line to Bay City Belt Line
Leased Nov. 22, 1893, Bay City Belt Line
Amend May 5, 1898, to reduce capital to $1,200,000

Bought May 8, 1908, Caro & Lake Huron
Sold July 20, 1909, part of line to Detroit Belt Line
Conveyed Sept. 27, 1916, to Michigan Central

Detroit & Bay City Traction Co.
See Detroit Bay City Traction

The Detroit and Charlevoix Railroad Company
O: 005, 015, 020, 040, 069
Inc. Jan. 2, 1901; $525,000; Detroit
To own: 60 miles, Frederic(k) to Charlevoix
May have acquired Frederick & Charlevoix and the rights of Detroit, Charlevoix & Escanaba
Line completed Sept. 16, 1901, Frederic to East Jordan
Control May 2, 1907, by Michigan Central
Merged Sept. 20, 1916, into Michigan Central

Detroit and Chicago Railroad Company
O: 046, 058, 082
Inc. Nov. 19, 1888; $1,000,000
To reorganize: Chicago & Canada Southern
Control at inc. by Lake Shore & Michigan Southern
Line acquired at inc., Slocum Jct. to Fayette, Ohio
Sold Nov. 15, 1897, part of line to Detroit & Lima Northern
Merged Jan. 1, 1915, into New York Central

Detroit and Chicago Traction Company
P: 013, 038, 081, 082, and others not stated [holding company]
Inc.(S) Feb. 18, 1901; $4,000,000; Jackson
To own: Detroit, via Ann Arbor, Jackson, Albion, and Marshall, to Battle Creek, thence S to Indiana state line or to Lake Michigan or to both [construction company]
Control Aug. 1, 1901, at inc., of Calhoun County Railway
Control Sept. 18, 1901, at inc., of Detroit & Ann Arbor and Jackson & Ann Arbor
Control Oct. 10, 1901, at inc., of Jackson & Albion Electric
Control Oct. 25, 1901, at inc., of Battle Creek & Marshall Traction
Lapsed

Detroit and Cincinnati Railway Company
P: 046, 058, 082
Inc. Feb. 26, 1896; $500,000; Detroit
To own: 62 miles, Detroit to Ohio state line in Seneca twp., Lenawee co.
Renamed Feb. 18, 1897, as Detroit & Lima Northern

Detroit & Dearborn Street Railway Company (E)
P: 082
Inc.(S) March 11, 1891; $100,000; Detroit
To own: in Detroit, Springwells and Dearborn
Lapsed

Detroit & Flint Railway Company (E)
O: 025, 050, 063, 082
Inc.(S) Aug. 9, 1901; $250,000
To buy: Detroit, Rochester, Romeo & Lake Orion; Detroit, Lake Orion & Flint; North Detroit Electric; and Detroit, Utica & Romeo
Control at inc. by Detroit United Ry
Bought Aug. 28, 1901, Detroit, Lake Orion & Flint
Bought Oct. 10, 1901, North Detroit Electric Ry
Sold ca. 1901, to Detroit United Ry

The Detroit and Grand Trunk Junction Street Railway Company (H)
O: 082
Inc.(S) March 27, 1873; $150,000; Detroit
To own: in Detroit
Line opened Dec. 18, 1873
Reorganized Sept. 15, 1875, as Congress & Baker Street Ry

Detroit & Highland Park Railroad Company (E)
P: 082
Inc. July 11, 1912; $50,000
To own: 2.5 miles, in Detroit
Amend July 18, 1916, to increase capital to $100,000 and to revise route to 10 miles, add branch to sec 17, Springwells twp.
Lapsed

The Detroit and Howell Railroad Company
P: 033, 047, 081, 082
Inc. June 17, 1864; $400,000
To own: 48 miles, Detroit to Howell
Merged March 29, 1870, into Detroit, Howell & Lansing RR

The Detroit and Huron Railway Company
O: 032
Inc. Feb. 29, 1912; $148,000; Detroit
To own: 18.5 miles, Bad Axe to Cass City
Control at inc. by Grand Trunk Western
Line completed Sept. 28, 1913, Cass City to Bad Axe
Merged Nov. 1, 1928, into Grand Trunk Western

The Detroit and Ironton Railroad Company (E)
O: 082
Inc. June 11, 1921; $999,000; Dearborn
To own: Springwells twp. to Brownstown twp.
Leased Jan. 1, 1924, to Ford Transportation Co.
Amend Feb. 1, 1924, to revise route: Flat Rock to Springwells vil.
Amend April 13, 1925, to modify out-of-state route and increase capital to $15,000,000
Bought June 25, 1929, rail assets of Ford Transp. Co.
Lease assigned June 25, 1929, to Detroit, Toledo & Ironton
Merged Dec. 29, 1931, into Detroit, Toledo & Ironton

Detroit & Lake Orion Railway Company (E)
P: 050, 063, 082
Inc.(S) March 14, 1899; $300,000; Detroit
To own: Detroit to Lake Orion via Pontiac and Rochester
Renamed May 25, 1899, as Detroit, Rochester, Romeo & Lake Orion

Detroit & Lake St. Clair Railway (E)
O: 050, 082
Inc.(S) March 23, 1900; $25,000; Lakeside
To own: Mt. Clemens to Grosse Pointe Farms
Bought March 24, 1900, Detroit, Lake Shore & Mt. Clemens
Control July 1900, by Detroit & Port Huron Shore Line
Amend March 8, 1901, to change office to New Baltimore
Amend Feb. 5, 1923, to change office to Highland Park
Dissolved April 23, 1930

The Detroit and Lima Northern Railway Company
O: 046, 058, 082
Inc. Feb. 18, 1897; $500,000
To rename: Detroit & Cincinnati
Amend March 26, 1897, to increase capital to $5,000,000
Line opened May 25, 1897, Adrian to Tecumseh
Bought Nov. 15, 1897, part of line of Detroit & Chicago RR
Amend Nov. 17, 1897, to include line of Lima Northern
Bought apparently Nov. 1897, Lima Northern (deed dated July 6, 1896)
Amend July 30, 1898, to increase capital to $8,000,000
Line completed Aug. 18, 1898, Delray via Tecumseh to Ohio line
Receivership Sept. 6, 1898
Foreclosure sale May 23, 1901, to Detroit Southern

Detroit and Mackinac Railway Company
O: 001, 004, 006, 009, 016, 020, 035, 060, 065, 068, 069, 071, 072
Inc. Dec. 17, 1894; $3,000,000; Detroit, East Tawas
To reorganize: Detroit, Bay City & Alpena
Line acquired at inc., Alger to Alpena
Bought April 16, 1895, Alpena & Northern
Leased June 29, 1907, Erie & Michigan Ry & Navigation
Leased June 1, 1912, AuSable & Northwestern Ry Co.
Bought June 1, 1914, AuSable & Northwestern Ry Co.
Bought Jan. 1949, Erie & Michigan Ry & Navigation
Operating agreement, April 1, 1976, with state of Michigan
Active corporation

The Detroit and Maumee Railroad Company
P: 058, 082
Chartered Aug. 25, 1835; $1,000,000
To own: 55 miles, Detroit to Maumee Bay
Jt.Res. July 26, 1836, authorized State to receive proposals to buy
Amend charter March 13, 1837, to allow to vary route as needed but must pass through Havre
Amend charter April 6, 1838, to extend completion date
Lapsed

Detroit & Milwaukee—
O: 019, 025, 034, 041, 063, 070, 078, 082
Chartered Feb. 13, 1855, as Detroit & Milwaukee Railway Company; $10,000,000; Detroit
Consolidated April 19, 1855, Detroit & Pontiac and Oakland & Ottawa
Line acquired April 19, 1855, Detroit to Pontiac
Control 1857, by Great Western Ry (Canadian corp.)
Act Feb. 14, 1857, authorized stock transfer office in Gr. Britain
Amend charter Feb. 3, 1858, not found
Line completed Nov. 22, 1858, Detroit to Grand Haven
Act Jan. 29, 1859, authorized purchase of Port Huron & Milwaukee
Act Jan. 29, 1859, established legality of borrowing from foreign sources
Receivership begun April 10, 1860
Foreclosure sale Oct. 4, 1860, to Detroit & Milwaukee RR
Inc. Oct. 18, 1860, as Detroit & Milwaukee Railroad Company; $10,000,000; Detroit
To reorganize: Detroit & Milwaukee Ry
Control at inc. by Great Western Ry (Canadian corp.)
Act March 4, 1861, authorized D&M Ry to replace stock issued by D&M RR, but with limits on further issue
Receivership begun April 15, 1875
Foreclosure sale Sept. 4, 1878, to Detroit, Grand Haven & Milw.

The Detroit and Monroe Railway Company (E)
P: 058, 082
Inc. April 30, 1901; $1,000,000
To own: 49 miles, Detroit to Monroe and branches to Carleton, South Rockwood, Trenton and Wyandotte
Amend Dec. 24, 1901, to acquire Monroe Traction, Toledo & Monroe, and Toledo & Michigan (but acquisition not completed)
Lapsed

Detroit and Northern Railway Company (E?)
P: 050, 074
Inc. Oct. 15, 1897; $256,000
To own: 32 miles, Mt. Clemens to Marine City
Lapsed

Detroit and Northwestern— (E)
O: 063, 082
Inc.(S) March 15, 1899, as Detroit and Northwestern Railway Company; $500,000; Detroit
To own: Detroit to Pontiac and other villages and townships [and buy Pontiac & Sylvan Lake]
Bought March 31, 1899, Pontiac & Sylvan Lake and Grand River Elec.
Amend April 4, 1900, as Detroit & Northwestern Railway Company, to change office to Farmington Jct.
Sold May 1, 1901, to Detroit United Ry

Detroit and Petoskey Rail Road Company
P: 016, 024
Inc. Oct. 22, 1889; $208,000
To own: 26 miles, Wolverine to Petoskey
Lapsed

The Detroit and Pontiac Railroad Company
O: 063, 082
Chartered March 7, 1834; $100,000
To own: Detroit to Pontiac, with branch to Rochester
Amend charter March 26, 1835, to allow bank and extend date to start operations
Act March 22, 1837, authorized purchase by State
Act March 5, 1838, authorized State to issue $100,000 in stock for company
Line opened May 19, 1838, Detroit to Royal Oak
Amend charter April 20, 1839, to extend completion date
Charter forfeited March 7, 1840, for non-completion
Rechartered April 13, 1841, to reinstate corporation
To build from Detroit to Pontiac
Act Feb. 11, 1842, authorized repayment to State by state bonds, stock, etc.
Resolution March 8, 1843, not compelled to operate on first day of week
Line completed July 4, 1843, Detroit to Pontiac
Act March 11, 1844, authorized State to transfer its mortgage to Alfred Williams on payment of amount due State
Act March 20, 1850, authorized connection with Oakland & Ottawa, increase capital to $200,000, allowed further increase to $500,000
Act Feb. 13, 1855, authorized merger with Oakland & Ottawa and name change to Detroit & Milwaukee
Merged April 19, 1855, into Detroit & Milwaukee

The Detroit and Pontiac Railway Company (E)
P: 063, 082
Inc.(S) Jan. 28, 1897; $250,000; Birmingham
To own: Detroit to Pontiac
Acquired at inc., Oakland Ry
Amend Aug. 3, 1897, to increase capital to $300,000
Amend Aug. 10, 1897, to increase capital to $400,000
Amend Feb. 7, 1899, to increase capital to $500,000
Sold June 1, 1901, to Detroit United Ry

Detroit and Port Huron Railway Company
P: 050, 074, 082
Inc. Jan. 7, 1858; $500,000
To own: 55 miles, Detroit to Port Huron
Lapsed

Detroit & Port Huron Shore Line Railway Company (E)
O: 050, 074, 082 [holding company]
Inc.(S) May 15, 1899
To: not stated
Control July 1900, of City Electric Ry of Port Huron; Rapid RR; Rapid Ry; Detroit & Lake St. Clair; Detroit, Mt. Clemens & Marine City; and Port Huron, St. Clair & Marine City
Control July 1, 1901, by Detroit United Ry
Operations ended May 1, 1928, of all property controlled

Detroit & River St. Clair Railway Company (E)
O: 050 P: 074
Inc.(S) Aug. 1, 1895; $350,000; Algonac
To own: Marine City to Algonac, to New Baltimore, to Chesterfield, to Mt. Clemens
Receivership Jan. 9, 1897, James O. Tucker, receiver
Line opened July 4, 1898, Chesterfield to Algonac
Receivership ended Dec. 31, 1899
Sold Dec. 30, 1899, to Detroit, Mt. Clemens & Marine City

Detroit and Saginaw River Railroad Company
P: 009, 044, 050, 073, 079, 082
Inc. Oct. 23, 1871; $900,000
To own: 105 miles, Detroit to Saginaw River in Bay or Saginaw Cos.
Lapsed

Detroit & St. Clair River— (E)
P: 050, 074, 082
Inc. May 14, 1885, as Detroit & St. Clair River Railway Company; $320,000; St. Clair
To own: 40 miles, St. Clair via Marine City, New Baltimore, Mt. Clemens and Fraser to Detroit & Bay City near Warren
Amend May 15, 1889, to increase number of directors
Amend May 17, 1889, as Detroit and St. Clair River Railway Company, to change route: 40 miles, St. Clair via Marine City, New Baltimore and Mt. Clemens to Detroit

Amend Sept. 15, 1891, as The Detroit and St. Clair River Railway Company, to change route: Port Huron via St. Clair, Marine City and Mt. Clemens to Detroit; capital $1,200,000
Amend Sept. 3, 1892, to reduce number of directors
Amend Oct. 14, 1892, to change corporate life to 400 years
Lapsed

Detroit and St. Joseph Railroad Company
P: 011, 013, 038, 039, 080, 081, 082
Chartered June 29, 1832; $1,500,000; Detroit
To own: city of Detroit to mouth of St. Joseph River
Amend charter March 7, 1834, to extend dates for construction and opening of part of line
Amend charter Aug. 25, 1835, authorized bank at Ypsilanti
Joint Resolution July 26, 1836, authorized Governor to receive proposals to buy company
Sold April 22, 1837, to state of Michigan

Detroit & Shelby
See Shelby & Detroit

The Detroit and Shiawassee railroad company
P: 033, 047, 063, 078, 082
Chartered March 22, 1837; $500,000
To own: 85 miles, Detroit to Shiawassee
Amend charter April 6, 1838, to change western terminus to Biddle City (now Lansing)
Lapsed

Detroit and South Lyon Railway Company
P: 063, 082
Inc. Aug. 25, 1883; $280,000
To own: 35 miles, Detroit near Detroit, Grand Haven & Milwaukee depot to line of Michigan Air Line at South Lyon
Lapsed

The Detroit and State Line Railroad Company
P: 058, 082
Inc. Feb. 1, 1872; $800,000
To own: 60 miles, Detroit to Ohio state line
Merged May 29, 1872, into Toledo, Canada Southern & Detroit

Detroit & State Line Wabash Railroad Company
O: Reorganizing company
Inc. Feb. 19, 1889; $300,000; St. Louis
To reorganize part of Wabash, St. Louis & Pacific (Detroit-Butler)
Acquired no date, Mich. line of Detroit, Butler & St. Louis and of Wabash, St. Louis & Pacific (from purchasing committee which acquired it on April 26, 1886)
Merged May 23, 1889, into Wabash

The Detroit & Toledo Railway Company (E)
P: 058, 082
Inc. June 21, 1890; $400,000
To own: 50 miles, Detroit to Toledo
Lapsed

The Detroit and Toledo Shore Line Railroad Company (E)
O: 058, 082
Inc. March 16, 1899; $1,500,000; Monroe
To rename: Pleasant Bay Ry, and build Ohio state line to Detroit; also may acquire Toledo & Ottawa Beach (non-Mich. corp.)
Amend April 1, 1901, to change number of directors
Receivership Jan. 8, 1902 to July 6, 1903
Control Dec. 1902, 50% by Grand Trunk Western, 50% by Toledo, St. Louis & Western (non-Mich. corp.)
Amend July 6, 1903, to change number of directors
Line completed Sept. 8, 1903, River Rouge to Ohio state line
Amend Dec. 18, 1931, to increase capital to $3,000,000
Sold 50% share of TSL&W no date, to New York, Chicago & St. Louis (non-Mich. corp.)
Sold 50% share of NYC&SL no date, to Norfolk & Western
Sold 50% share of Norfolk & Western, no date, to Grand Trunk Western
Merged June 26, 1981, into Grand Trunk Western

Detroit and Western Railway Company
O: 082
Inc. Dec. 24, 1908; $50,000; Ecorse
To own: 5 miles, Detroit to Oakwood
Control 1915, by Wabash
Amend June 11, 1941, not found
Dissolved Nov. 20, 1958

The Detroit Ann Arbor and Adrian Railway Company (E)
P: 046, 081, 082
Inc.(S) June 29, 1901; $25,000; Detroit
To own: in Washtenaw, Wayne and Lenawee counties
Lapsed

Detroit, Armada and Northern Railway Company (E)
P: 050, 082
Inc.(S) Aug. 21, 1916; $25,000; Detroit
To own: 40 miles, Detroit to Hamtramck to Armada to Memphis
Lapsed

Detroit, Bay City and Alpena Railroad Company
O: 001, 004, 006, 035, 065 P: 009, 025, 063, 073, 082
Inc. March 31, 1883; $2,000,000; Detroit
To reorganize: Bay City & Alpena, and own: 269 miles, Detroit, via Bay City to Alpena
Line acquired at inc. Prescott to East Tawas
Bought May 17, 1886, Black River
Line completed Sept. 20, 1886, Alger to Alpena
Amend June 7, 1887, to own: 320 miles, same as above plus branches
Receivership Oct. 1, 1893, Don M. Dickinson, receiver
Foreclosure sale Nov. 8, 1894, to Detroit & Mackinac

Detroit, Bay City & Western Railroad Company
O: 009, 074, 076, 079
Inc. May 8, 1907: $450,000; Bay City
To own: 30 miles, Bay City to Caro
Line opened Oct. 10, 1910, Bay City to Caro
Amend July 29, 1911, to own: 40 miles, Bay City to Wilmot
Amend Aug. 30, 1913, to own: 60 miles, Bay City to Sandusky
Amend Jan. 20, 1915, to own: 72 miles, Bay City to Peck
Amend Jan. 20, 1916, to own: 100 miles, Bay City to Port Huron
Line completed Oct. 27, 1916, Bay City to Port Huron
Conveyed May 1, 1925, to Detroit, Caro & Sandusky

Detroit Bay City Traction Company (E)
P: 009, 044, 063, 079, 082
Inc. Oct. 1, 1904; $1,000,000
To own: 108 miles, Detroit, via Franklin, Pontiac, Oakwood, Southfield, Hadley, Lapeer, Mayville, Akron and Caro, to Bay City
Lapsed—may have conveyed rights to Bay City, Caro & Eastern

Detroit Belt Line Railroad Company
O: 082
Inc. April 17, 1909; $100,000
To own: 4.5 miles, Detroit Manufacturers RR to Detroit & Bay City
Bought July 20, 1909, line from Detroit & Bay City
Leased July 20, 1909, for corp. life, to Michigan Central
Conveyed Dec. 26, 1916, to Michigan Central

Detroit Belt Railroad Company
P: 082
Inc. Oct. 27, 1892; $2,000,000
To own: 20 miles, Detroit, Grand Haven & Milwaukee depot in Detroit, parallel to DGH&M, Grand Trunk, and Wabash RRs, to West Detroit, then to Delray
Amend Oct. 9, 1897, to build 45 miles, Delray to Detroit
Lapsed

The Detroit Belt Railway & Depot Company
P: 082
Inc. May 27, 1881; $1,500,000; Detroit
To own: 18 miles in Detroit
Lapsed

Detroit, Butler and St. Louis—
O: 046, 058, 081, 082
Inc. Jan. 27, 1880, as Detroit, Butler and St. Louis Railroad Company; $800,000; Detroit
To own: 80 miles, Detroit to Butler, Ind.
Amend Jan. 17, 1881, as The Detroit, Butler and St. Louis Railroad Company, to consolidate: Butler & Detroit (Ohio and Ind. corp.)
Merged June 13, 1881, into Wabash, St. Louis & Pacific
Foreclosure sale April 26, 1886, to Detroit & State Line Wabash

Detroit, Caro and Sandusky Railway Company
O: 076, 079
Inc. May 1, 1925; $400,000; Sandusky
To own: 50 miles, Caro to Roseburg (and to acquire Detroit, Bay City & Western)
Line abandoned 1953
Amend Nov. 2, 1953, to end corporate life Dec. 18, 1953

Detroit, Charlevoix and Escanaba Rail Road Company
P: 005, 015, 020, 040
Inc. March 5, 1887; $600,000; Charlevoix
To own: 60 miles, Charlevoix to Grayling
Amend filed Nov. 15, 1887, to own: 107 miles, Grayling via Charlevoix to Straits of Mackinac; and change capital to $2,000,000
Disposition uncertain. Part may have gone to Chicago & North Michigan in 1891; may have gone to David E. Ward for logging road (possibly as Frederic(k) & Charlevoix) or to Detroit & Charlevoix

Detroit Citizens' Street Railway Company (H, E)
O: 082
Inc.(S) Aug. 24, 1891; $4,000,000; Detroit
To own: in Detroit and adjacent counties, townships and villages [and to buy Detroit Street Ry and Grand River Ry]
Bought Sept. 16, 1891, Detroit Street Ry
Bought Oct. 1, 1891, Grand River Ry
Possibly leased 1896, Detroit Suburban Ry; and The Detroit Electric Ry
Control Jan. 4, 1897, of The Detroit Electric Ry (1896 corp.) and Fort Wayne & Belle Isle
Control April 3, 1899, at inc., of Metropolitan Ry
Sold Dec. 31, 1900, to Detroit United Ry

The Detroit City Railway Company (H, E)
O: 082
Inc.(S) May 9, 1863; $100,000; Detroit
Line opened Aug. 4, 1863
Amend June 4, 1867, to increase capital to $121,000 and revise route: in City of Detroit
Bought Sept. 6, 1876, Russell St., St. Aubin Ave. & Detroit & Milwaukee Jct. Ry
Amend July 14, 1877, to increase capital to $500,000
Acquire Nov. 1, 1881, Hamtramck Street Ry
Bought June 22, 1882, Congress & Baker Street Ry and Cass Avenue Ry
Amend May 19, 1888, to increase capital to $1,000,000
Amend Dec. 27, 1889, to increase capital to $3,000,000
Conveyed Nov. 25, 1890, to Detroit Street Railway

Detroit Connecting Railroad Company
P: 082
Inc. March 27, 1918; $500,000; Detroit
To own: 60 miles, Monguagon twp. NWly to Romulus, then to Plymouth and Northville, then via Orchard Lake to Pontiac, then Ely to Utica and Mt. Clemens
Lapsed

The Detroit, Delray & Dearborn Railroad Company
O: 082
Inc. Sept. 17, 1895; $50,000; Detroit
To own: 6 miles, Delray to Dearborn
Control at inc. by Michigan Central
Line completed Oct. 5, 1895, Delray to Dearborn
Amend Dec. 5, 1912, to increase capital to $500,000
Conveyed Sept. 29, 1916, to Michigan Central

Detroit Edison Co.
O: 058
Private industrial road
Newport

The Detroit, Eel River and Illinois Railroad Company
P: 046
Inc. Sept. 26, 1870; $204,000
To own: 17 miles, SW of Morenci (conn. with Detroit, Eel River & Indiana) NEly to Adrian in Lenawee co.
Lapsed

Detroit Electric Railway Company (H, E)
O: 082
Inc.(S) May 17, 1886; $25,000; Detroit
To own: in Detroit and vicinity
Line opened Sept. 1, 1886
Sold Nov. 1, 1892, to Detroit Suburban Ry

The Detroit Electric Railway Company (E)
O: 082
Inc.(S) July 9, 1896; $50,000; Detroit
To own: in Detroit and adjacent towns and villages
Amend July 14, 1896, to increase capital to $1,000,000
Bought July 29, 1896, The Detroit Ry
Possibly leased 1896, to Detroit Citizens' Street Ry
Control Jan. 4, 1897, by Detroit Citizens' Street Ry
Sold Dec. 31, 1900, to Detroit United Ry

Detroit, Flint & Saginaw Railway Company (E)
O: 073 P: 025, 079
Inc.(T) Nov. 5, 1903; $1,000,000; Frankenmuth
To own: 45 miles, Saginaw to Flint and Vassar
Line opened May 1, 1904, Saginaw to Bridgeport
Receivership begun Nov. 20, 1906, receiver Detroit Trust Co.
Foreclosure sale June 25, 1908, to owners of Saginaw & Flint
Sold Aug. 20, 1908, to Saginaw & Flint

Detroit, Flint River and Saginaw Valley Railway Company (E)
P: 025, 073
Inc.(T) Feb. 23, 1906; $35,000; Flint
To own: 35 miles, Flint to Saginaw
Lapsed

Detroit, Fort Wayne and Belle Isle Railway Company (E)
O: 082
Inc.(S) Feb. 28, 1898; $1,200,000; Detroit
To own: in Detroit and adjacent twps.; buy Ft.Wayne & Belle Isle
Control at inc. by Detroit Citizens Street Ry
Acquired April 1, 1898, Fort Wayne & Belle Isle Ry
Merged Dec. 31, 1900, to Detroit United Rys

DETROIT GRAND HAVEN & MILWAUKEE RAILWAY

Detroit, Grand Haven and Milwaukee Railway Company
O: 019, 025, 034, 041, 063, 070, 078, 082
Inc. Oct. 28, 1878; $1,500,000; Detroit
To reorganize: Detroit & Milwaukee at foreclosure
Control at inc. by Grand Trunk Ry of Canada
Line acquired at inc., Detroit & Milwaukee (Detroit—Grand Haven)
Lease Oct. 27, 1908, for 10 years, of Grand Rapids Terminal
Merged Nov. 1, 1928, into Grand Trunk Western

Detroit, Grand Rapids & Western Railroad Company
O: 019, 023, 029, 033, 034, 037, 041, 047, 054, 059, 063, 073, 081, 082
Inc. Nov. 30, 1896; $5,693,500; Detroit, Boston
To reorganize: Detroit, Lansing & Northern; and to consolidate Grand Rapids, Lansing & Detroit; Saginaw & Grand Rapids; Saginaw Valley & St. Louis; and Saginaw & Western
Amend Dec. 29, 1896, to restate routes
Acquired Jan. 1, 1897, lines of above named companies
Sold Dec. 7, 1899, to Pere Marquette
Foreclosure sale March 28, 1917, to Pere Marquette RR

Detroit, Hillsdale and Indiana Rail Road Company
O: 030, 038, 081 P: 012
Inc. Jan. 9, 1869; $800,000; Ypsilanti
To own: 80 miles, Ypsilanti through Hillsdale to NE corner state of Indiana; thence to Logansport, Ind.
Amend Oct. 30, 1869, to modify eastern terminus: to be "at or near Ypsilanti"
Line opened July 1871, Ypsilanti to Saline
Line completed Nov. 1871, Ypsilanti to Bankers
Foreclosure sale Jan. 28, 1875, to Detroit, Hillsdale & SW

The Detroit, Hillsdale & South Western Railroad Company
O: 030, 038, 081
Inc. Jan. 30, 1875 $3,350,000; Ypsilanti, Boston
To reorganize: Detroit, Hillsdale & Indiana at foreclosure
Acquired at inc., line: Ypsilanti to Bankers
Leased Sept. 5, 1881, in perpetuity, to Lake Shore & Michigan Southern
Amend June 18, 1959, to reduce number of directors from 9 to 7
Sold 1961 to Michigan Central
Dissolved March 28, 1961

Detroit, Howell and Lansing Railroad Company
P: 033, 047, 063, 081, 082
Inc. March 29, 1870; $700,000; Detroit
To consolidate: Detroit & Howell and Howell & Lansing
Merged March 16, 1871, into Detroit, Lansing & Lake Michigan

Detroit, Howell and Lansing Railway Company (E)
P: 033, 047, 063, 081, 082
Inc.(T) May 8, 1901; $500,000
To own: 85 miles, Detroit to Lansing, via Highland Park, Plymouth, Northville, Royal Oak, Farmington, Novi, South Lyon, Green Oak, Brighton, Howell, Fowlerville, Webberville and Williamston
Renamed Nov. 7, 1901, as Detroit, Howell, Lansing & Grand Rapids

Detroit, Howell, Lansing & Grand Rapids Railway Company (E)
P: 008, 019, 023, 033, 034, 041, 047, 063, 081, 082
Inc.(T) Nov. 7, 1901; Detroit
To rename: Detroit, Howell & Lansing; add route to Grand Rapids via Grand Ledge, Lake Odessa, and Lowell
Dissolved Aug. 31, 1914

Detroit, Jackson & Chicago Railway (E)
O: 038, 081, 082
Inc.(S) Jan. 12, 1907; $25,000; Detroit
To own: in Detroit, Dearborn, Ypsilanti, Ann Arbor, Jackson, and Saline
Control at inc. by Detroit United Ry
Bought Feb. 1, 1907, Detroit, Ypsilanti, Ann Arbor & Jackson
Bought July 19, 1907, Jackson, Ann Arbor & Detroit
Amend ca. 1916, approved Mich. RR Comm. June 22, 1916, to increase capital to $1,000,000
Amend Feb. 6, 1923, to change office to Highland Park
Sold Sept. 12, 1928, by Detroit United Ry to bond-holders
Amend Feb. 4, 1929, to change office to Jackson
Operations ended Sept. 4, 1929

Detroit, Lake Orion and Flint Railwa Company (E)
P: 025, 063
Inc.(T) Nov. 27, 1899; $250,000
To own: 32 miles, Oxford to Flint, (and to rename Detroit, Rochester, Romeo & Lake Orion)
Amend April 24, 1900, to change route: 45 miles, extend to Oxford, Orion, Oakland and Avon twps.
Acquired ca. 1901, Detroit, Rochester, Romeo & Lake Orion
Sold Aug. 28, 1901, to Detroit & Flint

Detroit, Lake Shore and Mt. Clemens Railway Company (E)
O: 050, 082
Inc.(T) July 3, 1896; $300,000
To own: 23 miles, Detroit to Mt. Clemens via Grosse Pointe Farms
Line opened Sept. 28, 1898
Sold March 24, 1900 to Detroit & Lake St. Clair Ry

Detroit, Lansing & Grand Rapids Railway Company (E)
P: not given
Inc.(S) July 13, 1909; $25,000; Detroit
To own: Detroit to Grand Rapids via Lansing
Lapsed

Detroit, Lansing & Lake Michigan—
O: 019, 023, 033, 034, 041, 047, 059, 063, 081, 082
Inc. March 16, 1871, as The Detroit, Lansing and Lake Michigan Railroad Company; $2,000,000; Detroit
To consolidate: Detroit, Howell & Lansing and Ionia & Lansing
Line acquired at inc., Lansing to Greenville
Line completed Nov. 30, 1871, West Detroit to Howard City
Received July 18, 1872, Patterson RR
Amend Oct. 1, 1872, as Detroit, Lansing & Lake Michigan Railroad Company, to consolidate: Ionia, Stanton & Northern
Receivership begun July 31, 1876
Foreclosure sale Dec. 14, 1876, to Detroit, Lansing & Northern

Detroit, Lansing & Northern Rail Road Company
O: 019, 023, 033, 034, 037, 041, 047, 054, 059, 063, 081, 082
Inc. Dec. 21, 1876; $4,410,000; Detroit, Ionia, Boston
To reorganize: Detroit, Lansing & Lake Michigan
Line acquired at inc., West Detroit to Howard City and branches
Control 1879, of Saginaw Valley & St. Louis
Amend Oct. 30, 1879, to extend line: to Big Rapids
Lease, no date, of Saginaw Valley & St. Louis
Control, June 7, 1883, at inc., of Saginaw & Western
Lease, July 1, 1883, for 30 years, of Saginaw & Western
Control, May 17, 1887, at inc., of Grand Rapids, Lansing & Detroit
Lease, 1888, of Grand Rapids, Lansing & Detroit
Joint lease, July 1, 1889, of Detroit Union RR Depot & Station
Joint control, Aug. 24, 1889, at inc., of Fort Street Union Depot
Joint lease, Dec. 10, 1889, of Fort Street Union Depot
Receivership begun April 1, 1896, Charles M. Heald, receiver
Foreclosure sale, Nov. 10, 1896, to Detroit, Grand Rapids & Western

Detroit, Lexington & Lake Huron Railway Company (E)
P: 044, 050, 074, 076, 082
Inc.(S) May 25, 1900; $25,000; Detroit
To own: Detroit to Lexington, via Hamtramck, Utica, Washington, Romeo, Almont, Imlay City, Capac, Yale, and Croswell
Lapsed

Detroit, Lincoln and Denver Railroad Company
P: 058, 082
Inc. Dec. 22, 1883; $800,000
To build: 40 miles, Detroit to Ohio state line
Lapsed

Detroit, Mackinac and Marquette—
O: 002, 017, 048, 049, 052, 077
Inc. Aug. 20, 1879, as Detroit, Mackinac and Marquette Railway Company; $1,200,000; Detroit
To own: 150 miles, Straits of Mackinac to Marquette
Reinc. Sept. 3, 1879, as The Detroit, Mackinac and Marquette Railroad Company; $1,200,000; Detroit
To own: 150 miles, Straits of Mackinac to Marquette
Line opened Oct. 1, 1880, Marquette to Onota
Amend July 18, 1881, as Detroit, Mackinac and Marquette Railroad Company; $5,250,000, to add: 48 mile branch, main line to St. Ignace
Line completed Dec. 19, 1881, Marquette to St. Ignace
Amend Feb. 23, 1882, to increase capital to $6,250,000
Amend June 11, 1883, as Detroit, Mackinac and Marquette Railroad, to add 30 mile branch, Marquette to Ishpeming and iron mines
Foreclosure sale Oct. 20, 1886, to Mackinaw & Marquette

Detroit Manufacturers Railroad Company
O: 082
Inc. Jan 27, 1902; $300,000; Detroit
To buy: Detroit Terminal Ry
Bought March 31, 1902, Detroit Terminal Ry
Leased April 1, 1902, for 25 years, to Michigan Central
Disposition uncertain

Detroit Metropolitan Street Railway Company (E)
P: 082
Inc.(S) Dec. 14, 1892; $25,000; Detroit
To own: in Detroit, Greenfield twp., and adjacent townships
Lapsed

The Detroit, Monroe and Toledo Railroad Company
O: 058, 082
Inc. March 6, 1855; $376,000; Detroit, Cleveland
To own: 47 miles, Detroit to state line in Erie twp., Monroe co.
Line completed July 1856, Detroit to Toledo
Leased July 1, 1856, in perpetuity, to Michigan Southern & North. Indiana
Act Jan. 28, 1857, authorized extension of line in Detroit
Act Feb. 17, 1857, authorized consolidation with Mich. South. & North. Ind.
Consolidated April 29, 1914, eff. Jan. 1, 1915, into New York Central

Detroit, Monroe & Toledo Shore Line Railway
See Detroit, Monroe & Toledo Short Line

Detroit, Monroe & Toledo Short Line Railway Company (E)
O: 058, 082
Inc. Dec. 9, 1902; $3,000,000
To own: 60 miles, Springwells to Toledo
Acquired at inc. Toledo & Monroe and Monroe Traction
Amend Dec. 9, 1902, to change N terminus to Detroit
Line completed 1904
Control March 1, 1906, by Detroit United Ry
Reorganized Sept. 20, 1928, as Eastern Michigan Toledo RR

Detroit, Mt. Clemens and Marine City Railway Company (E)
O: 050 P: 074
Inc.(S) March 9, 1899; $600,000; Detroit
To own: in Mt. Clemens, New Baltimore, Algonac and Marine City
Bought Dec. 30, 1899, Detroit & River St. Clair
Bought ca. 1899, Mt. Clemens & Lakeside Traction
Control July 1900, by Detroit & Port Huron Shore Line
Amend Feb. 26, 1901, to change office to New Baltimore
Amend Feb. 5, 1923, to change office to Highland Park and change number of directors
Dissolved, no date

Detroit, Mt. Clemens, Romeo & Armada Electric Railway Company (E)
P: 050
Inc.(S) Dec. 22, 1900; $25,000; Mt. Clemens
To own: 25 miles, Mt. Clemens to Armada and Romeo
Lapsed

Detroit Municipal Railway Company (E)
P: 082
Inc.(S) July 10, 1899; $25,000; Detroit
To own: in Detroit and vicinity [to buy Detroit Citizens' Street Ry]
Lapsed

Detroit, Plymouth & Northville Railway Company (E)
O: 082 P: 081
Inc.(S) April 19, 1898; $150,000; Plymouth
To own: in Detroit, Dearborn, Wayne, Plymouth, Northville, Ann Arbor and Ypsilanti
Line opened Feb. 14, 1899
Sold Nov. 25, 1906, to Jackson, Ann Arbor & Detroit

Detroit, Pontiac and Northern Railroad Company (E)
P: 063, 082
Inc. Dec. 13, 1892; $500,000
To own: 30 miles, Pontiac to Detroit
Lapsed

Detroit, Pontiac & Owosso Railway Company (E)
P: not given
Inc.(S) Feb. 26, 1914; $50,000; Detroit
To own: Detroit to Owosso
Lapsed

Detroit, Pontiac, Lapeer and Northern Railway Company (E)
P: 009, 044, 063, 079, 082
Inc.(T) June 4, 1901; $1,000,000; Detroit
To own: 110 miles, Detroit to Bay City, via Pontiac, Lapeer, Hadley, Mayville, Caro, and Akron
Lapsed

Detroit, Port Huron and Sarnia Railway Company
P: 050, 074, 082
Inc. Nov. 1, 1856; $1,200,000
To own: 60 miles, from Detroit to Port Huron twp., St. Clair co.
Lapsed

The Detroit Railroad and Tunnel Company
P: 082
Inc. Nov. 17, 1888; $1,500,000
To own: 5 miles, at Detroit River
Lapsed

The Detroit Railway Company (E)
O: 082
Inc.(S) Dec. 10, 1894; $1,000,000; Detroit
To own: in Detroit and adjacent counties and townships
Line opened July 1, 1895
Sold July 29, 1896, to The Detroit Electric Ry (1896 corp.)

Detroit Rapid Transit Company
Inc. March 21, 1921
Not a railroad

The Detroit River and Lake Erie Terminal Company
P: 082
Inc. Feb. 20, 1902; $100,000; Detroit
To own: 12 miles, 12th & Howard Sts. in Detroit to SE 1/4 sec 25, Monguagon twp., Wayne Co.
Lapsed

Detroit River Bridge Company
P: 082
Inc. Dec. 1, 1898; Detroit
To rename: Michigan Central Bridge Co.
Renamed March 30, 1905, as Michigan & Canada Bridge & Tunnel

Detroit River Marine Railway Company
P: 082
Chartered March 16, 1847
To build railway on docks on Detroit River
Disposition unknown; probably lapsed

Detroit River Railroad and Bridge Company
P: 082
Inc. Jan. 29, 1872; $250,000
To own: 4 miles, bank of Detroit River in Monguagon twp., via bridge, Grosse Isle, ferry or bridge to Canada shore
Merged Aug. 20, 1873, into Canada Southern Bridge Co.

Detroit River Railroad Tunnel Company
P: 082
Inc. June 10, 1871; $500,000
To own: Michigan Central depot in Detroit to Canadian boundary and Detroit & Milwwaukee depot in Detroit to Canadian boundary
Lapsed

Detroit River Railway
May be alternate name for Detroit River Street Railway

Detroit, River Rouge & Dearborn Street Railway
See Detroit, Rouge River & Dearborn Street

Detroit River Sectional Floating Dock, Dry Dock, and Marine Railway Company
P: 082
Chartered March 17, 1847
To own: marine railway
Amend Feb. 24, 1848, not found
Lapsed

The Detroit River Street Railway Company (H)
P: 082
Inc.(T) Jan. 17, 1872; $50,000
To own: west to east city limits along Detroit River
Lapsed

Detroit River Subways Company
P: 082
Inc. Dec. 19, 1925; $1,000,000
To own: 3 miles, Detroit SEly to Canadian boundary
Lapsed

Detroit River Terminal Railroad Company
P: 082
Inc. June 28, 1899; $500,000; Detroit
To own: 16 miles, Detroit to Slocum Jct.
Lapsed

Detroit River Tunnel Company
O: 082
Inc. June 9, 1905; $3,000,000; Detroit
To consolidate Michigan & Canada Bridge & Tunnel and Michigan Bridge & Tunnel (Canadian corp.)
Control at inc. by Michigan Central
Leased Jan. 1, 1907, eff. Jan. 1, 1904, for 999 years to Michigan Central
Line completed Oct. 16, 1910
Sold April 30, 1985, to Canadian National Rys and Canadian Pacific

Detroit, Rochester, Romeo and Lake Orion Railway Company (E)
O: 063, 082
Inc.(S) May 25, 1899; $500,000; Detroit
To own: in Detroit, Pontiac, Royal Oak, Rochester, and Orion; also Pontiac, Royal Oak, Troy, Orion, Avon, Oakland, Warren and Sterling twps., and to rename Detroit & Lake Orion
Amend Nov. 16, 1899, to add Oakland twp. to termini
Line opened Nov. 18, 1899
Amend Dec. 8, 1900, to change termini
Conveyed ca. 1901, to Detroit, Lake Orion & Flint

Detroit, Romeo & Port Huron rail road Company
P: 050, 074, 082
Chartered March 18, 1848; $100,000
To rename: Shelby & Detroit
Amend charter Feb. 13, 1855, to increase capital to $2,000,000 and extend completion dates
Lapsed

Detroit, Rouge River and Dearborn Railway Company (E)
P: 082
Inc. May 3, 1889; $100,000
To own: 10 miles, Detroit to Dearborn
May have been renamed Detroit, Rouge River & Dearborn Street Ry

Detroit, Rouge River & Dearborn Street Railway Company (E)
P: 082
Inc.(S) March 13, 1893; $25,000; Springwells
To own: in Springwells twp.
Franchise acquired March 23, 1893, of Detroit, Springwells & Dearborn
Sold June 5, 1893, to Fort Wayne & Belle Isle

Detroit Service-at-Cost Railway Company (E)
P: 082
Inc.(S) Jan. 14, 1921; $25,000; Detroit
To own: in city of Detroit
Lapsed

Detroit Shipbuilding Co.
O: 082
Private industrial road
Detroit

Detroit Southern Railroad Company
O: 046, 058, 082
Inc. May 25, 1901; $17,000,000; Detroit
To buy: Detroit & Lima Northern at foreclosure sale
Amend May 25, 1901, to increase number of directors
Acquired at inc., line: Delray via Tecumseh to Ohio state line
Amend Oct. 28, 1901, to change number of directors
Foreclosure sale, May 1, 1905, to Detroit, Toledo & Ironton

The Detroit, Springwells and Dearborn Railway Company (E)
P: 082
Inc.(T) Nov. 30, 1891; $100,000
To own: 7-8 miles, from Springwells twp. to Dearborn twp.
Amend April 16, 1892; no changes in articles
Amend June 4, 1892, to change number of directors
Franchise transferred March 23, 1893, to Detroit, Rouge River & Dearborn Street Ry

The Detroit Street Railway Company (H, E)
O: 082
Inc.(S) Nov. 25, 1890; $3,000,000; Detroit
To own: in city of Detroit and adjacent villages and townships (and reorganize Detroit City Railway Co.)
Acquired at inc., Detroit City
Sold Sept. 16, 1891, to Detroit Citizens' Street Ry

Detroit Suburban Railway Company (E)
O: Holding company
Inc.(S) Oct. 29, 1892; $200,000; Detroit
To own: in city of Detroit and adjacent villages and townships (and to consolidate Jefferson Ave. Ry, Highland Park Ry, Detroit Elec. Ry, and Gratiot Ave. Ry)
Acquired Nov. 1, 1892, Detroit Electric Ry, East Detroit & Grosse Point, Jefferson Avenue Ry Co., and Gratiot Avenue Ry
Acquired Nov. 1, 1892, franchise of North Detroit & Chene
Acquired Feb. 1, 1893, Highland Park Ry
Possibly leased 1896, to Detroit Citizens' Street Ry
Merged Dec. 31, 1900, into Detroit United Ry

The Detroit Suburban Street Railway Company (E)
P: 082
Inc.(S) Dec. 24, 1890; $500,000; Detroit
To own: in Detroit and Wyandotte and adjoining suburbs
Conveyed May 3, 1892, to Wyandotte & Detroit River Ry

Detroit Terminal Railroad Company
O: 082
Inc. Dec. 7, 1905; $2,000,000; Detroit
To own: 25 miles, Detroit River East of city of Detroit, around said city, to the Detroit River West of said city
Owned at inc. 50% by Grand Trunk Western, 25% by Michigan Central, 25% by The Lake Shore and Michigan Southern Ry Co.
Amend Feb. 19, 1907, to change number of directors
Merged May 31, 1984, into Consolidated Rail Corp.

Detroit Terminal Railway Company
O: 082
Inc.(T) July 23, 1901; $75,000
To buy: Detroit Transit Ry
Bought Sept. 23, 1901, Detroit Transit Ry
Sold March 31, 1902, to Detroit Manufacturers RR

Detroit, Toledo & Ironton—
O: 046, 058, 082 Office: Detroit
Inc. May 2, 1905, as Detroit, Toledo and Ironton Railway Company; $25,000,000
To buy: Detroit Southern at foreclosure sale
Acquired at inc., line: Delray via Tecumseh to Ohio state line
Control June 1, 1905, of Ann Arbor Railroad Company
Amend Nov. 22, 1905, to increase number of directors
Control ended Nov. 25, 1910, of Ann Arbor Railroad Company
Foreclosure sale, Feb. 1914
Inc. Feb. 20, 1914, as Detroit, Toledo and Ironton Railroad Company; $12,500,000
To buy: Detroit, Toledo & Ironton Ry at foreclosure
Lease May 1, 1916, of Toledo-Detroit
Control Oct. 1916, of Toledo-Detroit
Control July 10, 1920, by Henry Ford
Control sold June 27, 1927, by Ford to Pennroad Corp.
Lease June 25, 1929, of Detroit & Ironton
Control sold Feb. 28, 1931, by Pennroad to Wabash RR
Amend Nov. 14, 1931, to change director's rights and increase capital to $25,000,000
Consolidated Dec. 29, 1931, Toledo-Detroit and Detroit & Ironton
Control Aug. 29, 1963, of Ann Arbor Railroad Company
Control sold June 26, 1965, by Wabash RR to Pennsylvania Co.
Merged June 14, 1983, into Grand Trunk Western

Detroit, Toledo & Jackson Railway Company
P: 038, 046, 058
Inc. June 5, 1881; $500,000
To own: 42 miles, Milan to Jackson
Lapsed

Detroit, Toledo & Milwaukee Railroad Company
O: 003, 008, 013, 030, 038, 039, 046, 058
Inc. July 22, 1897; $1,500,000; Toledo
To rename: Toledo & Milwaukee
Acquired at inc., line: Allegan to Dundee
Leased Jan. 6, 1899, eff. Jan. 1, 1899, to Cincinnati Northern
Lease cancelled Dec. 31, 1901, by Cincinnati Northern
Control, early 1902, 50% Michigan Central, 50% Lake Shore & Michigan Southern
Leased Jan. 1, 1905, in perpetuity, to Michigan Central and Lake Shore & MS
Sold Sept. 1, 1913, part of line (Battle Creek-Allegan) to Michigan & Chicago Ry
Amend April 17, 1916, to reduce capital to $1,060,000 and change route to be Dundee to 3.4 miles W of Battle Creek
Merged Aug. 1, 1969, into Penndel Co.

The Detroit Transit Railroad Company
P: 082
Inc. April 1, 1892; $200,000
To own: 24 miles, Fort Sreet Union Depot at 8th St., Detroit, to Walker and Wight Sts. at Detroit Terminal Ry
Lapsed

Detroit Transit Railway Company
O: 082
Inc.(T) Sept. 10, 1872; $50,000
To own: Detroit & Milwaukee Ry south of Jefferson Ave., easterly near Detroit River to one mile east of Detroit city limits in Hamtramck twp.
Conveyed Sept. 23, 1901, to Detroit Terminal Ry

Detroit Transportation Corp., city of Detroit
O: 082
Line opened July 31, 1987 [Detroit People Mover]
Active corp.

Detroit Union Bridge Company
P: 082
Inc. March 4, 1898; $2,000,000
To build railroad bridge over Detroit River at Detroit
Owned 50% by Grand Trunk Ry of Canada and 50% by Wabash
Lapsed

The Detroit Union Railroad Depot & Station Company
O: 082
Inc.(UD) June 9, 1881; $3,000,000; Detroit
To own: railroad freight and passenger depots in Detroit
Line completed 1882, Delray to 18th Street, Detroit
Operating control April 12, 1882, of Detroit, Western Transit & Junction
Amend April 17, 1882, to reduce capital to $2,000,000
Leased July 1, 1889, jointly to Detroit, Lansing & Northern, Flint & Pere Marquette, and Wabash
Amend Dec. 14, 1891, to increase capital to $2,500,000
Merged Oct. 13, 1954, eff. Jan. 1, 1955, into Penndel Co.

Detroit United Railway Company (E)
O: 025, 044, 058, 063, 081, 082
Inc.(S) Dec. 28, 1900; $12,500,000; Detroit
To buy: Detroit Electric; Detroit, Fort Wayne & Belle Isle; Detroit Citizens Street; and Detroit Suburban
Consolidated Dec. 31, 1900, Detroit Citizens' Street Ry; Detroit, Fort Wayne & Belle Isle; Detroit Suburban; and Detroit Electric (1896 corp.)
Bought Feb. 20, 1901, Wyandotte & Detroit River
Bought May 1, 1901, Detroit & Northwestern
Bought June 1, 1901, Detroit & Pontiac Ry
Control July 1, 1901, of Detroit & Port Huron Shore Line
Control Aug. 9, 1901, at inc., of Detroit & Flint
Bought ca. 1901, Detroit & Flint Ry
Amend Jan. 21, 1902, to change number of directors
Control March 1, 1906, of Detroit, Monroe & Toledo Short Line
Amend March 18, 1908, to change number of directors
Control Oct. 6, 1913, at inc., of Detroit, Almont & Northern
Control March 20, 1916, at inc., of Highland Park & Royal Oak
Amend not found, to increase capital to $25,000,000
Part sold May 15, 1922, to city of Detroit, Dept. of Street Rys
Amend Feb. 6, 1923, to change office to Highland Park and change number of directors
Receivership begun March 10, 1925, A. L. Drum receiver
Operations ended May 1, 1928, on Detroit & Port Huron Shore Line properties
Control sold Sept. 12, 1928, of Detroit, Jackson & Chicago to that road's bondholders
Control ended Sept. 12, 1928, of Detroit, Monroe & Toledo Short Line
Reorganized Sept. 12, 1928, part as Eastern Michigan Rys

Detroit, Utica & Romeo Railway Company (E)
O: 050, 063, 082
Inc. Aug. 10, 1898; $300,000
To own: 30 miles, Detroit to Romeo
Line opened 1901
Sold June 20, 1901, to North Detroit Electric

Detroit, Western Transit and Junction Railroad Company
O: 082
Inc. May 2, 1881; $500,000; Detroit
To own: 8 miles in Detroit
Amend March 2, 1882, to modify route in Detroit
Amend March 17, 1882, to reduce route
Operating agreement April 12, 1882, by Detroit Union Railroad Depot & Station
Disposition uncertain

Detroit Western Transit Railway Company
P: 082
Inc.(T) Nov. 8, 1872; $50,000
To own: 1.5 miles in Detroit
Lapsed

The Detroit, Ypsilanti & Ann Arbor Railway Company (E)
O: 081, 082
Inc.(S) Nov. 2, 1897; $400,000; Detroit
To own: in Ann Arbor, Ypsilanti, Detroit and other villages and townships
Bought at inc. Ann Arbor & Ypsilanti Electric
Amend Dec. 20, 1897, to add Pittsfield twp. to route
Line opened Dec. 24, 1897
Conveyed March 25, 1901, to Detroit, Ypsilanti, Ann Arbor & Jackson

Detroit, Ypsilanti, Ann Arbor and Jackson Railway Company (E)
O: 038, 081, 082
Inc.(S) Jan. 22, 1901; $2,600,000; Dearborn
To own: Detroit to Jackson
Bought March 25, 1901, Ypsilanti & Saline and Detroit, Ypsilanti & Ann Arbor
Control Nov. 1, 1901, of Lansing City Electric
End control March 15, 1904, of Lansing City Electric
Sold Feb. 1, 1907, to Detroit, Jackson & Chicago

Dewing and Son (Lumber Co.) (Gauge 3')
O: 067
Private logging road
Ashton

Dewing, W. G., and Sons Lumber Co.
Owned Allegan & Lake Shore

Diamond Lumber Co.
O: 066
Private logging road
Ontonagon

Division Street and Reed's Lake Railway Company (H)
P: 041
Inc.(S) April 7, 1874; $35,000
To own: in Grand Rapids from Division Ave. to Reeds Lake
Lapsed

The Division Street Railway Company (H)
O: 041
Inc.(S) Aug. 5, 1873; $25,000; Grand Rapids
To own: in Grand Rapids, on Division from Monroe to Hall, then E on Hall to Jefferson
Line opened Sept. 1, 1873
Amend July 14, 1882, to extend line and increase capital to $50,000
Merged 1886, into Street Ry of Grand Rapids

Dix Avenue Railway (E)
[May have been colloquial name of an extension of Detroit Electric (1886 corp.)] No corporate articles located.

Dollar Bay Lumber Co.
O: 031
Private logging road; Dollar Bay

[Robert] Dollar Lumber Co.
O: 048
Private logging road
Dollarville northwesterly
Built ca. 1885

Dowagiac Railway Company (E)
P: 011, 014
Inc.(S) Sept. 17, 1908; $200,000; Benton Harbor
To own: Indiana state line, via Cassopolis and Dowagiac, to Benton Harbor
Lapsed

Dow Chemical Co.
O: 056
Private industrial road; Midland
In Midland

DULUTH SOUTH SHORE AND ATLANTIC

Duluth, South Shore & Atlantic—
O: 002, 007, 017, 027, 031, 042, 048, 049, 052, 066, 077
Inc. Dec. 22, 1886, as The Duluth, South Shore and Atlantic Railway Company; $22,000,000; Marquette
To consolidate: Mackinaw & Marquette; Sault Ste. Marie & Marquette; Wisconsin, Sault Ste. Marie & Mackinac; and Duluth, Superior & Michigan (non-Mich. corp.)
Acquired at inc., line: St. Ignace to L'Anse and branches
Lease, Feb. 15, 1887, in perpetuity, of Marquette, Houghton & Ontonagon
Control Feb. 28, 1887, 25% of Sault Ste. Marie Bridge Co

Control ca. 1888, by Canadian Pacific
Amend July 26, 1888, to change number of directors
Line completed Sept. 16, 1888, Sault Ste. Marie to Wisconsin line
Bought July 17, 1890, Marquette, Houghton & Ontonagon and Marquette & Western
Control Oct. 20, 1890, at inc., of Lake Mich. & Lake Superior
Control March 12, 1900, 50% of Ste. Marie Union Depot Co.
Reinc. (Minn. corp.) Oct. 18, 1949, as Duluth, South Shore and Atlantic Railroad Company; Minneapolis
To consolidate: Duluth, South Shore & Atlantic and Mineral Range
Consolidated Nov. 1, 1949, Duluth, South Shore & Atlantic and Mineral Range
Acquired Sept. 1, 1952, part of Sainte Marie Union Depot Co.
Agreement March 15, 1960, eff. Dec. 30, 1960, to consolidate Minneapolis, St. Paul & Sault Ste. Marie and Wisconsin Central and rename new company as Soo Line
Renamed Jan. 1, 1961, as Soo Line RR

Duncan, J. W.
O: 016
Private lumbering tramway
Graded from "water mill" to Duncan Bay in 1852; not known if built

Dunham, Peters and Co. (Gauge 3')
O: 043
Private logging road; Chase
5 miles, in T17W R11W
Built 1881-82

E

East Detroit and Grosse Pointe Railway Company (E)
O: 082
Inc.(S) May 7, 1887; $100,000; Detroit
To own: Detroit to Hamtramck and Grosse Pointe twps.
Line opened Jan. 15, 1888
Sold Nov. 1, 1892, to Detroit Suburban Ry

Eastern & Northwestern—
P: 011, 012, 014, 030, 039, 046, 058, 075, 080
Inc. Nov. 15, 1899, as The Eastern & North Western Railway Company; $880,000; Benton Harbor
To own: 110 miles, Benton Harbor and St. Joseph to South line of Hillsdale co. near West county line
Amend March 24, 1900, as The Eastern and North Western Railway Company, to own: 160 miles, Benton Harbor and St. Joseph to Lake Erie in Monroe co., and increase capital to $1,280,000
Lapsed

Eastern Michigan Railways Company (E)
O: 025, 050, 063, 082
Inc.(S) Aug. 25, 1928; capital not stated; Highland Park
To own: Detroit to Flint, Pontiac, Wyandotte, Farmington, and Northville
Acquired at inc. part of Detroit United Ry
Operations ended Aug. 25, 1931
Assets conveyed Aug. 4, 1938, to Eastern Michigan Transportation (not RR)

Eastern Michigan Toledo Railroad Company (E)
O: 058, 082
Inc.(S) Sept. 20, 1928; $500,000
To reorganize: Detroit, Monroe & Toledo Shore Line [sic]
Acquired at inc. Detroit, Monroe & Toledo Short Line
Receivership begun June 18, 1931, John Collins, receiver
Operations ended Oct. 5, 1932

East Jordan & Southern Railroad Company
O: 005, 015
Inc. July 3, 1901; $250,000; East Jordan
To buy: 20 mile line of East Jordan Lumber Co. Ry (East Jordan SEly)
Line completed Oct. 1, 1901, East Jordan to Bellaire
Line abandoned 1961

East Jordan Lumber Co.
O: 005, 015
Private logging road
Sold July 1901, to East Jordan & Southern

The East Saginaw and Ann Arbor Rail Road Company
P: 025, 047, 073, 081
Inc. Oct. 28, 1869; $2,000,000
To own: 85 miles, East Saginaw to Ann Arbor via Chesaning, Corunna, Shiawasseetown, Newburg, Byron and Howell
Lapsed

East Saginaw and St. Clair Railroad Company
O: 073 P: 044, 074, 079
Inc. Oct. 9, 1872; $1,000,000
To own: 95 miles, South Saginaw via Vassar to St. Clair River
Control at inc. by Flint & Pere Marquette
Line opened 1874, in Saginaw
Consolidated Nov. 2, 1888, into Flint & Pere Marquette

East Saginaw City Railway Company (H)
O: 073
Inc.(T) Nov. 20, 1863; $60,000; East Saginaw
To own: in Saginaw, on Washington from Flint & Pere Marquette to city limits
Line opened 1865
Amend July 8, 1865, to extend on Washington and Mackinaw sts.
Amend Aug. 15, 1865, to extend on Water, Jefferson, Genesee and Bristol sts.
Disposition uncertain

East Saginaw Railway Company (H)
P: 073
Inc.(S) filed June 11, 1878
Articles not found

East Saginaw Street Railway Company (H)
P: 073
Inc.(S) June 4, 1886; $25,000
To own: in East Saginaw and adjoining cities and townships
Amend July 30, 1886, to increase capital to $50,000
Disposition uncertain

East Shore and Southwestern Railway Company
P: 011, 080
Inc.(T) March 7, 1905; $25,000
To own: 25 miles, Benton Harbor to South Haven
Lapsed

Electric Depot Company
P: 082
Inc.(Not RR) June 11, 1901 ; $50,000; Detroit
To operate union freight and passenger depots and stations
Lapsed

The Electric Railway Company (E)
P: 041
Inc.(S) July 9, 1890; $400,000
To own: in Grand Rapids; Grand Rapids, Paris and Wyoming twps.
Lapsed

Elgin Terminal Railway Company
P: 011
Inc. Feb. 7, 1913; $250,000
To own: St. Joseph and Benton Harbor Sly to Indiana state line in sec 22 T8S R20W
Lapsed

Elkhart and Lake Michigan Railroad Company
P: 011, 014
Inc. Jan. 3, 1868; $300,000
To own: 32 miles, Benton Harbor via Sodus, Berrien Springs, and Niles to Indiana state line in Milton twp., Cass co.
Lapsed. Grade used by Elkhart, Niles & Lake Michigan, but apparently no formal title transfer

Elkhart, Niles and Lake Michigan Rail Road Company
P: 011, 014
Inc. June 16, 1880; $1,000,000
To own: 38 miles, Benton Harbor via Niles and Edwardsburg to Indiana state line in Ontwa twp., Cass co.
Amend Aug. 15, 1881, to change southern terminus to Milton twp., Cass co.
Consolidated May 23, 1882, into Cincinnati, Wabash & Michigan

Elk Rapids, Williamsburg and Southern Railroad Company
P: 005, 028
Inc. June 10, 1889; $300,000
To own: 9 miles, Elk Rapids to Williamsburg
Lapsed. Route used by Chicago & North Michigan, but apparently no formal title transfer

Elk Short Line Railroad Company
P: 005
Inc. March 19, 1906; $8,000; Elk Rapids
To own: 1 mile, sec 20 to sec 28 T29N R9W
Lapsed

Emmet Lumber Co.
O: 024
Private logging road
7 miles, Wheeling northerly
Built 1903

Empire & South Eastern Railroad
O: 010, 045
Private logging road
Owned by T. Wilce Co.
10.7 miles, Empire to Empire Jct.
Built 1900

Epworth League Railway Company
O: 053
Inc.(T) March 9, 1895; $15,000
To own: 4 miles, Ludington via Lincoln Lake to Hamlin Lake
Line opened 1895, Ludington to Epworth
Renamed July 13, 1901, as Ludington & Northern

The Erie and Kalamazoo Railroad Company
O: 046, 058 P: 013, 030, 038
Chartered April 22, 1833; $1,000,000; Adrian
To own: Port Lawrence via Adrian to Kalamazoo River

Amend charter March 7, 1834, to extend time for completion
Amend charter March 26, 1835, authorize bank at Adrian or Tecumseh
Amend charter March 28, 1836, to amend banking powers
Control March 28, 1836, at inc., of Palmyra & Jacksonburgh
Line completed Nov. 2, 1836, Toledo to Adrian
Amend charter March 22, 1845, not found
Amend charter May 18, 1846, to change west terminus to Adrian
Leased Aug. 1, 1849, in perpetuity to Michigan Southern
Apparently sold April 1, 1976, rail assets to Consolidated Rail

Erie & Michigan Railway & Navigation Company
O: 035 P: 006
Inc. June 14, 1904; $250,000; Alabaster
To own: 28 miles, docks at Alabaster to Detroit & Mackinac Ry in sec 2 T21N R7E, and Alabaster to Michigan Central at Standish
Line opened 1906
Leased June 29, 1907, for 10 years to Detroit & Mackinac
Amend Jan. 14, 1929, to restate route
Amend Jan. 12, 1942, to change par value from $100 to $10
Sold Jan. 1949, to Detroit & Mackinac

Escanaba and Lake Superior—
O: 021, 022, 052, 055
Inc.(T) Nov. 17, 1898, as Escanaba & Lake Superior Railway Company; $72,000
To own: 60 miles, Escanaba to south line T45N, R28W and Flat Rock to Little Bay de Noquet
Reinc. Feb. 9, 1900, as Escanaba and Lake Superior Railroad Company; $693,000
To build: 70 miles, from Escanaba to T43N, R30W
Line completed Dec. 28, 1900, Wells to Channing
Bought April 1, 1901, rights of Escanaba & Lake Superior Ry
Amend May 29, 1907, to change number of directors to 7
Operating agreement, March 10, 1980, Mich. lines of Chicago, Milwaukee, St. Paul & Pacific
Bought Sept. 29, 1980, Mich. lines of Chicago, Milwaukee, St. Paul & Pacific
Sold Sept. 1982, line (Channing-Ontonagon) to state of Michigan
Sold July 1983, line (Iron Mountain-Channing) to state of Michigan
Active corporation

Escanaba and Lake Superior Railway Company
O: 021, 022, 055 P: 027, 036, 052
Inc. Nov. 24, 1880; $2,000,000
To own: 250 miles, sec 34, T39N, R24W, to mouth of Montreal River in Ontonagon co., and branch to Houghton
Control no date, by Chicago & North Western
Line completed 1882, Narenta to Metropolitan
Amend July 1, 1882, to add branch: sec 3 T41N R28W to sec 20 T40N R30W, total 270 miles
Merged July 1, 1882, into Chicago & North Western

The Escanaba Electric Street Railway Company (E)
O: 021
Inc.(S) Dec. 9, 1891; $50,000; Escanaba
To own: in Escanaba
Line opened 1892
Sold Aug. 13, 1909, to Escanaba Traction

The Escanaba, Frankfort and Southeastern Railroad Company
O: Reorganizing company
Inc. June 12, 1895; $160,000
To reorganize: Frankfort & South Eastern
Sold Oct. 15, 1895, to Ann Arbor RR Co.

Escanaba, Iron Mountain and Western Railroad Company
O: 021, 022, 055
Inc. Jan. 4, 1890; $2,500,000
To own: 90 miles, Escanaba to Crystal Falls via Iron River and Florence, Wisc.
Line completed 1891, North Escanaba to Loop Line Jct.
Leased May 15, 1891, to Chicago & North Western
Merged Oct. 7, 1947, into Chicago & North Western

Escanaba Lumber Co.
O: 049
Private logging road; Corinne
Bought Dec. 17, 1910, line of Manistique Lumbering Co.
See also Lake Michigan & Superior

Escanaba Traction Company (E)
O: 021
Inc.(T) filed Aug. 3, 1909; Escanaba
To: reorganize Escanaba Electric Street Ry and consolidate utility company
Bought Aug. 13, 1909, Escanaba Electric Street Ry
Operations ended May 1932

Escanaba, Twin Cities and Western Rail Road Company
P: 021, 022, 055
Inc. Jan. 3, 1889; $3,000,000
To own: 350 miles, Escanaba to St. Paul, Minn. (40 miles in Mich.)
Lapsed

Escanaba Western Railroad Company
P: 021
Inc. July 21, 1893; $100,000
To own: 7 miles, Escanaba Wly to point on Minneapolis, St. Paul & S.S.M.
Lapsed

Evart & Osceola Railroad
O: 067
Private logging road
Line opened 1878, 7 miles, Evart to sec 14 T18N R9W

F

Fair Haven Wooden Railroad
O: 074
Private tramway
NW 1/4 sec 23 to NW 1/4 sec 1 T3N R15E
In use late 1850s

Fenn Valley Railway Company
P: not given
Inc. July 11, 1978; $50,000; Grand Rapids
To operate in Michigan
Renamed Aug. 7, 1980, Wasepi Ry

The Fenton and Grand Blanc Railroad Company
P: 025
Inc. Sept. 15, 1871; $80,000
To own: 10 miles, Fenton to Grand Blanc
Lapsed

Fenton, Long Lake and Flint Railway Company (E)
P: 025
Inc.(T) Feb. 23, 1906; $16,000; Flint
To own: Flint to Grand Blanc, Fenton, and Holly
Lapsed

Ferrin, M. B. (Lumber Co.) (Gauge 3')
O: 040
Private logging road
8 miles, South Boardman
Built 1884

Ferry and Sons
O: 070
Private logging tramway
Bought 1855-56, Gilbert Tramway (5 miles in T7N R15W)

Flat River and Houghton Lake Railroad Company
P: 018, 034, 037, 054, 059, 072
Inc. Dec. 2, 1871; $1,000,000
To own: 90 miles, Flat River, Ionia co. to Houghton Lake
Lapsed

Fletcher, Pack and Co. (Gauge 3')
O: 001
Private logging road; Alpena
In Alcona co.

———

O: 004
Private logging road
Alpena to Hubbard Lake

Flint and Fentonville Railroad Company
P: 025
Inc. Jan. 3, 1863; $200,000
To own: 16 miles, Flint to Fentonville
Renamed Aug. 8, 1863, as Flint & Holly

Flint & Great Lakes Railroad Company
P: 025
Inc. May 28, 1917; $100,000
To own: 5 miles, sec 16 T7N R7E to sec 30 T8N R7E
Lapsed

The Flint and Holly Rail Road Company
O: 025, 063
Inc. Aug. 8, 1863; $300,000
To rename: Flint & Fentonville; line 17 miles, Flint to Holly
Line completed Nov. 1, 1864, Flint to Holly
Merged May 30, 1868, into Flint & Pere Marquette

Flint and Lansing Railway Company
P: 025, 033, 078
Inc. Oct. 23, 1872; $1,500,000
To own: 47.5 miles, Flint to Lansing
Lapsed

Flint & Pere Marquette—
O: 009, 018, 025, 026, 032, 037, 043, 044, 051, 053, 056, 058, 063, 067, 073, 074, 076, 079, 082
Inc. Jan. 21, 1857, as Flint and Pere Marquette Railway Company; $5,500,000; East Saginaw
To own: 170 miles, Flint to Pere Marquette in Mason co. (now Ludington)
Amend Aug. 3, 1857, same rights
Act Feb. 15, 1859, authorized consolidation with Genesee & Oakland
Line opened Jan. 20, 1862, Saginaw to Mt. Morris
Amend May 30, 1868, to consolidate: Flint & Holly; increase capital to $1,100,000
Control Dec. 16, 1868, of Bay City & East Saginaw
Amend Feb. 1, 1872, to consolidate: Holly, Wayne & Monroe; Cass River; Flint River; and Bay City & East Saginaw; increase capital to $3,500,000
Amend Sept. 18, 1872, to extend line: Otter Lake to Caro
Control Oct. 31, 1872, at inc., of East Saginaw & St. Clair

Line completed Dec. 1, 1874, Monroe to Ludington
Control Sept. 4, 1877, at inc., of Saginaw & Clare County
Control March 25, 1879, at inc., of Saginaw & Mt. Pleasant
Receivership begun July 1, 1879, Henry C. Potter, receiver
Control June 19, 1880, at inc., of Manistee
Foreclosure sale Aug. 18, 1880
Inc. Aug. 24, 1880, as Flint and Pere Marquette Railroad Company; $6,500,000
To reorganize: Flint & Pere Marquette Ry
Amend Nov. 2, 1888, as The Flint and Pere Marquette Railroad Company; $10,000,000: to consolidate: Saginaw & Clare County; Saginaw & Mt. Pleasant; East Saginaw & St. Clair; and Manistee
Bought April 1, 1889, Port Huron & Northwestern
Joint lease July 1, 1889, of Detroit Union RR Depot & Station
Joint control Aug. 24, 1889, at inc., of Fort St. Union Depot
Joint lease Dec. 10, 1889, of Fort St. Union Depot
Amend May 20, 1891, to add branch: Novi via Delray to Detroit
Control March 29, 1893, at inc., of Monroe & Toledo
Bought Aug. 27, 1897, Monroe & Toledo
Sold Dec. 6, 1899, to Pere Marquette
Foreclosure sale March 28, 1917, to Pere Marquette

Flint and Saginaw Traction Company (E)
P: 025, 073
Inc.(T) June 16, 1904; $35,000
To own: 35 miles, Flint to Saginaw
Lapsed

Flint Belt Railroad Company
O: 025
Inc. May 20, 1921; $1,000,000
To own: 8.25 miles in Genesee co.
Line opened 1922
Merged Nov. 30, 1955, into Chesapeake & Ohio

Flint City Railway Company (E)
P: 025
Inc.(S) March 17, 1891; $50,000; Flint
To build: in Flint
Lapsed

The Flint River Railroad Company
O: 025, 044
Inc. Nov. 3, 1871; $250,000
To own: 16 miles, Flint & Pere Marquette line in Genesee co. to Otter Lake
Line completed Oct. 8, 1872, McGrew to Otter Lake
Merged Feb. 1, 1872, into Flint & Pere Marquette

Flint, Saginaw & Bay City Railway Company
P: 009, 025, 073
Inc.(S) Sept. 23, 1901; $200,000; Saginaw
To own: Flint to Saginaw to Bay City
Lapsed

Flint Street Railway Company (E)
P: 025
Inc.(S) Nov. 8, 1890; $40,000
To own: in Flint
Lapsed

Flushing Railroad Company
P: 025
Inc. Aug. 30, 1886; $80,000
To own: 10 miles, Flint to Flushing
Lapsed

Ford Motor Co.
O: 007, 052
Private logging road; Pequaming
Line L'Anse easterly
Bought ca. 1920 line of Hebard & Thurber; abandoned ca. 1946

Ford Transportation Company
O: 082
Inc.(Not RR) June 9, 1923; $100,000; Dearborn
To: own railroad equipment and facilities
Lease Jan. 1, 1924, of Detroit & Ironton
Amend March 12, 1926, to restate rights and increase capital to $500,000
Railroad assets sold June 25, 1929, to Detroit & Ironton
Dissolved Sept. 10, 1929

The Fort Gratiot and Lexington Railroad Company
P: 074, 076
Inc. April 24, 1872; $200,000
To own: 20 miles, Grand Trunk depot in Port Huron to Lexington
Amend Dec. 11, 1872, to change northern terminus to Lexington twp.
Lapsed

Fort Street and Elmwood Railway Company (H)
O: 082
Inc.(T) Feb. 4, 1865; $100,000
To own: 5 miles, in Detroit, Fort Wayne to Elmwood Ave.
Line opened Sept. 6, 1865
Renamed Jan. 17, 1882, as Fort Wayne & Elmwood Ry

Fort Street Union Depot Company
O: 082
Inc.(UD) filed Aug. 24, 1889; Detroit

Control at inc. jointly by Detroit, Lansing & Northern; Flint & Pere Marquette; Wabash; and Canadian Pacific
Leased Dec. 10, 1889, to four above companies
Line completed Jan. 1893, 18th St. to 3rd St., Detroit
Disposition uncertain

Fort Wayne and Belle Isle Railway Company (H, E)
O: 082
Inc.(S) May 14, 1892; $250,000; Detroit
To reorganize: Fort Wayne & Elmwood
Bought July 1, 1892, Fort Wayne & Elmwood
Bought June 5, 1893, Detroit, Rouge River & Dearborn Street Ry
Amend July 16, 1895, to increase capital to $300,000
Amend March 24, 1896, to increase capital to $400,000
Control Jan. 4, 1897, by Detroit Citizens' Street Ry
Sold April 1, 1898, to Detroit, Fort Wayne & Belle Isle

Fort Wayne and Elmwood Railway Company (H)
O: 082
Inc.(T) Jan. 17, 1882; $156,000; Detroit
To rename: Fort Street & Elmwood Railway
Amend Jan. 24, 1888, to increase capital to $250,000
Sold July 1, 1892, to Fort Wayne & Belle Isle

Fort Wayne and Jackson Railroad Company
O: 012, 030, 038
Inc. Dec. 31, 1879; $3,000,000; Jackson
To reorganize: Fort Wayne, Jackson & Saginaw
Acquired at inc., line: Jackson to Fort Wayne
Leased Aug. 24, 1882, indefinitely to Lake Shore & Michigan Southern
Consolidated Dec. 31, 1981, into United RR Corp.

The Fort Wayne, Jackson and Saginaw Railroad Company
O: 012, 030, 038
Inc. Jan. 26, 1869; $1,500,000; Jackson
To consolidate: Jackson, Fort Wayne & Cincinnati and Fort Wayne, Jackson & Saginaw (Ind. corp.)
Line completed Jan. 17, 1870, Jackson to Fort Wayne
Foreclosure sale Dec. 3, 1879, to Fort Wayne & Jackson

Foster, Blackman and Co. (Gauge 4')
O: 043
Private logging road; Baldwin
5 miles, Baldwin River in T18N R13W
Built 1881

A[mos] Fox and Co.
O: 015
Private lumbering tramway
In Charlevoix
Built ca. 1867

The Frankfort and South Eastern Railroad Company (Gauge 3')
O: 010, 051 P: 083
Inc. Nov. 9, 1885; $100,000; Frankfort
To own: 20 miles, Frankfort to Upper Weldon Bridge, Weldon twp. or to Grand Rapids & Indiana Ry in Wexford co.
Amend Nov. 2, 1887, to change to standard guage
Amend Sept. 22, 1888, to change eastern terminus
Line completed Nov. 25, 1889, Frankfort to Beecher
Sold May 15, 1892, to Toledo, Ann Arbor & North Michigan
Foreclosure sale June 1, 1895, to Escanaba, Frankfort & Southeastern

Frankfort, Crystal Lake and Glenn Arbor Rail Road Company
P: 010, 045
Inc. March 3, 1890; $400,000
To own: 44 miles, Frankfort around Crystal Lake to Glenn Arbor with branch to Gilmore twp.
Lapsed

Franklin Mining Co.
O: 031
Private mining gravity tram way
0.8 miles, top of hill to stamp mill
Built 1860

Frederic(k) & Charlevoix Railroad
O: unknown
Private logging road
May have been conveyed to Detroit & Charlevoix

Frost, S., and Co.
O: 059
Private logging road
Stanton

Frost Shingle Co.
O: 031
Private logging road
Withey

The Fruitport and Lake Shore Rail Road Company
P: 061, 070
Inc. Jan. 29, 1870; $500,000
To own: 22 miles, Fruitport to Holland
Lapsed

Fuller, P. S., and Co.
O: 027
Private logging road
Watersmeet

Fulton Street & Reed's Lake Railway Company
P: 041
Inc.(S) Sept. 10, 1875; $25,000; Grand Rapids
To own: in Grand Rapids, from Fulton St. to Reeds Lake
Lapsed

G

Garden Bay Railway Company
O: 021, 077
Inc.(S) Oct. 27, 1915; $25,000
To own: 13.7 miles, line of Van Harbor Land & Lumber
Acquired May 14, 1915, line from Van Harbor Land & Lumber
Operations discontinued June 15, 1917

Gebhart and Estabrook (Lumber Co.) (Gauge 3')
O: 018
Private logging road
Clare co.

Genesee and Oakland Rail Road Company
P: 025, 063
Chartered April 3, 1848; $250,000
To build: Pontiac to Flint
Amend charter Feb. 13, 1855, to build: also from Flint to Saginaw county
Amend charter Feb. 3, 1858, to extend time for incorporation
Amend charter Feb. 15, 1859, to authorize consolidation into Flint & Pere Marquette
Lapsed

Gerrish, Winfield Scott
Owned Lake George & Muskegon River

Gibbs, J. H. (Gauge 3')
O: 059
Private logging road; Edmore
In T12N R6W?

The Gibralter and Clinton railroad company
P: 046, 058, 082
Chartered March 22, 1837; $400,000
To build: 40 miles, Gibralter to Clinton
Lapsed

Gilbert Tramway
O: 070
Private logging tramway
Line built ca. 1853, 5 miles in T7N R15W
Sold 1855-56 to Ferry and Sons

Gilchrist, F. W.
O: 004
Private logging pole-rail tramway
In use ca. 1878

The Gladstone Street Railway Company (E)
P: 021
Inc.(S) March 11, 1889; $25,000; Gladstone
To own: in Gladstone
Lapsed

The Glencoe, Pinconning and Lake Shore Railroad Company
O: 009
Inc. March 17, 1876; $120,000; Bay City
To own: 15 miles, SW cor sec 31 T17N R3E to Saginaw River at or near mouth of Pine River
Owned by George Campbell & Co.
Line opened 1874, Glencoe to Pinconning
Renamed April 30, 1879, as Pinconning

Glen Arbor Railroad
O: 045
Private road

Globe Train Railway Company
P: 031
Inc.(T) July 17, 1866; $50,000; Portage twp.
To own: W line sec 9 T54N R34W north to shore of Portage Lake in sec 34 T55N R34W
Lapsed

Gogebic & Iron Counties Railway & Light Company (E)
O: 027
Inc.(S) Oct. 6, 1910; $350,000; Bessemer
To consolidate Gogebic Street Ry and a power company
Acqired at inc., Gogebic Street Ry
Also inc. Nov. 26, 1910 (Wisc. corp.) as Gogebic and Iron Counties Railway & Light Co.; $100,000; Bessemer
Amend Dec. 13, 1910, to increase capital to $700,000
Renamed Feb. 8, 1911, as Ironwood & Bessemer Railway & Light

Gogebic and Montreal River Railroad Company
O: 027
Inc. Dec. 5, 1883; $600,000
To own: 15 miles, East branch of Montreal River in T47N R47W to east end of Sunday Lake
Leased Sept. 1, 1886, 999 years, to Penokee RR (non-Mich. corp.)
Line completed June 6, 1887, Ironwood to Bessemer
Lease assigned May 31, 1888, to Wisconsin Central
Amend June 25, 1888, to extend branches to various mines
Disposition uncertain

Gogebic Street Railway Company (E)
O: 027
Inc.(S) Sept. 14, 1910; $325,000; Bessemer
To own: in Wakefield, Bessemer, and Ironwood
Acquired at inc., Twin City General Electric
Merged Nov. 26, 1910, into Gogebic & Iron Counties

Gram, John C.
See AuSable Lumber Co.

Grand Haven and Southeastern Railway Company
P: 070
Inc. Nov. 4, 1897; $100,000; Grand Haven
To own: 4 miles, Grand Haven to north line Grand Haven twp.
Lapsed

Grand Haven Lumber Co.
O: 059
Private logging road; Grand Haven
Line built 1882, 10 miles, T10 & 11N R6W
Abandoned ca. 1886

Grand Haven Railroad Company
O: 003, 061, 070 P: 008, 013, 039
Inc. Sept. 21, 1878; $800,000; Allegan
To reorganize Michigan Lake Shore
Line acquired at inc., Allegan to Muskegon
Amend May 20, 1881, to extend line from Allegan to Battle Creek
Merged July 16, 1881, into Chicago & West Michigan

The Grand Haven Street Railway Company (E)
O: 070
Inc.(S) April 30, 1895; $25,000; Grand Haven
To own: in Grand Haven
Line opened June 1895
Amend Feb. 18, 1903, to increase capital to $100,000
Conveyed no date, probably to Grand Rapids, Grand Haven & Muskegon
Dissolved Feb. 1, 1904

The Grand Rapids and Bay City Railroad Company
P: 009, 029, 041, 056, 059
Inc. Aug. 3, 1871; $2,000,000
To own: 100 miles, Bay City to Grand Rapids
Lapsed

Grand Rapids & Belding Railway Company (E)
P: 041, 059
Inc.(T) Dec. 24, 1900; not given; Grand Rapids
To rename Grand Rapids, Belding & Greenville
Lapsed

Grand Rapids and Chicago Railroad Company
P: 003, 011, 041, 080
Inc. Sept. 10, 1887; $1,500,000
To own: 110 miles, Grand Rapids to Indiana state line in Berrien co.
Lapsed

Grand Rapids and Chicago Railway Company (E)
P: 003, 011, 041, 070
Inc. March 18, 1902; $1,000,000; Allegan
To own: 125 miles, Grand Rapids to Allegan, Kalamazoo, South Haven, St. Joseph and Benton Harbor
Renamed Aug. 4, 1904, as Grand Rapids & Kalamazoo Valley

The Grand Rapids and Holland Railroad Company
P: 041, 070
Inc. Feb. 20, 1871; $250,000
To own: 26 miles, Grand Rapids to Holland
Merged Oct. 25, 1871, into Chicago & Michigan Lake Shore

Grand Rapids & Indiana—
O: 003, 005, 015, 016, 024, 028, 039, 040, 041, 043, 054, 057, 059, 061, 067, 069, 070, 072, 075, 083
Inc. Aug. 1, 1855, as Grand Rapids and Indiana Railroad Company; $2,096,000; Grand Rapids
To consolidate: Grand Rapids & Indiana (Ind. corp.) and Grand Rapids & Southern
Amend June 26, 1857, as The Grand Rapids and Indiana Rail Road Company, to consolidate: Grand Rapids & Fort Wayne (Ind. corp.) and Grand Rapids & Mackinaw
Line opened Dec. 23, 1867, Grand Rapids to Cedar Springs
Receivership begun Jan. 19, 1869, Jessie L. Williams, receiver
Lease June 1, 1871, of Cincinnati, Richmond & Ft. Wayne (Ind. corp.)
Receivership ended June 20, 1871; control to Continental Improvement Co.
Lease Jan. 1, 1874, of Mansfield, Coldwater & Lake Michigan (Mich. lines)
Line completed May 1874, Fort Wayne to Petoskey
Lease Jan. 1, 1879, of Allegan & South Eastern
Amend March 3, 1880, to increase capital to $5,000,000
Lease cancelled Oct. 19, 1882, eff. Dec. 31, 1882, of Allegan & South East.
Lease Jan. 1, 1883, for 50 years, of Traverse City RR
Amend July 2, 1884, to consolidate: Grand Rapids, Indiana & Mackinaw
Lease June 9, 1886, for 99 yrs, of Muskegon, Grand Rapids & Indiana
Acquired Jan. 17, 1888, Bay View, Little Traverse & Mackinac

Foreclosure sale June 10, 1896
Inc. July 7, 1896, as Grand Rapids & Indiana Railway Company; $6,000,000
To reorganize Grand Rapids & Indiana RR
Received July 25, 1896, Grand Rapids & Indiana RR
Bought June 11, 1917, eff. May 1, 1917, Traverse City RR
Bought May 1, 1917, Muskegon, Grand Rapids & Indiana
Merged Dec. 1, 1953, into Penndel Co.

Grand Rapids & Ionia Railway Company
P: 034, 041
Inc. Nov. 3, 1903; $1,000,000; Detroit
To own 32 miles, Grand Rapids to Ionia
Amend July 14, 1904, to change names of incorporating officers
Amend Jan. 7, 1914, to change number of directors
Lapsed

The Grand Rapids and Kalamazoo Electric Railway Company (E)
P: 003, 008, 039, 041
Inc.(S) Jan. 26, 1899; $100,000; Detroit
To own: Grand Rapids to Kalamazoo
Lapsed

Grand Rapids & Kalamazoo Valley Railway Company (E)
P: 003, 039, 041
Inc. Aug. 4, 1904; $1,000,000; Kalamazoo
To rename: Grand Rapids & Chicago Ry, and to build 55 miles, Grand Rapids to Kalamazoo
Amend Aug. 4, 1904, to modify rights
Amend March 20, 1905, to increase capital to $2,000,000
Lapsed

Grand Rapids and Lake Michigan Railroad Company
P: 041, 070
Inc. Oct. 21, 1889; $750,000
To own: 25 miles, Grand Rapids to Holland
Lapsed

The Grand Rapids and Lake Shore Railroad Company
P: 041, 051, 053, 061, 062, 064
Inc. Feb. 3, 1869; $800,000
To own: 50 miles, Grand Rapids, via Lamont, Eastmanville, Union, Crawville, and Muskegon, to Whitehall
Amend Feb. 3, 1870, to change northern terminus to Pentwater
Amend May 21, 1870, as Grand Rapids and Lake Shore Railroad, to change northern terminus to Manistee
Merged Aug. 15, 1870, into Chicago & Michigan Lake Shore

Grand Rapids and Mackinaw Rail Road Company
P: 005, 015, 024, 028, 040, 041, 054, 059, 067, 083
Inc. May 22, 1857; $1,720,000
To own: 215 miles, Grand Rapids to Straits of Mackinac
Merged June 26, 1857, into Grand Rapids & Indiana

Grand Rapids and Mineral Springs Railroad Company
P: 041
Inc. May 4, 1889; $60,000
To own: 3 miles, Grand Rapids to Indian Mounds, in sec. 3, Wyoming twp.
Amend July 1, 1889, to own: 3 miles, SE cor sec 35, Walker twp. to jct. Lake Shore & Mich. South.—Chicago & West Mich. in sec 3, Wyoming twp.
Lapsed

The Grand Rapids and Northern Railway Company
P: 005, 015, 024, 028, 040, 041, 043, 054, 062, 067, 083
Inc. Dec. 16, 1856; $1,600,000
To own: 170 miles, Grand Rapids to Little Traverse Bay
Lapsed

Grand Rapids and North Western Railroad Company
P: 041, 053, 061, 062, 064, 070
Inc. Jan. 16, 1908; $3,000,000; Grand Rapids
To own: 95 miles, Grand Rapids to Ludington
Lapsed

Grand Rapids and Reeds Lake Street Railway Company (H)
O: 041
Inc.(S) Feb. 6, 1874; $35,000; Grand Rapids
To own: Grand Rapids to Reed's Lake
Amend Feb. 6, 1875, to restate route: in city and twp. of Grand Rapids
Line opened July 29, 1875
Sold July 20, 1880, to Reeds Lake Street Ry

Grand Rapids and Saginaw Railroad Company
P: 029, 034, 041
Inc. March 15, 1871; $1,500,000
To own: 30 miles, Grand Rapids to Kiddville, Ionia co.
Amend June 21, 1871, to change eastern terminus to St. Louis
Amend May 28, 1873, to change eastern terminus to Saginaw
Lapsed

Grand Rapids and Southern Rail Road Company
P: 003, 039, 041, 075
Inc. May 29, 1855; $696,000; Sturgis
To own: 87 miles, Grand Rapids to Indiana state line south of Sturgis
Merged Aug. 1, 1855, into Grand Rapids & Indiana

Grand Rapids & South Michigan Traction Company (E)
P: 013, 039, 041
Inc.(S) June 23, 1903; $1,300,000; Battle Creek
To own: Battle Creek to Grand Rapids, via Hickory Corners, Gull Lake, Milo, Prairieville, Orangeville, Gun Lake, Bowens Mills, Corning, and Bowen Station, with branch from Gull Lake via Richland to Kalamazoo
Lapsed

Grand Rapids, Belding and Greenville Railway Company
P: 034, 041, 059
Inc.(T) June 24, 1899; $100,000
To own: Mill Creek near Grand Rapids to Belding and Greenville
Renamed Dec. 24, 1900, as Grand Rapids & Belding

The Grand Rapids, Belding and Greenville Railway Company
P: 034, 059
Inc. Jan. 6, 1905; $600,000
To own: 19 miles, Saranac to Greenville
Amend Jan. 7, 1914, to change number of directors
Lapsed

Grand Rapids, Belding & Ionia Railway Company (E)
P: 034, 041
Inc.(S) Aug. 8, 1901; $100,000; Grand Rapids
To own: Grand Rapids to Ionia, via East Grand Rapids, Lowell, and Belding
Dissolved Dec. 30, 1914

Grand Rapids, Belding & Saginaw Railroad Company
O: 034, 059 P: 008
Inc. Sept. 26, 1898; $352,000
To own: 44 miles, Greenville via Belding, Lowell and Freeport to Hastings
Bought May 1, 1899, Lowell & Hastings
Line acquired at purchase, Lowell to Freeport
Line opened Jan. 1, 1900, Freeport to Belding
Control 1900, by Pere Marquette
Sold May 6, 1903, to Pere Marquette
Foreclosure sale, March 24, 1917, to Pere Marquette

Grand Rapids Belt Line Railroad Company
P: 041
Inc. Sept. 24, 1891; $200,000
To own: 4 miles in Grand Rapids
Lapsed

Grand Rapids, Chicago & St. Louis Railroad Company
P: 003, 011, 041, 070, 080
Inc. March 25, 1890; $1,000,000
To own: 80 miles, Grand Rapids to Benton Harbor via Holland
Lapsed

Grand Rapids City Railway Company (H)
P: 041
Inc.(T) May 20, 1864; $50,000
To build: 2 miles, Detroit & Milwaukee depot to Jefferson & Fulton Sts.
Lapsed

Grand Rapids Electric Railway Company (E)
P: 003, 008, 012, 013, 018, 023, 026, 030, 033, 034, 037, 039, 041, 054, 059, 070
Inc. March 24 1903; $2,000,000
To own: 250 miles, Grand Rapids to some point on Lake Huron with branch to Lansing
Bought Jan. 10, 1906, rights of Central Michigan RR
Amend June 20, 1907, to own: 250 miles, Grand Haven to Grand Rapids, thence to Gladwin; also branch Ohio state line in Amboy twp. to Battle Creek to a connection with first line
Some rights may have been sold to Battle Creek, Coldwater & Southern
Lapsed

The Grand Rapids, Grand Haven and Muskegon Railway Company (E)
O: 041, 061, 070
Inc.(S) March 6, 1899; $100,000; Grand Rapids
To own: Grand Rapids to Grand Haven and Muskegon
Control no date, by United Light & Power
Amend Nov. 20, 1900, to restate route in more detail; change number of directors
Amend Nov. 20, 1900, to increase capital to $1,100,000
Line opened Feb. 8, 1902
May have acquired Grand Haven Street Ry
End control May 1925, by United Light & Power
Receivership July 29, 1926
Abandoned April 18, 1928

The Grand Rapids, Grayling and Alpena Railroad Company
P: 004, 018, 020, 037, 041, 054, 057, 059, 060, 068, 072
Inc. May 4, 1891; $1,000,000
To own: 110 miles, Lake City to Alpena
Lapsed

Grand Rapids, Greenville & Alpena Railroad Company
P: 004, 018, 020, 037, 054, 059, 060, 068, 072
Inc. June 26, 1872; $2,000,000
To own: 160 miles, Greenville to Alpena
Cons. July 24, 1872, Grand Rapids, Rockford & Greenville
Lapsed

Grand Rapids, Greenville and Bay City Railroad Company
P: 041, 059
Inc. June 1, 1880; $200,000
To own: 18 miles, Rockford to Greenville
Lapsed

Grand Rapids, Holland & Chicago Railway Company (E)
O: 003, 041, 070
Inc.(S) July 18, 1904; $1,350,000; Holland
To own: in Wyoming twp., Zeeland, Holland, and Saugatuck; and acquire Grand Rapids, Holland & Lake Michigan
Bought Aug. 1, 1904, Grand Rapids, Holland & Lake Michigan
Leased Jan. 1, 1916, to Michigan Ry
Lease assigned April 10, 1919, to Michigan RR
Lease cancelled eff. Jan. 1, 1924
Foreclosure sale Oct. 20, 1926, to Hyman-Michael Co. [to scrap]
Operations ended Nov. 15, 1926
Part of line sold 1927, by Hyman-Michael Co. to United Suburban Ry
Dissolved Dec. 30, 1926

Grand Rapids, Holland and Lake Michigan Rapid Railway Company (E)
O: 003, 041, 070P: 061
Inc.(T) Feb. 24, 1900; $500,000; Detroit
To own: 32 miles, Grand Rapids to Macatawa Park, Ottawa Park, and townships in Allegan, Kent, Muskegon and Ottawa cos. (and to consolidate Saugatuck, Douglas & Lake Shore and Holland & Lake Michigan)
Acquired at inc. Saugatuck, Douglas & Lake Shore and Holland & Lake Michigan
Amend Dec. 8, 1900, to change number of directors
Amend Jan. 6, 1902, to increase capital to $1,000,000
Amend Feb. 10, 1903, to change number of directors
Sold Aug. 1, 1904, to Grand Rapids, Holland & Chicago

Grand Rapids, Indiana and Mackinaw Railroad Company
O: 016, 024
Inc. Feb. 18, 1881; $256,000
To own: 32 miles, Bay View to Mackinaw City
Line completed July 3, 1882, Kegomic to Mackinaw City
Merged July 2, 1884, into Grand Rapids & Indiana

The Grand Rapids, Indiana and Manistee Rail Road Company
P: 043, 051, 053, 067
Inc. Sept. 23, 1885; $450,000
To own: 55 miles, Milton Jct. to Manistee
Lapsed

Grand Rapids, Kalamazoo and South Haven Traction Company (E)
P: 003, 039, 041, 080
Inc. Aug. 22, 1901; $800,000; Allegan
To own: 100 miles, Grand Rapids to South Haven, Kalamazoo and Saugatuck
Lapsed

Grand Rapids, Kalkaska & Southeastern Railroad Company
O: 040, 057 P: 005, 020, 028
Inc. Aug. 30, 1897; $250,000; Grand Rapids
To own: 30 miles, Van Buren [now Rapid City] to Lake City
Amend Oct. 4, 1897, to change line: 52 miles, Elk Rapids via Van Buren and Kalkaska to Grayling, and increase capital to $416,000
Line completed Jan. 10, 1898, Rapid City to Stratford
Leased, ca. 1898, for 10 years, to Chicago & West Michigan
Control, 1903, by Chicago & West Michigan
Dissolved Sept. 14, 1924

Grand Rapids, Lansing and Detroit Railroad Company
O: 023, 034, 041
Inc. May 13, 1887; $450,000
To own: 53 miles, Grand Rapids to Grand Ledge
Control at inc. by Detroit, Lansing & Northern
Leased 1888, to Detroit, Lansing & Northern
Line completed Aug. 1888, Grand Rapids to Grand Ledge
Merged Feb. 1, 1896, eff. Jan. 1, 1897, into Detroit, Grand Rapids & Western

The Grand Rapids, Newaygo and Lake Shore Rail Road Company
O: 041, 061, 062 P: 051, 053, 064
Inc. Sept. 8, 1869; $1,000,000; Grand Rapids
To own: 80 miles, Grand Rapids via Newaygo to shore of Lake Michigan in Mason or Oceana co.
Line opened May 9, 1872, Grand Rapids to Sparta
Amend June 16, 1875, as Grand Rapids, Newaygo and Lake Shore Railroad, to own: 110 miles, S limits of Grand Rapids to Manistee
Line completed Sept. 24, 1875, Grand Rapids to White Cloud
Merged July 16, 1881, into Chicago & West Michigan

The Grand Rapids Rail Road Company
P: 041
Inc. Nov. 26, 1855; $30,000
To own: 3.5 miles in Kent co.
Lapsed

The Grand Rapids Railroad Company
P: 041
Inc. Jan. 31, 1871; $150,000
To own: 10 miles, Plums Mills on Grand Rapids & Indiana via E bank Grand River to point on Kalamazoo, Allegan & Grand Rapids Ry in Kent co.
Merged April 24, 1873, into Michigan Northern Ry (1873 inc.)

Grand Rapids Railroad Company (E)
O: 041
Inc.(S) April 11, 1927; $10,000; Grand Rapids
To own: street railway in Grand Rapids
Acquired at inc. Grand Rapids Railway
Amend May 24, 1927, to increase capital to $300,000
Operations ended Aug. 25, 1935
Dissolved Aug. 27, 1937

Grand Rapids Railway Company (E)
O: 041
Inc.(S) April 17, 1900; $4,000,000; Grand Rapids
To own: in City of Grand Rapids
Acquired at inc., Consolidated Street Ry
Amend Jan. 28, 1902, to change number of directors
Apparently acquired ca. 1906, South Grand Rapids Street
Conveyed April 11, 1927, property to Grand Rapids RR
Dissolved June 15, 1927

Grand Rapids, Rockford and Greenville Railroad Company
P: 041, 059
Inc. Nov. 10, 1870; $300,000
To own: 18 miles, Greenville to Rockford
Merged July 24, 1872, into Grand Rapids, Greenville & Alpena

The Grand Rapids, Spring Lake and Grand Haven Rapid Transit Company (E)
P: 041, 070
Inc. April 10, 1900; $500,000; Grand Rapids
To own: 32 miles, Grand Rapids to Grand Haven
Lapsed

Grand Rapids Street Railway Company (H)
O: 041
Inc.(T) Oct. 22, 1864; $60,000
To own: from Detroit & Milwaukee depot to Jefferson St.
Line opened May 10, 1865
Sold Dec. 31, 1869, to Street Ry of Grand Rapids

Grand Rapids Terminal Belt Railway Company
P: 041
Inc. Dec. 20, 1905; $100,000; Grand Rapids
To own: 10 miles, Pere Marquette and Lake Shore & Mich. South. crossing in Wyoming twp., easterly to Grand Trunk line North & East of Reeds Lake
Lapsed

Grand Rapids Terminal Railroad Company
O: 041
Inc. Aug. 9, 1904; $50,000; Detroit
To own: 2.22 miles in Grand Rapids
Line completed Jan. 1906
Amend Oct. 8, 1908, to revise route
Leased Oct. 27, 1908, for 10 years, to Detroit, Grand Haven & Milwaukee
Merged Nov. 1, 1928, into Grand Trunk Western

Grand Rapids Transfer and Junction Railroad Company
O: 041
Inc. Feb. 1, 1882; $8,000
To own: 1 mile from Chicago & West Mich. at Front St. to River Ave., Grand Rapids
Line completed June 1, 1882
Verbal lease 1886, to Chicago & West Michigan
Probably conveyed to Chicago & West Michigan, but no record of transfer found

The Grand Rapids, Traverse Bay & Mackinac Railroad Company
P: 005, 015, 024, 040, 041, 054, 057, 059, 067, 083
Inc. Sept. 1, 1856; $3,000,000
To own: 200 miles, Grand Rapids to or near Little Traverse Bay, then to Straits of Mackinac
Lapsed

Grand River and Muskegon Rail Road Company
P: 061, 070
Inc. Jan. 26, 1857; $200,000
To own: 20 miles from Detroit & Milwaukee in Ottawa co., via Muskegon to mouth of Muskegon River
Lapsed

The Grand River Electric Railroad Company (E)
O: 082
Inc.(S) March 8, 1898; $50,000; Detroit
To own: in Greenfield twp., Wayne co.
Line opened June 30, 1898
Sold March 31, 1899, to Detroit & Northwestern Ry

Grand River Railroad Company (E)
P: 041, 070
Inc. Oct. 10, 1891; $500,000
To own: 45 miles, Grand Rapids to Grand Haven with branch to Reeds Lake
Amend Nov. 28, 1892, to build: 62 miles, Grand Haven via Grand Rapids to Belding with branch to Reeds Lake
Lapsed

The Grand River Railway Company (H)
O: 082
Inc.(S) Nov. 29, 1890; $1,000,000
To reorganize: Grand River Street Ry
Sold Oct. 1, 1891, to Detroit Citizens' Street Ry

The Grand River Street Railway Company (H)
O: 082
Inc.(T) Feb. 12, 1869; $50,000
To own: in city of Detroit
Line opened Oct. 23, 1868
Amend Aug. 2, 1888, to increase capital to $100,000
Amend Dec. 27, 1889, to increase capital to $1,000,000
Possible transfer Jan. 17, 1890, to Grand River Ry
Reorganized Nov. 29, 1890, as Grand River Ry

Grand River Valley Railroad Company
O: 008, 023, 033, 038, 041
Chartered May 4, 1846; $1,000,000; Jackson
To own: 95 miles, Jackson to Grand Rapids
Amend charter March 17, 1847, to delete some incorporators
Act Feb. 3, 1858, granted right-of-way on Jackson-Lansing RR line
Act March 15, 1861, granted right-of-way over unimproved State land, and to extend completion dates
Act March 17, 1863, extended completion dates
Act March 20, 1863, granted Amboy, Lansing & Traverse Bay authority to buy company so long as Grand River Valley route not materially changed
Acquired Aug. 4, 1864, operating rights on Jackson, Lansing & Saginaw (Jackson to Rives Jct.)
Line opened July.4, 1868, Rives Jct. to Eaton Rapids
Line completed Jan. 1, 1870, Rives Jct. to Grand Rapids
Leased Aug. 15, 1870, for corp. life, to Michigan Central
Reinc. April 25, 1894, as The Grand River Valley Railroad; $1,000,000
To surrender state charter (retained same rights)
Merged Sept. 15, 1916, into Michigan Central

Grand Traverse Railroad Company
P: 005, 015, 028
Inc. Sept. 17, 1907; $450,000; Traverse City
To own: 56 miles, Traverse City to Charlevoix
Lapsed

Grand Trunk Corporation
O: Holding company
Inc. Nov. 18, 1971
To rename Grand Trunk Inds. and to acquire Grand Trunk Western
Acquired Dec. 30, 1971, Grand Trunk Western and other non-Mich. properties
Active corporation

Grand Trunk Industries, Incorporated
O: Holding company
Inc. Sept. 21, 1970 (Dela. corp.)
Renamed Nov. 18, 1971, as Grand Trunk Corp.

The Grand Trunk Rail Road Company of Michigan
P: 008, 011, 023, 033, 047, 050, 063, 080
Inc. May 26, 1868; $2,000,000
To own: 240 miles, Ridgeway via Lansing to St. Joseph, then via Niles to Indiana state line, then to Chicago
Amend Oct. 20, 1869, to allow directors to alter route
Lapsed

Grand Trunk Railway Company of Canada
O: Holding company
Inc. (Canadian corp.)
Lease July 5, 1860, eff. July 1, 1859, 999 years, of Chicago, Detroit & Canada Grand Trunk Junction
Control Nov. 23, 1875, at inc., of Michigan Air Line Ry
Control Nov. 1878, at inc., of Detroit, Grand Haven & Milwaukee
Control Jan. 7, 1880, at inc., of Chicago & Grand Trunk
Control Nov. 23, 1886, at inc., of St. Clair Tunnel
Control Aug. 1, 1888, of Toledo, Saginaw & Muskegon
Control Nov. 22, 1900, at inc., of Grand Trunk Western
Lease Dec. 28, 1900, eff. Jan. 1, 1901, 99 years, of Cincinnati, Saginaw & Mackinaw
Control Aug. 29, 1910, at inc., of Bay City Terminal
Conveyed eff. Jan. 1, 1923, to Canadian National Ry

The Grand Trunk Railway Company of Michigan
P: 011, 012, 013, 014, 033, 038, 047, 050, 063, 074, 075, 081
Inc. Dec. 21, 1866; $2,000,000; Jackson
To build 210 miles, Ridgeway via Romeo, Rochester, Pontiac, Pinckney, Jackson, Concord, Homer, Tekonsha, Union City, Colon, Three Rivers, Vandalia, Cassopolis and Niles to Indiana state line in Berrien co., then to Chicago
Amend June 1, 1868, to remove bylaw 8
Merged July 14, 1868, into Michigan Air Line RR

Grand Trunk Western—
O: 009, 013, 014, 019, 023, 025, 029, 032, 033, 034, 038, 039 041, 044, 047, 050, 059, 061, 063, 070, 073, 074, 075, 078 079, 082
Inc. Nov. 20, 1900, as Grand Trunk Western Railway Company; $6,000,000; Detroit
To reorganize: Port Huron & Indiana and Indiana & Illinois (Ind. corp.) and Chicago Lake County (Ill. corp.)
Line acquired at inc., Port Huron to Chicago
Control at inc. by Grand Trunk Ry of Canada
Control Dec. 7, 1905, 50% of Detroit Terminal
Control Feb. 28, 1907, of Chicago & Kalamazoo Terminal
Control Dec. 1, 1910, of Pontiac, Oxford &Northern
Control Feb. 29, 1912, at inc., of Detroit & Huron
Control eff. Jan. 1, 1923, by Canadian National Ry
Reinc. May 9, 1928, as Grand Trunk Western Railroad Company; $37,500,000
To consolidate: Grand Trunk Western Ry; Toledo, Saginaw & Muskegon; Pontiac, Oxford & Northern; Chicago, Detroit & Canada Grand Trunk Junction; Michigan Air Line Ry; Chicago & Kalamazoo Terminal; Grand Rapids Terminal; Bay City Terminal; Detroit, Grand Haven & Milwaukee; and Detroit & Huron
Consolidated Nov. 1, 1928, lines named
Lease assigned Nov. 15, 1928, eff. Jan. 1, 1929, of Cincinnati, Saginaw & Mackinaw by Grand Trunk Ry of Canada
Amend Oct. 18, 1929, to change capital structure
Amend Jan. 16, 1932, to change number of directors
Amend May 1, 1933, to change number of directors
Bought Jan. 1, 1943, Cincinnati, Saginaw & Mackinaw
Consolidated Aug. 23, 1955, Muskegon Ry & Navigation
Control Dec. 30, 1971, to Grand Trunk Corp.
Bought April 1, 1976, some lines from Penn Central Transp. Co.
Consolidated June 26, 1981, eff. Oct. 1, 1981, Detroit & Toledo Shore Line
Consolidated June 14, 1983, eff. Dec. 29, 1983, Detroit, Toledo & Ironton
Sold Aug. 1984, line (Wixom-Walled Lake) to Coe Rail
Sold Sept. 4, 1987, some lines to Central Michigan
Active corporation

Grass Lake and Manistee River Railroad Company (Gauge 3')
O: 020, 040
Inc. Feb. 4, 1886; $52,000; Manistee
To own: 13 miles, sec 33 T25N R5W and sec 17 T25N R4W to Manistee River in sec 35 T26N R6W
Line opened Sept. 3, 1886, 8 miles
Abandoned 1892

Gratiot Avenue Railway Company (E)
P: 082
Inc.(S) Dec. 8, 1891; $25,000; Detroit
To own: in Detroit and adjoining townships
Line opened May 25, 1891, by private parties that owned company
Merged Nov. 1, 1892, into Detroit Suburban Ry

Gratiot Electric Railway Company (E)
O: 074
Inc.(S) April 11, 1887; $25,000; Port Huron
To own: Fort Gratiot to Huronia Beach
Control at inc., by Port Huron Ry
Conveyed May 19, 1892, to City Electric Ry of Port Huron (1892 corp.)

Gratwick, Smith and Fryer Lumber Co.
Owned Crapo Lake & Northwestern

Grayling & Charlevoix Railroad Company
P: 005, 015, 020, 040, 069
Inc. March 24, 1891; $700,000
To own: 78 miles, Grayling and Frederic to Charlevoix
Lapsed

Grayling, Twin Lakes and Northeastern Railroad Company
O: 020, 060, 068, 069
Inc. July 24, 1891; $240,000
To own: 30 miles, Grayling to Twin Lakes
Control at inc. by Michigan Central
Line completed 1892, Grayling to Lewiston
Conveyed July 13, 1901, to Jackson, Lansing & Saginaw

Green Bay and Western Railroad
Wisc. corp.
Controlled April 5, 1982, at inc., Michigan & Western

Greenville, Stanton and St. Louis Railroad Company
P: 059
Inc. Sept. 29, 1871; $200,000
To own: 12 miles, Greenville to Stanton
Lapsed

Greenwood Lumber Co.
O: 066
Private logging road
Ontonagon

Grosse Ile Railway Company (E)
P: 082
Inc. April 19, 1910; $40,000
To own: 5 miles, Detroit Monroe & Toledo Short Line .6 mi S of Wyandotte S city limits thence E to Grosse Ile, thence S to Michigan Central station
Lapsed

H

Haak, J. A. (Gauge 3')
O: 043
Private logging road; Chase
3 miles, probably in T18N R11W
Built ca. 1881

Hackley and Hume
O: 018
Private logging road [also known as Long Lake & Muskegon River]
12 miles, T21N R4W to sec 1 T20N R5W
Built 1883

Hale, S[ylvester] and C. D.
O: 035
Private logging road; Tawas City
Tawas City Westerly

Hall, Edmund (Gauge 3')
O: 018
Private logging road
Clare co.

Hall and Manning Road (Gauge 3' 6")
O: 043
Private logging road
Lake co.

Hamtramck and Grosse Pointe Railway Company (H)
O: 082
Inc.(S) Nov. 2, 1887; $25,000; Detroit
To build: in Hamtramck and vicinity
Rights apparently conveyed, May 1891, to Jefferson Ave.

The Hamtramck Street Rail Way Company (H)
O: 082
Inc.(S) Aug. 29, 1868; $10,000
To own: in Detroit on Jefferson Ave., from Detroit City Ry to E city limits
Line opened Sept. 6, 1868
Transferred Nov. 1, 1881, to Detroit City Ry

Hancock and Calumet Railroad Company (Gauge 3' until ca. 1900, then standard)
O: 031, 042
Inc. Dec. 27, 1884; $300,000; Hancock
To own: 18 miles, Portage Lake bridge via Torch Lake and Lake Linden to Red Jacket
Line completed Dec. 1, 1885, Hancock to Calumet
Amend June 18, 1886; $350,000; to change: northern terminus to Allouez Mine, Keweenaw co.
Amend May 23, 1899, to add: 50 miles; branches to Lake Linden, to various mines, and to Lake Superior in Keweenaw co.
Control June 1, 1901, by Mineral Range RR
Conveyed Jan. 1, 1935, to Mineral Range RR

Hannah, Lay and Co.
O: 028
Private logging road
Traverse City

Harbor Beach and Port Hope Railroad Company
O: 032
Inc. March 25, 1903; $100,000
To own: 8 miles, Harbor Beach to Port Hope
Control at inc. by Pere Marquette
Line completed Oct. 1903, Harbor Beach to Port Hope
Conveyed Dec. 21, 1903, into Pere Marquette

The Harbor Springs Railway Company (Gauge 2' 6")
O: 024
Inc.(T) Dec. 10, 1900; $30,000; Harbor Springs
To own: 16 miles, Harbor Springs to Cross Village
Amend March 29, 1901, to permit route in village of Harbor Springs
Abandoned 1910
Dissolved Jan. 17, 1912

Haring & Lake City
O: 057, 083
Private logging road

Harris [Levi O. & Henry H.] Brothers
O: 001
Private logging tramway
Harrisville to sec 10 T26N R9E

Harrisville & Hubbard Lake
See R. A. Alger & Co.

Harroun, H. M. (Gauge 3')
O: 062
Private logging road
Newaygo co.

Hart and Horning
O: 062
Private logging road
Woodville

Hastings, Lowell and Northern Michigan Railroad Company
P: 008, 034, 041
Inc. May 18, 1883; $300,000
To own: 32 miles, Hastings to Smyrna
Bought Aug. 29, 1883, part of rights of Kalamazoo, Lowell & Northern Michigan
Sold May 31, 1887, to Lowell & Hastings

The Havre Branch rail-road company
P: 058
Chartered March 28, 1836; $100,000
To build: from Havre in Monroe co., westerly to Maumee Branch RR or to Erie & Kalamazoo RR
Act March 20, 1837, authorized State to purchase company
Amend charter March 24, 1840, to build: from state line near Havre to Southern RR at Monroe
Amend charter Feb. 16, 1844, to extend completion dates
Lapsed

Haynes and Sessions
O: 059
Private logging tram road
Near Stanton

Hazelton and Gerrish
See Lake George & Muskegon River

Hebard [Charles S. and Edward] and Thurber [H. C.]
O: 007
Private logging road; Pequaming
L'Anse easterly
Built ca. 1879; sold ca. 1920 to Ford Motor Co.

Hecla and Torch Lake Railroad Company (Gauge 4' 1")
O: 031
Inc. Jan. 6, 1868; $150,000; Calumet
To own: 12 miles, sec 23 Calumet twp. [Hecla Mine] to Dollar Bay, Houghton co., with branch to Torch Lake
Owned by Calumet & Hecla Co.
Converted to private ore road

Hecla Belt Line Railroad Company
O: 009
Inc. March 19, 1902; $175,000
To own: 20 miles, sec 14 T14N R5E to sec 25 T14N R4E
Conveyed Dec. 30, 1912, to Bay City & Battle Creek
Dissolved Dec. 15, 1913

Hecla Train Railway Company
P: 031
Inc.(T) June 1, 1867; $150,000; Calumet twp.
To own: 11 miles, Hecla Mine (sec 23 T56N R33W) SEly to Torch Lake, then SWly to Portage Lake near Dollar Bay
Lapsed

"Hemlock Central"
See Harbor Springs Ry

Hermansville and Western— (Gauge 3' 6")
O: 055
Inc. Sept. 2, 1881, as The Hermansville and Western Railway Company; $40,000; Hermansville
Owned by Wisconsin Land & Lumber Co. (Herman J. L. Meyer)
To own: 10 miles, Hermansville to Menominee River
Amend May 14, 1883, as Hermansville and Western Railway Company, to change capital to $150,000; to change to standard guage, and to own: 15 miles, Hermansville to Menominee River in sec 6 T38N R28W
Abandoned

Hersey Gravel Co.
O: 067
Private industrial road
Hersey

The Highland Park and Royal Oak Railroad Company (E)
P: 063, 082
Inc. March 20, 1916; $50,000; Highland Park
To own: 6 miles, sec 12 Greenfield twp. to Royal Oak
Controlled at inc., by Detroit United Ry
Sold Feb. 5, 1917, to Detroit, Almont & Northern

Highland Park Railway Company (E)
P: 082
Inc.(S) May 11, 1886; $50,000; Detroit
To build: in vicinity of Detroit
Line opened Sept. 18, 1886
Sold Feb. 1, 1893, to Detroit Suburban Ry

Hillsdale County Railway Company
O: 012, 030
Inc. Jan. 27, 1976; $300,000; Hillsdale
To own: RR in Hillsdale and Branch counties
Operating agreement April 1, 1976, with state of Michigan
Amend Jan. 3, 1978, to change number of directors
Active corporation

The Hobart and Manistee River Rail Road Company (Gauge 3')
O: 043P: 067, 083
Inc. July 11, 1879; $60,000; Manistee
To own: 15 miles, S. Branch Manistee River to Hobart on Grand Rapids & Ind.
Owned by John Canfield
Line opened Sept. 1, 1879, 9.2 miles
Abandoned 1890

The Holland and Lake Michigan Railway Company(E)
O: 070
Inc.(S) June 21, 1897; $150,000; Holland
To build: in Holland city and township
Line opened June 27, 1898
Merged Feb. 24, 1900, into Grand Rapids, Holland & Lake Michigan

Holland South Shore Railway Company (E)
P: 070
Inc. July 26, 1890; $60,000
To build: 5 miles, city of Holland to Black Lake
Lapsed

Holly, Wayne & Monroe Railway Company
O: 058, 063, 082
Inc. Nov. 15, 1865; $1,000,000
To own: 65 miles from Detroit & Milwaukee RR at Holly to Monroe
Line completed Jan. 1, 1872, Holly to Monroe
Merged Feb. 1, 1872, into Flint & Pere Marquette

Holmes, William, and Son (Gauge 3')
O: 036
Private logging road
Iron Co.

Holt Lumber Co.
O: 066
Private logging road
Bruces Crossing

Hope & Tittabawassee
See Tittabawassee & Hope

Hopkins Manufacturing Co.
Owned Bear Lake Lumber Co. (Bear Lake & Eastern and Bear Lake Train Ry)

Horr, R. G.
O: 065
Private logging tram road
5 miles, near Summit

Houghton and L'Anse Railroad Company
P: 007, 031
Inc. June 1, 1881; $1,000,000
To own: 33 miles, Houghton to L'Anse
Merged Feb. 1, 1883, into Marquette, Houghton & Ontonagon

Houghton and Ontonagon Railroad Company
P: 007, 031, 052, 066
Inc. Jan. 15, 1870; $560,000
To own: 70 miles, Ontonagon to T48N R29W
Amend July 13, 1871; $1,200,000; to change east terminus to Marquette, 110 miles
Amend Aug. 22, 1872, to change east terminus to Champion
Merged May 25, 1872, apparently eff. Aug. 22, 1872, into Marquette, Houghton & Ontonagon

The Houghton and Rockland Railroad Company
P: 031, 066
Inc. Aug. 18, 1883; $360,000
To own: 45 miles, Portage Lake in sec 5 T54N R33W to Rockland
Lapsed

Houghton, Chassell & Southwestern Railroad Company
O: 031, 066
Inc.(T) March 22, 1909; $50,000; Chassell
To own: 20 miles, 5th St. and Duluth, South Shore & Atlantic in Chassell to sec 11 T51N R38W
Owned by C. H. Worcester
Abandoned

The Houghton County Street Railway Company (E)
O: 031, 042
Inc.(S) July 26, 1899; $25,000; Houghton
To own: Houghton to Hancock, Laurium and Red Jacket; to Allouez Mine; Laurium to Lake Linden, Schoolcraft and Torch Lake; through Osceola, Quincy and Franklin twps. to Houghton
Line opened 1900
Amend Aug. 7, 1900, to increase capital to $750,000 and change office to Hancock
Amend May 22, 1901, to increase capital to $1,250,000
Amend Aug. 2, 1904, to change number of directors
Amend March 22, 1907, to restructure capital
Amend Aug. 6, 1907, to change office to Houghton
Conveyed Sept. 1, 1908, to Houghton County Traction

Houghton County Traction Company (E)
O: 031, 042
Inc.(S) July 24, 1908; $25,000; Houghton
To own, S. Kearsarge Mine to Mohawk Mine
Acquired Sept. 1, 1908, Houghton County Street Ry
Amend Sept. 1, 1908, to revise capital structure and increase capital to $1,250,000
Amend Oct. 28, 1908, to restate specifics of route and change number of directors
Operations ended May 21, 1932
Dissolved Aug. 10, 1933

Houghton Lake & Barker City
See Roscommon Lumber Co.

Houghton Lake and Eastern Railroad Company
P: 020, 072
Inc. Oct. 27, 1877; $300,000
To own: 35 miles, Houghton Lake (sec 11 T22N R3W) to line of Jackson, Lansing & Saginaw, and branch to lake in sec 28 T21N R2W and branch to lake in sec 1 T21N R2W and branches N and S on shore of Houghton Lake
Lapsed

Houghton Lumber Co.
O: 031
Private logging road
Houghton

Houghton Rail Road Company
P: 031
Inc. Sept. 7, 1860; $8,000; Houghton
To own: 2 miles, Portage Lake to Isle Royale Mine
Lapsed

Hovey, S. P., and Co.
O: 043
Private logging road
Baldwin area

Howell and Lansing Rail Road Company
P: 033, 047
Inc. June 23, 1868; $570,000
To own: 33 miles, Howell to Lansing
Merged March 29, 1870, into Detroit, Howell & Lansing

Hoyt, Jesse
O: 018
Private logging road
2 miles, west of Farwell
Built ca. 1878

—

O: 018
In T20N R3W

The Hudson and Jackson Railroad Company
P: 038, 046
Inc. Sept. 28, 1870; $300,000
To own: 30 miles, Hudson to Jackson
Lapsed

Hudson Motor Car Co.
O: 082
Private industrial road; Detroit

Hungerford Lake Railroad
O: 062
Private logging road; Big Rapids
Owned by Stewart Ives
4.5 miles, Hungerford in T15N R11W
Built 1879

HURON AND EASTERN

Huron & Eastern Railway Company
O: 032, 073, 076, 079
Inc. March 25, 1985; $400,000; not stated
To: operate a railroad in Michigan
Bought March 27, 1986, line (Kinde-Croswell) from CSX Transportation
Bought Dec. 22, 1988, line (Saginaw-Bad Axe) from CSX Transportation
Active corporation

Huron & Michigan Railway Company
P: 029, 034, 041, 059, 073
Inc. May 19, 1903; $2,300,000
To own: 100 miles, Grand Rapids to Saginaw
Lapsed

Huron & Western Railroad Company
O: 009
Inc. May 26, 1902; $88,000
To own: 11 miles, sec 15 T14N R5E to east line T14N R3E in Bay co.
Sold Aug. 6, 1903, to Pere Marquette

Huron Handle and Mfg. Co.
O: 071
Private logging road

—

See also Onaway & North Michigan, and Lobdell and Bailey

Huron Portland Cement Co.
O: 004
Private industrial road

I

Indiana & Lake Michigan—
O: 011
Inc. June 25, 1887, as The Indiana and Lake Michigan Railway of Michigan Company; $600,000
To own: 28 miles, St. Joseph southeasterly to Indiana state line
Amend Aug. 8, 1887, as Indiana and Lake Michigan Railway Company; $800,000
To consolidate: Indiana & Lake Michigan (Ind. corp.)
Operating agreement June 4, 1889, by Terre Haute & Indianapolis
Line completed Aug. 4, 1890, St. Joseph to South Bend
Leased Aug. 4, 1890, 99 years, eff. Jan. 6, 1890, to Terre Haute & Indpls.

Foreclosure sale, Dec. 8, 1898, to M. G. Bulkley and M. L. Scudder, and subsequently to St. Joseph, South Bend & Southern
Lease cancelled Feb. 28, 1899, by Terre Haute & Indianapolis
Conveyed Jan. 20, 1899, to St. Joseph, South Bend & Southern

Indiana and Michigan Railroad Company
P: 011
Inc. June 9, 1881 (Ind. corp.)
Merged July 16, 1881, into Chicago & West Michigan

The Indiana, Illinois and Iowa Railroad Company
O: 011
Inc. Sept. 15, 1898 (Ill., Ind., and Iowa corp.); $4,000,000; Chicago
To: consolidate non-Michigan companies
Lease Feb. 23, 1900, 50 years, of St. Joseph, South Bend & Southern
Line acquired at lease, St. Joseph to South Bend
Lease assigned March 15, 1905, of St. Joseph, South Bend & Southern, to Michigan Central
Merged April 6, 1906, into Chicago, Indiana & Southern

Indiantown & Southern Railroad
O: 055
Private logging road
Menominee co.

Ingalls, White Rapids & Northern— (Gauge 3')
O: 055
Inc. Sept. 17, 1886, as Ingalls, White Rapids and Northern Railway Company; $100,000
To own: 18 miles, C&NW in SW1/4sec 35 T35N R27W via Menominee River to sec 35 T37N R28W
Foreclosure sale July 6, 1889
Reinc. Sept. 2, 1889, as Ingalls, White Rapids and Northern Railroad Company; $120,000
Sold Dec. 17, 1894, eff. Jan. 1, 1895, to Wisconsin & Michigan

Inland Lime and Stone Co. (E)
O: 077
Private ore road
Owned by Inland Steel Co.
Port Inland
Operations ended Dec. 1989

Interstate Railway Company
P: 011
Inc.(T) Dec. 18, 1900; $350,000; Berrien Springs
To own: 32 miles, Benton Harbor to Niles to Indiana state line
Lapsed

InterUrban Railway Company of Saginaw, Michigan (E)
O: 009, 073
Inc.(T) March 6, 1895; $200,000
To own: Saginaw to Bay City and West Bay City
Leased Jan. 3, 1899, to Saginaw Valley Traction Co.
Control 1903, by Saginaw-Bay City Ry & Light
Conveyed ca. 1910 to Saginaw-Bay City Ry

The Ionia and Lansing Rail Road Company
O: 019, 023, 033, 034, P: 041, 059, 062, 064
Inc. Nov. 13, 1865; $300,000; Ionia
To own: 34 miles, Ionia to Lansing
Amend Jan. 13, 1869; $1,200,000; to own: 125 miles, Lansing to mouth of Pentwater River
Line opened Nov. 18, 1869, Lansing to Portland
Merged March 16, 1871, into Detroit, Lansing & Lake Michigan

The Ionia and Owosso Railway Company
P: 019, 034, 078
Inc. Dec. 23, 1903; $1,500,000
To own: 45 miles, Ionia to Owosso
Amend Jan. 7, 1914, to change number of directors
Lapsed

Ionia and Stanton Railroad Company
P: 034, 059
Inc. Dec. 29, 1869; $180,000
To own: 22 miles, Ionia to Stanton
Disposition unknown

The Ionia, Stanton and Northern Rail road Company
P: 034, 037, 054, 059, 067
Inc. July 16, 1872; $500,000; Ionia
To own: 62 miles, 3 mis. N of Ionia via Sheridan and Stanton to Chippewa on Flint & Pere Marquette line in Osceola co.
Merged Oct. 1, 1872, into Detroit, Lansing & Lake Michigan

The Iron Bay Rail Road Company
P: 052
Inc. March 6, 1866; $100,000
To own: 3.5 miles, Marquette to T47N R24W to conn. with Peninsula Branch RR
Lapsed

The Iron Mountain and Wisconsin State Line Rail Road Company
P: 021, 052, 055
Inc. June 27, 1856; $2,700,000
To own: 90 miles, Marquette co. to Delta co.
Lapsed

The Iron Mountain Rail Road Company
O: 052
Inc. Feb. 15, 1855; $400,000
To own: 25 miles, Marquette to west line T47N R28W
Line opened Aug. 1857, Marquette to Ishpeming
Sold Dec. 31, 1858, to Bay De Noquet & Marquette

Iron Mountain Railway Company
P: 052
Inc. March 10, 1855; $140,000
To own: 14 miles, mines of Jackson Iron Mountain to Marquette
Lapsed

Iron Range & Huron Bay Railroad Company
P: 007, 052
Inc. June 27, 1890; $500,000; Detroit
To own: 50 miles, Huron Bay to Michigamme
Amend Sept. 2, 1891, to increase capital to $1,000,000
Built but not operated, subsequently abandoned

Iron Range Railway Company
O: 052
Inc. Aug. 13, 1887; $250,000
To own: 30 miles, Chicago & North Western in Ishpeming to Michigamme with branch to Champion Mine
Control at inc. by Chicago & North Western
Line completed Aug. 10, 1888, Ishpeming to Republic
Sold June 10, 1889, to Chicago & North Western

Iron River Railway Company
O: 027, 036
Inc. Oct. 8, 1886; $800,000
To own: 100 miles, Chicago & North Western in Iron River to Wisconsin state line in Ontonagon co.
Control at inc. by Chicago & North Western
Line completed Sept. 1, 1887, Iron River to Watersmeet
Sold June 10, 1889, to Chicago & North Western

Iron River, Stambaugh & Crystal Falls Street Railway Company (E)
O: 036
Inc.(S) Feb. 28, 1914; $300,000; Iron River
To own: in Iron River, Stambaugh, Crystal Falls and Bates twp.
Line opened ca. 1913
Amend July 27, 1916, to change number of directors
Operations ended 1921

Ironwood and Bessemer Railway and Light Company (E)
O: 027
Inc. (Wisc. corp.) Feb. 8, 1911; $700,000; Ashland, Wisc.
To rename: Gogebic & Iron Counties Ry & Light (and acquire its rights)
Amend April 27, 1912, to change some corporate rights
Amend Dec. 19, 1912, to increase capital to $900,000
Amend Jan. 18, 1915, to change some corporate rights
Amend Feb. 15, 1917, to change capital structure and corporate rights
Amend Jan. 25, 1921, to increase capital to $1,500,000
Transferred ca. 1922, to Lake Superior District Power

Ironwood and Hurley Street Railway Company (H)
P: 027
Inc.(S) Dec. 10, 1886; $25,000; Ironwood
To own: in Ironwood twp.
Lapsed

Ironwood Electric Railway Company (E)
P: 027
Inc. not found
To: not found
Merged possibly, into Twin City General Electric Co.

The Ishpeming and Negaunee Railroad Company (E)
P: 052
Inc.(S) Sept. 19, 1890; $200,000
To own: in Ishpeming and adjoining townships
Lapsed

Ishpeming, L'Anse and Ontonagon Railroad Company
P: 007, 031, 052, 066
Inc. Jan. 6, 1885; $1,000,000
To own: 80 miles, Ishpeming to Ontonagon
Lapsed

Island Mining Co.
O: 042
Private ore road
2.75 miles on Isle Royale
Built about 1875

Isle Royale Copper Co.
O: 031
Private ore road
Isle Royale Mine to stamp mill

Ithaca and Alma Rail Road Company
O: 029
Inc. March 21, 1882; $60,000; Alma
To own: 7.5 miles, Ithaca to Alma
Line completed Dec. 28, 1882, Alma to Ithaca
Operated by Saginaw Valley & St. Louis
Conveyed, 1897, to Ann Arbor RR Co.

Ives, Stewart
Owned Hungerford Lake RR

J

The Jackson & Adrian Electric Railway Company (E)
P: 038, 046
Inc.(S) March 22, 1899; $50,000; Adrian
To own: Jackson to Adrian
Lapsed

Jackson and Albion Electric Railway Company (E)
P: 013, 038
Inc.(S) Oct. 10, 1901; $350,000; Jackson
To own: in Jackson and Calhoun counties [construction co.]
Control at inc., by Detroit & Chicago Traction
Conveyed no date, to Jackson & Battle Creek Traction

Jackson and Ann Arbor Railway Company (E)
P: 038, 081
Inc.(S) Sept. 18, 1901; $100,000; Jackson
To own: in Jackson and Washtenaw counties [construction co.]
Control at inc., by Detroit & Chicago Traction
Amend Sept. 11, 1905, to increase capital to $500,000
Sold Nov. 25, 1906, to Jackson, Ann Arbor & Detroit

LIMITED TRAINS
JACKSON & BATTLE CREEK
TRACTION COMPANY
THIRD RAIL SYSTEM

Jackson and Battle Creek Traction Company (E)
O: 013, 038
Inc.(S) May 17, 1902; $900,000; Jackson
To own: Jackson to Battle Creek
Acquired no date, property of Battle Creek & Marshall Traction, Calhoun County, and Jackson & Albion Electric
Amend Oct. 28, 1902, to increase capital to $1,500,000
Amend Jan. 21, 1903, to change office to Sheridan twp., Calhoun co.
Line opened May 17, 1903
Leased May 1, 1906, to Michigan United Rys
Dissolved Oct. 11, 1915

Jackson and Cincinnati Railway Company
O: 038, 046
Inc. Aug. 9, 1895; $160,000
To own: 20 miles, Addison to Jackson
Line completed April 25, 1896, Addison Jct. to Jackson
Sold June 1, 1898, to Cincinnati Northern

The Jackson and Eastern Railroad Company
P: 038, 047, 063, 081, 082
Inc. March 30, 1880; $1,000,000
To own: 80 miles, Jackson, via Waterloo, Unadilla and Pinckney, to Detroit
Lapsed

Jackson and Northern Railroad Company (Gauge 3')
O: 038
Inc.(T) Nov. 7, 1891; $12,000; Jackson
To own: Jackson to village of Portage (sec 11, Blackman twp.)
Reinc. Oct. 10, 1921
To continue corporate life
Abandoned

Jackson and Ohio Railroad Company
P: 030, 038, 046
Inc. Jan. 18, 1884; $600,000
To own: 40 miles, Jackson to Ohio state line (to Bryan, Ohio)
Merged Jan. 20, 1886, into Cincinnati, Jackson & Mackinaw RR

Jackson and Suburban Traction Company (E)
O: 038
Inc.(S) Sept. 27, 1900; $300,000; Jackson
To own: Jackson to Grass Lake
Acquired at inc., Jackson Street Ry
Conveyed April 25, 1904, to Jackson Consolidated Traction

Jackson and Tindle, Inc.
O: 024
Private logging road
Pellston to Pleasant, Center and Readmond twps.
Built 1903

Jackson, Ann Arbor and Detroit Railway Company (E)
O: 038, 081, 082
Inc. March 31, 1906; $1,900,000
To own: 90 miles, Detroit via Ypsilanti and Ann Arbor to Jackson with branch Wayne to Plymouth
Acquired Nov. 25, 1906, Detroit, Plymouth & Northville and Jackson & Ann Arbor
Sold July 19, 1907, to Detroit, Jackson & Chicago

Jackson, Ann Arbor and Detroit Traction Company (E)
P: 038, 081, 082
Inc.(S) May 6, 1903; $2,500,000; Scio twp.
To own: Jackson to Detroit
Lapsed

Jackson City Railway Company (H)
O: 038
Inc.(S) Aug. 24, 1881; $50,000

To own: in Jackson
Line opened 1886
Conveyed 1891, to Jackson Street Ry

Jackson Consolidated Traction Company (E)
O: 038
Inc.(S) April 19, 1904; $1,000,000; Jackson
To own: in Jackson, also Jackson to Grass Lake
Acquired at inc., Jackson & Suburban Traction
Acquired no date, Wolf Lake Ry & Resort
Control May 9, 1907, by Michigan United Rys
Sold Aug. 1, 1908, to Michigan United Rys
Dissolved Oct. 11, 1915

The Jackson, Fort Wayne and Cincinnati Railroad Company
P: 012, 030, 038
Inc. July 2, 1868; $500,000; Jackson
To own: 45 miles, Jackson to Indiana state line (to Fort Wayne)
Merged Jan. 26, 1869, into Fort Wayne, Jackson & Saginaw

Jackson Iron Co.
O: 021
Private industrial road
Fayette

Jackson, Lansing and Saginaw Railroad Company
O: 006, 009. 016, 019, 020, 033, 038, 065, 069, 072, 073, 078
Inc. Feb. 20, 1865; $1,500,000; Jackson
To rename Lansing & Jackson RR; build: 115 miles, Jackson via Lansing and Saginaw to Saginaw River
Granted Aug. 4, 1864, operating rights to Grand River Valley (Jackson to Rives Jct.)
Line opened Dec. 1865, Jackson to Mason
Rights acquired Oct. 26. 1866, of Amboy, Lansing & Traverse Bay from Lansing north
Amend Dec. 25, 1866, to build 280 miles, Jackson, via Saginaw and Traverse Bay, to Straits of Mackinac
Act Feb. 7, 1867, confirmed above action
Bought Jan. 4, 1867, Amboy, Lansing & Traverse Bay
Agreement filed Dec. 6, 1867, to allow Grand River Valley use of line Jackson to Rives. Jct.
Act March 8, 1869, to change northern terminus to Lake Superior
Amend March 1, 1871; $2,500,000; to operate line, 285 miles, Jackson via Lansing and Saginaw to Straits of Mackinac
Leased Sept. 1, 1871, for corp. life, to Michigan Central
Amend March 6, 1872, to reduce number of directors
Line completed Dec. 18, 1881, Jackson to Mackinaw City
Consolidated July 13, 1901, Grayling, Twin Lakes & Northeastern and Saginaw Bay & Northwestern
Merged Sept. 27, 1916, into Michigan Central

Jackson Main Street Railway
See Main Street Ry

The Jackson Rapid Transportation Company (E)
O: 038
Inc.(S) April 15, 1935
To own: in Jackson
Dissolved Nov. 7, 1936

Jackson Street Railway Company (E)
O: 038
Inc.(S) March 3, 1891; $150,000
To own: in Jackson and adjoining townships
Acquired no date, Jackson City Ry
Receivership June 26, 1897, William A. Foote, receiver
Conveyed Sept. 27, 1900, to Jackson & Suburban Traction

Jackson Transportation Company (E)
O: 038
Inc.(S) March 19, 1929
To own: in Jackson
Line acquired at inc., from Michigan Electric Ry
Abandoned June 27, 1936

The Jackson Union Rail Road Company
P: 038
Inc. July 13, 1855; $90,000
To own: 11 miles, Jackson to Napoleon
Lapsed

Jeannott, P., & Co. (Gauge 3')
O: 062
Private logging road
8 miles, White River northerly
Built 1882

Jefferson Avenue Railway
P: Unknown
Inc. filed March 13, 1881. Articles not located

The Jefferson Avenue Railway Company (E)
O: 082
Inc. May 30, 1891; $100,000
To own: 10 miles, Detroit to Lake St. Clair
Line opened Sept. 7, 1891
Conveyed Nov. 1, 1892, to Detroit Suburban Ry

Jennings & Northeastern Railroad (Gauge 3')
O: 057
Private logging road
Missaukee co.

Jenson, L., Co.
O: probably 027
Private logging road
Ruby Spur

Jerome and Williams (Gauge 3')
O: 054
Private logging road; Saginaw
9 miles, Chippewa River T15N R8W to T16N R8W
Bought ca. 1883 from J. and G. Wentworth

Jonesville, Marshall and Grand River Railroad Company
P: 013, 030
Inc. Feb. 28, 1867; $1,000,000
To own: 35 miles, Jonesville through Litchfield, Homer, Marshall, to north line Calhoun co.
Lapsed

Jonesville Railroad Company
P: 030
Chartered April 1, 1840; $50,000
To own: Jonesville to Indiana state line
Lapsed

Just. W. J., and Bros. (Gauge 3')
O: 059
Private logging road
Edmore

K

The Kalamazoo, Allegan and Grand Rapids Rail Road Company
O: 003, 039, 041
Inc. April 27, 1868; $800,000; Kalamazoo
To consolidate: Kalamazoo & Allegan and Kalamazoo & Grand Rapids
Line completed March 1, 1869, Kalamazoo to Grand Rapids
Leased Sept. 21, 1869, for 999 years, to Lake Shore & Michigan Southern
Amend May 5, 1943, to change number of directors
Merged June 15, 1982, eff. Aug. 12, 1982, into United RR

The Kalamazoo and Allegan Rail Road Company
P: 003, 039
Inc. June 17, 1867; $300,000; Kalamazoo
To own: 24 miles, Kalamazoo to Allegan via Otsego
Merged April 27, 1868, into Kalamazoo, Allegan & Grand Rapids

Kalamazoo and Grand Rapids Railroad Company
P: 003, 039, 041
Inc. Nov. 25, 1867; $500,000; Kalamazoo
To own: 50 miles, Kalamazoo to Grand Rapids
Merged April 27, 1868, into Kalamazoo, Allegan & Grand Rapids

Kalamazoo and Grand River rail road Company
P: 003, 039, 041
Chartered March 17, 1847; $600,000
To own: Kalamazoo to Grand Rapids
Lapsed

The Kalamazoo and Lake Michigan rail-road Company
P: 039, 080
Chartered March 28, 1836; $400,000; Kalamazoo
To own: 40 miles, Kalamazoo to mouth of South Black River
Lapsed

Kalamazoo and Lake Michigan Railway Company (E)
P: 011, 039, 080
Inc.(T) Nov. 26, 1900; $60,000; Benton Harbor
To own: 50 miles, Benton Harbor, via Coloma, Watervliet, Hartford, Lawrence, Paw Paw, and Oshtemo, to Kalamazoo
Amend April 18, 1901, to increase capital to $100,000
Amend July 17, 1902, to add branch to South Haven
Dissolved May 12, 1914

Kalamazoo and Schoolcraft Rail Road Company
O: 039
Inc. June 4, 1866; $200,000
To own: 14 miles, Kalamazoo to Schoolcraft
Line completed May 3, 1867, Kalamazoo to Schoolcraft
Merged Aug. 14, 1869, into Kalamazoo & White Pigeon

The Kalamazoo and South Haven Rail Road Company
O: 039, 080
Inc. April 2, 1869; $500,000; Kalamazoo, Detroit
To own: 40 miles, Kalamazoo to South Haven
Leased July 1, 1870, in perpetuity, to Michigan Central
Line completed Jan. 2, 1871, Kalamazoo to South Haven
Amend March 15, 1889, to reduce number of directors
Merged Sept. 27, 1916, into Michigan Central

Kalamazoo and White Pigeon Railroad Company
O: 039, 075
Inc. Aug. 14, 1869; $1,000,000
To consolidate: Schoolcraft & Three Rivers and Kalamazoo & Schoolcraft
Control at inc. by Lake Shore & Michigan Southern
Line acquired at inc., Kalamazoo to White Pigeon
Leased May 1, 1897, in perpetuity, to Lake Shore & Michigan Southern
Merged April 29, 1914, eff. Jan. 1, 1915, into New York Central

Kalamazoo City and County Street Railway Company (E)
P: 039
Inc.(S) July 18, 1890; $100,000
To own: in Kalamazoo city and county
Lapsed

Kalamazoo, Elkhart & South Bend Traction Railroad Company (E)
P: 014, 039, 075
Inc. (Ind. corp.) Dec. 22, 1905; $15,000; Elkhart, Ind.
To own: South Bend, via Mishawaka, Elkhart, Union, Mottville, Constantine, Three Rivers, Parkville, Vicksburg and Austin, to Kalamazoo
Lapsed

Kalamazoo, Gull Lake and Northern Railroad Company (E)
P: 008. 039
Inc. July 3, 1906; $200,000
To own 20 miles, Kalamazoo via Richland to N line sec 25 T1N R10W and branch Richland to Gull Lake thence NWly to sec 2 T1W R10W
Lapsed

Kalamazoo, Lake Shore & Chicago Railroad
Operating name for property owned by Southwestern Michigan Railroad Co.

Kalamazoo, Lake Shore and Chicago Railway Company (E)
O: 011, 039, 080
Inc.(T) June 6, 1906; $500,000; Kalamazoo
To rename Kalamazoo, Lake Shore & Chicago Traction
Acquired ca. 1907, part of line of Michigan Central
Leased April 15, 1907, for 25 years, from Pere Marquette [South Haven—Lawton]
Lease June 1, 1911, for 5 years, to Michigan United Rys
Lease (6/1911) assigned Jan. 1, 1912, to Michigan United Traction
Lease (6/1911) assigned Aug. 1, 1914, to Michigan Ry
Lease (6/1911) cancelled May 31, 1916
Abandoned

Kalamazoo Lake Shore and Chicago Traction Company (E)
P: 003, 011, 039, 080
Inc.(S) April 12, 1905; $500,000; Kalamazoo
To own: Kalamazoo to South Haven, Benton Harbor, and Saugatuck
Renamed June 6, 1906, as Kalamazoo, Lake Shore & Chicago Ry

The Kalamazoo, Lowell and Northern Michigan Railroad Company (Gauge 3')
P: 008, 034, 039, 041
Inc. Oct. 10, 1871; $600,000; Kalamazoo
To own: 68 miles, Kalamazoo via Hastings and Lowell to Smyrna in Ionia co.
Amend Aug. 1, 1874, to change gauge to 3'
Sold rights, Aug. 29, 1883, from Hastings north, to Hastings, Lowell & Northern Michigan
Sold rights, Dec. 31, 1884, from Hastings south, to Chicago, Kalamazoo & Saginaw

Kalamazoo, Paw Paw and Lake Michigan Railroad Company
P: 011, 039, 080
Inc. Nov. 20, 1885; $300,000
To own: 32-35 miles, Kalamazoo to mouth of St. Joseph River
Lapsed

Kalamazoo River Railroad Company
P: 003, 039
Chartered May 18, 1846; $500,000
To own: Kalamazoo to mouth of Kalamazoo River
Lapsed

Kalamazoo Street Railway Company (H)
O: 039
Inc.(S) Feb. 2, 1884; $100,000
To own: in Kalamazoo
Line opened 1885
Apparently conveyed to Citizens' Street Ry

Kalamazoo Transportation Company (E)
O: 039
Inc.(S) March 18, 1929
To own: in Kalamazoo
Line acquired at inc., from Michigan Electric
Operations ended Nov. 2, 1932

Kellogg and Sawyer (Lumber Co.) (Gauge 3')
O: 003
Private logging road; Office: Leroy
1.5 miles, Dunningville to NE cor sec 26 T3N R14W, about 1873

——

O: 067
5 miles, Leroy to sec 9 T18N R9W, built 1882

Kennedy, D. A.
O: 004
Private logging tramway
5000 ft, woods to ? River
In use 1878

Kent, Barry, Eaton Connecting Railway Company
O: 008, 023, 041
Inc. Oct. 28, 1978; $336,000; Detroit

To own: RR in Kent, Barry and Eaton counties
Contract July 15, 1979, with state of Michigan to operate from Bowen to Vermontville
Inactive corporation

Kent County Street Railway Company (E)
P: 041
Inc.(T) May 23, 1889; $1,000
To own: in any city, village or town in Kent co.
Amend Aug. 20, 1889, to increase capital to $50,000
Lapsed

The Keweenaw and Cliff Rail Road of Lake Superior Company
P: 042
Inc. March 10, 1864; $500,000
To own: 20 miles, Lac la Belle to Cliff Mine
Lapsed

Keweenaw Central Railroad Company
O: 031, 042
Inc. April 25, 1905; $1,000,000
To acquire: 32 miles, line of Lac la Belle & Calumet
Owned by Keweenaw Copper Co.
Line acquired at inc., Mohawk to Phoenix
Abandoned

Keweenaw Copper Co.
Owned Keweenaw Central RR

Killmaster Railroad Company
P: 001
Inc. July 11, 1893; $25,000
To own: 3 miles, Detroit, Bay City & Alpena line (sec 22 T26N R8E) to Killmaster (sec 25 T26N R8E)
Renamed July 17, 1893, as Lake Huron & Western

Klise, A. B. [Lumber Co.] (Gauge 3')
Owned Cecil Bay Lumber Co. and Sturgeon Bay Lumber Co.

Kneeland-Bigelow Co.
O: 069
Private logging road
Otsego co.

L

Lac la Belle and Calumet Rail Road Company (Gauge 3')
O: 031, 042
Inc. March 28, 1883; $150,000
To own: 31 miles, Lac la Belle to Calumet
Line opened no date, Mohawk to Phoenix
Renamed April 25, 1905, as Keweenaw Central

Lake County Railroad Company
O: 043P: 053
Inc. June 28, 1880; $300,000
Office: Ludington
To own: 14 miles
Abandoned

Lake George and Muskegon River Railroad Company
O: 018
Inc. Dec. 26, 1876; $60,000; Muskegon
To own: 7.5 miles, Lake George (sec 16 T18N R5W) to Muskegon River (sec 21 T19N R6W)
Amend Feb. 16, 1878; to extend main line from NW end Lake George SEly to sec 17 thence to NE corner sec 21 thence SEly to NE corner sec 24, 3.5 miles, and branch NE end Lake George (in sec 8) Ely to E sec line thence NEly to NE corner sec 9, 2 miles
Converted Nov. 28, 1881, to private logging road
Sold 1886, right-of-way to Toledo, Ann Arbor & Cadillac

The Lake Harbor Railroad Company
P: 061
Inc. July 1, 1892; $50,000
To own: 5 miles, Lake Michigan to Muskegon Lake (sec 25 T9N R17W)
Lapsed

Lake Huron and Southwestern Railway Company (Gauge 3')
O: 035, 065
Inc.(T) April 15, 1878; $70,000
To own: 26 miles, Tawas Bay to line T21N R4E
Line opened 1878, Tawas City to Prescott
Foreclosure sale Oct. 1, 1879, to Charles H. Prescott
Sold Feb. 12, 1880, to Tawas & Bay County

Lake Huron & Western Railroad Company
P: 001
Inc. July 17, 1893; $25,000
To rename Killmaster RR
Lapsed

Lake Independence Lumber Co.
O: 052
Private logging road
Big Bay

Lake Michigan and Eastern Railway Company
P: 011, 014
Inc.(S) Feb. 21, 1901; $25,000; Benton Harbor
To own: in Benton Harbor, St. Joseph, Dowagiac, Eau Clair and adjoining twps
Amend March 18, 1901; to add South Bend, Mishawaka and Elkhart to route
Lapsed

Lake Michigan and Kalamazoo Railway Company
P: 011, 039, 080
Inc.(S) July 23, 1910; $25,000; Benton Harbor
To own: 53 miles, St. Joseph, via Benton Harbor, Coloma, Watervliet, Hartford, Lawrence, and Paw Paw, to Kalamazoo
Lapsed

Lake Michigan and Lake Superior Railway Company
O: 021, 052
Inc. Oct. 20, 1890; $500,000
To own: 90 miles, Little Bay de Noquet to Duluth, South Shore & Atlantic Ry, Richmond twp., Marquette co.
Control at inc. by Duluth, South Shore & Atlantic
Disposition uncertain

Lake Michigan & Northern
O: 049
Private logging road
Mackinac co.

Lake Michigan & Superior Railroad
O: 077
Private logging road
See Escanaba Lumber Co.

Lake Michigan Division of the Toledo & South Haven Railroad
See Toledo & South Haven

Lake Mining Co.
O: 066
Private ore road
Lake Mine

The Lake Shore and Michigan Southern Railway Company
O: 003, 012, 013, 023, 030, 033, 038, 039, 041, 046, 058, 075, 081, 082
Inc. April 6, 1869; $30,000,000; Cleveland
To consolidate: Michigan Southern & Northern Indiana and Lake Shore (Ohio and Penn. corp.)
Line acquired at inc., constituents
Consolidated June 22, 1869, Buffalo & Erie (N.Y. and Penn. corp.)
Lease Sept. 21, 1869, for 999 years, of Kalamazoo, Allegan & Grand Rapids
Control Aug. 14, 1869, at inc., of Kalamazoo & White Pigeon
Control 1873, of Northern Central Michigan
Control and lease Nov. 1879, of Chicago & Canada Southern
Lease Sept. 5, 1881, in perpetuity, of Detroit, Hillsdale & South Western
Lease Aug. 24, 1882, indefinitely, of Fort Wayne & Jackson
Amend charter (of Michigan Southern) June 8, 1883; to change some rights
Control 1888, 50% of Lansing Transit Ry
Control Nov. 19, 1888, of Detroit & Chicago RR
Control Dec. 1, 1889, of Sturgis, Goshen & St. Louis
Control 1890, 16.5% of Battle Creek & Sturgis
Lease Feb. 1, 1890, part (Findley-Sturgis) of Battle Creek & Sturgis
Lease May 1, 1897, in perpetuity, of Kalamazoo & White Pigeon; and for corp. life, of Northern Central Michigan
Control 1902, 50% of Detroit, Toledo & Milwaukee
Lease Jan. 1, 1905, in perpetuity, of 50% Detroit, Toledo & Milwaukee
Lease July 1, 1905, 25 years, 50% of Lansing Manufacturers
Control Dec. 7, 1905, 25% of Detroit Terminal
Control April 6, 1906, at inc., of Chicago, Indiana & Southern
Merged Jan. 1, 1915, into New York Central

Lake Shore Railroad Company of Western Michigan
P: 003, 011, 061, 070, 080
Inc. June 25, 1869; $3,000,000
To own: 90 miles, St. Joseph to Muskegon River
Merged July 12, 1869, into Chicago & Michigan Lake Shore

Lake Shore Railway Company
P: 011
Inc.(S) Feb. 20, 1901; $25,000
To own: Benton Harbor and St. Joseph to Berrien Springs via Stevensville and Baroda
Lapsed

Lake Superior and Ishpeming—
O: 002, 052, 077
Inc. Feb. 17, 1893, as The Lake Superior and Ishpeming Railway Company; $150,000; Ishpeming
To own: 18.5 miles, Lake Superior near Marquette to Ishpeming and iron mines in vicinity
Amend Sept. 12, 1895, as The Lake Superior and Ishpeming Railway Company; to change capital to $1,000,000
Line opened Aug. 12, 1896, Presque Isle to Ishpeming

Control no date, by Cleveland Cliffs Iron Co.
Amend Aug. 17, 1923, as Lake Superior and Ishpeming Railroad Company; $1,500,000; Marquette; to consolidate Munising, Marquette & SE
Amend Aug. 6, 1941; to increase capital to $4,300,000
Amend April 25, 1949; to revise name to Lake Superior & Ishpeming Railroad Company
Amend April 26, 1976; to change number of directors
Amend Aug. 25, 1977; to change number of directors
Amend April 25, 1983; to change number of directors
Active corporation

Lake Superior District Power Company
O: 027
Inc.(Not RR) not found
Bought ca. 1922, Ironwood & Bessemer Ry & Light
Rail operations ended Sept. 1932

Lake Superior Iron and Chemical Co.
O: 048
Private industrial road
Newberry northeasterly and McMillan southwesterly
Bought 1910, part of Manistique
Sold 1924, to Charcoal Iron Co. of America

Lake Superior Iron and Coal Co.
O: 027
Private industrial road
Wakefield

Lake Superior Iron Mountain Railroad Company
P: 052
Inc. July 26, 1862; $200,000
To own: 20 miles, Marquette to near Jackson, Cleveland, and Lake Superior Mines
Lapsed

Lake Superior Lumber Co.
O: 066
Private logging road
Ontonagon co.

The Lake Superior Rail Road Company
P: 018, 025, 037, 043, 053, 056, 063, 067, 073
Inc. Jan. 28, 1857; $5,000,000
To own: 190 miles, Pontiac to Pere Marquette (now Ludington) via Goodrich, Flint, Saginaw, and Midland
Lapsed

Lake Superior Ship Canal Railway & Iron Company
P: 021, 022, 056
Inc. May 14, 1877; $8,000,000
To own: 45 miles, Menominee iron range to point on Green Bay on Chicago & North Western line
Amend May 14, 1878; to remove railroad rights; change capital to $4,000,000
Lapsed

Lake Superior Southern Railway Company
P: 007, 036, 052
Inc. April 3, 1905; $750,000; Oshkosh, Wisc.
To own: 85 miles, Huron Bay to Lake Michigammi, then to Wisc. state line
Lapsed

Lake Train Railway Company
O: 043
Inc.(T) April 8, 1875; $2,500
To own: 2.5 miles, Foremans Mill, Yates twp., Lake co. to Foreman station on Flint & Pere Marquette

Lakes Superior and Michigan Air Line Rail Road Company
P: 021, 052
Inc. April 11, 1864; $2,000,000
To own: 50 miles, Marquette twp. to Little Bay de Noc
Lapsed

Lakewood Street Railway Company (E)
P: 061
Inc.(S) June 27, 1913; $25,000,000; Lakewood
To own in Dalton and Fruitwood twps.
Lapsed

L'Anse & Ontonagon Railroad Company
P: 007, 031, 066
Inc. Feb. 21, 1865; $200,000
To own: 40 miles, L'Anse Bay to Ontonagon
Lapsed

L'Anse Bay Railroad Company (Gauge probably 3')
P: 007
Inc. Sept. 18, 1912; $20,000
To own: 5 miles, L'Anse to sec 5 T50N R32W
Lapsed

Lansing, Alma, Mt. Pleasant and Northern Railroad Company
P: 019, 029, 033, 037
Inc. Feb. 5, 1884; $544,000
To own: 68 miles, Lansing to Mt. Pleasant
Renamed May 5, 1886, as Toledo, Ann Arbor & Mount Pleasant

The Lansing & Battle Creek Traction Company (E)
P: 013, 023, 033
Inc.(S) Feb. 4, 1905; $50,000; Battle Creek
To own: Battle Creek to Lansing
Amend Feb. 15, 1905; to change number of directors
Lapsed

The Lansing and Jackson Rail Road Company
P: 033, 038
Inc. Dec. 22, 1863; $300,000; Jackson
To own: 36 miles, Lansing via Mason and Leslie to Jackson
Renamed Feb. 20, 1865, as Jackson, Lansing & Saginaw

The Lansing & Jackson Railway Company
P: 033, 038
Inc.(S) March 30, 1905; $1,450,000; Lansing
To own: Lansing to Jackson [construction company]
Merged May 1, 1906, to Michigan United Rys

Lansing and Lake Michigan Railroad Company
P: 003, 008, 023, 033, 070
Inc. May 3, 1872; $3,000,000
To own: 80 miles, Lansing to Lake Michigan at Holland
Lapsed

Lansing & Northeastern Railway Company (E)
O: 033, 078 P: 025, 073
Inc.(S) Jan. 22, 1910; $500,000; Detroit
To own: in Lansing, Owosso, Flint, and Saginaw
Control at inc. by Michigan United Rys
Line completed July 8, 1911
Leased Jan. 1, 1912, to Michigan United Railways
Lease assigned April 1, 1912, to Michigan United Traction
Lease assigned Jan. 1, 1916, to Michigan Railway
Operations ended May 16, 1929

The Lansing & Northern Railway Company
P: not given
Inc.(T) Aug. 1, 1900; $60,000; Lansing
To: not given [apparently to acquire property for Lansing, St. Johns & St. Louis (1900 corp.)]
Lapsed

Lansing and St. Johns Railroad Company
P: 019, 033
Inc. Sept. 27, 1871; $200,000
To own: 20 miles, Lansing to St. Johns
Lapsed

Lansing and Southeastern Railway Company (E)
P: 033, 038, 081
Inc.(S) Dec. 27, 1900; $100,000; Chelsea
To own: 45 miles, Chelsea, via Mason, to Lansing
Lapsed

The Lansing and Suburban Traction Company (E)
O: 019, 033
Inc.(S) March 8, 1904; $1,000,000; Lansing
To own: in Lansing
Control March 15, 1904, of Lansing City Electric
Bought March 26, 1904, Lansing, St. Johns & St. Louis (1900 corp.)
Merged May 1, 1906, to Michigan United Railways

Lansing City Electric Railway Company (E)
O: 033
Inc.(S) Oct. 13, 1892; $100,000; Lansing
To own: in Lansing [and reorganize Lansing City Ry]
Control Nov. 1, 1901, by Detroit, Ypsilanti, Ann Arbor & Jackson
Control March 15, 1904, by Lansing & Suburban Traction
Merged May 1, 1906, into Michigan United Rys

Lansing City Railway Company (H)
O: 033
Inc.(S) Nov. 21, 1885; $50,000
To own: in Lansing and adjacent towns
Reorganized Oct. 13, 1892, as Lansing City Electric

The Lansing Connecting Railroad Company
P: 033
Inc. Jan. 24, 1914; $50,000; Lansing
To own: .75 mile, Grand Trunk Ry in sec 22 T4N R2W NWly to Pere Marquette RR
Lapsed

The Lansing, Dexter and Ann Arbor Electric Railway Company (E)
P: 033, 047, 081
Inc.(S) Feb. 13, 1899; $250,000
To own: Lansing to Ann Arbor
Lapsed

The Lansing, Dexter and Ann Arbor Railway Company (E)
P: 033, 047, 081
Inc.(S) Dec. 22, 1897; $250,000; Lansing
To own: Lansing to Dexter
Amend Feb. 28, 1898; to change route to: Lansing to Ann Arbor
Lapsed

Lansing Manufacturers Railroad Company
O: 033
Inc. July 29, 1904; $100,000
To own: 6 miles, North Lansing to South Lansing
Leased July 1, 1905, 25 years, 50% to Michigan Central, 50% to Lake Shore & Michigan Southern
Merged Aug. 1, 1969, into Penndel Co.

Lansing, St. Johns and Mackinac Railroad Company
P: 019, 029, 033, 037
Inc. April 29, 1869; $800,000; Lansing
To own: 80 miles, Lansing to Mt. Pleasant
Lapsed

Lansing, Saint Johns and Northern Railroad Company
P: 019, 029, 033
Inc. Feb. 21, 1888; $500,000
To own: 47 miles, Lansing to Ithaca
Lapsed

The Lansing, St. Johns and St. Louis Railway Company (E)
P: 019, 029, 033
Inc.(S) Dec. 8, 1897; $250,000; Lansing
To own: Lansing to St. Johns and Maple Rapids, thence to Ithaca and St. Louis
Probably lapsed, but may have reincorporated as next company below

Lansing, St. Johns and St. Louis Railway Company (E)
O: 019, 033 P: 029
Inc.(S) April 10, 1900; $500,000; Lansing
To own: Lansing to Alma
Cons. no date, Crystal Lake Ry
Operated Jan. 12, 1902 to March 26, 1904, by Michigan Suburban
Sold March 26, 1904, to Lansing & Suburban Traction

Lansing Southern Railroad Company
O: 033
Inc. Aug. 29, 1907; $50,000; Lansing
To own: 2.36 miles, sec 6 T2N R1W to sec 16 T2N R1W
Control at inc. by Michigan United Rys
Line completed 1909
Operations ended May 18, 1929

The Lansing Street Railway Company (H)
P: 033
Inc.(S) June 20, 1876; $25,000; Lansing
To own: in Lansing
Lapsed

Lansing Transit Railway Company
P: 033
Inc.(T) April 30, 1886; $50,000
To own: 2 miles, Grand & Ottawa Sts. to Jackson, Lansing & Saginaw line, in Lansing
Lapsed

Lansing Transit Railway Company
O: 033
Inc. Aug. 31, 1886; $50,000
To own: 2 miles, Grand St., Lansing to Jackson, Lansing & Saginaw Ry
Amend April 30, 1887; to modify route
Control 1888, 50% by Michigan Central, 50% by Lake Shore & Michigan Southern
Leased Feb. 18, 1888, eff. Sept. 15, 1887, 99 years, to Michigan Central
Merged Aug. 1, 1969, into Penndel Co.

Lansing Transportation Company (E)
O: 033
Inc.(S) March 19, 1929; not stated
To own: in Lansing
Acquired at inc., part of Michigan Electric Railway
Operations ended April 15, 1933

Lapeer and Holly Railroad Company
P: 044, 063
Inc. Aug. 21, 1872; $200,000
To own: 25 miles, Lapeer to Holly
Lapsed

Lapeer and Northern Railroad Company
O: 044
Inc. Oct. 18, 1872; $150,000
To own: 14 miles, Detroit & Bay City line in Lapeer to North Branch
Controlled apparently by Detroit & Bay City from inc.
Line opened 1872, Lapeer to northeast of Lapeer
Abandoned by ca. 1880

Lapeer and Port Austin Railroad Company
P: 032, 044, 076, 079
Inc. Aug. 5, 1872; $600,000
To own: 70 miles, Lapeer to Port Austin
Lapsed

La Plaisance Bay Harbor Company, The president, directors and company of
O: 058
Chartered April 19, 1825; not known; Monroe
Facilities at La Plaisance Bay (Monroe co.)
To own: 0.5-mile railroad line
Conveyed Sept. 15, 1840, to "Southern" line of state of Michigan

Lawton, Paw Paw and South Haven Railroad Company
P: 080
Inc. Jan. 8, 1868; $220,000; not given
To own: 27 miles, Paw Paw to South Haven
Lapsed

Leelanau Transit Company
O: 045
Inc. May 23, 1919; $200,000
To buy: Traverse City, Leelanau & Manistique (24.04 miles, Hatch's to Northport plus .4 miles in Traverse City)
Leased June 9, 1919, to Manistee & Northeastern
Lease assigned Nov. 30, 1955, to Chesapeake & Ohio
Lease cancelled no date, to Chesapeake & Ohio
Active corporation

Lenawee County Railroad Company
O: 046
Inc. March 9, 1977; $300,000; Adrian
To own: in Lenawee co.
Operating agreement Oct. 1, 1977, with state of Michigan
Amend Dec. 5, 1977; to change voting rights
Amend Jan. 3, 1978; to change number of directors
Operations ended Sept. 30, 1990
Inactive corporation

Lewiston and Southeastern Railroad Company (Gauge 3')
O: 060, 068
Inc. May 25, 1896; $60,000; Lewiston
To own: 15 miles, Lewiston to sec 9 T27N R2E in Oscoda co.
Abandoned 1910

Lexington & Utica Railroad Company
P: 050, 074, 076
Inc. Dec. 17, 1883; $520,000
To own: 60 miles, Lexington to Utica
Lapsed

Lima Northern Railway Company
O: 046
Inc. March 27, 1895 (Ohio corp.)
Sold July 6, 1896, to Detroit & Lima Northern, but apparently not conveyed until Nov. 1897

Limpert and Howe
O: 027
Private logging road
Thomaston

Lobdell and Bailey
O: 071
Private logging road; Onaway
Onaway southeasterly to sec 6 T33N R3E

———

See also Onaway & North Michigan and Huron Handle & Mfg. Co.

Long, A. B., and Sons (Gauge 3' 10")
O: 054, 059
Private logging road
6 miles, sec 11 T12N R7W to T13N R7W, built 1882

Long Lake & Muskegon River
See Hackley & Hume

Long Lake, Durand and Corunna Electric Street Railway Company (E)
P: 078
Inc.(S) Nov. 16, 1898; $50,000; Commerce
To own: in Genesee and Shiawassee cos.
Lapsed

Loud [Henry M.], Gay [A. F.] and Co.
O: 035
Private lumbering tramway
AuSable, 3000 ft. mill to dock
Built 1870
Sold 1876, to Oscoda Salt & Lumber Co.

Loud, George A., Henry N., and Edward F.
Owned Au Sable & Northwestern

Loud, H[enry] M. and Sons Lumber Co.
O: 035
Private lumbering tramway
AuSable
Bought 1887, from Oscoda Salt & Lumber Co.

Louden, Anderson and Co.
O: 059
Private logging tram road
In Montcalm co.

Lowell and Hastings Railroad Company
O: 041 P: 008
Inc. May 2, 1887; $200,000; Grand Rapids
To own: 21 miles, Lowell to Hastings
Bought May 31, 1887, Hastings, Lowell & Northern Michigan
Line opened Dec. 1887, Lowell to Freeport
Sold May 1, 1899, to Grand Rapids, Belding & Saginaw

Ludington and Northern Railway Company
O: 053
Inc.(T) July 13, 1901; $15,000; Ludington
To rename Epworth League Ry
Line acquired at inc., Ludington to Epworth
Renew inc. Jan. 26, 1925; to continue corp. existence for 30 years
Renew inc. Feb. 1, 1955; to continue corp. existence for 30 years
Amend May 10, 1955; to increase capital to $120,000
Amend May 13, 1975; to change term of corp. existence to "perpetual"
Active corporation

The Ludington Southern Railway Company
P: 041, 053, 061, 062, 064, 070
Inc. June 18, 1906; $640,000
To own: 80 miles, Grand Rapids to Ludington, with termini in Michigan, Illinois, and Wisconsin
Lapsed

Lynes, S. D., and Co.
O: 018
Private logging road
Tobacco River

M

Mackinac and Chicago Railroad Company
P: 003, 011, 080
Inc. April 30, 1872; $1,500,000
To own: 75 miles, Montieth, via Otsego, Lawrence, Berrien Springs, New Troy and Three Oaks, to Indiana state line in Three Oaks twp.
Lapsed

Mackinac Transportation Company
Operated railroad car ferries between Mackinaw City and St. Ignace
Inc.(Not RR) Oct. 10, 1881
Owned 33% by Michigan Central, 33% by Grand Rapids & Indiana, 33% by Duluth, South Shore & Atlantic
Amend Nov. 8, 1901; to change corp. office to Mackinaw City
Renew inc. Sept. 22, 1911; to extend corp. life 30 years
Amend Feb. 24, 1914; to change corp. office to St. Ignace
Operations ended 1984

The Mackinaw and Lake Superior Railroad Company
P: 002, 017, 048, 049, 052, 077
Inc. June 30, 1873; $2,000,000
To own: 150 miles, Straits of Mackinac to Marquette Harbor
Lapsed

Mackinaw and Marquette Railroad Company
O: Reorganizing company
Inc. Dec. 18, 1886
To reorganize Detroit, Mackinac & Marquette
Conveyed Dec. 22, 1886, to Duluth, South Shore & Atlantic

Macomb and Saginaw railroad Company
P: 025, 044, 050, 063, 073
Chartered Aug. 24, 1835; $1,000,000
To own: 90 miles, Mt. Clemens to Saginaw City
Amend charter March 30, 1840; authorized substituting turnpike road for railroad
Lapsed

Main Street Railway Company (H)
P: 038
Inc.(S) Nov. 12, 1873; $40,000
To own: in Jackson, from E to W end Main St.
Lapsed

Mancelona and North Western Rail Way Company
O: 005
Inc.(T) May 5, 1892; $8,000
To own: 8 miles, Mancelona NWly to "Cedar River Valley"
Abandoned

Mancelona Handle Co. (Gauge 3')
O: 005
Private logging road
Mancelona

Manchester & Homer Railroad Company
P: 013, 038, 081
Inc. Dec. 12, 1870; $350,000
To own: 38 miles, Manchester to Homer
Lapsed

Manistee & Grand Rapids Railroad Company
O: 043, 051, 053, 067 P: 041, 061, 062, 064
Inc. filed Nov. 11, 1889; $1,000,000
To own: 100 miles, Manistee to Grand Rapids
Line opened Dec. 20, 1892, Manistee to Peacock
Amend Sept. 16, 1904; to change route: 110 miles, add branch to Luther
Line completed Jan. 1, 1906, Manistee to Marion
Foreclosure sale Sept. 12, 1913, to Michigan East & West

The Manistee & Luther Railroad Company (Gauge 3')
O: 043, 051, 083
Inc. March 24, 1886; $400,000
To own: 40 miles, East Lake to Luther
Abandoned Nov. 30, 1913

Manistee and Northeastern—
O: 010, 020, 028, 040, 045, 051, 083
Inc. Jan. 7, 1887, as Manistee and Northeastern Rail Road Company; $600,000; Manistee
To own: 75 miles, Manistee to Grand Traverse
Line opened Nov. 20, 1888, Manistee to Nessen City
Amend Jan. 7, 1892, as Manistee and North-Eastern Railroad Company; to increase capital to $2,000,000
Line completed July 1, 1892, Manistee to Traverse City
Amend Jan. 30, 1904, as Manistee and Northeastern Railroad Company; to change number of directors
Amend Feb. 24, 1909, as The Manistee and Northeastern Railroad Company; to add branch from Kaleva to sec 3 T26N R6W
Leased June 9, 1919, Leelanau Transit
Receiver's sale Dec. 16, 1925
Inc. Sept. 4, 1926, as Manistee & Northeastern Railway Company
To reorganize Manistee & Northeastern RR
Control Dec. 1931, by Pere Marquette
Merged Nov. 30, 1955, into Chesapeake & Ohio

The Manistee, Filer City & East Lake Railway Company (E)
O: 051
Inc.(S) Aug. 24, 1892; $150,000; Manistee
To own in Manistee and adjacent townships
Line opened 1892
Conveyed ca. 1905, to Northern Michigan Traction

Manistee Light and Traction Company (E)
O: 051
Inc.(S) June 28, 1907; $1,000,000; Manistee
To consolidate: Northern Michigan Traction Co. and a power co.
Line acquired at inc., line of Northern Michigan Traction
Conveyed ca. 1912, to Manistee Ry

Manistee Railroad Company
O: 051, 053
Inc. May 31, 1880; $400,000; Saginaw
To own: 22 miles, from Flint & Pere Marquette in T18N R15W to Manistee River
Control at inc. by Flint & Pere Marquette
Line completed Dec. 31, 1881, Walhalla to Manistee
Merged Nov. 2, 1888, into Flint & Pere Marquette

Manistee Railway Company (E)
O: 051
Inc.(S) Oct. 27, 1912; $25,000; Manistee
To own: street railway in Manistee
Acquired ca. 1912, line of Manistee Light & Traction
Operations ended Aug. 26, 1921
Dissolved Dec. 28, 1922

The Manistee Street Railway Company (H)
P: 051
Inc.(S) Dec. 4, 1882; $25,000
To own: in Manistee
Lapsed

Manistee Tram Railway Company (Gauge 3')
O: 043, 051
Private logging road
Manistee and Lake cos.

Manistique and Lake Superior Railroad Company
O: 002, 077
Inc. July 21, 1909; $250,000; Manistique
To own: 60 miles, Manistique to Shingleton and Doty
Bought Aug. 1, 1909, Manistique & Northern (line: Manistique to Shingleton)
Control April 1911, by Ann Arbor
Abandoned 1968

Manistique and Northern Railroad Company
O: 002, 077
Inc. Jan. 9, 1908; $1,100,000
To reorganize Manistique, Marquette & Northern
Line acquired at inc., Manistique to Shingleton
Sold Aug. 1, 1909, to Manistique & Lake Superior
Dissolved Aug. 24, 1914

The Manistique and Northwestern Railway Company
O: 002, 077 P: 052
Inc. April 25, 1891; $1,600,000
To own: 80 miles, Manistique to Negaunee and Ishpeming
Line completed Dec. 31, 1898, Manistique to Shingleton
Sold May 1, 1902, to Manistique, Marquette & Northern

Manistique Lumbering Co.
O: 002, 077
Private logging road
Acquired Sept. 1910, line of Manistique Ry
Sold Dec. 17, 1910, to Escanaba Lumber Co.

Manistique, Marquette and Northern Railroad Company
O: 002, 077
Inc. March 24, 1902; $2,000,000
To own: 60 miles, Manistique to Shingleton, with branch Scotts Camp northwesterly 20 miles
Bought May 1, 1902, Manistique & Northwestern
Line acquired at purchase, Manistique to Shingleton
Foreclosure sale Sept. 21, 1905, to Union Trust Co.
Conveyed Jan. 9, 1908, to Manistique & Northern

Manistique Pulp and Paper Co.
O: 077
Private industrial road
Manistique

The Manistique Railway Company
O: 002, 048, 049, 077
Inc. Sept. 15, 1886; $100,000
To own: 12.5 miles, north line sec 4 T45N R13W via Seney to SE¼ SE¼ sec 3 T47N R13W
Control at inc., by Alger, Smith & Co.
Line opened Oct. 20, 1886, Seney to Hoist
Amend Oct. 18, 1889; to own 60 miles, Grand Marais to Manistique; increase capital to $500,000
Foreclosure sale Sept. 1910, to Manistique Lumbering Co.
Sold 1910, part of line to Lake Superior Iron & Chemical; abandoned remainder

Mansfield, Coldwater and Lake Michigan Rail Road Company
O: 003 P: 008, 012, 013, 030
Inc. Dec. 28, 1870; $4,000,000
To merge: Mansfield, Coldwater & Lake Michigan Ry (Ohio corp.) and Ohio & Michigan
Line opened Sept. 1871, Allegan to Montieth
Leased Jan. 1, 1874,, to Grand Rapids & Indiana
Foreclosure sale Aug. 28, 1877, Michigan property to Allegan & South Eastern; Ohio property to Pennsylvania RR

Maple Rapids and Lansing Railroad Company
P: 019, 033
Inc. Dec. 21, 1880; $230,000
To own: 23 miles, Maple Rapids to line of Detroit, Lansing & Northern in southern Clinton or northern Ingham co.
Lapsed

Maple Rapids & Southern Rail Road Company
P: 019
Inc. Sept. 24, 1877; $70,000
To own: 8 miles, Maple Rapids to line of Detroit & Milwaukee RR
Lapsed

Marlborough Railroad Company
O: 043
Inc. July 13, 1906; $25,000
To own: 1 mile, Marlborough Jct. to Marlborough
Control at inc. by Pere Marquette
Conveyed no date, to Pere Marquette

Marquette and Chicago Rail Road Company
P: 052
Inc. April 18, 1860; $500,000
To own: 20 miles, Marquette to Lake Superior Mine
Control at inc., by Cleveland Iron Mining Co.
Lapsed

Marquette & Huron Mountain Railroad Company
O: 052
Inc. Dec. 1, 1962; $208,000; Marquette
To buy 23.74 miles, West Yard to Big Bay, and build 1.5 miles, West Yard to Marquette
Status uncertain

Marquette & Iron Range Railroad Company
P: 052
Inc. Oct. 15, 1895; $160,000
To own: 20 miles, Marquette to T47N R27W
Lapsed

Marquette and Ontonagon Railroad Company
O: 052 P: 007, 031, 066
Inc. Dec. 27, 1862; $2,000,000
To own: 125 miles, Marquette, via Lake Superior, Iron Mountain, and L'Anse Bay, to Ontonagon
Bought no date, Marquette & Ontonagon Ry
Amend April 28, 1871; to consolidate Bay de Noquet & Marquette
Amend Aug. 22, 1872; to change W terminus to W line sec 9 T47N R30W
Apparently merged May 25, 1872, into Marquette, Houghton & Ontonagon

Marquette and Ontonagon Railway Company
P: 007, 031, 052, 066
Inc. Jan. 7, 1857; $1,000,000
To own: 100 miles, Marquette, Houghton and Ontonagon cos.
Amend April 7, 1857; to change route, Marquette to Ontonagon
Leased ca. 1857 to Bay De Noquet & Marquette
Line opened July 1865, Winthrop Jct. to Lake Michigammi
Sold no date, to Marquette & Ontonagon RR

Marquette and Peninsula Railway Company
P: 052
Inc. May 25, 1871; $150,000
To own: 12 miles, Marquette to T46N R25W
Lapsed

Marquette and Southeastern Railway Company
O: 002, 052, 077
Inc. Oct. 1, 1900; $1,000,000; Marquette
To own: 85 miles, Marquette near Presque Isle to Manistique
Control at inc. by Cleveland Cliffs Iron Co.
Line completed July 1, 1902, Marquette to Lawson
Amend Aug. 7, 1905; to add: branch from Marquette near Presque Isle to just north of Lake Independence
Merged April 22, 1911, into Munising, Marquette & Southeastern

Marquette and State Line Rail Road Company
P: 052, 055
Inc. Jan. 14, 1857; $2,000,000
To own: 75 miles, Marquette to Wisconsin state line
Merged March 21, 1857, to form Chicago, St. Paul & Fond du Lac

Marquette and Western Railroad Company
O: 052
Inc. Oct. 3, 1883; $1,250,000
To own: 25 miles, Marquette to Ishpeming
Line completed June 9, 1884, Marquette to Ishpeming
Leased May 1885, in perpetuity, to Marquette, Houghton & Ontonagon
Sold July 17, 1890, to Duluth, South Shore & Atlantic

The Marquette, Champion and Chicago Railway Company
P: 052
Inc. Oct. 1, 1889; $2,000,000
To own: 33 miles, Marquette to Champion
Lapsed

Marquette City and Presque Isle Railway Company (E)
O: 052
Inc.(S) Aug. 2, 1890; $25,000; Marquette
To own: City of Marquette to Presque Isle Park
Amend March 7, 1891; to increase capital to $100,000
Amend Sept. 23, 1891; to increase capital to $200,000
Line opened 1891
Sold April 18, 1921, to Marquette City Ry

Marquette City Railway Company (E)
O: 052
Inc.(S) April 18, 1921; $200,000; Marquette
To reorganize: Marquette City & Presque Isle
Amend March 6, 1923; not found
Operations ended April 19, 1935

Marquette County Electric Railway Company (E)
O: 052
Inc.(S) Feb. 27, 1917; $25,000; Ishpeming
To buy: street ry from Marquette Co. Gas & Electric
Acquired at inc., line of Marquette Co. Gas & Electric
Operations ended Aug. 20, 1927

Marquette County Gas and Electric Company (E)
O: 052
Inc. (Maine corp.) Nov. 15, 1906; not stated; Ishpeming
To operate electric railway (no termini given)
Acquired at inc., Marquette County Gas Light & Traction
Conveyed Feb. 27, 1917, to Marquette Co. Electric Ry

Marquette County Gas Light and Traction Company (E)
O: 052
Inc.(T) Sept. 30, 1904; $400,000; Ishpeming
To consolidate Negaunee & Ishpeming Street Ry & Elec. and a power co.
Line acquired at inc., of Negauee & Ishpeming Street Ry & Elec.
Conveyed Nov. 15, 1906, to Marquette Co. Gas & Electric

Marquette, Houghton & Ontonagon—
O: 007, 031, 052 P: 066
Inc. May 25, 1872, apparently eff. Aug. 22, 1872, as Marquette, Houghton & Ontonagon Railroad Company; $2,400,000
To consolidate: Marquette & Ontonagon RR and Houghton & Ontonagon
Line opened Dec. 1872, Champion to L'Anse
Amend Nov. 21, 1873, as The Marquette, Houghton and Ontonagon Railroad Company; $5,000,000; to own: 102 miles, Marquette to Ontonagon
Amend Feb. 1, 1883, as The Marquette, Houghton and Ontonagon Railroad Company; $5,065,000; to consolidate: Hougton & L'Anse
Consolidated Feb. 1, 1883, Houghton & L'Anse
Lease May 1885, in perpetuity, of Marquette & Western
Control June 30, 1888, at inc., of Negaunee & Palmer
Leased Feb. 15, 1887, in perpetuity, to Duluth, South Shore & Atlantic
Sold July 17, 1890, to Duluth, South Shore & Atlantic

The Marquette Iron Range Cable Transit and Railway Company
P: 052
Inc. May 11, 1886; $2,000,00
To own: 50 miles, Marquette to Lake Michigamme [sic] with branch to Republic
Lapsed

Marquette, Negaunee & Ishpeming Interurban Railway Company (E)
P: 052
Inc.(S) May 31, 1907; $25,000; Marquette
To own: Marquette to Negaunee
Lapsed

Marquette, Sault Ste. Marie and Mackinac Railroad Company
P: 002, 048, 049, 052, 077
Inc. Dec. 16, 1872; $6,000,000
To own: 200 miles, Marquette to St. Marys River, with branch to Straits of Mackinac
Lapsed

The Marshall and Coldwater Railroad Company
P: 012, 013, 023, 034, 059
Inc. Sept. 3, 1870; $200,000
To own: 25 miles, Marshall to Coldwater
Amend July 6, 1871; to change route: to build 40 miles, Coldwater to Peninsular Ry in Walton twp.; capital $350,000
Amend Sept. 6, 1871; to change N terminus to Muir; route 80 miles; capital $650,000
Amend Dec. 7, 1871; to change north terminus to Elm Hall; route 110 miles; capital $900,000
Renamed Sept. 5, 1874, as Coldwater, Marshall & Mackinaw

The Marshall and Northern Railroad Company
P: 013, 023
Inc. March 7, 1902; $200,000
To own: 50 miles, sec 35 Tekonsha twp. to Sunfield
Lapsed

Mashek Chemical and Iron Co.
O: 021
Private logging road
Wells

The Mason and Oceana Railroad Company (Gauge 3')
O: 053, 064 P: 041, 062
Inc. Aug. 3, 1886; $150,000; Buttersville
To own: 30 miles, Butters & Peters Mill to sec 30 T16N R16W
Line opened Jan. 6, 1887, Buttersville to Crystal Valley
Amend May 31, 1901; to own: 70 miles, Buttersville via sec 25 T14N R15W to Newaygo; capital $280,000
Amend March 22, 1902; to own: 95 miles, Buttersville via sec 19 T12N R12W to Grand Rapids; capital $380,000
Line completed June 1, 1903, Buttersville to Maple
Abandoned Dec. 1, 1909

Mathinson and White (Gauge 3')
O: unknown
Private logging road; Grand Rapids

Maumee Branch Railroad Company
P: 011, 012, 014, 030, 046, 058, 075
Chartered Aug. 22, 1835; $100,000
To own: mouth of Maumee River to Erie & Kalamazoo RR
Amend charter Aug. 25, 1835; authorized extension through S tier of counties to Lake Michigan
Amend charter June 21, 1837; to own from Manhattan, Ohio via Havre Branch RR to Erie & Kalamazoo RR; capital $1,500,000
Lapsed

McCoy, Daniel (Gauge 3')
O: 043
Private logging road
Lake co.

McCoy, D. M., Lumber Co.
O: 049
Private logging road
Rexton

McIntyre and Co. (Gauge 3')
O: 036
Private logging road
Iron co.

McKnight Brothers and Tinker
O: 017
Private industrial tram road
In Sault Ste. Marie
Bought line ca. 1846, from American Fur Co.
Conveyed ca. 1847, to Chippewa Portage

McMillan, C. V., Lumber Co.
O: 066
Private logging road
Ontonagon co.
Sold Aug. 1, 1906, to Ontonagon RR

McNaughton, John
Owned Mecosta RR

The Mecosta Railroad Company (Gauge 3')
O: 054
Inc. Oct. 25, 1882; $50,000
To own: 12 miles, NE 1/4 sec 36 T15N R10W (Muskegon River) to SE 1/4 sec 21 T15N R8W (Horsehead Lake)
Owned by John Sweet
Line opened March 1, 1883
Amend July 15, 1885; to add 6 mile branch; capital $100,000
Ownership sold, July 1886, to John McNaughton
Abandoned 1888

The Medina and Canandaigua Railroad Company
P: 046
Chartered April 5, 1838; $100,000
To own: Morenci to point in Lenawee co.
Lapsed

Medusa Portland Cement Co.
O: 015
Private industrial road
West of Charlevoix

Menasha Woodenware Co.
O: 066
Private logging road
Ontonagon

The Menominee and Escanaba Railway Company
P: 021, 055
Inc.(S) June 19, 1905; $300,000; Menominee
To own: Menominee, via Daggett, to Escanaba
Dissolved April 16, 1915

Menominee and Marinette Light and Traction Company (E)
O: 055
Inc.(S) June 6, 1903; $560,000; Menominee
To consolidate: Menominee Electric Light, Railway & Power and Marinette Gas Electric Light & Street Ry (Wisc. corp)
Line acquired at inc., of Menominee El. Light, Ry & Power
Amend July 20, 1908; to increase capital to $1,000,000
Amend March 25, 1914; to increase capital to $1,250,000

Amend July 18, 1922; to change office to Milwaukee
Amend Sept. 4, 1923; to change annual meeting requirements
Operations ended 1928
Amend May 3, 1933; to change annual meeting requirements
Amend Dec. 12, 1933; to extend corporate life 30 years
Merged Dec. 23, 1953, into Wisconsin Public Service

Menominee & Northern Railroad Company
P: 055
Inc. Oct. 16, 1893; $500,000
To own: 55 miles, Menominee to North line sec 3 T38N R28W
Possibly sold Jan. 1, 1895, to Wisconsin & Michigan

Menominee and St. Paul Railway Company
O: 055
Inc. June 9, 1899; $500,000
To own: 10 miles, Menominee to Wisconsin state line
Control at inc. by Ann Arbor RR Co.
Amend May 17, 1927; to change number of directors
Operations ended Nov. 30, 1958

The Menominee and Sault Ste. Marie Railway Company
P: 017, 021, 049, 055, 077
Inc. April 20, 1885; $2,000,000
To own: 200 miles, Wisconsin state line to Sault Ste. Marie
Merged March 22, 1887, into Minneapolis, Sault Ste. Marie & Atlantic

Menominee Branch Railroad Company
O: 055
Inc. July 2, 1883; $300,000
To own: 8 miles, Menominee River to Green Bay at Menominee with branch to sec 35 T32N R27W
Line completed Jan. 1884, in Menominee
Merged Dec. 7, 1886, into Milwaukee & Northern

Menominee Electric Light, Railway and Power Company (E)
O: 055
Inc.(S) filed April 13, 1892; $110,000
To own: in Menominee (and cons. Men. El. Ry & Pwr. and power co.)
Line acquired at inc., of Menominee El. Ry & Power
Res. May 28, 1903; to confirm street ry rights (1899 P.A. no. 96)
Merged June 6, 1903, into Menominee & Marinette Lt. & Tract.

Menominee Electric Railway and Power Company (E)
O: 055
Inc.(S) April 4, 1891; $110,000; Menominee
To own: street ry in Menominee
Line opened ca. 1891
Merged April 13, 1892, into Menominee El. Light Ry & Power

Menominee Range Street Railway Company (E)
P: 022
Inc.(S) Sept. 11, 1901; Iron Mountain
To own: in Iron Mountain, Norway, and adjacent townships
Lapsed

Menominee River Railroad Company
O: 022, 036, 055
Inc. Feb. 9, 1875; $400,000; Chicago
To own: 50 miles, Michigamme River to Chicago & NW line in T38N R26W
Amend Aug. 25, 1875; to change capital to $500,000
Control 1877, by Chicago & North Western
Line opened 1877, Powers to Quinnesec
Amend Dec. 16, 1879; to add branch, sec 30 T40N R30W NWly to sec 20 T40N R30W, 2.7 miles
Amend Oct. 15, 1880; to consolidate Menominee Ry (Wisc. corp.); capital $165,000
Amend May 20, 1881; to add branch, Brule, Wisc. to Lake Superior in Ontonagon co.
Line completed 1882, Powers to Crystal Falls
Amend June 30, 1882; to add 60 miles, Crystal Falls to Keweenaw Bay; capital $1,500,000
Merged July 1, 1882, into Chicago & North Western

The Menominee Street Railway Company (H)
P: 055
Inc.(S) Sept. 10, 1888; $50,000; Menominee
To own: in Menominee
Lapsed

Mercer, DeLatrie Lumber Co.
O: 066
Private logging road
Barclay

Merrill and Ring Logging Co.
O: unknown
Private logging road; Saginaw

Metropolitan Electric Railway Company (E)
P: 082
Inc.(S) Oct. 12, 1885; $50,000; Detroit
To own: in Detroit and vicinity
Lapsed

The Metropolitan Railway Company (E)
P: 082
Inc.(S) April 3, 1899; $25,000; Detroit
To own: in Detroit and vicinity
Control at inc. by Detroit Citizens' Street Ry
Apparently lapsed

Meyer, Herman, J. L.
See Wisconsin Land & Lumber Co.

Michigan, State of
See "Central," "Northern," "Southern," University of Michigan, and Western Michigan University

———

Bought various dates, lines of Ann Arbor, Chesapeake & Ohio, Escanaba & Lake Superior, Penn Central Transportation and Soo Line to be operated by agreements with Detroit & Mackinac, Hillsdale County, Kent-Barry-Eaton Connecting, Lenawee County, Michigan Interstate, Michigan Northern, Soo Line RR, and Tuscola & Saginaw Bay

Michigan Air Line Extension Rail Road Company
P: 050, 074
Inc. Nov. 13, 1869; $1,000,000
To own: 28 miles, Ridgeway to St. Clair then to New Baltimore
Lapsed

The Michigan Air Line Railroad Company
O: 012, 013, 014, 038, 050, 075 P: 063, 081
Inc. July 2, 1868, eff. July 14; $4,000,000; Jackson
To consolidate: Grand Trunk Ry of Michigan and Grand Trunk Ry of Northern Indiana (Ind. corp.) [to form line Ridgway to Chicago]
Acquired no date, Niles & South Bend
Line opened Dec. 9, 1869, Ridgeway to Romeo
Consolidated Oct. 8, 1870, St. Joseph Valley (Ind. corp.)
Leased Jan. 1, 1870, eff. Feb. 1871, for 999 years, to Michigan Central
Line completed Feb. 1871, Jackson to Niles
Leased April 13, 1872, line Jackson east, to St. Clair River, Pontiac & Jackson
Foreclosure sale April 28, 1875, line Pontiac east, and conveyed to Michigan Air Line Ry
Amend Oct. 19, 1898; to change capital to $1,000,000
Merged Sept. 27, 1916, into Michigan Central

The Michigan Air Line Railway Company
O: 038, 047, 050, 063 P: 081
Inc. Nov. 18, 1875; $300,000
To reorganize: part of Michigan Air Line RR and St. Clair & Chicago Air Line
Control at inc. by Grand Trunk Ry of Canada
Line acquired at inc., Ridgeway to Romeo
Amend July 22, 1880; to change termini to Ridgeway and 1 mile west of Detroit & Milwaukee at Pontiac
Amend Jan. 21, 1882; to own: 105 miles, Ridgeway to Jackson via Pontiac; capital $1,002,000
Bought Oct. 25, 1882, part of line of Toledo, Ann Arbor & Grand Trunk
Line completed Jan. 1, 1884, Ridgeway to Jackson
Amend Oct. 16, 1889; to reduce number of directors
Merged Nov. 1, 1928, into Grand Trunk Western

Michigan Alkali Co.
O: unknown
Private logging road

The Michigan & Canada Bridge & Tunnel Company
P: 082
Inc. March 30, 1905; $2,000,000
To rename Detroit River Bridge Co.
Merged June 9, 1905, into Detroit River Tunnel Co.

Michigan and Chicago Railway Company (E)
O: 003. 008, 013, 039, 041 P: 011, 009, 073, 078, 080
Inc. Aug. 23, 1912; $3,000,000
To own: 51.645 miles, Grand Rapids to Kalamazoo; to rename Michigan & Chicago Westbound Ry
Amend Dec. 19, 1912; to revise route: 183 miles, to add branch from 17 miles N of Kalamazoo to Battle Creek, branch from same point to Allegan, with line Kalamazoo to Benton Harbor, with branch Paw Paw to South Haven
Amend April 24, 1913; to add: branch Plainwell to Otsego and branch Yorkville to Gull Lake and increase capital to $6,000,000
Amend Nov. 17, 1913; to revise route: 233 miles, to add line Owosso to Bay City
Renamed March 19, 1914, as Michigan Ry

Michigan and Chicago Westbound Railway Company (E)
P: 003, 039, 041
Inc. July 22, 1909; $3,000,000
To own: 51.645 miles, Grand Rapids to Kalamazoo
Renamed Aug. 23, 1912, as Michigan & Chicago Ry

Michigan & Indiana Railway Company (E)
P: 011
Inc.(S) June 25, 1898; $25,000; Berrien Springs
To own: in Benton Harbor, St. Joseph, Niles, Berrien Springs, Buchanan, and adjoining townships
Lapsed

The Michigan & Indiana Traction Company (E)
P: 013, 023, 033
Inc.(S) Oct. 20, 1903; $200,000; Battle Creek
To own: in Battle Creek, Grand Ledge, and Lansing
Lapsed

Michigan and Mackinaw Railroad Company
O: Reorganizing company
Inc. July 15, 1891; $1,280,000
To acquire: Michigan Div. of Cincinnati, Jackson & Mackinaw RR at foreclosure
Merged July 17, 1891, into Cincinnati, Jackson & Mackinaw Ry

Michigan & Northwestern Railway Company
Act of Feb. 15, 1859, authorized Flint & Pere Marquette to change name—name not used

Michigan and Ohio Car Ferry Co.
Inc.(Not RR) Nov. 24, 1897

Michigan & Ohio Electric Railway Company (E)
P: 058, 082
Inc.(S) July 21, 1900; $200,000; Detroit
To own: in Detroit, Dundee, and Maybee, and adjacent townships
Lapsed

The Michigan and Ohio Railroad Company
O: 003, 008, 013, 030, 038, 039, 046, 058
Inc. June 25, 1883; $8,000,000
To consolidate: Toledo & Milwaukee Ry and Toledo & Michigan (Ohio corp.)
Line completed Nov. 29, 1883, Allegan to Dundee
Foreclosure sale Nov. 4, 1886, to Cincinnati, Jackson & Mackinaw
Sold March 25, 1887, to Cincinnati, Jackson & Mackinaw RR

The Michigan and Ohio Railway Company
P: 008, 013, 030, 041, 070
Inc. Sept. 15, 1873; $15,000,000
To merge: Ohio & Grand Haven and Portsmouth, Columbus & Michigan (Ohio corp.); line: Grand Haven to Portsmouth, Ohio
Lapsed

Michigan & Western Railroad Company
P: not stated
Inc. April 5, 1982; $2,640,000
To own: in Michigan
Control at inc. by Green Bay & Western
Apparently lapsed

Michigan Central—
O: 003, 005, 006, 008, 009, 011, 012, 013, 014, 016, 019, 020, 023, 026, 032, 033, 038, 039, 041, 044, 050, 056, 058, 060, 063, 065, 069, 072, 073, 074, 075, 078, 079, 080, 081, 082
Chartered March 28, 1846, as Michigan Central Rail Road Company; $2,200,000; Detroit and Boston
To own line: Detroit, via Ypsilanti, Ann Arbor, Dexter, Jackson, Marshall, Battle Creek, Kalamazoo to some point in the state of Michigan on or near Lake Michigan, accessible to steam boats navigating said Lake
Bought Sept. 24, 1846, "Central" line from state of Michigan
Line acquired Sept. 24, 1846, Detroit to Kalamazoo
Amend charter March 16, 1847; to change fiscal year and annual meeting date
Amend charter April 3, 1848; to allow company to control other companies to connect line to Chicago
Line completed May 1852, Detroit to Chicago
Amend charter Feb. 13, 1855; to increase number of directors and other changes
Amend charter Feb. 10, 1859; to limit certain powers
Lease July 1, 1870, in perpetuity, of Kalamazoo & South Haven
Lease Aug. 15, 1870, for corp. life, of Grand River Valley
Lease Feb. 1871, for corp. life, of Michigan Air Line RR
Lease Sept. 1, 1871, for corp. life, of Jackson, Lansing & Saginaw
Amend charter April 1, 1879; to change annual meeting date
Lease March 10, 1881, for corp. life, of Detroit & Bay City
Operating agreement Dec. 12, 1882, of Canada Southern Ry
Lease Feb. 15, 1883, of Saginaw Bay & Northwestern
Control May 28, 1883, of Saginaw Bay & Northwestern
Amend charter June 8, 1883; to modify minor corporate rights
Lease Feb. 18, 1888, 99 years, of Lansing Transit
Lease Feb. 1, 1890, in perpetuity, of Bay City & Battle Creek and Battle Creek & Sturgis
Control 1890, 83.5% of Battle Creek & Sturgis
Control July 24, 1891, at inc., of Grayling, Twin Lakes & Northeastern
Amend charter May 31, 1893; to modify corporate rights
Control Oct. 11, 1894, at inc., of Buchanan & St. Joseph River
Control Sept. 19, 1895, at inc., of Detroit, Delray & Dearborn
Reinc. Dec. 4, 1901, as The Michigan Central Railroad Company; $18,738,000; to surrender charter
Lease March 31, 1902, 25 years, of Detroit Manufacturers RR
Control early 1902, 50% of Detroit, Toledo & Milwaukee
Lease Jan. 1, 1904, 999 years, of Canada Southern Ry
Amend May 5, 1904; to change number of directors
Lease Jan. 1, 1905, in perpetuity, 50% of Detroit, Toledo & Milwaukee
Lease assigned March 15, 1905, eff. Feb. 23, 1900, for 50 years, of St. Joseph, South Bend & Southern, by Indiana, Illinois & Iowa
Control June 9, 1905, at inc., of Detroit River Tunnel
Lease July 1, 1905, 25 years, 50% of Lansing Manufacturers
Control Dec. 8, 1905, 25% of Detroit Terminal
Lease Jan. 2, 1906, for corp. life, of Toledo, Canada Southern & Detroit
Control 1906, of Chicago, Kalamazoo & Saginaw
Lease Jan. 1, 1907, eff. Jan. 1, 1904, for 999 years, of Detroit River Tunnel Co.
Control May 2, 1907, of Detroit & Charlevoix

Lease July 20, 1909, for corp. life, of Detroit Belt Line
Consolidated June 19, 1912, Buchanan & St. Joseph River
Consolidated Sept. 15, 1916, Grand River Valley
Consolidated Sept. 20, 1916, Detroit & Charlevoix
Consolidated Sept. 27, 1916, Kalamazoo & South Haven; Bay City & Battle Creek; Michigan Air Line RR; Detroit & Bay City; Toledo, Canada Southern & Detroit; and Jackson, Lansing & Saginaw
Consolidated Sept. 29, 1916, Detroit, Delray & Dearborn
Consolidated Dec. 26, 1916, Detroit Belt Line
Leased Feb. 1, 1930, 999 years, to New York Central
Bought 1961, Detroit, Hillsdale & South Western
Conveyed April 1, 1976, some rail properties to Consolidated Rail
Conveyed Oct. 24, 1978, rail properties to Penn Central Corp.
Disposition uncertain

Michigan Central Bridge Company
P: 082
Inc. Dec. 19, 1895
To own: 3 miles and bridge over Detroit River in Wayne co.
Renamed Dec. 1, 1898, as Detroit River Bridge Co.

Michigan Central Traction Company, Limited (E)
P: 013, 023, 033
Inc. (partnership) June 23, 1902; $750,000; Battle Creek
To own: Battle Creek, via Bellevue, Olivet, Charlotte and Grand Ledge, to Lansing
Lapsed

Michigan City, Lakeside and St. Joe Electric Railway Company (E)
P: 011
Inc. June 14, 1912; $750,000; St. Joseph
To own: 30 miles, St. Joseph to New Buffalo then SWly to Indiana state line
Lapsed

Michigan East & West Railway Company
O: 043, 051, 053, 067
Inc. Nov. 25, 1913; $1,000,000
To reorganize: Manistee & Grand Rapids
Line acquired at inc., of Manistee & Grand Rapids
Abandoned 1916

Michigan Electric Railway Company (E)
P: 011
Inc.(S) April 12, 1901; $25,000; St. Joseph
To own: St. Joseph to Indiana state line toward Michigan City
Lapsed

Michigan Electric Railway Company (E)
O: 013, 019, 033, 038, 039, 078
Inc.(S) Aug. 2, 1923; $7,903,800; Jackson
To acquire Michigan United Rys
Lease assigned no date, of Michigan United Rys, by Michigan Ry
Conveyed March 18, 1929, part of line to Kalamazoo Transportation
Conveyed March 19, 1929, part of line to Battle Creek Transportation
Conveyed March 19, 1929, part of line to Jackson Transportation
Conveyed March 19, 1929, part of line to Lansing Transportation
Conveyed March 20, 1929, part to Michigan Electric Shares
Dissolved Dec. 14, 1929

Michigan Electric Shares Corporation
O: Liquidating company
Inc.(Not RR) March 20, 1929
[To dispose of rail property of Michigan United Ry]
Acquired at inc., part of line of Michigan Electric Ry
Dissolved June 19, 1933

Michigan Extension Railway Company
P: 012, 013, 014, 019, 025, 033, 038, 039, 047, 063, 074, 075, 078
Inc. March 1, 1878; $6,900,000
To own: 203 miles, Indiana state line in Cass co. (connect with Indiana Extension Ry) to Port Huron
Lapsed

Michigan Forest Products Co.
O: 017
Private logging road
Strongs

Michigan, Indiana and St. Louis Railroad Company
P: 075
Inc. May 30, 1882; $2,500,000
To consolidate: Sturgis & Indiana; Michigan, Indiana & St. Louis (Ind. corp.); and Danville, Indiana & Michigan (Ill. corp.)
Lapsed

Michigan-Indiana Traction Company (E)
P: 012, 013
Inc.(S) Sept. 27, 1911; $750,000; Battle Creek
Route not specified, but Battle Creek and Coldwater named as points
Dissolved Jan. 14, 1915

Michigan Interstate Railway Company
O: 010, 018, 019, 029, 037, 047, 051, 057, 058, 067, 078, 081, 083

Inc. Aug. 27, 1977; $399,993
To: operate in Michigan
Operating agreement Oct. 1, 1977, with state of Michigan
Amend Nov. 8, 1979, to increase capital $120,000 (for preferred stock)
Active corporation

Michigan Inter-Urban Railway Company (E)
P: 012, 013
Inc.(S) July 13, 1901; $700,000
To own: Battle Creek to Coldwater via Union City
Lapsed

The Michigan Lake Shore Rail Road Company
O: 003, 061, 070 P: 010, 028, 051, 053, 064
Inc. Feb. 5, 1869; $500,000; Grand Rapids
To own: 22 miles, Ferrysburg to Holland
Amend Sept. 29, 1869; to consolidate Muskegon & Ferrysburg and Allegan & Holland
Amend Oct. 29, 1869; to extend northern terminus to Traverse City; capital $1,800,000
Line opened Dec. 1869, Muskegon to Ferrysburg
Line completed Aug. 29, 1870, Allegan to Muskegon
Foreclosure sale June 19, 1878, to Grand Haven

Michigan Light & Traction Company (E)
P: 003, 011, 039, 041, 080
Inc.(S) Aug. 20, 1909; $25,000; Detroit
To own: Grand Rapids, to Kalamazoo, to New Buffalo, to Chicago
Dissolved Nov. 1, 1910

Michigan Limestone and Chemical Co.
O: 071
Private quarry road
At Calcite
Built 1907
Active road

Michigan Logging Co.
O: 027
Private logging road
Lake Gogebic

Michigan Midland—
P: 019, 025, 033, 034, 041, 047, 050, 070, 074, 078
Inc. May 19, 1870, as Michigan Midland Rail Road Company; $3,000,000
To own: 102 miles, St. Clair to Lansing
Amend Dec. 28, 1871, as Michigan Midland Railroad Company; to own: 200 miles, St. Clair to mouth of Black Lake, Holland twp.; capital $6,000,000
Sold Nov. 12, 1873, to Michigan, Midland & Canada

Michigan, Midland and Canada Railroad Company
O: 050, 074
Inc. Sept. 17, 1872; $400,000
To own: 15 miles, St. Clair to Chicago, Detroit & Canada Grand Trunk Jct. line (at Lenox)
Bought Nov. 12, 1873, Michigan Midland
Line completed Dec. 7, 1873, St. Clair to Ridgeway
Operating agreement Dec. 12, 1882, by Canada Southern
Control 1882, by Canada Southern
Foreclosure sale Feb. 23, 1906, to St. Clair & Western

The Michigan Northern Rail Road Company
P: 003, 005, 016, 024, 028, 039, 040, 041, 043, 054, 059, 062, 067, 075, 083
Inc. March 11, 1869; $2,500,000; Kalamazoo
To own: 294 miles, Sturgis twp. through Grand Rapids to Traverse Bay then to Straits of Mackinac
Lapsed

The Michigan Northern Railroad Company
P: 043, 062, 064
Inc. Aug. 25, 1887; $400,000
To own: 50 miles, Chase via Lilley Jct. to Hart
Lapsed

Michigan Northern Railroad Company
P: 008, 009, 019, 023, 029, 034, 037, 039, 056
Inc. Oct. 17, 1919; $3,000,000
To own: 235 miles, Bay City to Kalamazoo and branch, Sunfield via Lansing to Maple Rapids
Lapsed

The Michigan Northern Railway Company
P: 004, 018, 020, 037, 041, 059, 060, 068, 072
Inc. April 11, 1873; $2,000,000
To own: 200 miles, Plums Mill, Kent co. via Greenville to Alpena
Consolidated April 24, 1873, Grand Rapids RR (1871 inc.)
Lapsed

Michigan Northern Railway Company
O: 005, 015, 016, 024, 028, 040, 041, 054, 059, 067, 069, 083
Inc. March 18, 1976; $80,000; Cadillac
To operate in above-named counties
Operating agreement April 1, 1976, with state of Michigan
Agreement cancelled Oct. 1, 1984
Apparently active company

Michigan, Ohio & Indiana Railroad Company
P: 058
Inc. May 24, 1905; $50,000; Dundee
To own: 5 miles, Petersburg to Dundee
Lapsed

Michigan Railroad Company (E)
O: 003, 008, 009, 013, 025, 039, 041, 070, 073
Inc. April 10, 1919; $5,000,000
To acquire Michigan Ry (143 miles, Grand Rapids to Kalamazoo, Allegan to Battle Creek, Flint to Bay City with branch to Frankenmuth)
Acquired at inc., lines of Michigan Ry (Flint-Bay City, Kalamazoo-Grand Rapids, Battle Creek-Allegan)
Lease at inc., assigned by Michigan Ry, of Grand Rapids, Holland & Chicago
Conveyed Nov. 1, 1923, part to Saginaw Transit
Lease cancelled Jan. 1, 1924, of Grand Rapids, Holland & Chicago
Receivership Oct. 28, 1924
Foreclosure sale March 7, 1929
Operations ended June 16, 1929
Dissolved Dec. 14, 1929

Michigan Railway Company (E)
O: 003, 008, 009, 013, 019, 025, 033, 038, 039, 041, 070, 073, 078
Inc. March 19, 1914; $6,000,000
To rename Michigan & Chicago Ry, and acquire all rights plus to add line Saginaw to Flint with branch to Frankenmuth, 268 miles
Control at inc., by Commonwealth Power Ry & Light
Acquired at inc., Saginaw & Flint and Saginaw-Bay City
Lease Aug. 1, 1914, of Kalamazoo, Lake Shore & Chicago Ry
Leases assigned Jan. 1, 1916, by Michigan United Traction and Michigan United Rys, all lines
Lease Jan. 1, 1916, of Grand Rapids, Holland & Chicago
Lease cancelled May 31, 1916, of Kalamazoo, Lake Shore & Chicago
Lease assigned April 10, 1919, of Grand Rapids, Holland & Chiago, to Michigan RR
Conveyed April 10, 1919, part to Michigan RR (Flint-Bay City, Kalamazoo-Grand Rapids, Battle Creek-Allegan)
Leases assigned 1921, of Michigan United Traction and Michigan United Ry lines, to Michigan United Ry
Dissolved June 22, 1921

Michigan Railway Company
O: Reorganizing holding company
Inc. Jan. 6, 1880; $2,089,500
To buy lines: Lansing and west from Chicago & Lake Huron and Peninsular at foreclosure
Merged Jan. 7, 1880, into Chicago & Grand Trunk

Michigan Railway and Light Company (E)
P: 078
Inc.(S) Aug. 8, 1905; $100,000; Owosso
To own: in Owosso and Corunna and adjacent townships
Lapsed

Michigan Shore and Eastern Railway Company
P: 003, 011, 070, 080
Inc. Jan. 29, 1903; $1,000,000; Benton Harbor
To own: 125 miles, from Indiana state line in Bertrand twp., via Niles, Buchanan, Berrien Springs, Benton Harbor, Coloma, South Haven, and Saugatuck, to Holland; and to buy South Haven & Eastern; Milwaukee, Benton Harbor & Columbus; and Benton Harbor Coloma & Paw Paw Lake Train Ry
Lapsed

Michigan Shore Railroad, Inc.
O: 061
Inc. Sept. 27, 1990; $100,000; Greenville
To operate railroad in Muskegon county
Control at inc. by Rail-Tex Corp.
Bought Dec. 12, 1990; line (in Muskegon) from Central Michigan
Active corporation

The Michigan Southern and Northern Indiana Rail Road Company
O: 012, 030, 038, 046, 058, 075, 081, 082
Inc. April 25, 1855; $12,000,000
To consolidate: Northern Indiana (Ind. corp.) and Michigan Southern
Line acquired at inc. Toledo to Chicago with branches
Lease July 1, 1856, in perpetuity, of Detroit, Monroe & Toledo
Act Feb. 17, 1857; authorized consolidation of Detroit, Monroe & Toledo
Leased Nov. 21, 1864, part of line to St. Joseph Valley
Merged April 6, 1869, into Lake Shore & Michigan Southern

The Michigan Southern Railroad Company
O: 012, 030, 038, 046, 058, 075, 081
Chartered May 9, 1846; $500,000; Monroe
To buy: "Southern" line and Palmyra & Jacksonburgh from state of Michigan
Bought Dec. 28, 1846, "Southern" line from state of Michigan
Line acquired Dec. 28, 1846, Monroe to Hillsdale

Amend charter March 24, 1849; changed payments to State and completion dates
Amend charter March 31, 1849; changed completion dates
Lease Aug. 1, 1849, in perpetuity, of Erie & Kalamazoo
Amend charter April 1, 1850; authorized stock and bonds, changed completion dates and terminii, altered repayment to state, set rates
Line opened Oct. 4, 1851, Monroe to South Bend
Line completed May 1852, Monroe to Chicago
Amend charter Feb. 13, 1855; authorized consolidation with Northern Indiana; new corp. to be named Michigan Southern & Northern Indiana
Merged April 25, 1855, into Michigan Southern & Northern Indiana

Michigan Suburban Railroad Company (E)
O: 019, 033
Inc. Dec. 30, 1901; $200,000; Port Huron
To own: 18 miles, Lansing to St. Johns
Operated Jan. 12, 1902 to March 26, 1904, Lansing, St. Johns & St. Louis
Lapsed

Michigan Terminal Railway Company
P: 041, 061
Inc. filed April 14, 1893
To own: 45 miles, Muskegon to Grand Rapids
Lapsed

Michigan Terminal Transfer Railway Company
P: 011
Inc. April 7, 1905; $100,000; Benton Harbor
To own: 2 miles, Indiana, Illinois & Iowa depot in Benton Harbor NWly to Higman Park
Lapsed

Michigan Traction Company (E)
O: 013, 039
Inc.(S) Dec. 31, 1896; $500,000; Kalamazoo
To own: Kalamazoo to Battle Creek
Amend Dec. 7, 1897; to change number of directors
Control Oct. 1, 1898, of Citizens Street Ry of Battle Creek and Citizens Street Ry [of Kalamazoo]
Acquired no date, Citizens Street of Battle Creek and Citizens Street [of Kalamazoo]
Line opened Aug. 2, 1900
Merged May 1, 1906, into Michigan United Rys
Dissolved Oct. 11, 1915

Michigan Traction Extension Company (E)
P: 013, 039
Inc.(S) Sept. 2, 1903; $25,000; Kalamazoo
To own: street rys in Kalamazoo and Battle Creek
Merged May 1, 1906, into Michigan United Rys

Michigan Traction Extension Company (E)
P: unknown
Inc.(S) filed March 31, 1906, but not located

Michigan United Railways Company (E)
O: 013, 019, 033, 038, 039
Inc.(S) March 31, 1906; $5,000,000; Kalamazoo
To own: St. Johns, to Lansing, to Jackson, to Battle Creek, to Kalamazoo
Leased May 1, 1906, Jackson & Battle Creek Traction and Lansing & Jackson
Cons. May 1, 1906, Lansing & Suburban Traction; Lansing City Electric; Michigan Traction Extension; and Michigan Traction
Control May 9, 1907, of Jackson Consolidated Traction
Control Aug. 29, 1907, at inc., of Lansing Southern
Amend June 20, 1908; to increase capital to $7,000,000
Bought Aug. 1, 1908, Jackson Consolidated Traction
Control Jan. 22, 1910, at inc., of Lansing & Northeastern
Amend March 7, 1910; to change number of directors
Bought ca. 1911, Owosso & Corunna Electric
Lease June 1, 1911, of Kalamazoo, Lake Shore & Chicago
Lease Jan. 1, 1912, of Lansing & Northeastern
Lease assigned Jan. 1, 1912, of Kalamazoo, Lake Shore & Chicago, to Michigan United Traction
Leases assigned April 1, 1912, all leases, to Michigan United Traction
Leased April 1, 1912, all lines to Michigan United Traction
Leased Jan. 1, 1916, all owned lines to Michigan Ry
Amend Sept. 21, 1922; to change office to Jackson
Conveyed 1923, owned lines and some leased lines to Michigan Electric Ry
Dissolved April 12, 1924

Michigan United Traction Company (E)
O: 013, 019, 033, 038, 039, 078
Inc.(S) Dec. 27, 1911; $100,000; Kalamazoo
To own: street rys in Michigan
Lease Jan. 1, 1912, of Kalamazoo, Lake Shore & Chicago
Lease April 1, 1912, rail lines of Michigan United Ry
Lease assigned Aug. 1, 1914, of Kalamazoo, Lake Shore & Chicago to Michigan Ry
Leases assigned Dec. 31, 1915, all lines, to Michigan Ry
Dissolved Dec. 31, 1915

Michigan West Shore Traction Company (E)
P: 003, 011, 041, 080
Inc.(S) March 6, 1901; $1,000,000; South Haven
To own: Grand Rapids to New Buffalo
Lapsed

Michigan-Wisconsin Transportation Company
Inc.(Not RR) June 8, 1983; $500,000; Ludington
To operate rail- and car-ferry in Michigan and to ports in Wisconsin

Midland & Hubbard Railroad Copany
O: 056
Inc. Sept. 21, 1893; $80,000; Midland
To own: 9 miles, Midland to Hubbard
Abandoned

Midland & Northern Railway Company
P: 009, 056
Inc. Jan. 17, 1894; $25,000; Midland
To own: 3 miles, center sec 12 T15N R2E to N branch Kawkawlin River
Lapsed

Midland Gravel Co.
O: 054
Private industrial road
Millbrook

The Midland Train Railway Company (Gauge 3')
O: 056
Inc.(T) Oct. 23, 1885; $12,000; Midland
To own: 12 miles, SE 1/4 post sec 21 T14N R2E (Midland co.), southwest to center of sec 36 T13N R1E
Abandoned

Mid-Michigan Railroad, Inc.
O: 029, 034, 041, 059, 073
Inc. Dec. 16, 1987; $10,000; Greenville
To operate a railroad
Control at inc. by Rail-Tex Corp.
Bought Dec 18, 1987, line (Elmdale-Greenville, Paines-Elwell) from CSX Transportation
Active corporation

Mills and Leighton (Gauge 3')
O: 080
Private logging road
Van Buren co.

Milwaukee & Northern—
O: 007, 022, 031, 036, 052, 055, 066
Inc. June 5, 1880 (Wisc. corp.), as Milwaukee & Northern Railroad Company
Amend Dec. 7, 1886, as The Milwaukee and Northern Railroad Company; $8,000,000; to consolidate: Republic Branch and Menominee Branch
Line completed Nov. 20, 1887, Wisconsin state line to Champion
Bought June 20, 1890, Ontonagon & Brule River
Control Sept. 1890, by Chicago, Milwaukee & St. Paul
Sold June 23, 1893, to Chicago, Milwaukee & St. Paul

Milwaukee, Benton Harbor & Columbus Railway Company
O: 011
Inc. April 6, 1897; $600,000; Benton Harbor
To consolidate: St. Joseph Valley and Benton Harbor & South Eastern (Ind. corp.)
Line completed Oct. 4, 1897, Benton Harbor to Berrien Springs
Merged May 6, 1903, into Pere Marquette

Milwaukee, Lake Shore and Western Railway Company
O: 027, 066
Inc. May 31, 1872 (Wisc. corp.)
Amend Feb. 13, 1883; $10,000,000; to consolidate Wisc. corp. and Vieux Desert & Lake Superior
Line opened Sept. 23, 1883, Wisconsin state line to Watersmeet
Amend June 11, 1884; to extend routes; capital $10,000,000
Line completed 1884, Watersmeet to Ironwood
Control no date, by Chicago & North Western
Sold Aug. 19, 1893, to Chicago & North Western

Mineral Range & L'Anse Bay Railroad Company (Gauge 3')
P: 007, 031
Inc. June 9, 1871; $200,000
To own: 45 miles, head of Keweenaw Bay via Houghton to N line Calumet twp.
Renamed Oct. 25, 1872, as Mineral Range RR

Mineral Range Railroad Company (Gauge 3' until 1898, then standard)
O: 007, 031, 042, 066
Inc. Oct. 25, 1872; $400,000; Hancock
To rename: Mineral Range & L'Anse Bay and change line to 100 miles, Copper Harbor to Ontonagon River
Line completed Oct. 11, 1873, Hancock to Calumet
Amend Feb. 15, 1899; to change gauge and extend line to Copper Harbor and to Ontonagon River
Amend April 9, 1901; to change capital to $800,000
Control June 1, 1901, of Hancock & Calumet
Amend Oct. 22, 1901; to change number of directors
Control no date, by Duluth, South Shore & Atlantic
Lease 1902, of Mohawk Mining Co. RR
Amend Dec. 22, 1902; to increase capital to $1,200,000
Amend Feb. 24, 1910; to increase capital to $1,500,000
Lease assigned 1917, of Mohawk Mining Co., to Copper Range
Acquired Jan. 1, 1935, Hancock & Calumet
Merged Nov. 1, 1949, into Duluth, South Shore & Atlantic

Mineral Range Railway Company
P: 027, 031, 042, 066
Inc. Dec 27, 1864; $1,200,000
To own: 150 miles, Lac la Belle, Keweenaw co. to Big Montreal River at west state line
Lapsed

Minneapolis, St. Paul and Sault Ste. Marie—
O: 017, 021, 027, 049, 055, 077
Inc. June 11, 1888, as Minneapolis, St. Paul and Sault Ste. Marie Railway Company; $21,000,000; Minneapolis
To consolidate: Minneapolis, Sault Ste. Marie & Atlantic and three non-Mich.corps.
Line acquired at inc., Sault Ste. Marie to Wisconsin state line
Control 1890, by Canadian Pacific
Control March 15, 1900, at inc., 50% of Sainte Marie Union Depot
Amend Sept. 17, 1907; to increase capital to $42,000,000
Lease April 1, 1909, of Wisconsin Central
Amend Sept. 18, 1917; to change annual meeting date
Reinc. July 18, 1944, as Minneapolis, St. Paul and Sault Ste. Marie Railroad Company
Acquired Sept. 1, 1952, part of Sainte Marie Union Depot Co.
Merged Jan. 1, 1961, into Soo Line RR

Minneapolis, Sault Ste. Marie and Atlantic Railway Company
O: 017, 021, 049, 055, 077
Inc. March 22, 1887; $12,000,000
To consolidate: MSSM & A (Wisc. corp.) and Menominee & Sault Ste. Marie
Control March 16, 1887, at inc., 25% of Sault Ste. Marie Bridge Co.
Line completed Jan. 1, 1888, Sault Ste. Marie to Wisconsin state line
Merged June 11, 1888, into Minneapolis, St. Paul & Sault Ste. Marie

Minor, John S.
O: 060
Private logging road
Montmorency co.

The Missaukee Railroad Company
P: 057, 083
Inc. Feb. 12, 1878; $500,000
To own: 30 miles, Cadillac to lake on secs 4 & 5 T24N R5W
Lapsed

Mitchell Brothers (William and Austin) (Gauge 3')
O: 057
Private logging road
Missaukee co. and Kalkaska
See also Jennings & Northeastern

Mohawk Mining Co.
O: 042
Private ore road
Leased 1902, to Mineral Range RR
Lease assigned 1917, to Copper Range
Dissolved (not RR)

The Monroe and Ann Arbor rail-road Company
P: 058, 081
Chartered March 28, 1836; $300,000
To own: 33 miles, Monroe to Ann Arbor
Lapsed

The Monroe & Toledo Railway Company
O: 058
Inc. March 28, 1893; $128,000
To own: 16 miles, Flint & Pere Marquette north of Monroe to Ohio state line in sec 6 T9S R8E
Control at inc. by Flint & Pere Marquette
Amend April 22, 1896; to increase capital to $200,000
Line completed Nov. 15, 1896, Monroe to Alexis
Sold Aug. 27, 1897, to Flint & Pere Marquette

The Monroe and Ypsilanti Rail-road Company
P: 058, 081
Chartered March 28, 1836; $400,000
To own: Monroe to Ypsilanti
Amend charter March 13, 1840; to extend completion dates
Amend charter March 19, 1845; to extend corporate rights, extend completion dates
Lapsed

Monroe Connecting Railway Company
P: 058
Inc. May 31, 1917; $100,000
To own: 2.5 miles, Detroit, Monroe & Toledo Shore Line N of Monroe SWly to same line S of Monroe
Lapsed

Monroe, Dundee and Lake Erie Railway Company
P: 058
Inc.(T) March 26, 1896; $400,000
To own: Monroe to Dundee
Lapsed

Monroe Traction Company (E)
P: 058
Inc.(T) April 13, 1901; $10,000
To own: 4.5 miles, Monroe to N city limits
Conveyed Dec. 9, 1902, to Detroit, Monroe & Toledo Short Line

The Montague Pentwater and Manistee Railroad Company
P: 051, 053, 061, 064
Inc. July 7, 1871; $600,000
To own: 65 miles, Montague to Manistee
Merged Oct. 25, 1871, into Chicago & Michigan Lake Shore

Moon, Robert A. (Gauge 3')
O: 062
Private logging road; Big Rapids
7 miles, Muskegon River to T16N R11W
Built 1879

Moore and Cody
See Cody [L. J.] and Moore

Moores, J. Henry
Owned West Branch & Moorestown

The Mottville and White Pigeon railroad Company
P: 075
Chartered April 5, 1838; $100,000
To own: Mottville to Indiana state line
Lapsed

Mount Clemens and Lakeside Electric Street Railway and Dock Company (E)
O: 050
Inc.(S) Oct. 16, 1894; $25,000
To own: in Mt. Clemens and Clinton, Harrison and Erin twps.
Line completed at merger
Merged June 13, 1895, into Mt. Clemens & Lakeside Traction

The Mt Clemens and Lakeside Traction Company (E)
O: 050
Inc.(S) June 13, 1895; $100,000; Lakeside (Harrison twp.)
To own: in Mt. Clemens and Chesterfield, Clinton, Harrison and Erin twps.
Consolidated at inc., Mt. Clemens & Lakeside Electric and Mt. Clemens Street
Line opened Sept. 28, 1898, Detroit city limits to Mt. Clemens
Conveyed ca. 1899, to Detroit, Mt. Clemens & Marine City

The Mount Clemens Street Railway Company (H)
O: 050
Inc.(S) July 26, 1893; $25,000
To own: in Mt. Clemens
Line opened no date
Merged June 13, 1895, into Mt. Clemens & Lakeside Traction

Mount Pleasant and Western Railroad Company
P: 037, 054
Inc. March 14, 1887; $400,000
To own: 40 miles, Mt. Pleasant to Big Rapids
Lapsed

Mudgett, D. B.
O: 001
Private logging tramway
Near Harrisville

Munising, Marquette and Southeastern Railway Company
O: 002, 052, 077
Inc. April 22, 1911, eff. June 27, 1911; $1,870,000
To consolidate: Munising and Marquette & Southeastern
Control at inc., by Cleveland Cliffs Iron Co
Line acquired at inc., Munising to Little Lake and Marquette
Merged Aug. 17, 1923, into Lake Superior & Ishpeming

Munising Railway Company
O: 002, 052, 077
Inc. July 3, 1895; $870,000
To own: 38 miles, Grand Island or Munising Bay to C & NW at Little Lake; branch #1 25 miles, main line near Munising Bay to T49N R15W; branch #2 24 miles, main line in T46N R19W to Delta Lbr Co Ry in T43N R17W
Line opened Nov. 30, 1897, Munising to Little Lake
Control 1899, by Cleveland Cliffs Iron Co
Amend Nov. 14, 1905; to add: 7.3 miles, Little Lake to Austin and Princeton Mines
Merged June 27, 1911, into Munising, Marquette & Southeastern

Murphy and Dorr
O: 018
Private logging road
In T20N R3W

Muskegon and Big Rapids Railroad Company
P: 054, 061, 064
Inc. Aug. 24, 1871; $500,000
To own: 50 miles, Muskegon to Big Rapids
Merged July 27, 1872, into Chicago & Michigan Lake Shore

The Muskegon and Ferrysburg Rail Road Company
P: 061, 070
Inc. May 6, 1868; $250,000
To own: 17 miles, Ferrysburg to Muskegon Harbor
Merged Sept. 29, 1869, into Michigan Lake Shore

The Muskegon and Greenville Railroad Company
P: 041, 059, 061
Inc. Oct. 18, 1870; $1,000,000
To own: 47.5 miles, Muskegon via Cedar Springs to Ionia & Lansing line in Montcalm co.
Lapsed

The Muskegon, Grand Rapids and Indiana Railroad Company
O: 041, 061, 070
Inc. Jan. 18, 1886; $350,000; Grand Rapids
To own: 40 miles, Muskegon to Grand Rapids
Leased June 9, 1886, 99 years, to Grand Rapids & Indiana
Line completed Dec. 1, 1886, Muskegon Jct. to Muskegon
Sold June 17, 1917, eff. May 1, 1917, to Grand Rapids & Indiana
Dissolved April 4, 1918

Muskegon Lake—
O: 061
Inc. Nov. 15, 1879, as Muskegon Lake Railroad Company; $40,000
To own: 5 miles, Muskegon to mouth of Muskegon Lake
Amend Nov. 15, 1880, as The Muskegon Lake Railroad Company; to change capital to $75,000
Line completed 1881, Muskegon to Port Sherman
Control 1886, by Chicago & West Michigan
Sold Oct. 1, 1900, to Pere Marquette

Muskegon, Ludington and Manistee Railway Company (E)
P: 051, 053, 061, 064
Inc.(S) May 29, 1913; $ 1,500,000; Muskegon
To own: Muskegon to Ludington to Manistee
Lapsed

The Muskegon Railway Company (H, E)
O: 061
Inc.(S) Sept. 14, 1882; $25,000; Muskegon
To own: in Muskegon
Line opened Nov. 25, 1882
Amend Dec. 4, 1882; to change office to Lakeside
Amend Feb. 3, 1883; to increase capital to $50,000
Amend April 23, 1890; to increase capital to $100,000 and change corp. rights
Conveyed Jan. 5, 1897, to Muskegon Street Ry

Muskegon Railway and Navigation Company
O: 061
Inc. March 21, 1918; $500,000
To own: 10 miles, in Muskegon
Line completed 1923
Merged Aug. 23, 1955, into Grand Trunk Western

The Muskegon River and Cat Creek Rail Road Company (Gauge 4')
O: 067
Inc. Nov. 13, 1878; $32,000
To own: 4 miles, N bank Muskegon River (sec 16 T17N R9W) to sec 32 T18N R9W
Abandoned

Muskegon River and Rose Lake Railway Company (Gauge 3')
O: 067
Inc. April 29, 1878; $60,000
To own: 13 miles, Muskegon River (T18N R8W) NWly to Rose Lake
Line opened, Dec. 28, 1878, 7.5 miles
Abandoned 1881

Muskegon Street Railway Company (H)
P: 061
Inc.(S) Oct. 28, 1880; $25,000
To own: in Muskegon
Disposition unclear

Muskegon Street Railway Company (E)
O: 061
Inc.(S) Jan. 5, 1897; $100,000
To own in Muskegon, Muskegon Hts., North Muskegon, and Muskegon and Norton twps.
Acquired, at inc., Muskegon Ry
Amend Jan. 29, 1897; to increase capital to $250,000
Conveyed Jan. 19, 1901, to Muskegon Traction

Muskegon Terminal Railway Company
P: 041, 061
Inc. Aug. 19, 1892; $450,000
To own: 45 miles, Muskegon to Grand Rapids
Lapsed

Muskegon Traction and Lighting Company (E)
O: 061
Inc.(S) Feb. 19, 1901; $600,000; Muskegon
To consolidate: Muskegon Traction and a power company
Acquired at inc., Muskegon Traction
Owned at inc. by American Traction & Lighting
Amend Feb. 3, 1903; to increase capital to $700,000
Operations ended Oct. 10, 1929
Renamed Nov. 25, 1930, as Muskegon Gas Co.

Muskegon Traction Company (E)
O: 061
Inc.(S) Jan. 19, 1901; $150,000; Muskegon
To own: street ry in Muskegon and Muskegon Co.
Acquired at inc., Muskegon Street Ry (1897 corp.)
Conveyed Feb. 19, 1901, to Muskegon Traction & Lighting

The Muskrat Lake and Clam River Rail Road Company (Gauge 3')
O: 057
Inc. July 29, 1881; $40,000
To own: 10 miles, Muskrat Lake (sec 6 T22N R7W) to Clam River (NE 1/4 SE 1/4 sec 33 T22N R7W)
Line opened Jan. 1, 1882, 5.0 miles
Conveyed 1886, to Cody [L. J.] and Moore

N

Nahma & Northern
O: 002, 021
Private logging road
Owned by Bay De Noquet Lumber Co.
Nahma northerly
Line begun ca. 1881; abandoned ca. 1951

Nason, C. F.
O: 041
Private logging road
Near Cedar Springs

National Railroad Passenger Corporation
O: 011, 039, 080
Inc. (Dela. corp)
To operate rail passenger service
Began operations May 1, 1971
Bought April 1, 1976, line Kalamazoo to Indiana state line from Penn Central Transp. Co.
Active corporation

Naubinway Logging Co. (Gauge 3')
O: 049
Private logging road
Mackinac co.

Negaunee and Ishpeming Street Railway Company (E)
P: 052
Inc.(S) July 31, 1891; $100,000; Negaunee
To own: in Ishpeming and Negaunee
Merged May 5, 1892, into Negaunee & Ishpeming Street Ry & Electric

Negaunee & Ishpeming Street Railway and Electric Company (E)
O: 052
Inc.(S) undated, filed May 5, 1892; $100,000; Negaunee
To consolidate: Negaunee & Ishpeming St. Ry and a power co.
Amend Nov. 29, 1892; to increase capital to $150,000
Line opened July 1893
Merged Sept. 30, 1904, into Marquette Co. Gas Light & Traction

Negaunee & Palmer Railroad Company
O: 052
Inc. June 29, 1888; $100,000
To own: 10 miles, Negaunee to Palmer
Control at inc. by Marquette, Houghton & Ontonagon
Apparently transferred to Marquette, Houghton & Ontonagon

Neil, Robert (Gauge 3')
O: 062
Private logging road
Newaygo co.

Nester Logging Railroad
O: unknown
Private logging road

Nevin, D[avid]
O: 001
Private logging tramroad
Near Harrisville

The Newaygo Railroad Company
P: 041, 062
Inc. Feb. 2, 1886; $500,000; Newaygo
To own: 20 miles, Grand Rapids & Indiana at Cedar Springs to Newaygo
Lapsed

Newberry Lumber and Coal Co.
O: 048
Private industrial road
Newberry northeasterly
Bought 1929, line of Charcoal Iron Co. of America
Operations ended 1945

New Buffalo & Lakeside Railroad Company
P: 011
Inc. Dec. 26, 1913; $100,000
To own: 7 miles, Lakeside to New Buffalo then to Indiana state line to connect to line to Michigan City
Sold May 31, 1928, to Riviera Co. (not RR)
Dissolved May 31, 1928

New Mexico Central & Northern Railway Company
P: not Michigan
Inc. Feb. 27, 1882
To own: 250 miles, in New Mexico
Reinc. Feb. 25, 1884
To own: 250 miles, in New Mexico
Amend July 1, 1886; to own: 550 miles, Pueblo, Colo. to White Oaks, N.M. to Corpus Christi, Tex.; capital $8,000,000
Lapsed

The New York Central Railroad Company
O: 003, 005, 006, 008, 009, 011, 012, 013, 014, 016, 019, 020, 023, 026, 030, 032, 033, 038, 039, 040, 041, 044, 046, 050, 056, 058, 060, 063, 065, 069, 072, 073, 074, 075, 078, 079, 080, 081, 082
Inc. April 29, 1914, eff. Jan. 1, 1915; New York City
To consolidate: Lake Shore & Michigan Southern; Detroit, Monroe & Toledo; Kalamazoo & White Pigeon; Northern Central Michigan; New York Central & Hudson River (N.Y. corp.); Detroit & Chicago; Chicago, Indiana & Southern (Ind. and Ill. corp.); Dunkirk, Allegheny Valley & Pittsburg (N.Y. and Penn. corp.); Terminal Ry of Buffalo (N.Y. corp.); Swan Creek Ry of Toledo (Ohio corp.); and Geneva, Corning & Southern (N.Y. and Penn. corp.)
Bought June 11, 1915, Sturgis, Goshen & St. Louis
Leased Feb. 1, 1930, Michigan Central; Cleveland, Cincinnati, Chicago & St. Louis; and Chicago, Kalamazoo & Saginaw
Lease assigned Feb. 1, 1930, of Detroit, Toledo & Milwaukee by Michigan Central
Lease assigned July 1, 1930, of Lansing Manufacturers by Michigan Central
Merged Jan. 12, 1962, eff. Feb. 1, 1968, into Pennsylvania New York Central Transportation Co.

Nicholas, Church and Co.
O: unknown
Private logging road; Greenville

Niles and Buchanan Railway Company (E)
P: 011
Inc.(S) Nov. 12, 1904; $25,000; Niles
To own: from Niles to Buchanan
Merged Feb. 7, 1906, into Southern Michigan Ry

The Niles and South Bend Rail Road Company
P: 011
Inc. April 20, 1869; $36,000; Niles
To own: 4.5 miles, Niles to Indiana state line
Conveyed no date, to Michigan Air Line RR

Nirvana & Luther Railroad Company (Gauge 3')
P: 043
Inc. May 2, 1883; $52,000
To own: 13 miles, Nirvana on Flint & Pere Marquette to Luther
Lapsed

Norfolk and Western Railway Company
O: 046, 058, 081, 082
Chartered Jan. 15, 1896 (Va. corp.)
Consolidated March 1, 1961, eff. Oct. 16, 1964, New York, Chicago & St. Louis
Lease Oct. 16, 1964, of Wabash
Control March 31, 1970, of Wabash RR
Stock exchange June 1, 1982, with Norfolk Southern Corp.
Active corporation

Norfolk Southern Corporation
O: Holding company
Inc. July 23, 1980 (Va. corp.)
Stock exchange June 1, 1982, of Norfolk & Western Ry and Southern Ry
Active corporation

North Branch and Sauble River Railroad Company (Gauge 3')
O: 053
Inc. June 1, 1888; $50,000
To own: 12 miles, North branch Pere Marquette River in sec 21 T18N R15W to sec 5 T19N R15W
Owned by Danaher and Melendy
Lapsed

North Detroit & Chene
[Organizers obtained a franchise in Hamtramck twp., but company apparently never incorporated. Franchise transferred Nov. 1, 1892, to Detroit Suburban.]

North Detroit Electric Railway Company
O: 082
Inc.(S) July 21, 1899; $50,000; Detroit
To build: in Hamtramck twp. and other cities, villages & twps.
Line opened 1900
Amend Dec. 8, 1900; to change office to Hamtramck twp.
Amend Jan. 14, 1901; to change number of directors
Bought June 20, 1901, Detroit, Utica & Romeo
Sold Oct. 10, 1901, to Detroit & Flint

"Northern" line of state of Michigan
P: 019, 025, 034, 041, 044, 070, 074, 078
Enacted March 20, 1837
To own: Palmer or near mouth of Black River, St. Clair co. to either navigable waters of Grand River, Kent co. or on Lake Michigan, Ottawa co.
Rights assigned March 17, 1847, to Port Huron & Lake Michigan

The Northern Central Michigan Rail Road Company
O: 013, 023, 030, 033, 038
Inc. Nov. 11, 1866; $1,500,000
To own: 80 miles, Lansing to Eaton Rapids, Albion, Homer, and Amboy, Hillsdale co.
Rights acquired Jan. 12, 1867, of Amboy, Lansing & Traverse Bay south of Michigan Avenue, Lansing
Amend Sept 1, 1868; to increase directors from 7 to 9
Line opened Jan. 7, 1872, Jonesville to Albion
Line completed Jan. 13, 1873, Jonesville to Lansing
Control 1873, by Lake Shore & Michigan Southern
Leased May 1, 1897, for corp. life, to Lake Shore & Michigan Southern
Merged Jan. 1, 1915, into New York Central

Northern Indiana Railway Company (E)
O: 011
Inc. (Ind. corp.)
Cons. 1930, Southern Michigan Ry
Bankruptcy Dec. 31, 1931
Operations ended May 30, 1934

Northern Iron Rail Road—
P: 052
Inc. Feb. 3, 1862, as Northern Iron Rail Road Company; $200,000
To own: 20 miles, Lake Superior in Marquette twp. to Negaunee twp.
Amend Oct. 1, 1864, as Northern Iron Rail Road Company of Lake Superior; to change capital to $500,000, also number of directors
Lapsed

Northern Lumber Co.
O: 052
Private logging road
Birch

The Northern Michigan Central Railway Company
P: 005, 015, 016, 018, 020, 024, 029, 037, 040, 047, 057, 063, 069, 073, 078
Inc. Aug. 19, 1881; $3,360,000
To own: 210 miles, New Hudson (connection with Toledo, Ann Arbor & Grand Trunk) NWly via Owosso to Mackinaw City
Lapsed

Northern Michigan Power Company
P: not specified
Inc. (Maine corp.) Jan. 2, 1913
To operate street ry in Michigan
No record found of operations

The Northern Michigan Rail Road Company
P: 050, 082
Inc. Feb. 9, 1867; $200,000; Utica
To own: 17 miles, crossing of Detroit & Milwaukee and Grand Trunk rys (now Milwaukee Jct.) to Warren then to Utica
Lapsed

The Northern Michigan Rail Road Company
P: 006, 009, 016, 017, 020, 021, 024, 026, 031, 049, 052, 056, 060, 065, 066, 068, 069, 072, 073, 077
Inc. Nov. 18, 1867; $2,500,000; Detroit
To own: 400 miles, West state line, along S shore Lake Superior Ely to Straits of Mackinac, then to Saginaw
Lapsed

The Northern Michigan Railroad Company
P: 027, 031, 066
Inc. Oct. 12, 1888; $1,000,000
To own: 70 miles, Houghton via Rockland to Watersmeet
Renamed Jan. 23, 1899, as Copper Range

Northern Michigan Railroad Company
P: 017, 049
Inc. April 12, 1901; $1,000,000
To own: St. Ignace to Sault Ste. Marie
Lapsed

Northern Michigan Railway Company
P: 009, 044, 050, 073, 079, 082
Inc. May 26, 1869; $2,000,000
To own: 100 miles, Bay City to Detroit, via Vassar, Columbiaville, Lapeer, Almont, Romeo and Utica
Lapsed

Northern Michigan Traction Company (E)
O: 051
Inc.(S) March 29, 1905; $100,000; Manistee
To own: in Manistee and adjacent territory
Acquired ca. 1905, Manistee, Filer City & East Lake
Merged June 28, 1907, into Manistee Light & Traction

Northern Pacific Railway
Minn. corp.
Leased Jan. 1, 1890, Wisconsin Central Ry
Lease cancelled Sept. 26, 1893, of Wisconsin Central Ry

The Northern Rapid Transit Construction Company
Inc.(Not RR) Aug. 30, 1905

Northland Lumber Co.
O: 031
Private logging road
Pori

North Park Bridge Company
P: 041
Inc. April 4, 1902; $25,000; Grand Rapids
To own: 650 feet, North Park to Walker twp.
Dissolved Sept. 1, 1922, filed Jan. 29, 1923

The North Park Street Railway Company (E)
O: 041
Inc.(S) Aug. 21, 1889; $100,000
To own: in Grand Rapids twp.
Line opened Summer 1890
Amend May 21, 1894; to change number of directors
Conveyance uncertain, but became part of Grand Rapids Ry

Northwest Copper Co.
O: 042
Private mining road
1200 ft, Northwest Mine to stamp mill
Built 1857

Northwestern Cooperage and Lumber Co.
O: 002
Private logging road
Alger co.

The North Western Grand Trunk Railway Company
O: 025, 044, 074
Inc. Aug. 23, 1879; $1,500,000
To reorganize: Port Huron & Lake Michigan at foreclosure
Line acquired at inc., Port Huron to Flint
Merged Jan. 7, 1880, into Chicago & Grand Trunk

Northwestern Land and Lumber Co.
O: 036
Private logging road
Gibbs City

Northwestern Lumber Co.
O: 036
Private logging road

Norwich Mining Co.
O: 066
Private mining tramway
2 miles, mine to stamp mill

O

The Oakdale Park Street Railway Company
P: 041
Inc.(T) Feb. 19, 1889; $5,000; Grand Rapids
To own: in Paris twp., Kent co.
Lapsed

Oakland and Ottawa Rail Road Company
P: 019, 025, 034, 041, 063, 070, 078
Chartered April 3, 1848; $2,500,000
To own: Pontiac via Fentonville to Lake Michigan in Ottawa co.
Act March 20, 1850; authorized Detroit & Pontiac to connect with company
Amend charter March 26, 1851; authorized to issue bonds
Act Feb. 13, 1855; authorized merger into Detroit & Milwaukee
Merged April 19, 1855, into Detroit & Milwaukee

The Oakland Railway Company (E)
O: 063, 082
Inc.(S) Jan. 19, 1895; $50,000; Royal Oak
To own: from Royal Oak, one line to Highland Park and Detroit, another line to Pontiac and Orchard Lake; also lines to Southfield, Franklin, and Orchard Lake, and via Troy Corners and Big Beaver to Rochester
Line opened Feb. 8, 1896
Conveyed Jan. 28, 1897, to Detroit & Pontiac Ry

Ogemaw Springs Railroad
O: 065
Private logging road
Owned by C. H. Plummer
South of Beaver Lake
About 1881

Ohio and Central Michigan Railroad Company
P: 012, 030
Inc. Dec. 1, 1884; $375,000
To own: 25 miles, Coldwater to Ohio state line in sec 12 T9S R3W
Lapsed

Ohio and Grand Haven Railroad Company
P: 003, 008, 013, 023, 030, 039, 070
Inc. Jan. 3, 1873; $2,000,000
To own: 175 miles, Grand Haven to Ohio state line near E line Hillsdale co.
Lapsed, but rights may have been conveyed to Michigan & Ohio Ry

Ohio & Lake Superior Rail Road Company
P: 002, 007, 009, 016, 017, 024, 025, 031, 047, 049, 052, 058, 060, 063, 065, 066, 068, 073, 081, 082
Inc. Nov. 29, 1865; $6,000,000
To own: 700 miles, Toledo, Ohio via Saginaw and Straits of Mackinac to Crow Wing, Minn., with branches to Detroit, Sault Ste. Marie, Marquette, Ontonagon, and Superior City
Lapsed

Ohio & Michigan Interurban Railway Company (E)
P: 058, 081
Inc.(T) Dec. 21, 1908; $1,000,000
To own: 46 miles, Ann Arbor to Ohio state line, via Milan and Petersburg
Renamed Feb. 1, 1909, as Ohio Northern & Michigan

The Ohio & Michigan Railway Company
P: 003, 008, 012, 013, 030, 039
Inc. May 10, 1870; $800,000
To own: 95 miles, Ohio state line in Amboy, Hillsdale co. via Coldwater to Allegan
Merged Dec. 28, 1870, into Mansfield, Coldwater & Lake Michigan

Ohio and Michigan Sand and Gravel Co.
O: 047
Private industrial road
Chilson

Ohio & Michigan Traction Company (E)
P: 058, 081
Inc.(T) June 6, 1903; $1,650,000
To own: 45 miles, Toledo to Ann Arbor
Merged June 24, 1904, into Toledo, Ann Arbor & Detroit

The Ohio & Morenci Railroad Company
O: 046
Inc. Aug. 3, 1933; not given; Morenci (Ohio corp.)
To own: 21 miles, Sylvania twp. (Ohio) via Morenci to Wakefield Corners
Bought no date, part of Toledo & Western
Withdrawn Dec. 28, 1954, from Michigan activity

Ohio & Southern Michigan Railway Company
P: 012, 013, 030, 038, 039, 075
Inc.(S) June 4, 1907; $1,500,000; Hillsdale
To own: South Camden to Jackson; also Camden via Coldwater to Kalamazoo
Lapsed

Ohio Dock Horse Railroad
O: 070
Private logging road
In T6N R14W

Ohio Northern & Michigan Railroad Company
P: 058, 081
Inc.(T) Feb. 1, 1909
To rename Ohio & Michigan Interurban
Lapsed

Ohio, Quincy and Grand Haven Railroad Company
P: 003, 008, 012, 013, 039, 070
Inc. April 3, 1872; $2,000,000
To own: 150 miles, Grand Haven to Quincy
Lapsed

Olivet & South Eastern Railway Company
P: 023
Inc. Sept. 9, 1896, not given
To own: 2.5 miles, Ainger to Olivet
Lapsed

Olivet Railway Company
P: 023
Inc. April 16, 1890; $20,000
To own: 2.33 miles, Olivet to Grand Trunk Olivet station
Lapsed

Onaway & North Michigan Railway Company
O: 071
Inc. Aug. 9, 1901; $50,000; Onaway
To own: 5.5 miles, in and near Onaway
Dissolved Dec. 31, 1930

Onota Charcoal Co.
O: 002
Private lumbering road
Onota south
Built ca. 1890

The Ontonagon and Brule River Railroad Company
O: 066 P: 036
Inc. Sept. 8, 1880; $1,000,000
To own: 80 miles, Ontonagon to intersection Brule River and E line T42N R36W
Amend April 1, 1881; to change number of directors
Line opened Aug. 14, 1882, Ontonagon to 20 mile east
Sold June 20, 1890, to Milwaukee & Northern
Dissolved Jan. 22, 1934

Ontonagon and Flintsteel Railway Company
P: 066
Inc.(T) Aug. 2, 1909; $10,000
To own: sec 25 T52N R40W (Ontonagon Lumber Co.) to sec 3 T51N R39W
Dissolved Dec. 17, 1921

Ontonagon and Montreal River Railroad Company
P: 066
Inc. Feb. 14, 1880; $400,000
To own: 50 miles, Ontonagon River near Rockland SWly to Montreal River
Lapsed

Ontonagon & Southwestern Railway Company
P: 066
Inc. July 30, 1904; $200,000; Ontonagon
To own: 25 miles, Ontonagon to SW corner T50N R43W
Lapsed

Ontonagon and State Line Rail Road Company
P: 027, 066
Inc. June 25, 1856; $2,000,000
To own: 80 miles, Ontonagon to Wisconsin state line
Merged March 27, 1857, into Chicago, St. Paul & Fond du Lac

Ontonagon Fibre Co.
O: 066
Private logging road
Ontonagon

The Ontonagon, Gogebic and Wisconsin Railroad Company
P: 027, 066
Inc. Aug. 26, 1882; $3,000,000
To own: 70 miles, Ontonagon to Wisconsin state line S of Lake Gogebic
Lapsed

Ontonagon, Gogebic & Wisconsin State Line
See The Ontonagon, Gogebic and Wisconsin Railroad Company

Ontonagon Railroad Company
O: 066
Inc.(T) Oct. 24, 1904; $1,000; Ontonagon
To own: 1325 feet in Ontonagon
Amend April 6, 1906; to own: 6.65 miles, easterly terminus C. V. McMillan logging RR (Halfway Creek in sec 12 T51N R41W) to Wly terminus at Chicago, Milwaukee, St. Paul & Pacific (in sec 25 T52N R40W) and increase capital to $30,000
Amend Dec. 21, 1914; to increase number of directors
Abandoned May 7, 1931
Dissolved May 21, 1936

Ontonagon Southern Railroad Company
P: 027, 031, 066
Inc. Sept. 4, 1907; $400,000
To own: 50 miles, Wisc. state line in R37W Nly and NWly to Mass
Lapsed

The Osceola, Lake and Wexford Railroad Company
O: 043, 083
Inc. May 18, 1892; $80,000
To own: 10 miles, Olga, Lake co. to Hoxeyville, Wexford co.
Abandoned

The Oscoda and AuSable Street Railway Company (H)
P: 035
Inc.(S) Oct. 27, 1890; $30,000; Oscoda
To own: Oscoda to AuSable
Lapsed

Oscoda Salt and Lumber Co.
O: 035
Private logging tramway; AuSable
AuSable, at mill and dock
Bought 1876, line from Loud, Gay & Co.
Sold 1887, line to H. M. Loud & Sons

Osterhout and Fox Lumber Co.
O: 043
Private logging road
Deer Lake

Ottawa Beach and Southern Railway Company (E)
P: 058
Inc.(S) Sept. 15, 1905; $100,000; Monroe
To own: in Erie, Lasalle and Monroe twps.
Merged Oct. 25, 1906, into Toledo, Ottawa Beach & Northern

Ovid and Traverse Bay Rail Road Company
P: 019, 029
Inc. April 17, 1882; $1,000,000
To own: 28 miles, Ovid to Alma
Lapsed

Owosso and Big Rapids Railroad Company
P: 029, 037, 054, 059, 078
Inc. June 26, 1869; $2,000,000
To own: 81 miles, Owosso, via Shiawassee, Gratiot, Montcalm, Isabella and Mecosta cos., to Big Rapids
Renamed Dec. 22, 1871, as Owosso & North Western

Owosso & Corunna Electric Company (E)
O: 078
Inc.(S) Jan. 29, 1898; $150,000; Owosso
To own: in Owosso, Corunna and Caledonia twp. (and consolidate Owosso & Corunna Traction and a power company)
Acquired March 14, 1898, Owosso & Corunna Traction Co.
Receivership begun April 30, 1908
Sold 1911, to Michigan United Rys

The Owosso and Corunna Electric Street Railway Company (E)
P: 078
Inc.(S) Oct. 5, 1895; $50,000; Owosso
To own: street ry in Owosso and Corunna
Renamed Nov. 20, 1895, as Owosso & Corunna Traction

Owosso & Corunna Street Railway Company (E)
P: 078
Inc.(S) Sept. 2, 1891; $50,000; Owosso
To own: Owosso to Corunna
Foreclosure sale Nov. 25, 1895, to Owosso & Corunna Traction

Owosso & Corunna Traction Company (E)
O: 078
Inc.(S) Nov. 20, 1895; $150,000; Owosso
To rename: Owosso & Corunna Electric Street Ry
Bought Nov. 25, 1895, Owosso & Corunna Street
Line opened 1895
Merged March 14, 1898, into Owosso & Corunna Electric Co.

The Owosso and North Western Railroad Company
P: 010, 018, 019, 029, 037, 043, 051, 054, 067, 078, 083
Inc. Dec. 22, 1871; $2,000,000
To rename: Owosso & Big Rapids; line 150 miles, Owosso via Alma to Frankfort
Sold 1883, to Toledo, Ann Arbor & North Michigan

The Owosso City Electric Railway Company (E)
P: 078
Inc.(S) July 21, 1890; $50,000
To own: in Owosso and adjoining towns
Lapsed

Oxford & Almont Div. of Toledo and Port Austin RR
See Toledo & Port Austin

Oxford and Port Austin Rail Road Company
P: 032, 044, 063, 079
Inc. July 25, 1879; $672,000
To own: 84 miles, Oxford to Port Austin
Renamed Dec. 30, 1879, as Pontiac, Oxford & Port Austin

P

Packard, Alfred H., Jr.
O: 080
Private logging horse road
4 miles, sec 2 T2S R17W to sec 28 T1S R17W, about 1880
3 miles, Covert to sec 8 T2S R17W, about 1880

Painter, Parks and Thompson
O: 070
Private logging road
13 miles, Spring Lake
Built 1883-84

Paint River Railway Company
O: 036
Inc. May 28, 1890; $120,000
To own: 15 miles, Chicago & North Western at Crystal Falls to Hemlock Mine
Control at inc. by Chicago & North Western
Line completed 1891, Crystal Falls to Hemlock Mine
Sold June 4, 1891, to Chicago & North Western

Palmer, Nichols and Co.
See Paris & Pere Marquette River

The Palmyra and Jacksonburgh rail-road Company
O: 046 P: 038, 081
Chartered March 28, 1836; $300,000
To own: 46 miles, Palmyra via Tecumseh and Clinton to Jacksonburgh
Control at chartering by Erie & Kalamazoo
Amend charter June 22, 1837; authorized state to issue stock to assist company
Resolution April 6, 1838; state to require additional security for loan
Line opened Aug. 9, 1838, Palmyra to Tecumseh
Act April 1, 1840; authorized state to loan iron
Act April 9, 1841; state to release loan security if part of line conveyed to state
Act April 13, 1841; repealed Act of April 1, 1840
Act Feb. 11, 1842; authorized means of repaying state loan
Sold 1844, to state of Michigan for use by "Southern" line
Act Feb. 22, 1845; provided for completion to Tecumseh
Res. March 3, 1845; authorized to let contracts for completion
Act May 9, 1846; authorized sale of company to Michigan Southern
Resolution March 21, 1849; authorized state to settle with company

Pampa Land Co.
O: 031
Private logging road
Winona

The Paris & Pere Marquette River Railroad Company (Gauge 3' 1")
O: 043, 054, 062
Inc. June 15, 1882; $48,000
To own: 12 miles, Paris to West line sec 2 T16N R12W
Owned by Palmer, Nichols & Co.
Line opened, July 19, 1884, Upper Paris west 16 miles
Abandoned 1889

Patten Timber Co.
O: 036
Private logging road
Amasa

Patterson Rail Road Company
O: 034
Inc. Sept. 21, 1870; $50,000
To own: 2 miles, Patterson Mills to Kiddville
Evidently donated July 18, 1872, to Detroit, Lansing & Lake Michigan

Paw Paw Rail Road Company (Gauge 3' after conveyance)
O: 080
Inc. April 25, 1857; $20,000; Paw Paw
To own: 4.28 miles, Paw Paw to Michigan Central RR in Antwerp twp.
Act Feb. 11, 1859; authorized specific fares
Line completed Sept. 1867, Lawton to Paw Paw
Conveyed Sept. 9, 1886, to Toledo & South Haven
Merged March 7, 1887, into Toledo & South Haven

The Paw Paw Valley Railway Company
P: 011, 039, 080
Inc. Oct. 27, 1869; $400,000
To own: 50 miles, Schoolcraft, via Lawton, Paw Paw, Lawrence, Hartford, Watervliet, and Benton Harbor, to St. Joseph
Lapsed

Pelton's Logging Road (Gauge 3' 6")
O: 043
Private logging road
Lake Co.

Peninsula—
O: 021, 052 P: 007, 031, 055, 066
Inc. Feb. 3, 1862, as The Peninsula Railroad Company (of Michigan); $1,000,000
To own: 125 miles, Marquette twp. on Lake Superior to mouth of Menominee River
Amend May 23, 1863, as Peninsula Rail Road Company of Michigan; to own: 150 miles, Wisc. state line near mouth of Menominee River via Little Bay de Noquet to iron mines in Marquette co. and to Marquette; capital $2,500,000
Amend June 20, 1863, as Peninsula Railroad Company of Michigan; to rename
Amend June 30, 1863; to change route, (1) from Wisc. state line near mouth of Menominee River via Little Bay de Noquet to Ontonagon, (2) branch from main line to Marquette, (3) branch from main line to Portage Lake, Houghton co.; capital $4,000,000
Line completed Sept. 1864, Escanaba to Negaunee
Merged Oct. 21, 1864, into Chicago & North Western

The Peninsula Branch Railroad Company of Michigan
P: 052
Inc. Oct. 17, 1865; $150,000
To own: 10 miles, village of Harvey to a point on Chicago & North Western RR
Lapsed

Peninsular—
O: 013, 014, 023, 033, 039
Inc. Aug. 13, 1865, as The Peninsular Railway Company; $500,000; Battle Creek
To own: 44 miles, Battle Creek to Lansing
Amend Jan 3, 1868, as The Peninsular Railway; $900,000; to consolidate: Peninsular Railway Extension Co.
Line opened Dec. 1869, Battle Creek to Lansing
Amend undated, filed April 30, 1870, as Peninsular Railway Company; to consolidate: Peninsular RR of Indiana and Peninsular Ry of Illinois
Line completed Oct. 13, 1873, Lansing to Valparaiso, Ind.
Merged July 30, 1878, into Chicago & Lake Huron

Peninsular Railway Extension Company
P: 013, 014, 039
Inc. Oct. 23, 1866; $750,000; Battle Creek
To own: 64 miles, Battle Creek to state line, Milton twp., Cass co.
Merged Jan. 3, 1868, into Peninsular Ry

Penn Central Company
O: 003, 005, 006, 008, 009, 011, 012, 013, 014, 015, 016, 019, 020, 023, 024, 026, 028, 030, 032, 033, 038, 039, 040, 041, 044, 046, 050, 054, 056, 058, 059, 061, 063, 065, 067, 069, 070, 072, 073, 075, 078, 079, 080, 081, 082, 083
Inc. Feb. 28, 1968
To rename Pennsylvania New York Central Transp. Co.
Conveyed Oct. 1, 1969, rail operations to Penn Central Transp. Co.
Bankruptcy started June 21, 1970
Active company

The Penn Central Corporation
O: holding company and non-railroad business
Inc. Oct. 24, 1978
To rename Penn Central Transportation Co.
Acquired at inc. rail properties of Penn Central Transportation; Penndel Co.; Pennsylvania Co.; Connecting Ry; Cleveland, Cincinnati, Chicago & St. Louis; and Michigan Central

Amend June 15, 1979, to restate articles
Sold Sept. 1980, part to state of Michigan
Amend filed Dec. 7, 1981, to restate articles
Cons. Dec. 31, 1981, Cleveland, Cincinnati, Chicago & St. Louis
Sold Sept. 1982, part to state of Michigan
Sold Feb. 15, 1984, part to state of Michigan
Sold ca. 1984, part to Southern Michigan RR Society
Active corporation

Penn Central Transportation Company
O: *See* Penn Central Co.
Inc. Oct. 1, 1969 (Dela. corp.)
Owned at inc. Penndel Co. and Pennsylvania Co.
Acquired Oct. 1, 1969, rail operations of Penn Central Co.
Bankruptcy entered June 21, 1970
Conveyed April 1, 1976, part rail assets to Consolidated Rail and Grand Trunk Western
Conveyed April 1, 1976, line (Kalamazoo-Ind. state line) to National Rail Passenger Corp.
Renamed Oct. 24, 1978, Penn Central Corp.

Penndel Co.
O: Holding company
Inc. Nov. 20, 1953 (Dela. corp.)
Owned at inc. by Pennsylvania RR
Cons. Dec. 1, 1953, Grand Rapids & Indiana
Cons. Oct. 13, 1954, eff. Jan. 1, 1955, Detroit Union RR Depot & Station
Sold 1963, line (Missaukee Jct. to Lake City and Falmouth) to Cadillac & Lake City
Owned Feb. 28, 1968, by Penn Central Co.
Cons. July 1, 1969, Battle Creek & Sturgis
Cons. Aug. 1, 1969, Detroit, Toledo & Milwaukee; Lansing Manufacturers; and Lansing Transit
Owned Oct. 1, 1969, by Penn Central Transportation Co.
Conveyed Oct. 24, 1978, rail properties to Penn Central Corp.

Pennsalt Railroad Company
O: 082
Inc. Oct. 8, 1901; $25,000; Wyandotte
To own: 1 mile, Detroit River at Ecorse-Monguagon twp. line to Detroit Southern RR
Renamed Aug. 17, 1908, as Wyandotte Southern

Pennsylvania Company
O: Holding company
Inc. April 7, 1870 (Penn. corp.)
Owned at inc. by Pennsylvania RR
Control 1928, of Wabash
Owned Feb. 28, 1968, by Penn Central Co.
Owned Oct. 1, 1969, by Penn Central Transportation Co.
Control transferred March 31, 1970, of Wabash to Norfolk & Western
Conveyed Oct. 24, 1978, rail properties to Penn Central Corp.

Pennsylvania-Detroit Railroad Company
O: 058, 082
Inc. Feb. 20, 1917; $5,000,000
To own: 25 miles, Ohio state line near Ann Arbor RR to Carleton; 26 miles Carleton to Third St., Detroit; 26 miles from near River Rouge around Detroit to Detroit River
Control at inc. by Pennsylvania RR
Line opened 1922
Leased Jan. 1, 1923, 999 years, to Pennsylvania RR
Merged July 1, 1924, into Pennsylvania, Ohio & Detroit

Pennsylvania New York Central Transportation Company
O: Organizing company
Inc. Jan. 12, 1962, eff. Feb. 1, 1968
To consolidate: Pennsylvania RR and New York Central
Line acquired Feb. 1, 1968, constituent companies, but retained predecessor names until renaming (next line)
Renamed Feb. 28, 1968, as Penn Central Co.

The Pennsylvania, Ohio and Detroit Railroad Company
O: 058, 082
Inc. June 7, 1924, eff. July 1, 1924
To consolidate: Pennsylvania-Detroit and other non-Mich. cos.
Control, at inc., by Pennsylvania RR
Leased April 29, 1926, to Pennsylvania RR
Merged Oct. 26, 1955, into Connecting Ry

The Pennsylvania Railroad Company
O: 003, 005, 015, 016, 024, 028, 039, 040, 041, 054, 057, 058, 059, 061, 067, 069, 070, 072, 075, 082, 083
Chartered Feb. 25, 1847, filed Aug. 5, 1922 (Penn. corp.)
Control April 7, 1870, at inc., of Pennsylvania Co.
Owned July 22, 1901, at inc., Connecting Ry
Control Feb. 20, 1917, at inc., of Pennsylvania-Detroit
Leased Jan. 1, 1923, Pennsylvania-Detroit
Control June 7, 1924, at inc., of Pennsylvania, Ohio & Detriot
Leased April 29, 1926, Pennsylvania, Ohio & Detroit
Merged Jan. 12, 1962, eff. Feb. 1, 1968, into Pennsylvania New York Central Transp. Co.

Pentwater and Manistee Railroad Company
O: Reorganizing company
Inc. Oct. 31, 1899; Grand Rapids
To rename Pere Marquette RR (1899 corp.)
Reinc. Nov. 1, 1899, as Pere Marquette RR

The Peoples Railway Company of Detroit
P: 082
Inc.(S) May 25, 1901; $25,000; Detroit
To own: in Detroit
Lapsed

Pere Marquette and Big Rapids Railroad Company
P: 043, 053, 054, 062
Inc. May 6, 1892; $360,000
To own: 45 miles, Ludington to Big Rapids
Lapsed

Pere Marquette International Bridge Company
P: 082
Inc. Feb. 23, 1903; $500,000
To own: 10 miles, bridge over Detroit River from near S end of Grosse Isle to Amherstburg, Ont.
Lapsed

Pere Marquette

Pere Marquette—
O: 003, 005, 008, 009, 010, 011, 015, 018, 019, 023, 024, 025, 026, 028, 029, 032, 033, 034, 037, 040, 041, 043, 044, 045, 047, 051, 053, 054, 056, 057, 058, 059, 061, 062, 063, 064, 067, 070, 073, 074, 076, 079, 080, 081, 082
Inc. Sept. 20, 1899, as Pere Marquette Railroad Company; $150,000; Detroit
To own: 33 miles, Pentwater to Manistee
Control at inc. jointly by : Flint & Pere Marquette; Detroit, Grand Rapids & Western; and Chicago & West Michigan
Renamed Oct. 31, 1899, as Pentwater & Manistee
Reinc. Nov. 1, 1899, as Pere Marquette Railroad Company; to consolidate Flint & Pere Marquette; Detroit, Grand Rapids & Western; Chicago & West Michigan; capital $28,000,000
Received Dec. 6, 1899, Flint & Pere Marquette
Received Dec. 7, 1899, Chicago & West Michigan and Detroit, Grand Rapids & Western
Control Jan. 1900, of Saginaw, Tuscola & Huron
Lease Feb. 1900, 999 years, of Saginaw, Tuscola & Huron
Control 1900, of Grand Rapids, Belding & Saginaw
Bought Oct. 1, 1900, Muskegon Lake
Control March 26, 1903, at inc., of Harbor Beach & Port Hope
Control March 30, 1903, at inc., of Pere Marquette of Indiana
Bought April 1, 1903, South Haven & Eastern
Amend May 6, 1903; to increase number of directors
Bought May 6, 1903, Milwaukee, Benton Harbor & Columbus; Grand Rapids, Belding & Saginaw; Sanilac; Bay City Belt Line; and Saginaw, Tuscola & Huron
Bought May 7, 1903, Benton Harbor, Coloma & Paw Paw Lake
Bought Aug. 6, 1903, of Huron & Western
Lease Dec. 17, 1903, of Lake Erie & Detroit River (Canadian corp.)
Bought Dec. 21, 1903, Harbor Beach & Port Hope
Amend July 9, 1904; to change number of directors
Control July 1904, of Chicago, Cincinnati & Louisville (Ind. corp.)
Control June 21, 1905, of Toledo Ry & Terminal (Ohio corp.)
Control July 16, 1906, at inc., of Marlborough RR
Lease April 15, 1907, part [Lawton-South Haven] to Kalamazoo, Lake Shore & Chicago
Consolidated Aug. 12, 1907, Pere Marquette of Indiana
Control Sept. 1907, by Cincinnati, Hamilton & Dayton
Control ended Dec. 4, 1907, of Toledo Ry & Terminal
Control ended May 1912, by Cincinnati, Hamilton & Dayton
Leased cancelled May 31, 1916, of part to Kalamazoo, Lake Shore & Chicago Ry
Reinc. March 12, 1917, as Pere Marquette Railway Company; $68,675,000; to reorganize Pere Marquette RR
Foreclosure sale March 15, 1917, to Pere Marquette Ry
Bought March 26, 1917, Chicago & North Michigan
Amend May 18, 1927; to restate routes and mileage
Amend May 18, 1927; to restate capital structure
Control May 1929, by Chesapeake & Ohio
Control Dec. 1931, of Manistee & Northeastern
Amend May 17, 1932; to change number of directors
Merged Feb. 19, 1946, eff. April 1, 1947, into Chesapeake & Ohio

Pere Marquette Railroad Company of Indiana
O: 011
Inc. Feb. 23, 1903 (Ind. corp.)
To own: 46 miles, New Buffalo to Ind.-Ill. state line near Hammond, Ind.
Control at inc. by Pere Marquette
Line opened Dec. 15, 1903, Alfred to Porter, Ind.
Merged Aug. 12, 1907, into Pere Marquette
Foreclosure sale March 27, 1917, to Pere Marquette Ry

The Pere Marquette Transportation Company
Inc.(Not RR) Sept. 2, 1896
To carry cars, freight and passengers on Great Lakes
Owned by Flint & Pere Marquette
Apparently dissolved April 5, 1906

The Peters Manistee Train Railway Company
O: 051, 053
Inc.(T) Aug. 3, 1883; $25,000
Office: Manistee
To own: 4 miles, sec 13 T20N R17W to Manistee Lake sec 19 T21N R17W
Amend Oct. 24, 1885; to change capital to $50,000
Abandoned

The Peters Train Railway Company
O: 051
Inc.(T) March 9, 1878; $50,000
To own: 6 miles, sec 27 T21N R15W to Manistee River sec 35 T22N R15W
Abandoned 1882

Petoskey & Harbor Springs Railroad Company
P: 024
Inc. July 30, 1901; $64,000
To own: 8 miles, Petoskey to Harbor Springs
Lapsed

The Petoskey and Harbor Springs Railway Company
P: 024
Inc.(S) Sept. 17, 1901; $25,000; Petoskey
To own: in Petoskey, Harbor Springs, and adjoining areas
Lapsed

The Petoskey, Harbor Springs and Northern Railway Company
P: 024
Inc.(S) Sept. 25, 1900; $25,000
To own: not stated
Lapsed

The Petoskey, Harbor Springs and Shore Railway Company
P: 024
Inc.(S) Sept. 26, 1899; $25,000
To own: in Petoskey, Harbor Springs, and adjoining territory
Dissolved Sept. 25, 1900

Pickeral Lake & Muskegon River Railroad
O: 062
Private logging road
Owned by Ryerson, Hills & Co.
2.5 miles, Pickeral Lake to Newaygo
Built 1878

The Pinconning Railroad Company
O: 009, 026
Inc. April 30, 1879; $200,000
To own: 20 miles, SE corner sec 19 T17N R5E to Tittabawassee River in sec 12 T17N R1E, and to rename Glencoe, Pinconning & Lake Shore
Line acquired at inc., Pinconning to west
Renamed Nov. 18, 1880, as Saginaw Bay & Northwestern

Piqua Handle and Manufacturing Co.
O: 052
Private logging road
Michigamme

Pittsburgh and Lake Superior Railway Company
P: 052
Inc. Sept. 5, 1884; $600,000
To own: 5 miles, Palmer Nly to Negaunee
Lapsed

Platt and Miller (Gauge 3' 6")
O: 001
Private logging road; Detroit
6 miles, Alcona westward
Built 1880

The Pleasant Bay Railway Company
P: 058
Inc. Feb. 1898; $100,000
To own: 10 miles, Ohio state line in Erie twp. to mouth of Otter twp.
Renamed March 16, 1899, as Detroit & Toledo Shore Line

Plummer, C. H.
O: 065
Private logging road
6 miles, Edwards Lake
Built 1878
———
Owned Ogemaw Springs RR

Pontiac and Detroit Railway, President, Directors and Company of the
P: 063, 082
Chartered July 31, 1830; $100,000; Pontiac
To own: Pontiac to Detroit
Lapsed

Pontiac and Flint Electric Railway Company (E)
P: 025, 063
Inc.(T) Nov. 26, 1900; $50,000; Saginaw
To own: 30 miles, Pontiac to Flint via Drayton Plains, Waterford, Clarkston, Springfield, and Grand Blanc
Dissolved April 24, 1901

Pontiac and Genesee Railroad Company
P: 025, 063
Chartered May 15, 1846; $500,000
To own: Pontiac to Flint
Amend charter March 30, 1848; to increase capital to $1,500,000
Lapsed

Pontiac and Orchard Lake Street Rail Road Company (E)
P: 063
Inc.(S) Oct. 21, 1889; $50,000; Pontiac
To own: street railroad
Lapsed

Pontiac and Oxford Rail Road Company
P: 063
Inc. May 13, 1879; $112,000
To build 14 miles, Pontiac to Oxford
Lapsed

The Pontiac and Southern Railroad Company
P: 063, 082
Inc. March 7, 1883; $240,000
To own: 30 miles, Pontiac to Wayne
Lapsed

The Pontiac and Sylvan Lake Railway Company (E)
O: 063
Inc.(T) July 8, 1895; $50,000; Pontiac
To own: 10 miles, in Pontiac and adjoining towns
Line opened Oct. 1, 1895
Sold March 31, 1899, to Detroit & Northwestern

Pontiac Belt Railroad Company
P: 063
Inc. Jan. 25, 1923; $80,000
To own: 6.5 miles, sec 3 Bloomfield twp. Nly to sec 2 Pontiac twp. thence Wly to sec 13 Waterford twp
Dissolved March 30, 1941

Pontiac, Orion & Detroit Railway Company (E)
P: 063
Inc.(S) July 13, 1900
To own: Pontiac to Lake Orion and Oxford
Lapsed

The Pontiac, Oxford and Northern Railroad Company
O: 032, 044, 063, 079
Inc. Sept. 19, 1889; $1,000,000
To reorganize Pontiac, Oxford & Port Austin
Line acquired at inc., Pontiac to Caseville
Amend Sept. 17, 1902, to reduce number of directors
Control Dec. 1, 1910, by Grand Trunk Western
Merged Nov. 1, 1928, into Grand Trunk Western

Pontiac, Oxford and Port Austin Railroad Company
O: 032, 044, 063, 079
Inc. Dec. 30, 1879; $800,000
To rename Oxford & Port Austin; and build 100 miles, Pontiac via Oxford to Port Austin
Amend Sept. 24, 1881; to change line to be Pontiac to Caseville; capital $1,500,000
Line completed Oct. 8, 1883, Pontiac to Caseville
Foreclosure sale, June 5, 1889, to Pontiac, Oxford & Northern

Portage Lake and Keweenaw Railroad Company
P: 031, 042
Inc. Oct. 28, 1868; $200,000
To own: 25 miles, Portage Lake to Calumet Mine, then to Allouez Mine, then to Cliff Mine
Lapsed

Portage Lake & Manistee River (Gauge 3' 1")
O: 020
Private logging road
Owned by Salling-Hanson Lumber Co.
Sec 8 T26N R4W to sec 31 T27N R4W
Built 1883

Portage Lake & Muskegon River Railroad (Gauge 3')
O: 020
Private logging road
Owned by D. A. Blodgett and Byrne

Portage Lake Mining Co.
O: 031
Private mining road
Mine to top of hill
Built 1865

Portage Lake Railway (Gauge 3' 1/2")
O: unknown
Private logging road

Portage Lake Train Railway Company
P: 031
Inc.(T) Aug. 13, 1865
To own: Portage Lake, through Houghton, to Grand Portage Copper Mines
Lapsed

Portage Railroad Company
P: 031
Inc. July 30, 1888; $100,000
To own: 6 miles, sec 28 T53N R32W to sec 17 T53N R32W with branch to stone quarry
Lapsed

Port Huron and Detroit Railroad Company
O: 074
Inc. Sept. 1, 1917; $15,000; Port Huron
To own: 14 miles, Port Huron to Marine City
Control at inc. by Thomas L. Handy
Line completed Aug. 1, 1918, Marysville to Marine City
Sold Dec. 1984, to Chesapeake & Ohio

Port Huron & Gratiot Street Railway Copany (H)
O: 074
No inc. articles located
Line opened Oct. 8, 1866
Merged April 5, 1877, into Port Huron Ry

Port Huron & Indiana Railway Company
O: Reorganizing company
Inc. Nov. 19, 1900; $1,000,000
To reorganize Michigan lines of Chicago & Grand Trunk
Merged Nov. 20, 1900, into Grand Trunk Western

Port Huron and Lake Michigan Rail Road Company
O: 025, 044, 074 P: 019, 034, 041, 070, 078
Chartered Jan. 30, 1847; $2,000,000; Port Huron
To own: Port Huron to Lake Michigan near mouth of Grand River
Rights received March 17, 1847, of "Northern" line of state of Michigan
Amend charter April 7, 1851; to extend completion dates
Rechartered Feb. 13, 1855
To own: Port Huron to Lake Michigan at or near mouth of Grand River; capital $8,000,000; boat operation authorized
Bought June 26, 1862, Port Huron & Milwaukee, at foreclosure
Line opened Nov. 1869, Port Huron to Emmet
Line completed Dec. 12, 1871, Port Huron to Flint
Merged July 30, 1878, into Chicago & Lake Huron
Foreclosure sale June 21, 1879, to North Western Grand Trunk

Port Huron & Lexington Railway Company
P: 073, 074, 076, 079
Inc. May 3, 1894; $200,000
To own: 20 miles, Port Huron to Lexington
Renamed Jan. 17, 1899, as Port Huron, Lexington & Western

Port Huron and Milwaukee Railway Company
P: 025, 044, 074, 078
Inc. Nov. 29, 1855; $4,000,000; Port Huron
To own: 90 miles, Port Huron to Detroit & Milwaukee Ry in Shiawassee co.
Act Feb. 5, 1857; authorized to issue stock in Great Britain
Act Jan. 29, 1859; authorized sale of company to Detroit & Milwaukee
Foreclosure sale, June 26, 1862, to Port Huron & Lake Michigan

Port Huron and Northern Railway Company (E)
P: 074
Inc.(S) Feb. 29, 1912; $100,000; Detroit
To own: Port Huron to Lexington and Croswell
Dissolved May 18, 1922

Port Huron and Northwestern Railway Company (Gauge 3' until 1899, then standard)
O: 032, 044, 073, 074, 076, 079 P: 009, 050, 082
Inc. March 21, 1878; $400,000; Port Huron
To own: 100 miles, Port Huron to Port Austin
Line opened May 12, 1879, Port Huron to Croswell
Amend Jan. 9, 1880, as The Cass City Branch of the Port Huron and Northwestern Railway Company; to add: branch 80 miles, Kingsley via Brockway Center and Cass City to Caseville; capital added $320,000
Amend Nov. 27, 1880; to add lines: 45 miles, Marlette to Bay City; and 55 miles, Port Huron to Detroit; capital added $400,000
Amend March 2, 1881; to add line: 46 miles, Marlette to East Saginaw; capital added $184,000
Amend March 22, 1882; to add line: 36 miles, Palms to Port Austin; capital added $144,000
Amend Sept. 13, 1882; to consolidate: Port Huron & Southwestern; capital $1,000,000
Line completed Dec. 11, 1882, Port Huron to Port Austin
Amend March 9, 1883; to increase number of directors
Sold April 1, 1889, to Flint & Pere Marquette
Foreclosure sale March 28, 1917, to Pere Marquette

The Port Huron and Owosso Railroad Company
P: 025, 044, 074, 078
Inc. March 1, 1869; $1,000,000
To own: Owosso, via Flint and Lapeer, to Port Huron
Lapsed

Port Huron and Port Austin Electric Railway Company (E)
P: 032, 074, 076
Inc.(S) July 21, 1899; $25,000; Detroit
To own: Port Huron to Port Austin, Port Hope, Harbor Beach, Forestville, Lexington, Port Sanilac, and various twps.
Lapsed

Port Huron and Saginaw Valley Railroad Company
P: 044, 073, 074, 079
Inc. Jan. 13, 1873; $1,000,000
To own: 100 miles, Port Huron to Saginaw River
Lapsed

Port Huron and St. Clair River Railroad Company
P: 074
Inc. Oct. 16, 1890; $200,000
To own: 20 miles, Port Huron to Marine City
Lapsed

Port Huron and Southwestern Railway Company (Gauge 3')
P: 044, 074
Inc. Jan. 27, 1882; $160,000
To own: 32 miles, Port Huron to Almont
Merged Sept. 13, 1882, into Port Huron & Northwestern

Port Huron Electric Railway Company (E)
O: 074
Inc.(S) Aug. 4, 1886; $25,000; Port Huron
To buy Port Huron Ry
Acquired at inc., Port Huron Ry
Conveyed May 19, 1892, to City Elect Ry of Port Huron (1892 corp)

Port Huron, Lexington & Western Railway Company
P: 009, 044, 073, 074, 079
Inc. Jan. 17, 1899
To rename Port Huron & Lexington, and to build Port Huron to Saginaw City and Bay City
Lapsed

Port Huron Railroad Tunnel Company
P: 074
Inc. Oct. 8, 1886; $1,000,000
To own: 1.5 mile tunnel under St. Clair River
Merged Nov. 9, 1886, into St. Clair Tunnel Co.

Port Huron Railway Company (H, E)
O: 074
Inc.(S) April 5, 1877; $50,000; Port Huron
To buy City RR and Port Huron & Gratiot Street
Acquired at inc. City RR and Port Huron & Gratiot Street
Control April 11, 1887, at inc., of Gratiot Electric Ry
Conveyed Aug. 4, 1886, to Port Huron Electric

The Port Huron St. Clair and Marine City Railway Company (E)
O: 074
Inc.(S) April 12, 1899; $300,000; Port Huron
To own: Port Huron to Marine City
Control at inc. by City Electric of Port Huron (1892 corp.)
Control July 1900, by Detroit & Port Huron Shore Line
Amend Feb. 5, 1923; to change office to Highland Park

Port Huron Southern Railroad Company
O: 074
Inc. Jan. 11, 1900; $50,000; Port Huron
To own: 6 miles, Port Huron southerly to St. Clair River
Control at inc. by Thomas L. Handy
Line completed Jan. 1901
Disposition uncertain
Dissolved April 13, 1923

Port Sheldon and Grand Rapids railroad company
P: 041, 070
Chartered Dec. 30, 1837; $250,000
To own: from Pigeon Lake on Lake Michigan to Kent in Kent co.
Amend charter April 10, 1839; to extend completion date, confer other rights
Lapsed

Potter, W[illiam] H. and E[dward] K.
O: 004
Private logging tramway
In Alpena, mill to dock
Used ca. 1878

Potts, J[ohn] E.
O: 060, 068
Private logging road
Bear Lake

Potts, J[ohn] E., Salt and Lumber Co. (Gauge 3')
O: 068
Private logging road; McKinley
14 miles, McKinley southwesterly
Built 1884
Transfer 1887, to Potts Logging Ry

The Potts Logging Railway Company (Gauge 3')
O: 001, 035, 060, 065, 068
Inc.(T) July 27, 1887; $50,000
To own: 50 miles, north bank AuSable River in sec 15 T26N R4E to north line Oscoda co., also from same beginning to Damon, with branches as needed
Acquired at inc., line of J. E. Potts Salt & Lumber Co.
Amend Aug. 23, 1888; to own: 150 miles, Potts post office to north line of Montmorency co., branch Potts to Damon, branch Potts to AuSable
Sold July 15, 1891, to Au Sable & Northwestern

Pryor, James, and Son
O: 031
Private logging road; Houghton

Q

Quay, D., and Son
O: 049
Private logging road
Moran

Quincy and Torch Lake Railroad Company (Gauge 3')
O: 031
Inc. June 27, 1888; $50,000; Calumet
To own: 8 miles, Quincy Mine to shore of Torch Lake in sec 23 T55N R33W
Owned by Quincy Mining Co.
Amend Nov. 21, 1888; to shorten route to 6 miles, same termini
Dissolved Feb. 23, 1927
Converted no date, to private ore road
Abandoned

Quincy Mining Co.
O: 031
Private mining incline road
0.4 mile, rockhouse to mill
Built 1879
——
Owned Quincy & Torch Lake

Quinnesec & Western Railway Company
O: 055 P: 022
Inc. April 6, 1905; $120,000; Menominee
To own: 7 miles, Everett to Wisconsin state line at Menominee River in sec 25 T37N R29W; also 8 miles, Quinnesec via Iron Mountain to Menominee River on west boundary of Breitung twp.
Line completed Dec. 1904, Everett to Menominee River
Sold June 14, 1905, to Wisconsin & Michigan

R

Rail-Tex Corporation
Texas holding corp.
Control of Mid-Michigan and Michigan Shore

Raisin River Railroad Company
P: 058
Inc. Nov. 20, 1900; $50,000; Detroit
To own: 3 miles, Maybee to Raisin River Stone Quarry
Lapsed

The Rapid Railroad Company (E)
O: 050, 074 P: 082
Inc. Jan. 5, 1898; $1,000,000
To own: 48 miles, Clinton twp., Macomb co. to Port Huron
Amend Dec. 31, 1912; to change route, 63 miles, Gratiot Ave. at Detroit city limits to Port Huron
Control July 1900, by Detroit & Port Huron Shore Line
Abandoned

The Rapid Railway Company (E)
O: 050, 074, 082
Inc.(S) Feb. 28, 1894; $250,000; Detroit
To own: in Michigan
Line opened July 14, 1895, Detroit city limits to Mt. Clemens
Control July 1900, by Detroit & Port Huron Shore Line
Amend March 8, 1901; to change office to New Baltimore
Amend Feb. 5, 1923; to change office to Highland Park
Amend Feb. 26, 1924; to extend corporate life
Abandoned

"Rapid Railway System"
Operating name used for properties controlled by Detroit & Port Huron Shore Line

Rapid River and Eastern Rail Road Company (Gauge 3')
O: 005, 040
Inc. Aug. 13, 1892; $120,000
To own: 15 miles, Torch Lake (sec 7 T28N R8W) to Kalkaska
Abandoned

The Ravenna and Spring Lake Narrow Gauge Rail Road Company (Gauge 3')
P: 061
Inc. Oct. 1879; $20,000
To own: 5 miles, sec 36 T9N R16W to T9N R15W
Lapsed

The Reed's Lake Electric Railway Company of Grand Rapids (E)
P: 041
Inc.(S) April 11, 1890; $50,000
To own: in Grand Rapids and Grand Rapids twp.
Lapsed

Reeds Lake, Grand Rapids and Soldiers Home Suburban Railway Company (H)
P: 041
Inc. May 14, 1889; $60,000; Grand Rapids
To own: 7.5 miles, Reeds Lake via Grand Rapids to Soldiers Home
Lapsed

Reeds Lake Street Railway Company (H)
O: 041
Inc.(S) July 2, 1880; $25,000
To buy Grand Rapids & Reeds Lake Street Ry
Bought July 20, 1880, Grand Rapids & Reeds Lake Street Ry
Sold 1886, to Street Ry of Grand Rapids

Republic Branch Railroad Company
P: 022, 052
Inc. Sept. 21, 1881; $500,000
To own: 50 miles, Montreal River in sec 9 T39N R30W to line of Marquette, Houghton & Ontonagon RR

Amend June 10, 1887; to add: 10 mile branch to Duluth, South Shore & Atlantic near Champion
Merged Dec. 7, 1886, into Milwaukee & Northern

Riverdale and Lake Michigan Railroad Company
P: 010, 029, 067, 083
Inc. Nov. 28, 1884; $1,740,000
To own: 116 miles, Riverdale to Frankfort
Lapsed

River Raisin and Grand River railroad Company
P: 023, 034, 038, 041, 046, 058
Chartered Aug. 22, 1835; $1,500,000
To own: 150 miles, River Raisin to Grand Rapids
Act Feb. 3, 1858; authorized right-of-way over state land
Lapsed

River Raisin and Lake Erie rail-road company
O: 058 P: 046
Chartered March 28, 1836; $300,000
To own: LaPlaisance Bay on Lake Erie via Monroe and Dundee to Erie & Kalamazoo RR at Blissfield, plus two branches
Resolution March 21, 1837; authorized state to begin proceedings against company
Act March 31, 1840; authorized state to purchase completed road
Sold Sept. 17, 1840, to state of Michigan for "Southern" line
Act April 9, 1841; ordered investigation of property
Resolution April 13, 1841; property bought by state became part of "Southern" line

River Rouge Railway Company (E)
P: 082
Inc.(S) May 16, 1905; $25,000; Ecorse twp.
To own: in Wayne co.
Amend Feb. 6, 1923; to change office to Highland Park
Lapsed

Riverside Park Railway Company of Saginaw, Michigan (E)
P: 073
Inc.(S) June 30, 1894; $25,000
To own: Saginaw City to Spaulding twp.
Lapsed

Robinson Lumber Co.
O: 068
Private logging road
Oscoda co.

Rochester, Almont and Northern Railroad Company (Gauge 3')
P: 044, 050, 063
Inc. June 5, 1879; $100,000
To own: 20 miles, Rochester via Lakeville to Almont
Lapsed

Rochester and Romeo Railroad Company
P: 050, 063
Inc. Aug. 9, 1869; $50,000
To own: 6 miles, Rochester to Romeo
Lapsed

The Rochester and St. Clair Railway Company
P: 050, 063
Inc. Jan. 9, 1900; $150,000; Detroit
To own: 18 miles, Rochester to Lenox twp.
Lapsed

Rockland Mining Co.
O: 066
Private mining tramway
Rockland Mine to stamp mill
Built 1856

Rogers, Bartlett R.
O: 011
Private logging horse road
Sec 11 to sec 3 T7S R20W

The Romeo and Almont Rail Road Company
P: 044, 050
Inc. Jan. 28, 1870; $100,000
To own: 9 miles, Romeo to Almont
Lapsed

The Romeo and Mt. Clemens Railroad Company
P: 050
Chartered April 16, 1833; $150,000
To own: 15 miles, Mt. Clemens to Romeo
Lapsed

The Romeo and Western Railroad Company
P: 033, 038, 047, 050, 063, 081
Inc. July 11, 1870; $200,000
To build 14 miles, Romeo to Oxford
Amend July 11, 1871; to increase capital $2,000,000; modify route to 95 miles, Romeo, via Lakeville, Oxford, Clarkston, to Jackson
Lapsed

Roscommon Lumber Co.
O: 072
Private logging road; Grand Haven
(also known as Houghton Lake & Barker City)
13 miles, Houghton Lake to Barker City (T21N R1W)
Built 1882

——

O: 018
In T20N R3W

Rosebush Ranch Co.
O: 036
Private logging road
Amasa

Roxburgh, James
O: 043
Private logging road
Forman to Forman's Mill

Ruddock, Nuttal and Co. (Gauge 3')
O: 051
Private logging road; Chicago
4 miles, Stronach to sec 5 T20N R16W
Built 1882

Rumsey Lumber Co. (Gauge 3' 1")
O: 062
Private logging road
3 miles, in T16N R11W
Built 1884

Russell Street, St. Aubin Avenue and Detroit and Milwaukee Junction Railway Company (H)
O: 082
Inc.(S) Aug. 5, 1874; $30,000
To own: Detroit to Grand Trunk RR in Hamtramck twp., and to buy St. Aubin Avenue Street Ry
Line opened Nov. 25, 1874
Sold Sept. 6, 1876, to Detroit City Ry

Ryerson [Martin], Hills [Charles] and Co.
Owned Pickeral Lake & Muskegon River

———

O: 062
Private logging road
Sec 1 T12N R13W to sec 21 T13N R13W

S

Saginaw & Bay City Railway Company (E)
P: 009, 073
Inc.(T) Oct. 25, 1894; $500,000
To own: 15 miles, Saginaw to Bay City
Lapsed

The Saginaw and Bay City Rapid Transit Company (E)
P: 009, 073
Inc.(S) Jan. 23, 1895; $100,000
To own: Saginaw to Bay City
Lapsed

Saginaw and Clare County Railroad Company
O: 018
Inc. Sept. 4, 1877; $160,000; East Saginaw
To build 20 miles, Clare via Farwell to Lake George and branch to lake in sec 17 T19N R4W
Control at inc. by Flint & Pere Marquette
Line completed Sept. 30, 1880, Clare to Harrison
Amend March 21, 1883; to own: 30 miles, Clare via Farwell to sec 13 T20N R3W; capital $500,000
Merged Nov. 2, 1888, into Flint & Pere Marquette

Saginaw and Flint Railway Company (E)
O: 025, 073
Inc.(T) Aug. 20, 1908; $100,000; Flint
To own: 24 miles, Saginaw to Flint, via Bridgeport, Frankenmuth, Clio and Mt. Morris; with branch, Frankenmuth to Vassar
Control at inc. by Commonwealth Power Ry & Light
Acquired at inc. Detroit, Flint & Saginaw
Line opened Nov. 23, 1908
Amend Sept. 28, 1909; to increase capital to $1,000,000
Rail assets conveyed March 19, 1914, to Michigan Ry
Dissolved March 19, 1914

Saginaw and Frankenmuth Railway Company (E)
P: 073
Inc.(T) Aug. 16, 1898; $50,000; Saginaw
To own: 14 miles, Saginaw to Frankenmuth
Lapsed

The Saginaw and Genesee railroad company
P: 025, 073
Chartered March 22, 1837; $400,000
To own: 40 miles, Saginaw City to line of Northern in Genesee co.
Amend charter April 20, 1839; authorized borrowing; extended completion dates
Lapsed

Saginaw and Grand Rapids Railroad Company
O: 029, 059 P: 041
Inc. Oct. 22, 1878; $1,000,000; Saginaw
To own: 70 miles, St. Louis to Grand Rapids
Control at inc., by Saginaw Valley & St. Louis
Line opened March 1879, St. Louis to Alma
Leased no date, to Saginaw Valley & St. Louis
Merged Feb. 1, 1896, eff. Jan. 1, 1897, into Detroit, Grand Rapids & Western
Saginaw and Lansing Rail Road Company
P: 033, 073, 078
Inc. Aug. 9, 1855; $1,250,000
To own: 56 miles, East Saginaw to Lansing
Lapsed

Saginaw & Montcalm Railway Company (Gauge 3')
P: 029, 059, 073
Inc. May 20, 1871; $200,000
To own: 46 miles, East Saginaw, via St. Louis and Alma, to Elm Hall
Lapsed

Saginaw and Mount Pleasant Railroad Company (Gauge 3', standard ca. 1888)
O: 037, 056
Inc. Feb. 11, 1879; $100,000; East Saginaw
To own: 14 miles, Coleman to Mt. Pleasant
Control at inc. by Flint & Pere Marquette
Line completed Dec. 15, 1879, Coleman to Mt. Pleasant
Merged Nov. 2, 1888, into Flint & Pere Marquette

Saginaw and St. Clair River Rail Road Company
P: 044, 073, 074, 079
Inc. March 10, 1870; $3,000,000
To own: 100 miles, East Saginaw to St. Clair
Lapsed

Saginaw and Southwestern Railway Company
P: 019, 073, 078
Inc.(T) May 20, 1905; $50,000; Saginaw
To own: 50 miles, Saginaw to St. Johns, via St. Charles, Chesaning, Oakley and Elsie
Renamed July 8, 1905, Saginaw Bay South Western

The Saginaw and Western Railroad Company
O: 029, 059
Inc. June 5, 1883; $675,000
To reorganize Chicago, Saginaw & Canada (line 50 miles, St. Louis to Howard City)
Control at inc. by Detroit, Lansing & Northern
Line acquired at inc., St. Louis to Lakeview
Leased July 1, 1883, 30 years, to Detroit, Lansing & Northern
Line completed Aug. 1886, St. Louis to Howard City
Merged Feb. 1, 1896, eff. Jan. 1, 1897, into Detroit, Grand Rapids & Western

Saginaw Bay and Northwestern Rail Road Company
O: 006, 009, 026
Inc. Nov. 18, 1880; $300,000
To buy Pinconning RR and build line, Mt. Forest to sec 22 T19N R3E and sec 18 T18N R3E to sec 2 T18N R3E
Line acquired at inc., Pinconning to west
Leased Feb. 15, 1883, to Michigan Central
Control May 28, 1883, by Michigan Central
Conveyed July 13, 1901, to Jackson, Lansing & Saginaw

Saginaw-Bay City Railway and Light Company
O: Holding company
Inc.(Not RR) 1903
Articles not located
Control, no date, of Bay Cities Consolidated, Saginaw Valley Traction, Bay City Traction & Electric, InterUrban Ry, and three utility companies

Saginaw-Bay City Railway Company (E)
O: 009, 073
Inc.(T) Dec. 30, 1909; $2,600,000; Bay City
To rename Bay City Traction & Electric (and buy Saginaw Valley Traction)
Acquired no date, InterUrban Ry and Saginaw Valley Traction
Conveyed March 19, 1914, to Michigan Ry
Bankruptcy Aug. 10, 1921
Dissolved Sept. 22, 1923

Saginaw Bay South Western Railway Company
P: 019, 034, 073, 078
Inc.(T) July 8, 1905; $100,000; Saginaw
To rename Saginaw & Southwestern; to own: 100 miles, Bay City to Woodbury, via Saginaw, St. Charles, Chesaning, Oakley, St. Johns, Elsie, and Portland
Lapsed

Saginaw City Street Railway
See Saginaw Street Ry (1864 corp.)

Saginaw Consolidated Street Railway Company of Saginaw, Michigan (E)
O: 073
Inc.(S) Oct. 29, 1894; $150,000; Saginaw
To own: Saginaw to Saginaw and Jamestown twps.
Acquired at inc., line of undetermined company
Merged Jan. 3, 1899, into Saginaw Valley Traction

Saginaw Lumber & Salt Co.
O: unknown
Private logging road; Saginaw

Saginaw, Owosso & Lansing Railroad Company
P: 019, 033, 073, 078
Inc. Dec. 28, 1906; $600,000
To own: 60 miles, Saginaw via Owosso to Lansing
Lapsed

Saginaw Southern Railway Company
P: 073
Inc.(T) Jan. 4, 1900; $50,000; Saginaw
To own: 30 miles, Saginaw to Chesaning
Amend May 14, 1900; to change route: 50 miles, Saginaw to Durand, via Chesaning
Lapsed

Saginaw Street Railroad Company (H)
P: 073
Inc.(S) Feb. 20, 1868
To own: in Saginaw
Lapsed

Saginaw Street Railway Company (H)
[Articles written Saginaw City Street Railway Company, but word "City" lined out before filing.]
O: 073
Inc.(S) April 21, 1864; $50,000
To own: in Saginaw City
Line opened April 4, 1865
Disposition uncertain

Saginaw Street Railway Company (H)
O: 073
Inc.(S) Feb. 2, 1886; $30,000; Saginaw
To own: Saginaw to East Saginaw and adjoining townships
Disposition uncertain

Saginaw Suburban Railway Company (E)
P: 009, 025, 073
Inc.(T) March 3, 1898; $100,000; Saginaw
To own: 30 miles, Saginaw to Flint
Amend Aug. 15, 1898; to change route: 50 miles, Bay City via Saginaw to Flint
Amend Sept. 14, 1898; to extend to Bay City suburbs
Lapsed

Saginaw Transit Company (E)
O: 073
Inc.(S) Aug. 9, 1923; $1,479,000; Saginaw
To own: in Saginaw
Acquired Nov. 1, 1923, part of Michigan RR
Operations ended Oct. 9, 1931

Saginaw, Tuscola and Huron Railroad Company (Gauge 3', standard in 1891)
O: 032, 073, 079
Inc. Feb. 14, 1881; $600,000
To own: 60 miles, East Saginaw to Bad Axe and Caseville
Line opened April 4, 1882, Saginaw to Sebewaing
Line completed July 1, 1886, Saginaw to Bad Axe
Amend May 21, 1891; to change to standard gauge
Control Jan. 1900, by Pere Marquette
Leased Feb. 1900, to Pere Marquette
Sold May 6, 1903, to Pere Marquette

Saginaw Union Street Railway Company (H)
O: 073
Inc.(S) Oct. 4, 1887; $50,000
To own: in Saginaw, East Saginaw, and adjoining territory
Amend Aug. 3, 1889; to increase capital to $200,000
Disposition uncertain

Saginaw Valley and St. Louis Railroad Company
O: 029, 073
Inc. May 16, 1871; $300,000
To own: 34 miles, East Saginaw to St. Louis via Saginaw
Line completed Jan. 1, 1873, Paines to St. Louis
Amend July 22, 1878; to own: 91 miles, extend from St. Louis to Grand Rapids and branch St. Louis to Mt. Pleasant; $1,000,000
Control Oct. 23, 1878, at inc., of Saginaw & Grand Rapids
Control 1879, by Detroit, Lansing & Northern
Amend June 14, 1882; to own: 63 miles, East Saginaw via Alma to Grand Rapids; 22 miles, St. Louis to Mt. Pleasant; and 6.5 miles, Alma to Ithaca
Operated Dec. 28, 1882, Ithaca & Alma
Leased no date, to Detroit, Lansing & Northern
Merged Jan. 1, 1897, into Detroit, Grand Rapids & Western

Saginaw Valley Traction Company (E)
O: 009, 073
Inc.(S) Jan. 3, 1899; $1,100,000; Saginaw
To acquire Saginaw Consol. Street, InterUrban, and Union Street
Acquired at inc., 3 companies above
Control 1903, by Saginaw-Bay City Ry & Light
Transferred ca. 1910, to Saginaw-Bay City Ry

St. Aubin Avenue Street Railway Company (H)
P: 082
Inc.(S) Aug. 26, 1873; $30,000
To own: Detroit to junction of Detroit & Milwaukee and Grand Trunk RRs (now Milwaukee Jct.)
Renamed Aug. 5, 1874, as Russell St., St. Aubin & etc.

The St. Clair and Chicago Air Line Railroad Company
O: 047, 050, 063
Inc. July 20, 1872; $1,700,000
To rename St. Clair River, Pontiac & Jackson
Line leased at inc., Ridgeway to Romeo
Foreclosure sale April 8, 1875, to Michigan Air Line Ry

The St. Clair and Romeo Rail-road Company
P: 050, 074
Chartered March 26, 1836; $100,000
To own: 26 miles, Palmer in St. Clair co. to Romeo
Amend charter March 6, 1840; to extend completion dates
Lapsed

St. Clair & Western Railroad Company
O: 050, 074
Inc. Sept. 24, 1906; $120,000
To reorganize Michigan Midland & Canada
Control at inc. by Canada Southern Ry
Line acquired at inc., St. Clair to Ridgeway
Abandoned Sept. 23, 1932 (ICC approval)
Dissolved Dec. 27, 1949

St. Clair City Railway Company (H)
[Articles originally written St. Clair City Street Railway Company, but word "Street" lined out before filing]
P: 074
Inc.(S) June 10, 1869; $10,000; St. Clair
To own: in St. Clair
Lapsed

The St. Clair River, Pontiac and Jackson Railroad Company
O: 047, 050, 074 P: 038, 063
Inc. April 5, 1872; $1,200,000
To own: 120 miles, St. Clair River in St. Clair co. via Pontiac to Jackson

Leased April 13, 1872, in perpetuity, part Michigan Air Line RR
Line acquired by lease, Ridgeway to Romeo
Renamed July 20, 1872, as St. Clair & Chicago Air Line

St. Clair Tunnel Company
O: 074
Inc. Nov. 9, 1886; $2,000,000; Detroit and Montreal
To consolidate Port Huron RR Tunnel and St. Clair Frontier Tunnel (Canadian company)
Control at inc. by Grand Trunk Ry of Canada
Line completed Oct. 24, 1891
Merged March 31, 1958, into Canadian National
Dissolved March 31, 1958

St. Helen, Houghton Lake & Western
See Henry Stephens & Co.

The St. Helen's Lake and Southern Railroad Company (Gauge 3' 6")
O: 072
Inc. Jan. 9, 1883; $72,000
To own: 18 miles, St. Helen's station to center sec 17 T21N R2W
Abandoned

The St. Ignace, Sault Ste. Marie and Northern Railway Company
P: 017, 049
Inc. March 24, 1888; $250,000; Sault Ste. Marie
To own: 25 miles, St. Ignace to point on Minneapolis, Sault Ste. Marie & Atlantic between Trout Lake and Pine River
Lapsed

St Joe River Traction Company (E)
P: 011, 014, 039, 080
Inc.(S) Oct. 4, 1904; $750,000; Benton Harbor
To own: Indiana state line, via Cassopolis, to Benton Harbor, with branch to Kalamazoo
Merged Jan. 23, 1906, into Benton Harbor-St. Joe Ry & Light

The St. Joseph and Benton Harbor Street Railway Company (H)
O: 011
Inc.(S) Sept. 24, 1881; $25,000; St. Joseph
To own: St. Joseph to Benton Harbor and adjoining townships
Reinc.(S) Nov. 10, 1884
To own: St. Joseph to Benton Harbor
Amend Jan. 19, 1889; to increase capital to $100,000
Amend April 12, 1892; to change number of directors
Amend May 3, 1892; to restate articles
Line opened 1892
Merged Oct. 10, 1900, into Benton Harbor & St. Joseph Elect. Ry & Light

St. Joseph and Benton Harbor Street Train Railway Company (H)
P: 011
Inc.(T) Dec. 31, 1888; $50,000
To own: in Benton Harbor and St. Joseph
Lapsed

The St. Joseph and Lake Shore Street Railway Company (H)
P: 011
Inc.(S) Feb. 10, 1894; $75,000; St. Joseph
To own: St. Joseph to St. Joseph and Lincoln townships
Lapsed

St. Joseph County Division of the Toledo & South Haven Railroad
See Toledo & South Haven

St. Joseph Division of the Toledo & South Haven Railroad
See Toledo & South Haven

St. Joseph Rail Road Company
P: 011
Chartered April 2, 1850; $500,000
To own: St. Joseph to point on Michigan Central RR
Lapsed

St. Joseph River Rail Road Company
P: 011, 014
Inc. Oct. 18, 1867; $500,000
To own: 30 miles, St. Joseph via Berrien Springs and Niles to Ontwa twp., Cass co.
Lapsed

St. Joseph, South Bend & Southern Railroad Company
O: 011
Inc. Jan. 20, 1899 (Ind. corp.); $750,000
To buy at foreclosure Indiana & Lake Michigan
Leased Feb. 23, 1900, 50 years, to Indiana, Illinois & Iowa RR
Lease assigned, March 15, 1905, to Michigan Central
Disposition uncertain

St. Joseph Terminal Railroad Company
P: 011
Inc. May 15, 1909; $50,000
To own: 5 miles, S city limits St. Joseph to Benton Harbor, and to buy RR property of F. P. Graves
Lapsed

St. Joseph Valley Rail Road Company
O: 075 P: 011, 014
Chartered April 3, 1848; $1,000,000
To own: St. Joseph via Cassopolis to any point in St. Joseph co.

Line opened 1855, Constantine to Three Rivers
Act March 15, 1861; to extend completion dates & authorize use of state land
Act March 17, 1863; to extend completion dates
Leased Nov. 21, 1864, part of Michigan Southern & Northern Indiana
Act March 18, 1865; to authorize purchase of company by Schoolcraft & Three Rivers RR
Sold Aug. 14, 1869, to Schoolcraft & Three Rivers RR

St. Joseph Valley— (Gauge 3')
O: 011
Inc. Jan. 27, 1880, as St. Joseph Valley Rail Road Company; $140,000
To own: 14 miles, Berrien Springs to Indiana state line in Bertrand twp.
Amend Dec. 2, 1881; to own: 30 miles, St. Joseph to Indiana state line; capital $300,000
Amend June 2, 1884, as The St. Joseph Valley Railroad Company; to consolidate South Bend & St. Joseph (Ind. corp.); $400,000
Line completed Sept. 1, 1888, Buchanan to Berrien Springs
Foreclosure sale, May 7, 1889
Reinc. July 29, 1889, as St. Joseph Valley Railway Company
To reorganize St. Joseph Valley RR; capital $300,000
Merged April 6, 1897, into Milwaukee, Benton Harbor & Columbus

The St. Louis, Sturgis and Battle Creek Railroad Company
O: 012, 013, 075
Inc. Jan. 3, 1884; $1,000,000
To own: 40 miles, Battle Creek to Sturgis
Line completed Jan. 1889, Battle Creek to Sturgis
Receivership begun March 14, 1889, William K. Ackerman, receiver
Foreclosure sale, Sept. 11, 1889, to Battle Creek & Sturgis

The St. Mary's and Minneapolis Railroad Company
P: 002, 007, 017, 027, 031, 036, 048, 052, 066, 077
Inc. Oct. 8, 1881; $10,000,000
To build 300 miles, St. Marys River to Montreal River
Lapsed

The Saint Mary's Falls Railway Company
P: 017
Inc. Aug. 13, 1887; $100,000
To own: 5 miles, St. Marys Straits in sec 10 T47N R1W to mouth of Mission Creek
Lapsed

Sainte Marie Union Depot Company
O: 017
Inc.(UD) March 12, 1900; $75,000; Sault Ste. Marie
To operate station in Sault Ste. Marie
Control at inc., 50% by Duluth, South Shore & Atlantic, 50% by Minneapolis, St. Paul & Sault Ste. Marie
Line completed Jan. 1, 1902
Conveyed Sept. 1, 1952, to DSS&A and MStP&SSM
Dissolved Feb. 2, 1953

Salina Street Railway Company (H)
P: 073
Inc.(T) Nov. 23, 1863
To own: Washington & Mackinaw Sts. N to N twp. line
Lapsed

Salling-Hanson Lumber Co.
O: 020
Private logging road
Crawford co.

———

Owned Portage Lake & Manistee River

Sanilac Railroad Company
O: 076
Inc. Oct. 11, 1901; $56,000
To own: 7 miles, Carsonville to Sanilac Center
Line completed June 1, 1903, Poland to Sandusky
Merged May 6, 1903, into Pere Marquette

Sands, Louis (Gauge 3' 2")
O: 051
Private logging road
Manistee co.

Saugatuck and South Haven Railway Company
P: 003, 080
Inc. Dec. 3, 1898; $176,000
To own: 22 miles, Saugatuck to South Haven
Lapsed

The Saugatuck, Douglas and Lake Shore Railway Company (E)
O: 003
Inc.(S) Feb. 12, 1898; $120,000; Saugatuck
To own: Saugatuck to Douglas and adjoining towns
Line opened Aug. 19, 1899
Conveyed Feb. 24, 1900, to Grand Rapids, Holland & Lake Michigan

Sault Ste. Marie and Lake Huron Railway Company
P: 017, 049
Inc. Nov. 16, 1916; $300,000; Sault Ste. Marie
To own: 36 miles, Sault Ste. Marie via Pickford to Les Cheneaux Islands
Lapsed

Sault Ste. Marie and Marquette Railroad Company
P: 017
Inc. Feb. 5, 1880; $300,000
To own: 35 miles, Sault Ste. Marie to line of Detroit, Mackinac & Marquette
Merged Dec. 22, 1886, into Duluth, South Shore & Atlantic

Sault Ste. Marie and Southwestern Railway Company
P: 002, 017, 022, 036, 048, 052, 077
Inc. Feb. 3, 1885; $12,000,000
To own: 250 miles, Sault Ste. Marie to Wisconsin state line in T43N R37W
Merged April 29, 1885, into Canada, LaCrosse & Southwestern

Sault Ste. Marie Bridge Company
O: 017
Inc. Feb. 19, 1881; $100,000
To own: 5 miles, bridge from point in Chippewa Co. to Canadan bank, St. Marys River·
Amend Feb. 28, 1887
To consolidate Sault Ste. Marie Bridge (Canadian corp.)
Control March 16, 1887, 25% Duluth, South Shore & Atlantic, 25% Minneapolis, Sault Ste. Marie & Atlantic, 50% Canadian Pacific Ry
Line completed 1888
Active corporation

Sault Ste. Marie Railway Company
P: 017
Inc. Nov. 5, 1897; $100,000
To own: 6 miles in Sault Ste. Marie
Lapsed

The Sault Ste. Marie Street Railway Company (H)
O: 017
Inc.(S) Aug. 17, 1887; $25,300; Sault Ste. Marie
To own: in Sault Ste. Marie
Line opened 1888
Conveyed 1901, to Trans-St. Mary's Traction

The Sault Ste. Marie Terminal Railway Company
P: 017
Inc.(UD) Oct. 14, 1901; $100,000; Sault Ste. Marie
To own: in Sault Ste. Marie
Dissolved Feb. 13, 1941

Sault Ste. Marie Traction Company (E)
O: 017
Inc.(S) Jan. 11, 1919; $200,000; Sault Ste. Marie
To buy Trans-St Mary's Traction
Acquired at inc., Trans-St. Mary's Traction
Amend May 24, 1928; to reduce capital to $25,000
Operations ended July 8, 1931

Sawyer, Goodman Co.
O: 066
Private logging road
Ontonagon

Schneider and Brown Lumber Co.
O: 027
Private logging road
Jack Spur

The Schoolcraft and Three Rivers Rail Road Company
O: 039, 075
Inc. June 1, 1855; $130,000; Schoolcraft
To own: 13 miles, at or near Schoolcraft to at or near Three Rivers
Act March 18, 1865; authorized purchase of St. Joseph Valley RR
Line completed May 3, 1867, Schoolcraft to Three Rivers
Consolidated Aug. 14, 1869, St. Joseph Valley RR
Merged Aug. 14, 1869, into Kalamazoo & White Pigeon

Scott and Howe Lumber Co.
O: 027
Private logging road
Ironwood

Seaman & Webster (Gauge 3')
O: 043
Private logging road
Chase

Shaw Box, Crane and Hoist Co.
O: 061
Private industrial road
Muskegon

The Shelby and Belle River Rail-road Company
P: 044, 050
Chartered March 26, 1836; $100,000
To own: 25 miles, Shelby, Macomb Co. to Belle River, Lapeer co.
Lapsed

The Shelby and Detroit Railroad Company
O: 050, 082
Chartered March 7, 1834; $100,000
To own: 23 miles, Shelby in Macomb co. to Detroit
Amend charter Aug. 25, 1835; to extend commencement date
Amend charter May 4, 1846; to own: Detroit via Utica and Romeo to Port Huron; extended completion date; increased capital to $1,000,000
Amend charter March 18, 1848; authorized renaming as Detroit, Romeo & Port Huron; extended completion date

Amend charter April 7, 1851; authorized lease to Detroit & Pontiac; changed S terminus
Amend charter Feb. 13, 1855; to extend completion dates; increase capital to $2,000,000 (as Detroit, Romeo & Port Huron)
Operations ended ca. 1845

Sheldon and Co.
O: 017
Private logging road
Chippewa co.

The Shiawassee and Vernon Rail Way Company
P: 078
Inc. Aug. 11, 1856; $10,000; Shiawasseetown
To own: Shiawasseetown to Vernon
Lapsed

Sibley Quarry Co.
O: 082
Private industrial road
Sibley

Silkman [John H.] and Hart
O: 005
Private lumbering tramway
5 miles, Torch Lake to Grand Traverse Bay (sec 24 T31N R9W)
Built 1869

Slaght, N.
O: 059
Private logging road; Greenville
In Montcalm co.

Smith & Hull (Lumber Co.)
O: 010
Private logging road
Frankfort

Smith, Benjamin F.
O: 035
Private mining wooden road
Alabaster (T21N R7E); quarry to dock
Built mid-1860s

Smith [George E.] Lumber Co.
O: 040
Private logging road
Kalkaska

Smith, H.
O; 059
Private logging road
3 miles, Lakeview to Townline Lake in T12N R8W

Solvay Process Co.
O: 082
Private industrial road
Sibley

Soo-Detour Railway Company
P: 017
Inc. May 8, 1901; $500,000
To own: 53 miles, Sault Ste. Marie to Detour
Lapsed

Soo Line Corporation
O: Holding company
Inc. 1984 (Minn. corp.)
Control at inc., by Canadian Pacific Ry
Exchange Dec. 31, 1984, stock for Soo Line RR
Bought Feb. 19, 1985, The Milwaukee Road, Inc.
Conveyed Jan. 1, 1986, rail assets of The Milwaukee Road, Inc. to Escanaba & Lake Superior
Active (non-Mich.) holding company

Soo Line Railroad Company
O: 002, 007, 017, 021, 027, 031, 048, 049, 052, 055, 066, 077
Inc. Dec. 30, 1960, eff. Jan. 1, 1961
To rename Duluth, South Shore & Atlantic
Control at inc., by Canadian Pacific Ry
Consolidated Jan. 1. 1961, Wisconsin Central and Minneapolis, St. Paul & Sault Ste. Marie
Line acquired at inc., constituent lines
Exchange Dec. 31, 1984, stock for Soo Line Corp.
Sold Oct. 11, 1987, part (Lake States Transp. Div.) to Wisconsin Central Ltd.
Active (non-Mich.) corporation

Soo-Snows Railway Company (E)
P: 017, 049
Inc.(S) Nov. 15, 1916; $250,000; Sault Ste. Marie
To own: in Sault Ste. Marie
Lapsed

Soo Street Railway Company (E?)
P: 017
Inc.(S) April 12, 1887; $100,000; Sault Ste. Marie
To own: Sault Ste. Marie and vicinity
Lapsed

South Bend and Benton Harbor Railroad Company
P: 011
Inc. Jan. 20, 1886; $500,000
To own: 27 miles, Indiana state line to Benton Harbor
Lapsed

South Bend & St. Joseph Railroad Company
Inc. not found (Ind. corp.)
Merged June 2, 1884, into St. Joseph Valley

South Bend and Southern Michigan Railway Company (E)
P: 011
Inc.(S) Feb. 12, 1901; $25,000; Niles
To own: Indiana state line to Niles to St. Joseph and Benton Harbor
Cons. Sept. 8, 1902, South Bend Northern (Ind. corp.)
Line opened Aug. 3, 1903
Merged Feb. 7, 1906, into Southern Michigan

South Bend, Niles and Saint Joseph Railroad Company
P: 011
Inc. Aug. 8, 1884; $300,000
To own: 32 miles, St. Joseph via Berrien Springs and Niles to Indiana state line
Lapsed

South Boardman (Lumber Co.) (Gauge 3')
O: 040
Private logging road
Kalkaska co.

South Branch Railroad
See Butters and Peters

South-Eastern and North-Western Transcontinental Railway Company
P: 011, 014
Inc. Dec. 6, 1890; $500,000; Benton Harbor
To own: 50 miles, mouth of St. Joseph River to Indiana state line via Dowagiac
Lapsed

South Eastern Michigan Railway Company
P: 046, 058, 082
Inc. May 16, 1871; $600,000
To own: 65 miles, Monguagon twp., Wayne co. to Ohio state line in Medina twp., Lenawee co.
Merged July 11, 1871, into Chicago & Canada Southern

"Southern" line of state of Michigan
O: 030, 046, 058 P: 011, 012, 014, 075
Enacted March 20, 1837
To own: navigable waters of River Raisin via Monroe to New Buffalo
Acquired Sept. 15, 1840, La Plaisance Bay Harbor Co.
Accepted Sept. 17, 1840, line of River Raisin & Lake Erie
Line opened Nov. 23, 1840, Monroe to Adrian
Line completed Sept. 25, 1843, Monroe to Hillsdale
Bought 1844, Palmyra & Jacksonburgh
Sold Dec. 28, 1846, to Michigan Southern

Southern Electric Railway Company (E)
P: 009, 073
Inc.(T) Oct. 9, 1911; $200,000; Flint
To own: 17 miles, Saginaw to Bay City
Lapsed

Southern, Kent and Pacific Railroad Company
P: not given
Inc. March 12, 1981; $70,000; Grand Rapids
To operate RR in United States
Status not known

The Southern Michigan Railroad Society
O: 046
Inc.(Not RR) Aug. 10, 1982; Adrian
Bought ca. 1984, part (Lenawee Jct.-Clinton) from Penn Central Transp.
Active non-profit corporation

Southern Michigan Railway Company (E)
O: 011
Inc. Feb. 7, 1906; $2,000,000; South Bend
To consolidate Niles & Buchanan and South Bend & Southern Michigan
Line completed May 16, 1906
Merged 1930, into Northern Indiana Ry
Dissolved July 1, 1930

The Southern Michigan Traction Company (E)
P: 003, 039, 041
Inc.(S) filed Aug. 22, 1901; $50,000; Grand Rapids
To own: Grand Rapids to Kalamazoo
Lapsed

South Grand Rapids Street Railway Company (E)
O: 041
Inc.(S) Nov. 1, 1888; $25,000; Grand Rapids
To own: in Grand Rapids, Wyoming twp., and Paris twp.
Amend Sept. 16, 1890; to increase number of directors
Apparently conveyed ca. 1906, to Grand Rapids Ry

South Haven & Eastern Railroad Company
O: 080
Inc. May 18, 1894; $300,000
To own: 37 miles, South Haven to Lawton via Hartford, Lawrence and Paw Paw
Acquired at inc., Toledo & South Haven
Sold April 1, 1903, to Pere Marquette

The South Haven and Lake Shore Railway Company (E)
P: 003, 080
Inc. May 10, 1901; $176,000; South Haven
To build 22 miles, South Haven to Saugatuck
Lapsed

South Haven and Paw Paw Lake Electric Railway Company (E)
P: 011, 080
Inc.(S) Dec. 17, 1900; $150,000; South Haven
To own: South Haven to Paw Paw Lake
Lapsed

South Haven Traction Company (E)
P: 080
Inc.(T) July 1, 1905; $800,000; South Haven
To own: 37 miles, Saugatuck via South Haven to Watervliet
Lapsed

South Lyons and Northern Railway Company
P: 025, 047, 063, 081
Inc. May 3, 1890; $400,000
To own: 40 miles, Leland via South Lyons to Flint
Lapsed

The South Park and Crystal Springs Street Railway Company (E)
P: 041
Inc.(T) Nov. 1, 1889; $50,000
To own: 2 miles, in Grand Rapids
Amend July 7, 1891; to extend line
Lapsed

Southwestern Michigan Railroad Company
O: 080 P: 003, 008, 039
Inc. March 28, 1978; $50,000
To operate RR in Allegan, Barry and Kalamazoo counties
Rail operations under name of Kalamazoo, Lake Shore & Chicago Railroad
Bought Aug. 18, 1986, line (Hartford-Paw Paw) from CSX Transportation
Bought Feb. 1990, line (in Hartford) from CSX Transportation
Active corporation

Spies-Thompson Lumber Co.
O: 066
Private logging road
Ontonagon co.

Spring Harbor & Boyne Falls Railroad Company (Gauge 3')
P: 015
Inc. May 15, 1882; $30,000
To own: 6 miles, Spring Harbor to Grand Rapids & Indiana in sec 10 T32N R5W
Lapsed

Springwells, Ecorse and Wyandotte Railway Company (E)
P: 082
Inc.(T) May 31, 1887; $10,000
To own: 10 miles, Springwells via Ecorse twp. to Wyandotte
Lapsed

Stafford, E. H., Manufacturing Co. (Gauge 3')
O: 049
Private logging road
Sand Bay, Bois Blanc Island

Standard Gravel Co.
O: 063
Private industrial road; Pontiac

Staples [H. E.] and Covell [Lyman T.] (Gauge 3')
O: 061, 064
Private logging road; Whitehall
Oceana and Muskegon cos.

State Lumber Co.
O: 040
Private logging road
Kalkaska co.

Stearns & Culver Lumber Co. (Gauge 3')
O: 007
Private logging road
L'Anse

Steel(e), William (Gauge 3')
O: 059
Private logging road; Wyman
14.5 miles, Six Lakes to T12N R6W, built 1882

Stephens, Henry and Co.
O: 072
Private logging road; St. Helen
8 miles, St. Helen
(also known as St. Helen, Houghton Lake & Western)
Built 1883, abandoned ca. 1896

Stimson, Thomas D. (Gauge 3')
O: 061
Private logging road; Muskegon
See Big Rapids & Western

Stratton, D. A.
O: 031
Private logging road
Atlantic (Mine)

Street Rail Road Company of East Saginaw (H)
P: 073
Inc.(S) June 10, 1878; $25,000
To own: in East Saginaw
Lapsed

The Street Railway Co. of Grand Rapids Company (H)
O: 041
Inc.(S) Dec. 31, 1869; $50,000; Grand Rapids
To buy line Jefferson & Fulton to Detroit & Milwaukee depot
Acquired at inc., Grand Rapids Street Ry
Amend Dec. 3, 1883; to increase capital $400,000
Amend July 13, 1886; to increase number of routes operated
Acquired 1886, Division Street; Reeds Lake Street; and West Side Street
Merged Oct. 25, 1890, into Valley City Street & Cable

The Street Railway Company of Ludington (H)
P: 053
Inc.(S) Nov. 26, 1889; $25,000; Ludington
To own: in Ludington
Lapsed

The Street Railway Construction Company
P: 041
Inc.(S) Oct. 2, 1886; $25,000; Grand Rapids
To own: Grand Rapids to Grand Rapids and Paris twps.
[May have served as a construction company in Grand Rapids area]
Lapsed

Sturgeon Bay Lumber Co. (Gauge 3')
O: 024
Private logging road
Owned by A. B. Klise
8 miles, Sturgeon Bay easterly

The Sturgis and Indiana Railway Company
P: 075
Inc. April 4, 1882; $50,000
To own: 5 miles, Sturgis SWly to Indiana state line
Merged May 30, 1882, into Michigan, Indiana & St. Louis

The Sturgis and Mansfield Railroad Company
P: 075
Inc. April 13, 1870; $100,000
To own: 6 miles, Sturgis to Indiana state line in SE corner Fawn River twp. (toward Orland, Ind.)
Lapsed

The Sturgis and State Line Railway Company
P: 075
Inc. Dec. 28, 1886; $120,000
To own: 6 miles, Sturgis southwesterly to Indiana state line to connect with Indiana & Western
Merged July 1, 1887, into Canada & St. Louis

Sturgis, Goshen and St. Louis Railway Company
O: 075
Inc. Oct. 29, 1889; $2,000,000; Cleveland
To reorganize Canada & St. Louis
Line acquired at inc., Sturgis to Goshen, Ind.
Control Dec. 1, 1889, by Lake Shore & Michigan Southern
Sold June 11, 1915, to New York Central

The Sturgis, Indiana and Ohio Railway Company
P: 039, 075, 080
Inc. Jan. 12, 1889; $1,500,000
To own: 100 miles, South Haven to Indiana state line southeast of Fawn River
Lapsed

The Superior Terminal Railway Company
P: 052
Inc. Jan. 27, 1893; $85,000
To own: 8 miles, Lake Superior Mine in Ishpeming to same in Tilden twp.
Dissolved Dec. 1, 1931

Sweet, John
Owned Mecosta RR

T

Tahquamenon Boat Service, Inc.
O: 048
Private tourist road; Newberry
Operates "Toonerville Trolley," 5 miles, Soo Jct. to sec 11 T46N R8W
Converted from private logging road
Active operation

Tawas and Bay County Railroad Company (Gauge 3' 2")
O: 006, 035, 065
Inc. Feb. 12, 1880; $160,000
To own: 40 miles, East Tawas to Jackson, Lansing & Saginaw RR near Bay co. line; also to buy Lake Huron & Southwestern
Line acquired at inc., Tawas City to Prescott
Sold July 11, 1882, to Bay City & Alpena

Taylor, Fred F.
Owned Wood Lake Logging

Terre Haute and Indianapolis Railroad Company
Inc. Ind. corp.
Operating agreement June 4, 1889 of Indiana & Lake Michigan
Lease Aug. 4, 1890, 99 years, eff. Jan. 6, 1890 of Indiana & Lake Michigan
Lease cancelled Feb. 28, 1899, of Indiana & Lake Michigan

Thayer Lumber Co.
O: 057
Private logging road
Stratford

Thomas, Herbert (Gauge 3')
O: 043
Private logging road; Chase
3.5 miles, Chase to T18 R11W, built 1882

Thomas Log & Lumber Co.
O: 059
Private logging road
Montcalm co.

Thompson & Wells Co.
O: 066
Private logging road
Ontonagon

Thumb Railway Company
P: 032, 050, 074, 076
Inc. April 8, 1912; $2,000,000; Capac
To own: 90 miles, Mt. Clemens to Bad Axe
Amend Jan. 14, 1913; to change number of directors
Dissolved April 30, 1924

Tittabawassee & Hope (Gauge 3')
O: 056
Private logging road
Owned by Wright [A. W.] and Ketchem
22 miles, Averill to T16N R1E
Built 1881-83, abandoned 1888

Tittabawassee Railroad Company
P: 056
Inc. May 5, 1931; $600,000
To own: 11.1 miles in Midland co.
Dissolved Sept. 24, 1935

The Toledo, Adrian & Jackson Railway Company (E)
P: 038, 046, 058
Inc.(T) Nov. 24, 1900; $70,000
To own: 55 miles, Jackson to Ohio state line, via Napoleon, Brooklyn, Tecumseh, Adrian, Palmyra, and Blissfield; and 15 miles, Hudson to Ohio state line via Morenci
Lapsed

Toledo & Ann Arbor—
O: 058, 081
Inc. undated, filed Nov. 23, 1877, as Toledo and Ann Arbor Railroad Company; $750,000; Toledo
To own: Ann Arbor to Toledo
Bought May 1, 1878, Toledo & State Line (Ohio corp.)
Amend May 11, 1878, as The Toledo and Ann Arbor Railroad Company; to consolidate Toledo & State Line (Ohio corp.)
Line opened June 1878, Toledo to Ann Arbor
Amend July 5, 1878; to increase capital to $1,500,000
Merged Oct. 14, 1880, into Toledo, Ann Arbor & Grand Trunk

Toledo and Cadillac Railroad Company
P: 018, 037, 057, 067, 083
Inc. Jan. 20, 1886; $630,000
To own: 63 miles, Mt. Pleasant to Cadillac
Possible affiliation with Toledo, Ann Arbor & Cadillac, but not of record

The Toledo and Jackson Electric Railway Company (E)
P: 038, 046, 058
Inc.(T) Aug. 21, 1905; $100,000; Tecumseh
To own: 65 miles, Ohio state line to Jackson, via Deerfield, Britton, Tecumseh, and Brooklyn
Lapsed

Toledo and Michigan Electric Railway Company (E)
P: 012, 030, 046
Inc. March 24, 1903; $450,000
To own: 56 miles, Adrian to Coldwater
Amend July 17, 1903; to increase capital to $1,500,000
Lapsed

The Toledo and Michigan Terminal Railway Company
P: 058
Inc. April 24, 1901; $200,000
To own: 25 miles, Toledo to Monroe
Lapsed

The Toledo and Milwaukee Railroad Company
O: Reorganizing company
Inc. June 18, 1897; $1,500,000
To buy Michigan division of Cincinnati, Jackson & Mackinaw Ry
Renamed July 22, 1897, as Detroit, Toledo & Milwaukee

The Toledo and Milwaukee Railway Company
P: 003, 008, 013, 030, 038, 039, 046, 058
Inc. Aug. 6, 1879; $1,500,000
To own: 144 miles, Ohio state line (on Ann Arbor RR) to Allegan
Acquired March 13, 1883, Allegan & South Eastern
Line acquired March 13, 1883, Allegan to Montieth
Merged June 25, 1883, into Michigan & Ohio

Toledo and Monroe Railway Company (E)
O: 058
Inc. March 23, 1898; $450,000
To own: 22 miles, Toledo to Monroe

Amend Nov. 18, 1899; to clarify route and capital structure
Line opened April 1, 1901
Sold Dec. 9, 1902, to Detroit, Monroe & Toledo Short Line

Toledo & Northern Railroad Company of Michigan
P: 058
Inc. Dec. 18, 1869; $125,000
To own: 15 miles, Monroe to Ohio state line
Lapsed

Toledo & Northwestern Railway Company
P: 013, 023
Inc. Sept. 28,1897; $200,000
To own: 24 miles, Albion to Charlotte
Amend April 1, 1898; to extend 18 miles, Albion to Hanover; capital $350,000
Lapsed

Toledo and Port Austin Railroad Company, Oxford and Almont Division of the (Gauge 3')
P: 063, 074
Inc. April 21, 1879; $60,000
To own: 14 miles, Oxford to Almont
Lapsed

Toledo and Saginaw Bay Railway Company
P: 037, 044, 063, 079
Inc. Aug. 15, 1881; $1,600,000
To own: 120 miles, Pontiac to Caseville
Lapsed

Toledo & South Haven— (Gauge 3')
P: 080
Inc. Jan. 29, 1876, as Bangor & South Haven Division of the Toledo and South Haven Railroad Company; $44,000
To own: not stated
Disposition uncertain

——

O: 080
Inc. Feb. 2, 1876, as Van Buren Division of the Toledo and South Haven Railroad Company
To own: 22 miles, Lawton via Paw Paw and Lawrence to Black River at Bangor
Line opened Oct. 1, 1877, Paw Paw to Lawrence
Amend June 26, 1882, as name next above; to change western terminus to Chicago & West Michigan RR at Hartford
Amend Sept. 9, 1886, as Toledo and South Haven Railroad Company; $250,000; to own: 36 miles, Lawton via Paw Paw, Lawrence and Hartford to South Haven (and consolidate Van Buren and Lake Michigan divs.)
Bought Sept. 9, 1886, Paw Paw RR
Line acquired at inc., Lawton to Hartford
Amend March 7, 1887; to consolidate Paw Paw RR
Line completed July 27, 1887, Lawton to South Haven
Receivership June 11, 1890, J. Ihling, receiver
Sold May 23, 1894, to South Haven & Eastern

——

P: 075
Inc. Dec. 2, 1876, as St. Joseph County Division of the Toledo & South Haven Railroad Company; $30,000
To own: 5 miles, Centerville to Grand Rapids & Indiana RR
Lapsed

——

P: 039, 075, 080
Inc. March 11, 1882, as The St. Joseph Division of the Toledo and South Haven Railroad Company; $250,000
To own: 35 miles, Lawton via Parkville and Centreville to Grand Rapids & Indiana RR in St. Joseph co.
Lapsed

——

P: 080
Inc. Nov. 8, 1884, as The Lake Michigan Division of the Toledo and South Haven Railroad Company; $64,000
To own: 16 miles, Hartford to South Haven
Conveyed Sept. 9, 1886, to Toledo & South Haven

The Toledo & Western Railroad Company (E)
O: 046
Inc. Dec. 10, 1906 (Ohio corp.); $10,000; Sylvania, Ohio
To own: Toledo to Pioneer, Ohio; with branch Allen Jct. to Adrian
Line acquired Jan. 1, 1907, Toledo & Western Ry
Amend Jan. 11, 1907; to increase capital to $2,000,000
Leased ca. 1907, Adrian Street Ry
Control March 28, 1907, by Toledo Ry & Light
Sold no date part to Ohio & Morenci
Sold ca. 1935 RR part in Michigan to Blissfield
Abandoned (in Mich.) 1936

The Toledo and Western Railway Company (E)
O: 046
Inc. Dec. 26, 1899 (Ohio corp.); $1,800,000; Toledo, Adrian
To own: Toledo to Morenci
Line opened Dec. 25, 1901
Line completed Nov. 1, 1903
Receivership July 2, 1906, Charles E. Franklin, receiver
Foreclosure sale, Jan. 1, 1907, to Toledo & Western RR

Toledo, Ann Arbor and Cadillac Railway Company
P: 018, 037, 057, 067, 083
Inc. June 17, 1886; $1,260,000; Toledo
To own: 63 miles, Mt. Pleasant to Cadillac
Bought 1886, right-of-way of Lake George & Muskegon River
Merged Dec. 21, 1887, into Toledo, Ann Arbor & North Michigan
Foreclosure sale July 2, 1895, to Ann Arbor

The Toledo, Ann Arbor and Detroit Railroad Company (E)
P: 058
Inc.(T) June 24, 1904; $1,500,000
To consolidate Ohio & Michigan Traction and Toledo & North Western (Ohio corp.)
Foreclosure sale Nov. 1907, to Toledo, Ann Arbor & Jackson

The Toledo, Ann Arbor and Grand Trunk Railway Company
O: 058, 063, 081 P: 047, 078
Inc. Oct. 14, 1880; $1,900,000; Toledo
To own: Toledo to Pontiac (to consolidate Toledo & Ann Arbor and Toledo, Ann Arbor & North Eastern)
Line acquired at inc., Toledo to Ann Arbor
Line opened Aug. 1881, Ann Arbor to South Lyon
Amend. Aug. 12, 1882; to change line to 98 miles, Toledo to Durand
Sold Oct. 25, 1882, part of rights to Michigan Air Line Ry
Merged May 19, 1884, into Toledo, Ann Arbor & North Michigan
Foreclosure sale July 2, 1895, to Ann Arbor

The Toledo, Ann Arbor and Jackson Railroad Company (E)
O: 058 P: 081
Inc.(T) Sept. 15, 1911; $500,000
To own: 50 miles, Ann Arbor to Toledo [and buy Toledo, Ann Arbor & Detroit]
Line opened March 4, 1913, Toledo to Petersburg
Renamed April 28, 1915, as Toledo-Detroit

Toledo, Ann Arbor and Lake Michigan Railway Company
O: 010, 051, 083
Inc. March 5, 1888; $1,200,000; Toledo
To own: 60 miles, Cadillac to Frankfort
Amend April 18, 1889; $3,000,000; to add 34 mile branch sec 34 T25N R13W to Glen Arbor, 22 mile branch sec 34 T25N R13W to Traverse City, 33 mile branch sec 34 T25N R13W to Manistee
Line completed Nov. 17, 1889, Cadillac to Beecher
Sold April 16, 1890, to Toledo, Ann Arbor & North Michigan
Foreclosure sale, July 2, 1895, to Ann Arbor

Toledo, Ann Arbor & Mackinaw Railway Company
P: 005, 015, 020, 024, 040, 057, 067, 069, 083
Inc. Jan. 20, 1891; $2,800,000; Toledo
To own: 141 miles, Marion to Straits of Mackinac
Lapsed

Toledo, Ann Arbor and Mt. Pleasant Railway Company
O: 029, 037
Inc. May 5, 1886; Toledo
To rename Lansing, Alma, Mt. Pleasant & Northern (Line 21 miles, St. Louis to Mt. Pleasant via Alma)
Line completed June 1886, Alma to Mt. Pleasant
Merged Nov. 30, 1886, into Toledo, Ann Arbor & North Michigan
Foreclosure sale July 2, 1895, to Ann Arbor

Toledo, Ann Arbor and North Eastern Railroad Company
P: 063, 081
Inc. Sept. 9, 1878; $500,000; Toledo
To own: 33 miles, Ann Arbor to Pontiac
Merged Oct. 14, 1880, into Toledo, Ann Arbor & Grand Trunk

The Toledo, Ann Arbor and Northern Rail Road Company
P: 047, 058, 078, 081
Inc. Oct. 22, 1869; $1,000,000; Ann Arbor
To own: 100 miles, Ohio state line in Monroe co. (from line of Toledo & Northern), via Ann Arbor, to Owosso
Foreclosure sale Sept. 28, 1875 to Benjamin P. Crane
Sold June 9, 1877, by Crane to James M. Ashley
Sold Nov. 23, 1877, by Ashley to Toledo & Ann Arbor

Toledo, Ann Arbor & North Michigan—
O: 010, 018, 019, 029, 037, 047, 051, 057, 058, 067, 078, 081, 083
Inc. Oct. 28, 1882, as Toledo, Ann Arbor & North Michigan Railway Company; $1,740,000; Toledo
To own: 87 miles, St. Louis via Alma, Ithaca and Owosso to Toledo, Ann Arbor & Grand Trunk near South Lyon
Bought 1883, Owosso & North Western
Amend May 19, 1884, as The Toledo, Ann Arbor & North Michigan Railway Company; $3,640,000; to own: Toledo to St. Louis and consolidate Toledo, Ann Arbor & Grand Trunk
Line opened Aug. 1884, Owosso to St. Louis
Amend Nov. 30, 1886, eff. Jan. 1, 1887, as The Toledo, Ann Arbor and North Michigan Railway; $4,040,000; to own: Toledo to Mt. Pleasant and consolidate Toledo, Ann Arbor & Mt. Pleasant

Amend Dec. 21, 1887, as The Toledo, Ann Arbor and North Michigan Railway Company; $5,300,000; to own: Toledo to Cadillac and consolidate Toledo, Ann Arbor & Cadillac
Operated 1888-1889, Toledo, Saginaw & Mackinaw RR Co.
Line completed Nov. 17, 1889, Toledo to Beecher
Bought April 16, 1890, Toledo, Ann Arbor & Lake Michigan
Amend April 16, 1890, as Toledo, Ann Arbor and North Michigan Railway Company; $8,000,000; to own: 377 miles, Toledo to Copemish with 4 branches
Bought May 15, 1892, Frankfort & South Eastern
Receivership begun April 27, 1893, Wellington R. Burt, receiver
Foreclosure sale July 2, 1895
Conveyed Oct. 14, 1895, to Ann Arbor RR Co.

Toledo, Ann Arbor and Saginaw Rail Road Company
P: 025, 047, 058, 073, 081
Inc. June 29, 1866; $1,000,000
To own: 100 miles, Toledo to Saginaw or Flint via Ann Arbor and Fenton
Lapsed

Toledo, Canada Southern and Detroit Railway Company
O: 058, 082
Inc. May 29, 1872; $2,000,000
To consolidate Detroit & State Line and Junction Ry (Ohio corp.)
Control at inc. by Canada Southern Ry Co.
Line completed Sept. 1, 1873, West Detroit to Toledo
Operating agreement Dec. 12, 1882, by Michigan Central
Leased Jan. 2, 1906, for corp. life to Michigan Central
Merged Sept. 27, 1916, into Michigan Central

Toledo-Detroit Railroad Company
O: 058
Inc.(T) April 28, 1915
To rename Toledo, Ann Arbor & Jackson
Line completed Dec. 15, 1915, Toledo to Dundee
Leased May 1, 1916, to Detroit, Toledo & Ironton
Control Oct. 1916, by Detroit, Toledo & Ironton
Amend Sept. 22, 1930; to set dissolution of company
Merged Dec. 29, 1931, into Detroit, Toledo & Ironton
Dissolved Sept. 15, 1932

The Toledo, Marshall & Northern Railroad Company
P: 013, 023, 034, 059
Inc. Oct. 13, 1884; $800,000
To own: 87 miles, Marshall to Elm Hall (and to buy Coldwater, Marshall & Mackinaw)
Lapsed

Toledo Michigan and Lake Huron Rail Road Company
P: 013, 023, 034, 037, 059
Inc. Dec. 13, 1906
To rename Coldwater, Marshall & Mackinaw
Lapsed

The Toledo, Monroe and Detroit Electric Railway Company (E)
P: 058, 082
Inc.(S) March 15, 1894; $100,000; Monroe
To own: Monroe to Detroit
Lapsed

Toledo, Ottawa Beach and Northern Railway Company (E)
O: 058
Inc.(T) Oct. 25, 1906; $1,500,000
To consolidate Ottawa Beach & Southern and Toledo & Point Place (Ohio corp.)
Leased Jan. 17, 1907, to Toledo Ry & Light
Line completed March 31, 1907
Operations ended Oct. 17, 1927
Dissolved April 24, 1930

Toledo Railway and Light Co.
O: Holding company
Inc. no date (Ohio corp.)
Lease Jan. 17, 1907, of Toledo, Ottawa Beach & Northern
Control March 28, 1907, of Toledo & Western RR

The Toledo, Saginaw and Mackinaw Railroad Company
O: 009, 025, 073, 078 P: 006, 016, 020, 060, 065, 068, 069
Inc. June 28, 1887; $2,500,000
To own: 250 miles, Durand via Saginaw to Mackinaw City
Line opened Oct. 23, 1888, Durand to Flushing
Operated 1888-1889, by Toledo, Ann Arbor & North Michigan
Sold Dec. 31, 1889, to Cincinnati, Saginaw & Mackinaw

Toledo, Saginaw and Muskegon Railway Company
O: 029, 041, 059, 061, 070 P: 009, 073
Inc. Jan. 22, 1886; $2,800,000
To own: 140 miles, Muskegon eastwardly
Amend Feb. 13, 1886; to own: 156 miles and to fix eastern terminus at Bay City
Line opened Sept. 24, 1887, Ashley to Carson City
Line completed Aug. 1, 1888, Ashley to Muskegon
Control Aug. 1, 1888, by Grand Trunk Ry of Canada
Merged Nov. 1, 1928, into Grand Trunk Western

The Toledo, Ypsilanti and Saginaw Air Line Rail Road Company
P: 058, 063, 082
Inc. Nov. 27, 1869; $1,500,000
To own: 75 miles, Bedford twp., Monroe co. to Holly
Lapsed

"Toonerville Trolley"
See Tahquamenon Boat Service, Inc.

Towle, James
O: 059
Private logging road
6 miles in T10N R7W
Built 1882

Trans-Michigan Street Rail Road Company (E)
P: 003, 080
Inc.(S) Oct. 15, 1906; $100,000; Allegan
To own: Allegan to South Haven
Lapsed

Trans-St. Mary's Traction Company (E)
O: 017
Inc.(S) Oct. 14, 1901; $100,000; Sault Ste. Marie
To own: in Sault Ste. Marie and to international boundary
Acquired 1901, Sault Ste. Marie Street Ry
Amend Jan. 13, 1903; to increase capital to $500,000
Sold Jan. 11, 1919, to Sault Ste. Marie Traction
Dissolved Dec. 18, 1919

Trap Rock Valley
O: 031
Private ore road
Owned by Calumet & Hecla Co.
Abandoned

The Traverse City and Leelanau Railroad Company
P: 028, 045
Inc. Jan. 10, 1900; $300,000
To own: 35 miles, Traverse City to Northport
Lapsed

Traverse City and Peninsula Railroad Company
P: 028
Inc. Dec. 12, 1903; $500,000; Traverse City
To own: 20 miles, Traverse City to Old Mission
Lapsed (*See* letter Feb. 13, 1913, filed Feb. 20, 1913)

The Traverse City and Peninsula Traction Company
Inc. June 28, 1905
Not a railroad

Traverse City, Kalkaska and Grayling Rail Road Company
P: 040
Inc. Nov. 27, 1888; $200,000
To own: 18 miles, Manistee River in sec 36 T27N R5W to Kalkaska
Lapsed

Traverse City, Leelanau and Manistique—
O: 028, 045
Inc. Nov. 20, 1901, as Traverse City, Leelanau and Manistique Railroad Company; $500,000
To own: 30 miles, Traverse City to Northport
Line completed 1906, Hatchs to Northport
Foreclosure sale April 17, 1907, to Union Trust Co.
Reinc. Sept. 14, 1908, as Traverse City, Leelanau and Manistique Railway Company; $278,000
To reorganize Traverse City, Leelanau & Manistique RR
Sold May 23, 1919, rail assets to Leelanau Transit
Dissolved Oct. 26, 1926, eff. Oct. 31, 1926

Traverse City, Peninsula and Old Mission Electric Railroad Company (E)
P: 028
Inc. Nov. 30, 1894; $160,000; Traverse City
To own: 20 miles, Traverse City to Old Mission
Amend Sept. 26, 1899; to add 20 miles, Old Mission to Traverse City via west shore and increase capital to $440,000
Amend Oct. 2, 1899; to add 30 miles, Traverse City to Northport; increase capital to $500,000
Lapsed

Traverse City Railroad Company
O: 028
Inc. Aug. 2, 1871; $160,000; Traverse City
To own: 20 miles, Traverse City to Fife Lake
Amend Nov. 21, 1871; to increase capital to $205,000
Line completed Dec. 1872, Walton Jct. to Traverse City
Controlled at completion by Pennsylvania Co.
Leased Jan. 1, 1883, 50 years, to Grand Rapids & Indiana
Sold June 11, 1917, eff. May 1, 1917, to Grand Rapids & Indiana
Dissolved May 2, 1918

Traverse City Street Railway Company (E)
P: 028
Inc.(S) Sept. 20, 1907; $25,000; Traverse City
To own: in Traverse City
Lapsed

Traverse Traction Co.
Inc. June 17, 1905
Not a railroad

The Tri-State Railways Company of Michigan (E)
P: 012, 030, 038, 046, 075
Inc.(S) Sept. 3, 1913; $100,000; Hillsdale
To own: Adrian to Elkhart; Jonesville to Pioneer, Ohio; and Adrian to Jackson
Lapsed

Trout Creek Lumber Co. (Gauge 3')
O: 066
Private logging road
Trout Creek

Trowbridge, John, and Brothers
Owned Corlies & Thunder Bay

Troy and Rochester railroad company
P: 063
Chartered March 12, 1844; $100,000
To own: Rochester to line of Detroit & Pontiac
Lapsed

Turner, Joe
O: 006
Private logging road
Turnerville

Turpenine, H. V.
O: 027
Private logging road
Bessemer

Tuscola and Saginaw Bay Railway Company
O: 005, 010, 015, 018, 019, 024, 028, 029, 032, 037, 040, 047, 051, 057, 067, 069, 073, 078, 079, 081, 083
Inc. April 26, 1977; $220,000
To operate RR in Michigan
Operates rail lines under contract with state of Michigan
Active corporation

Twin City General Electric Company (E)
O: 027
Inc.(S) April 15, 1893; $400,000; Ironwood
To consolidate Twin City Ry (1889 corp.) and a power company
May have aquired rights of Ironwood Electric Ry
Conveyed Sept. 14, 1910, to Gogebic Street Ry

Twin City Railway Company (E)
O: 027
Inc.(S) Nov. 27, 1889; $25,000; Ironwood
To own: street ry in Ironwood and Vaughn twp., Wisc.
Amend Aug. 1, 1891; to increase capital to $75,000
Line opened ca. 1893
Merged April 15, 1893, into Twin City General Electric Co.

Twin City Railway Company (E)
O: 011
Inc.(S) Aug. 21, 1928; $150,000; Benton Harbor
To own: street ry in St. Joseph and Benton Harbor [and to buy Benton Harbor-St. Joe Ry & Light]
Acquired at inc., Benton Harbor-St. Joe Ry & Light
Operations ended Sept. 1935
Dissolved Jan. 30, 1936

Tyoga Lumber Co.
O: 002
Private logging road
4 miles, Tyoga (sec 14 T47N R22W) to sec 25 T48N R22W
Built 1906; abandoned 1907

U

Underwood Veneer Co.
O: 027
Private logging road
In T45&46N R45&46W

Union Bay & Nonesuch Railroad
O: 066
Private ore road
Ontonagon co.

Union Depot Company of Durand, Michigan
P: 078
Inc.(UD) Nov. 9, 1888; $25,000
To own: union depot in Durand
Lapsed

Union Electric Company (E)
P: 011
Inc.(S) June 15, 1892
To merge Peoples Electric Light & Power (power company) and Union Street Ry of Benton Harbor & St. Joseph
Lapsed

The Union Street Railway Company (E)
P: 009
Inc.(S) Sept. 27, 1890; $100,000; Bay City
To own: Bay City to West Bay City
Disposition uncertain

Union Street Railway Company of Benton Harbor and St. Joseph, Michigan (E)
P: 011
Inc.(S) May 31, 1892; $50,000; Benton Harbor
To own: street ry in Benton Harbor, St. Joseph, and Benton, St. Joseph and Lincoln twps.
Merged June 15, 1892, into Union Electric Co.

Union Street Railway Company of Saginaw, Michigan (E)
O: 073
Inc.(S) Sept. 30, 1893; $300,000; Saginaw
To own: in Saginaw
Merged Jan. 3, 1899, into Saginaw Valley Traction

Union Traction Company (E)
P: 025, 073
Inc.(T) June 23, 1902; $50,000; Saginaw
To own: 35 miles, Saginaw to Flint
Lapsed

United Logging Co.
O: 027
Private logging road
Watersmeet

United Railroad Corporation
O: Holding company
Inc. Nov. 23, 1981 (Dela. corp.)
Owned at inc. by Consolidated Rail Corp.
To operate railroads
Consolidated Dec. 18, 1981, Chicago, Kalamazoo & Saginaw, and non-Mich. companies
Consolidated Dec. 31, 1981, Fort Wayne & Jackson
Consolidated June 15, 1982, eff. Aug. 12, 1982, Kalamazoo, Allegan & Grand Rapids
Active holding company

United States Gypsum Co.
O: 017
Private ore road
Raco

United States Steel Co.
O: 049
Private ore road
Port Dolomite

United Suburban Railway Company (E)
O: 041
Inc. filed June 1927
To: [articles not located]
Acquired 1927, part of Grand Rapids, Holland & Chicago
Operations ended June 25, 1932

United Traction Company (E)
O: 009, 073
Inc.(S) Aug. 1, 1903; $250,000; Bay City
To own: in Bay City and Saginaw [reorganize Bay Cities Consolidated Ry]
Merged Dec. 1, 1903, into Bay City Traction & Electric

University of Michigan (E)
O: 081
Spur to power plant, Ann Arbor

Upper Michigan Logging Co.
O: 017
Private logging road
Seewhy

Upper Peninsula & Green Bay Railway Company
P: 007, 022, 031, 036, 052, 066
Inc. Sept. 4, 1979; $50,000
To operate: 208 miles, Green Bay to Champion and Ontonagon
Lapsed

Utica and Lexington Rail-road Company
P: 050, 074, 076
Inc. Dec. 10, 1883; $520,000
To own: 60 miles, Utica to Lexington
Lapsed

V

The Valley City Street and Cable Railway Company (C, H, E)
O: 041
Inc.(S) June 6, 1887; $100,000
To own: in Grand Rapids
Amend June 27, 1887; to increase capital to $200,000
Amend Feb. 25, 1888; to change number of directors
Line opened April 16, 1888
Amend July 5, 1888; to change number of directors
Amend Jan. 16, 1889; to increase capital to $600,000
Consolidated Oct. 25, 1890, Street Ry of Grand Rapids
Amend July 1, 1891; to increase capital to $2,000,000
Renamed July 1, 1891, as Consolidated Street Ry

Valley City Street Cable Railway Company of Grand Rapids (C)
P: 041
Inc.(S) Feb. 25, 1885; $100,000; Grand Rapids
To: [articles not located]
[This company may have been the original name of Valley City Street and Cable Ry, and that company may have been a variant successor name of this company.]

Van Buren Division of the Toledo & South Haven RR
See Toledo & South Haven

Van Harbor & Northern Railway Company
O: 021
Private logging road
Owned by Van Harbor Land & Lumber Co.
Garden Peninsula

Van Harbor Land & Lumber Co.
O: 021
Private logging road
Conveyed May 14, 1915, rail property to Garden Bay Ry
See also Van Harbor & Northern

Vieux Desert and Lake Superior Railroad Company
P: 021, 022, 027, 036, 055, 066
Inc. Aug. 4, 1881; $2,000,000
To own: 230 miles, Lac Vieux Desert to Union Bay, and branches to Montreal River and to mouth of Escanaba River
Merged Feb. 13, 1883, into Milwaukee, Lake Shore & Western

VonPlaten, Fox Co.
O: 036
Private logging road
Pentoga

VonPlaten Lumber Co.
O: 022
Private logging road
Iron Mountain

W

Wabash—
O: 046, 058, 082
Inc. May 23, 1889, as The Wabash Railroad Company; $52,000,000; Detroit
To consolidate Detroit, State Line & Wabash; Wabash Western; and non-Mich. companies
Joint lease July 1, 1889, of Detroit Union RR Depot & Station
Joint control Aug. 24, 1889, at inc., of Fort St. Union Depot
Joint lease Dec. 10, 1889, of Fort St. Union Depot
Amend March 13, 1906; to increase capital to $102,000,000
Amend Jan. 26, 1907; to increase capital to $118,500,000
Foreclosure sale, July 21, 1915
Reinc. (Ind. corp.) Oct. 22, 1915, as Wabash Railway Company; Detroit; $143,460,000; to reorganize Wabash RR
Control 1915, of Detroit & Western
Control May 19, 1925, of Ann Arbor RR Co.
Control 1928, by Pennsylvania Co.Receivership 1933
Reinc. (Ohio corp.) Dec. 31, 1941, as Wabash Railroad Company
To reorganize Wabash Railway
Amend May 22, 1945; to change stock rights
Amend May 22, 1956; to change stock voting rights
Control Aug. 31, 1963, of Ann Arbor RR Co. transferred to Detroit, Toledo & Ironton
Leased March 17, 1961, eff. Oct. 16, 1964, to Norfolk & Western
Control transferred March 31, 1970, by Pennsylvania Co. to Norfolk & Western
Amend May 22, 1973; to change voting rights
Active corporation

The Wabash, St. Louis and Pacific Railway Company
O: 046, 058, 082
Inc. Nov. 10, 1879 (Ind. corp.)
Reinc. June 13, 1881, eff. July 1, 1881
To consolidate Detroit, Butler & St. Louis and Wabash, St. Louis & Pacific; capital $563,250
Line completed Aug. 15, 1881, Delray to Ohio state line
Receivership May 29, 1884
Foreclosure sale no date, to Wabash Western
Foreclosure sale April 26, 1886, to Detroit & State Line Wabash
Operations transferred March 31, 1887, to Wabash Western

The Wabash Western Railway Company
O: 046, 058, 082
Inc. March 8, 1886 (Mo. corp.)
Operations agreement March 31, 1887, of Wabash, St. Louis & Pacific
Merged May 23, 1889, into Wabash

Wallace Stone Co. (Gauge 3')
O: 032
Private industrial road
Bayport

Ward, David E.
O: 020
Private logging road
See also Frederic[k] & Charlevoix

Ware and Tucker
O: 043
Private logging road
3 miles, Chase to T17N R11W
Built 1881

Wasepi Railway Company
P: not given
Inc. Aug. 7, 1980
To rename Fenn Valley
Lapsed

Weatherwax Lumber Co.
O: 070
Private logging road
In T6N R13W

Weidman & Son Lumber Co.
O: 066
Private logging road
Trout Creek

Wells Lumber Co.
O: 055
Private logging road; Menominee

Wells, Stone and Co.
Operated A. W. Wright Lumber Co. road

Wentworth, J. and G. (Gauge 3')
O: 054
Private logging road
8 miles, Chippewa River (T15N R8W) to T16N R8W
Built 1882; sold ca. 1883 to Jerome and Williams

West Bay City Street Railway Company (E)
O: 009
Inc.(S) Sept. 26, 1887; $100,000
To own: in West Bay City and to Bay City
Merged no date, into Bay Cities Consolidated

West Branch and Moorestown Rail Road Company (Gauge 3')
O: 057
Inc. Feb. 9, 1882; $100,000; Moorestown
To own: 12 miles, West Branch Muskegon River in sec 23 T23N R6W Nly to Moorestown, and further
Owned by J. Henry Moores
Line opened July 1882, 7.5 miles
Abandoned

West Michigan Interurban Railway Company (E)
P: 041, 061, 064
Inc.(S) March 27, 1903; $100,000; Muskegon
To own: Grand Rapids to Muskegon to Hart
Lapsed

West Michigan Lumber Co.
O: 062
Private logging road
Newaygo co.

West Michigan Railway Company (E)
P: 011, 014, 039, 080
Inc. Aug. 4, 1905; $700,000; Benton Harbor
To own: 85 miles, Benton Harbor to Dowagiac and Cassopolis, and Benton Harbor to Paw Paw and Kalamazoo, plus terminals in Illinois and Wisconsin [and acquire West Michigan Traction]
Amend Aug. 21, 1922; to dissolve company
Dissolved Aug. 31, 1922

West Michigan Traction Company (E)
P: 003, 011, 014, 039, 080
Inc. July 27, 1901; $1,000,000; Benton Harbor
To own: 90 miles, Benton Harbor to Kalamazoo and branches to Dowagiac, Cassopolis, Decatur, Paw Paw and Allegan
Foreclosure sale, no date, to West Michigan Ry

Western Michigan University (C)
O: 039
Operated cable railway, 1908 to 1947

Weston, Isaac M.
O: 062
Private logging horse tram
Newaygo co.

Westphalia, Hubbardston and Northern Rail Road Company
P: 019, 034
Inc. Sept. 1, 1869; $160,000
To own: 19 miles, Hubbardston, via Pewamo and Westphalia, to point on Ionia & Lansing line
Lapsed

West Side Street Railway Company of Grand Rapids (H)
O: 041
Inc.(S) May 15, 1878; $25,000; Grand Rapids
To own: on Scribner St., from Bridge to Webster
Line opened 1878
Merged 1886, into Street Ry of Grand Rapids

Wetzell Brothers
O: 062
Private logging road
Lumberton

White and Friant
O: 059
Private logging road
Six Lakes
Built 1881; abandoned 1886

White, Friant & Letellier (Gauge 3')
O: 067
Private logging road
5 miles in Osceola co.

The White Pigeon and State Line Railroad Company
P: 075
Inc. July 24, 1869; $50,000
To own: 4 miles, White Pigeon southerly to Indiana state line (thence to Goshen, Ind.)
Lapsed

White River Railroad Company
O: 062
Inc. Nov. 13, 1879; $130,000
To own: 13 miles, White Cloud to Crooked Lake
Control at inc. by Chicago & West Michigan
Line opened April 1, 1880, White Cloud to Mud Lake
Leased April 1, 1880, 999 years, to Chicago & West Michigan
Sold Feb. 7, 1884, to Chicago & West Michigan

Whitney [David J.] and Remick
O: 037
Private logging road; Detroit
6 miles, Pine River in T13N R6W
Built 1878

Whitney [David, Jr.] and Stinchfield
O: 059
Private logging road
7 miles, Six Lakes to T11N R6W
Built 1878

Wilhelm & Brothers (Gauge 3')
O: unknown
Private logging road; Highland

Wilkie
O: 002
Private quarry tramway
Quarry to dock
In sec 27 T47N R19W
Operated in 1870s

Wilkinson, Joseph N.
O: 011
Private logging horse road
3 miles, sec 17 to sec 14 T7W R20W
Built about 1854

Willard, W. F. (Gauge 3')
O: 080
Private logging road; Ferrysburg
5 miles, Grand River in T8N R16W
Built 1881

Wilson, Luther and Wilson Logging (Gauge 3')
O: 043
Private logging road; Luther
7 miles in T19N R11W
Built 1883

Wing, W. D., Co., Ltd.
Owned Wingleton & Wolf Lake

Wingleton & Wolf Lake (Gauge 3')
O: 043
Private logging road
Owned by W. D. Wing Co., Ltd.
9-12 miles in T18&19N R13W
Built 1883

Winona & Luther Railroad
See Nirvana & Luther

Winsor Street Railway Company (H)
P: 041
Inc.(S) March 21, 1874; $6,250; Grand Rapids
To own: in Grand Rapids
Lapsed

Wisconsin and Lake Superior Rail Road Company
P: 007, 022, 027, 031, 052, 055, 066
Inc. Dec. 8, 1866; $2,000,000
To own: 300 miles, mouth of Menominee River Nly to Keweenaw Bay then Nly to mineral range at Houghton then NEly and SWly along range to Bayfield, Wisc.
Lapsed

Wisconsin & Michigan—
O: 022, 055
Inc. (Wisc. corp.) Oct. 17, 1893, as Wisconsin & Michigan Railway Company; $1,500,000; Menominee
To own: line in Wisconsin (25 miles, Marinette to Menominee River)
Bought Dec. 17, 1894, eff. Jan. 1, 1895, Ingalls, White Rapids & Northern
Bought Aug. 3, 1894, eff. Jan. 1, 1895, Menominee & Northern
Line opened Jan. 1, 1895, Fisher to Faithorn Jct.
Bought July 3, 1902, Wisconsin, Michigan & Northern
Bought June 14, 1905, Quinnesec & Western
Foreclosure sale Nov. 6, 1917, to W&M RR
Reinc. March 26, 1918, as Wisconsin & Michigan Railroad Company (Wisc. corp.); $1,500,000; Menominee
To reorganize Wisconsin & Michigan Ry
Operations ended July 1, 1938
Dissolved Feb. 6, 1939

Wisconsin Central—
O: 027
Inc. June 17, 1887, (Wisc. corp.) as Wisconsin Central Railway Company
To: not stated
Lease May 31, 1888, of Gogebic & Montreal River
Line acquired at lease, Ironwood to Bessemer
Leased Jan. 1, 1890, to Northern Pacific
Lease cancelled Sept. 26, 1893, by Northern Pacific
Leased April 1, 1909, 99 years, to Minneapolis, St. Paul & Sault Ste. Marie
Reinc. Feb. 19, 1954, as Wisconsin Central Railroad Company (Minn. corp.); $1,000; Minneapolis
To: not given
Merged Jan. 1, 1961, into Soo Line RR

Wisconsin Central, Ltd.
O: 002, 007, 017, 021, 027, 031, 048, 049, 052, 055, 066, 077
Inc. March 13, 1987 (Ill. corp.); $15,000,000; Rosemont, Ill.
To operate a railroad
Control, at inc., by Wisconsin Central Transportation Corp.
Bought Oct. 11, 1987, Michigan lines of Soo Line RR
Active corporation

Wisconsin Central Transportation Corporation
O: Holding company
Inc. not found
Owned 1987, at inc., Wisconsin Central Ltd.

Wisconsin Land and Lumber Co.
O: 002, 048, 077
Private logging road
Control Oct. 21, 1909, of Blaney & Southern
Bought July 1, 1925, Blaney & Southern
Also owned Hermansville & Western

Wisconsin, Michigan & Northern Railway Company
O: 022, 055
Inc. Nov. 12, 1898; $130,000
To own: 16 miles, Faithorn Jct. to Quinnessec
Sold July 3, 1902, to Wisconsin & Michigan

Wisconsin, Sault Ste. Marie & Mackinac Railway Company
P: 007, 027, 031, 052, 066
Inc. Sept. 4, 1886; $2,600,000
To own: 130 miles, Montreal River in sec 5 T47N R47W to Marquette
Merged Dec. 22, 1886, into Duluth, South Shore & Atlantic

Wolf Lake Railway and Resort Company, Ltd.
O: 038
Inc.(partnership) May 7, 1902; $30,000; Jackson
To own resort on Wolf Lake, Grass Lake twp., and electric ry between resort and Jackson & Suburban Traction line
Conveyed no date, to Jackson Consolidated Traction

Wood Lake Logging Railroad (Gauge 3')
O: 059
Private logging road
Owned by Fred F. Taylor
4 miles, Hiram to T11N R10W
Built 1882

Worcester, C. H., Co.
O: 002
Private logging road
Cusino
See also Houghton, Chassell & Southwestern

Wright [Ammi W.] and Ketchum
Owned Tittabawassee & Hope, office Saginaw

Wright, A[mmi] W., Lumber Co.
O: 026, 072
Private logging road; Saginaw
Operated by Wells, Stone & Co.
25 miles, Sugar River (sec 13 T20N R2W) toT21N R2W

Wright, F. N., & Co. (Gauge 3')
O: 059
Private logging road; Greenville
1.5 miles, secs 19 & 20 T11N R6W
Built 1883

Wyandotte and Detroit River Railway Company (E)
O: 082
Inc.(S) May 3, 1892; $250,000
To own: in Wyandotte, Trenton, and Ecorse and Monguagon twps.
Acquired at inc., Detroit Suburban Street Ry
Line opened June 1, 1892
Sold Feb. 20, 1901, to Detroit United Ry

Wyandotte Southern Railroad Company
O: 082
Inc. Aug. 17, 1908; Wyandotte
To rename Pennsalt RR
Active corporation

Wyandotte Terminal Railroad Company
O: 082
Inc. Sept. 14, 1904; $15,000
To own: 1.5 miles, Detroit Southern RR to Detroit River
Line completed June 1905
Amend Oct. 15, 1921; to increase capital to $500,000
Amend April 25, 1939; to change number of directors
Amend April 28, 1942; to change number of directors
Amend Nov. 24, 1942; to change number of directors
Line abandoned 1982
Dissolved no date, filed March 28, 1983

Wyman [Charles], Buswell and Co.
O: 059
Private logging road; Grand Haven
6 miles in T12N R6W

O: 062
Rogue River in T11N 12W to T11N R11W

Y

Ypsilanti & Saline Electric Railway Company (E)
O: 081
Inc.(S) April 21, 1899; $25,000; Ypsilanti
To own: Ypsilanti to Saline
Line opened May 20, 1899
Sold March 25, 1901, to Detroit, Ypsilanti, Ann Arbor & Jackson

The Ypsilanti and Tecumseh Railroad Company
P: 046, 081
Chartered April 3, 1838; $200,000
To own: 25 miles, Ypsilanti to Tecumseh
Act April 6, 1838; authorized state to negotiate loan to company
Res. April 16, 1839; directed State Treasurer to pay $15,000 to co.
Act April 1, 1840; named commissioners to settle up with company
Res. April 13, 1841; authorized commissioners to settle with co.
Act Feb. 11, 1842; authorized means of settling with state
Res. Jan. 29, 1853; state authorized to settle claims with company
Lapsed

Z

Zenith Lumber Co.
O: 007
Private logging road
Baraga

CORPORATE FAMILY TREES

The corporate family trees that follow diagram the antecedents of Michigan's major railroad companies. The diagrams include all Michigan corporations, but do not include, in all cases, all non-Michigan companies.

The following selected data are shown:

1. Name of the company. Chapter 2 gives the correct legal name of the company and for all corporate data.
2. Date of incorporation and, if not a Michigan company, state of incorporation.
3. Lease of the company to another or a successor company.
4. Financial control or ownership of the company by another or a successor company.
5. Date and method of disposition of the company.

A solid line between a company and a successor company indicates that the first company was transferred by sale, consolidation, or reorganization entirely to the successor. A dashed line indicates that the first company was controlled by or leased to a second company but was not later transferred to that second company.

A line to the top of a company indicates that the transfer took place at the inception of the company. A line from the bottom of the company indicates that the transfer took place at the demise of the company. A line from the side indicates the event took place during the life of the company.

COMPANIES

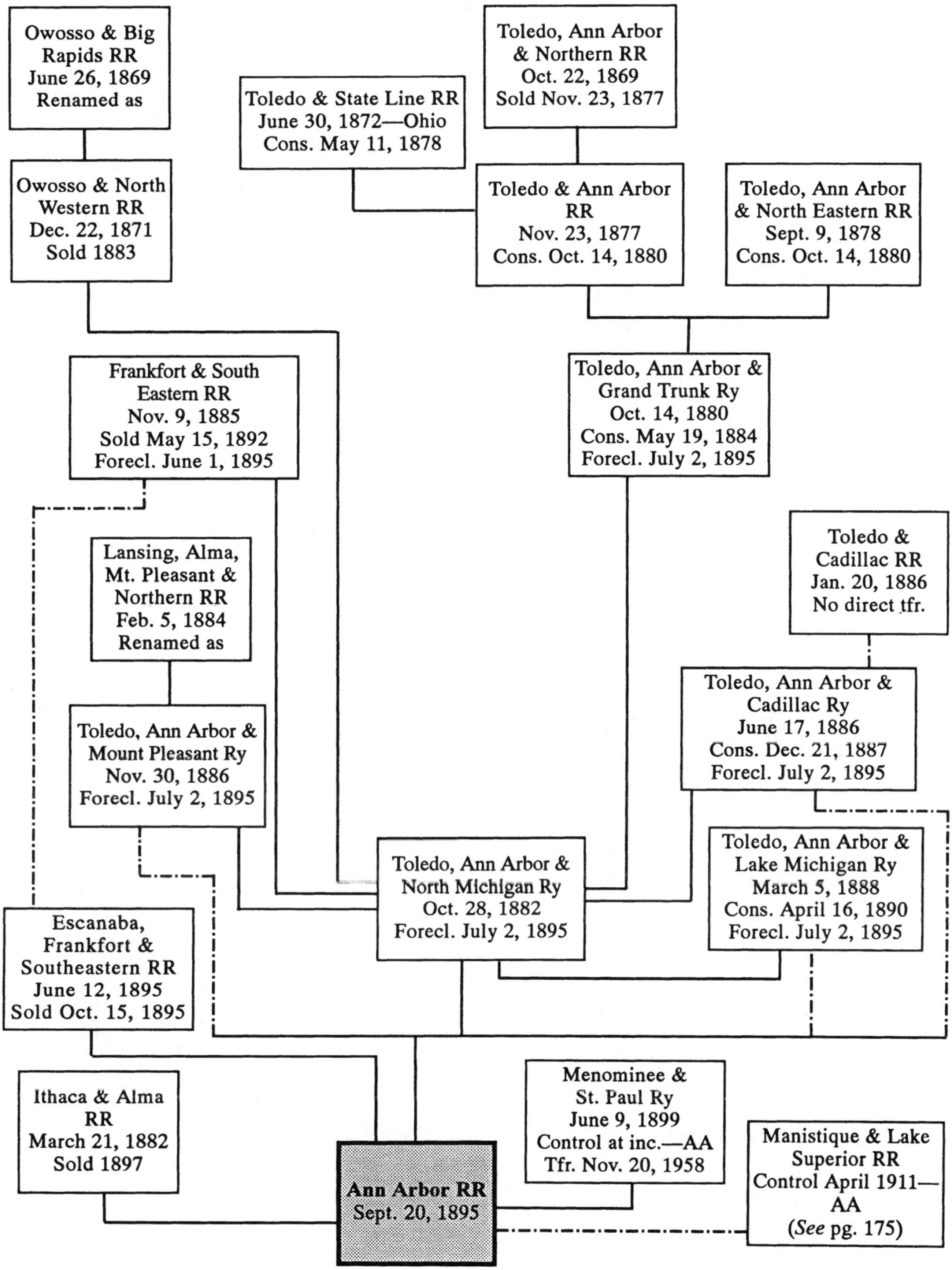
Owosso & Big Rapids RR June 26, 1869 Renamed as
Toledo & State Line RR June 30, 1872—Ohio Cons. May 11, 1878
Toledo, Ann Arbor & Northern RR Oct. 22, 1869 Sold Nov. 23, 1877
Owosso & North Western RR Dec. 22, 1871 Sold 1883
Toledo & Ann Arbor RR Nov. 23, 1877 Cons. Oct. 14, 1880
Toledo, Ann Arbor & North Eastern RR Sept. 9, 1878 Cons. Oct. 14, 1880
Frankfort & South Eastern RR Nov. 9, 1885 Sold May 15, 1892 Forecl. June 1, 1895
Toledo, Ann Arbor & Grand Trunk Ry Oct. 14, 1880 Cons. May 19, 1884 Forecl. July 2, 1895
Toledo & Cadillac RR Jan. 20, 1886 No direct tfr.
Lansing, Alma, Mt. Pleasant & Northern RR Feb. 5, 1884 Renamed as
Toledo, Ann Arbor & Cadillac Ry June 17, 1886 Cons. Dec. 21, 1887 Forecl. July 2, 1895
Toledo, Ann Arbor & Mount Pleasant Ry Nov. 30, 1886 Forecl. July 2, 1895
Toledo, Ann Arbor & North Michigan Ry Oct. 28, 1882 Forecl. July 2, 1895
Toledo, Ann Arbor & Lake Michigan Ry March 5, 1888 Cons. April 16, 1890 Forecl. July 2, 1895
Escanaba, Frankfort & Southeastern RR June 12, 1895 Sold Oct. 15, 1895
Ithaca & Alma RR March 21, 1882 Sold 1897
Menominee & St. Paul Ry June 9, 1899 Control at inc.—AA Tfr. Nov. 20, 1958
Ann Arbor RR Sept. 20, 1895
Manistique & Lake Superior RR Control April 1911—AA (*See* pg. 175)

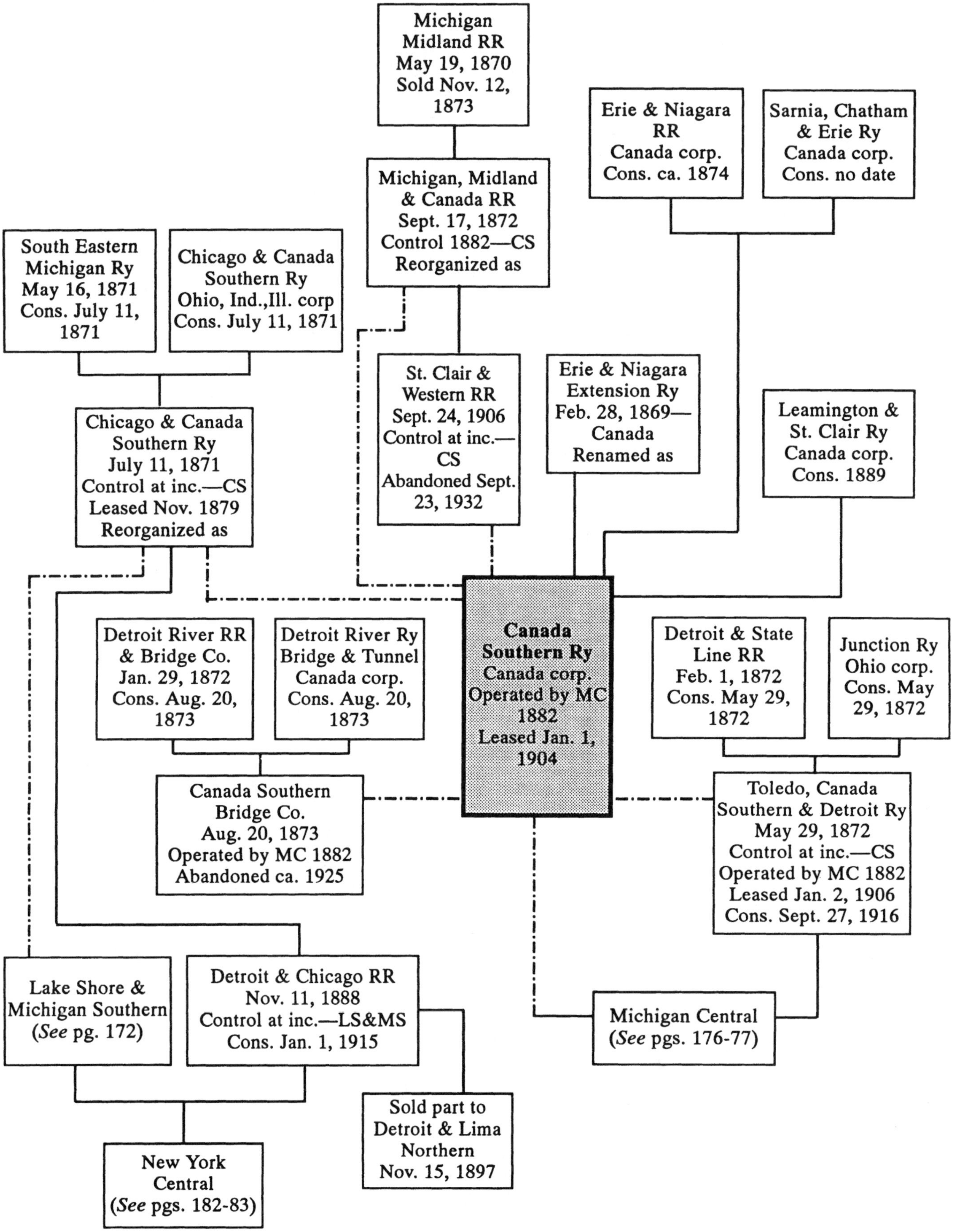
Michigan Midland RR May 19, 1870 Sold Nov. 12, 1873
Michigan, Midland & Canada RR Sept. 17, 1872 Control 1882—CS Reorganized as
Erie & Niagara RR Canada corp. Cons. ca. 1874
Sarnia, Chatham & Erie Ry Canada corp. Cons. no date
South Eastern Michigan Ry May 16, 1871 Cons. July 11, 1871
Chicago & Canada Southern Ry Ohio, Ind.,Ill. corp Cons. July 11, 1871
St. Clair & Western RR Sept. 24, 1906 Control at inc.—CS Abandoned Sept. 23, 1932
Erie & Niagara Extension Ry Feb. 28, 1869—Canada Renamed as
Leamington & St. Clair Ry Canada corp. Cons. 1889
Chicago & Canada Southern Ry July 11, 1871 Control at inc.—CS Leased Nov. 1879 Reorganized as
Detroit River RR & Bridge Co. Jan. 29, 1872 Cons. Aug. 20, 1873
Detroit River Ry Bridge & Tunnel Canada corp. Cons. Aug. 20, 1873
Canada Southern Ry Canada corp. Operated by MC 1882 Leased Jan. 1, 1904
Detroit & State Line RR Feb. 1, 1872 Cons. May 29, 1872
Junction Ry Ohio corp. Cons. May 29, 1872
Canada Southern Bridge Co. Aug. 20, 1873 Operated by MC 1882 Abandoned ca. 1925
Toledo, Canada Southern & Detroit Ry May 29, 1872 Control at inc.—CS Operated by MC 1882 Leased Jan. 2, 1906 Cons. Sept. 27, 1916
Lake Shore & Michigan Southern (*See* pg. 172)
Detroit & Chicago RR Nov. 11, 1888 Control at inc.—LS&MS Cons. Jan. 1, 1915
Michigan Central (*See* pgs. 176-77)
Sold part to Detroit & Lima Northern Nov. 15, 1897
New York Central (*See* pgs. 182-83)

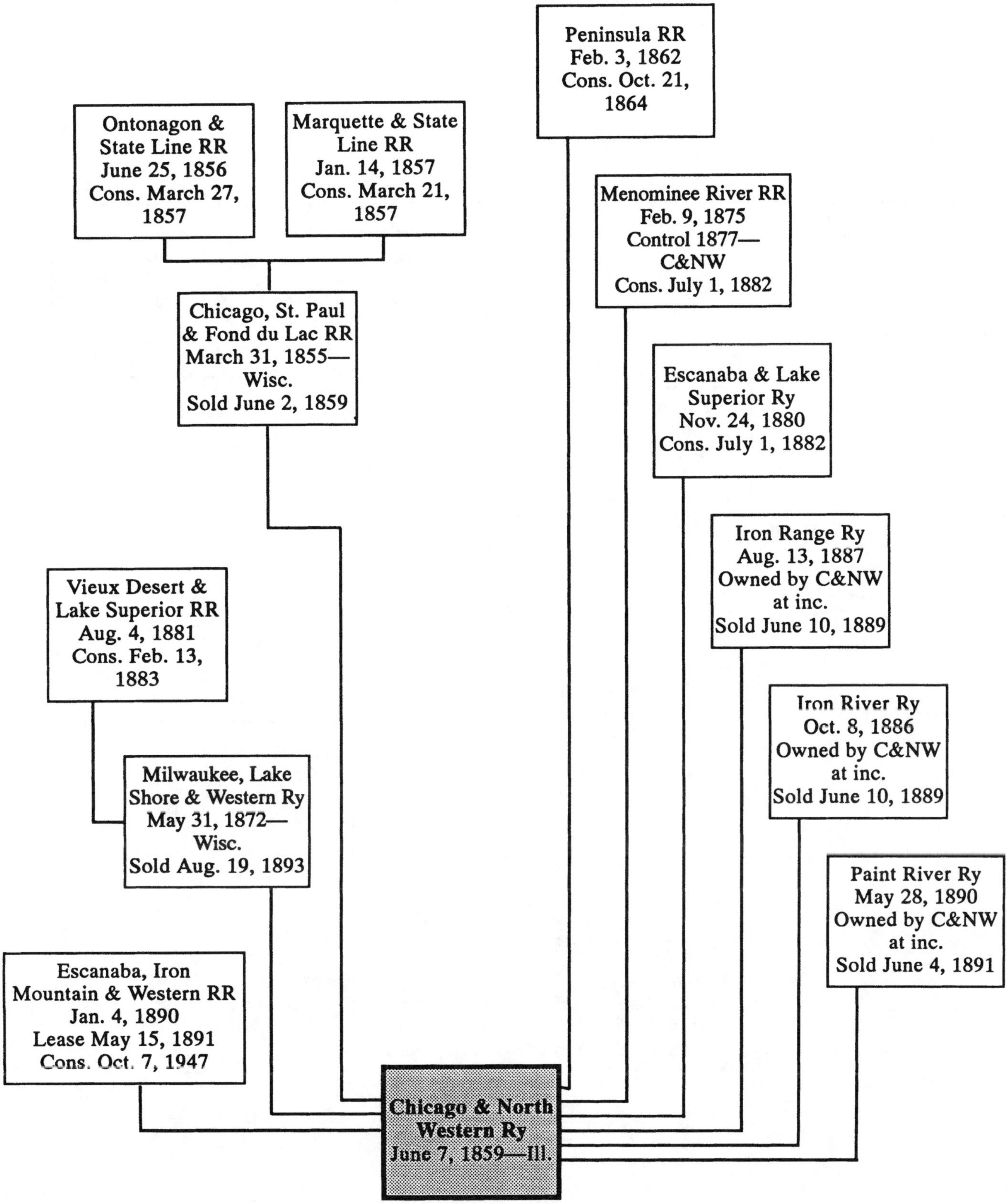
Peninsula RR Feb. 3, 1862 Cons. Oct. 21, 1864
Ontonagon & State Line RR June 25, 1856 Cons. March 27, 1857
Marquette & State Line RR Jan. 14, 1857 Cons. March 21, 1857
Menominee River RR Feb. 9, 1875 Control 1877—C&NW Cons. July 1, 1882
Chicago, St. Paul & Fond du Lac RR March 31, 1855—Wisc. Sold June 2, 1859
Escanaba & Lake Superior Ry Nov. 24, 1880 Cons. July 1, 1882
Iron Range Ry Aug. 13, 1887 Owned by C&NW at inc. Sold June 10, 1889
Vieux Desert & Lake Superior RR Aug. 4, 1881 Cons. Feb. 13, 1883
Iron River Ry Oct. 8, 1886 Owned by C&NW at inc. Sold June 10, 1889
Milwaukee, Lake Shore & Western Ry May 31, 1872—Wisc. Sold Aug. 19, 1893
Paint River Ry May 28, 1890 Owned by C&NW at inc. Sold June 4, 1891
Escanaba, Iron Mountain & Western RR Jan. 4, 1890 Lease May 15, 1891 Cons. Oct. 7, 1947
Chicago & North Western Ry June 7, 1859—Ill.

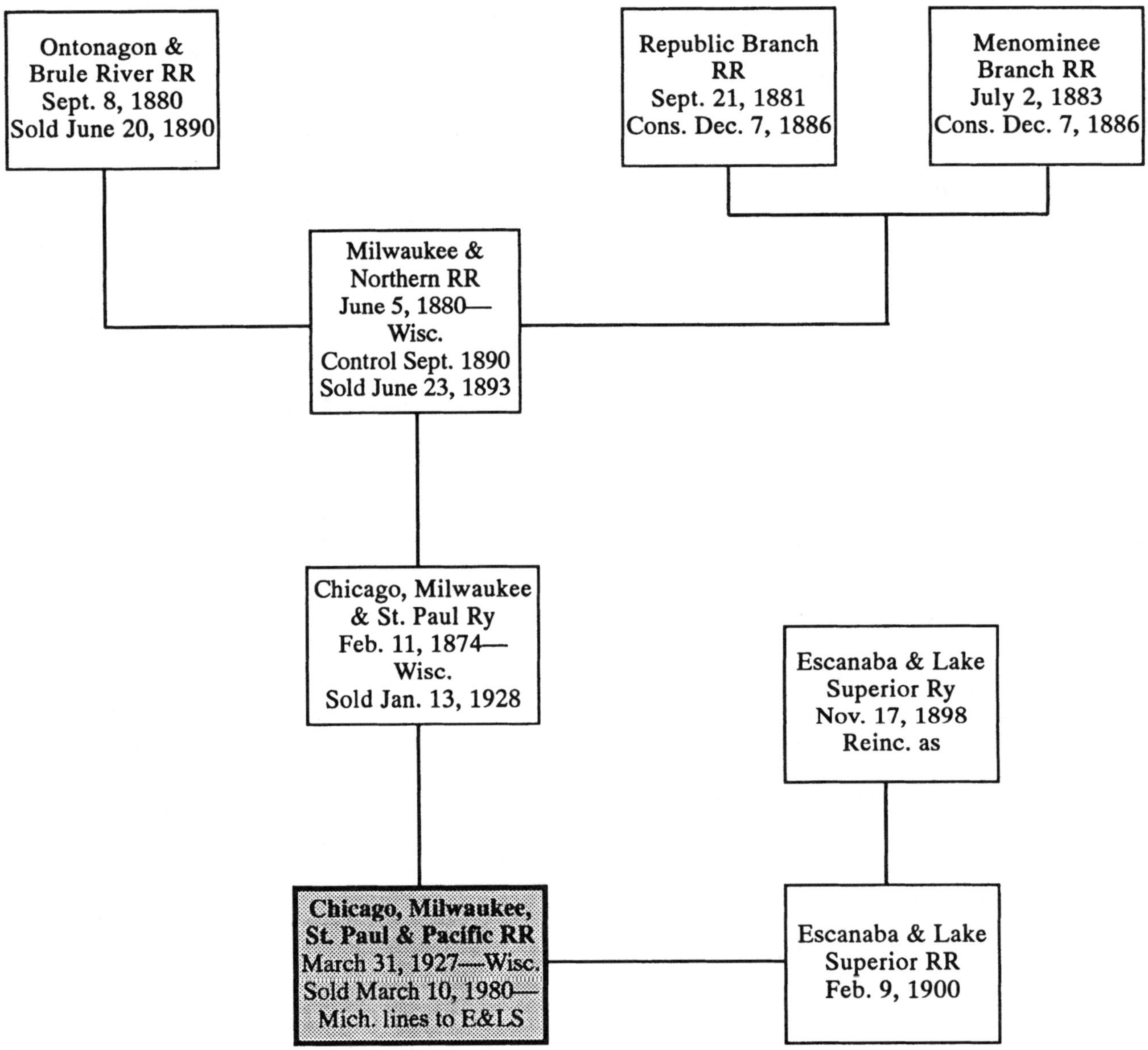
Ontonagon & Brule River RR Sept. 8, 1880 Sold June 20, 1890
Republic Branch RR Sept. 21, 1881 Cons. Dec. 7, 1886
Menominee Branch RR July 2, 1883 Cons. Dec. 7, 1886
Milwaukee & Northern RR June 5, 1880—Wisc. Control Sept. 1890 Sold June 23, 1893
Chicago, Milwaukee & St. Paul Ry Feb. 11, 1874—Wisc. Sold Jan. 13, 1928
Escanaba & Lake Superior Ry Nov. 17, 1898 Reinc. as
Chicago, Milwaukee, St. Paul & Pacific RR March 31, 1927—Wisc. Sold March 10, 1980—Mich. lines to E&LS
Escanaba & Lake Superior RR Feb. 9, 1900

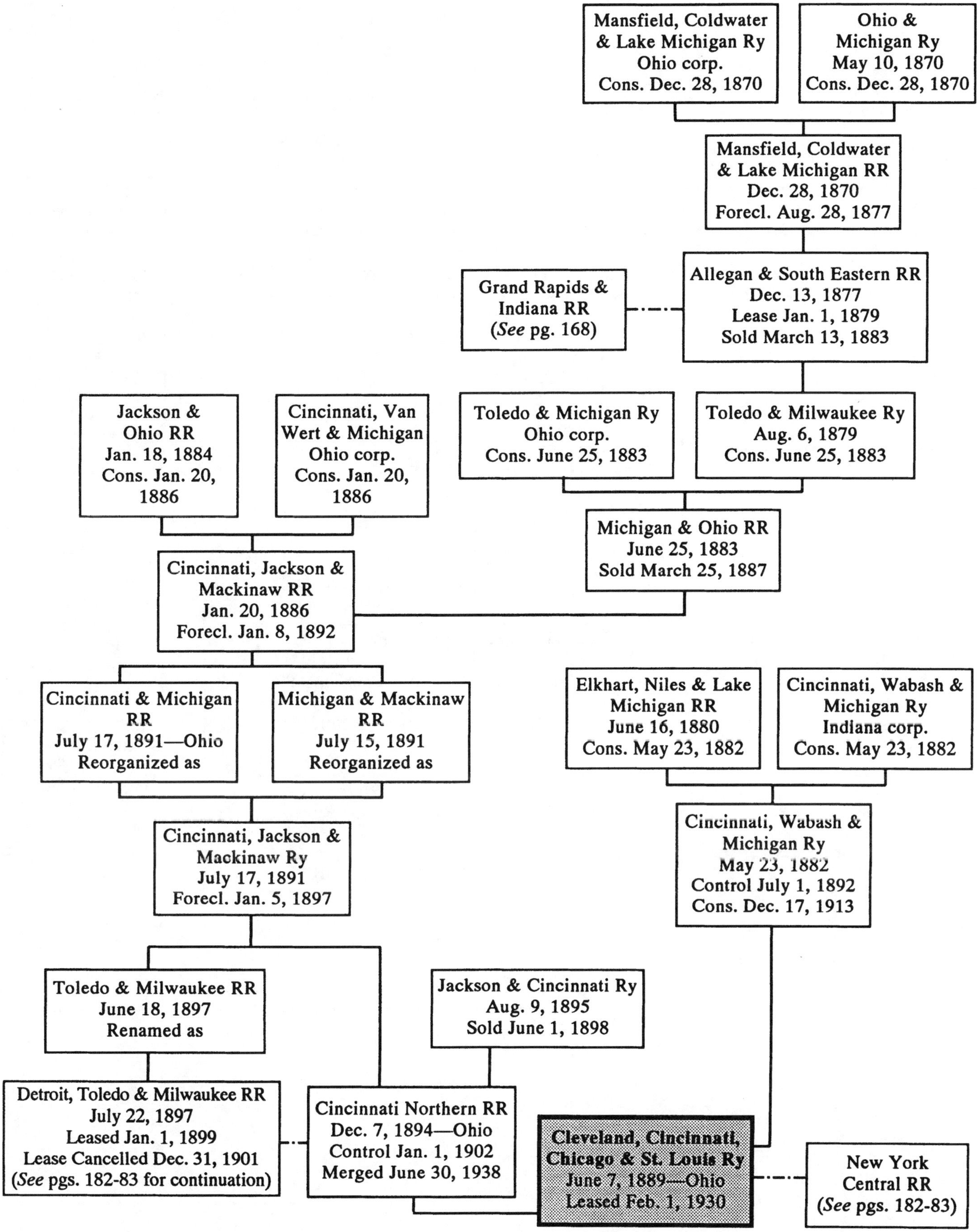
Mansfield, Coldwater & Lake Michigan Ry Ohio corp. Cons. Dec. 28, 1870
Ohio & Michigan Ry May 10, 1870 Cons. Dec. 28, 1870
Mansfield, Coldwater & Lake Michigan RR Dec. 28, 1870 Forecl. Aug. 28, 1877
Grand Rapids & Indiana RR (*See* pg. 168)
Allegan & South Eastern RR Dec. 13, 1877 Lease Jan. 1, 1879 Sold March 13, 1883
Jackson & Ohio RR Jan. 18, 1884 Cons. Jan. 20, 1886
Cincinnati, Van Wert & Michigan Ohio corp. Cons. Jan. 20, 1886
Toledo & Michigan Ry Ohio corp. Cons. June 25, 1883
Toledo & Milwaukee Ry Aug. 6, 1879 Cons. June 25, 1883
Michigan & Ohio RR June 25, 1883 Sold March 25, 1887
Cincinnati, Jackson & Mackinaw RR Jan. 20, 1886 Forecl. Jan. 8, 1892
Cincinnati & Michigan RR July 17, 1891—Ohio Reorganized as
Michigan & Mackinaw RR July 15, 1891 Reorganized as
Elkhart, Niles & Lake Michigan RR June 16, 1880 Cons. May 23, 1882
Cincinnati, Wabash & Michigan Ry Indiana corp. Cons. May 23, 1882
Cincinnati, Jackson & Mackinaw Ry July 17, 1891 Forecl. Jan. 5, 1897
Cincinnati, Wabash & Michigan Ry May 23, 1882 Control July 1, 1892 Cons. Dec. 17, 1913
Toledo & Milwaukee RR June 18, 1897 Renamed as
Jackson & Cincinnati Ry Aug. 9, 1895 Sold June 1, 1898
Detroit, Toledo & Milwaukee RR July 22, 1897 Leased Jan. 1, 1899 Lease Cancelled Dec. 31, 1901 (*See* pgs. 182-83 for continuation)
Cincinnati Northern RR Dec. 7, 1894—Ohio Control Jan. 1, 1902 Merged June 30, 1938
Cleveland, Cincinnati, Chicago & St. Louis Ry June 7, 1889—Ohio Leased Feb. 1, 1930
New York Central RR (*See* pgs. 182-83)

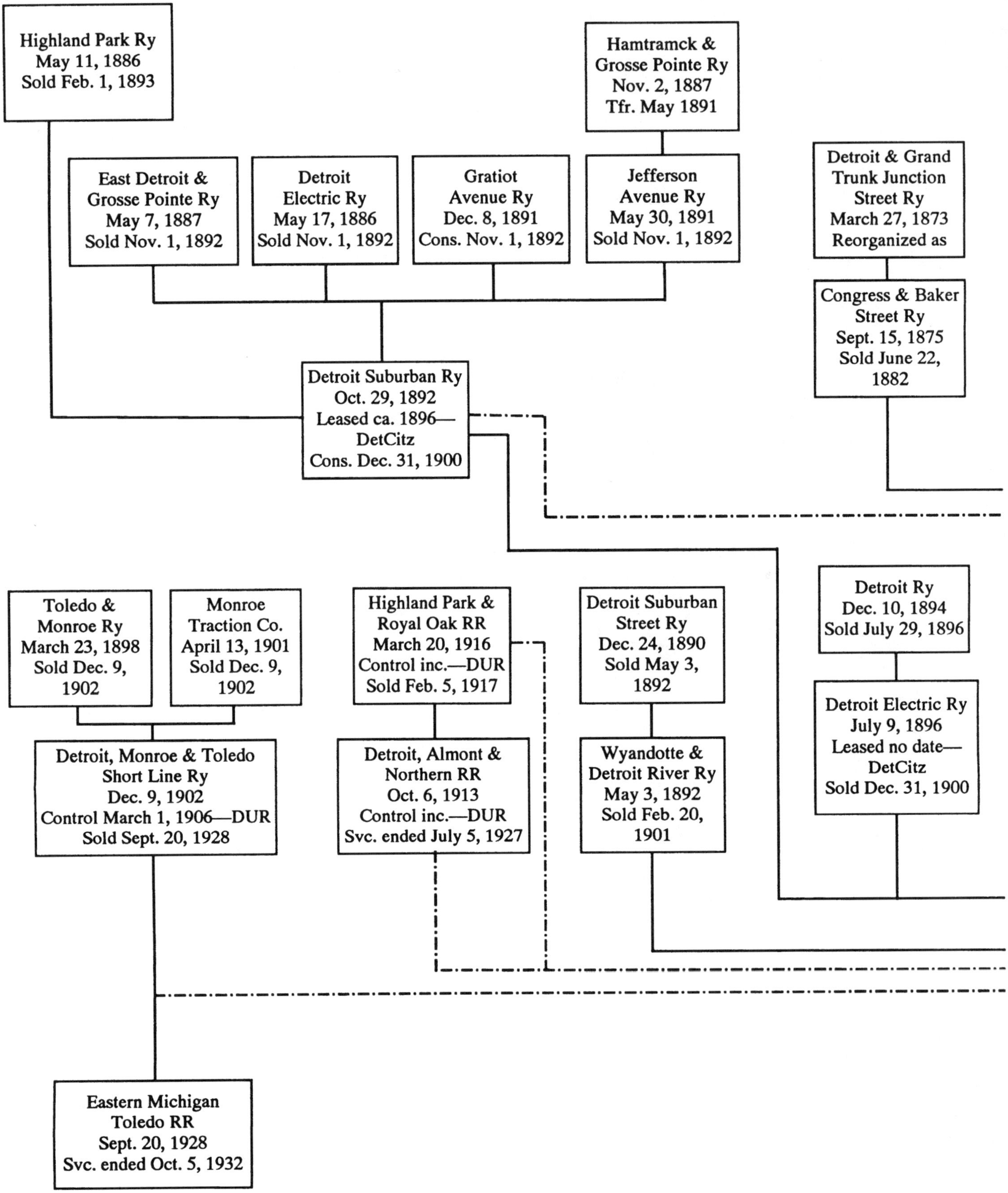
Highland Park Ry
May 11, 1886
Sold Feb. 1, 1893
Hamtramck & Grosse Pointe Ry
Nov. 2, 1887
Tfr. May 1891
East Detroit & Grosse Pointe Ry
May 7, 1887
Sold Nov. 1, 1892
Detroit Electric Ry
May 17, 1886
Sold Nov. 1, 1892
Gratiot Avenue Ry
Dec. 8, 1891
Cons. Nov. 1, 1892
Jefferson Avenue Ry
May 30, 1891
Sold Nov. 1, 1892
Detroit & Grand Trunk Junction Street Ry
March 27, 1873
Reorganized as
Congress & Baker Street Ry
Sept. 15, 1875
Sold June 22, 1882
Detroit Suburban Ry
Oct. 29, 1892
Leased ca. 1896—DetCitz
Cons. Dec. 31, 1900
Toledo & Monroe Ry
March 23, 1898
Sold Dec. 9, 1902
Monroe Traction Co.
April 13, 1901
Sold Dec. 9, 1902
Highland Park & Royal Oak RR
March 20, 1916
Control inc.—DUR
Sold Feb. 5, 1917
Detroit Suburban Street Ry
Dec. 24, 1890
Sold May 3, 1892
Detroit Ry
Dec. 10, 1894
Sold July 29, 1896
Detroit, Monroe & Toledo Short Line Ry
Dec. 9, 1902
Control March 1, 1906—DUR
Sold Sept. 20, 1928
Detroit, Almont & Northern RR
Oct. 6, 1913
Control inc.—DUR
Svc. ended July 5, 1927
Wyandotte & Detroit River Ry
May 3, 1892
Sold Feb. 20, 1901
Detroit Electric Ry
July 9, 1896
Leased no date—DetCitz
Sold Dec. 31, 1900
Eastern Michigan Toledo RR
Sept. 20, 1928
Svc. ended Oct. 5, 1932

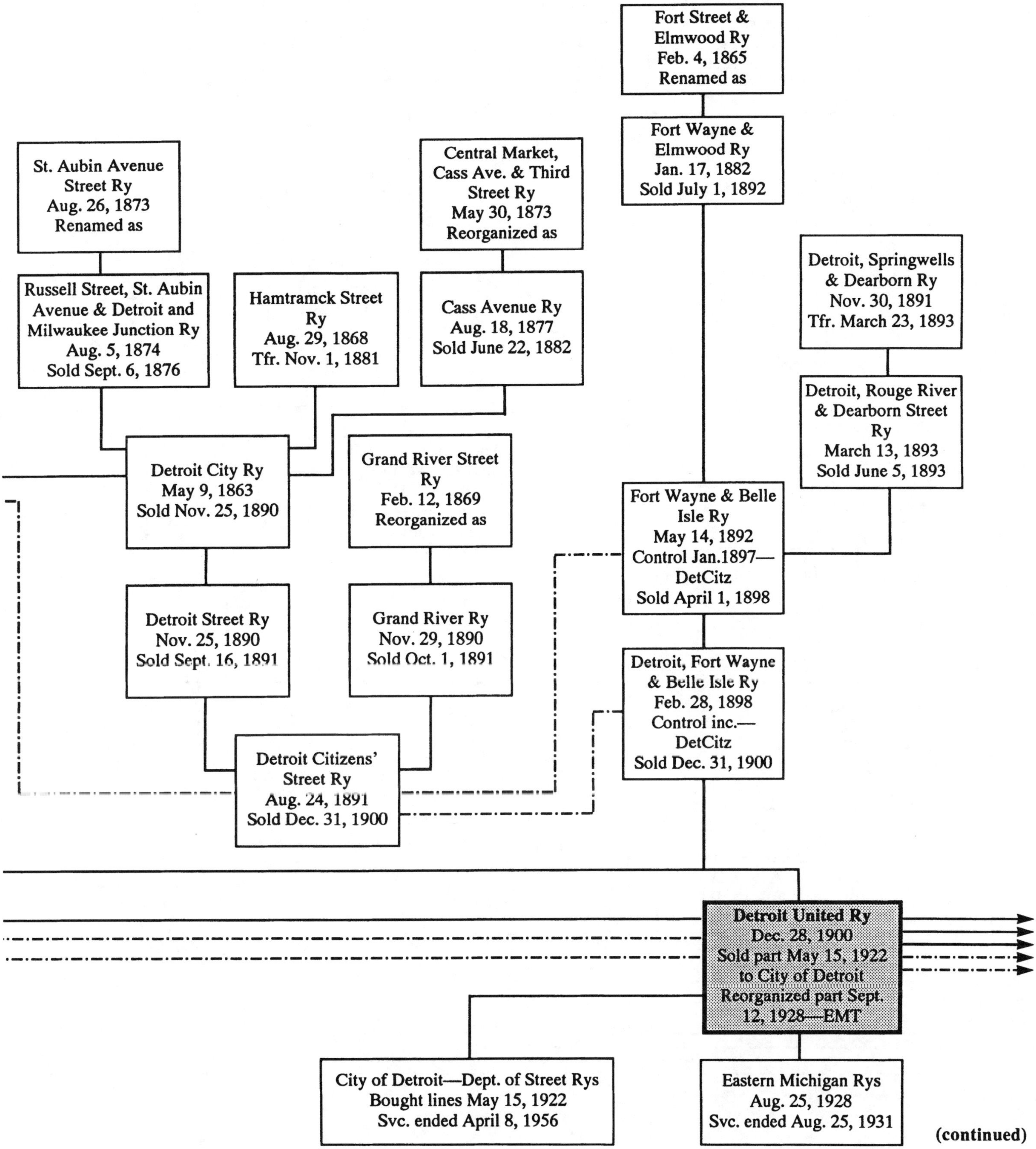
Fort Street & Elmwood Ry Feb. 4, 1865 Renamed as
Fort Wayne & Elmwood Ry Jan. 17, 1882 Sold July 1, 1892
St. Aubin Avenue Street Ry Aug. 26, 1873 Renamed as
Central Market, Cass Ave. & Third Street Ry May 30, 1873 Reorganized as
Russell Street, St. Aubin Avenue & Detroit and Milwaukee Junction Ry Aug. 5, 1874 Sold Sept. 6, 1876
Hamtramck Street Ry Aug. 29, 1868 Tfr. Nov. 1, 1881
Cass Avenue Ry Aug. 18, 1877 Sold June 22, 1882
Detroit, Springwells & Dearborn Ry Nov. 30, 1891 Tfr. March 23, 1893
Detroit, Rouge River & Dearborn Street Ry March 13, 1893 Sold June 5, 1893
Detroit City Ry May 9, 1863 Sold Nov. 25, 1890
Grand River Street Ry Feb. 12, 1869 Reorganized as
Fort Wayne & Belle Isle Ry May 14, 1892 Control Jan.1897—DetCitz Sold April 1, 1898
Detroit Street Ry Nov. 25, 1890 Sold Sept. 16, 1891
Grand River Ry Nov. 29, 1890 Sold Oct. 1, 1891
Detroit, Fort Wayne & Belle Isle Ry Feb. 28, 1898 Control inc.—DetCitz Sold Dec. 31, 1900
Detroit Citizens' Street Ry Aug. 24, 1891 Sold Dec. 31, 1900
Detroit United Ry Dec. 28, 1900 Sold part May 15, 1922 to City of Detroit Reorganized part Sept. 12, 1928—EMT
City of Detroit—Dept. of Street Rys Bought lines May 15, 1922 Svc. ended April 8, 1956
Eastern Michigan Rys Aug. 25, 1928 Svc. ended Aug. 25, 1931

(continued)

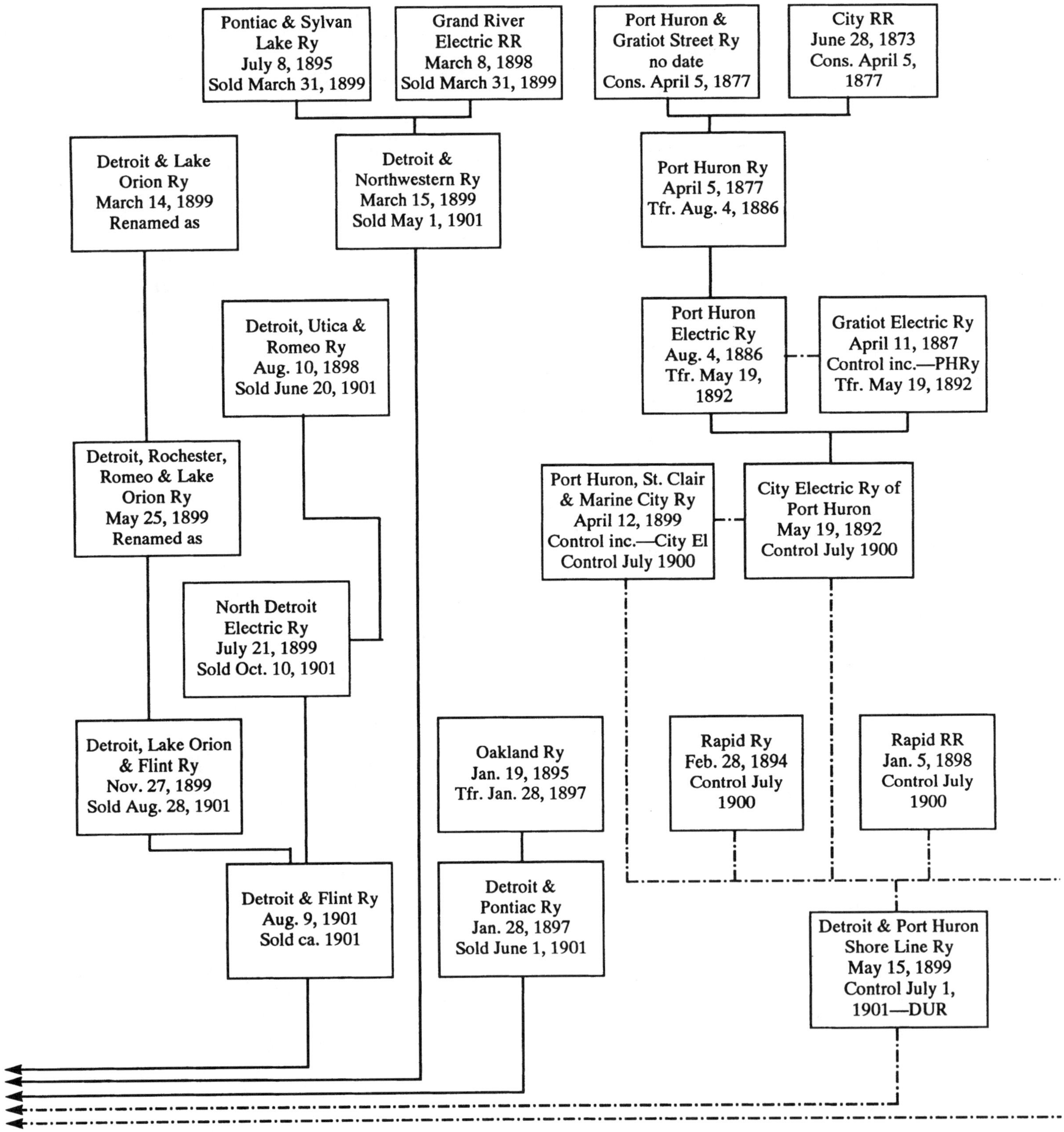
Pontiac & Sylvan Lake Ry July 8, 1895 Sold March 31, 1899
Grand River Electric RR March 8, 1898 Sold March 31, 1899
Port Huron & Gratiot Street Ry no date Cons. April 5, 1877
City RR June 28, 1873 Cons. April 5, 1877
Detroit & Lake Orion Ry March 14, 1899 Renamed as
Detroit & Northwestern Ry March 15, 1899 Sold May 1, 1901
Port Huron Ry April 5, 1877 Tfr. Aug. 4, 1886
Detroit, Utica & Romeo Ry Aug. 10, 1898 Sold June 20, 1901
Port Huron Electric Ry Aug. 4, 1886 Tfr. May 19, 1892
Gratiot Electric Ry April 11, 1887 Control inc.—PHRy Tfr. May 19, 1892
Detroit, Rochester, Romeo & Lake Orion Ry May 25, 1899 Renamed as
Port Huron, St. Clair & Marine City Ry April 12, 1899 Control inc.—City El Control July 1900
City Electric Ry of Port Huron May 19, 1892 Control July 1900
North Detroit Electric Ry July 21, 1899 Sold Oct. 10, 1901
Detroit, Lake Orion & Flint Ry Nov. 27, 1899 Sold Aug. 28, 1901
Oakland Ry Jan. 19, 1895 Tfr. Jan. 28, 1897
Rapid Ry Feb. 28, 1894 Control July 1900
Rapid RR Jan. 5, 1898 Control July 1900
Detroit & Flint Ry Aug. 9, 1901 Sold ca. 1901
Detroit & Pontiac Ry Jan. 28, 1897 Sold June 1, 1901
Detroit & Port Huron Shore Line Ry May 15, 1899 Control July 1, 1901—DUR

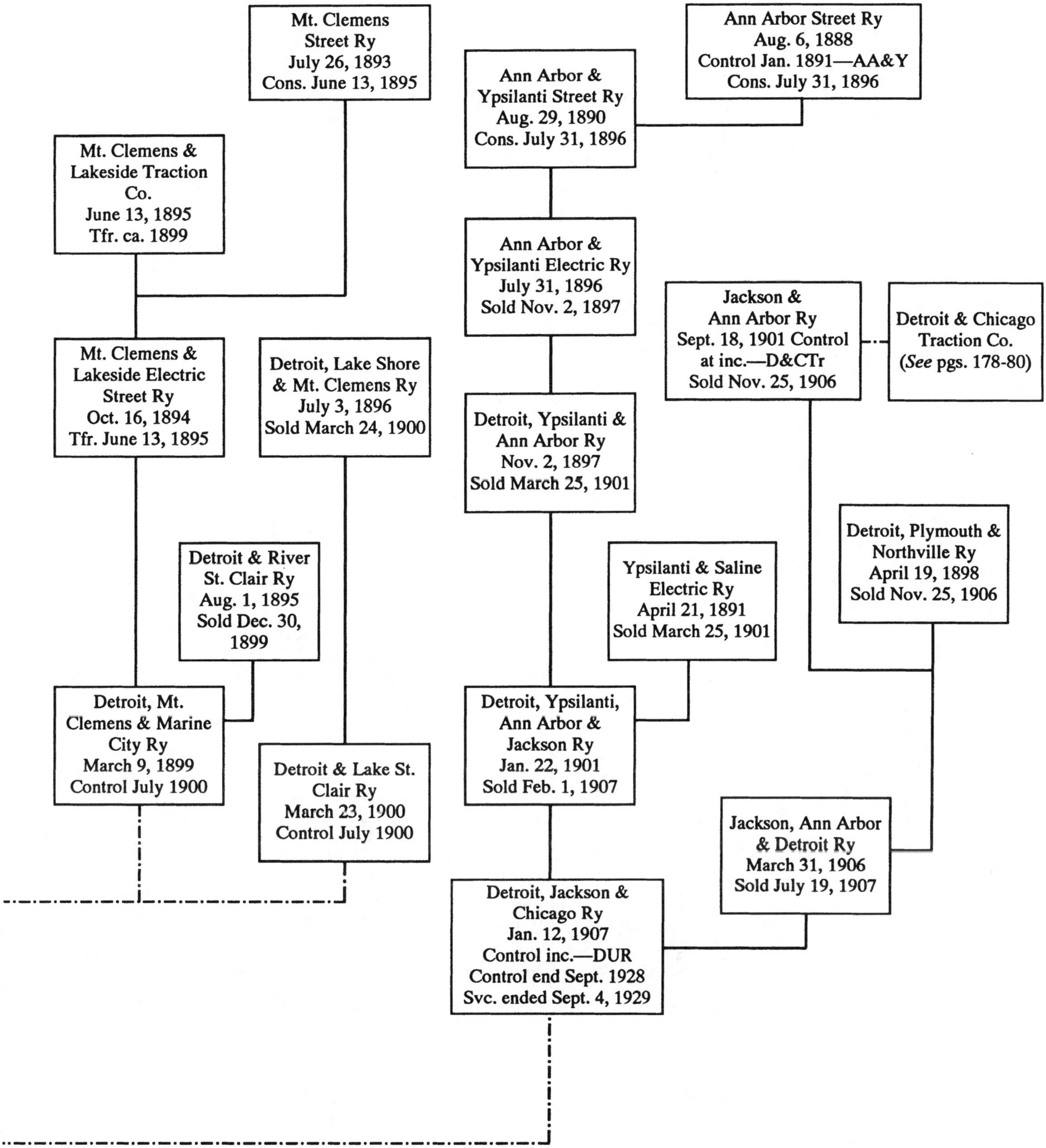
Mt. Clemens Street Ry
July 26, 1893
Cons. June 13, 1895
Mt. Clemens & Lakeside Traction Co.
June 13, 1895
Tfr. ca. 1899
Mt. Clemens & Lakeside Electric Street Ry
Oct. 16, 1894
Tfr. June 13, 1895
Detroit, Lake Shore & Mt. Clemens Ry
July 3, 1896
Sold March 24, 1900
Detroit & River St. Clair Ry
Aug. 1, 1895
Sold Dec. 30, 1899
Detroit, Mt. Clemens & Marine City Ry
March 9, 1899
Control July 1900
Detroit & Lake St. Clair Ry
March 23, 1900
Control July 1900
Ann Arbor Street Ry
Aug. 6, 1888
Control Jan. 1891—AA&Y
Cons. July 31, 1896
Ann Arbor & Ypsilanti Street Ry
Aug. 29, 1890
Cons. July 31, 1896
Ann Arbor & Ypsilanti Electric Ry
July 31, 1896
Sold Nov. 2, 1897
Detroit, Ypsilanti & Ann Arbor Ry
Nov. 2, 1897
Sold March 25, 1901
Jackson & Ann Arbor Ry
Sept. 18, 1901 Control at inc.—D&CTr
Sold Nov. 25, 1906
Detroit & Chicago Traction Co.
(See pgs. 178-80)
Detroit, Plymouth & Northville Ry
April 19, 1898
Sold Nov. 25, 1906
Ypsilanti & Saline Electric Ry
April 21, 1891
Sold March 25, 1901
Detroit, Ypsilanti, Ann Arbor & Jackson Ry
Jan. 22, 1901
Sold Feb. 1, 1907
Jackson, Ann Arbor & Detroit Ry
March 31, 1906
Sold July 19, 1907
Detroit, Jackson & Chicago Ry
Jan. 12, 1907
Control inc.—DUR
Control end Sept. 1928
Svc. ended Sept. 4, 1929

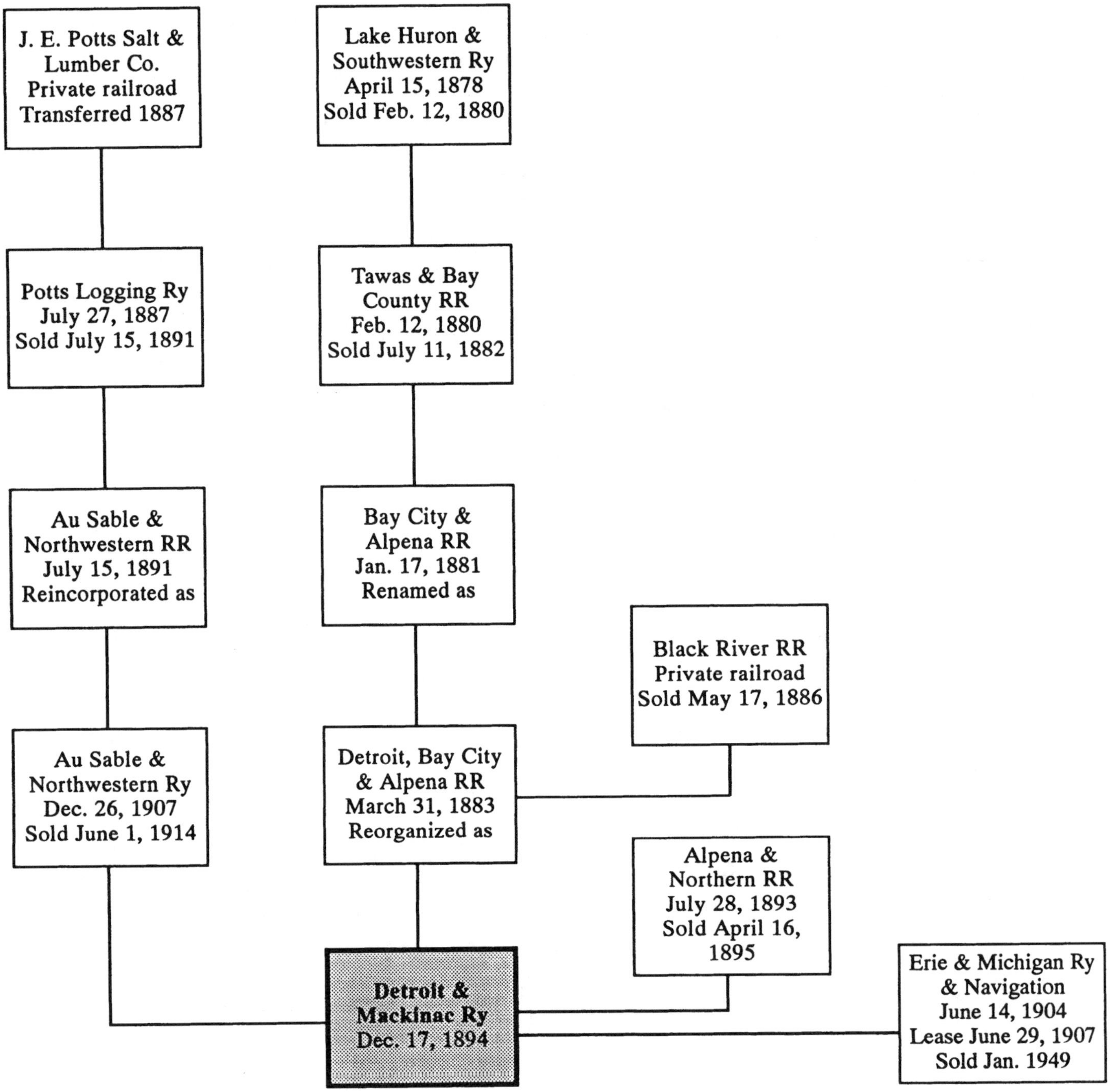
J. E. Potts Salt & Lumber Co. Private railroad Transferred 1887
Potts Logging Ry July 27, 1887 Sold July 15, 1891
Au Sable & Northwestern RR July 15, 1891 Reincorporated as
Au Sable & Northwestern Ry Dec. 26, 1907 Sold June 1, 1914
Lake Huron & Southwestern Ry April 15, 1878 Sold Feb. 12, 1880
Tawas & Bay County RR Feb. 12, 1880 Sold July 11, 1882
Bay City & Alpena RR Jan. 17, 1881 Renamed as
Detroit, Bay City & Alpena RR March 31, 1883 Reorganized as
Black River RR Private railroad Sold May 17, 1886
Alpena & Northern RR July 28, 1893 Sold April 16, 1895
Detroit & Mackinac Ry Dec. 17, 1894
Erie & Michigan Ry & Navigation June 14, 1904 Lease June 29, 1907 Sold Jan. 1949

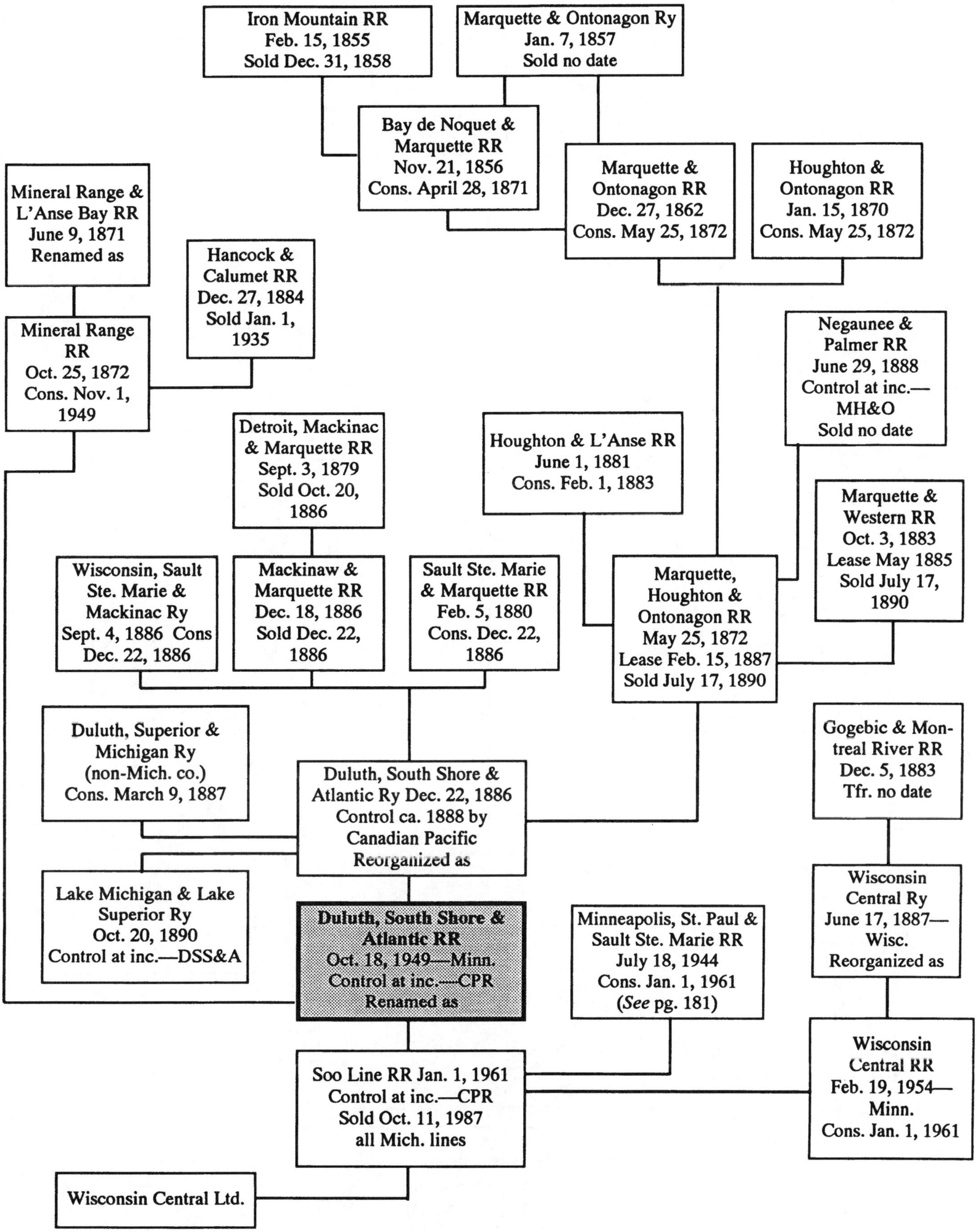
Iron Mountain RR
Feb. 15, 1855
Sold Dec. 31, 1858
Marquette & Ontonagon Ry
Jan. 7, 1857
Sold no date
Bay de Noquet & Marquette RR
Nov. 21, 1856
Cons. April 28, 1871
Marquette & Ontonagon RR
Dec. 27, 1862
Cons. May 25, 1872
Houghton & Ontonagon RR
Jan. 15, 1870
Cons. May 25, 1872
Mineral Range & L'Anse Bay RR
June 9, 1871
Renamed as
Hancock & Calumet RR
Dec. 27, 1884
Sold Jan. 1, 1935
Mineral Range RR
Oct. 25, 1872
Cons. Nov. 1, 1949
Negaunee & Palmer RR
June 29, 1888
Control at inc.—MH&O
Sold no date
Detroit, Mackinac & Marquette RR
Sept. 3, 1879
Sold Oct. 20, 1886
Houghton & L'Anse RR
June 1, 1881
Cons. Feb. 1, 1883
Marquette & Western RR
Oct. 3, 1883
Lease May 1885
Sold July 17, 1890
Wisconsin, Sault Ste. Marie & Mackinac Ry
Sept. 4, 1886 Cons Dec. 22, 1886
Mackinaw & Marquette RR
Dec. 18, 1886
Sold Dec. 22, 1886
Sault Ste. Marie & Marquette RR
Feb. 5, 1880
Cons. Dec. 22, 1886
Marquette, Houghton & Ontonagon RR
May 25, 1872
Lease Feb. 15, 1887
Sold July 17, 1890
Duluth, Superior & Michigan Ry
(non-Mich. co.)
Cons. March 9, 1887
Duluth, South Shore & Atlantic Ry Dec. 22, 1886
Control ca. 1888 by Canadian Pacific
Reorganized as
Gogebic & Montreal River RR
Dec. 5, 1883
Tfr. no date
Lake Michigan & Lake Superior Ry
Oct. 20, 1890
Control at inc.—DSS&A
Duluth, South Shore & Atlantic RR
Oct. 18, 1949—Minn.
Control at inc.—CPR
Renamed as
Minneapolis, St. Paul & Sault Ste. Marie RR
July 18, 1944
Cons. Jan. 1, 1961
(*See* pg. 181)
Wisconsin Central Ry
June 17, 1887—Wisc.
Reorganized as
Soo Line RR Jan. 1, 1961
Control at inc.—CPR
Sold Oct. 11, 1987
all Mich. lines
Wisconsin Central RR
Feb. 19, 1954—Minn.
Cons. Jan. 1, 1961
Wisconsin Central Ltd.

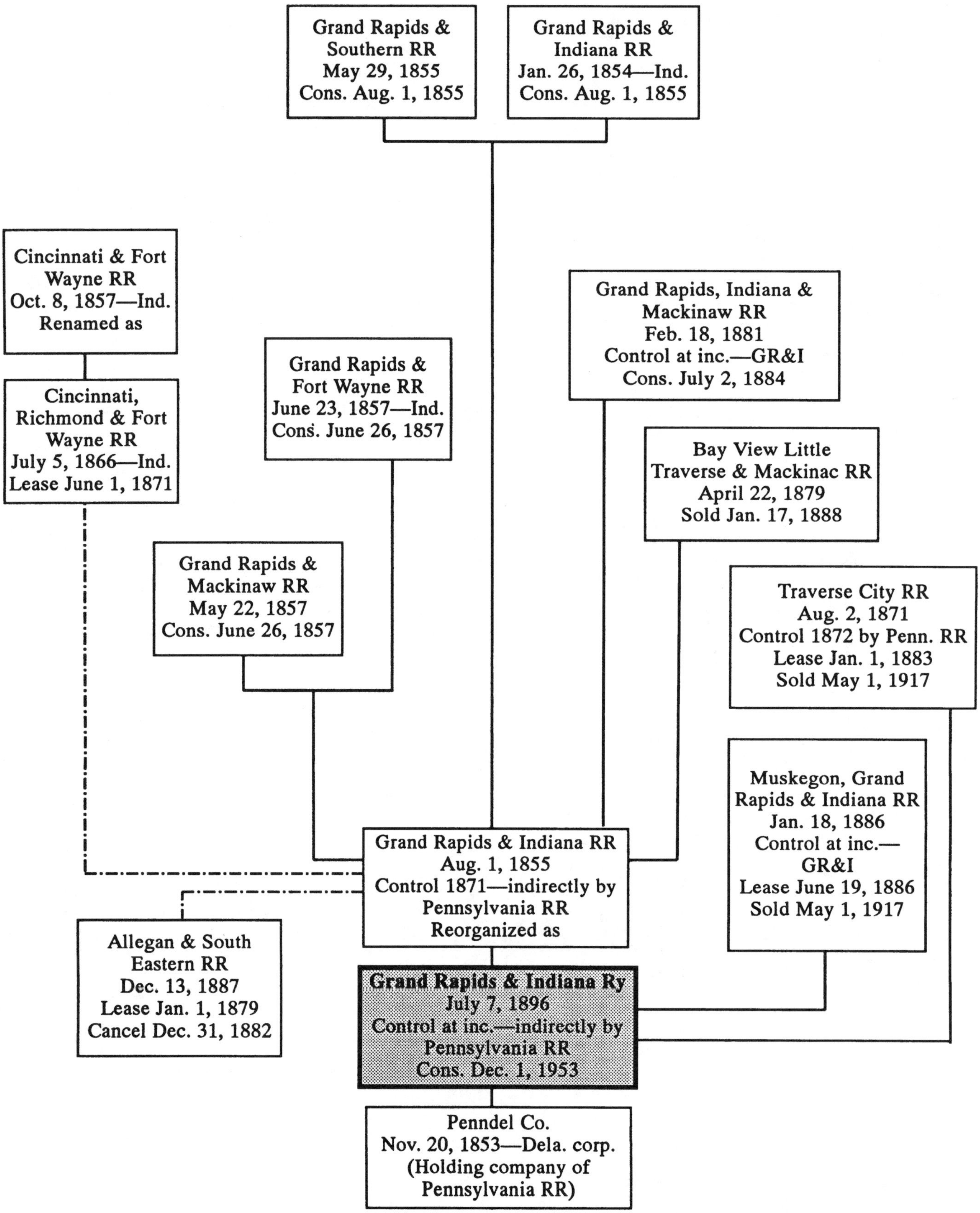
Grand Rapids & Southern RR
May 29, 1855
Cons. Aug. 1, 1855
Grand Rapids & Indiana RR
Jan. 26, 1854—Ind.
Cons. Aug. 1, 1855
Cincinnati & Fort Wayne RR
Oct. 8, 1857—Ind.
Renamed as
Cincinnati, Richmond & Fort Wayne RR
July 5, 1866—Ind.
Lease June 1, 1871
Grand Rapids & Fort Wayne RR
June 23, 1857—Ind.
Cons. June 26, 1857
Grand Rapids & Mackinaw RR
May 22, 1857
Cons. June 26, 1857
Grand Rapids, Indiana & Mackinaw RR
Feb. 18, 1881
Control at inc.—GR&I
Cons. July 2, 1884
Bay View Little Traverse & Mackinac RR
April 22, 1879
Sold Jan. 17, 1888
Traverse City RR
Aug. 2, 1871
Control 1872 by Penn. RR
Lease Jan. 1, 1883
Sold May 1, 1917
Muskegon, Grand Rapids & Indiana RR
Jan. 18, 1886
Control at inc.—GR&I
Lease June 19, 1886
Sold May 1, 1917
Grand Rapids & Indiana RR
Aug. 1, 1855
Control 1871—indirectly by Pennsylvania RR
Reorganized as
Allegan & South Eastern RR
Dec. 13, 1887
Lease Jan. 1, 1879
Cancel Dec. 31, 1882
Grand Rapids & Indiana Ry
July 7, 1896
Control at inc.—indirectly by Pennsylvania RR
Cons. Dec. 1, 1953
Penndel Co.
Nov. 20, 1853—Dela. corp.
(Holding company of Pennsylvania RR)

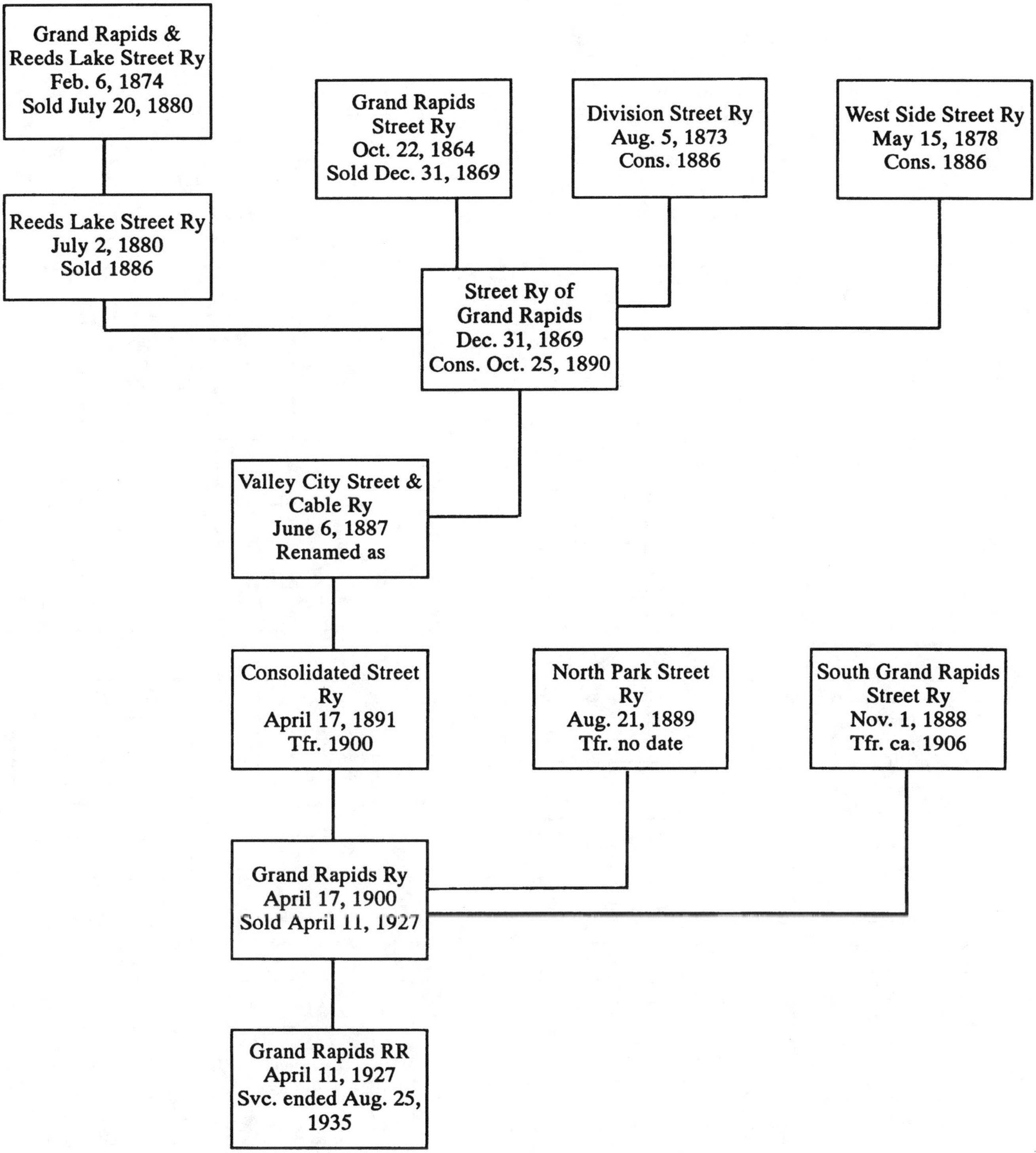
Grand Rapids & Reeds Lake Street Ry Feb. 6, 1874 Sold July 20, 1880
Grand Rapids Street Ry Oct. 22, 1864 Sold Dec. 31, 1869
Division Street Ry Aug. 5, 1873 Cons. 1886
West Side Street Ry May 15, 1878 Cons. 1886
Reeds Lake Street Ry July 2, 1880 Sold 1886
Street Ry of Grand Rapids Dec. 31, 1869 Cons. Oct. 25, 1890
Valley City Street & Cable Ry June 6, 1887 Renamed as
Consolidated Street Ry April 17, 1891 Tfr. 1900
North Park Street Ry Aug. 21, 1889 Tfr. no date
South Grand Rapids Street Ry Nov. 1, 1888 Tfr. ca. 1906
Grand Rapids Ry April 17, 1900 Sold April 11, 1927
Grand Rapids RR April 11, 1927 Svc. ended Aug. 25, 1935

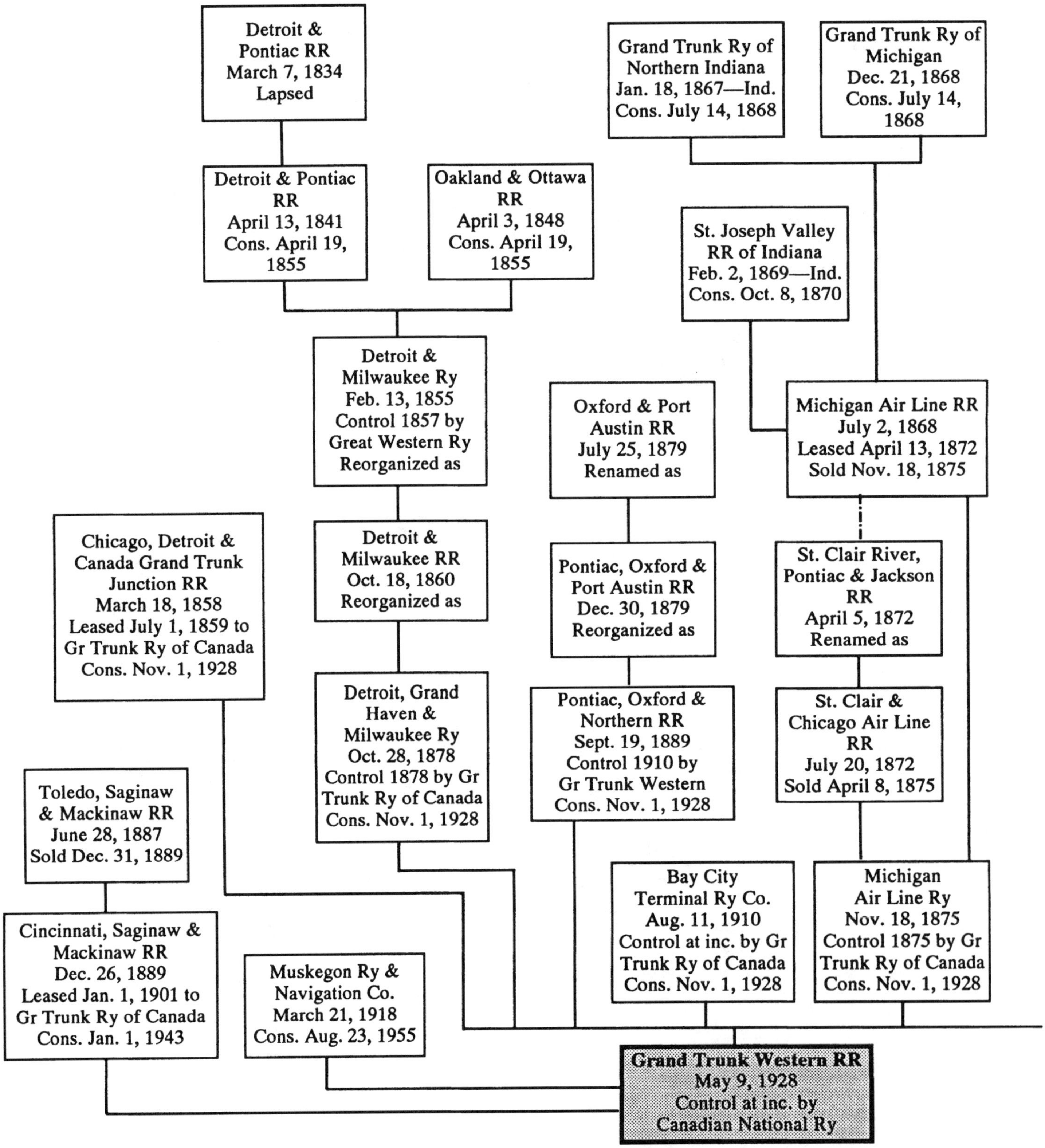
Detroit & Pontiac RR March 7, 1834 Lapsed
Grand Trunk Ry of Northern Indiana Jan. 18, 1867—Ind. Cons. July 14, 1868
Grand Trunk Ry of Michigan Dec. 21, 1868 Cons. July 14, 1868
Detroit & Pontiac RR April 13, 1841 Cons. April 19, 1855
Oakland & Ottawa RR April 3, 1848 Cons. April 19, 1855
St. Joseph Valley RR of Indiana Feb. 2, 1869—Ind. Cons. Oct. 8, 1870
Detroit & Milwaukee Ry Feb. 13, 1855 Control 1857 by Great Western Ry Reorganized as
Oxford & Port Austin RR July 25, 1879 Renamed as
Michigan Air Line RR July 2, 1868 Leased April 13, 1872 Sold Nov. 18, 1875
Chicago, Detroit & Canada Grand Trunk Junction RR March 18, 1858 Leased July 1, 1859 to Gr Trunk Ry of Canada Cons. Nov. 1, 1928
Detroit & Milwaukee RR Oct. 18, 1860 Reorganized as
Pontiac, Oxford & Port Austin RR Dec. 30, 1879 Reorganized as
St. Clair River, Pontiac & Jackson RR April 5, 1872 Renamed as
Detroit, Grand Haven & Milwaukee Ry Oct. 28, 1878 Control 1878 by Gr Trunk Ry of Canada Cons. Nov. 1, 1928
Pontiac, Oxford & Northern RR Sept. 19, 1889 Control 1910 by Gr Trunk Western Cons. Nov. 1, 1928
St. Clair & Chicago Air Line RR July 20, 1872 Sold April 8, 1875
Toledo, Saginaw & Mackinaw RR June 28, 1887 Sold Dec. 31, 1889
Bay City Terminal Ry Co. Aug. 11, 1910 Control at inc. by Gr Trunk Ry of Canada Cons. Nov. 1, 1928
Michigan Air Line Ry Nov. 18, 1875 Control 1875 by Gr Trunk Ry of Canada Cons. Nov. 1, 1928
Cincinnati, Saginaw & Mackinaw RR Dec. 26, 1889 Leased Jan. 1, 1901 to Gr Trunk Ry of Canada Cons. Jan. 1, 1943
Muskegon Ry & Navigation Co. March 21, 1918 Cons. Aug. 23, 1955
Grand Trunk Western RR May 9, 1928 Control at inc. by Canadian National Ry

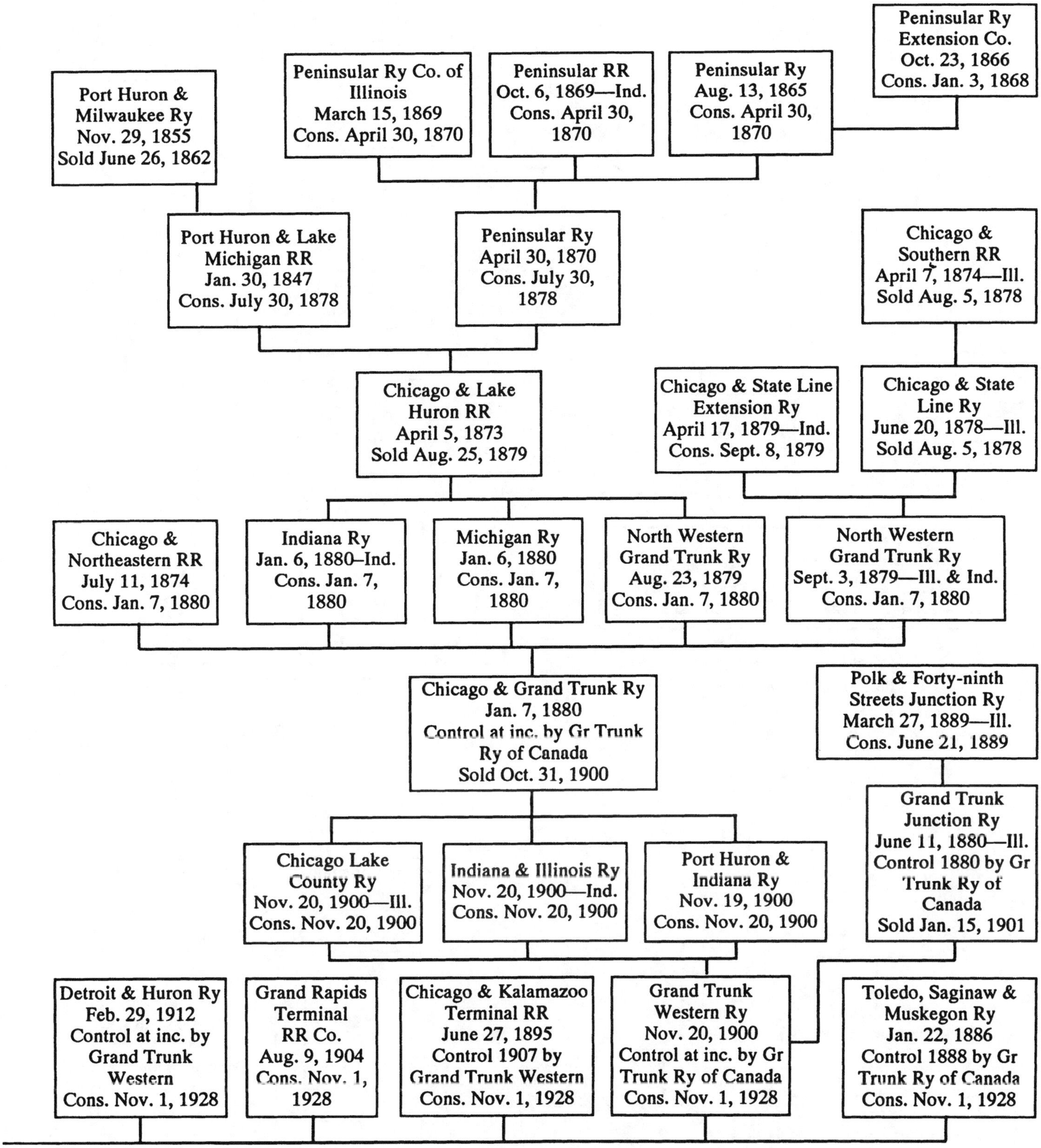
Port Huron & Milwaukee Ry Nov. 29, 1855 Sold June 26, 1862
Peninsular Ry Co. of Illinois March 15, 1869 Cons. April 30, 1870
Peninsular RR Oct. 6, 1869—Ind. Cons. April 30, 1870
Peninsular Ry Aug. 13, 1865 Cons. April 30, 1870
Peninsular Ry Extension Co. Oct. 23, 1866 Cons. Jan. 3, 1868
Port Huron & Lake Michigan RR Jan. 30, 1847 Cons. July 30, 1878
Peninsular Ry April 30, 1870 Cons. July 30, 1878
Chicago & Southern RR April 7, 1874—Ill. Sold Aug. 5, 1878
Chicago & Lake Huron RR April 5, 1873 Sold Aug. 25, 1879
Chicago & State Line Extension Ry April 17, 1879—Ind. Cons. Sept. 8, 1879
Chicago & State Line Ry June 20, 1878—Ill. Sold Aug. 5, 1878
Chicago & Northeastern RR July 11, 1874 Cons. Jan. 7, 1880
Indiana Ry Jan. 6, 1880–Ind. Cons. Jan. 7, 1880
Michigan Ry Jan. 6, 1880 Cons. Jan. 7, 1880
North Western Grand Trunk Ry Aug. 23, 1879 Cons. Jan. 7, 1880
North Western Grand Trunk Ry Sept. 3, 1879—Ill. & Ind. Cons. Jan. 7, 1880
Chicago & Grand Trunk Ry Jan. 7, 1880 Control at inc. by Gr Trunk Ry of Canada Sold Oct. 31, 1900
Polk & Forty-ninth Streets Junction Ry March 27, 1889—Ill. Cons. June 21, 1889
Chicago Lake County Ry Nov. 20, 1900—Ill. Cons. Nov. 20, 1900
Indiana & Illinois Ry Nov. 20, 1900—Ind. Cons. Nov. 20, 1900
Port Huron & Indiana Ry Nov. 19, 1900 Cons. Nov. 20, 1900
Grand Trunk Junction Ry June 11, 1880—Ill. Control 1880 by Gr Trunk Ry of Canada Sold Jan. 15, 1901
Detroit & Huron Ry Feb. 29, 1912 Control at inc. by Grand Trunk Western Cons. Nov. 1, 1928
Grand Rapids Terminal RR Co. Aug. 9, 1904 Cons. Nov. 1, 1928
Chicago & Kalamazoo Terminal RR June 27, 1895 Control 1907 by Grand Trunk Western Cons. Nov. 1, 1928
Grand Trunk Western Ry Nov. 20, 1900 Control at inc. by Gr Trunk Ry of Canada Cons. Nov. 1, 1928
Toledo, Saginaw & Muskegon Ry Jan. 22, 1886 Control 1888 by Gr Trunk Ry of Canada Cons. Nov. 1, 1928

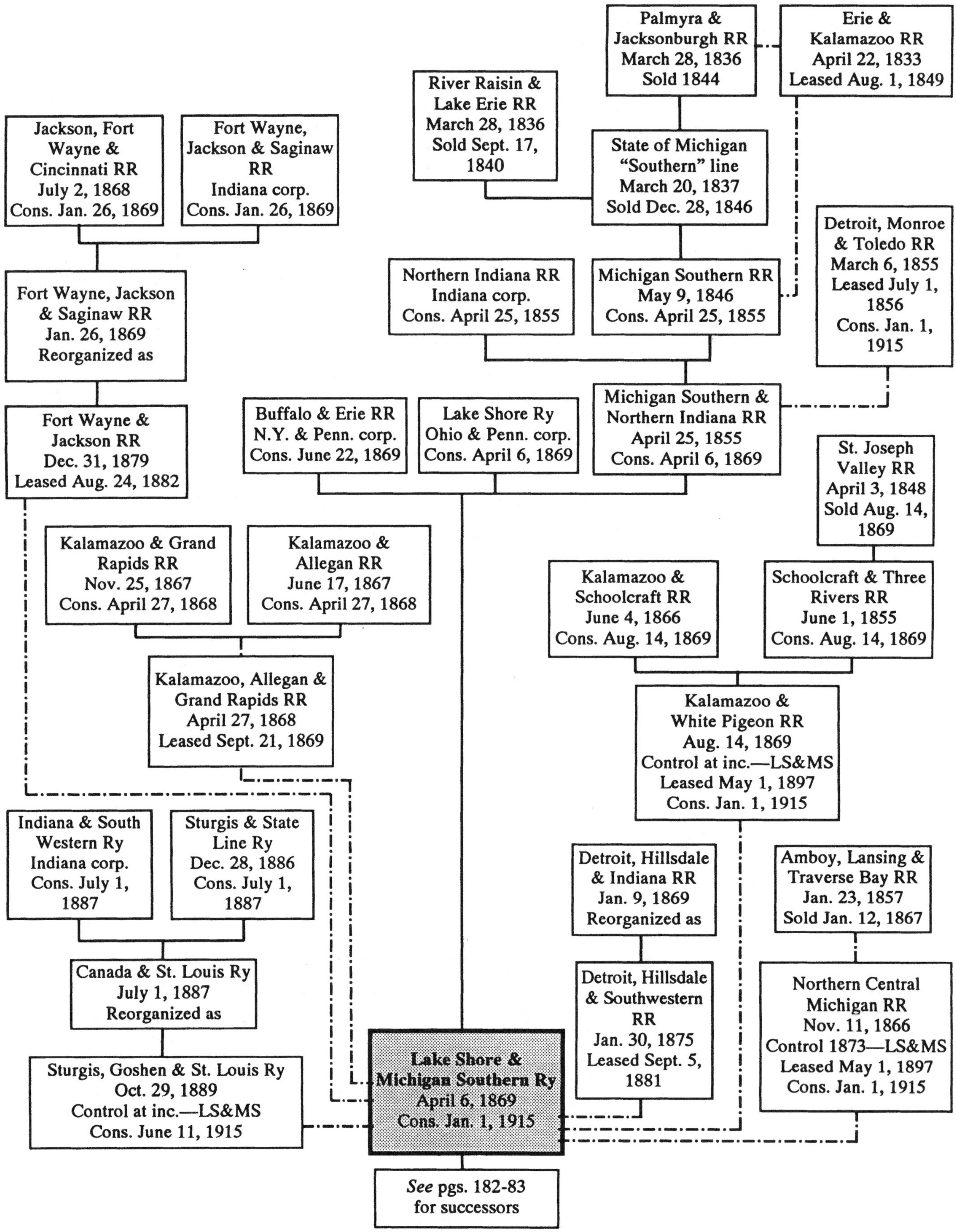
Palmyra & Jacksonburgh RR March 28, 1836 Sold 1844
Erie & Kalamazoo RR April 22, 1833 Leased Aug. 1, 1849
River Raisin & Lake Erie RR March 28, 1836 Sold Sept. 17, 1840
Jackson, Fort Wayne & Cincinnati RR July 2, 1868 Cons. Jan. 26, 1869
Fort Wayne, Jackson & Saginaw RR Indiana corp. Cons. Jan. 26, 1869
State of Michigan "Southern" line March 20, 1837 Sold Dec. 28, 1846
Detroit, Monroe & Toledo RR March 6, 1855 Leased July 1, 1856 Cons. Jan. 1, 1915
Northern Indiana RR Indiana corp. Cons. April 25, 1855
Michigan Southern RR May 9, 1846 Cons. April 25, 1855
Fort Wayne, Jackson & Saginaw RR Jan. 26, 1869 Reorganized as
Michigan Southern & Northern Indiana RR April 25, 1855 Cons. April 6, 1869
Fort Wayne & Jackson RR Dec. 31, 1879 Leased Aug. 24, 1882
Buffalo & Erie RR N.Y. & Penn. corp. Cons. June 22, 1869
Lake Shore Ry Ohio & Penn. corp. Cons. April 6, 1869
St. Joseph Valley RR April 3, 1848 Sold Aug. 14, 1869
Kalamazoo & Grand Rapids RR Nov. 25, 1867 Cons. April 27, 1868
Kalamazoo & Allegan RR June 17, 1867 Cons. April 27, 1868
Kalamazoo & Schoolcraft RR June 4, 1866 Cons. Aug. 14, 1869
Schoolcraft & Three Rivers RR June 1, 1855 Cons. Aug. 14, 1869
Kalamazoo, Allegan & Grand Rapids RR April 27, 1868 Leased Sept. 21, 1869
Kalamazoo & White Pigeon RR Aug. 14, 1869 Control at inc.—LS&MS Leased May 1, 1897 Cons. Jan. 1, 1915
Indiana & South Western Ry Indiana corp. Cons. July 1, 1887
Sturgis & State Line Ry Dec. 28, 1886 Cons. July 1, 1887
Detroit, Hillsdale & Indiana RR Jan. 9, 1869 Reorganized as
Amboy, Lansing & Traverse Bay RR Jan. 23, 1857 Sold Jan. 12, 1867
Canada & St. Louis Ry July 1, 1887 Reorganized as
Detroit, Hillsdale & Southwestern RR Jan. 30, 1875 Leased Sept. 5, 1881
Northern Central Michigan RR Nov. 11, 1866 Control 1873—LS&MS Leased May 1, 1897 Cons. Jan. 1, 1915
Lake Shore & Michigan Southern Ry April 6, 1869 Cons. Jan. 1, 1915
Sturgis, Goshen & St. Louis Ry Oct. 29, 1889 Control at inc.—LS&MS Cons. June 11, 1915
See pgs. 182-83 for successors

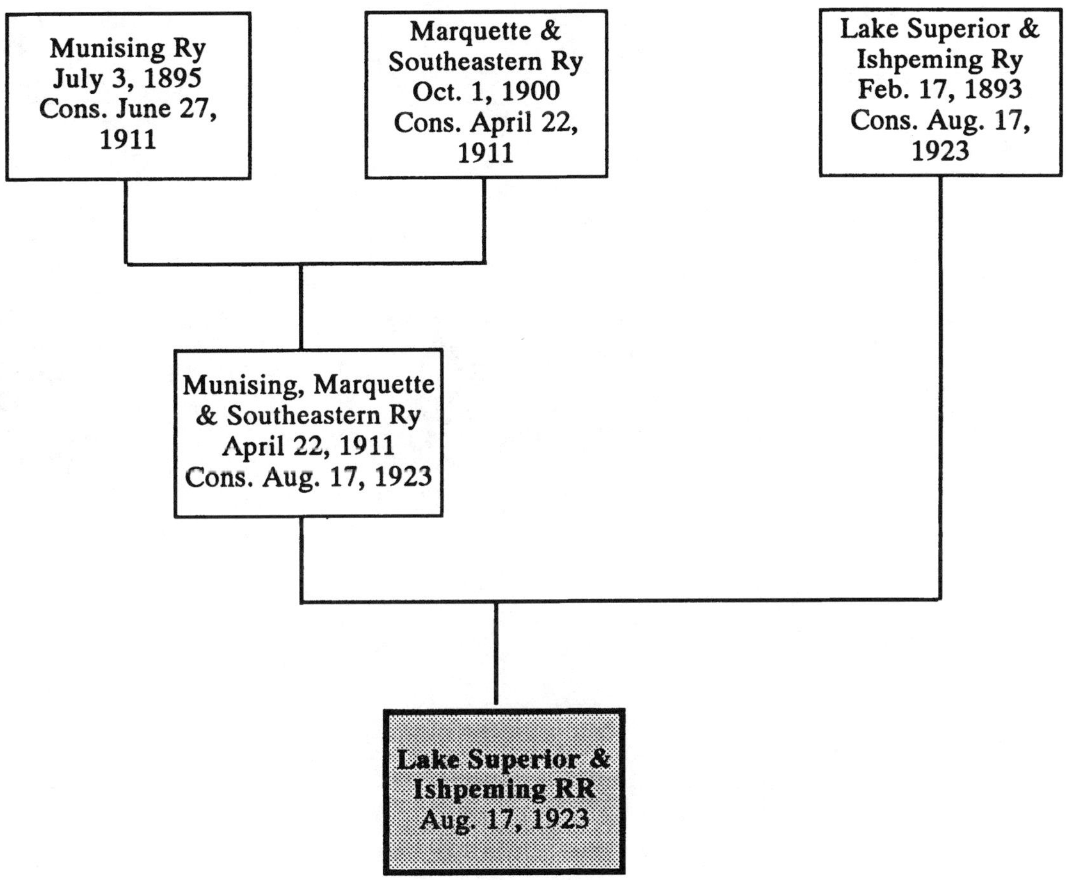
Munising Ry
July 3, 1895
Cons. June 27, 1911
Marquette & Southeastern Ry
Oct. 1, 1900
Cons. April 22, 1911
Lake Superior & Ishpeming Ry
Feb. 17, 1893
Cons. Aug. 17, 1923
Munising, Marquette & Southeastern Ry
April 22, 1911
Cons. Aug. 17, 1923
Lake Superior & Ishpeming RR
Aug. 17, 1923

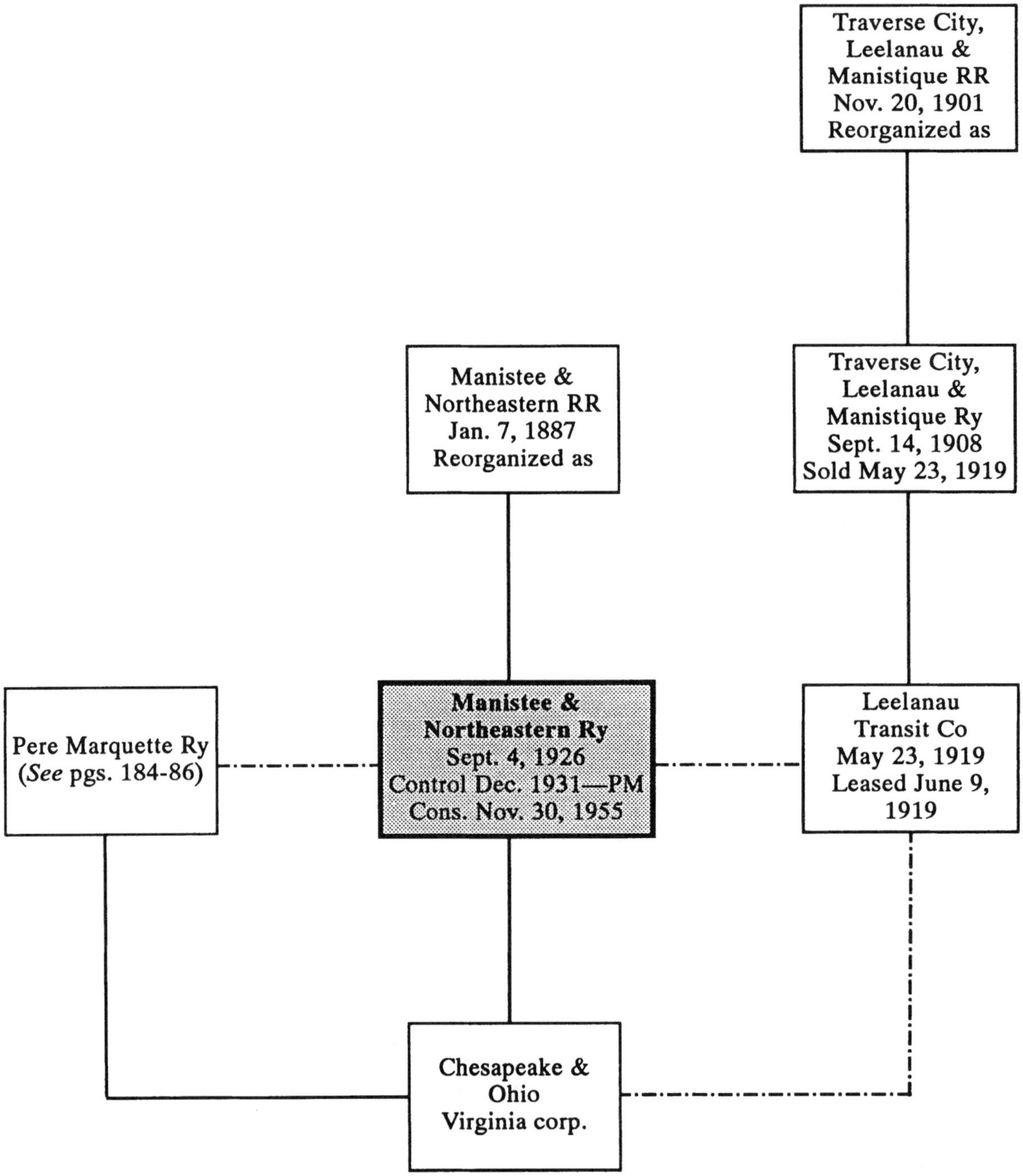
Traverse City,
Leelanau &
Manistique RR
Nov. 20, 1901
Reorganized as
Manistee &
Northeastern RR
Jan. 7, 1887
Reorganized as
Traverse City,
Leelanau &
Manistique Ry
Sept. 14, 1908
Sold May 23, 1919
Pere Marquette Ry
(*See* pgs. 184-86)
Manistee &
Northeastern Ry
Sept. 4, 1926
Control Dec. 1931—PM
Cons. Nov. 30, 1955
Leelanau
Transit Co
May 23, 1919
Leased June 9,
1919
Chesapeake &
Ohio
Virginia corp.

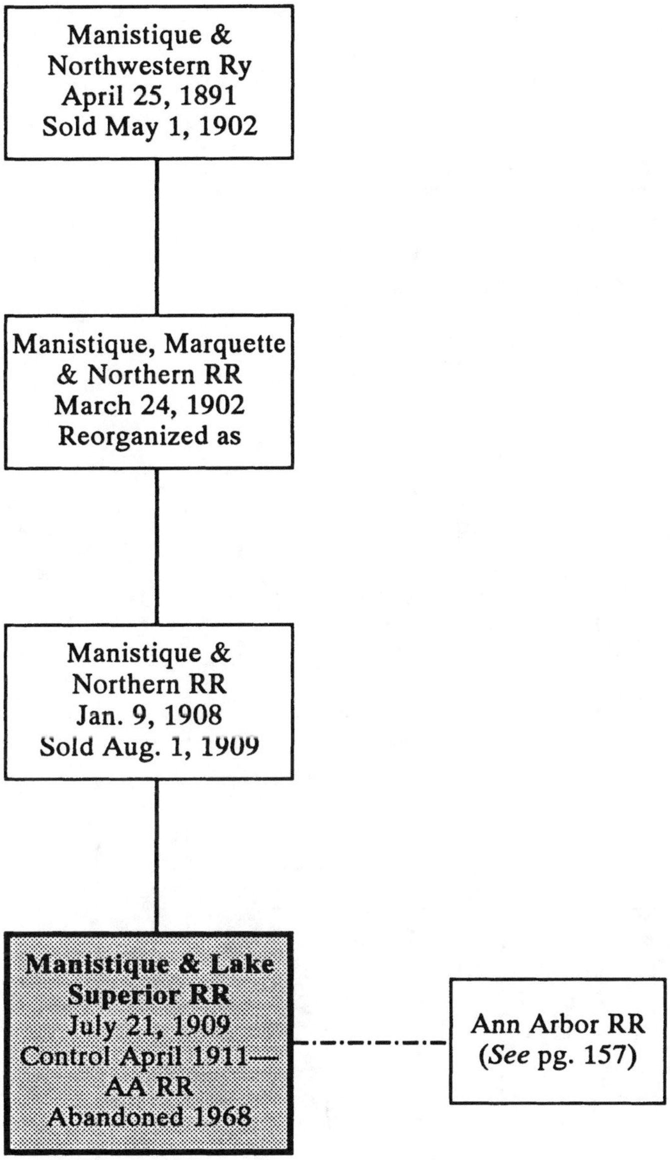
Manistique & Northwestern Ry
April 25, 1891
Sold May 1, 1902
Manistique, Marquette & Northern RR
March 24, 1902
Reorganized as
Manistique & Northern RR
Jan. 9, 1908
Sold Aug. 1, 1909
Manistique & Lake Superior RR
July 21, 1909
Control April 1911—AA RR
Abandoned 1968
Ann Arbor RR
(*See* pg. 157)

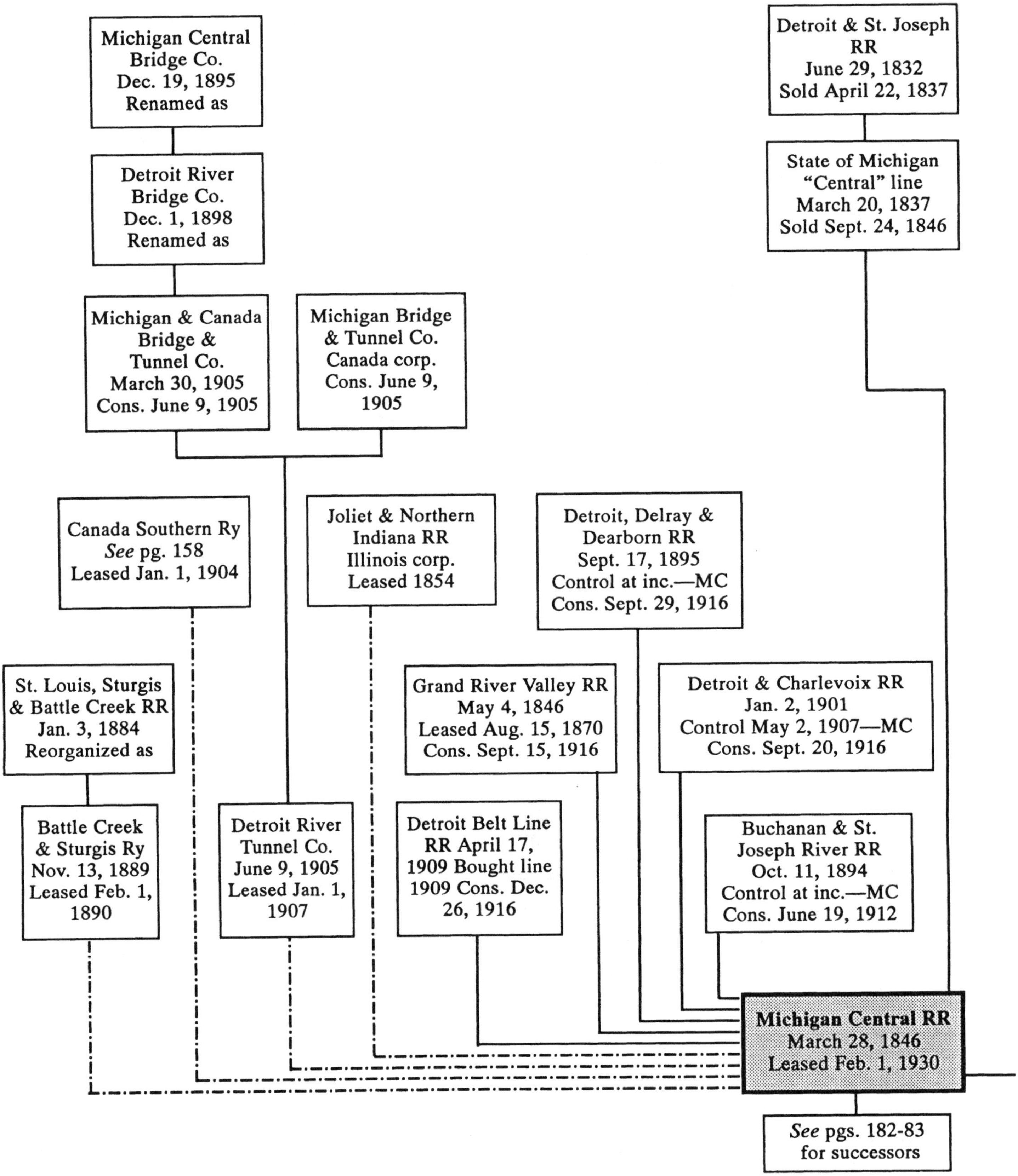
Michigan Central Bridge Co. Dec. 19, 1895 Renamed as
Detroit River Bridge Co. Dec. 1, 1898 Renamed as
Michigan & Canada Bridge & Tunnel Co. March 30, 1905 Cons. June 9, 1905
Michigan Bridge & Tunnel Co. Canada corp. Cons. June 9, 1905
Detroit & St. Joseph RR June 29, 1832 Sold April 22, 1837
State of Michigan "Central" line March 20, 1837 Sold Sept. 24, 1846
Canada Southern Ry See pg. 158 Leased Jan. 1, 1904
Joliet & Northern Indiana RR Illinois corp. Leased 1854
Detroit, Delray & Dearborn RR Sept. 17, 1895 Control at inc.—MC Cons. Sept. 29, 1916
St. Louis, Sturgis & Battle Creek RR Jan. 3, 1884 Reorganized as
Grand River Valley RR May 4, 1846 Leased Aug. 15, 1870 Cons. Sept. 15, 1916
Detroit & Charlevoix RR Jan. 2, 1901 Control May 2, 1907—MC Cons. Sept. 20, 1916
Battle Creek & Sturgis Ry Nov. 13, 1889 Leased Feb. 1, 1890
Detroit River Tunnel Co. June 9, 1905 Leased Jan. 1, 1907
Detroit Belt Line RR April 17, 1909 Bought line 1909 Cons. Dec. 26, 1916
Buchanan & St. Joseph River RR Oct. 11, 1894 Control at inc.—MC Cons. June 19, 1912
Michigan Central RR March 28, 1846 Leased Feb. 1, 1930
See pgs. 182-83 for successors

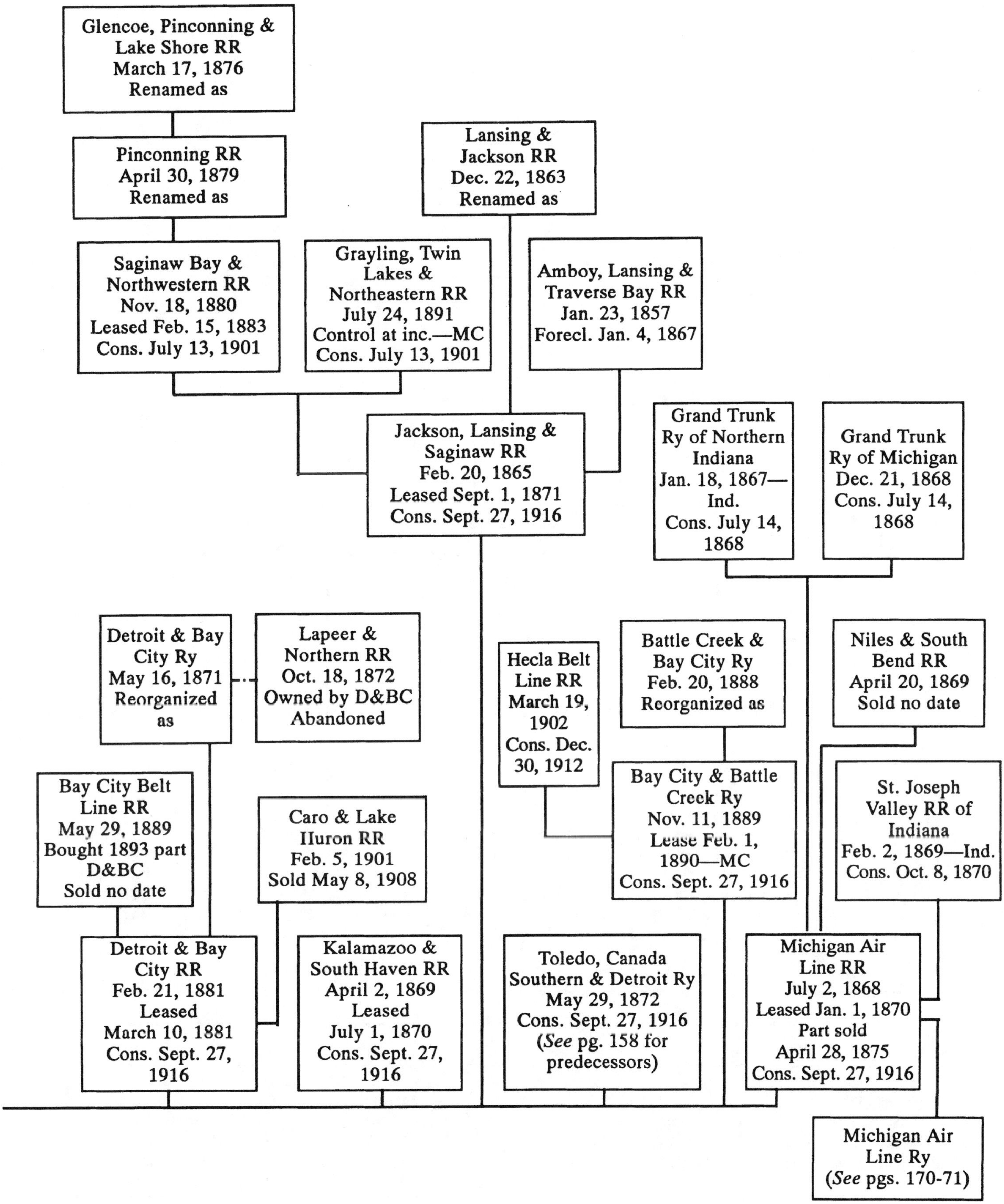
Glencoe, Pinconning & Lake Shore RR March 17, 1876 Renamed as
Pinconning RR April 30, 1879 Renamed as
Lansing & Jackson RR Dec. 22, 1863 Renamed as
Saginaw Bay & Northwestern RR Nov. 18, 1880 Leased Feb. 15, 1883 Cons. July 13, 1901
Grayling, Twin Lakes & Northeastern RR July 24, 1891 Control at inc.—MC Cons. July 13, 1901
Amboy, Lansing & Traverse Bay RR Jan. 23, 1857 Forecl. Jan. 4, 1867
Jackson, Lansing & Saginaw RR Feb. 20, 1865 Leased Sept. 1, 1871 Cons. Sept. 27, 1916
Grand Trunk Ry of Northern Indiana Jan. 18, 1867—Ind. Cons. July 14, 1868
Grand Trunk Ry of Michigan Dec. 21, 1868 Cons. July 14, 1868
Detroit & Bay City Ry May 16, 1871 Reorganized as
Lapeer & Northern RR Oct. 18, 1872 Owned by D&BC Abandoned
Hecla Belt Line RR March 19, 1902 Cons. Dec. 30, 1912
Battle Creek & Bay City Ry Feb. 20, 1888 Reorganized as
Niles & South Bend RR April 20, 1869 Sold no date
Bay City Belt Line RR May 29, 1889 Bought 1893 part D&BC Sold no date
Caro & Lake Huron RR Feb. 5, 1901 Sold May 8, 1908
Bay City & Battle Creek Ry Nov. 11, 1889 Lease Feb. 1, 1890—MC Cons. Sept. 27, 1916
St. Joseph Valley RR of Indiana Feb. 2, 1869—Ind. Cons. Oct. 8, 1870
Detroit & Bay City RR Feb. 21, 1881 Leased March 10, 1881 Cons. Sept. 27, 1916
Kalamazoo & South Haven RR April 2, 1869 Leased July 1, 1870 Cons. Sept. 27, 1916
Toledo, Canada Southern & Detroit Ry May 29, 1872 Cons. Sept. 27, 1916 (*See* pg. 158 for predecessors)
Michigan Air Line RR July 2, 1868 Leased Jan. 1, 1870 Part sold April 28, 1875 Cons. Sept. 27, 1916
Michigan Air Line Ry (*See* pgs. 170-71)

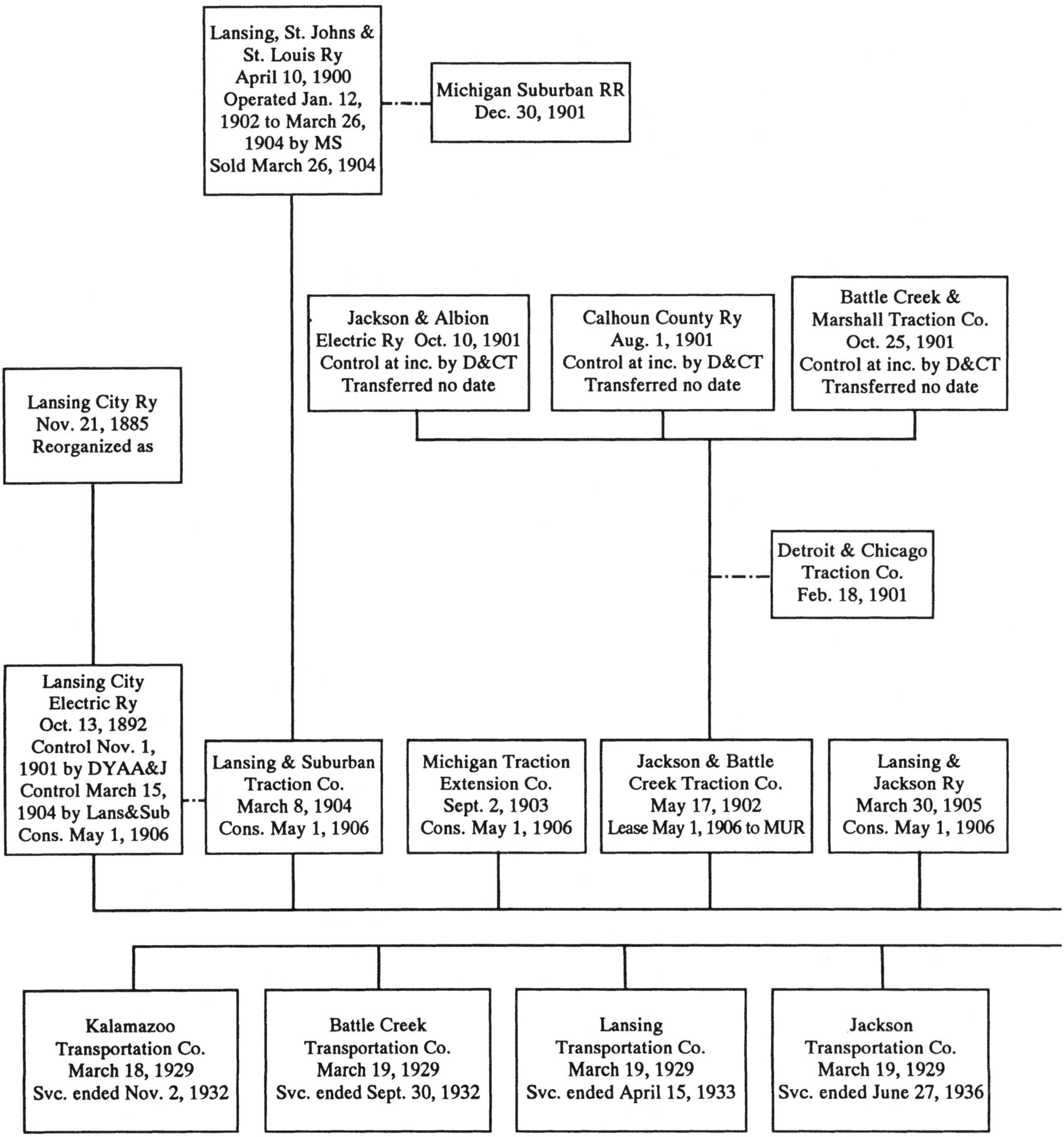
Lansing, St. Johns & St. Louis Ry April 10, 1900 Operated Jan. 12, 1902 to March 26, 1904 by MS Sold March 26, 1904
Michigan Suburban RR Dec. 30, 1901
Jackson & Albion Electric Ry Oct. 10, 1901 Control at inc. by D&CT Transferred no date
Calhoun County Ry Aug. 1, 1901 Control at inc. by D&CT Transferred no date
Battle Creek & Marshall Traction Co. Oct. 25, 1901 Control at inc. by D&CT Transferred no date
Lansing City Ry Nov. 21, 1885 Reorganized as
Detroit & Chicago Traction Co. Feb. 18, 1901
Lansing City Electric Ry Oct. 13, 1892 Control Nov. 1, 1901 by DYAA&J Control March 15, 1904 by Lans&Sub Cons. May 1, 1906
Lansing & Suburban Traction Co. March 8, 1904 Cons. May 1, 1906
Michigan Traction Extension Co. Sept. 2, 1903 Cons. May 1, 1906
Jackson & Battle Creek Traction Co. May 17, 1902 Lease May 1, 1906 to MUR
Lansing & Jackson Ry March 30, 1905 Cons. May 1, 1906
Kalamazoo Transportation Co. March 18, 1929 Svc. ended Nov. 2, 1932
Battle Creek Transportation Co. March 19, 1929 Svc. ended Sept. 30, 1932
Lansing Transportation Co. March 19, 1929 Svc. ended April 15, 1933
Jackson Transportation Co. March 19, 1929 Svc. ended June 27, 1936

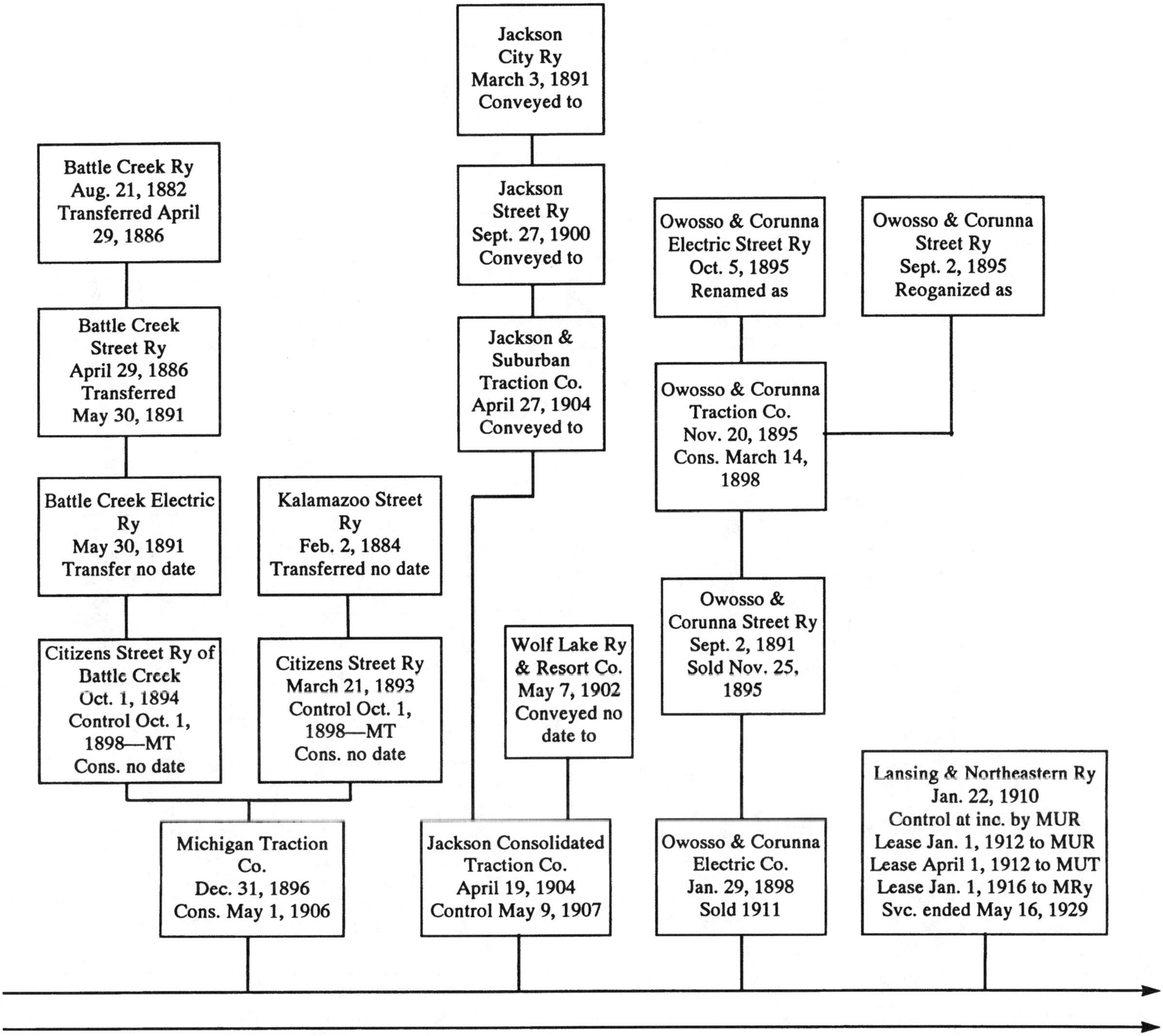
Jackson City Ry March 3, 1891 Conveyed to
Jackson Street Ry Sept. 27, 1900 Conveyed to
Jackson & Suburban Traction Co. April 27, 1904 Conveyed to
Battle Creek Ry Aug. 21, 1882 Transferred April 29, 1886
Battle Creek Street Ry April 29, 1886 Transferred May 30, 1891
Battle Creek Electric Ry May 30, 1891 Transfer no date
Kalamazoo Street Ry Feb. 2, 1884 Transferred no date
Citizens Street Ry of Battle Creek Oct. 1, 1894 Control Oct. 1, 1898—MT Cons. no date
Citizens Street Ry March 21, 1893 Control Oct. 1, 1898—MT Cons. no date
Michigan Traction Co. Dec. 31, 1896 Cons. May 1, 1906
Wolf Lake Ry & Resort Co. May 7, 1902 Conveyed no date to
Jackson Consolidated Traction Co. April 19, 1904 Control May 9, 1907
Owosso & Corunna Electric Street Ry Oct. 5, 1895 Renamed as
Owosso & Corunna Street Ry Sept. 2, 1895 Reoganized as
Owosso & Corunna Traction Co. Nov. 20, 1895 Cons. March 14, 1898
Owosso & Corunna Street Ry Sept. 2, 1891 Sold Nov. 25, 1895
Owosso & Corunna Electric Co. Jan. 29, 1898 Sold 1911
Lansing & Northeastern Ry Jan. 22, 1910 Control at inc. by MUR Lease Jan. 1, 1912 to MUR Lease April 1, 1912 to MUT Lease Jan. 1, 1916 to MRy Svc. ended May 16, 1929

(continued)

MICHIGAN UNITED

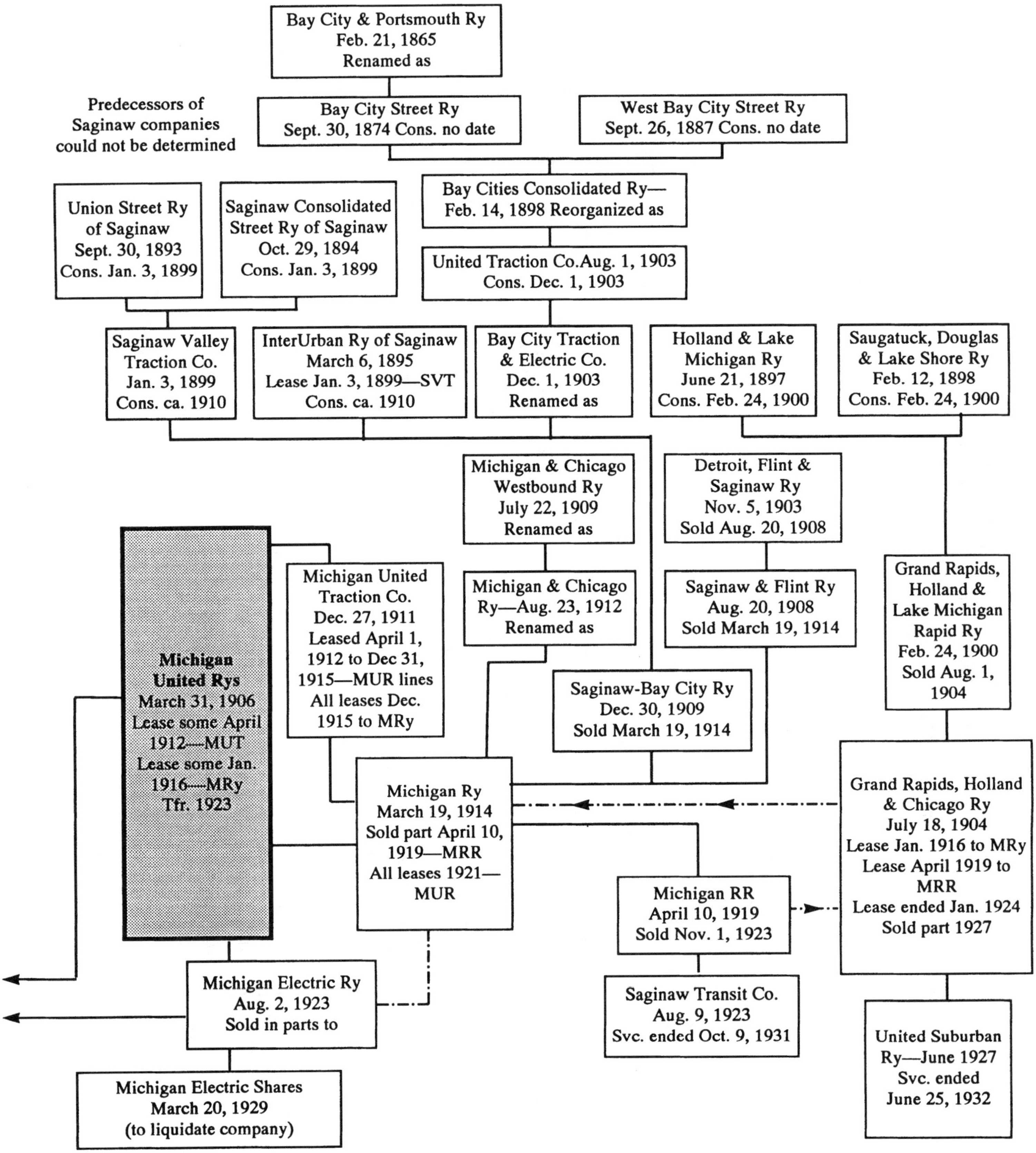

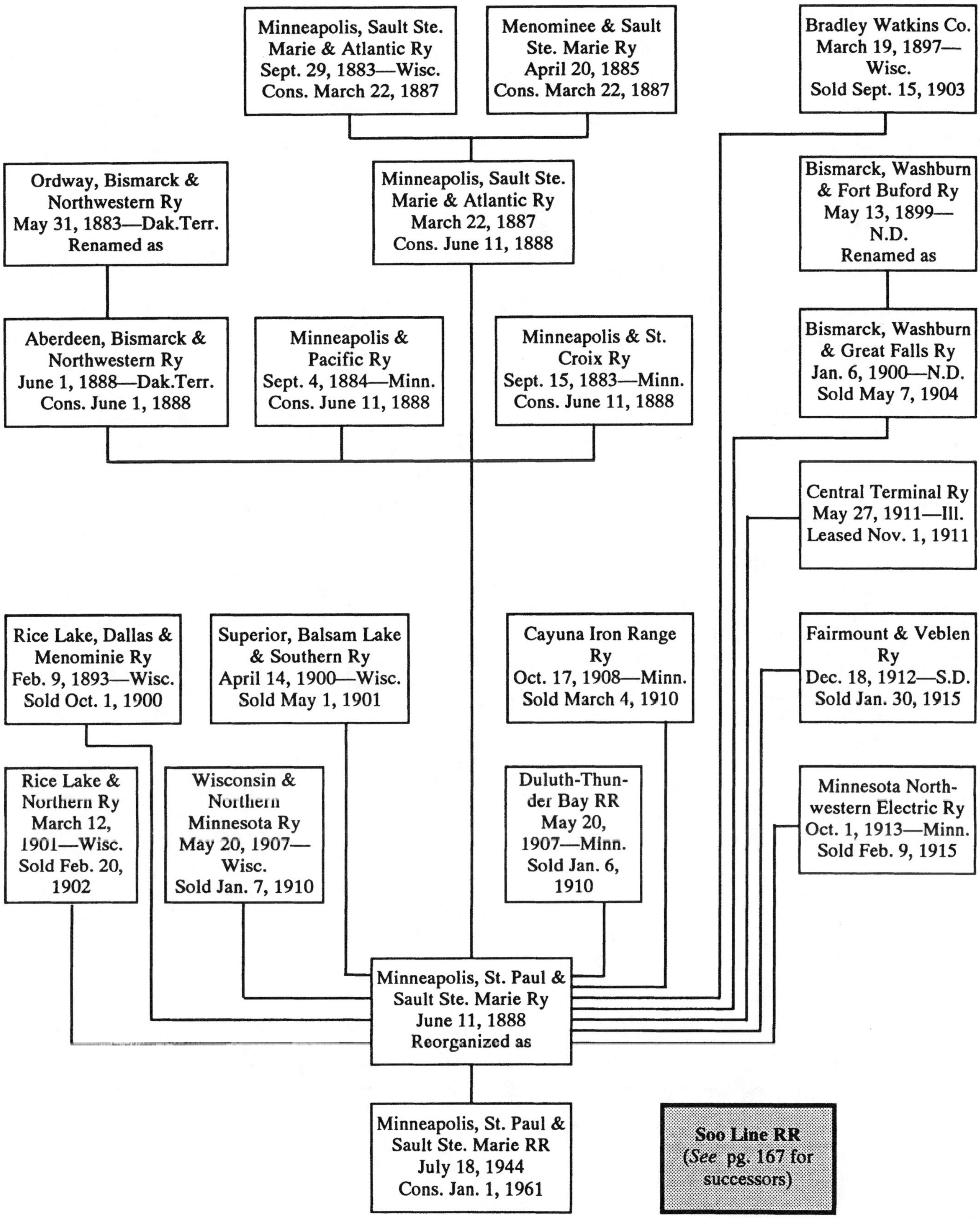
Minneapolis, Sault Ste. Marie & Atlantic Ry Sept. 29, 1883—Wisc. Cons. March 22, 1887
Menominee & Sault Ste. Marie Ry April 20, 1885 Cons. March 22, 1887
Bradley Watkins Co. March 19, 1897—Wisc. Sold Sept. 15, 1903
Ordway, Bismarck & Northwestern Ry May 31, 1883—Dak.Terr. Renamed as
Minneapolis, Sault Ste. Marie & Atlantic Ry March 22, 1887 Cons. June 11, 1888
Bismarck, Washburn & Fort Buford Ry May 13, 1899—N.D. Renamed as
Aberdeen, Bismarck & Northwestern Ry June 1, 1888—Dak.Terr. Cons. June 1, 1888
Minneapolis & Pacific Ry Sept. 4, 1884—Minn. Cons. June 11, 1888
Minneapolis & St. Croix Ry Sept. 15, 1883—Minn. Cons. June 11, 1888
Bismarck, Washburn & Great Falls Ry Jan. 6, 1900—N.D. Sold May 7, 1904
Central Terminal Ry May 27, 1911—Ill. Leased Nov. 1, 1911
Rice Lake, Dallas & Menominie Ry Feb. 9, 1893—Wisc. Sold Oct. 1, 1900
Superior, Balsam Lake & Southern Ry April 14, 1900—Wisc. Sold May 1, 1901
Cayuna Iron Range Ry Oct. 17, 1908—Minn. Sold March 4, 1910
Fairmount & Veblen Ry Dec. 18, 1912—S.D. Sold Jan. 30, 1915
Rice Lake & Northern Ry March 12, 1901—Wisc. Sold Feb. 20, 1902
Wisconsin & Northern Minnesota Ry May 20, 1907—Wisc. Sold Jan. 7, 1910
Duluth-Thunder Bay RR May 20, 1907—Minn. Sold Jan. 6, 1910
Minnesota Northwestern Electric Ry Oct. 1, 1913—Minn. Sold Feb. 9, 1915
Minneapolis, St. Paul & Sault Ste. Marie Ry June 11, 1888 Reorganized as
Minneapolis, St. Paul & Sault Ste. Marie RR July 18, 1944 Cons. Jan. 1, 1961
Soo Line RR (*See* pg. 167 for successors)

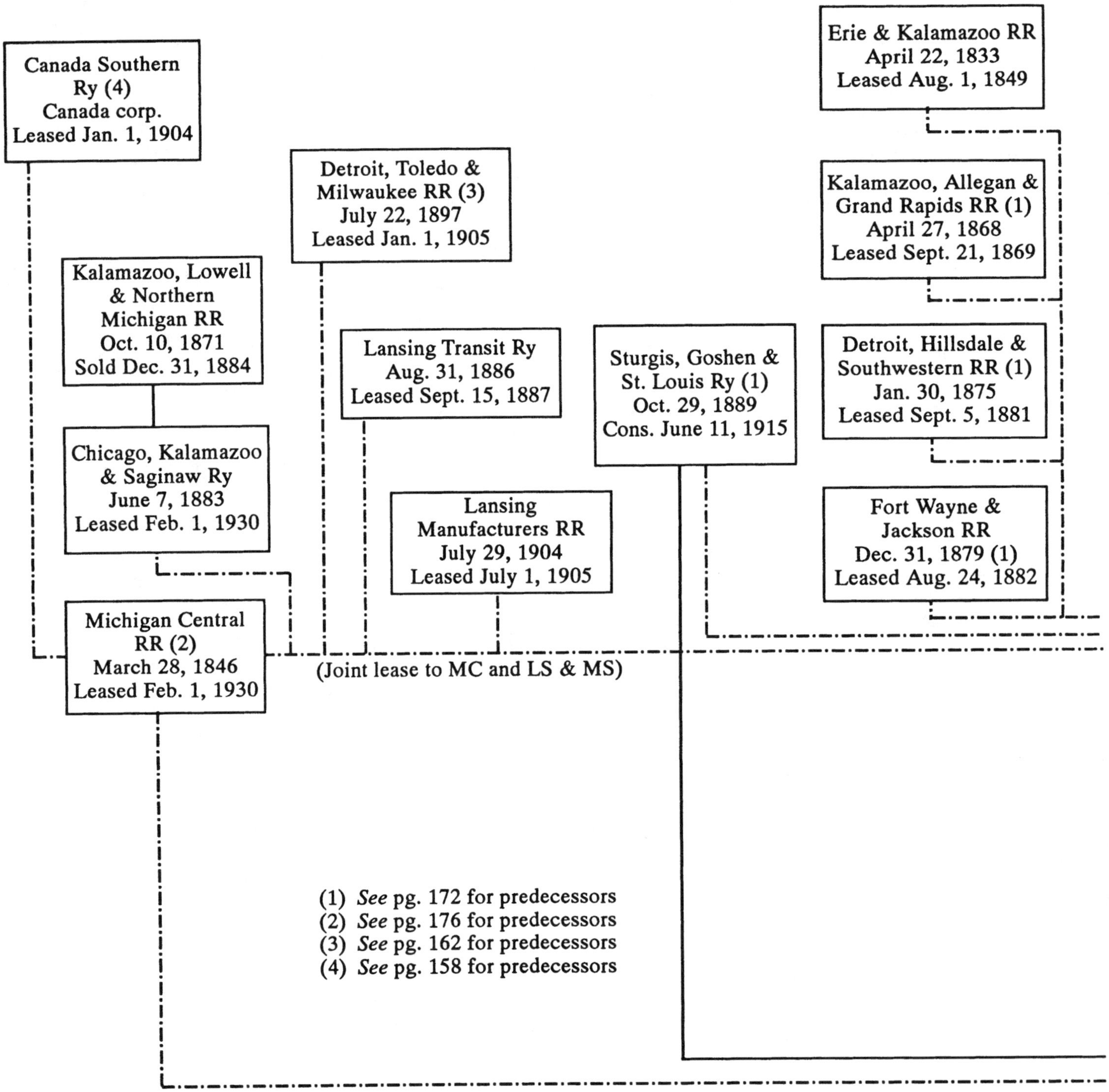

(1) *See* pg. 172 for predecessors
(2) *See* pg. 176 for predecessors
(3) *See* pg. 162 for predecessors
(4) *See* pg. 158 for predecessors

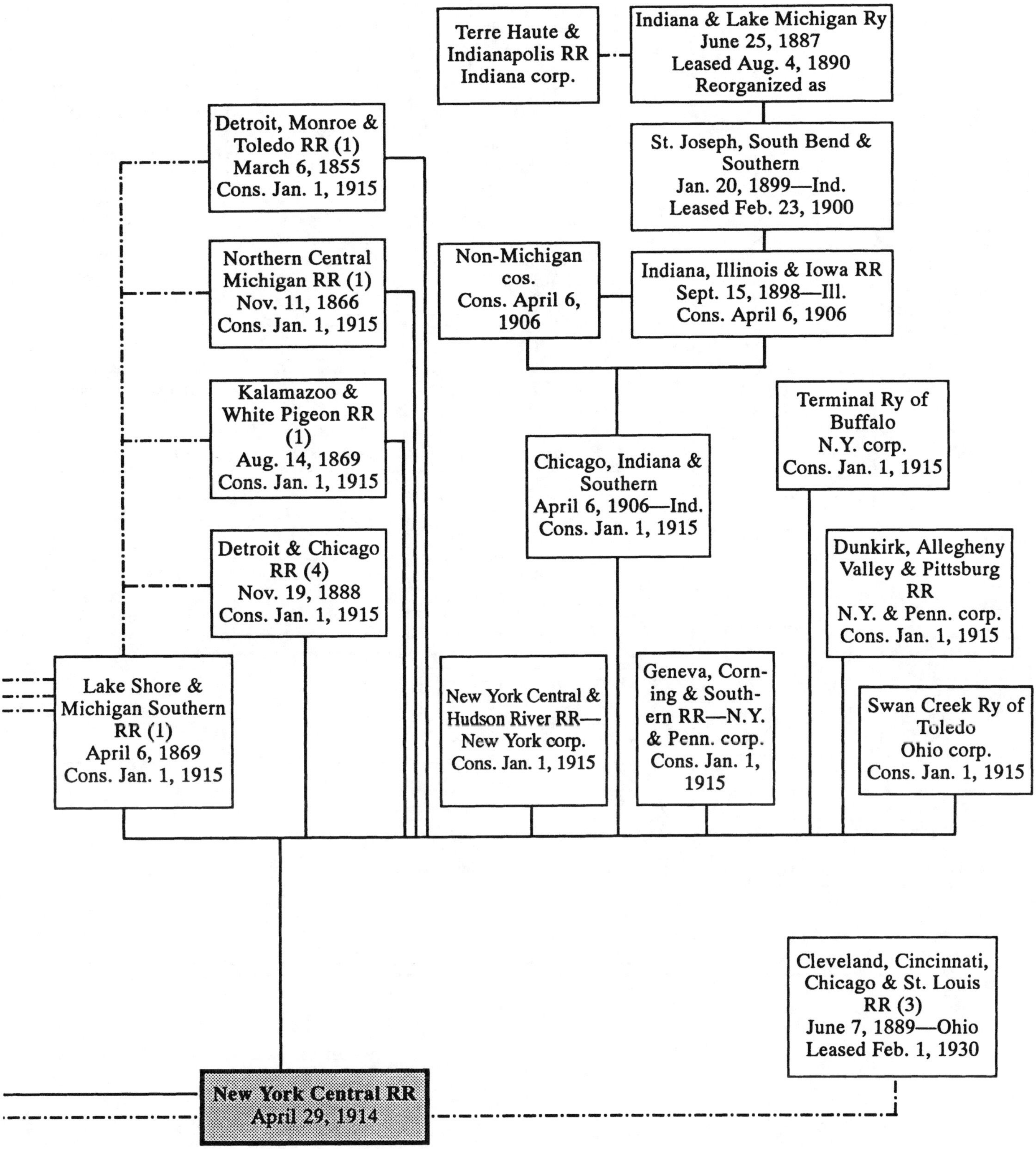
Terre Haute & Indianapolis RR Indiana corp.
Indiana & Lake Michigan Ry June 25, 1887 Leased Aug. 4, 1890 Reorganized as
St. Joseph, South Bend & Southern Jan. 20, 1899—Ind. Leased Feb. 23, 1900
Detroit, Monroe & Toledo RR (1) March 6, 1855 Cons. Jan. 1, 1915
Northern Central Michigan RR (1) Nov. 11, 1866 Cons. Jan. 1, 1915
Non-Michigan cos. Cons. April 6, 1906
Indiana, Illinois & Iowa RR Sept. 15, 1898—Ill. Cons. April 6, 1906
Kalamazoo & White Pigeon RR (1) Aug. 14, 1869 Cons. Jan. 1, 1915
Terminal Ry of Buffalo N.Y. corp. Cons. Jan. 1, 1915
Chicago, Indiana & Southern April 6, 1906—Ind. Cons. Jan. 1, 1915
Detroit & Chicago RR (4) Nov. 19, 1888 Cons. Jan. 1, 1915
Dunkirk, Allegheny Valley & Pittsburg RR N.Y. & Penn. corp. Cons. Jan. 1, 1915
Lake Shore & Michigan Southern RR (1) April 6, 1869 Cons. Jan. 1, 1915
New York Central & Hudson River RR—New York corp. Cons. Jan. 1, 1915
Geneva, Corning & Southern RR—N.Y. & Penn. corp. Cons. Jan. 1, 1915
Swan Creek Ry of Toledo Ohio corp. Cons. Jan. 1, 1915
Cleveland, Cincinnati, Chicago & St. Louis RR (3) June 7, 1889—Ohio Leased Feb. 1, 1930
New York Central RR April 29, 1914

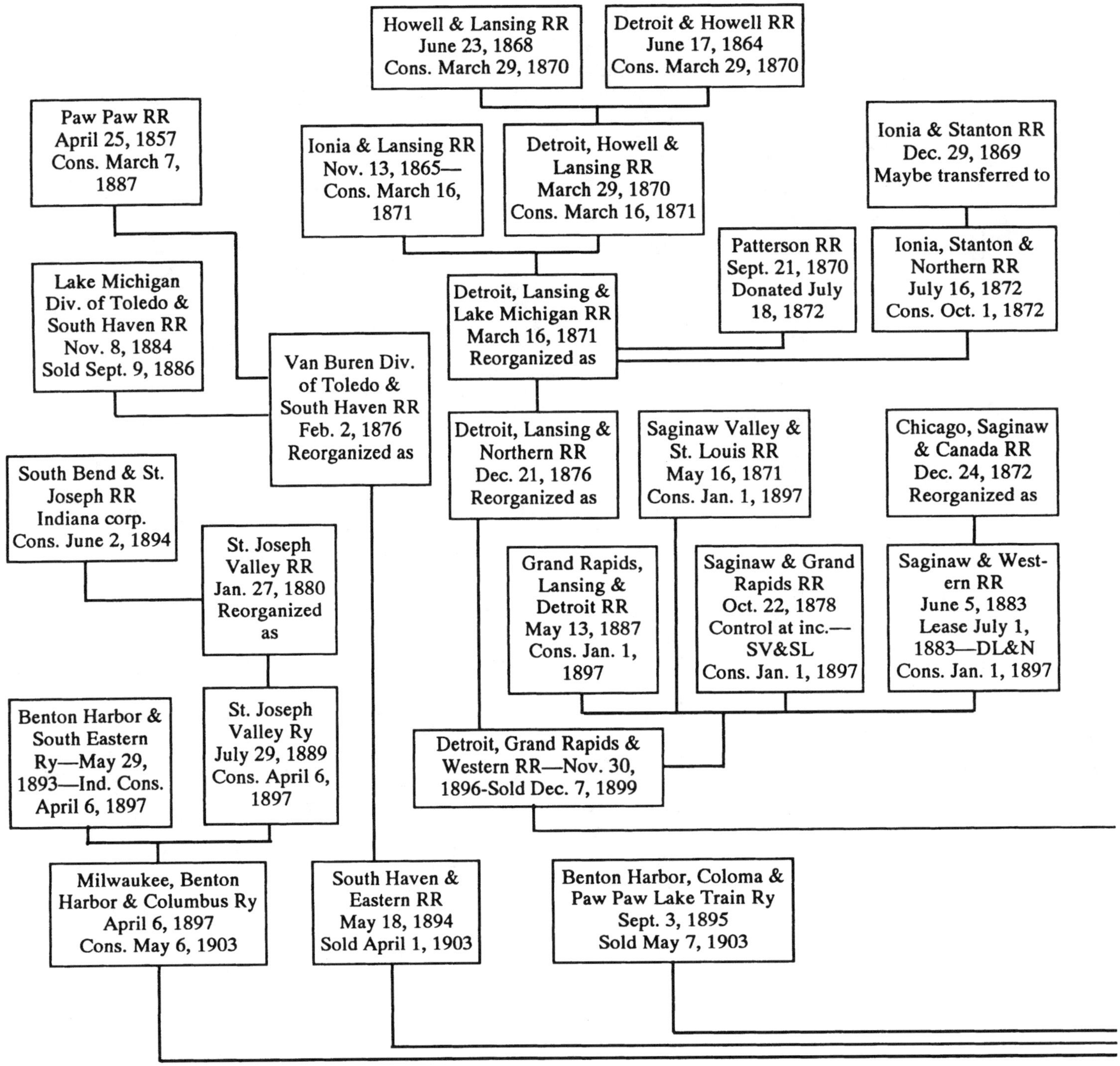
Howell & Lansing RR June 23, 1868 Cons. March 29, 1870
Detroit & Howell RR June 17, 1864 Cons. March 29, 1870
Paw Paw RR April 25, 1857 Cons. March 7, 1887
Ionia & Lansing RR Nov. 13, 1865— Cons. March 16, 1871
Detroit, Howell & Lansing RR March 29, 1870 Cons. March 16, 1871
Ionia & Stanton RR Dec. 29, 1869 Maybe transferred to
Patterson RR Sept. 21, 1870 Donated July 18, 1872
Ionia, Stanton & Northern RR July 16, 1872 Cons. Oct. 1, 1872
Lake Michigan Div. of Toledo & South Haven RR Nov. 8, 1884 Sold Sept. 9, 1886
Detroit, Lansing & Lake Michigan RR March 16, 1871 Reorganized as
Van Buren Div. of Toledo & South Haven RR Feb. 2, 1876 Reorganized as
Detroit, Lansing & Northern RR Dec. 21, 1876 Reorganized as
Saginaw Valley & St. Louis RR May 16, 1871 Cons. Jan. 1, 1897
Chicago, Saginaw & Canada RR Dec. 24, 1872 Reorganized as
South Bend & St. Joseph RR Indiana corp. Cons. June 2, 1894
St. Joseph Valley RR Jan. 27, 1880 Reorganized as
Grand Rapids, Lansing & Detroit RR May 13, 1887 Cons. Jan. 1, 1897
Saginaw & Grand Rapids RR Oct. 22, 1878 Control at inc.— SV&SL Cons. Jan. 1, 1897
Saginaw & Western RR June 5, 1883 Lease July 1, 1883—DL&N Cons. Jan. 1, 1897
Benton Harbor & South Eastern Ry—May 29, 1893—Ind. Cons. April 6, 1897
St. Joseph Valley Ry July 29, 1889 Cons. April 6, 1897
Detroit, Grand Rapids & Western RR—Nov. 30, 1896-Sold Dec. 7, 1899
Milwaukee, Benton Harbor & Columbus Ry April 6, 1897 Cons. May 6, 1903
South Haven & Eastern RR May 18, 1894 Sold April 1, 1903
Benton Harbor, Coloma & Paw Paw Lake Train Ry Sept. 3, 1895 Sold May 7, 1903

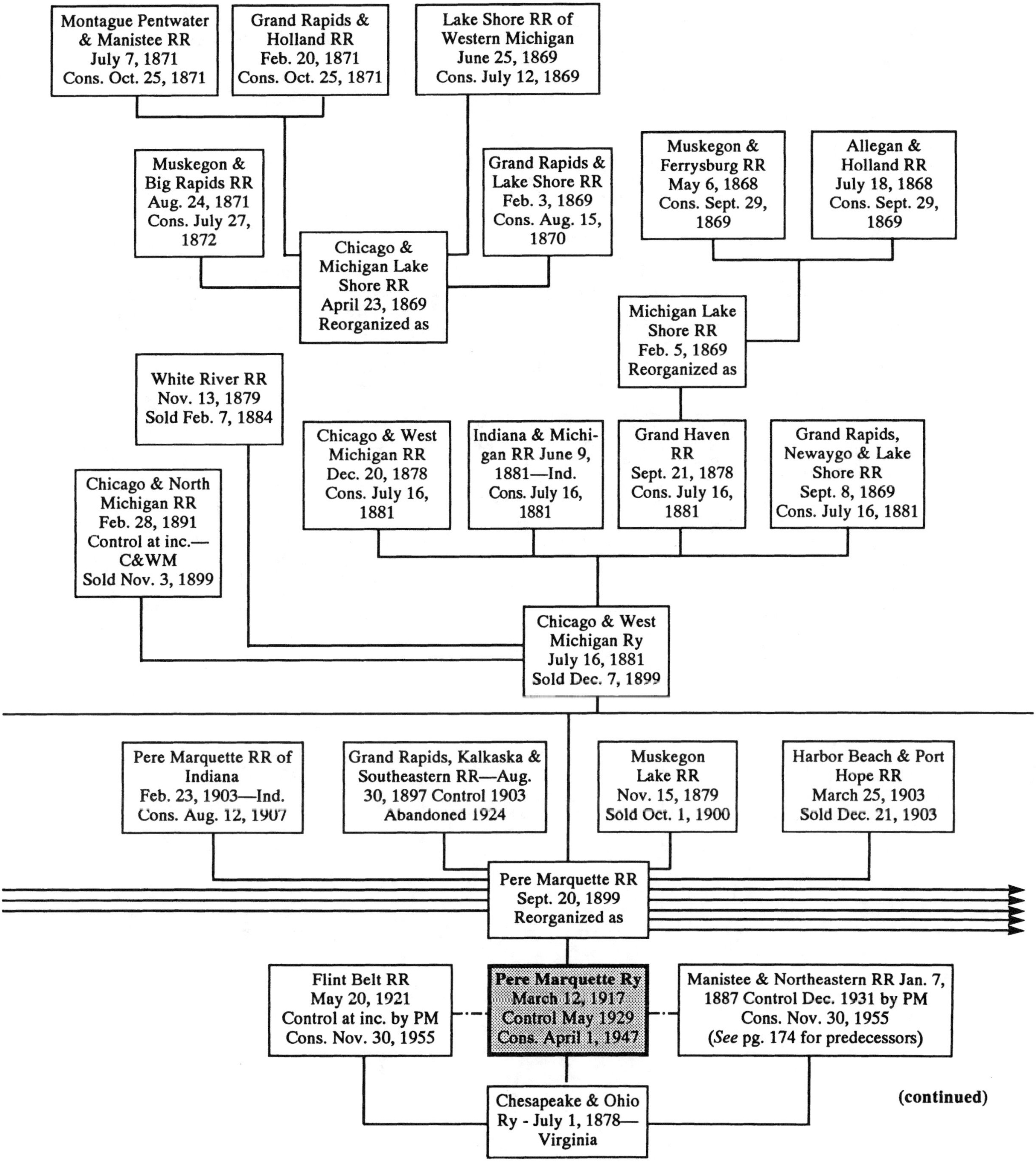
Montague Pentwater & Manistee RR July 7, 1871 Cons. Oct. 25, 1871
Grand Rapids & Holland RR Feb. 20, 1871 Cons. Oct. 25, 1871
Lake Shore RR of Western Michigan June 25, 1869 Cons. July 12, 1869
Muskegon & Big Rapids RR Aug. 24, 1871 Cons. July 27, 1872
Grand Rapids & Lake Shore RR Feb. 3, 1869 Cons. Aug. 15, 1870
Muskegon & Ferrysburg RR May 6, 1868 Cons. Sept. 29, 1869
Allegan & Holland RR July 18, 1868 Cons. Sept. 29, 1869
Chicago & Michigan Lake Shore RR April 23, 1869 Reorganized as
Michigan Lake Shore RR Feb. 5, 1869 Reorganized as
White River RR Nov. 13, 1879 Sold Feb. 7, 1884
Chicago & West Michigan RR Dec. 20, 1878 Cons. July 16, 1881
Indiana & Michigan RR June 9, 1881—Ind. Cons. July 16, 1881
Grand Haven RR Sept. 21, 1878 Cons. July 16, 1881
Grand Rapids, Newaygo & Lake Shore RR Sept. 8, 1869 Cons. July 16, 1881
Chicago & North Michigan RR Feb. 28, 1891 Control at inc.— C&WM Sold Nov. 3, 1899
Chicago & West Michigan Ry July 16, 1881 Sold Dec. 7, 1899
Pere Marquette RR of Indiana Feb. 23, 1903—Ind. Cons. Aug. 12, 1907
Grand Rapids, Kalkaska & Southeastern RR—Aug. 30, 1897 Control 1903 Abandoned 1924
Muskegon Lake RR Nov. 15, 1879 Sold Oct. 1, 1900
Harbor Beach & Port Hope RR March 25, 1903 Sold Dec. 21, 1903
Pere Marquette RR Sept. 20, 1899 Reorganized as
Flint Belt RR May 20, 1921 Control at inc. by PM Cons. Nov. 30, 1955
Pere Marquette Ry March 12, 1917 Control May 1929 Cons. April 1, 1947
Manistee & Northeastern RR Jan. 7, 1887 Control Dec. 1931 by PM Cons. Nov. 30, 1955 (*See* pg. 174 for predecessors)
Chesapeake & Ohio Ry - July 1, 1878— Virginia

(continued)

PERE MARQUETTE

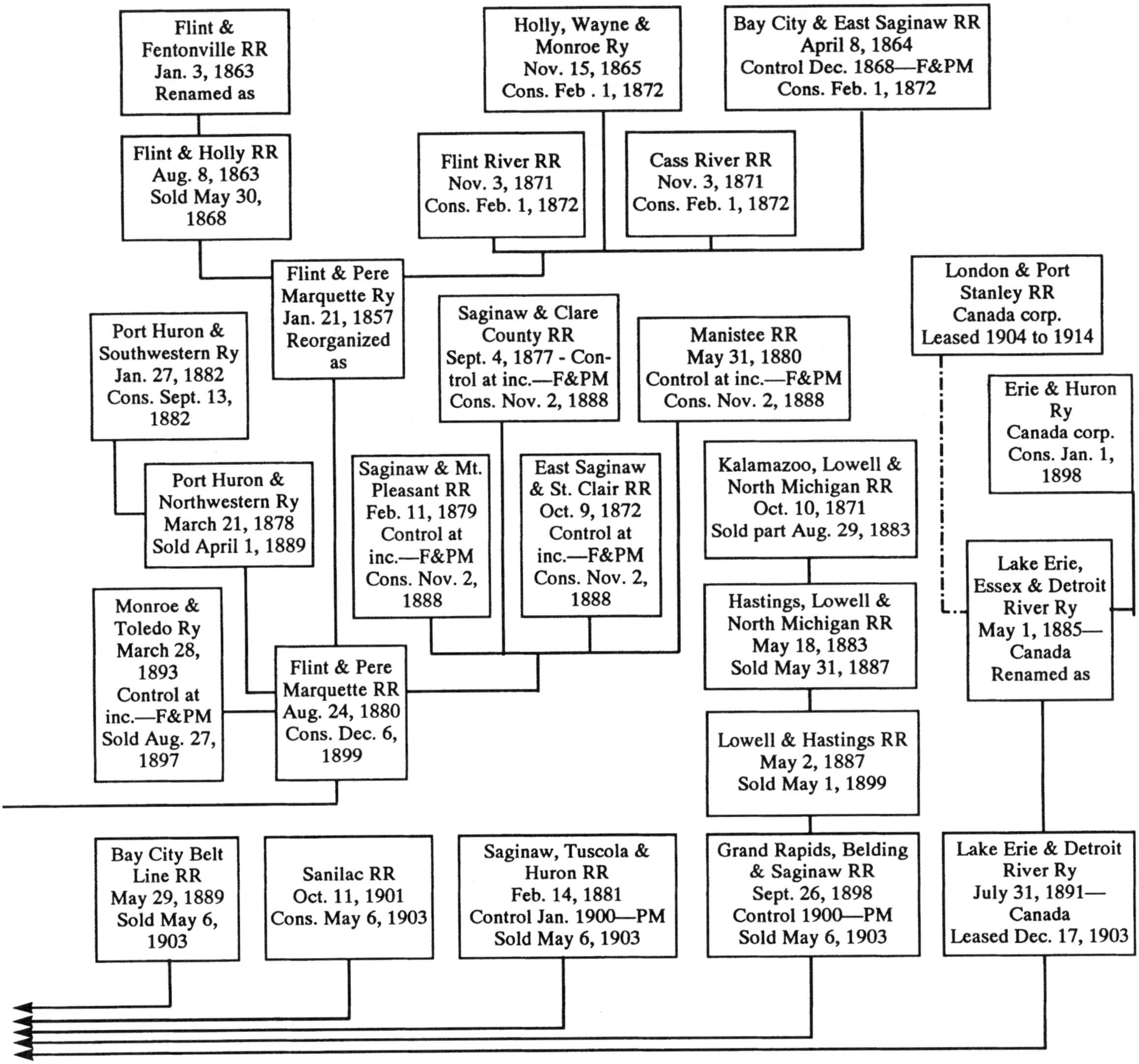

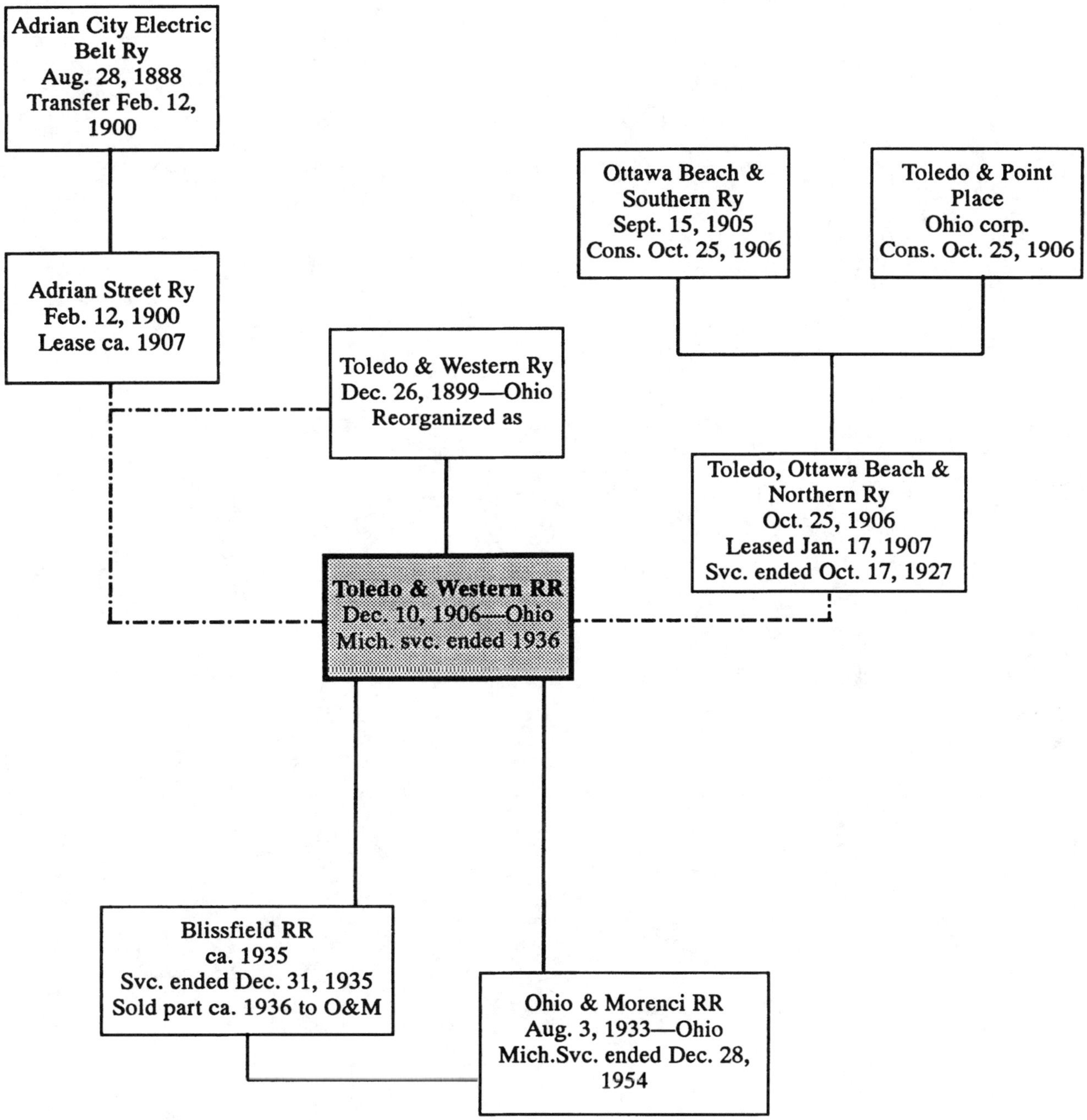
Adrian City Electric Belt Ry Aug. 28, 1888 Transfer Feb. 12, 1900
Adrian Street Ry Feb. 12, 1900 Lease ca. 1907
Ottawa Beach & Southern Ry Sept. 15, 1905 Cons. Oct. 25, 1906
Toledo & Point Place Ohio corp. Cons. Oct. 25, 1906
Toledo & Western Ry Dec. 26, 1899—Ohio Reorganized as
Toledo, Ottawa Beach & Northern Ry Oct. 25, 1906 Leased Jan. 17, 1907 Svc. ended Oct. 17, 1927
Toledo & Western RR Dec. 10, 1906—Ohio Mich. svc. ended 1936
Blissfield RR ca. 1935 Svc. ended Dec. 31, 1935 Sold part ca. 1936 to O&M
Ohio & Morenci RR Aug. 3, 1933—Ohio Mich.Svc. ended Dec. 28, 1954

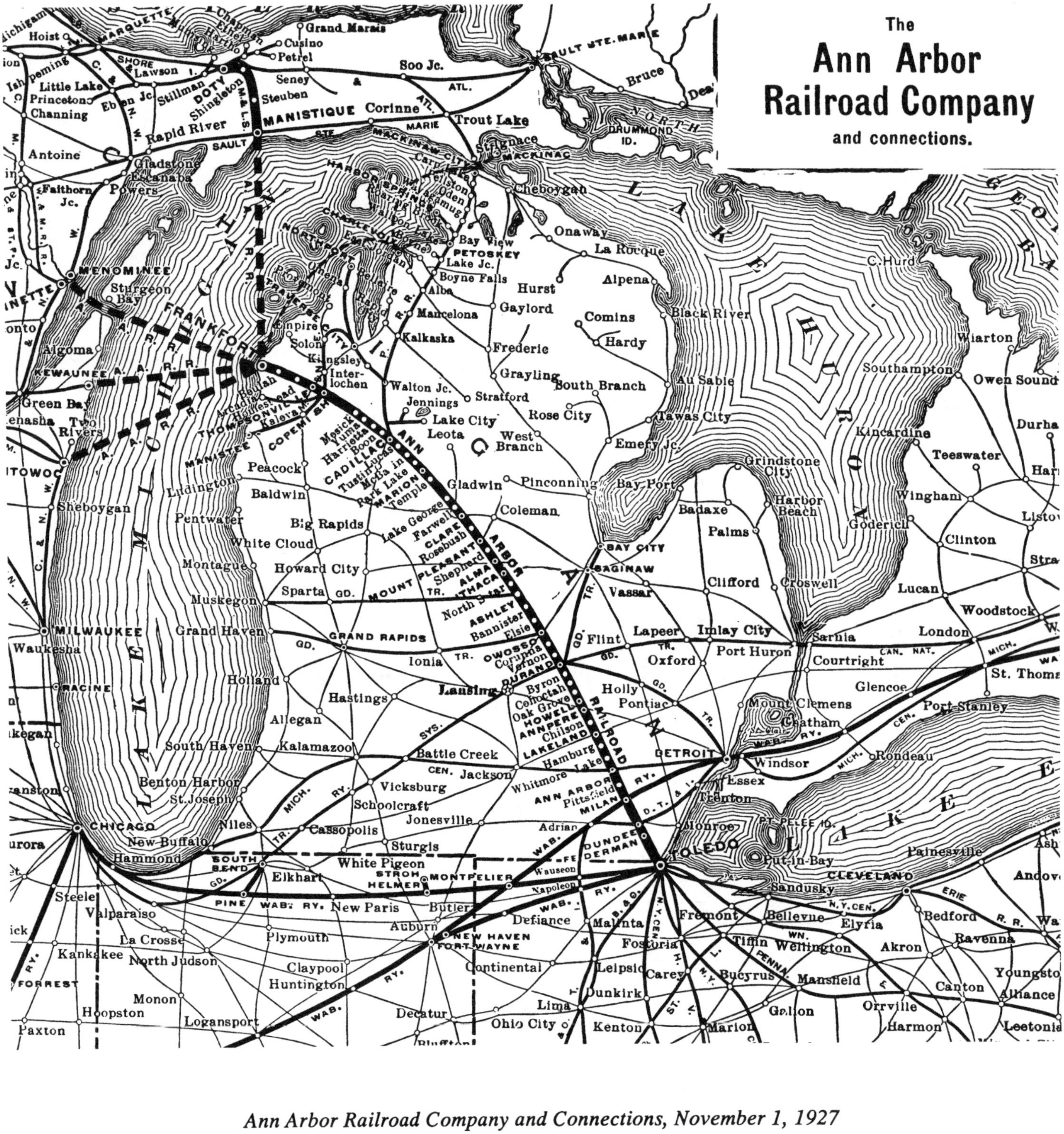

Ann Arbor Railroad Company and Connections, November 1, 1927

CHRONOLOGY OF CORPORATE ACTIONS

This chapter is a listing, in chronological order, of changes in the corporate organization of Michigan railroad corporations. The dates given in the left column are those of the date of the document or the event. Dates followed by an asterisk are reported by sources as the filing date of the event even if the actual document has not been located. If the document had a different effective date, that date is given after the name of the company involved.

The column next to the left is the event or action covered in the document. A list of standard terms and abbreviations is shown below.

STANDARD TERMS AND ABBREVIATIONS USED

A-Char.	Amend charter
A-Cons.	Amend corporate articles of second named to effect consolidation of first named into second named
A-Inc.	Amend corporate articles of any type of corporation
Act	Act of Michigan Legislature
Agree	Agreement
Bank.	Bankruptcy entered
Char.	Chartered
Con.Res.	Concurrent Resolution
Cons.	Consolidated, merged—first named into second named
Diss.	Coporation dissolved
Don.	Donated
Exch.	Stock exchanged
F.Sale	Sold at foreclosure
Inc.	Incorporated (General Ry. Act)
Jt.Res.	Joint Resolution
Lease	Lease—first named to second named
O.Inc.	Incorporated (other than as a railroad company)
Opg.Ag.	Operating agreement
Partn.	Partnership agreement
Rec.	Receivership begun
Reinc.	Reincorporated (Gen. Ry. Act)
Res.	Resolution of Legislature
S.Inc.	Incorporated (Street Ry. Act)
Sale	Sale of property—first named to second named
T.Inc.	Incorporated (Train Ry. Act)
Tfr.	Transfer of property
UD.Inc.	Incorporated (Union Depot Act)
X-	. . . cancelled; . . . expired
$	Financial control
With.	Withdrew as Michigan corporation

In the right column are the names of the companies involved. The names used in this part are not the full legal names but are sufficient to locate the company in Chapter 2 of this work.

To the right of the name, in parentheses, is a finding aid for the documentation of the action. A number of early entries are by acts of the state or territorial legislature; the date given is that of approval by the governor, with the Local Acts volume and page number. If the act was published as a Local Act, that is so shown. Resolutions show the date adopted, with the volume and page number of the resolution.

Later entries give the date the document was filed with the Michigan Secretary of State, and now stored at the State Record Center, Lansing. (In Dept. of Commerce boxed records, when the document was found in a folder other than that of the named company, the folder name is shown in brackets after the box number.)

A - Department of Commerce, Corporation and Securities Lot 756, with the folio and page in which recorded.

B - Department of Commerce, Corporation and Securities Lot 120, with the box number in which found.

C - Department of Commerce, Corporation and Securities Lot 102, with the box number in which found.

D - Department of Commerce, Corporation and Securities Lot 105, with the box number in which found.

E - Department of Commerce, Corporation and Securities Lot 106, with the box number in which found.

F - Department of Commerce, Corporation and Securities Lot 107, with the box number in which found.

G - Department of Commerce, Corporation and Securities Lot 108, with the box number in which found.

H - Department of Commerce, Corporation and Securities Lot 109, with the box number in which found.

J - Departmentt of Commerce, Corporation and Securities Lot 110, with the box number in which found.

Michigan Department of Transportation, Lansing.

K - Current records microfiche.

1825

4/19	Char.	La Plaisance Bay Harbor Co. (Terr. Laws, II, 262-264)

1830

7/31	Char.	Pontiac & Detroit (Terr. Laws, III, 844-847)

1832

6/29	Char.	Detroit & St. Joseph (Terr. Laws, III, 960-966)

1833

4/16	Char.	Romeo & Mt. Clemens (Terr. Laws, III, 1028-1033)
4/22	Char.	Erie & Kalamazoo (Terr. Laws, III, 1125-1131)

1834

3/7	Char.	Shelby & Detroit (Terr. Laws, III, 1303-1308)
3/7	Char.	Detroit & Pontiac (Terr. Laws, III, 1287-1293)
3/7	A-Char.	Detroit & St. Joseph (Terr. Laws, III, 1296)
3/7	A-Char.	Erie & Kalamazoo (Terr. Laws, III, 1392-1397)

1835

3/26	A-Char.	Detroit & Pontiac (Terr. Laws, III, 1387-1392)
3/26	A-Char.	Erie & Kalamazoo (Terr. Laws, III, 1392-1397)
8/22	Char.	River Raisin & Grand River (Terr. Laws, IV, 112-122)
8/22	Char.	Maumee Branch RR (Terr. Laws, IV, 156-161)
8/24	Char.	Macomb & Saginaw (Terr. Laws, IV, 124-134)
8/25	A-Char.	Detroit & St. Joseph (Terr. Laws, IV, 142-147)
8/25	Char.	Detroit & Maumee (Terr. Laws, IV, 148-153)
8/25	A-Char.	Maumee Branch RR (Terr. Laws, IV, 153-155)
8/25	A-Char.	Shelby & Detroit (Terr. Laws, IV, 155)

1836

3/24	Char.	Allegan & Marshall (1836 Acts, 287-297)
3/26	Char.	Shelby & Belle River (1836 Acts, 267-277)
3/26	Char.	St. Clair & Romeo (1836 Acts, 307-317)
3/26	Char.	Constantine & Niles (1836 Acts, 369-378)
3/28	Char.	Monroe & Ypsilanti (1836 Acts, 277-287)
3/28	Char.	Clinton & Adrian (1836 Acts, 297-307)

3/28	Char.	Palmyra & Jacksonburgh (1836 Acts, 318-328)
3/28	Char.	Kalamazoo & Lake Michigan (1836 Acts, 328-338)
3/28	Char.	Havre Branch (1836 Acts, 338-348)
3/28	Char.	Monroe & Ann Arbor (1836 Acts, 348-358)
3/28	Char.	River Raisin & Lake Erie (1836 Acts, 358-369)
3/28	A-Char.	Erie & Kalamazoo (1836 Acts, 378-379)
7/26	Res.	Detroit & Maumee and Detroit & St. Joseph (Jt. Res. not found)

1837

3/13	A-Char.	Detroit & Maumee (1837 Acts No. 35, 53)
3/20	Act	Legislature created Internal Improvement Program (and "Central," "Southern," and "Northern" lines) and authorized purchase of Havre Branch (1837 Acts No. 67, 130-133)
3/21	Res.	River Raisin & Lake Erie (1837 Res. No. 73, 299)
3/22	Char.	Gibralter & Clinton (1837 Acts, No. 59, 217-225)
3/22	Act	Re: Detroit & Pontiac (1837 Acts, No. 70, 282-284)
3/22	Char.	Detroit & Shiawassee (1837 Acts, No. 111, 227-235)
3/22	Char.	Saginaw & Genesee (1837 Acts, No. 118, 269-277)
4/22	Sale	Detroit & St. Joseph to State of Michigan
6/21	A-Char.	Maumee Branch RR (Special 1837 Acts, No. 6, 309)
6/22	A-Char.	Palmyra & Jacksonburgh (Special 1837, Acts No. 16, 319-321)
12/30	Char.	Port Sheldon & Grand Rapids (1838 Acts, No. 12, 16-24)

1838

3/5	Act	Re: Detroit & Pontiac (1838 Acts, No. 20, 66-69)
3/31	Char.	Auburn & Lapeer (1838 Acts, No. 74, 145-153)
4/3	Char.	Ypsilanti & Tecumseh (1838 Acts, No. 84, 175-183)
4/5	Char.	Mottville & White Pigeon (1838 Acts, No. 94, 196-205)
4/5	Char.	Medina & Canandaigua (1838 Acts, No. 96, 212-220)
4/6	A-Char.	Detroit & Shiawassee (1838 Acts, No. 106, 235-236)
4/6	A-Char.	Detroit & Maumee (1838 Acts, No. 117, 247-248)
4/6	Act	Re: Allegan & Marshall (1838 Acts, No. 121, 252-255)
4/6	Act	Re: Ypsilanti & Tecumseh (1838 Acts, No. 124, 259-262)
4/6	Res.	Re: Palmyra & Jacksonburgh (1838 Res. No. 13, 287)

1839

4/10	A-Char.	Port Sheldon & Grand Rapids (1839 Acts, No. 42, 68-70)

4/16	Res.	Re: Ypsilanti & Tecumseh (1839 Res. No. 24, 259)
4/20	A-Char.	Saginaw & Genesee (1839 Acts, No. 109, 206)
4/20	A-Char.	Detroit & Pontiac (1839 Acts, No. 111, 207)

1840

3/6	A-Char.	St. Clair & Romeo (1840 Acts, No. 24, 29-30)
3/13	A-Char.	Monroe & Ypsilanti (1840 Acts, No. 37, 41-42)
3/24	A-Char.	Havre Branch (1840 Acts, No. 68, 120-121)
3/30	A-Char.	Macomb & Saginaw (1840 Acts, No. 86, 137-138)
3/31	Act	Re: River Raisin & Lake Erie (1840 Acts, No. 100, 153-155)
4/1	Char.	Jonesville RR (1840 Acts, No. 103, 158-162)
4/1	Act	Re: Ypsilanti & Tecumseh (1840 Acts, No. 113, 170-171)
4/1	Act	Palmyra & Jacksonburgh (1840 Acts, No. 115, 172-173)
9/15	Tfr.	La Plaisance Bay Harbor Co. to State of Michigan
9/17	Sale	River Raisin & Lake Erie to State of Michigan

1841

4/9	Act	Re: Palmyra & Jacksonburgh (1841 Acts, No. 56, 139-140)
4/9	Res.	Re: River Raisin & Lake Erie (1841 Res. No. 16, 214)
4/13	Char.	Detroit and Pontiac (action not found)
4/13	Act	Re: Palmyra & Jacksonburgh (1841 Acts, No. 81, 178)
4/13	Res.	Re: River Raisin & Lake Erie (1841 Res. No. 24, 218)
4/13	Res.	Re: Ypsilanti & Tecumseh (1841 Res. No. 27, 219)

1842

2/11	Act Re:	Palmyra & Jacksonburgh and Ypsilanti & Tecumseh and Allegan & Marshall and Detroit & Pontiac (1842 Acts, No. 22, 26-27)

1843

3/8	Res.	Re: Detroit & Pontiac (1843 Res. No. 25, 233)

1844

2/16	A-Char.	Havre Branch (1844 Acts, No. 12, 11)
3/11	Act	Re: Detroit & Pontiac (1844 Acts, No. 81, 116-117)
3/12	Char.	Troy & Rochester (1844 Acts, No. 86, 125-132)
n.d.	Sale	Palmyra & Jacksonburgh to State of Michigan (for "Southern")

1845

2/22	Act	Re: Palmyra & Jacksonburgh (1845 Acts, No. 14, 12-13)
3/3	Res.	Re: Palmyra & Jacksonburgh (1845 Res. No. 11, 158)
3/19	A-Char.	Monroe & Ypsilanti (1845 Acts, No. 43, 54)
3/22	A-Char.	Erie & Kalamazoo (1845 Acts, No. 67, 85-89)

1846

3/28	Char.	Michigan Central (1846 Acts, No. 42, 37-64)
5/4	Char.	Grand River Valley (1846 Acts, No. 98, 111-119)
5/4	Char.	Battle Creek & Grand Rapids (1846 Acts, No. 104, 145-153)
5/4	A-Char.	Shelby & Detroit (1846 Acts, No. 105, 153-154)
5/9	Char.	Michigan Southern (1846 Acts, No. 113, 170-194)
5/15	Char.	Pontiac & Genesee (1846 Acts, No. 137, 227-235)
5/18	Char.	Kalamazoo River RR (1846 Acts, No. 154, 276-284)
5/18	A-Char.	Erie & Kalamazoo (1846 Acts, No. 158, 288-290)
9/24	Sale	State of Michigan "Central" to Michigan Central
12/28	Sale	State of Michigan "Southern" to Michigan Southern

1847

1/30	Char.	Port Huron & Lake Michigan (1847 Acts, No. 5, 5-19)
2/25	Char.	Pennsylvania RR (Penn. corp.) (filed 8/5/1922; K)
3/16	A-Char.	Michigan Central (1847 Acts, No. 71, 86)
3/16	Char.	Detroit River Marine (1847 Acts, No. 72, 87-90)
3/17	Char.	Chippewa Portage Co. (1847 Acts, No. 75, 97-101)
3/17	Char.	Kalamazoo & Grand River (1847 Acts, No. 82, 106-114)
3/17	Char.	Detroit River Sectional Floating Dock, etc. (1847 Acts, No. 86, 126-129)
3/17	A-Char.	Grand River Valley (1847 Acts, No. 87, 129-30)

1848

2/24	A-Char.	Detroit River Sectional Floating Dock, etc. (1848 Acts, No. 46, 45)
3/18	Char.	Detroit, Romeo & Port Huron (1848 Acts, No. 87, 98-99) (Rename Shelby & Detroit)
3/30	A-Char.	Pontiac & Genesee (1848 Acts, No. 152, 197-204)
4/3	A-Char.	Michigan Central (1848 Acts, No. 197, 276-277)
4/3	Char.	St. Joseph Valley (1848 Acts, No. 199, 278-292)
4/3	Char.	Genesee & Oakland (1848 Acts, No. 202, 294-308)
4/3	Char.	Oakland & Ottawa (1848 Acts, No. 234, 351-366)

1849

3/21	Res.	Re: Palmyra & Jacksonburgh (1849 Res. No. 28, 379)
3/24	A-Char.	Michigan Southern (1849 Acts, No. 128, 130-134)
3/31	A-Char.	Michigan Southern (1849 Acts, No. 214, 261)
8/1	Lease	Erie & Kalamazoo to Michigan Southern

1850

3/20	Act Re:	Detroit & Pontiac (1850 Acts, No. 96, 83-84)
4/1	A-Char.	Michigan Southern (1850 Acts, No. 195, 195-200)
4/2	Char.	St. Joseph RR (1850 Acts, No. 274, 308-322)

1851

3/26	A-Char.	Oakland & Ottawa (1851 Acts, No. 56, 58-59)
4/7	A-Char.	Shelby & Detroit (1851 Acts, No. 131, 166-167)
4/7	A-Char.	Port Huron & Lake Michigan (1851 Acts, No. 137, 170)

1853

1/29	Res.	Re: Ypsilanti & Tecumseh (1853 Res. No. 11, 200-201)

1855

2/13	A-Char.	Detroit, Romeo & Port Huron (1855 Acts, No. 137, 297-300)
2/13	A-Char.	Michigan Southern (1855 Acts, No. 138, 300-303)
2/13	A-Char.	Michigan Central (1855 Acts, No. 139, 304-305)
2/13	Char.	Detroit & Milwaukee (1855 Acts, No. 140, 305-308)
2/13	Char.	Port Huron & Lake Michigan (1855 Acts, No. 158, 368-391)
2/13	A-Char.	Genesee & Oakland (1855 Acts, No. 167, 419)
2/15	Inc.	Iron Mountain RR (filed 2/22; A,1:1-2; B,14[MarqHou&Ont])
3/6	Inc.	Detroit, Monroe & Toledo (filed 4/26; A,1:22-25)
3/10	Inc.	Iron Mountain Ry (filed 3/14; A,1:3-4)
3/31	Inc.	Chicago, St. Paul & Fond du Lac (Wisc. corp.)
4/19	Cons.	Detroit & Pontiac and Oakland & Ottawa into Detroit & Milwaukee
4/25	Inc.	Michigan Southern & Northern Indiana (filed 5/18; A,6:279-285)
5/29	Inc.	Grand Rapids & Southern (filed 5/31; A,1:28-31; B,13)
6/1	Inc.	Schoolcraft & Three Rivers (filed 6/6; A,1:32-34)
7/13	Inc.	Jackson Union RR (filed 7/20; A,1:41-44; B,14)
8/1	Inc.	Grand Rapids & Indiana (filed 9/1; A,1:51-54; B,13)
8/9	Inc.	Saginaw & Lansing (filed 9/8; A,1:58-60; B,15)

11/26	Inc.	Grand Rapids RR (filed 2/5/1856; A,1:75-77; B,13)
11/29	Inc.	Port Huron & Milwaukee (filed 12/6; A,1:73-75; B,15)

1856

6/25	Inc.	Ontonagon & State Line (filed 8/20; A,1:92-94; B,12[ChiStPaul&Fond])
6/27	Inc.	Iron Mountain & Wisconsin State Line (filed 7/3; A,1:92-94; B,14)
7/1	Lease	Detroit, Monroe & Toledo to Michigan Southern & Northern Indiana (filed 8/23/1856; B,13[DM&T])
8/11	Inc.	Shiawassee & Vernon (filed 8/13; A,6:188-190; B,15)
9/1	Inc.	Grand Rapids, Traverse Bay & Mackinac (filed 12/29; A,1:98-100; B,13)
11/1	Inc.	Detroit, Port Huron & Sarnia (filed 3/27/1858; A,1:179-181; B,13)
11/21	Inc.	Bay De Noquet & Marquette (filed 12/27; A,1:96-98; B,12)
12/8	Inc.	Amboy & Traverse Bay (filed 1/12/1857; A,1:105-107; B,12)
12/16	Inc.	Grand Rapids & Northern (filed 1/5/1857; A,1:100-103; B,13)

1857

1/7	Inc.	Marquette & Ontonagon Ry (filed 2/6; A,1:120-121; B,14)
1/14	Inc.	Marquette & State Line (filed 1/16; A,1:109-110; B,12 [ChiStPaul&Fond])
1/21	Inc.	Flint & Pere Marquette (filed 1/22; A,1:110-112; B,13)
1/23	Inc.	Amboy, Lansing & Traverse Bay (filed 1/29; A,1:112-116; B,12)
1/26	Inc.	Grand River & Muskegon (filed 2/21; A,1:118-120; B,13)
1/28	Inc.	Lake Superior RR (filed 2/2; A,1:117-118; B,14)
1/28	Act Re:	Detroit, Monroe & Toledo (1857 Acts, No. 18, 15-16)
2/5	Act Re:	Port Huron & Milwaukee (1857 Acts, No. 59, 156)
2/14	Act Re:	Detroit & Milwaukee (1857 Acts, No. 123, 344)
2/17	Act Re:	Detroit, Monroe & Toledo (1857 Acts, No. 154, 403)
3/21	A-Cons.	Marquette & State Line into Chicago, St. Paul & Fond du Lac (filed 5/19; A,1:144-146; B,12[CSP&F])
3/27	A-Cons.	Ontonagon & State Line into Chicago, St. Paul & Fond du Lac (filed 5/18; A,1:147-149; B,12[CSP&F])
4/7	A-Inc.	Marquette & Ontonagon Ry (filed 4/10; A,1:132-133; B,14)
4/25	Inc.	Paw Paw RR (filed 9/16; A,1:169-172; B,15(Toledo&SoHvn))
5/22	Inc.	Grand Rapids & Mackinaw (filed 6/8; A,1:149-151; B,13[GR&Ind])
6/26	A-Cons.	Grand Rapids & Mackinaw and Grand Rapids & Fort Wayne (Ind.corp) into Grand Rapids & Indiana (filed 7/30; A,1:161-164; B,13[GR&I])
8/3	A-Inc.	Flint & Pere Marquette (filed 8/4; A,1:164-166; B,13)
n.d.	Lease	Marquette & Ontonagon to Bay De Noquet & Marquette

Articles of acceptance (of land grant)

Grand Rapids & Indiana A,1:122-124
Flint & Pere Marquette A,1:124-125
Amboy, Lansing & Traverse Bay A,1:126-127
Bay De Noquet & Marquette A,1:127
Marquette & State Line A,1:128
Detroit & Milwaukee A,1:128-129
Ontonagon & State Line A,1:129-130
Port Huron & Lake Michigan A,1:130-131
Marquette & Ontonagon A,1:131

1858

1/7	Inc.	Detroit & Port Huron (filed 3/26; A,1:177-179; B,12)
2/3	A-Char.	Genesee & Oakland (1858 Acts, No. 12, 28)
2/3	A-Char.	Detroit & Milwaukee (1858 Acts, No. 14, 42)
2/3	Act Re:	River Raisin & Grand River (1858 Acts, No. 16, 43)
2/3	A-Char.	Grand River Valley (1858 Acts, No. 16, 43)
3/18	Inc.	Chicago, Detroit & Canada Grand Trunk Junction (filed 3/25; A,1:174-177)
12/31	Sale	Iron Mountain RR to Bay De Noquet & Marquette (filed 4/5/1859; A,1:222-225; B,12[B&M])

1859

1/29	Act Re:	Detroit & Milwaukee and Port Huron & Milwaukee (1859 Acts, No. 34, 32-33)
1/29	Act Re:	Detroit & Milwaukee (1859 Acts, No. 37, 36-37)
2/10	A-Char.	Michigan Central (1859 Acts, No. 95, 250-252)
2/11	Act Re:	Paw Paw RR (1859 Acts, No. 108, 268)
2/15	Act Re:	Iron Mountain (1859 Acts, No. 216, 764)
2/15	Act Re:	Flint & Pere Marquette and Genesee & Oakland (1859 Acts, No. 258, 1073-1075)
6/2	F.Sale	Chicago, St. Paul & Fond du Lac to Chicago & North Western
7/1	Lease	Chicago, Detroit & Canada Grand Trunk Junction to Grand Trunk Ry of Canada

1860

4/10	Rec.	Detroit & Milwaukee
4/18	Inc.	Marquette & Chicago (filed 4/19; A,1:284-285; B,14)
9/7	Inc.	Houghton RR (filed 9/24; A,1:310-312; B,13)
10/4	F.Sale	Detroit & Milwaukee Ry to Detroit & Milwaukee RR (filed 10/22)
10/18	Inc.	Detroit & Milwaukee RR (filed 10/22)

1861

3/4	Act Re:	Detroit & Milwaukee (1861 Acts, No. 94, 126-127)
3/15	Act Re:	Grand River Valley and St. Joseph Valley (1861 Acts, No. 159, 240-241)

1862

2/3	Inc.	Peninsula RR (filed 4/22; A,1:352-354; B,12[C&NW])
2/3	Inc.	Northern Iron (filed 4/23; A,1:354-356; B,15)
6/26	F.Sale	Port Huron & Milwaukee to Port Huron & Lake Michigan
7/26	Inc.	Lake Superior Iron Mountain (filed 7/28; A,1:361-363; B,14)
12/27	Inc.	Marquette & Ontonagon RR (filed 1/2/1863; A,1:380-381; B,14 [MarqHou&Ont])

1863

1/3	Inc.	Flint & Fentonville (filed 1/7; A,1:384-385; B,13[F&PM])
3/17	Act Re:	Grand River Valley and St. Joseph Valley (1863 Acts, No. 111, 169)
3/20	Act Re:	Amboy, Lansing & Traverse Bay and Grand River Valley (1863 Acts, No. 207, 360-361)
5/9	S.Inc.	Detroit City (filed 5/12; B,12)
5/23	A-Inc.	Peninsula (filed 5/26; A,1:425-427; B,12[C&NW])
6/20	A-Inc.	Peninsula (filed 7/14; A,1:438-440; B,12[C&NW])
6/30	A-Inc.	Peninsula (filed 9/15; A,1:449-451; B,12[C&NW])
8/8	Inc.	Flint & Holly (filed 10/16; A,1:464-467; B,13[F&PM])
11/20	T.Inc.	East Saginaw City Ry (filed 11/30; B,13)
11/23	T.Inc.	Salina Street Ry (filed 12/8; B,15)
12/22	Inc.	Lansing & Jackson RR (filed 2/23/1864; A,1:565-568; B,14[JackLans&Sag])

1864

1/21	T.Inc.	Corlies & Thunder Bay Train (filed 1/26; A,1:524-525; B,12)
3/10	Inc.	Keweenaw & Cliff of Lake Superior (filed 3/16; A,1:597-600; B,14)
4/8	Inc.	Bay City & East Saginaw (filed 4/8; A,1:634-636; B,13[F&PM])
4/11	Inc.	Lakes Superior & Michigan Air Line (filed 5/18; B,14)
4/21	S.Inc.	Saginaw Street Ry (filed 5/13; B,15[SaginawConsol])
5/20	T.Inc.	Grand Rapids City Ry (filed 6/30; A,2:88-89; B,13)
6/17	Inc.	Detroit & Howell (filed 9/21; A,2:113-119; B,13[DetGRW])
10/1	A-Inc.	Northern Iron of Lake Superior (filed 11/3; A,2:131-132; B,15)
10/21	Cons.	Peninsula to Chicago & North Western (filed 1/7/1865; A,2:163-170; rerecorded A,5:181-188; B,12[C&NW])
10/22	T.Inc.	Grand Rapids Street Ry (filed 10/28; A,2:129-130; B,13)

11/21	Lease	Michigan Southern & Northern Indiana (part: White Pigeon-Constantine) to St. Joseph Valley
12/27	Inc.	Mineral Range Ry (filed 1/19/1865; A,2:174-177; rerecorded A,5:189-191)

1865

2/4	T.Inc.	Fort Street & Elmwood (filed 2/9; A,2:182-183; B,13[FtWayne&Elm])
2/20	Inc.	Jackson, Lansing & Saginaw (filed 2/24; A,2:197-200; B,14)
2/21	T.Inc.	Bay City & Portsmouth (filed 2/22; A,2:192-193; B,12[BayCyStRy])
2/21	Inc.	L'Anse & Ontonagon (filed 2/23; A,2:195-197; B,14)
3/18	Act	Re: St. Joseph Valley and Schoolcraft & Three Rivers (1865 Acts, No. 229, 488)
7/8	A-Inc.	East Saginaw City (filed 7/12; B,13)
8/13	T.Inc.	Portage Lake Train Ry (filed 8/14; A,2:259-261; B,15)
8/13	Inc.	Peninsular (filed 10/3; A,2:292-295; B,12[Chi&LHuron])
8/15	A-Inc.	East Saginaw City (filed 8/17; B,13)
9/1	Inc.	Chicago & Michigan Grand Trunk (filed 9/8; A,2:269-285)
10/17	Inc.	Peninsula Branch (filed 10/27; A,2:307-309; B,15)
11/13	Inc.	Ionia & Lansing (filed 2/26/1866; A,2:369-371; B,13[DetGR&W])
11/15	Inc.	Holly, Wayne & Monroe (filed 11/17; A,2:320-322; B,13[Flint&PM])
11/29	Inc.	Ohio & Lake Superior (filed 12/2; A,2:322-324; B,15)

1866

3/6	Inc.	Iron Bay RR (filed 3/19; A,2:378-379; B,14)
6/4	Inc.	Kalamazoo & Schoolcraft (filed 6/9; A,2:415-417)
6/29	Inc.	Toledo, Ann Arbor & Saginaw (filed 8/15; A,2:430-437; rerecorded A,2:438-444; B,15)
7/17	T.Inc.	Globe Train Ry (filed 8/23; A,2:445-446; B,13)
8/30	S.Inc.	Ann Arbor Street (filed 10/1; B,12)
10/23	Inc.	Peninsular Ry Extension (filed 1/3/1868; A,3:78-85; B,12 [Chi&LHuron])
10/26	Tfr.	Amboy, Lansing & Traverse Bay rights to Jackson, Lansing & Saginaw (filed 10/29; A,2:467-469; B,14[Jackson,Lans&Sag])
10/27	T.Inc.	Calumet Train (filed 11/3; A,2:473; B,12)
11/11	Inc.	Northern Central Michigan RR (filed 11/12; A,2:477-478; B,15)
12/8	Inc.	Wisconsin & Lake Superior (filed 12/13; A,2:493-494; B,16)
12/21	Inc.	Grand Trunk Ry of Michigan (filed 1/19/1867; A,2:509-521)
12/25	A-Inc.	Jackson, Lansing & Saginaw (filed 1/25/1867; A,2:523-526; B,14)

1867

1/4	F.Sale	Amboy, Lansing & Traverse Bay to Jackson, Lansing & Saginaw
1/12	Tfr.	Amboy, Lansing & Traverse Bay rights to Northern Central Michigan (filed 1/14; A,2:502-503; B,15[NorthCentMich])

1/18	T.Inc.	Calumet Train Ry (filed 6/18; A,2:585-587; B,12)
2/7	Act	Jackson, Lansing & Saginaw (1867 Acts, No. 10)
2/9	Inc.	Northern Michigan RR (filed 2/19; A,2:531-533; B,15)
2/28	Inc.	Jonesville, Marshall & Grand River (filed 1/13/1869; A,3:269-272; B,14)
6/1	T.Inc.	Hecla Train Ry (filed 6/18; A,2:587-589; B,13)
6/4	A-Inc.	Detroit City Ry (filed 8/12; A,2:614-615; B,12)
6/17	Inc.	Kalamazoo & Allegan (filed 6/18; A,2:590-592)
10/18	Inc.	St. Joseph River (filed 11/21; A,3:40-44; B,15)
11/18	Inc.	Northern Michigan RR (filed 12/12; A,3:61-65; B,15)
11/25	Inc.	Kalamazoo & Grand Rapids (filed 1/3/1868; A,3:76-77)

1868

1/3	A-Cons.	Peninsular Ry Extension into Peninsular (filed 2/17; A,3:106-108; B,12[Chi&LHuron])
1/3	Inc.	Elkhart & Lake Michigan (filed 1/15; A,3:101-105; B,13)
1/6	Inc.	Hecla & Torch Lake (filed 3/8; A,3:118-120; B,13)
1/8	Inc.	Lawton, Paw Paw & South Haven (filed 5/9; A,3:142-145; B,14)
2/20	S.Inc.	Saginaw Street RR (filed 3/14; B,15)
2/28	Inc.	Canada Southern (Canadian corp.)
4/27	Inc.	Kalamazoo, Allegan & Grand Rapids (filed 6/3; A,3:177-182)
5/6	Inc.	Muskegon & Ferrysburg (filed 1/22/1869; A,3:278-281; B,13[GrandHvn])
5/26	Inc.	Grand Trunk RR of Michigan (filed 7/1; A,3:194-196; B,13[DetGrHvn&Milw])
5/30	A-Cons.	Flint & Holly into Flint & Pere Marquette (filed 9/2; A,3:231-234; B,13[F&PM])
6/1	A-Inc.	Grand Trunk Ry of Michigan (filed 6/2; A,3:150-174)
6/23	Inc.	Howell & Lansing (filed 6/23; A,3:188-191; B,13[DetGR&W])
7/2	Inc.	Jackson, Fort Wayne & Cincinnati (filed 9/26; A,3: 246-251)(correction to articles filed 1/19/1869; A,3:351)
7/2	Inc.	Michigan Air Line RR (filed 8/25; A,3:227-228)
7/18	Inc.	Allegan & Holland (filed 7/29; A,3:211-214)
8/29	S.Inc.	Hamtramck Street Ry (filed 5/15/1869; B,13)
9/1	A-Inc.	Northern Central Michigan (filed 10/2; A,3:252; B,15)
10/28	Inc.	Portage Lake & Keweenaw (filed 12/4; A,3:256-258; B,15)
11/10	$	Bay City & East Saginaw by Flint & Pere Marquette

1869

1/9	Inc.	Detroit, Hillsdale & Indiana (filed 2/3; A,3:292-298; B,13[DetHill&SW])
1/13	A-Inc.	Ionia & Lansing (filed 2/5; A,3:299-306; B,13[DetGR&W])

1/19	Rec.	Grand Rapids & Indiana
1/26	Inc.	Fort Wayne, Jackson & Saginaw (filed 4/6; A,3:359-362)
2/3	Inc.	Grand Rapids & Lake Shore (filed 2/11; A,3:310-313; B,12[Chi&MichLkSh])
2/5	Inc.	Michigan Lake Shore (filed 2/16; A,3:313-316; B,13[GrHvn])
2/12	T.Inc.	Grand River Street (filed 2/27; B,13)
3/1	Inc.	Port Huron & Owosso (filed 5/24; A,5:236-238; B,15)
3/8	Act	Jackson,Lansing & Saginaw (1869 Acts, No. 261, A,2:267-268)
3/11	Inc.	Michigan Northern RR (filed 3/11; A,3:339-340; B,14)
4/2	Inc.	Kalamazoo & South Haven (filed 4/15; B,14)
4/6	Inc.	Lake Shore & Michigan Southern (filed 6/2; A,6:190-194)
4/6	Inc.	Air Line Ry of Michigan (filed 4/28; A,3:372-374; B,12)
4/9	Inc.	Detroit, Adrian, Logansport & St. Louis (filed 5/11; A,3:384-388; B,12)
4/20	Inc.	Niles & South Bend (filed 4/28; A,3:369-371; B,15)
4/23	Inc.	Chicago & Michigan Lake Shore (filed 4/24; A,3:363-365; B,12)
4/29	Inc.	Lansing, St. Johns & Mackinac (filed 5/4; A,3:379-383; B,14)
5/26	Inc.	Northern Michigan Ry (filed 7/9; A,3:421-424; B,15)
6/10	S.Inc.	St. Clair City (filed 6/14; B,15)
6/22	A-Cons.	Buffalo & Erie (not Mich. corp.) into Lake Shore & Michigan Southern (filed 8/13; A,6:198-207)
6/25	Inc.	Lake Shore of Western Michigan (filed 7/3; A,3:408-410; B,12[Chi&MichLkSh])
6/26	Inc.	Owosso & Big Rapids (filed 8/16; A,5:239-241; B,15 [Owosso&NW])
7/12	A-Cons.	Lake Shore of Western Michigan into Chicago & Mich. Lake Shore (filed 7/19; A,6:195-197; B,12[C&MLS])
7/24	Inc.	White Pigeon & State Line (filed 7/26; A,3:435-437; B,16)
8/9	Inc.	Rochester & Romeo (filed 8/17; A,3:454-455; B,15)
8/14	Inc.	Kalamazoo & White Pigeon (filed 9/24; A,6:208-212)
9/1	Inc.	Westphalia, Hubbardston & Northern (filed 11/4; A,3:493-497)
9/8	Inc.	Grand Rapids, Newaygo & Lake Shore (filed 9/11; A,3:469-470; B,13)
9/21	Lease	Kalamazoo, Allegan & Grand Rapids to Lake Shore & Michigan Southern
9/29	A-Cons.	Allegan & Holland and Muskegon & Ferrysburg into Michigan Lake Shore (filed 10/13; A,6:213-217; B,13[GrandHvn])
10/20	A-Inc.	Grand Trunk RR of Michigan (filed 3/19/1870; A,5:385-396)
10/22	Inc.	Toledo, Ann Arbor & Northern (filed 11/26; A,3:515-525; B,15[ToledoAA&NMich])
10/27	Inc.	Paw Paw Valley (filed 10/30; A,3:486-488; B,15)
10/28	Inc.	East Saginaw & Ann Arbor (filed 11/30; A,3:526-532; B,13)
10/29	A-Inc.	Michigan Lake Shore (filed 11/9; A,3:500-511; B,13[GrHvn])

10/30	A-Inc.	Detroit, Hillsdale & Indiana (filed 11/3; A,3:489-492; B,13[DetHill&SW])
11/13	Inc.	Michigan Air Line Extension RR (filed 1/15/1870; A,3:563-565)
11/27	Inc.	Toledo, Ypsilanti & Saginaw Air Line (filed 1/25/1870; A,3:568-573; B,15)
12/18	Inc.	Toledo & Northern (filed 1/12/1870; A,3:557-560; B,15)
12/20	Inc.	Deer Creek & Marble Quarry (filed 1/29/1870; A,3:575-577; B,12)
12/29	Inc.	Ionia & Stanton (filed 12/29; A,3:543-545)
12/31	S.Inc.	Street Ry of Grand Rapids (filed 12/31; B,15)

1870

1/15	Inc.	Houghton & Ontonagon (filed 1/17; A,3:566-567; B,14[MarH&O])
1/28	Inc.	Romeo & Almont (filed 2/1; A,3:578-579)
1/29	Inc.	Fruitport & Lake Shore (filed 3/4; A,3:593-595; B,13)
2/3	A-Inc.	Grand Rapids & Lake Shore (filed 3/4; A,3:591-592; B,12[Chi&MichLkSh])
3/10	Inc.	Saginaw & St. Clair River (filed 4/25; A,3:630-632; B,15)
3/29	Inc.	Detroit, Howell & Lansing (filed 4/11; A,3:618-620; B,13[DetGR&W])
4/7	O.Inc.	Pennsylvania Co. (PA corp.)
4/13	Inc.	Sturgis & Mansfield (filed 5/11; A,3:635-637; B,15)
4/30	A-Cons.	Peninsular RR (Indiana corp.) and Peninsular Ry (Illinois corp.) into Peninsular (filed 4/30; A,7:303-306)
5/10	Inc.	Ohio & Michigan Ry (filed 5/21; A,4:3-7; B,14[MansfCold&M])
5/19	Inc.	Michigan Midland (filed 7/4; A,4:22-23; B,14)
5/21	A-Inc.	Grand Rapids & Lake Shore (filed 6/4; A,4:8-9; B,12 [Chi&MichLkSh])
6/21	A-Inc.	Chicago & North Western (filed 6/28; A,4:18-19)
7/1	Lease	Kalamazoo & South Haven to Michigan Central
7/11	Inc.	Romeo & Western (filed 7/12; A,4:26-27; B,15)
8/15	A-Cons.	Grand Rapids & Lake Shore into Chicago & Michigan Lake Shore (filed 9/24; A,4:58-59; B,12[C&MLS])
8/15	Lease	Grand River Valley to Michigan Central
9/3	Inc.	Marshall & Coldwater (filed 9/22; A,4:54-56; B,15[Toledo Mich&LkHur])
9/15	Inc.	Adrian & Detroit (filed 9/30; A,4:60-62; B,12)
9/21	Inc.	Patterson RR (filed 10/3; A,4:68-69; B,15)
9/26	Inc.	Detroit, Eel River & Illinois (filed 12/7; A,4:91-93; B,12)
9/28	Inc.	Hudson & Jackson (filed 10/3; A,4:63-67; B,13)
10/8	Cons.	St. Joseph Valley (Indiana corp.) into Michigan Air Line RR (filed 10/11; A,4:71-73)
10/18	Inc.	Muskegon & Greenville (filed 10/29; A,4:76-79; B,14)
11/5	Inc.	Canada Southern & Chicago (filed 11/28; A,4:86-88; B,12)

11/10	Inc.	Grand Rapids, Rockford & Greenville (filed 2/24/1871; A,4:134-137; B,13[GRGreenv&Alp])
12/12	Inc.	Manchester & Homer (filed 12/29; A,4:102-104)
12/28	Inc.	Mansfield, Coldwater & Lake Michigan (filed 5/23/1871; A,4:202-208; B,14)

1871

1/31	Inc.	Grand Rapids RR (filed 2/2; A,4:121-123; B,14[MichNo])
2/—	Lease	part of Michigan Air Line RR to Michigan Central
2/20	Inc.	Grand Rapids & Holland (filed 4/17; A,4:166-170; B,12[Chi&MichLkSh])
3/1	A-Inc.	Jackson, Lansing & Saginaw (filed 5/13; A,4:188-189; B,14)
3/15	Inc.	Grand Rapids & Saginaw (filed 7/5; A,4:226-230; B,13)
3/16	Inc.	Detroit, Lansing & Lake Michigan (filed 4/11; A,4:151-165; B,13[DetGR&W])
4/28	A-Cons.	Bay De Noquet & Marquette into Marquette & Ontonagon RR (filed 8/24; A,4:253-255; B,12[Bay]; B,14[MarqH&O])
5/16	Inc.	Saginaw Valley & St. Louis (filed 5/18; A,4:192-194; B,15)
5/16	Inc.	South Eastern Michigan (filed 5/19; A,4:194-195; B,12 [Det&Chi])
5/16	Inc.	Detroit & Bay City (filed 5/22; A,4:197-198; B,12)
5/20	Inc.	Saginaw & Montcalm (filed 5/23; A,4:209-210; B,15)
5/25	Inc.	Marquette & Peninsula (filed 5/31; A,4:211-212; B,14)
6/9	Inc.	Mineral Range & L'Anse Bay (filed 11/3; A,4:308-309; B,14[MinRge])
6/10	Inc.	Detroit River RR Tunnel (filed 8/31; A,4:251-252; B,12)
6/20	X-Rec.	Grand Rapids & Indiana
6/21	A-Inc.	Grand Rapids & Saginaw (filed 7/5; A,4:226-230)
7/6	A-Inc.	Marshall & Coldwater (filed 7/14; A,4:233-234; B,15 [ToledoMich&LkHur])
7/7	Inc.	Montague, Pentwater & Manistee (filed 7/11; A,4:231-232; B,12[Chi&MichLkSh])
7/11	Inc.	Chicago & Canada Southern (filed 10/28; A,4:297-302; B,12[Det&Chi])
7/11	A-Inc.	Romeo & Western (filed 8/25; A,4:256-257)
7/13	A-Inc.	Houghton & Ontonagon (filed 1/25/1872; A,4:382-383; B,14[MarqH&O])
8/2	Inc.	Traverse City RR (filed 10/30; A,4:303-305)
8/3	Inc.	Grand Rapids & Bay City (filed 9/4; A,4:260-268; B,13)
8/24	Inc.	Muskegon & Big Rapids (filed 12/7; A,4:334-336; B,12 [Chi&MichLkSh])
9/1	Lease	Jackson, Lansing & Saginaw to Michigan Central
9/6	A-Inc.	Marshall & Coldwater (filed 1/9/1872; A,4:366-367; B,15[ToledoMich&LkHur])
9/15	Inc.	Fenton & Grand Blanc (filed 9/16; A,4:272-273; B,13)
9/27	Inc.	Lansing & St. Johns (filed 10/6; A,4:280-281; B,14)
9/29	Inc.	Greenville, Stanton & St. Louis (filed 9/30: A,4:278-280; B,13)

10/7	Inc.	Adrian & State Line (filed 4/24/1872; A,4:451-454; B,12)
10/10	Inc.	Kalamazoo, Lowell & Northern Michigan (filed 11/20; A,4:320-326; B,14)
10/17	Inc.	Carson City & Palo (filed 11/23; A,4:327-329; B,12)
10/21	A-Inc.	Detroit & Bay City (filed 1/3/1872; A,4:364; B,12)
10/23	Inc.	Detroit & Saginaw River (filed 10/30; A,4:306-307; B,12)
10/25	A-Cons.	Grand Rapids & Holland into Chicago & Michigan Lake Shore (filed 12/19; A,4:344-350; B,12[Chi&MLS])
10/25	A-Cons.	Montague, Pentwater & Manistee into Chicago & Michigan Lake Shore (filed 12/19; A,4:351-357; B,12[Chi&MLS])
11/3	Inc.	Flint River (filed 12/6; A,4:332; B,13[Flint&PM])
11/3	Inc.	Cass River (filed 12/12; A,4:338-339; B,13[Flint&PM])
11/21	A-Inc.	Traverse City RR (filed 2/6/1872; A,4:385; rerecorded A,4:641)
12/2	Inc.	Flat River & Houghton Lake (filed 12/7; A,4:333-334; B,13)
12/6	Inc.	Canada, Michigan & Chicago (filed 2/8/1872; A,4:386-387; B,12)
12/7	A-Inc.	Marshall & Coldwater (filed 1/9/1872; A,4:368-369; B,15 [ToledoMich&LkHur])
12/22	Inc.	Owosso & North Western (filed 12/29; A,4:360-361; B,15)
12/28	A-Inc.	Michigan Midland (filed 1/6/1872; A,4:365-366; B,14)

1872

1/17	T.Inc.	Detroit River Street Ry (filed 1/20; A,4:376-377; B,13)
1/29	Inc.	Detroit River RR & Bridge (filed 2/26; A,4:398-399)
2/1	Inc.	Detroit & State Line (filed 3/19; A,4:418-419)
2/1	A-Cons.	Bay City & East Saginaw; Flint River; Holly, Wayne & Monroe; and Cass River into Flint & Pere Marquette (filed 6/4; A,4:495-501; B,13[F&PM])
3/6	A-Inc.	Jackson, Lansing & Saginaw (filed 3/7; B,14)
4/3	Inc.	Ohio, Quincy & Grand Haven(filed 4/29; A,4:457-459; B,15)
4/5	Inc.	St. Clair River, Pontiac & Jackson (filed 4/8; A,4:434-436; B,15[StClair&ChgoAirL])
4/13	Lease	part Michigan Air Line RR to St. Clair River, Pontiac & Jackson
4/24	Inc.	Fort Gratiot & Lexington (filed 4/30; A,4:461-463; B,13)
4/30	Inc.	Mackinac & Chicago (filed 5/1; A,4:464-466; B,14)
5/3	Inc.	Lansing & Lake Michigan (filed 5/16; A,4:478-479; B,14)
5/25	Inc.	Marquette, Houghton & Ontonagon (filed 9/2; A,4:606-613; B,14)
5/29	Inc.	Toledo, Canada Southern & Detroit (filed 7/10; A,4:546-550; refiled 8/2; A,4:575-580; B,15)
5/31	Inc.	Milwaukee, Lake Shore & Western (Wisc. corp.)
6/20*	S.Inc.	Detroit River Ry (filing date shown, articles not found)
6/26	Inc.	Grand Rapids, Greenville & Alpena (filed 7/22; A,4:568-569; B,13)

7/16	Inc.	Ionia, Stanton & Northern (filed 7/17; A,4:561-562; B,13[DetGR&W])
7/18	Tfr.	Patterson RR to Detroit, Lansing & Lake Michigan
7/20	Inc.	St. Clair & Chicago Air Line (filed 10/2; A,6:160-164; B,15)
7/24	Cons.	Grand Rapids, Rockford & Greenville into Grand Rapids, Greenville & Alpena (filed 12/16; A,5:302-307; B,13[GRGreenv&Alp])
7/27	A-Cons.	Muskegon & Big Rapids into Chicago & Michigan Lake Shore (filed 10/24; A,5:264-269; B,12[Chi&MLS])
8/5	Inc.	Lapeer & Port Austin (filed 8/13; A,4:588-589; B,14)
8/21	Inc.	Lapeer & Holly (filed 8/28; A,4:598-599; B,14)
8/22	A-Inc.	Marquette & Ontonagon RR (filed 9/2; A,4:605; B,14[MarH&O])
8/22	A-Inc.	Houghton & Ontonagon (filed 9/5; A,4:618; B,14[MarH&O])
9/10	T.Inc.	Detroit Transit Ry (filed 9/21; B,13)
9/17	Inc.	Michigan, Midland & Canada (filed 9/21; A,4:626-627; B,14)
9/18	A-Inc.	Flint & Pere Marquette (filed 10/14; A,5:256-257; B,13)
10/1	A-Cons.	Ionia, Stanton & Northern into Detroit, Lansing & Lake Michigan (filed 12/11; A,5:297-300; B,13[DetGR&W])
10/9	Inc.	East Saginaw & St. Clair (filed 10/31; A,5:274-275; B,13[Flint&PM])
10/18	Inc.	Lapeer & Northern (filed 10/23; A,5:262-263; B,14)
10/23	Inc.	Flint & Lansing (filed 10/28; A,5:270-271; B,13)
10/25	Inc.	Mineral Range (filed 11/8; A,5:282-283; B,14)
11/8	T.Inc.	Detroit Western Transit Ry (filed 11/9; B,13)
12/11	A-Inc.	Fort Gratiot & Lexington (filed 3/6/1873; A,5:409-411; B,13)
12/16	Inc.	Marquette, Sault Ste. Marie & Mackinac (filed 12/23; A,5:318-319; B,14)
12/24	Inc.	Chicago, Saginaw & Canada (filed 1/4/1873; A,5:325-326; B,15[Saginaw&W])

1873

1/3	Inc.	Ohio & Grand Haven (filed 1/4; A,5:327-328; B,14[Mich&Ohio])
1/13	Inc.	Port Huron & Saginaw Valley (filed 1/16; A,5:344-349; B,15)
3/26	Inc.	Cincinnati & Great Northern (filed 4/3; A,5:441-444; B,12)
3/27	S.Inc.	Detroit & Grand Trunk Junction (filed 6/16; B,12)
4/5	Inc.	Chicago & Lake Huron (filed 8/15; A,6:85-90; B,12)
4/11	Inc.	Michigan Northern Ry (filed 4/18; A,5:458-459; B,14)
4/24	Cons.	Grand Rapids into Michigan Northern (filed 8/19; A,6:91-95; B,14[MichNo])
5/14	A-Inc.	Detroit & Bay City (filed 5/31; A,5:493; B,12)
5/28	A-Inc.	Grand Rapids & Saginaw (filed 6/7; A,6:6-7; B,13)
5/30	S.Inc.	Central Market, Cass Ave. & Third St. (filed 5/31; B,12[CassAve])

6/7	Cons.	Cincinnati & Great Northern into Cincinnati & Great Northern (Ohio corp.) (filed 9/23; A,6:139-148; B,12)
6/28	S.Inc.	City RR (filed 9/16; B,12)
6/30	Inc.	Mackinaw & Lake Superior (filed 7/1; A,6:35-36; B,14)
6/30	A-Inc.	Chicago, Saginaw & Canada (filed 8/22; A,6:99-102; B,15 [Saginaw&W])
8/5	S.Inc.	Division Street Ry. (filed 8/9; B,13)
8/20	Inc.	Canada Southern Bridge Co. (filed 9/23; A,6:149-153)
8/26	S.Inc.	St. Aubin Ave. Street Ry (filed 9/15; B,15[RussellSt])
9/15	Inc.	Michigan & Ohio Ry (filed 4/1/1874; A,6:384-390; B,14)
11/12	S.Inc.	Main Street Ry (filed 11/15; B,14)
11/12	Sale	Michigan Midland to Michigan Midland & Canada (B,14)
11/21	A-Inc.	Marquette, Houghton & Ontonagon (filed 3/16/1874; A,6:362-363; B,14)

1874

1/1	Lease	Mansfield, Coldwater & Lake Michigan (Michigan lines) to Grand Rapids & Indiana
2/6	S.Inc.	Grand Rapids & Reeds Lake Street Ry (filed 2/9; B,13)
2/11	Inc.	Chicago, Milwaukee & St. Paul (Wisc. corp.)
3/21	S.Inc.	Winsor Street Ry (filed 3/28; B,16)
4/7	S.Inc.	Division Street & Reed's Lake Ry (filed 4/14; B,13)
7/11	Inc.	Chicago & Northeastern (filed 8/12; A,6:488-489)
8/1	A-Inc.	Kalamazoo, Lowell & Northern Michigan (filed 11/9; A,6:548)
8/5	S.Inc.	Russell Street, St. Aubin Avenue & Detroit & Milwaukee Junction (filed 8/7; B,15)
9/5	Inc.	Coldwater, Marshall & Mackinaw (filed 12/22; A,6:590-591; B,15[ToledoMich&LkHur])
9/30	T.Inc	Bay City Street Ry (filed 11/20, B,12; refiled 1/2/75)
12/15	Inc.	Alpena & Michigan South-western (filed 2/23/1875; A,6:656-657; B,12)

1875

1/28	F.Sale	Detroit, Hillsdale & Ind. to Detroit, Hillsdale & SW (*See* Inc. 1/30; A,6:615-619)
1/30	Inc.	Detroit, Hillsdale & South-Western (filed 1/30; A,6:615-619; B,12)
2/6	A-Inc.	Grand Rapids & Reeds Lake (filed 2/17; B,13)
2/9	Inc.	Menominee River RR (filed 2/16; A,6:645-646; B,12[C&NW])
4/8	F.Sale	St. Clair & Chicago Air Line to Michigan Air Line Ry
4/8	T.Inc.	Lake Train Ry (filed 4/15; B,14)
4/15	Rec.	Detroit & Milwaukee
4/28	F.Sale	part Michigan Air Line RR to Michigan Air Line Ry
6/16	A-Inc.	Grand Rapids, Newaygo & Lake Shore (filed 3/15/1877; A,7:473-475; B,13)

8/25	A-Inc.	Menominee River RR (filed 9/2; A,7:146; B,12[C&NW])
9/10	S.Inc.	Fulton Street & Reed's Lake Ry (filed 9/18; B,13)
9/15	S.Inc.	Congress & Baker Street Ry (filed 9/17; B,12)
9/28	F.Sale	Toledo, Ann Arbor & Northern
11/18	Inc.	Michigan Air Line Ry (filed 11/23; A,7:200-203)
11/27	T.Inc.	Bear Lake Train Ry (filed 1/19/1876; B,12)

1876

1/29	Inc.	Toledo & South Haven [Bangor & South Haven Div.](filed 2/2; A,7:278-280; B,12[B&SHDivT&SH])
1/29	Inc.	Alpena & South-Western (filed 1/31; A,7:271-272; B,12)
2/2	Inc.	Toledo & South Haven [Van Buren Div.] (filed 4/21; A,7:330-332; B,15)
3/17	Inc.	Glencoe, Pinconning & Lake Shore (filed 3/22; A,7:310-311; B,14[JacksonLans&Sag])
6/20	S.Inc.	Lansing Street Ry (filed 6/20; B,14)
7/31	Rec.	Detroit, Lansing & Lake Michigan
9/6	Sale	Russell Street, etc. to Detroit City
11/11	Rec.	Chicago & Michigan Lake Shore
11/14	A-Inc.	Coldwater, Marshall & Mackinaw (filed 1/17/1877; A,7:452; B,15[ToledoMich&LkHur])
12/2	Inc.	Toledo & South Haven [St. Joseph Co. Division] (filed 4/30/1877; A,7:492-493; B,15[St.JosCoDivT&SH])
12/14	F.Sale	Detroit, Lansing & Lake Michigan to Detroit, Lansing & Northern (*See* Inc. 12/21; A,7:433-439)
12/21	Inc.	Detroit, Lansing & Northern (filed 12/27; A,7:433-439; B,12[DetGR&W])
12/26	Inc.	Lake George & Muskegon River (filed 12/29; A,7:440-441; B,14)

1877

4/5	S.Inc.	Port Huron Ry (filed 4/12; B,15)
5/—	Rec.	Central Market, Cass Avenue & Third Street
5/14	Inc.	Lake Superior Ship Canal Railway & Iron Co. (filed 5/15; A,7:514-516; B,14)
7/14	A-Inc.	Detroit City (filed 7/17; B,12)
8/18	S.Inc.	Cass Avenue Ry (filed 8/23; B,12)
8/28	F.Sale	Mansfield, Coldwater & Lake Michigan part to Allegan & South Eastern and part to Pennsylvania (*See* Inc. 1/22/1878; A,8:61-62)
9/4	Inc.	Saginaw & Clare County (filed 9/4; A,7:590-591; B,13 [Flint&PM])
9/24	Inc.	Maple Rapids & Southern (filed 10/15; B,14)
10/27	Inc.	Houghton Lake & Eastern (filed 10/29; A,7:645-646; B,13)
11/20	Rec.	Chicago, Saginaw & Canada

11/23	Inc.	Toledo & Ann Arbor (filed 11/23; A,7:673-676; B,15[ToledoAA&NoMich])
12/13	Inc.	Allegan & South-Eastern (filed 1/22/1878; A,8:61-62)

1878

2/12	Inc.	Missaukee RR (filed 2/14; A,8:91-92; B,14)
2/16	A-Inc.	Lake George & Muskegon River (filed 6/7; A,8:174-175; B,14)
3/1	Inc.	Michigan Extension Ry (filed 3/6; A,8:108-110; B,14)
3/9	T.Inc.	Peters Train Ry (filed 3/21; B,15)
3/21	Inc.	Port Huron & Northwestern (filed 3/23; A,8:118-119; B,15)
4/15	T.Inc.	Lake Huron & Southwestern (filed 3/4/1879; B,14)
4/29	Inc.	Muskegon River & Rose Lake (filed 5/2; A,8:136-137; B,14)
5/1	Sale	Toledo & State Line to Toledo & Ann Arbor
5/11	A-Cons.	Toledo & Ann Arbor (filed 5/24; A,8:163-167; B,15[ToledoAA&NoMich])
5/14	A-Inc.	Lake Superior Ship Canal Railway & Iron Co. (filed 5/18; A,8:156-160; B,14)
5/15	S.Inc.	West Side Street Ry of Grand Rapids (filed 1/25/1881; B,16)
6/10	S.Inc.	Street RR of East Saginaw (filed 6/14; B,15)
6/11*	S.Inc.	East Saginaw Ry (filing date shown; articles not found)
6/19	F.Sale	Michigan Lake Shore to Grand Haven (*See* Inc. 9/21; A,8:236-242)
7/1	Inc.	Chesapeake & Ohio (Virginia corp.)
7/5	A-Inc.	Toledo & Ann Arbor (filed 8/1; A,8:212-214; B,15[ToledoAA&NoMich])
7/22	A-Inc.	Saginaw Valley & St. Louis (filed 7/24; A,8:196-197; B,15)
7/30	Cons.	Peninsular and Port Huron & Lake Michigan into Chicago & Lake Huron
9/4	F.Sale	Detroit & Milwaukee to Detroit, Grand Haven & Milwaukee (*See* Inc. 10/28; A,8:256-259)
9/9	Inc.	Toledo, Ann Arbor & North-Eastern (filed 9/26; A,8:234-235; B,15[ToledoAA&NoMich])
9/21	Inc.	Grand Haven (filed 9/27; A,8:236-242; B,13)
10/22	Inc.	Saginaw & Grand Rapids (filed 10/23; A,8:254-255; B,15)
10/28	Inc.	Detroit, Grand Haven & Milwaukee (filed 10/28; A,8:256-257 and 11/8; A,8:264-268; B,13)
11/13	Inc.	Muskegon River & Cat Creek (filed 11/19; A,8:279-281; B,14)
11/15	F.Sale	Chicago & Michigan Lake Shore to Chicago & West Michigan (*See* Inc. 12/20; A,8:300-304)
12/20	Inc.	Chicago & West Michigan (filed 12/28; A,8:300-304; B,12[Chi&MichLkSh])

1879

n.d.	Lease	Bay City Street to Detroit & Bay City
1/1	Lease	Allegan & Southeastern to Grand Rapids & Indiana
2/11	Inc.	Saginaw & Mt. Pleasant (filed 3/25; A,8:337-338; B,13[Flint&PM])
4/1	A-Char.	Michigan Central (1879 P.Acts, No. 21, 17-18)

4/21	Inc.	Toledo & Port Austin [Oxford & Almont Div. of] (filed 6/9; A,8:386-387; B,15[Oxf&AlDivT&PA])
4/22	Inc.	Bay View Little Traverse & Mackinac (filed 5/2; A,8:355-356; B,12)
4/30	Inc.	Pinconning (filed 5/2; A,8:357-358; B,14[JackLans&Sag])
5/13	Inc.	Pontiac & Oxford (filed 6/20; A,8:399-400; B,15)
6/5	Inc.	Rochester, Almont & Northern (filed 6/12; A,8:393-395; B,15)
6/21	F.Sale	Port Huron & Lake Michigan to North Western Grand Trunk (*See* Inc. 8/23; A,8:444-449, 459)
7/1	Rec.	Flint & Pere Marquette
7/11	Inc.	Hobart & Manistee River (filed 7/19; A,8:416; B,13)
7/25	Inc.	Oxford & Port Austin (filed 7/28; A,8:419-420)
8/6	Inc.	Toledo & Milwaukee Ry (filed 8/8; A,8:429-431; B,12[CinJack&M])
8/20	Inc.	Detroit, Mackinac & Marquette (filed 8/21; A,8:440-441; B,13)
8/23	Inc.	North Western Grand Trunk (filed 8/26; A,8:444-449, 459)
8/25	F.Sale	Chicago & Lake Huron to Michigan Ry, Indiana Ry, and North Western Grand Trunk (*See* Inc. 1/6/1880; A,8:539-541)
9/3	Inc.	Detroit, Mackinac & Marquette (filed 9/4; A,8:451-452; B,13[DulSS&A])
10/1	F.Sale	Lake Huron & Southwestern to Tawas & Bay County
10/—	Inc.	Ravenna & Spring Lake Narrow Gauge (filed 10/15; B,15)
10/30	A-Inc.	Detroit, Lansing & Northern (filed 12/8; A,8:511)
11/—	Lease	Chicago & Canada Southern to Lake Shore & Mich. Sou.
11/10	Inc.	Wabash, St. Louis & Pacific (Indiana corp.)
11/13	Inc.	White River (filed 11/14; A,8:498-499; B,16)
11/15	Inc.	Muskegon Lake (filed 12/18; A,8:517-519; B,14)
11/17	Inc.	Croswell & Peck (filed 12/29; A,8:520-521; B,12)
11/23	Inc.	Capac & Northern (filed 11/29; A,8:504; B,12)
12/3	F.Sale	Fort Wayne, Jackson & Saginaw to Fort Wayne & Jackson (*See* Inc. 12/31; A,8:535-537)
12/16	A-Inc.	Menominee River RR (filed 12/18; A,8:516-517; B,12[C&NW])
12/30	Inc.	Pontiac, Oxford & Port Austin (filed 1/15/1880; A,8:543-544)
12/31	Inc.	Fort Wayne & Jackson (filed 1/5/1880; A,8:535-537)

1880

1/6	Inc.	Michigan Ry (filed 1/7; A,8:539-541)
1/7	Inc.	Chicago & Grand Trunk (filed 4/6; A,8:670-689)
1/9	A-Inc.	Port Huron & Northwestern (filed 1/21; A,8:554; B,15)
1/27	Inc.	St. Joseph Valley (filed 2/4; A,8:571-572; B,14[MilwBH&C])
1/27	Inc.	Detroit, Butler & St. Louis (filed 2/11; A,8:598-599; B,16[Wabash])

2/5	Inc.	Sault Ste. Marie & Marquette (filed 2/6; A,8:589-590; B,13[DulSS&A])
2/12	Inc.	Tawas & Bay County (filed 2/19; A,8:612-613; B,15)
2/14	Inc.	Ontonagon & Montreal River (filed 2/26; A,8:621-623; B,15)
3/3	A-Inc.	Grand Rapids & Indiana (filed 12/8/1881; A,10:172-174; B,13)
3/30	Inc.	Jackson & Eastern (filed 3/31; A,8:653-654; B,14)
4/1	Lease	White River to Chicago & West Michigan
5/21	Inc.	Bay View & Crooked Lake (filed 9/28; A,9:204-206; B,12)
5/31	Inc.	Manistee RR (filed 6/19; A,9:67-68; B,13[Flint&PM])
6/1	Inc.	Grand Rapids, Greenville & Bay City (filed 7/23; A,9:110-111; B,13)
6/5	Inc.	Milwaukee & Northern (Wisconsin corp.)
6/16	Inc.	Elkhart, Niles & Lake Michigan (filed 6/19; A,9:64-66; B,12[CinWab&Mich])
6/28	Inc.	Lake County RR (filed 9/8; A,9:152-153; B,14)
7/2	S.Inc.	Reeds Lake Street Ry (filed 7/6; B,15)
7/20	Sale	Grand Rapids & Reeds Lake Street to Reeds Lake Street
7/22	A-Inc.	Michigan Air Line Ry (filed 8/14; A,9:129-133)
8/18	F.Sale	Flint & Pere Marquette RR to Flint & Pere Marquette Ry (*See* Inc. 8/24; A,9:140-145)
8/20	Sale	Grand Rapids & Reeds Lake to Reeds Lake Street
8/24	Inc.	Flint & Pere Marquette Ry (filed 8/31; A,9:140-145; B,13)
9/8	Inc.	Ontonagon & Brule River (filed 9/10; A,9:203-204; B,15)
10/14	Inc.	Toledo, Ann Arbor & Grand Trunk (filed 10/15; A,9:223-226, 260-263; B,15[ToledoAA&NoMich])
10/15	A-Cons.	Menominee Ry (Wisc. corp.) into Menominee River (filed 11/15; A,9:281-285; B,12[C&NW])
10/28	S.Inc.	Muskegon Street Ry (filed 11/9; B,14)
11/15	A-Inc.	Muskegon Lake (filed 12/7; A,9:309-310; B,14)
11/18	Inc.	Saginaw Bay & Northwestern (filed 11/27; A,9:291-292; B,14[JacksonLans&Sag])
11/24	Inc.	Escanaba & Lake Superior Ry (filed 11/26; A,9:289-290; B,12[C&NW])
11/27	A-Inc.	Port Huron & Northwestern (filed 12/10; A,9:310-311; B,15)
12/21	Inc.	Maple Rapids & Lansing (filed 1/21/1881; A,9:356-357; B,14)

1881

1/17	Inc.	Bay City & Alpena (filed 1/18; A,9:352-353)
1/17	A-Inc.	Detroit, Butler & St. Louis (filed 5/25; A,9:517-522; B,16[Wabash])
1/20	Inc.	Buckley & Douglas (filed 9/6; A,10:39-40; B,12)
2/12	F.Sale	Detroit & Bay City Ry to Detroit & Bay City RR (*See* Inc. 2/21; A,9:393-396)
2/14	Inc.	Saginaw, Tuscola & Huron (filed 2/24; A,9:397; B,15)

2/18	Inc.	Grand Rapids, Indiana & Mackinaw (filed 2/19; A,9:381-382; B,13[GR&I])
2/19	Inc.	Sault Ste. Marie Bridge Co. (filed 2/24; A,9:387-388)
2/21	Inc.	Detroit & Bay City RR (filed 2/26; A,9:393-396; B,12)
3/2	A-Inc.	Port Huron & Northwestern (filed 10/28; A,10:128-129; B,15)
3/10	Lease	Detroit & Bay City to Michigan Central
3/13*	Inc.	Jefferson Avenue Ry (filing date shown, articles not found)
4/1	A-Inc.	Ontonagon & Brule River (filed 4/9; A,9:426; B,15)
4/20	A-Inc.	Chicago & West Michigan (filed 5/2; A,9:458-459; B,12[Chi&MichLkSh])
5/2	Inc.	Detroit, Western Transit & Junction (filed 5/2; A,9:459-460; B,13)
5/20	A-Inc.	Menominee River RR (filed 5/23; A,9:513-515; B,12[C&NW])
5/20	A-Inc.	Grand Haven (filed 5/24; A,9:515-517; B,13)
5/27	Inc.	Detroit Belt Ry & Depot (filed 5/31; A,9:529-530; B,12)
6/1	Inc.	Houghton & L'Anse (filed 6/4; A,9:535-536; B,14[MarH&O])
6/5	Inc.	Detroit, Toledo & Jackson (filed 6/15; A,9:580-581; B,13)
6/9	UD.Inc.	Detroit Union RR Depot & Station (filed 6/11; A,9:557-559; B,13)
6/13	Reinc.	Wabash, St. Louis & Pacific (eff. 7/1) (filed 9/10; A,10:51-53; B,16[Wabash])
7/16	A-Cons.	Grand Haven and Grand Rapids, Newaygo & Lake Shore and Indiana & Michigan (Indiana corp.) into Chicago & West Michigan (filed 10/1; A,10:72-95, 98-102; B,12[C&WM])
7/18	A-Inc.	Detroit, Mackinac & Marquette (filed 7/20; A,9:621; B,13[DulSS&A])
7/29	Inc.	Muskrat Lake & Clam River (filed 9/21; A,10:59-61; B,14)
8/4	Inc.	Vieux Desert & Lake Superior (filed 9/28; A,10:65-67; B,14[MilwLkSh&W])
8/15	Inc.	Toledo & Saginaw Bay (filed 8/16; A,9:685-686; B,15)
8/15	A-Inc.	Elkhart, Niles & Lake Michigan (filed 9/29; A,10:71-72; B,12[CinWab&Mich])
8/19	Inc.	Northern Michigan Central (filed 8/23; A,10:26-27; B,15)
8/24	S.Inc.	Jackson City Ry (filed 8/27; B,14)
9/2	Inc.	Hermansville & Western (filed 9/6; A,10:43-46; B,13)
9/5	Lease	Detroit, Hillsdale & SW to Lake Shore & Michigan Southern
9/21	Inc.	Republic Branch (filed 9/28; A,10:67-68; B,14[Milw&N])
9/24	A-Inc.	Pontiac, Oxford & Port Austin (filed 10/7; A,10:107-109)
9/24	S.Inc.	St. Joseph & Benton Harbor Street (filed 9/30; B,15)
10/8	Inc.	St. Mary's & Minneapolis (filed 10/12; A,10:111-112; B,15)
10/10	O.Inc.	Mackinac Transportation Co. (filed 10/12; A,10:112-114)
11/1	Sale	Hamtramck Street to Detroit City
11/28	Tfr.	Lake George & Muskegon River to private owners
12/2	A-Inc.	St. Joseph Valley (filed 1/19/1882; A,10:214-215; B,14 [MilwBH&Col])

1882

1/17	T.Inc.	Fort Wayne & Elmwood (filed 2/3; B,13)
1/20	Inc.	Bear Lake & Eastern (filed 1/24; A,10:222-223; B,12)
1/21	A-Inc.	Michigan Air Line Ry (filed 3/29; A,10:335-340)
1/27	Inc.	Port Huron & Southwestern (filed 1/28; A,10:227-228; B,15[PortHur&NW])
2/1	Inc.	Grand Rapids Transfer & Junction (filed 2/2; A,10:232-233; B,13)
2/9	Inc.	West Branch & Moorestown (filed 2/20; A,10:267-269; B,16)
2/23	A-Inc.	Detroit, Mackinac & Marquette (filed 2/27; A,10:276-277; B,13[DulSS&A])
2/27	Inc.	New Mexico Central & Northern (filed 6/2; A,10:436-438; B,15)
3/2	A-Inc.	Detroit, Western Transit & Junction (filed 3/14; A,10:316; B,13)
3/11	Inc.	Toledo & South Haven [St. Joseph Div.] (filed 3/16/1883; A,12:77-79; B,15[StJosDivT&SH])
3/17	A-Inc.	Detroit, Western Transit & Junction (filed 3/18; A,10:324-325; B,13)
3/21	Inc.	Ithaca & Alma (filed 4/15; A,10:358-359; B,14)
3/22	A-Inc.	Port Huron & Northwestern (filed 10/7; A,10:581; B,15)
4/4	Inc.	Sturgis & Indiana (filed 4/11; A,10:350-351; B,14[MichInd&Stur])
4/12	Opg.Ag.	Detroit, Western Transit & Junction by Detroit Union RR Depot
4/17	Inc.	Ovid & Traverse Bay (filed 4/26; A,10:372-373; B,15)
4/17	A-Inc.	Detroit Union RR Depot (filed 4/19; A,10:363-366, 368-369; B,13)
4/26	Inc.	Bay City & Midland (filed 5/2; A,10:379-380; B,12)
5/15	Inc.	Spring Harbor & Boyne Falls (filed 5/20; A,10:410-411; B,15)
5/23	Inc.	Cincinnati, Wabash & Michigan (filed 8/11; A,10:524-529; B,12)
5/30	Inc.	Michigan, Indiana & St. Louis (filed 10/21; A,10:605-611; B,14)
6/14	A-Inc.	Saginaw Valley & St. Louis (filed 6/24; A,10:473-474; B,15)
6/15	Inc.	Paris & Pere Marquette River (filed 7/20; A,10:498-499; B,15)
6/22	Sale	Congress & Baker and Cass Avenue to Detroit City
6/26	A-Inc.	Toledo & South Haven [Van Buren Div. of] (filed 8/4; A,10:521-522; B,15)
6/30	A-Inc.	Menominee River RR (filed 7/5; A,10:482; B,12[C&NW])
7/1	A-Inc.	Escanaba & Lake Superior Ry (filed 7/5; A,10:483; B,12[C&NW])
7/1	A-Cons.	Menominee River and Escanaba & Lake Superior into Chicago & North Western (filed 9/19; A,10:564-569; B,12[C&NW])
7/11	Sale	Tawas & Bay County to Bay City & Alpena
7/14	A-Inc.	Division Street Ry (filed 7/17, B,13)
8/12	A-Inc.	Toledo, Ann Arbor & Grand Trunk(filed 8/14; A,10:541-542; refiled 10/24; A,10:613-631; B,15[ToledoAA&NoMich])
8/21	S.Inc.	Battle Creek Ry (filed 8/28; B,12)

8/23	Inc.	Central Michigan Ry (filed 8/23; A,10:544-545; B,12)
8/24	Lease	Fort Wayne & Jackson to Lake Shore & Michigan Southern
8/26	Inc.	Ontonagon, Gogebic & Wisconsin (filed 9/14; A,10:558-559; B,15)
9/13	A-Cons.	Port Huron & Southwestern into Port Huron & Northwestern (filed 12/9; A,10:665-666; B,15[PtHur&NW])
9/14	S.Inc.	Muskegon Ry (filed 9/15; B,14)
10/18	Inc.	Cadillac & Evart (filed 10/24; A,10:631-633; B,12)
10/25	Inc.	Mecosta RR (filed 10/26; A,10:635-636; B,14)
10/28	Inc.	Toledo, Ann Arbor & North Michigan (filed 11/16; A,10:652-654; B,15)
12/4	S.Inc.	Manistee Street Ry (filed 12/6; B,14)
12/4	A-Inc.	Muskegon Ry (filed 12/6; B,14)
12/12	Opg.Ag.	Canada Southern (and subsidiaries) by Michigan Central
12/31	X-Lease	Allegan & Southeastern by Grand Rapids & Indiana

1883

1/1	Lease	Traverse City RR to Grand Rapids & Indiana
1/9	Inc.	St. Helen's Lake & Southern (filed 1/11; A,12:22-23; B,15)
2/1	A-Cons.	Houghton & L'Anse to Marquette, Houghton & Ontonagon (filed 4/19; A,12:130-145; B,14[MarqH&O])
2/3	A-Inc.	Muskegon Ry (filed 2/6; B,14)
2/13	A-Cons.	Vieux Desert & Lake Superior into Milwaukee, Lake Shore & Western (filed 5/4; A,12:168-181; B,14[MLS&W])
2/15	Lease	Saginaw Bay & Northwestern to Michigan Central
3/7	Inc.	Pontiac & Southern (filed 3/19; A,12:81-82; B,15)
3/9	A-Inc.	Port Huron & Northwestern (filed 3/13; A,12:73; B,15)
3/13	Sale	Allegan & South Eastern to Toledo & Milwaukee (B,12[CJ&M])
3/21	A-Inc.	Saginaw & Clare County (filed 4/11; A,12:123-124)
3/28	Inc.	Lac la Belle & Calumet (filed 4/4; A,12:115-116)
3/31	Inc.	Detroit, Bay City & Alpena (filed 4/2; A,12:110-112)
4/3	T.Inc.	Arcadia & Betsey River Train Ry (filed 4/10; B,12)
5/2	Inc.	Nirvana & Luther (filed 5/16; A,12:193-195; B,15)
5/10	F.Sale	Chicago, Saginaw & Canada to Saginaw & Western (*See* Inc. 6/5; A,12:215-218)
5/14	A-Inc.	Hermansville & Western (filed 7/16; A,12:266-269; B,13)
5/18	Inc.	Hastings, Lowell & Northern Michigan (filed 7/9; A,12:255-257; B,13)
5/28	$	Saginaw Bay & Northwestern by Michigan Central
5/30	Inc.	Allegan & Lake Shore (filed 6/9; A,12:225-226; B,12)
6/5	Inc.	Saginaw & Western (filed 6/7; A,12:215-218; B,15)

6/7	Inc.	Chicago, Kalamazoo & Saginaw (filed 7/3; A,12:252-253)
6/8	A-Char.	Michigan Central (1883 P.Acts, No. 188, 205-206)
6/8	A-Char.	Michigan Southern (now Lake Shore & Michigan Southern) (1883 P.Acts, No. 189, 206-207)
6/11	A-Inc.	Detroit, Mackinac & Marquette (filed 6/18; A,12:240; B,13[DulSS&A])
6/22	T.Inc.	Adrian City Train & Street Ry (filed 6/23; B,12)
6/25	Inc.	Michigan & Ohio RR (filed 10/9; A,12:363-375; B,12[CJ&M])
7/1	Lease	Saginaw & Western to Detroit, Lansing & Northern
7/2	Inc.	Menominee Branch RR (filed 7/9; A,12:258-259; B,14[Milw&N])
8/3	T.Inc.	Peters Manistee Train Ry (filed 11/2; B,15)
8/18	Inc.	Houghton & Rockland (filed 9/1; A,12:318-319; B,13)
8/25	Inc.	Detroit & South Lyon (filed 9/19; A,12:349-350; B,12)
8/29	Sale	Kalamazoo, Lowell & North Michigan, partial rights to Hastings, Lowell & North Michigan
10/3	Inc.	Marquette & Western (filed 10/12; A,12:383-384; B,14)
10/4	Inc.	Canada, LaCrosse & Southwestern RR (filed 10/20; A,12:408-409; B,12)
11/21	A-Inc.	Bay City Street (filed 11/24; B,12)
12/3	A-Inc.	Street Ry of Grand Rapids (filed 12/6; B,15)
12/5	Inc.	Gogebic & Montreal River (filed 12/27; A,12:470-471; B,13)
12/10	Inc.	Utica & Lexington (filed 12/13; A,12:458-459; B,16)
12/17	Inc.	Lexington & Utica (filed 12/20; A,12:465-466; B,14)
12/22	Inc.	Detroit, Lincoln & Denver (filed 12/26; A,12:468-469; B,12)

1884

1/3	Inc.	St. Louis, Sturgis & Battle Creek (filed 1/7; A,12:489-491)
1/18	Inc.	Jackson & Ohio (filed 1/19; A,12:500-501; B,12[CinJ&M])
2/2	S.Inc.	Kalamazoo Street Ry (filed 2/4; B,14)
2/5	Inc.	Lansing, Alma, Mt. Pleasant & Northern (filed 2/12; A,12:518-521; B,15[ToledoAA&NoMich])
2/7	Sale	White River to Chicago & West Michigan
2/25	Reinc.	New Mexico Central & Northern (filed 3/1; A,12:528-530; B,15)
5/19	A-Cons.	Toledo, Ann Arbor & Grand Trunk into Toledo, Ann Arbor & North Michigan (filed 7/29; A,12:652-669; B,15[ToledoAA&NoMich])
5/29	Rec.	Wabash, St. Louis & Pacific
6/2	A-Cons.	South Bend & St. Joseph (Indiana corp.) into St. Joseph Valley (filed 6/12; A,12:636-638; B,14[MilwBH&Col])
6/11	A-Inc.	Milwaukee, Lake Shore & Western (filed 6/12; A,12:639-640; B,14)
7/2	A-Cons.	Grand Rapids, Indiana & Mackinaw into Grand Rapids & Indiana (filed 10/7; A,14:8-10; B,13[GR&I])

7/17	Inc.	Coldwater & Central Michigan (filed 9/17; A,12:695-696; B,12)
8/8	Inc.	South Bend, Niles & St. Joseph (filed 8/9; A,12:678-679; B,15)
9/5	Inc.	Pittsburgh & Lake Superior (filed 9/11; A,12:683-684; B,15)
10/13	Inc.	Toledo, Marshall & Northern (filed 10/17; A,14:18-19; B,15[ToledoMich&LkHur])
10/18	Sale	Coldwater, Marshall & Mackinaw to Toledo, Marshall & Northern (filed 10/22; B,15[ToledoMich&LkHur])
11/8	Inc.	Toledo & South Haven [Lake Michigan Div. of] (filed 11/25; A,14:30-31; B,14[LMDivT&SH])
11/10	S.Inc.	St. Joseph & Benton Harbor Street Ry (filed 11/12; B,15)
11/28	Inc.	Riverdale & Lake Michigan (filed 12/5; A,14:37-38; B,15)
12/1	Inc.	Ohio & Central Michigan (filed 12/5; A,14:38-40; B,15)
12/18	Inc.	Cadillac, Manistee Valley & Lake Michigan (filed 12/29; A,14:57-59; B,12)
12/27	Inc.	Hancock & Calumet (filed 1/14/1885; A,14:69; B,13)
12/31	Sale	Kalamazoo, Lowell & North Michigan, partial rights to Chicago, Kalamazoo & Saginaw

1885

1/6	Inc.	Ishpeming, L'Anse & Ontonagon (filed 1/13; A,14:67-68; B,14)
2/3	Inc.	Sault Ste. Marie & Southwestern (filed 2/19; A,14:103-105; B,12[CanadaLaCr&SW])
2/25	S.Inc.	Valley City Street Cable Ry (filed 2/28; B,16)
4/20	Inc.	Menominee & Sault Ste. Marie (filed 4/20; A,14:145-146)
4/29	Inc.	Canada, LaCrosse & Southwestern Ry (filed 8/10; A,14:233-267; B,12)
5/—	Lease	Marquette & Western to Marquette, Houghton & Ontonagon
5/14	Inc.	Detroit & St. Clair River (filed 6/5; A,14:205-207; B,12)
7/15	A-Inc.	Mecosta RR (filed 11/16; A,14:324; B,14)
9/16	Inc.	Crawford & Manistee River (filed 9/28; A,14:294-297; B,12)
9/23	Inc.	Grand Rapids, Indiana & Manistee (filed 10/14;A,14:302-304; B,13)
10/12	S.Inc.	Metropolitan Electric Ry (filed 10/13; B,14)
10/23	T.Inc.	Midland Train Ry (filed 11/30; B,14)
10/24	A-Inc.	Peters Manistee Train (filed 11/24; B,15)
11/9	Inc.	Frankfort & South Eastern (filed 12/2; A,14:336-337; B,13[EscFr&SE])
11/11	Inc.	Arms Lake (filed 11/14; A,14:319-320; B,12)
11/20	Inc.	Kalamazoo, Paw Paw & Lake Michigan (filed 12/3; A,14:341-344; B,14)
11/21	S.Inc.	Lansing City Ry (filed 12/30; B,14)

1886

n.d.	Sale	Division Street; Reeds Lake Street; and West Side Street to Street Ry of Grand Rapids
1/1	Sale	Bay City Street Ry to Detroit & Bay City

1/18	Inc.	Muskegon, Grand Rapids & Indiana (filed 2/12; A,14:421-423; B,14)
1/20	Inc.	South Bend & Benton Harbor (filed 1/22; A,14:384-385; B,15)
1/20	Inc.	Toledo & Cadillac (filed 1/26; A,14:397-398; B,15)
1/20	Inc.	Cincinnati, Jackson & Mackinaw (filed 3/12; A,14:449-457; B,12)
1/22	Inc.	Toledo, Saginaw & Muskegon (filed 1/25; A,14:386-387; B,15)
2/2	Inc.	Newaygo RR (filed 2/10; A,14:418-420; B,15)
2/2	S.Inc.	Saginaw Street Ry (filed 2/3; B,15[SagConsol])
2/4	Inc.	Grass Lake & Manistee River (filed 6/16; A,14:564-565; B,13)
2/6	Inc.	Bay City, Caro & Port Huron (filed 2/15; A,14:423-425; B,12)
2/13	A-Inc.	Toledo, Saginaw & Muskegon (filed 2/16; A,14:426; B,15)
3/8	Inc.	Wabash Western (Missouri corp.)
3/24	Inc.	Manistee & Luther (filed 3/26; A,14:468-469)
4/26	F.Sale	Detroit, Butler & St. Louis to Detroit, St. Louis & Western (*See* Inc. 2/19/1889; A,18:93-95; B,16[Wabash])
4/27	Inc.	Chicago & Canada Pacific (filed 6/17; A,14:565-566; B,12)
4/29	S.Inc.	Battle Creek Street (filed 5/4; B,12)
4/30	T.Inc.	Lansing Transit Ry (filed 4/30; B,14)
5/5	Inc.	Toledo, Ann Arbor & Mt. Pleasant (filed 5/7; B,15(TAA&NM])
5/11	Inc.	Marquette Iron Range Cable Transit & Ry (filed 5/19; A,14:529-532; B,14)
5/11	S.Inc.	Highland Park Ry (filed 5/12; B,13)
5/17	Sale	Black River to Detroit, Bay City & Alpena
5/17	S.Inc.	Detroit Electric (filed 5/19; B,12)
6/4	S.Inc.	East Saginaw Street (filed 6/28; B,13)
6/9	Lease	Muskegon, Grand Rapids & Indiana to Grand Rapids & Indiana
6/17	Inc.	Toledo, Ann Arbor & Cadillac (filed 6/22; A,14:617-618; B,15[ToledoAA&NoMich])
6/18	A-Inc.	Hancock & Calumet (filed 7/6; A,14:583-585; B,13)
7/1	A-Inc.	New Mexico Central & Northern (filed 9/2; A,14:621-622; B,15)
7/13	A-Inc.	Street Ry of Grand Rapids (filed 8/31; B,15)
7/30	A-Inc.	East Saginaw Street (filed 9/3; B,13)
8/2	Inc.	Chicago & Canada Pacific (filed 8/19; A,14:611-612; B,12)
8/3	Inc.	Mason & Oceana (filed 8/9; A,14:602-603; B,14)
8/4	S.Inc.	Port Huron Electric Ry (filed 8/6; B,15)
8/25	Inc.	Alaska (filed 8/27; A,14:615-616; B,12)
8/30	Inc.	Flushing (filed 10/11; A,14:669-670; B,13)
8/31	Inc.	Lansing Transit Ry (filed 9/1; A,14:619-620)

9/1	Lease	Gogebic & Montreal River to Penokee
9/4	Inc.	Wisconsin, Sault Ste. Marie & Mackinac (filed 9/7; A,14:625-626; B,13[DulSS&A])
9/9	Cons.	Toledo & South Haven [Lake Michigan div.] into Toledo & South Haven (filed 9/11; A,14:639-641; B,15)
9/9	Sale	Paw Paw RR to Toledo & South Haven (filed 9/11; A,14:642-645)
9/9	A-Cons.	Toledo & South Haven (filed 9/11; A,14:646-647; B,15)
9/15	Inc.	Manistique Ry (filed 9/18; A,14;651-652; B,14)
9/17	Inc.	Ingalls, White Rapids & Northern (filed 10/2; A,14:664-665; B,14)
10/2	S.Inc.	Street Ry Construction Co. (filed 10/2; B,15)
10/8	Inc.	Port Huron RR Tunnel (filed 10/11; A,14:671-673; B,15[StClairTunnel])
10/8	Inc.	Iron River Ry (filed 10/11; A,14:673-674; B,12[C&NW])
10/20	F.Sale	Detroit, Mackinac & Marquette to Mackinaw & Marquette (*See* Inc. 12/18; A,16:24-26; B,13[DulSS&A])
11/4	F.Sale	Michigan & Ohio RR to Cincinnati, Jackson & Mackinaw (*See* Inc. 2/10/1887; A,16:315-316)
11/9	Inc.	St. Clair Tunnel Co. (filed 11/23; A,16:2-10; B,15)
11/30	A-Cons.	Toledo, Ann Arbor & Mt. Pleasant into Toledo, Ann Arbor & North Michigan (filed 1/26/1887, eff. 1/1/1887; A,16:85-99; B,15)
12/7	Cons.	Republic Branch and Menominee Branch into Milwaukee & Northern (filed 9/2/1887; A,16:490-498; B,14[Milw&N])
12/10	S.Inc.	Ironwood & Hurley Street Ry (filed 12/15; B,14)
12/18	Inc.	Mackinaw & Marquette (filed 12/20; A,16:24-26; B,14[DSS&A])
12/22	Inc.	Duluth, South Shore & Atlantic (filed 3/9/87; A,16:156-162; B,13)
12/28	Inc.	Sturgis & State Line (filed 12/29; A,16:34-35; B,15[SturgisGoshen&StL])

1887

1/7	Inc.	Manistee & Northeastern (filed 1/12; A,16:60-61; B,14)
1/17	Inc.	Colfax & Big Rapids (filed 2/1; A,16:106-107; B,12)
2/10	A-Inc.	Cincinnati, Jackson & Mackinaw RR (filed 5/7; A,16:315-316; B,12)
2/15	Lease	Marquette, Houghton & Ontonagon to Duluth, South Shore & Atlantic
2/28	A-Inc.	Sault Ste. Marie Bridge Co. (filed 3/16; A,16:172-179)
3/5	Inc.	Detroit, Charlevoix & Escanaba (filed 3/9; A,16:163-166; B,12)
3/5	Inc.	Allegan & State Line (filed 3/5; C,10)
3/7	A-Cons.	Paw Paw RR into Toledo & South Haven (filed 9/2; A,16:498-504; B,15)
3/14	Inc.	Mt. Pleasant & Western (filed 3/15; A,16:170-171; B,14)
3/22	Inc.	Minneapolis, Sault Ste. Marie & Atlantic (filed 3/30; A,16:200-236; B,14[MplsSP&SSM])
3/25	Sale	Michigan & Ohio RR to Cincinnati, Jackson & Mackinaw RR (filed 4/19; A,16:270-279; B,12[CJ&M])

4/1	Inc.	Big Rapids & Western (filed 5/5; A,16:307-309; B,12)
4/11	S.Inc.	Gratiot Electric (filed 4/21; B,13)
4/12	S.Inc.	Soo Street Ry (filed 4/14; B,15)
4/30	A-Inc.	Lansing Transit Ry (filed 5/3; A,16:300-302)
5/2	Inc.	Lowell & Hastings (filed 5/6; A,16:310-311; B,14)
5/3	A-Inc.	Battle Creek Street (filed 5/4; B,12)
5/7	S.Inc.	East Detroit & Grosse Pointe (filed 5/11; B,13)
5/13	Inc.	Grand Rapids, Lansing & Detroit (filed 5/17; A,16:327-329; B,13)
5/15	A-Inc.	Cincinnati, Jackson & Mackinaw RR (filed 5/25; A,16:346; B,12)
5/27	S.Inc.	Cable Street (filed 6/2; B,12)
5/31	Sale	Hastings, Lowell & North Michigan to Lowell & Hastings
5/31	T.Inc.	Springwells, Ecorse & Wyandotte Ry (filed 6/1; B,15)
6/6	S.Inc.	Valley City Street & Cable (filed 6/8; B,12[ConsSRofGR])
6/7	A-Inc.	Detroit, Bay City & Alpena (filed 6/8; A,16:369)
6/10	A-Inc.	Republic Branch (filed 6/25; A,16:384-385; B,14[Milw&N])
6/17	Inc.	Wisconsin Central Ry (Wisconsin corp.)
6/25	Inc.	Indiana & Lake Michigan (filed 6/28; A,16:392-394; B,14)
6/27	A-Inc.	Valley City Street & Cable (filed 7/12; B,12[ConsSRGR])
6/28	Inc.	Toledo, Saginaw & Mackinaw (filed 6/29; A,16:394-395; B,15)
7/1	Inc.	Canada & St. Louis (filed 11/17; A,16:566-573; B,15[SturgisGoshen&StL])
7/2	A-Inc.	Chicago & Grand Trunk (filed 10/7; A,16:533)
7/27	T.Inc.	Potts Logging Ry (filed 8/5; B,15)
8/8	A-Cons.	Indiana & Lake Michigan (Mich. corp.) into Indiana & Lake Michigan (Ind. corp.) (filed 3/30/1888; A,17:173-190; B,14)
8/13	Inc.	Iron Range Ry (filed 8/15; A,16:464-465; B,12[C&NW])
8/13	Inc.	St. Mary's Falls (filed 8/18; A,16:467-469; B,15)
8/25	Inc.	Michigan Northern (filed 9/9; A, 16:506-508; B, 14)
9/10	Inc.	Grand Rapids & Chicago (filed 9/17; A, 16:524-525; B, 13)
9/26	S.Inc.	West Bay City Street (filed 9/28; B, 16)
10/4	S.Inc.	Saginaw Union Street Ry (filed 10/5; B,15)
10/10	S.Inc.	City Street Ry of Grand Rapids (filed 10/11; B,12)
10/29	A-Inc.	Chicago, Kalamazoo & Saginaw (filed 12/10; A,16:606-609)
11/2	A-Inc.	Frankfort & South Eastern (filed 11/16; A,16:565; B,13[EscFr&SE])
11/2	S.Inc.	Hamtramck & Grosse Pointe (filed 11/3; B,13)
11/5	Inc.	Sault Ste. Marie Ry (filed 12/5; A,16:597-600; B,15)

11/15	A-Inc.	Detroit, Charlevoix & Escanaba (filed 1/16/1888; A,16:658-659)
12/9	A-Inc.	Chicago, Kalamazoo & Saginaw (filed 7/10/1888; A,17:543)
12/21	A-Cons.	Toledo, Ann Arbor & Cadillac into Toledo, Ann Arbor & North Michigan (filed 4/20/1888; A,17:238-253; B,15)

1888

1/5	S.Inc.	Benton Harbor Street (filed 2/4; B,12)
1/17	F.Sale	Bay View Little Traverse & Mackinac to Grand Rapids & Indiana
1/24	A-Inc.	Fort Wayne & Elmwood (filed 1/25; B,13)
2/18	Lease	Lansing Transit Ry to Michigan Central
2/20	Inc.	Battle Creek & Bay City (filed 2/21; A,17:64-69; B,12)
2/21	Inc.	Lansing, St. Johns & Northern (filed 2/23; A,17:75-76; B,14)
2/25	A-Inc.	Valley City Street & Cable (filed 5/21; B,12[ConsSRGR])
3/5	Inc.	Toledo, Ann Arbor & Lake Michigan (filed 3/29; A,17:169-170; B,15)
3/24	Inc.	St. Ignace, Sault Ste. Marie & Northern (filed 4/13; A,17:215-217; B,15)
5/19	A-Inc.	Detroit City (filed 6/29; B,12)
5/31	Lease	Gogebic & Montreal River by Penokee assigned to Wisconsin Central Ry
6/1	Inc.	North Branch & Sauble River (filed 6/8; A,17:323-324; B,15)
6/1	Inc.	Central Michigan (filed 9/7; A,17:581-582; B,12)
6/11	Inc.	Minneapolis, St. Paul & Sault Ste. Marie (filed 6/13; A,17:326-508; B,14)
6/25	A-Inc.	Gogebic & Montreal River (filed 7/3; A,17:534-536; B,13)
6/27	Inc.	Quincy & Torch Lake (filed 6/29; A,17:526-528; B,15)
6/29	Inc.	Negaunee & Palmer (filed 6/30; A,17:530-531; B,15)
7/5	A-Inc.	Valley City Street & Cable (filed 7/7; A,17:541-543; B,12[ConsSRGR])
7/26	A-Inc.	Duluth, South Shore & Atlantic (filed 8/20; A,17:556; B,13)
7/30	Inc.	Portage RR (filed 7/31; A,17:552-553; B,15)
8/2	A-Inc.	Grand River Street (filed 8/4; B,13)
8/6	S.Inc.	Ann Arbor Street (filed 1/5/1889; B,12)
8/23	A-Inc.	Potts Logging Ry (filed 9/28; B,15)
8/28	T.Inc.	Adrian City Electric Belt (filed 8/30; B,12)
9/5	Inc.	Columbus & Lake Michigan (filed 9/7; A,17:583-584; B,12[ColsLima&Milw])
9/10	S.Inc.	Menominee Street Ry (filed 9/19; B,14)
9/22	A-Inc.	Frankfort & South Eastern (filed 10/8; A,17:616; B,13[EscFr&SE])
9/25	Inc.	Chippewa Valley (filed 10/18; A,17:630-632; B,12)
9/25	F.Sale	Chicago & Canada Southern to Detroit & Chicago (*See* Inc. 11/19; A,17:662-664)
10/12	Inc.	Northern Michigan RR (filed 10/15; A,17:624-626)

11/1	S.Inc.	South Grand Rapids Street Ry (filed 11/2; B,15)
11/2	A-Cons.	Saginaw & Clare County and East Saginaw & St. Clair and Manistee and Saginaw & Mt. Pleasant into Flint & Pere Marquette (filed 1/31/1889; A,18:43-72; B,13[F&PM])
11/9	UD	Inc. Union Depot of Durand (filed 11/9; J,29)
11/17	Inc.	Detroit RR & Tunnel (filed 11/19; A,17:652-653)
11/19	Inc.	Detroit & Chicago (filed 11/24; A,17:662-664; B,12)
11/21	A-Inc.	Quincy & Torch Lake (filed 12/3; A,17:677-678; B,15)
11/27	Inc.	Traverse City, Kalkaska & Grayling (filed 12/3; A,17:675-676)
12/31	T.Inc.	St. Joseph & Benton Harbor Street Train (filed 1/3/1889; B,15)

1889

1/3	Inc.	Escanaba, Twin Cities & Western (filed 1/4; A,18:8-10; B,13)
1/3	Inc.	Columbus, Lima & Milwaukee (filed 4/23; A,18:166-184; B,12)
1/12	Inc.	Sturgis, Indiana & Ohio (filed 1/15; A,18:26-28; B,15)
1/16	A-Inc.	Valley City Street & Cable (filed 1/17; B,12[ConsSRGR])
1/19	A-Inc.	St. Joseph & Benton Harbor Street (filed 1/22; B,15)
2/19	Inc.	Detroit & State Line Wabash (filed 2/27; A,18:93-95)
2/19	T.Inc.	Oakdale Park Street Ry (filed 2/20; B,15)
3/11	S.Inc.	Gladstone Street Ry (filed 3/18; B,13)
3/14	Rec.	St. Louis, Sturgis & Battle Creek
3/15	A-Inc.	Kalamazoo & South Haven (filed 3/15; A,18:97; B,14)
4/1	Sale	Port Huron & Northwestern to Flint & Pere Marquette
4/18	A-Inc.	Toledo, Ann Arbor & Lake Michigan (filed 5/23; A,18:211-212; B,15)
5/3	Inc.	Detroit, Rouge River & Dearborn (filed 5/4; A,18:191-193; B,12)
5/4	Inc.	Grand Rapids & Mineral Springs (filed 5/8; A,18:193-194; B,13)
5/7	F.Sale	St. Joseph Valley RR to St. Joseph Valley Ry (*See* Inc. 7/29; A,18:282-288; B,14[MilwBH&Col])
5/14	Inc.	Reeds Lake, Grand Rapids & Soldiers Home Suburban (filed 5/16; A,18:207-209; B,15)
5/15	A-Inc.	Detroit & St. Clair River (filed 1/29/1890; B,12)
5/17	A-Inc.	Detroit & St. Clair River (filed 5/22; A,18:210-211; B,12)
5/23	Inc.	Wabash RR (filed 7/31; A,18:264-282)
5/23	T.Inc.	Kent County Street Ry (filed 5/24; B,14)
5/29	Inc.	Bay City Belt Line (filed 6/3; A,18:219-220; B,12)
6/4	Opg.Ag.	Indiana & Lake Michigan by Terre Haute & Indianapolis
6/5	F.Sale	Pontiac, Oxford & Port Austin to Pontiac, Oxford & Northern (*See* Inc. 9/19; A,18:333-336)
6/7	Inc.	Cleveland, Cincinnati, Chicago & St. Louis (Ohio corp. and filing)

6/10	Inc.	Elk Rapids, Williamsburg & Southern (filed 6/12; A,18:227-229; B,13)
6/10	Sale	Iron River and Iron Range to Chicago & North Western (filed 3/19/1890; B,12[C&NW])
6/29	A-Inc.	Bay City Belt Line (filed 7/30; A,18:262-263; B,12)
7/1	A-Inc.	Grand Rapids & Mineral Springs (filed 7/15; A,18:255; B,13)
7/1	Lease	Detroit Union RR Depot to 3 companies
7/6	F.Sale	Ingalls, White Rapids & Northern Ry to IWR&N RR (*See* Inc. 9/2; A,18:326-330)
7/10	A-Inc.	Chicago & West Michigan (filed 7/19; A,18:260-261; B,12)
7/29	Inc.	St. Joseph Valley Ry (filed 8/1; A,18:282-288)
8/3	A-Inc.	Saginaw Union Street Ry (filed 8/12; B,15)
8/17	F.Sale	Canada & St. Louis to Sturgis, Goshen & St. Louis
8/20	A-Inc.	Kent Country Street Ry (filed 3/3/1890; B,14)
8/21	S.Inc.	North Park Street Ry (filed 10/4; B,15)
8/24*	UD.Inc.	Fort St. Union Depot (filing date shown; articles not found)
9/2	Inc.	Ingalls, White Rapids & Northern RR (filed 9/18; A,18:326-330; B,14)
9/11	F.Sale	Battle Creek & Bay City to Bay City & Battle Creek (*See* Inc. 11/11; A,18:385-387)
9/11	F.Sale	St. Louis, Sturgis & Battle Creek to Battle Creek & Sturgis (*See* Inc. 11/13; A,18:388-390)
9/19	Inc.	Pontiac, Oxford & Northern (filed 9/24; A,18:333-336)
10/1	Inc.	Marquette, Champion & Chicago (filed 10/2; B,14)
10/16	A-Inc.	Michigan Air Line Ry (filed 10/18; A,18:357)
10/18	A-Inc.	Manistique Ry (filed 10/21; A,18:358-359; B,14)
10/21	S.Inc.	Pontiac & Orchard Lake Street (filed 10/29; B,15)
10/21	Inc.	Grand Rapids & Lake Michigan (filed 10/22; B,13)
10/22	Inc.	Detroit & Petoskey (filed 1/9/1890; B,12)
10/29	Inc.	Sturgis, Goshen & St. Louis (filed 5/29/1890; A,18:637-639; B,15)
11/1	T.Inc.	South Park & Crystal Springs Street (filed 11/6; B,15)
11/6	Inc.	Dead River (filed 11/11, B,12)
11/7	Rec.	Cincinnati, Jackson & Mackinaw
11/11	Inc.	Bay City & Battle Creek (filed 11/12; A,18:385-387; B,12[BatCrk&BayC])
11/11	Inc.	Manistee & Grand Rapids (filed 11/11; B,14[MichE&W])
11/13	Inc.	Battle Creek & Sturgis (filed 11/14; A,18:388-390)
11/26	S.Inc.	Street Ry of Ludington (filed 11/27; B,15)
11/27	S.Inc.	Twin City Ry (filed 12/4; J,28)
12/1	$ Sturgis,	Goshen & St. Louis by Lake Shore & Michigan Southern
12/10	Lease	Fort St. Union Depot to 4 companies
12/26	Inc.	Cincinnati, Saginaw & Mackinaw (filed 12/28; B,12)

12/27	A-Inc.	Grand River Street (filed 1/17/1890; B,13)
12/27	A-Inc.	Detroit City (filed 1/17/1890; B,12)
12/31	Sale	Toledo, Saginaw & Mackinaw to Cincinnati, Saginaw & Mackinaw

1890

1/1	Lease	Wisconsin Central Ry to Northern Pacific
1/4	Inc.	Escanaba, Iron Mountain & Western (filed 1/24; B,13)
2/1	Lease	Battle Creek & Sturgis to Michigan Central and Lake Shore & Michigan Southern
2/1	Lease	Bay City & Battle Creek to Michigan Central
2/4	Inc.	Benton Harbor Belt & Terminal (filed 2/24; B,12)
3/3	Inc.	Frankfort, Crystal Lake & Glenn Arbor (filed 3/20; B,13)
3/25	Inc.	Grand Rapids, Chicago & St. Louis (filed 3/27; B,13)
4/11	S.Inc.	Reed's Lake Electric Ry (filed 4/15; B,15)
4/16	A-Cons.	Toledo, Ann Arbor & Lake Michigan into Toledo, Ann Arbor & North Michigan (filed 5/22; A,18:633-635; B,15)
4/16	Inc.	Olivet Ry (filed 5/5; B,15)
4/23	A-Inc.	Muskegon Ry (two filed 4/24; B,14)
5/3	Inc.	South Lyons & Northern (filed 7/21; B,15)
5/28	Inc.	Paint River (filed 6/14; B,15)
6/11	Rec.	Toledo & South Haven
6/20	Sale	Ontonagon & Brule River to Milwaukee & Northern
6/21	Inc.	Detroit & Toledo (filed 6/26; B,12)
6/25	A-Inc.	Ann Arbor Street (filed 9/12; refiled 1/30/1891; B,12)
6/27	Inc.	Iron Range & Huron Bay (filed 6/30; B,14)
7/9	S.Inc.	Electric Ry (filed 7/10; B,13)
7/17	Sale	Marquette & Western and Marquette, Houghton & Ontonagon to Duluth, South Shore & Atlantic
7/18	S.Inc.	Kalamazoo City & County Street Ry (filed 7/21; B,14)
7/21	S.Inc.	Owosso City Electric (filed 8/7; B,15)
7/26	Inc.	Holland South Shore (filed 8/11; B,13)
8/2	S.Inc.	Marquette City & Presque Isle (filed 8/12; B,14)
8/4	Lease	Indiana & Lake Michigan to Terre Haute & Indianapolis
8/25	S.Inc.	Ann Arbor, Ypsilanti & Detroit Street (filed 8/26; B,12)
8/29	T.Inc.	Ann Arbor & Ypsilanti Street (filed 8/30; B,12)
9/—	$	Milwaukee & Northern by Chicago, Milwaukee & St. Paul
9/16	A-Inc.	South Grand Rapids Street (filed 9/22; B,15)

9/19	S.Inc.	Ishpeming & Negaunee (filed 11/7; B,14)
9/27	S.Inc.	Union Street Ry (filed 9/30; B,16)
10/16	Inc.	Port Huron & St. Clair River (filed 10/22; B,15)
10/20	Inc.	Lake Michigan & Lake Superior (filed 11/10; B,14)
10/25	Cons.	Street Ry of Grand Rapids into Valley City St & Cable
10/27	S.Inc.	Oscoda & AuSable Street (filed 10/28; B,15)
11/1	Opg.Ag.	Cincinnati, Saginaw & Mackinaw by Chicago & Grand Trunk (dated 10/2/1890)
11/8	S.Inc.	Flint Street (filed 11/12; B,13)
11/25	S.Inc.	Detroit Street (filed 12/1; B,13)
11/29	S.Inc.	Grand River Ry (filed 12/1; B,13)
12/6	Inc.	South-Eastern & North-Western Transcontinental (filed 12/9; B,15)
12/8	A-Inc.	Cincinnati, Saginaw & Mackinaw (filed 12/19; A,20:157-158; B,12)
12/24	S.Inc.	Detroit Suburban Street (filed 12/27; B,13)

1891

1/20	Inc.	Toledo, Ann Arbor & Mackinaw (filed 2/17; A,20:229-230; B,15)
1/31	$	Ann Arbor Street by Ann Arbor & Ypsilanti Street
2/10	Inc.	Baraga & Watersmeet (filed 2/11; A,20:219-221; B,12)
2/28	Inc.	Chicago & North Michigan (filed 3/2; A,20:241-242; B,12)
3/3	S.Inc.	Jackson Street Ry (filed 3/4; B,14)
3/7	A-Inc.	Marquette City & Presque Isle (filed 4/3; B,14)
3/11	S.Inc.	Detroit & Dearborn Street Ry (filed 3/14; B,12)
3/17	S.Inc.	Flint City Ry (filed 3/18; B,13)
3/24	Inc.	Grayling & Charlevoix (filed 3/30; A,20:281-283; B,13)
4/4	S.Inc.	Menominee Electric Ry & Power (filed 4/10; G,35)
4/25	Inc.	Manistique & Northwestern (filed 5/4; A,20:332-334; B,14)
5/4	Inc.	Grand Rapids, Grayling & Alpena (filed 5/11; A,20:345-348; B,13)
5/15	Lease	Escanaba, Iron Mountain & Western to Chicago & North Western
5/19	Inc.	Cheboygan & East Michigan (filed 7/6; A,20:403-406; B,12)
5/20	A-Inc.	Flint & Pere Marquette (filed 6/1; A,20:369-370)
5/21	A-Inc.	Saginaw, Tuscola & Huron (filed 6/1; A,20:370-371)
5/30	S.Inc.	Battle Creek Electric Ry (filed 6/1; B,12)
5/30	Inc.	Jefferson Avenue Ry (filed 6/3; A,20:371-372; B,14)
6/1	Lease	Chicago & North Michigan by Chicago & West Michigan
6/4	Sale	Paint River to Chicago & North Western

7/1	A-Inc.	Valley City Street & Cable (filed 7/11; B,12[ConsSRGR])
7/1	S.Inc.	Consolidated Street (filed 7/11; B,12)
7/7	A-Inc.	South Park & Crystal Springs Street (filed 7/8; B,15)
7/15	Inc.	Michigan & Mackinaw (filed 7/16; A,20:406-408; B,12[CJ&M])
7/15	Inc.	Au Sable & Northwestern (filed 7/17; A,20:410-412; B,12)
7/17	Inc.	Cincinnati & Michigan (Ohio corp.) (filed 7/18)
7/17	Inc.	Cincinnati, Jackson & Mackinaw Ry (filed 3/9/1892; A,20:639-648; B,12)
7/24	Inc.	Grayling, Twin Lakes & Northeastern (filed 7/25; A,20:414-416; B,13)
7/31	S.Inc.	Negaunee & Ishpeming Street (filed 11/23; B,14[MarCoGLT])
8/24	S.Inc.	Detroit Citizen's Street (filed 9/2; B,12)
9/2	A-Inc.	Iron Range & Huron Bay (filed 10/27; A,20:471-472; B,14)
9/2	S.Inc.	Owosso & Corunna Street (filed 9/11; B,15)
9/4	Inc.	Chicago, Lake Michigan & Eastern (filed 9/7; A,20:433-435; B,12)
9/15	A-Inc.	Detroit & St. Clair River (filed 10/1; A,20:449-450; B,12)
9/16	Sale	Detroit Street to Detroit Citizens'
9/23	A-Inc.	Marquette City & Presque Isle (filed 10/30; B,14)
9/24	Inc.	Grand Rapids Belt Line (filed 10/2; A,20:450-453; B,13)
10/1	Sale	Grand River Ry to Detroit Citizens'
10/10	Inc.	Grand River RR (filed 2/19/1892; A,20:609-610; B,13)
11/7	T.Inc.	Jackson & Northern (filed 11/10; B,14)
11/10	Inc.	Crystal Lake RR (filed 11/16; A,20:483-485; B,12)
11/30	T.Inc.	Detroit, Springwells & Dearborn (filed 12/2; B,13)
12/8	S.Inc.	Gratiot Avenue Ry (filed 12/9; B,13)
12/9	S.Inc.	Escanaba Electric Street Ry (filed 3/15/1892; B,13)
12/14	A-Inc.	Detroit Union RR Depot (filed 1/3/1892; B,13)

1892

1/7	A-Inc.	Manistee & Northeastern (filed 8/29; A,24:126-127; B,14)
1/8	F.Sale	Cincinnati, Jackson & Mackinaw to Michigan & Mackinaw and to Cincinnati & Michigan
4/1	Inc.	Detroit Transit RR (filed 4/4; A,20:684-687; B,13)
4/12	A-Inc.	St. Joseph & Benton Harbor Street (filed 4/16; B,15)
4/13	S.Inc.	Menominee Electric Light Ry & Power (filed 4/13; G,35)
4/16	A-Inc.	Detroit, Springwells & Dearborn (filed 4/16; B,13)
4/28	T.Inc.	Belding Street Ry & Improvement Co. (filed 5/4; B,12)
5/3	A-Inc.	St. Joseph & Benton Harbor Street (filed 5/6; B,15)

5/3	S.Inc.	Wyandotte & Detroit River (filed 5/7; B,16)
5/5	T.Inc.	Mancelona & North Western (filed 5/27; B,14)
5/5	S.Inc.	Negaunee & Ishpeming Street Ry & Electric (filed 5/5; B,14[MarqCoGL&T])
5/6	Inc.	Pere Marquette & Big Rapids (filed 6/10; A,24:53; B,15)
5/14	S.Inc.	Fort Wayne & Belle Isle (filed 5/23; B,13)
5/15	Sale	Frankfort & South Eastern to Toledo, Ann Arbor & North Michigan
5/18	Inc.	Osceola, Lake & Wexford (filed 5/21; A,24:38-39; B,15)
5/19	S.Inc.	City Electric Ry of Port Huron (filed 5/26; B,12)
5/31	S.Inc.	Union Street Ry of Benton Harbor & St. Joseph (filed 6/10; B,16)
6/4	A-Inc.	Detroit, Springwells & Dearborn (filed 6/10; B,13)
6/15	S.Inc.	Union Electric (filed 7/9; B,16)
7/1	Inc.	Lake Harbor RR (filed 8/1; A,24:90-91; B,14)
7/1	$	Cincinnati, Wabash & Michigan by Cleveland C. C. & St.L.
7/1	Sale	Fort Wayne & Elmwood to Fort Wayne & Belle Isle
7/12	S.Inc.	Capitol Street Ry (filed 7/14; B,12)
8/13	Inc.	Rapid River & Eastern (filed 8/16; A,24:104-106; B,15)
8/16	A-Inc.	Chicago & West Michigan (filed 9/3; A,24:134-135; B,12)
8/19	Inc.	Muskegon Terminal (filed 4/14/1893; A,24:340-341; B,14)
8/24	S.Inc.	Manistee, Filer City & East Lake (filed 9/1; B,14)
9/3	A-Inc.	Detroit & St. Clair River (filed 9/8; A,24:135-136; B,12)
10/13	S.Inc.	Lansing City Electric Ry (filed 10/28; B,14)
10/14	A-Inc.	Detroit & St. Clair River (filed 11/25; A,24:199-200; B,12)
10/27	Inc.	Detroit Belt (filed 11/2; A,24:186-187; B,12)
10/29	S.Inc.	Detroit Suburban Ry (filed 11/1; B,13)
11/1	Sale	Detroit Electric; Gratiot Avenue; Jefferson Avenue; and East Detroit & Grosse Pointe to Detroit Suburban
11/28	A-Inc.	Grand River RR (filed 11/28; A,24:203-204; B,13)
11/29	A-Inc.	Negaunee & Ishpeming Street Ry & Elec (filed 12/17; B,14[MarqCoGL&T])
12/13	Inc.	Detroit, Pontiac & Northern (filed 12/27; A,24:240-242; B,13)
12/14	S.Inc.	Detroit Metropolitan Street Ry (filed 12/14; B,13)
12/15	A-Inc.	City Electric Ry of Port Huron (filed 12/16; B,12)

1893

1/27	Inc.	Superior Terminal (filed 1/30; A,24:263-264; B,15)
2/1	Sale	Highland Park Ry to Detroit Suburban
2/17	Inc.	Lake Superior & Ishpeming (filed 2/24; A,24:292-293)

3/13	S.Inc.	Detroit, Rouge River & Dearborn Street (filed 3/15; B,13)
3/21	S.Inc.	Citizens Street Ry (filed 5/1; B,12)
3/28	Inc.	Monroe & Toledo (filed 3/30; A,24:322-323; B,14)
4/14*	Inc.	Michigan Terminal Ry (filing date shown; articles not found)
4/15	S.Inc.	Twin City General Electric Co. (filed 5/29; J,28)
4/26	Inc.	Boyne City & Southeastern (filed 5/3; A,24:357-358; B,12)
4/27	Rec.	Toledo, Ann Arbor & North Michigan
5/29	Inc.	Benton Harbor & South Eastern (Indiana corp.)
5/31	A-Char.	Michigan Central (1893 P.Acts, No. 179, 283-285)
6/5	Sale	Detroit, Rouge River & Dearborn Street to Fort Wayne & Belle Isle
6/23	Sale	Milwaukee & Northern to Chicago, Milw. & St. Paul
7/11	Inc.	Killmaster RR (filed 7/15; A,24:427-428; B,14)
7/17	Inc.	Lake Huron & Western (filed 7/20; A,24:430; B,14)
7/21	Inc.	Escanaba Western (filed 7/22; A,24:441-442; B,13)
7/26	S.Inc.	Mt. Clemens Street Ry (filed 8/4; B,14[MC&Lakeside])
7/28	Inc.	Alpena & Northern (filed 11/1; A,24:480-481; B,12)
8/19	Sale	Milwaukee, Lake Shore & Western to Chicago & NorthWestern
9/21	Inc.	Midland & Hubbard (filed 9/25; A,24:468-469; B,14)
9/26	X-Lease	Wisconsin Central Ry by Northern Pacific
9/30	S.Inc.	Union Street Ry of Saginaw (filed 10/9; B,16)
10/16	Inc.	Menominee & Northern (filed 10/28; A,24:476-477; B,14)
10/17	Inc.	Wisconsin & Michigan Ry (Wisc. corp.) (filed 7/11/1903; A,53:282-284)
11/22	Lease	Bay City Belt Line to Detroit & Bay City
11/22	Sale	part of Detroit & Bay City to Bay City Belt Line

1894

1/17	Inc.	Midland & Northern (filed 5/12; A,24:607-609; B,14)
2/10	S.Inc.	St. Joseph & Lake Shore Street (filed 4/9; B,15)
2/28	S.Inc.	Rapid Ry (filed 3/1; B,15)
3/10	S.Inc.	City & Suburban Traction (filed 3/20; B,12)
3/15	S.Inc.	Toledo, Monroe & Detroit Electric (filed 3/16; B,15)
4/25	Reinc.	Grand River Valley (filed 5/11; B,13)
5/3	Inc.	Port Huron & Lexington (filed 5/28; B,15[PtHurLex&W])
5/18	Inc.	South Haven & Eastern (filed 5/23; B,15)
5/21	A-Inc.	North Park Street Ry (filed 7/9; B,15)

6/30	S.Inc.	Riverside Park Ry of Saginaw (filed 7/11; B,15)
8/3	Sale	Menominee & Northern to Wisconsin & Michigan Ry (eff. 1/1/1895)
8/8	A-Inc.	Boyne City & Southeastern (filed 8/27; A,24:695-697; B,12)
8/16	A-Inc.	Ann Arbor Street (filed 8/18; B,12)
10/1	S.Inc.	Citizens Street Ry of Battle Creek (filed 10/8; B,12)
10/11	Inc.	Buchanan & St. Joseph River (filed 10/12; A,24:718-719; B,12)
10/16	S.Inc.	Mt. Clemens & Lakeside Electric Street Ry & Dock (filed 1/7/1895; B,14)
10/25	T.Inc.	Saginaw & Bay City Ry (filed 1/25/1895; B,15)
10/29	S.Inc.	Saginaw Consolidated Street (filed 10/30; B,15)
11/8	F.Sale	Detroit, Bay City & Alpena to Detroit & Mackinac (*See* Inc. 12/17; A,28:25-53)
11/30	Inc.	Traverse City, Peninsular & Old Mission Electric (filed 12/1; A,28:1-3)
12/7	Inc.	Cincinnati Northern (Ohio corp. and filing)
12/10	S.Inc.	Detroit Ry (filed 12/10; B,12)
12/17	Inc.	Detroit & Mackinac Ry (filed 12/29; A,28:25-53)
12/17	Sale	Ingalls, White Rapids & Northern to Wisconsin & Michigan Ry (eff. 1/1/1895)

1895

1/19	S.Inc.	Oakland Ry (filed 1/24; B,15)
1/23	S.Inc.	Saginaw & Bay City Rapid Transit (filed 2/6; B,15)
3/6	T.Inc.	InterUrban Ry of Saginaw (filed 3/8; B,14)
3/9	T.Inc.	Epworth League (filed 3/12; K)
3/27	Inc.	Lima Northern (Ohio filing)
4/16	Sale	Alpena & Northern to Detroit & Mackinac
4/30	S.Inc.	Grand Haven Street Ry (filed 5/2; B,13)
6/1	F.Sale	Frankfort & South Eastern to Escanaba, Frankfort & Southeastern (*See* Inc. 6/12; A,28:221-225)
6/12	Inc.	Escanaba, Frankfort & Southeastern (filed 7/9; A,28:221-225; B,13)
6/13	S.Inc.	Mt. Clemens & Lakeside Traction (filed 6/22; B,14)
6/27	Inc.	Chicago & Kalamazoo Terminal (filed 7/1; A,28:212-214)
7/2	F.Sale	Toledo, Ann Arbor & Cadillac; Toledo, Ann Arbor & Grand Trunk; Toledo, Ann Arbor & Lake Michigan; Toledo, Ann Arbor & Mt. Pleasant; Toledo, Ann Arbor & North Michigan to Ann Arbor (*See* Inc. 9/20; A,28:293-301)
7/3	Inc.	Munising Ry (filed 7/11; A,28:225-227)
7/8	T.Inc.	Pontiac & Sylvan Lake (filed 7/25; B,15)
7/16	A-Inc.	Fort Wayne & Belle Isle (filed 7/25; B,13)
8/1	S.Inc.	Detroit & River St. Clair (filed 9/21; B,12)
8/9	Inc.	Jackson & Cincinnati (filed 8/12; A,28:260-262; B,14)

9/3	T.Inc.	Benton Harbor, Coloma & Paw Paw Lake (filed 9/12; B,12)
9/5	Inc.	Arcadia & Betsey River (filed 9/25; A,28:301-303; B,12)
9/12	A-Inc.	Lake Superior & Ishpeming (filed 10/11; A,28:316-320)
9/17	Inc.	Detroit, Delray & Dearborn (filed 9/19; A,28:289-290; B,13)
9/20	Inc.	Ann Arbor (filed 9/21; A,28:293-301)
9/27	A-Inc.	Central Michigan (filed 9/30; A,28:307-308; B,12)
10/5	S.Inc.	Owosso & Corunna Electric St. (filed 10/11; H,15)
10/14	Tfr.	Toledo, Ann Arbor & North Michigan to Ann Arbor
10/15	Inc.	Marquette & Iron Range (filed 10/17; A,28:328-329; B,14)
10/15	Sale	Escanaba, Frankfort & Southeastern to Ann Arbor
11/20	S.Inc.	Owosso & Corunna Traction (filed 11/25; H,15)
11/25	F.Sale	Owosso & Corunna Street to Owosso & Corunna Traction
12/19	Inc.	Michigan Central Bridge Co (filed 1/23/1896; A,28:401-402)

1896

1/15	Inc.	Norfolk & Western (Virginia corp. filed 10/12/1964; K)
2/10	A-Inc.	Consolidated Street (filed 3/7; B,12)
2/26	Inc.	Detroit & Cincinnati (filed 3/7; A,28:469-471)
3/24	A-Inc.	Fort Wayne & Belle Isle (filed 5/25; B,13)
3/26	T.Inc.	Monroe, Dundee & Lake Erie (filed 3/30; B,14)
4/1	Rec.	Detroit, Lansing & Northern
4/22	A-Inc.	Monroe & Toledo (filed 4/22; A,28:552-554; B,14)
5/25	Inc.	Lewiston & Southeastern (filed 5/26; A,28:598-599; B,14)
6/10	F.Sale	Grand Rapids & Indiana RR to Grand Rapids & Indiana Ry (*See* Inc. 7/7; A,28:675-679; B,13)
7/3	T.Inc.	Detroit, Lake Shore & Mt. Clemens (filed 7/16; B,12)
7/7	Inc.	Grand Rapids & Indiana (filed 7/11; A,28:675-679)
7/9	S.Inc	Detroit Electric (filed 7/10; B,12)
7/14	A-Inc.	Detroit Electric (filed 7/31; B,12)
7/29	Sale	Detroit Ry to Detroit Electric
7/31	S.Inc.	Ann Arbor & Ypsilanti Electric (filed 8/20; B,12)
9/2	O.Inc.	Pere Marquette Transportation Co. (filed 9/11; A,28:719-721)
9/9	Inc.	Olivet & South Eastern (filed 10/12; A,28:730-731; B,15)
11/10	F.Sale	Detroit, Lansing & Northern to Detroit, Grand Rapids & Western (*See* Inc. 11/30; A,31:17-25)
11/30	Inc.	Detroit, Grand Rapids & Western (filed 12/4; A,31:17-25; B,12)
12/29	A-Inc.	Detroit, Grand Rapids & Western (filed 1/5/1897; A,31:37-38; B,12)
12/31	S.Inc.	Michigan Traction (filed 1/4/1897; B,14)

1897

n.d.	Sale	Ithaca & Alma to Ann Arbor
1/1	Cons.	Grand Rapids, Lansing & Detroit; Saginaw Valley & St. Louis: Saginaw & Grand Rapids; and Saginaw & Western into Detroit, Grand Rapids & Western
1/4	$	Detroit Electric and Fort Wayne & Belle Isle by Detroit Citizens'
1/5	F.Sale	Cincinnati, Jackson & Mackinaw, part to Toledo & Milwaukee and part to Cincinnati Northern (*See* Inc. 6/18; A,31:241-244)
1/5	S.Inc.	Muskegon Street Ry (filed 1/28; B,14)
1/9	Rec.	Detroit & River St. Clair
1/12	Inc.	Benton Harbor Elec. Ry & Transit (filed 1/13; A,31:38-41; B,12)
1/28	S.Inc.	Detroit & Pontiac (filed 1/30; B,12)
1/29	A-Inc.	Muskegon Street Ry (filed 2/6; B,14)
2/18	Inc.	Detroit & Lima Northern (filed 2/20; A,31:57-58)
3/26	A-Inc.	Detroit & Lima Northern (filed 4/10; A,31:130-132)
4/6	Inc.	Milwaukee, Benton Harbor & Columbus (filed 8/10; A,31:284-292; B,14)
5/1	Lease	Kalamazoo & White Pigeon and Northern Central Michigan to Lake Shore & Michigan Southern
6/18	Inc.	Toledo & Milwaukee RR (filed 6/21; A,31:241-244)
6/21	S.Inc.	Holland & Lake Michigan (filed 6/23; B,13)
6/26	Rec.	Jackson Street Ry
7/22	Inc.	Detroit, Toledo & Milwaukee (filed 9/7; A,31:312-313)
8/3	A-Inc.	Detroit & Pontiac (filed 8/12; B,12)
8/10	A-Inc.	Detroit & Pontiac (filed 8/12; B,12)
8/17	S.Inc.	Sault Ste. Marie Street Ry (filed 8/25; B,15)
8/21	S.Inc.	Benton Harbor & Eastman Springs (filed 8/24; B,12[BH&SJ])
8/27	Cons.	Monroe & Toledo into Flint & Pere Marquette
8/30	Inc.	Grand Rapids, Kalkaska & Southeastern (filed 9/14; A,31:315-316; B,13)
9/28	Inc.	Toledo & Northwestern (filed 10/6; A,31:331-333; B,15)
10/4	A-Inc.	Grand Rapids, Kalkaska & Southeastern (filed 10/14; A,31:338-339; B,13)
10/9	A-Inc.	Detrcit Belt (filed 11/16; A,31:359-361; B,12)
10/15	Inc.	Detroit & Northern (filed 11/12; A,31:353-356; B,12)
10/26	A-Inc.	Boyne City & Southeastern (filed 11/8; A,31:348-350; B,12)
11/2	S.Inc.	Detroit, Ypsilanti & Ann Arbor (filed 11/3; B,13)
11/4	Inc.	Grand Haven & Southeastern (filed 11/8; A,31:351-352; B,13)
11/15	Sale	part of Detroit & Chicago to Detroit & Lima Northern

11/17	A-Inc.	Detroit & Lima Northern (filed 12/22; A,31:384-385)
11/24	O.Inc.	Michigan & Ohio Car Ferry (filed 12/15; A,31:377-378)
12/7	T.Inc.	Bay, Tuscola & Huron (filed 12/23; B,12)
12/7	A-Inc.	Michigan Traction (filed 12/9; B,14)
12/8	S.Inc.	Lansing, St. Johns & St. Louis (filed 12/27; B,14)
12/20	A-Inc.	Detroit, Ypsilanti & Ann Arbor (filed 1/22/1898; B,13)
12/22	S.Inc.	Lansing, Dexter & Ann Arbor (filed 12/27; B,14)

1898

1/5	Inc.	Rapid RR (filed 1/6; A,31:392-393; B,15)
1/29	S.Inc.	Owosso & Corunna Electric (filed 1/31; H,15)
2/—	Inc.	Pleasant Bay (filed 3/29; A,31:467-469)
2/12	S.Inc.	Saugatuck, Douglas & Lake Shore (filed 2/14; B,15)
2/14	S.Inc.	Bay Cities Consolidated (filed 2/25; B,12)
2/28	S.Inc.	Detroit, Fort Wayne & Belle Isle (filed 3/1; B,13)
2/28	A-Inc.	Lansing, Dexter & Ann Arbor (filed 3/2; B,14)
3/3	T.Inc.	Saginaw Suburban (filed 3/8; B,15)
3/4	Inc.	Detroit Union Bridge Co. (filed 3/7; A,31:428-429; B,13)
3/8	S.Inc.	Grand River Electric (filed 3/17; B,13)
3/14	Cons.	Owosso & Corunna Traction to Owosso & Corunna Electric
3/23	Inc.	Toledo & Monroe (filed 3/25; A,31:462-463; B,15)
4/1	A-Inc.	Toledo & Northwestern (filed 11/8/1901; A,45:170-172; B,15)
4/1	Sale	Fort Wayne & Belle Isle to Detroit, Fort Wayne & Belle Isle
4/19	S.Inc.	Detroit, Plymouth & Northville (filed 5/28; B,13)
4/21	T.Inc.	Chicago, Detroit & Toledo (filed 4/23; B,12)
5/5	A-Inc.	Detroit & Bay City (filed 5/21; A,31:525; B,12)
6/1	Sale	Jackson & Cincinnati to Cincinnati Northern
6/25	S.Inc.	Michigan & Indiana Ry (filed 7/27; B,14)
7/30	A-Inc.	Detroit & Lima Northern (filed 8/23; A,31:582-585)
8/10	Inc.	Detroit, Utica & Romeo (filed 8/10; A,31:577-578; B,13)
8/15	A-Inc.	Saginaw Suburban (filed 9/1; B,15)
8/16	T.Inc.	Saginaw & Frankenmuth (filed 8/17; B,15)
9/14	A-Inc.	Saginaw Suburban (filed 9/16; B,15)
9/15	Inc.	Indiana, Illinois & Iowa (filed 10/7/1903; A,54:546-557; B,14)
9/26	Inc.	Grand Rapids, Belding & Saginaw (filed 11/15; A,31:648-649; B,13)

10/1	$	Citizens Street [Kalamazoo] and Citizens Street of Battle Creek by Michigan Traction
10/19	A-Inc.	Michigan Air Line RR (filed 11/4; A,31:627)
11/12	Inc.	Wisconsin, Michigan & Northern (filed 11/17; A,31:650-651; B,16)
11/16	S.Inc.	Long Lake, Durand & Corunna Electric Street (filed 11/17; B,14)
11/17	T.Inc.	Escanaba & Lake Superior (filed 12/5; B,13)
12/1	Inc.	Detroit River Bridge Co (filed 12/3; A,31:652)
12/3	Inc.	Saugatuck & South Haven (filed 12/15; A,31:663-664; B,15)
12/5	Inc.	Bloomfield & Orchard Lake (filed 12/9; B,12)
12/8	F.Sale	Indiana & Lake Michigan to St. Joseph, South Bend & Southern (*See* Inc. 1/20/1899; A,35:341-347)

1899

1/1	Lease	Detroit, Toledo & Milwaukee to Cincinnati Northern
1/3	S.Inc.	Saginaw Valley Traction (filed 1/4; B,15)
1/17	Inc.	Port Huron, Lexington & Western (filed 1/19; A,31:698-699; B,15)
1/20	Inc.	Columbus, Marshall & Northeastern (filed 2/28; A,35:13-17; B,12)
1/20	Inc.	St. Joseph, South Bend & Southern (Indiana corp.) (filed 8/12; A,35:341-347)
1/23	Inc.	Copper Range (filed 2/20; A,35:1-5)
1/26	S.Inc.	Grand Rapids & Kalamazoo Electric (filed 1/31; B,13)
2/7	A-Inc.	Detroit & Pontiac (filed 2/8; B,12)
2/13	S.Inc.	Lansing, Dexter & Ann Arbor Electric (filed 2/16; B,14)
2/15	A-Inc.	Mineral Range (filed 2/20; A,31:739-740; B,14)
2/28	X-Lease	Indiana & Lake Michigan by Terre Haute & Indianapolis
3/6	S.Inc.	Grand Rapids, Grand Haven & Muskegon (filed 3/7; B,13)
3/9	S.Inc.	Detroit, Mt. Clemens & Marine City (filed 3/22; B,12)
3/14	S.Inc.	Detroit & Lake Orion (filed 3/22; B,12[DetRoch&LO])
3/15	S.Inc.	Detroit & Northwestern (filed 3/22; B,12)
3/16	Inc.	Detroit & Toledo Shore Line (filed 4/14; A,35:83-84)
3/22	S.Inc.	Jackson & Adrian Electric (filed 4/5; B,14)
3/31	Sale	Pontiac & Sylvan Lake and Grand River Electric to Detroit & Northwestern
4/1	A-Inc.	Benton Harbor & Eastman Springs (filed 4/6; B,12[BH&SJ])
4/3	S.Inc.	Metropolitan Ry (filed 4/3; B,14)
4/12	S.Inc.	Port Huron, St. Clair & Marine City (filed 5/9; B,15)
4/21	S.Inc.	Ypsilanti & Saline Electric (filed 5/17; B,16)
5/1	Sale	Lowell & Hastings to Grand Rapids, Belding & Saginaw
5/15	S.Inc.	Detroit & Port Huron Shore Line (filed 5/17; not found)

5/23	A-Inc.	Hancock & Calumet (filed 6/3; A,35:138-139; B,13)
5/25	S.Inc.	Detroit, Rochester, Romeo & Lake Orion (filed 6/3; B,12)
6/9	Inc.	Menominee & St. Paul (filed 6/14; A,35:156-157; B,14)
6/24	T.Inc.	Grand Rapids, Belding & Greenville (filed 7/11; B,13)
6/28	Inc.	Detroit River Terminal (filed 7/7; A,35:200-201; B,13)
7/—	Rec.	Bay Cities Consolidated
7/10	S.Inc.	Detroit Municipal (filed 7/11; B,13)
7/21	S.Inc.	Port Huron & Port Austin Electric (filed 7/24; B,15)
7/21	S.Inc.	North Detroit Electric (filed 8/8; B,15)
7/26	S.Inc.	Houghton County Street Ry (filed 8/4; B,13)
9/20	Inc.	Pere Marquette (filed 9/21; A,35:469-471; B,15[Pentw&Man])
9/26	A-Inc.	Traverse City, Peninsula & Old Mission (filed 10/3; A,36:107-108)
9/26	S.Inc.	Petoskey, Harbor Springs & Shore (filed 9/29; B,15)
10/2	A-Inc.	Traverse City, Peninsula & Old Mission (filed 10/3; A,36:109-110)
10/31	Inc.	Pentwater & Manistee (filed 11/1; A,36:245-246; B,15)
11/1	Inc.	Pere Marquette (filed 11/1; A,36:247-251; B,15)
11/3	Sale	Chicago & North Michigan to Chicago & West Michigan
11/15	Inc.	Eastern & Northwestern (filed 11/17; A,36:311-313; B,13)
11/16	A-Inc.	Detroit, Rochester, Romeo & Lake Orion (filed 11/24; A,36:361-362; B,12)
11/18	A-Inc.	Toledo & Monroe (filed 11/22; A,36:336-337; B,15)
11/27	T.Inc.	Detroit, Lake Orion & Flint (filed 11/28; B,12)
12/6	Sale	Flint & Pere Marquette to Pere Marquette
12/7	Sale	Chicago & West Michigan and Detroit, Grand Rapids & Western to Pere Marquette
12/26	Inc.	Toledo & Western Ry (Ohio corp.) (filed 7/19/1904; A,59:418-420; B,15)
12/30	Sale	Detroit & River St. Clair to Detroit, Mt. Clemens & Marine City

1900

1/4	T.Inc.	Saginaw Southern (filed 1/8; B,15)
1/9	Inc.	Rochester & St. Clair (filed 1/19; A,37:89-91; B,15)
1/10	Inc.	Traverse City & Leelanau (filed 2/1; A,37:157-159; B,16)
1/11	Inc.	Port Huron Southern (filed 1/25; A,37:117-119; B,15)
2/9	Inc.	Escanaba & Lake Superior (filed 2/12; A,37:224-227)
2/12	S.Inc.	Adrian Street Ry (filed 2/13; B,12)
2/23	Lease	St. Joseph, South Bend & Southern to Indiana, Illinois & Iowa
2/24	T.Inc.	Grand Rapids, Holland & Lake Michigan (filed 2/26; B,13)

3/12	UD.Inc.	Sainte Marie Union Depot Co. (filed 3/15; B,15)
3/23	S.Inc.	Detroit & Lake St. Clair (filed 3/23; B,12)
3/24	A-Inc.	Eastern & Northwestern (filed 3/28; A,37:432-435; B,13)
3/24	Sale	Detroit, Lake Shore & Mt. Clemens to Detroit & Lake St. Clair
4/4	A-Inc.	Detroit & Northwestern (filed 3/22/1901; B,12)
4/10	Inc.	Grand Rapids, Spring Lake & Grand Haven Rapid Transit (filed 5/10; A,39:164-167; B,13)
4/10	S.Inc.	Lansing, St. Johns & St. Louis (filed 5/25; B,14)
4/17	S.Inc.	Grand Rapids Ry (filed 4/18; B,13)
4/24	A-Inc.	Detroit, Lake Orion & Flint (filed 4/30; B,13)
5/14	A-Inc.	Saginaw Southern (filed 5/18; A,39:217-218; B,15)
5/25	S.Inc.	Detroit, Lexington & Lake Huron (filed 5/31; B,12)
7/—	$	City Electric of Port Huron; Detroit & Lake St. Clair; Detroit, Mt. Clemens & Marine City; Port Huron, St. Clair & Marine City; Rapid RR; and Rapid Ry by Detroit & Port Huron Shore Line
7/13	S.Inc.	Pontiac, Orion & Detroit (filed 7/14, B,15)
7/21	S.Inc.	Michigan & Ohio Electric Ry (filed 7/30; B,14)
8/1	T.Inc.	Lansing & Northern (filed 8/1; B,14)
8/7	A-Inc.	Houghton County Street Ry (filed 8/17; A,40:77-78; B,13)
9/25	Diss.	Petoskey, Harbor Springs & Shore (filed 9/26; B,15)
9/25	S.Inc.	Petoskey, Harbor Springs & Northern (filed 9/26; B,15)
9/25	T.Inc.	Crystal Lake Ry (filed 10/30; B,12)
9/27	S.Inc.	Jackson & Suburban Traction (filed 9/28; B,14)
10/1	Inc.	Marquette & Southeastern (filed 10/3; A,40:207-209)
10/1	Sale	Muskegon Lake to Pere Marquette
10/8	Inc.	Alpena & Western (filed 2/20/1901; A,41:443-445; B,12)
10/10	S.Inc.	Benton Harbor & St. Joseph Electric Ry & Light (filed 10/11; B,12)
10/31	F.Sale	Chicago & Grand Trunk to Port Huron & Indiana and Indiana & Illinois (*See* Inc. 11/19; A,40:429-441)
11/19	Inc.	Port Huron & Indiana (filed 11/20; A,40:429-441)
11/20	Inc.	Raisin River (filed 11/21; A,40:441-443; B,15)
11/20	Inc.	Grand Trunk Western (filed 11/22; A,40:444-457)
11/20	A-Inc.	Grand Rapids, Grand Haven & Muskegon (2 filed 11/21; B,13)
11/24	T.Inc.	Toledo, Adrian & Jackson (filed 11/27; B,15)
11/26	T.Inc.	Pontiac & Flint Electric (filed 11/27; B,15)
11/26	T.Inc.	Kalamazoo & Lake Michigan Ry (filed 2/21/1901; B,14)
12/8	A-Inc.	Grand Rapids, Holland & Lake Michigan (filed 12/14; B,13)

12/8	A-Inc.	Detroit, Rochester, Romeo & Lake Orion (filed 12/20; B,12)
12/8	A-Inc.	North Detroit Electric (filed 12/20; B,15)
12/10	T.Inc.	Harbor Springs Ry (filed 1/14/1901; B,13)
12/17	S.Inc.	South Haven & Paw Paw Lake Electric (filed 12/20; B,15)
12/18	T.Inc.	Interstate Ry (filed 1/28/1901; B,14)
12/22	S.Inc.	Detroit, Mt. Clemens, Romeo & Armada (filed 12/24; B,12)
12/24	T.Inc.	Grand Rapids & Belding (filed 1/14/1901; B,13[GRBeld&S])
12/27	S.Inc.	Lansing & Southeastern (filed 12/29; B,14)
12/28	S.Inc.	Detroit United Ry (filed 12/31; B,13)
12/31	Cons.	Detroit Citizens' Street; Detroit, Fort Wayne & Belle Isle; Detroit Suburban; and Detroit Electric into Detroit United

1901

1/1	Lease	Cincinnati, Saginaw & Mackinaw to Grand Trunk Railway of Canada
1/2	Inc.	Detroit & Charlevoix (filed 1/3; A,41:120-122; B,12)
1/14	A-Inc.	North Detroit Electric (filed 1/15; B,15)
1/19	S.Inc.	Muskegon Traction (filed 1/19; H,2)
1/22	S.Inc.	Detroit, Ypsilanti, Ann Arbor & Jackson (filed 1/23;B,13)
2/5	Inc.	Caro & Lake Huron (filed 3/4; A,42:19-20; B,12)
2/12	S.Inc.	South Bend & Southern Michigan (filed 2/15; B,15)
2/18	S.Inc.	Detroit & Chicago Traction (filed 3/4; B,12)
2/19	S.Inc.	Muskegon Traction & Lighting (filed 2/26; H,2)
2/20	S.Inc.	Lake Shore Ry (filed 2/28; B,14)
2/20	Sale	Wyandotte & Detroit River to Detroit United
2/21	S.Inc.	Lake Michigan & Eastern (filed 3/1; B,14)
2/26	A-Inc.	Detroit, Mt. Clemens & Marine City (filed 3/14; B,12)
3/6	S.Inc.	Michigan West Shore Traction (filed 3/9; B,14)
3/8	A-Inc.	Rapid Ry (filed 3/11; B,15)
3/8	A-Inc.	Detroit & Lake St. Clair (filed 3/12; B,12)
3/15	Inc.	Alpena, Gaylord & Western (filed 3/25; A,42:140-142; B,12)
3/18	A-Inc.	Lake Michigan & Eastern (filed 5/27; B,14)
3/25	Sale	Ypsilanti & Saline and Detroit, Ypsilanti & Ann Arbor to Detroit, Ypsilanti, Ann Arbor & Jackson
3/29	A-Inc.	Harbor Springs Ry (filed 3/30; B,13)
4/1	A-Inc.	Detroit & Toledo Shore Line (filed 12/10; K)
4/9	A-Inc.	Mineral Range (filed 4/15; A,42:303; B,14)

4/12	S.Inc.	Michigan Electric Ry (filed 4/15; B,14)
4/12	Inc.	Northern Michigan RR (filed 5/4; A,42:481-483; B,15)
4/13	T.Inc.	Monroe Traction (filed 4/16; B,14)
4/18	A-Inc.	Kalamazoo & Lake Michigan Ry (filed 5/8; B,14)
4/24	Inc.	Toledo & Michigan Terminal (filed 4/24; A,42:369-371; B,15)
4/24	Diss.	Pontiac & Flint Electric (filed 4/27; B,15)
4/30	Inc.	Detroit & Monroe (filed 5/9; A,43:22-24; B,12)
5/1	Sale	Detroit & Northwestern to Detroit United
5/2	A-Inc.	Alpena & Western (filed 1/8/1902; B,12)
5/8	Inc.	Soo-Detour (filed 5/24; A,43:112-114; B,15)
5/8	T.Inc.	Detroit, Howell & Lansing (filed 5/13; B,12[DHL&GR])
5/10	Inc.	South Haven & Lake Shore (filed 5/14; A,43:44-47; B,15)
5/22	A-Inc.	Houghton County Street (filed 6/10; B,13)
5/23	F.Sale	Detroit & Lima Northern to Detroit Southern (*See* Inc. 5/25; A,43:129-200)
5/25	Inc.	Detroit Southern (filed 5/25; A,43:129-200)
5/25	S.Inc.	Peoples Ry of Detroit (filed 5/28; B,15)
5/25	A-Inc.	Detroit Southern (filed 6/10; A,43:214)
5/31	A-Inc.	Mason & Oceana (filed 8/12; A,44:160-162; B,14)
6/1	Sale	Detroit & Pontiac to Detroit United
6/1	$	Hancock & Calumet by Mineral Range
6/4	T.Inc.	Detroit, Pontiac, Lapeer & Northern (filed 9/6; B,12)
6/11	UD.Inc.	Benton Harbor Terminal (filed 6/12; B,12)
6/20	Sale	Detroit, Utica & Romeo to North Detroit Electric
6/26	A-Inc.	Alpena, Gaylord & Western (filed 7/2; A,43:411; B,12)
6/29	S.Inc.	Detroit, Ann Arbor & Adrian (filed 7/1; B,12)
7/1	$	Detroit & Port Huron Shore Line by Detroit United
7/3	Inc.	East Jordan & Southern (filed 7/9; A,43:462-463)
7/8	Inc.	Camden Southern (filed 7/10; A,43:464-466; B,12)
7/13	S.Inc.	Michigan Inter-Urban (filed 7/22; B,14)
7/13	Cons.	Saginaw Bay & Northwestern and Grayling, Twin Lakes & North Eastern into Jackson, Lansing & Saginaw
7/13	T.Inc.	Ludington & Northern (filed 7/18; K)
7/22	Inc.	Connecting Ry (Penn. corp.; B,15[Penna, Ohio & Detroit])
7/23	T.Inc.	Detroit Terminal (filed 7/26; B,13)
7/27	Inc.	West Michigan Traction (filed 7/29; A,44:57-60)
7/30	Inc.	Petoskey & Harbor Springs RR (filed 8/1; A,44:71-72; B,15)

8/1	S.Inc.	Calhoun County (filed 8/3; B,12)
8/8	S.Inc.	Grand Rapids, Belding & Ionia (filed 8/9; B,13)
8/9	Inc.	Onaway & North Michigan (filed 8/15; A,44:171-175)
8/9	S.Inc.	Detroit & Flint (filed 8/10; B,12)
8/22	Inc.	Grand Rapids, Kalamazoo & South Haven Traction (filed 8/22; 44:196-199; B,13)
8/22	S.Inc.	Southern Michigan Traction (filed 9/3; J,9)
8/28	Sale	Detroit, Lake Orion & Flint to Detroit & Flint
9/4	Sale	Detroit, Utica & Romeo to Detroit & Flint
9/11	S.Inc.	Menominee Range Street Ry (filed 9/13; B,14)
9/17	S.Inc.	Petoskey & Harbor Springs Ry (filed 9/18; B,15)
9/18	S.Inc.	Detroit & Ann Arbor (filed 9/20; B,12)
9/18	S.Inc.	Jackson & Ann Arbor (filed 9/20; B,14)
9/23	S.Inc.	Flint, Saginaw & Bay City (filed 10/22; B,13)
9/23	Sale	Detroit Transit to Detroit Terminal Ry (B,13[DTransit])
10/8	Inc.	Pennsalt (filed 10/12; A,44:475-478)
10/10	S.Inc.	Jackson & Albion Electric (filed 10/11; B,14)
10/10	Sale	North Detroit Electric to Detroit & Flint
10/11	Inc.	Sanilac (filed 11/20; A,45:262-263; B,15)
10/14	UD.Inc.	Sault Ste. Marie Terminal (filed 10/18; B,15)
10/14	S.Inc.	Trans-St. Mary's Traction (filed 10/18; B,16)
10/22	A-Inc.	Mineral Range (filed 10/26; A,45:93; B,14)
10/25	S.Inc.	Battle Creek & Marshall Traction (filed 10/28; B,12)
10/28	A-Inc.	Detroit Southern (filed 11/14; A,45:226)
11/1	$	Lansing City Electric by Detroit, Ypsilanti, Ann Arbor & Jackson
11/7	Inc.	Detroit, Howell, Lansing & Grand Rapids (filed 11/12; B,12)
11/8	A-Inc.	Mackinac Transportation (filed 4/2/1902; A,47:233-235)
11/20	Inc.	Traverse City, Leelanau & Manistique (filed 11/25; A,45:300-302; B,16)
12/4	Inc.	Michigan Central (filed 12/30; K)
12/24	A-Inc.	Detroit & Monroe (filed 12/28; A,45:514-515; B,12)
12/30	Inc.	Michigan Suburban (filed 1/11/1902; A,46:28-30; B,14)
12/31	X-Lease	Detroit, Toledo & Milwaukee by Cincinnati Northern

1902

1/1	$	Cincinnati Northern by Cleveland, Cincinnati, Chicago & St. Louis
1/6	A-Inc.	Grand Rapids, Holland & Lake Michigan Rapid (2/18; A,46:405-406; B,13)
1/8	Rec.	Detroit & Toledo Shore Line

1/12	Opg.Ag.	Lansing, St. Johns & St. Louis by Michigan Suburban
1/21	A-Inc.	Detroit United (filed 1/25; B,13)
1/27	Inc.	Detroit Manufacturers (filed 1/30; A,46:175-177; B,13)
1/28	A-Inc.	Grand Rapids Ry (filed 2/18; B,13)
2/20	Inc.	Detroit River & Lake Erie Terminal (filed 2/21; A,46:447-448; B,12)
2/28	O.Inc.	Belle Isle Scenic (filed 3/1; B,12)
3/7	Inc.	Marshall & Northern (filed 3/10; A,46:638-640; B,14)
3/18	Inc.	Grand Rapids & Chicago (filed 3/19; A,47:77-80; B,13 [GR&KalVal])
3/19	Inc.	Hecla Belt Line (filed 4/3; A,47:245-248; B,13)
3/22	A-Inc.	Mason & Oceana (filed 4/7; A,47:296-298; B,14)
3/24	Inc.	Manistique, Marquette & Northern (filed 4/1; A,47:230-232)
3/31	Sale	Detroit Terminal Ry to Detroit Manufacturers (B,13[DTerm])
4/1	Lease	Detroit Manufacturers to Michigan Central
4/4	Inc.	North Park Bridge Co. (filed 4/7; A,47:293-294; B,15)
5/1	Sale	Manistique & Northwestern to Manistique, Marquette & Northern
5/7	A-Inc.	Alpena, Gaylord & Western (filed 7/5; A,48:396)
5/7	Partn.	Wolf Lake Ry & Resort (filed 1/7/1904; B,14)
5/17	S.Inc.	Jackson & Battle Creek Traction (filed 5/19; B,14)
5/26	Inc.	Huron & Western (filed 5/27; A,48:97-99; B,13)
6/23	T.Inc.	Union Traction (filed 6/24; B 15)
6/23	Partn.	Michigan Central Traction (filed 12/31/1903; B,14)
7/3	Sale	Wisconsin, Michigan & Northern to Wisconsin & Michigan Ry
7/17	A-Inc.	Kalamazoo & Lake Michigan Ry (filed 10/11; B,14)
9/8	Cons.	South Bend Northern (Indiana corp.) into South Bend & Southern Michigan (filed 9/15; B,15)
9/17	A-Inc.	Pontiac, Oxford & Northern (filed 9/25; A,49:308)
9/27	T.Inc.	Blaney & Southern (filed 10/18; B,12)
10/28	A-Inc.	Jackson & Battle Creek Traction (filed 11/1; B,14)
12/9	Inc.	Detroit, Monroe & Toledo Short Line (filed 12/10; A,50:213-215; B,12)
12/9	A-Inc.	Detroit, Monroe & Toledo Short Line (filed 5/26/1903; A,50:373-374; B,12)
12/22	A-Inc.	Mineral Range RR (filed 1/6/1903; A,50:373-374; B,14)

1903

n.d.	F.Sale	Bay Cities Cons. to Bay City Traction & Light
1/13	A-Inc.	Trans-St. Mary's Traction (filed 1/31; B,16)
1/21	A-Inc.	Jackson & Battle Creek Traction (filed 11/24; B,14)

1/29	Inc.	Michigan Shore & Eastern (filed 2/4; A,51:53-57; B,14)
2/3	A-Inc.	Muskegon Traction & Lighting (filed 2/?; H,2)
2/10	A-Inc.	Chicago & Northwestern (filed 3/11; A,51:328-330; B,14)
2/10	A-Inc.	Grand Rapids, Holland & Lake Michigan (filed 5/5; B,13)
2/18	A-Inc.	Grand Haven Street (filed 4/21; B,13)
2/23	Inc.	Pere Marquette International Bridge Co. (filed 3/6; A,51:325-327; B,15)
2/23	Inc.	Pere Marquette RR of Indiana (Indiana corp.) (filed 3/30; A,51:522-524)
3/24	Inc.	Grand Rapids Electric (filed 5/19; A,52:384-386; B,13)
3/24	Inc.	Toledo & Michigan Electric (filed 5/26; B,15)
3/25	Inc.	Harbor Beach & Port Hope (filed 3/26; A,51:474-475; B,13)
3/27	S.Inc.	West Michigan Interurban (filed 5/12/1904; B,16)
4/1	Sale	South Haven & Eastern to Pere Marquette
5/6	S.Inc.	Jackson, Ann Arbor & Detroit Traction (filed 6/26; B,14)
5/6	A-Inc.	Alpena, Gaylord & Western (filed 6/15; A,53:14-15)
5/6	Sale	Milwaukee, Benton Harbor & Columbus; Grand Rapids, Belding & Saginaw; Sanilac; Bay City Belt Line; and Saginaw, Tuscola & Huron to Pere Marquette
5/6	A-Inc.	Pere Marquette (filed 10/27; A,55:165; B,12[Chi&MLS])
5/7	Sale	Benton Harbor, Coloma & Paw Paw Lake to Pere Marquette
5/19	Inc.	Huron & Michigan (filed 5/23; A,52:440-442; B,13)
5/28	Res.	Menominee El. Light, Ry & Power (filed 6/1; A,52:496-497)
6/6	T.Inc.	Ohio & Michigan Traction (filed 6/20; B,15[ToledoAA&Det])
6/6	S.Inc.	Menominee & Marinette Light & Traction (filed 7/1; G,35)
6/15	S.Inc.	Chicago, Michigan & Indiana (filed 6/16; B,12)
6/23	S.Inc.	Grand Rapids & South Michigan (filed 6/24; B,13)
7/6	A-Inc.	Detroit & Toledo Shore Line (filed 7/6; K)
7/17	A-Inc.	Toledo & Michigan Electric (filed 1/21/1907; A,75:125-126; B,15)
8/1	S.Inc.	United Traction (filed 8/13; B,15)
8/6	Sale	Huron & Western to Pere Marquette
9/2	S.Inc.	Michigan Traction Extension (filed 9/11; G,42)
9/10	Inc.	Cheboygan Southern (filed 10/2; A,54:476-479; B,12)
9/17	S.Inc.	Cadillac Traction (filed 9/25; B,12)
10/20	S.Inc.	Michigan & Indiana Traction (filed 10/21; B,14)
11/3	Inc.	Grand Rapids & Ionia (filed 11/12; A,55:296-298; B,12)
11/5	T.Inc.	Detroit, Flint & Saginaw (filed 11/27; B,13)
12/1	S.Inc.	Bay City Traction & Electric (filed 12/4; B,15)

12/12	Inc.	Traverse City & Peninsula (filed 12/19; A,55:585-588; B,16)
12/21	Sale	Harbor Beach & Port Hope to Pere Marquette
12/23	Inc.	Ionia & Owosso (filed 7/2/1904; A,59:418-420; B,14)

1904

1/1	Lease	Canada Southern by Michigan Central
1/30	A-Inc.	Manistee & Northeastern (filed 1/9/1909; A,87:121; B,14)
2/1	Diss.	Grand Haven Street (filed 2/1; B,13)
3/8	S.Inc.	Lansing & Suburban Traction (filed 3/9; B,14)
3/15	$	Lansing City Elec. by Lansing & Suburban Traction
3/24	Inc.	Delray Connecting (filed 3/15; K)
3/26	Sale	Lansing, St. Johns & St. Louis to Lansing Suburban Traction
4/19	S.Inc.	Jackson Consolidated Traction (filed 4/25; G,1)
4/30	S.Inc.	Battle Creek & Coldwater Electric (filed 5/4; B,12)
5/5	A-Inc.	Michigan Central (filed 5/11; A,58:514)
5/31	Inc.	Bay City & Port Huron (filed 6/11; A,59:227-229; B,12)
5/31	S.Inc.	Bessemer & Ironwood Interurban (filed 7/1; B,12)
6/14	Inc.	Erie & Michigan Ry & Navigation (filed 6/30; A,59:406-408; B,13)
6/16	T.Inc.	Flint & Saginaw Traction (filed 6/17; B,13)
6/23	Inc.	Battle Creek & Grand Rapids Inland Lakes-Traction (filed 6/25; A,59:359-362)
6/24	T.Inc.	Toledo, Ann Arbor & Detroit (filed 12/10; B,15)
7/9	A-Inc.	Pere Marquette (filed 7/15; A,59:478; B,12[Chi&MLS])
7/14	A-Inc.	Grand Rapids & Ionia (filed 3/3/1905; A,63:510; B,13)
7/18	S.Inc.	Grand Rapids, Holland & Chicago (filed 7/19; B,13)
7/21	Inc.	Adrian & Ann Arbor Electric (filed 7/23; A,59:571-574; B,12)
7/29	Inc.	Lansing Manufacturers RR (filed 8/30; A,60:301-302)
7/30	Inc.	Ontonagon & Southwestern (filed 8/6; A,60:121-123; B,15)
8/1	Sale	Grand Rapids, Holland & Lake Michigan to Grand Rapids, Holland & Chicago
8/2	A-Inc.	Houghton County Street (filed 8/15; B,13)
8/4	Inc.	Grand Rapids & Kalamazoo Valley (filed 8/5; A,60:107-108; B,13)
8/4	A-Inc.	Grand Rapids & Kalamazoo Valley (filed 8/5; B,13)
8/9	Inc.	Grand Rapids Terminal RR (filed 8/13; A,60:169-170)
8/15	T.Inc.	Bay City & Caro (filed 8/16; B,12)
9/14	Inc.	Adrian & Jackson Traction (filed 9/16; A,60:443-445; B,12)
9/14	Inc.	Wyandotte Terminal (filed 9/19; A,60:479-481)

9/16	A-Inc.	Manistee & Grand Rapids (filed 9/20; B,14[MichE&W])
9/30	T.Inc.	Marquette County Gas Light & Traction (filed 10/13; B,14)
10/1	Inc.	Detroit Bay City Traction Co. (filed 10/10; A,61:96-99; B,12)
10/4	S.Inc.	St. Joe River Traction Co. (filed 10/20; A,61:186-189)
10/13	Inc.	Ann Arbor Interurban (filed 10/17; A,61:165-167; B,12)
10/24	T.Inc.	Ontonagon RR (filed 10/27; B,15)
11/12	S.Inc.	Niles & Buchanan (filed 11/14; B,15)

1905

1/1	Lease	Detroit, Toledo & Milwaukee to Michigan Central and Lake Shore & Michigan Southern
1/6	Inc.	Grand Rapids, Belding & Greenville (filed 3/3; A,63:511-513; B,13)
1/24	Inc.	Delray Terminal (filed 2/7; A,63:180-182; B,12)
2/4	S.Inc.	Lansing & Battle Creek Traction (filed 2/14; B,14)
2/15	A-Inc.	Lansing & Battle Creek Traction (filed 3/2; B,14)
2/22	A-Inc.	Adrian Street (filed 2/24; B,12)
3/7	T.Inc.	East Shore & Southwestern (filed 3/13; B,13)
3/15	Lease	St. Joseph, South Bend & Southern by Indiana, Illinois & Iowa assigned to Michigan Central
3/17	Inc.	Boyne City, Gaylord & Alpena (filed 3/28; A,64:220-222; B,12)
3/20	A-Inc.	Grand Rapids & Kalamazoo Valley (filed 4/5; A,64:358-359; B,13)
3/29	S.Inc.	Northern Michigan Traction (filed 4/5; B,14[ManistL&T])
3/30	Inc.	Michigan & Canada Bridge & Tunnel (filed 4/5; A,64:289)
3/30	S.Inc.	Lansing & Jackson Ry (filed 5/1; B,14)
4/3	Inc.	Lake Superior Southern (filed 9/21; A,67:96-97; B,14)
4/6	Inc.	Quinnesec & Western (filed 6/7; A,65:392-394; B,15)
4/7	Inc.	Michigan Terminal Transfer (filed 4/12; A,64:372-375; B,14)
4/12	S.Inc.	Kalamazoo Lake Shore & Chicago Traction (filed 6/15; B,14)
4/25	Inc.	Keweenaw Central (filed 4/27; A,64:578-580)
5/1	F.Sale	Detroit Southern to Detroit, Toledo & Ironton (*See* Inc. 5/2; A,65:41-51)
5/2	Inc.	Detroit, Toledo & Ironton (filed 5/2; A,65:41-51)
5/16	S.Inc.	River Rouge (filed 5/18; B,15)
5/20	T.Inc.	Saginaw & Southwestern (filed 6/21; B,15[SagBaySW])
5/24	Inc.	Michigan, Ohio & Indiana (filed 5/27; A,65:301-303; B,14)
6/1	$	Ann Arbor by Detroit, Toledo & Ironton
6/9	Inc.	Detroit River Tunnel (filed 12/13; A,68:215-220)

6/14	Sale	Quinnesec & Western to Wisconsin & Michigan
6/19	S.Inc.	Menominee & Escanaba (filed 6/30; B,14)
7/1	Lease	Lansing Manufacturers RR to Michigan Central and New York Central
7/1	T.Inc.	South Haven Traction (filed 7/20; J,2)
7/8	T.Inc.	Saginaw Bay South Western (filed 8/31; B,15)
8/4	Inc.	West Michigan Ry (filed 8/5; A,66:331-334; B,16)
8/7	A-Inc.	Marquette & Southeastern (filed 8/11; A,66:371-372)
8/8	S.Inc.	Michigan Ry & Light (filed 8/17; B,14)
8/21	T.Inc.	Toledo & Jackson Electric (filed 9/5; B,15)
9/11	A-Inc.	Jackson & Ann Arbor (filed 9/14; B,14)
9/15	S.Inc.	Ottawa Beach & Southern (filed 9/16; B,15[ToledoOB&N])
9/21	T.Inc.	Coldwater Train (filed 9/26; B,12)
9/21	F.Sale	Manistique, Marquette & Northern to Union Trust Co. (*See* Inc. 1/17/1908; A,81:308-311)
10/23	Inc.	Battle Creek & Southeastern (filed 10/27; A,67:446-449; B,12)
11/14	A-Inc.	Munising Ry (filed 11/28; A,68:119-120)
11/22	A-Inc.	Detroit, Toledo & Ironton (filed 11/23; A,68:80-81)
12/7	Inc.	Detroit Terminal (filed 12/8; A,68:189-190)
12/20	Inc.	Grand Rapids Terminal Belt (filed 12/26; A,68:349-350; B,13)
12/22	Inc.	Kalamazoo, Elkhart & South Bend Traction (filed 1/2/1906; A,68:388-392)
12/30	Inc.	Chicago, Kalamazoo & Eastern (filed 1/12/1906; A,68:502-504; B,12)

1906

1/2	Lease	Toledo, Canada Southern & Detroit to Michigan Central
1/10	Sale	Central Michigan RR to Grand Rapids Electric (filed 1/25; B,12[CentMich])
1/23	S.Inc.	Benton Harbor-St. Joe Ry & Light (filed 1/25; C,10)
2/7	Inc.	Southern Michigan Ry (filed 2/8; B,15)
2/23	F.Sale	Michigan Midland & Canada to St. Clair & Western (*See* Inc. 9/24; A,73:87-89)
2/23	T.Inc.	Detroit, Flint River & Saginaw Valley (filed 2/24; B,12)
2/23	T.Inc.	Fenton, Long Lake & Flint (filed 2/24; B,13)
3/1	Sale	Detroit, Monroe & Toledo Short Line to Detroit United
3/8	S.Inc.	Detroit & Adrian Traction (filed 3/24; B,12)
3/13	A-Inc.	Wabash RR (filed 6/23; A,71:489-491; B,16)
3/19	Inc.	Elk Short Line (filed 3/21; A,70:137-138; B,13)
3/31	Inc.	Jackson, Ann Arbor & Detroit (filed 9/5; A,72:531-533; B,14)
3/31	S.Inc.	Michigan United (filed 3/31; B,14)

4/5	Diss.	Pere Marquette Trans. (filed 4/7; A,70:328)
4/6	Inc.	Chicago, Indiana & Southern (Indiana corp.)
4/6	A-Inc.	Ontonagon (filed 5/4; B,15)
5/1	Cons.	Lansing & Jackson; Lansing City Electric; Lansing & Suburban; Michigan Traction Extension; and Michigan traction into Michigan United Rys
5/1	Lease	Jackson & Battle Creek Traction to Michigan United Rys
6/6	T.Inc.	Kalamazoo, Lake Shore & Chicago (filed 10/12; B,14)
6/18	Inc.	Ludington Southern (filed 10/12; A,73:273-275; B,13)
6/27	Sale	Benton Harbor & St Joseph Elec. Ry & Light to Benton Harbor-St. Joe Ry & Light
7/2	Rec	Toledo & Western Ry
7/3	Inc.	Kalamazoo, Gull Lake & Northern (filed 7/14; A,72:111-114; B,14)
7/13	Inc.	Marlborough RR (filed 7/16; A,72:123-124; B,14)
9/24	Inc.	St. Clair & Western (filed 9/25; A,73:87-89; B,15)
10/15	S.Inc.	Trans-Michigan Street (filed 10/27; B,15)
10/18	A-Inc.	Chicago & North Western (filed 11/5; A,73:54; B,12)
10/25	T.Inc.	Toledo, Ottawa Beach & Northern (filed 10/27; B,15)
11/15	O.Inc.	Marquette County Gas & Electric Co. (Maine corp.) (filed 2/12/1907; A,75:484-486)
11/20	Rec.	Detroit, Flint & Saginaw (B,12[DetFlRiv&SagVal])
11/25	Sale	Jackson & Ann Arbor and Detroit, Plymouth & Northville to Jackson, Ann Arbor & Detroit
12/10	Inc.	Toledo & Western RR (Ohio corp.) (filed 4/10/1907; A,77:6-8; B,15)
12/13	Inc.	Toledo Michigan & Lake Huron (filed 12/31; A,74:490-491; B,15)
12/28	Inc.	Saginaw, Owosso & Lansing (filed 1/25/1907; A,75:215-218; B,15)

1907

1/1	Lease	Detroit River Tunnel by Michigan Central (eff. 1/1/1904)
1/1	F.Sale	Toledo & Western Ry to Toledo & Western RR
1/2	Sale	Au Sable & Northwestern to Loud partnership
1/11	A-Inc.	Toledo & Western RR (filed 4/10; A,77:8-9)
1/12	S.Inc.	Detroit, Jackson & Chicago (filed 1/14; B,12)
1/17	Lease	Toledo, Ottawa Beach & Northern to Toledo Railway & Light
1/26	A-Inc.	Wabash RR (filed 2/2; A,75:324-326; B,16)
2/1	Sale	Detroit, Ypsilanti, Ann Arbor & Jackson to Detroit, Jackson & Chicago
2/19	A-Inc.	Detroit Terminal (filed 3/1; A,76:60)
2/28	$	Chicago & Kalamazoo Terminal by Grand Trunk Western
3/22	A-Inc.	Houghton County Street (filed 3/28; B,13)

3/28	$	Toledo & Western RR by Toledo Railway & Light
4/15	Lease	Pere Marquette (part) to Kalamazoo, Lake Shore & Chicago
4/17	F.Sale	Traverse City, Leelanau & Manistique (*See* Inc. 9/19/1908; A,85:205-208)
5/2	$	Detroit & Charlevoix by Michigan Central
5/8	Inc.	Detroit, Bay City & West. (filed 5/13; A,77:374-376; B,12)
5/9	$	Jackson Cons. Traction by Michigan United Rys
5/29	A-Inc.	Escanaba & Lake Superior (filed 6/11; A,78:102)
5/31	S.Inc.	Marquette, Negaunee & Ishpeming Interurban (filed 6/1; B,14)
6/4	S.Inc.	Ohio & Southern Michigan (filed 6/6; B,15)
6/20	A-Inc.	Grand Rapids Electric (filed 1/18/1909; A,87:234-235; B,13)
6/29	Lease	Erie & Michigan Ry & Navigation to Detroit & Mackinac
6/28	S.Inc.	Manistee Light & Traction (filed 7/15; B,14)
7/19	Sale	Jackson, Ann Arbor & Detroit to Detroit, Jackson & Chicago
8/6	A-Inc.	Houghton County Street (filed 8/26; B,13)
8/12	Cons.	Pere Marquette of Indiana (Indiana corp.) into Pere Marquette (filed 12/11; A,81:3-42; B,12 [C&WM],B,12[PM])
8/29	Inc.	Lansing Southern (filed 9/11; A,79:373-374; B,14)
9/—	$	Pere Marquette by Cincinnati, Hamilton & Dayton
9/4	Inc.	Ontonagon Southern (filed 9/6; A,79:345-346; B,15)
9/17	Inc.	Grand Traverse (filed 9/23; A,79:487-491; B,13)
9/17	A-Inc.	Minneapolis, St. Paul & Sault Ste. Marie (filed 1/9/1909; A,87:129-133; B,14)
9/20	S.Inc.	Traverse City Street (filed 9/21; B,16)
11/—	F.Sale	Toledo, Ann Arbor & Detroit to Toledo, Ann Arbor & Jackson
12/14	S.Inc.	Calumet & Lac La Belle Traction (filed 12/28; B,12)
12/26	Inc.	Au Sable & Northwestern (filed 1/8/1908; A,81:233-235; B,12)

1908

1/9	Inc.	Manistique & Northern (filed 1/17; A,81:308-311; B,14)
1/16	Inc.	Grand Rapids & North Western (filed 1/31; A,81:414-417; B,13)
3/18	A-Inc.	Detroit United (filed 3/19; B,13)
4/30	Rec.	Owosso & Corunna Electric
5/8	Sale	Caro & Lake Huron to Detroit & Bay City
6/20	A-Inc.	Michigan United Rys (filed 6/24; B,14)
7/20	A-Inc.	Menominee & Marinette Light & Traction
7/24	S.Inc.	Houghton County Traction (filed 7/29; A,84:396-398)
8/1	Sale	Jackson Cons. Traction to Michigan United Rys

8/17	Inc.	Wyandotte Southern (filed 9/1; A,85:88-89)
8/20	T.Inc.	Saginaw & Flint (filed 8/21; B,15)
9/1	A-Inc.	Houghton County Traction (filed 9/12; B,13)
9/14	Inc.	Traverse City, Leelanau & Manistique Ry (filed 9/19; A,85:205-208; B,16)
9/17	S.Inc.	Dowagiac Ry (filed 9/19; B,13)
10/8	A-Inc.	Grand Rapids Terminal RR (filed 10/9; A,85:379-380)
10/27	Lease	Grand Rapids Terminal by Detroit, Grand Haven & Milwaukee
10/28	A-Inc.	Houghton County Traction (filed 11/20; B,13)
12/11	Inc.	Battle Creek, Coldwater & Southern (filed 12/18; A,86:450-453; B,12)
12/21	T.Inc.	Ohio & Michigan Interurban (filed 1/2/1909; B,15)
12/24	Inc.	Detroit & Western (filed 12/31; A,86:582-583; B,12)

1909

2/1	T.Inc.	Ohio, Northern & Michigan (filed 2/15; A,88:73-74; B,15)
2/24	A-Inc.	Manistee & Northeastern (filed 3/11; B,14)
3/22	T.Inc.	Houghton, Chassell & Southwestern (filed 3/30; B,13)
4/1	Lease	Wisconsin Central Ry to Minneapolis, St. Paul & Sault Ste. Marie
4/17	Inc.	Detroit Belt Line (filed 5/3; A,89:531-532; B,12)
5/10	A-Inc.	Benton Harbor-St. Joe Ry & Light (filed 5/29; A,90:243-245)
5/15	Inc.	St. Joseph Terminal (filed 6/3; A,90:290-292; B,15)
6/15	T.Inc.	Delta Traction (filed 7/8; B,12)
7/13	S.Inc.	Detroit, Lansing & Grand Rapids (filed 7/16; B,12)
7/20	Sale	Detroit & Bay City part to Detroit Belt Line
7/20	Lease	Detroit Belt Line to Michigan Central
7/21	Inc.	Manistique & Lake Superior (filed 7/23; A,91:333-336)
7/21	A-Inc.	Chicago & Kalamazoo Terminal (filed 7/22; A,91:315-316)
7/22	Inc.	Michigan & Chicago Westbound (filed 7/22; A,91:344-346)
8/1	Sale	Manistique & Northern to Manistique & Lake Superior
8/2	T.Inc.	Ontonagon & Flintsteel (filed 8/4; B,15)
8/3*	T.Inc.	Escanaba Traction (filing date shown; articles not found)
8/13	Sale	Escanaba Electric Street to Escanaba Traction
8/20	S.Inc.	Michigan Light & Traction (filed 8/24; B,14)
9/28	A-Inc.	Saginaw & Flint (filed 9/30; B,15)
10/21	$	Blaney & Southern by Wisconsin Land & Lumber
12/30	T.Inc.	Saginaw-Bay City (filed 2/18/1910; B,15)

1910

1/22	S.Inc.	Lansing & Northeastern (filed 2/3; B,14)
2/19	Inc.	Bay City, Caro & Eastern (filed 2/24; A,96:216-217; B,12)
2/24	A-Inc.	Mineral Range (filed 4/6; B,14)
3/7	A-Inc.	Michigan United Rys (filed 8/26/1915; B,14)
3/8	O.Inc.	Commonwealth Power Railway & Light (articles not found)
4/19	Inc.	Grosse Ile Ry (filed 5/4; A,98:202-203; B,13)
7/23	Inc.	Lake Michigan & Kalamazoo (filed 9/8; A,101:88-91; B,14)
8/1	Lease	part of Chicago, Kalamazoo & Saginaw to Chicago & Kalamazoo Terminal
8/11	Inc.	Bay City Terminal (filed 8/29; A,101:15-17; B,12)
8/25	A-Inc.	Battle Creek, Coldwater & Southern (filed 8/27; A,101:4; B,12)
9/—	F.Sale	Manistique Ry to Manistique Lumbering Company
9/14	S.Inc.	Gogebic Street (filed 10/6; B,13)
10/6	S.Inc.	Gogebic & Iron Counties Ry & Light (filed 11/14; B,13)
11/1	Diss.	Michigan Light & Traction (filed 11/4; B,14)
11/25	X-$	Detroit, Toledo & Ironton of Ann Arbor
11/26	Inc.	Gogebic & Iron Counties Ry & Light (Wisc. corp.) (filed 2/19/1915; A,146:337-342)
12/1	$	Pontiac, Oxford & Northern by Grand Trunk Western
12/13	A-Inc.	Gogebic & Iron Counties Ry & Light (filed 2/19/1915; A,146:342-345)

1911

n.d.	Sale	Owosso & Corunna Electric to Michigan United Rys
2/8	Inc.	Ironwood & Bessemer Ry & Light (Wisc. corp.) (filed 2/19/1915; A,146:345-347)
4/—	$	Manistique & Lake Superior by Ann Arbor
6/1	Lease	Kalamazoo, Lake Shore & Chicago to Michigan United Rys
6/27	Inc.	Munising, Marquette & Southeastern (filed 6/30; A,108:368-392)
7/29	A-Inc.	Detroit, Bay City & Western (filed 8/10; A,109:350-352; B,12)
9/15	T.Inc.	Toledo, Ann Arbor & Jackson (filed 9/21; B,15)
9/22	A-Inc.	Mackinac Transportation (filed 10/10; A,112:106-109)
9/27	S.Inc.	Michigan-Indiana Traction (filed 9/29; A,110:545-548; B,14)
10/9	T.Inc.	Southern Electric (filed 10/31; B,15)
12/27	S.Inc.	Michigan United Traction (filed 12/27; G,42)

1912

1/1	Lease	Lansing & Northeastern to Michigan United Rys
1/17	Diss.	Harbor Springs Ry (filed 1/18; A,113:460; B,13)

2/29	S.Inc.	Port Huron & Northern (filed 3/19; B,15)
2/29	Inc.	Detroit & Huron (filed 3/23; A,115:594-596; B,12)
4/1	Lease	Michigan United Rys lines to Michigan United Traction
4/8	Inc.	Thumb Ry (filed 4/23; A,116:477-480; B,15)
4/27	A-Inc.	Ironwood & Bessemer Ry & Light (filed 2/19/1915; A,146:347-350)
5/—	X-$	Pere Marquette by Cincinnati, Hamilton & Dayton
6/1	Lease	Au Sable & Northwestern to Detroit & Mackinac
6/14	Inc.	Michigan City, Lakeside & St. Joe Electric (filed 7/29; A,119:223-227; B,14)
6/19	Cons.	Buchanan & St. Joseph River into Michigan Central
7/11	Inc.	Detroit & Highland Park (filed 7/16; A,118:593-595; B,12)
8/23	Inc.	Michigan & Chicago (filed 8/29; A,120:59-61; B,14[MichRy])
9/18	Inc.	L'Anse Bay RR (filed 10/21; A,121:300-302; B,14)
10/27	S.Inc.	Manistee Ry (filed 3/10/1913; B,14)
12/5	A-Inc.	Detroit, Delray & Dearborn (filed 9/4/1913; A,131:157-158; B,13)
12/19	A-Inc.	Michigan & Chicago (filed 12/23; A,123:105-107; B,14[Mich])
12/19	A-Inc.	Ironwood & Bessemer Ry & Light (filed 2/19/1915; A,146:351-354)
12/31	A-Inc.	Rapid RR (filed 2/6/1913; A,124:435-436; B,15)
12/30	Sale	Hecla Belt to Bay City & Battle Creek

1913

1/2	O.Inc.	Northern Michigan Power Co. (filed 6/15/1914; A,139:375-391)
1/14	A-Inc.	Thumb Ry (filed 1/28; A,124:200-201; B,15)
2/7	Inc.	Elgin Terminal (filed 4/17; A,127:208-216; B,13)
4/24	A-Inc.	Michigan & Chicago (filed 6/4; A,128:492-494; B,14[Mich])
5/29	S.Inc.	Muskegon, Ludington & Manistee (filed 6/24; B,14)
6/27	S.Inc.	Lakewood Street Ry (filed 7/31; B,14)
8/30	A-Inc.	Detroit, Bay City & Western (filed 9/11; A,131:234-236; B,12)
9/1	Sale	part Detroit, Toledo & Milwaukee to Michigan & Chicago
9/3	S.Inc.	Tri-State of Michigan (filed 10/1; B,16)
9/12	F.Sale	Manistee & Grand Rapids to Michigan East & West (*See* Inc. 11/25; A,134:128-134)
10/6	Inc.	Detroit, Almont & Northern (filed 10/15; A,132:137-139; B,12)
11/17	A-Inc.	Michigan & Chicago (filed 12/26; A,134:123-125; B,14[Mich])
11/25	Inc.	Michigan East & West (filed 12/27; A,134:128-134; B,14)
12/15	Diss.	Hecla Belt Line (filed 7/20/1914; B,13)
12/17	Sale	Cincinnati, Wabash & Michigan to Cleveland, Cincinnati, Chicago & St. Louis
12/26	Inc.	New Buffalo & Lakeside (filed 4/18/1914; A,138:98-101; B,15)

1914

1/7	A-Inc.	Grand Rapids, Belding & Greenville (filed 1/13; A,134:398-399; B,13)
1/7	A-Inc.	Grand Rapids & Ionia (filed 1/13; A,134:399-400; B,13)
1/7	A-Inc.	Ionia & Owosso (filed 1/13; A,134:400-401; B,14)
1/24	Inc.	Lansing Connecting RR (filed 6/30; B,14)
2/20	Inc.	Detroit, Toledo & Ironton RR (filed 3/4; A,136:217-225)
2/24	A-Inc.	Mackinac Transportation (filed 11/6/1915; A,154:406-407)
2/26	S.Inc.	Detroit, Pontiac & Owosso (filed 7/10; B,13)
2/28	S.Inc.	Iron River, Stambaugh & Crystal Falls (filed 5/8; B,14)
3/19	Inc.	Michigan Ry (filed 3/21; A,137:91-94; B,14)
3/19	Diss.	Saginaw & Flint (filed 9/1; B,15)
3/25	A-Inc.	Menominee & Marinette Light & Traction (no filing date given; G,35)
5/12	Diss.	Kalamazoo & Lake Michigan Ry (filed 2/17/1915; B,14)
6/1	Sale	Au Sable & Northwestern to Detroit & Mackinac
8/24	Diss.	Manistique & Northern (filed 9/1; A,142:4)
8/31	Diss.	Detroit, Howell, Lansing & Grand Rapids (filed 9/8; B,13)
9/19	A-Inc.	Ann Arbor (filed 10/10; K)
11/12	S.Inc.	Albion, Charlotte, Northern (filed 12/4; B,12)
12/21	A-Inc.	Ontonagon (filed 3/8/1915; B,15)
12/30	Diss.	Grand Rapids, Belding & Ionia (filed 2/27/1915; A,146:482, B,13)

1915

n.d.	$	Detroit & Western by Wabash
1/1	Cons.	Detroit & Chicago; Kalamazoo & White Pigeon; Northern Central Michigan; Detroit, Monroe & Toledo; and Chicago, Indiana & Southern to New York Central
1/14	Diss.	Michigan-Indiana Traction (filed 1/28; A,145:460)
1/18	A-Inc.	Ironwood & Bessemer Ry & Light (filed 2/19; A,146:354-357; refiled 3/5/1921; A,237:31-35)
1/20	A-Inc.	Detroit, Bay City & Western (filed 8/6; A,151:572-575; B,12)
2/13	Diss.	Delta Traction (filed 2/25; B,12)
4/16	Diss.	Menominee & Escanaba (filed 4/19; B,14)
4/28	T.Inc.	Toledo-Detroit (filed 5/26; B,15)
5/14	Sale	Van Harbor & Northern to Garden Bay Ry
6/11	Sale	Sturgis, Goshen & St.Louis to New York Central
7/21	F.Sale	Wabash RR to Wabash Ry (*See* inc. 10/22; A,159:207-217)
10/11	Diss.	Jackson & Battle Creek Traction (filed 11/30; B,14)

10/11	Diss.	Jackson Consolidated Traction (filed 11/30; B,14)
10/11	Diss.	Michigan Traction (filed 11/30; B,14)
10/22	Inc.	Wabash Ry (filed 3/4/1916; A,159:207-217)
10/27	S.Inc.	Garden Bay (filed 2/2/1916; B,13)
12/24	A-Inc.	Delray Connecting (filed 2/19/1916; A,158:388-391)
12/31	Diss.	Michigan United Traction (filed 1/?/1916; G,42)

1916

1/1	Lease	Grand Rapids, Holland & Chicago to Michigan Ry
1/1	Lease	Lansing & Northeastern by Michigan United Rys to Michigan Ry
1/20	A-Inc.	Detroit, Bay City & Western (filed 5/29; A,163:211-213; B,12)
3/20	Inc.	Highland Park & Royal Oak (filed 4/8; A,161:31-33; B,13)
4/17	A-Inc.	Detroit, Toledo & Milwaukee (filed 8/3; A,166:25-26)
5/1	Lease	Toledo-Detroit to Detroit, Toledo & Ironton
5/31	X-Lease	Kalamazoo, Lake Shore & Chicago Ry by Michigan Ry
7/18	A-Inc.	Detroit & Highland Park (filed 8/18; A,166:344-345; B,12)
7/27	A-Inc.	Iron River, Stambaugh & Crystal Falls (filed 8/26; B,14)
8/21	S.Inc.	Detroit, Armada & Northern (filed 9/25; B,12)
9/15	Cons.	Grand River Valley into Michigan Central
9/20	Cons.	Detroit & Charlevoix into Michigan Central
9/27	Cons.	Kalamazoo & South Haven; Bay City & Battle Creek; Detroit & Bay City; Jackson, Lansing & Saginaw; Michigan Airline RR; and Toledo, Canada Southern & Detroit into Michigan Central
9/29	Cons.	Detroit, Delray & Dearborn into Michigan Central
11/16	Inc.	Sault Ste. Marie & Lake Huron (filed 1/31/1917; A,172:461-463; B,15)
11/15	S.Inc.	Soo-Snows (filed 1/31/1917; B,15)
12/26	Cons.	Detroit Belt Line into Michigan Central

1917

n.d.	Lease	Mohawk Mining Co. RR to Copper Range
2/5	Sale	Highland Park & Royal Oak to Detroit, Almont & Northern
2/15	A-Inc.	Ironwood & Bessemer Ry & Light (filed 3/5/1921; A,137:35-39)
2/20	Inc.	Pennsylvania-Detroit (filed 2/27; A,174:184-186; B,15)
2/27	S.Inc.	Marquette County Electric (filed 4/26; G,30)
3/12	Inc.	Pere Marquette Ry (filed 3/13; A,175:63-70; B,15)
3/15	F.Sale	Pere Marquette RR to Pere Marquette Ry

3/24	F.Sale	Grand Rapids, Belding & Saginaw to Pere Marquette
3/26	F.Sale	Chicago & North Michigan to Pere Marquette
3/27	F.Sale	Pere Marquette of Indiana to Pere Marquette
3/27	F.Sale	Port Huron & Northwestern to Pere Marquette
3/28	F.Sale	Chicago & West Michigan to Pere Marquette and Detroit, Grand Rapids & Western
5/1	Sale	Traverse City and Muskegon, Grand Rapids & Indiana to Grand Rapids & Indiana (eff. 5/1)
5/28	Inc.	Flint & Great Lakes (filed 6/1; A,178:479-480; B,13)
5/31	Inc.	Monroe Connecting (filed 6/8; A,179:129-131; B,14)
9/1	Inc.	Port Huron & Detroit (filed 9/28; A,182:436-438)
9/18	A-Inc.	Minneapolis, St. Paul & Sault Ste. Marie (filed 10/29; A,183:484; B,14)
11/6	F.Sale	Wisconsin & Michigan Ry (*See* Inc. 8/1/1918; A,192:585-600)

1918

3/21	Inc.	Muskegon Ry & Navigation (filed 5/22; A,190:469-471; B,14)
3/26	Inc.	Wisconsin & Michigan RR (Wisc. corp.) (filed 8/1; A,192:585-600)
3/27	Inc.	Detroit Connecting (filed 7/13; A,192:265-267; B,12)
4/4	Diss.	Muskegon, Grand Rapids & Indiana (filed 4/24; A,189:521-523; B,14)
4/18	A-Inc.	Delray Connecting (filed 4/26; A,189:578)
5/2	Diss.	Traverse City RR (filed 5/28; A,190:581-583)
6/18	A-Inc.	Cincinnati, Saginaw & Mackinaw (filed 7/12; A,192:233-234; B,12)

1919

1/11	S.Inc.	Sault Ste. Marie Traction (filed 1/30; H ?)
4/10	Inc.	Michigan RR (filed 4/17; A,200:262-264; B,14)
4/10	Lease	Grand Rapids, Holland & Chicago, by Michigan Ry, to Michigan RR
5/23	Inc.	Leelanau Transit Co. (filed 6/17; A,203:21-22)
6/9	Lease	Leelanau Transit Co. to Manistee & Northeastern
6/20	A-Inc.	Delray Connecting (filed 10/2; A,207:494-495)
10/17	Inc.	Michigan Northern RR (filed 3/20/1920; A,217:407-410; B,14)
12/18	Diss.	Trans-St. Mary's Traction (filed 1/20/1920; B,15)

1920 —— ————————————

1921

1/14	S.Inc.	Detroit Service-at-Cost (filed 1/17; B,13)
1/25	A-Inc.	Ironwood & Bessemer Ry & Light (filed 3/5; A,237:40-41)
4/18	S.Inc.	Marquette City Ry (filed 4/25; G,30)

5/20	Inc.	Flint Belt (filed 6/6; B,13)
6/11	Inc.	Detroit & Ironton (filed 6/23; B,12)
6/22	Diss.	Michigan Ry (filed 6/30; B,14)
8/10	Bank.	Saginaw-Bay City (filed 8/15; B,15)
10/10	Reinc.	Jackson & Northern (filed 11/10; B,14)
10/15	A-Inc.	Wyandotte Terminal (filed 10/19; A,242:119-120)
12/17	Diss.	Ontonagon & Flintsteel (filed 12/20; B,15)

1922

3/15	A-Inc.	Delray Connecting (filed 3/27; K)
5/15	Sale	Detroit United part to Department of Street Railways [City of Detroit]
5/18	Diss.	Port Huron & Northern (filed 5/22; B,15)
7/18	A-Inc.	Menominee & Marinette Light & Traction (no filing date given; G,35)
8/21	A-Inc.	West Michigan Ry (filed 11/10; B,16)
8/31	Diss.	West Michigan Ry (filed 9/13; B,16)
9/1	Diss.	North Park Bridge Co. (filed 1/29/1923; B,15)
9/21	A-Inc.	Michigan United Rys (filed 9/26; B,14)
12/28	Diss.	Manistee Ry (filed 1/3/1923; B,14)

1923

1/1	Lease	Pennsylvania-Detroit to Pennsylvania
1/25	Inc.	Pontiac Belt (filed 1/30; B,15)
2/5	A-Inc.	Detroit, Mt. Clemens & Marine City (filed 4/16; B,12)
2/5	A-Inc.	Detroit & Lake St. Clair (filed 7/7; B,12)
2/5	A-Inc.	Rapid Ry (filed 7/7; B,15)
2/5	A-Inc.	Port Huron, St. Clair & Marine City (filed 7/7; B,15)
2/6	A-Inc.	Detroit, Jackson & Chicago (filed 4/16; B,13)
2/6	A-Inc.	Detroit United (filed 3/3; B,13)
2/6	A-Inc.	River Rouge (filed 7/7; B,15)
3/6	A-Inc.	Marquette City Ry (filed 5/14; A,241:115-117)
4/13	Diss.	Port Huron Southern (filed 4/25; B,15)
5/13	S.Inc.	City Electric Ry of Port Huron (filed 5/24; B,12)
6/9	O.Inc.	Ford Transportation Co. (filed 6/15; F,10)
8/2	S.Inc.	Michigan Electric Ry (filed 8/3; B,14)
8/9	S.Inc.	Saginaw Transit (filed 9/10; B,15)
8/17	A-Cons.	Munising, Marquette & Southeastern into Lake Superior & Ishpeming (filed 11/22; K)

9/4	A-Inc.	Menominee & Marinette Light & Traction (no filing date given; G,35)
9/22	Diss.	Saginaw-Bay City (filed 9/22; B,15)
11/1	Sale	Michigan RR (part) to Saginaw Transit

1924

1/1	Lease	Detroit & Ironton to Ford Transportation Co.
1/1	X-Lease	Grand Rapids, Holland & Chicago by Michigan RR
2/1	A-Inc.	Detroit & Ironton (filed 4/11; B,12)
2/26	A-Inc.	Rapid Ry (filed 3/7; B,15)
3/18	Diss.	Benton Harbor & St. Joseph Electric (filed 3/18; B,12)
4/12	Diss.	Michigan United Rys (filed 4/25; B,14)
4/30	Diss.	Thumb Ry (filed 5/3; B,15)
6/7	Inc.	Pennsylvania, Ohio & Detroit (eff. 7/1) (filed 8/25; B,15)
7/1	Cons.	Pennsylvania-Detroit into Pennsylvania, Ohio & Detroit (filed 8/25; B,15)
9/14	Diss.	Grand Rapids, Kalkaska & Southeastern (filed 10/14; B,13)
10/28	Rec.	Michigan RR

1925

1/26	Inc.	Ludington & Northern (filed 3/10; K)
4/13	A-Inc.	Detroit & Ironton (filed 12/31/1926; B,12)
5/19	$	Ann Arbor by Wabash Ry
5/1	Inc.	Detroit, Caro & Sandusky (filed 5/28; B,12)
7/1	Sale	Blaney & Southern to Wisconsin Land & Lumber
12/19	Inc.	Detroit River Subways (filed 6/1/1926; B,13)

1926

4/29	Lease	Pennsylvania, Ohio & Detroit to Pennsylvania RR
5/19	A-Inc.	Ann Arbor (filed 7/26; K)
7/29	Rec.	Grand Rapids, Grand Haven & Muskegon
9/4	Inc.	Manistee & Northeastern (filed 9/4; B,14)
9/27	Lease	Cincinnati Northern to Cleveland, Cinci, Chi & St.Louis
10/20	F.Sale	Grand Rapids, Holland & Chicago to Hyman-Michael Co.
10/26	Diss.	Traverse City, Leelanau & Manistique (eff. 10/31; filed 1/6/1927; B,15; confirm dated 1/10/1927; filed 1/19/1927; B,15)
12/30	Diss.	Grand Rapids, Holland & Chicago (filed 12/16; B,13)

1927

2/23	Diss.	Quincy & Torch Lake (filed 3/5; B,15)
3/31	Inc.	Chicago, Milwaukee, St. Paul & Pacific (Wisc. corp., filed 6/8)
4/11	S.Inc.	Grand Rapids RR (filed 4/11; F,24)
4/11	Sale	Grand Rapids Ry to Grand Rapids RR
5/16	Diss.	Adrian Street (filed 5/25; B,12)
5/17	A-Inc.	Ann Arbor (filed 6/2; K)
5/17	A-Inc.	Menominee & St. Paul (filed 6/2; B,14)
5/18	A-Inc.	Pere Marquette (two filed 6/8; B,15)
5/24	A-Inc.	Grand Rapids RR (filed 5/24; F,24)
6/—	Inc.	United Suburban (articles not found)
6/15	Diss.	Grand Rapids Ry (filed 8/30; B,13)
12/30	Inc.	Connorville & Lake Superior (filed 2/25/1928; B,12)

1928

1/13	Tfr.	Chicago, Milwaukee & St. Paul to Chicago, Milwaukee, St. Paul & Pacific
5/9	Reinc.	Grand Trunk Western (filed 11/1; K)
5/24	A-Inc.	Sault Saint Marie Traction (filed 6/4; H,?)
5/31	Diss.	New Buffalo & Lakeside (filed 8/11; B,15)
8/21	S.Inc.	Twin City Ry (filed 8/22; B,15)
8/25	S.Inc.	City Contract (filed 9/12; B,12)
8/25	S.Inc.	Eastern Michigan (filed 9/12; B,13)
8/29	Diss.	Benton Harbor-St. Joe Ry (filed 8/29; C,10)
9/12	Sale	Detroit, Jackson & Chicago to bondholders
9/20	S.Inc.	Eastern Michigan Toledo (filed 9/22; B,13)
9/22	A-Inc.	Arcadia & Betsey River (filed 3/5/1929; B,12)
11/1	Cons.	Bay City Terminal; Chicago & Kalamazoo Terminal; Detroit, Grand Haven & Milwaukee; Detroit & Huron; Grand Rapids Terminal; Grand Trunk Western Ry; Michigan Air Line Ry; Pontiac, Oxford & Northern; Toledo, Saginaw & Muskegon; and Chicago, Detroit & Canada Grand Trunk Junction into Grand Trunk Western

1929

1/1	Lease	Cincinnati, Saginaw & Mackinaw to Grand Trunk Western by Grand Trunk Railway of Canada (dated 11/15/1928)
1/14	A-Inc.	Erie & Michigan Ry & Navigation (filed 6/14; B,13)
2/4	A-Inc.	Detroit, Jackson & Chicago (filed 2/11; B,13)
3/7	F.Sale	Michigan RR

3/18	S.Inc.	Kalamazoo Transportation Co. (filed 3/30; B,14)
3/19	S.Inc.	Battle Creek Transportation Co. (filed 3/30; B,12)
3/19	S.Inc.	Jackson Transportation Co. (filed 3/30; B, 14)
3/19	S.Inc.	Lansing Transportation Co. (filed 3/20; B, 14)
3/20	*O.Inc.	Michigan Electric Shares Corp. (filing date shown, articles not found)
5/—	$	Pere Marquette by Chesapeake & Ohio
6/25	Lease	Detroit & Ironton to Detroit, Toledo & Ironton
9/10	Diss.	Ford Transportation Co.
10/18	A-Inc.	Grand Trunk Western (filed 12/11; K)
11/18	A-Inc.	Chicago & North Western (filed 11/25; B,12)
12/14	Diss.	Michigan Electric Ry (filed 12/28; B,14)
12/14	Diss.	Michigan RR (filed 1/2/1930; B,14)

1930

n.d.	Cons.	Southern Michigan into Northern Indiana
2/1	Lease	Chicago, Kalamazoo & Saginaw; Cleveland, Cincinnati, Chicago & St. Louis; and Michigan Central to New York Central
4/23	Diss.	Detroit & Lake St. Clair (filed 4/4; B,12)
4/24	Diss.	Toledo, Ottawa Beach & Northern (filed 5/14; B,15)
5/20	A-Inc.	Ann Arbor (filed 5/21; K)
7/1	Diss.	Southern Michigan Ry (filed 9/30; B,15)
9/22	A-Inc.	Toledo-Detroit (filed 10/18/1932; B,15)
11/4	O.Inc.	Algonac Transit (filed 11/4; C,10)
12/31	Diss.	Onaway & North Michigan (filed 1/3/1931; B,15)

1931

5/5	Inc.	Tittabawassee (filed 5/8; B,15)
6/18	Rec.	Eastern Michigan Toledo
11/14	A-Inc.	Detroit, Toledo & Ironton (filed 2/8/1932; K)
12/—	$	Manistee & Northeastern by Pere Marquette
12/1	Diss.	Superior Terminal (filed 1/4/1932; B,15)
12/18	A-Inc.	Detroit & Toledo Shore Line (filed 4/25/1932; K)
12/29	Cons.	Toledo-Detroit and Detroit & Ironton into Detroit, Toledo & Ironton

1932

1/16	A-Inc.	Grand Trunk Western (filed 2/26; K)
5/17	A-Inc.	Pere Marquette (filed 6/2; B,15)
9/15	Diss.	Toledo-Detroit (filed 10/24; B,15)

1933

5/1	A-Inc.	Grand Trunk Western (filed 7/5; K)
5/3	A-Inc.	Menominee & Marinette Light & Traction (filing date not given; B,13)
6/19	Diss.	Michigan Electric Shares (articles not found)
8/3	Inc.	Ohio & Morenci (Ohio corp.)(filed 9/6; B,15)
8/10	Diss.	Houghton County Traction (filing date not given; B,13)
12/12	A-Inc.	Menominee & Marinette Light & Traction (filing date not given; G,35)

1934

1/22	Diss.	Ontonagon & Brule River (filed 2/12/1935; B,15)

1935

1/1	Sale	Hancock & Calumet to Mineral Range
1/15*	Inc.	Boyne City (filing date shown; B,12)
4/15	S.Inc.	Jackson Rapid Transportation (filed 6/7; B,14)
6/29	Bank.	Chicago, Milwaukee, St. Paul & Pacific
9/23	A-Inc.	Coldwater Train (filed 10/3; B,12)
9/24	Diss.	Tittabawas (filed 9/27; B,15)

1936

1/30	Diss.	Twin City Ry (filed 2/17; B,16)
5/21	Diss.	Ontonagon (filed 6/1; B,15)
11/7	Diss.	Jackson Rapid Transportation (filed 11/18; B,14)

1937

6/16	A-Inc.	Copper Range (filed 6/30; K)
8/27	Diss.	Grand Rapids RR (filed 8/27; F,24)

1938

2/10	A-Inc.	Delray Connecting (filed 2/28; A,241:577)
6/30	Cons.	Cincinnati Northern into Cleveland, Cincinnati, Chicago & St. Louis
8/4	Sale	Eastern Michigan to Eastern Michigan Transp.

1939

2/6	Diss.	Wisconsin & Michigan RR (filed 2/14, B,16)
4/25	A-Inc.	Wyandotte Terminal (filed 6/13; A,242:121-122)

1940 —— ————————————————

Date	Action	Entry
1941		
2/13	Diss.	Sault Ste. Marie Terminal (filed 2/20; B,15)
3/30	Diss.	Pontiac Belt (filed 5/20; B,15)
6/11	A-Inc.	Detroit & Western (filed 4/28/1942; A,242:116-118; B,12)
8/6	A-Inc.	Lake Superior & Ishpeming (filed 10/10; K)
12/31	Reinc.	Wabash RR (filed 10/20/1943; K)
1942		
1/12	A-Inc.	Erie & Michigan Ry & Nav (filed 5/14; B,13)
4/28	A-Inc.	Wyandotte Terminal (filed 5/25; A,242:125)
11/24	A-Inc.	Wyandotte Terminal (filed 2/4/1943; A,242:155-156)
1943		
1/1	Sale	Cincinnati, Saginaw & Mackinaw to Grand Trunk Western
5/5	A-Inc.	Kalamazoo, Allegan & Grand Rapids (filed 6/21; K)
1944		
7/18*	Reinc.	Minneapolis, St. Paul & Sault Ste. Marie (filing date)
1945		
5/22	A-Inc.	Wabash RR (filed 8/28; K)
11/26	X-Bank.	Chicago, Milwaukee, St. Paul & Pacific (filed 1/29/1946; eff. 1/1/1944; K)
1946	——	——————————————
1947		
4/1	Cons.	Pere Marquette into Chesapeake & Ohio (dated 2/19/1946) (filed 6/6; B,15)
10/7	Cons.	Escanaba, Iron Mountain & Western into Chicago & Northwestern
1948		
1949		
1/—	Sale	Erie & Michigan Ry & Navigation to Detroit & Mackinac
4/25	A-Inc.	Lake Superior & Ishpeming (filed 6/12; K)
10/18	Inc.	Duluth, South Shore & Atlantic (filed 12/1; K)
11/1	Cons.	Mineral Range to Duluth, South Shore & Atlantic
12/27	Diss.	St. Clair & Western (filed 12/29; B,15)
1950	——	——————————————

1951	——	——————————————
1952		
9/1	Sale	Sainte Marie Union Depot to Duluth, South Shore & Atlantic and Minneapolis, St. Paul & Sault Ste. Marie
1953		
2/2	Diss.	Sainte Marie Union Depot (filed 5/7; B,15)
11/2	A-Inc.	Detroit, Caro & Sandusky (filed 11/30; B,12)
11/20	O.Inc.	Penndel Co. (Pennsylvania Corp.)
12/1	Cons.	Grand Rapids & Indiana into Penndel (filed 9/27/1954; B,13)
12/23	Cons.	Menominee & Marinette Light & Traction into Wisconsin Public Service (filing date not given; G,35)
1954		
2/19	Reinc.	Wisconsin Central RR (Minn. corp.) (filed 4/6; B,16)
10/13	Cons.	Detroit Union RR Depot into Penndel
12/28	With.	Ohio & Morenci (filed 12/30; B,15)
1955		
2/1	Inc.	Ludington & Northern (filed 2/11; K)
5/10	A-Inc.	Ludington & Northern (filed 6/22; K)
8/23	Cons.	Muskegon Ry & Navigation into Grand Trunk Western
10/26	Cons.	Pennsylvania, Ohio & Detroit into Connecting (filed 5/31/1956; eff. 12/9/1956; B,15)
11/30	Cons.	Flint Belt and Manistee & Northeastern into Chesapeake & Ohio (filed 12/8; B,13[FB], B,14[M&NE])
11/30	Lease	Leelanau Transit by Manistee & Northeastern assigned to Chesapeake & Ohio
1956		
5/22	A-Inc.	Wabash RR (filed 6/18; K)
1957	——	——————————————
1958		
3/31	Cons.	St. Clair Tunnel to Canadian National (dated 2/18; filed 3/31; B,15)
3/31	Diss.	St. Clair Tunnel (filed 4/2; B,15)
11/20	Diss.	Detroit & Western (filed 11/24/1959; B,12)

1959

6/18	A-Inc.	Detroit, Hillsdale & South Western (filed 8/19; B,13)

1960

12/30	Inc.	Soo Line (filed 2/2/1961; K)

1961

1/1	Cons.	Wisconsin Central and Minneapolis, St. Paul & Sault Ste. Marie into Soo Line (filed 2/2; B,16)
3/28	Diss.	Detroit, Hillsdale & South Western (filed 9/1; B,13)

1962

12/1	Inc.	Marquette & Huron Mountain (filed 6/27/1963; K)

1963

3/5	Inc.	Cadillac & Lake City (Delaware corp.) (filed 3/8; K)
8/29	$	Wabash RR to Detroit, Toledo & Ironton of Ann Arbor

1964

10/16	Lease	Wabash RR by Norfolk & Western (filed 8/16/1965; K)

1965 —— ————————

1966 —— ————————

1967 —— ————————

1968

2/1	Cons.	New York Central and Pennsylvania into Pennsylvania, New York Central Transportation (dated 1/12/1962; filed 3/6/1968, K)
2/28	Inc.	Penn Central (filed 8/6; K)
3/20	A-Inc.	Delray Connecting (filed 5/3; K)

1969

7/1	Cons.	Battle Creek & Sturgis into Penndel Co.
8/1	Cons.	Detroit, Toledo & Milwaukee; Lansing Manufacturers; Lansing Transit into Penndel Co.

1970

3/31	$	Wabash by Pennsylvania Co. to Norfolk & Western
6/21	Bank.	Penn Central Co. and Penn Central Transp. Co.
9/21	O.Inc.	Grand Trunk Inds. (Delaware corp.)

1971

6/24	O.Inc.	Chicago Milwaukee corp. (Delaware corp.)
11/18	O.Inc.	Grand Trunk Corp.

1972

1/14	Exch.	Chicago, Milwaukee, St. Paul & Pacific to Chicago Milwaukee corp.
5/—	Inc.	Chicago & North Western Transportation
6/1	Exch.	Chicago & North Western to Chicago & North Western Transp.

1973

2/26	Inc.	Chessie System (Virginia corp.)
5/22	A-Inc.	Wabash RR (filed 8/2; K)
6/15	Exch.	Chesapeake & Ohio to Chessie System
10/15	Bank.	Ann Arbor
10/15	A-Inc.	Ann Arbor (filed 12/15; K)

1974

2/28	Reinc.	Cadillac & Lake City (Delaware corp.) (dated 2/7/1975; filed 10/5/1978; K)

1975

5/13	A-Inc.	Ludington & Northern (filed 5/19; K)

1976

1/27	Inc.	Hillsdale County RR (filed 1/29; K)
2/10	Inc.	Consolidated Rail (Pennsylvania corp.)(filed 3/31; K)
3/18	Inc.	Michigan Northern Ry (filed 3/22; K)
4/1	Sale	Penn Central Transportation and leased lines (part) to Consolidated Rail, Grand Trunk Western, and National RR Passenger
4/1	Sale	Ann Arbor (part) to State of Michigan and Grand Trunk Western
4/1	Opg.Ag.	State of Michigan with Consolidated Rail, Hillsdale County RR, and Michigan Northern
4/26	A-Inc.	Lake Superior & Ishpeming (filed 8/15/1978; K)
5/22	Inc.	Boyne Valley (filed 6/23; K)
6/21	Inc.	Adrian Clinton & Southern (filed 6/25; K)

1977

3/9	Inc.	Lenawee County RR (filed 3/15; K)
4/26	Inc.	Tuscola & Saginaw Bay (filed 5/31; K)
8/25	A-Inc.	Lake Superior & Ishpeming (filed 8/15/1978; K)

8/27	Inc.	Michigan Interstate Ry (filed 8/31; K)
10/1	Opg.Ag.	State of Michigan with Lenawee County RR, Michigan Interstate, and Tuscola & Saginaw Bay
12/5	A-Inc.	Lenawee County RR (filed 12/16; K)
12/19	Bank.	Chicago, Milwaukee, St. Paul & Pacific

1978

1/3	A-Inc.	Hillsdale County RR (filed 1/13; K)
1/3	A-Inc.	Lenawee County RR (filed 1/13; K)
3/28	Inc.	Southwestern Michigan (filed 3/29; K)
7/11	Inc.	Fenn Valley (filed 9/15; K)
10/24	Inc.	Penn Central Corp. (filed 10/23; K)
10/28	Inc.	Kent, Barry, Eaton Connecting (filed 11/2; K)

1979

2/6	Sale	Detroit, Toledo & Ironton (part) to Norfolk & Western
2/8	Sale	Detroit, Toledo & Ironton (part) to Lenawee County
6/15	A-Inc.	Penn Central Corp. (filed 8/6; K)
7/15	Opg.Ag.	State of Michigan with Kent, Barry, Eaton Connecting
9/4	Inc.	Upper Peninsula & Green Bay (filed 12/13; K)
11/8	A-Inc.	Michigan Interstate (filed 12/3; K)
12/28	Diss.	Copper Range (filed 4/22/1980; K)

1980

3/10	Opg.Ag.	Chicago, Milwaukee, St. Paul & Pacific (Mich. lines) by Escanaba & Lake Superior
7/—	Sale	Ann Arbor (part) to State of Michigan
7/23	Inc.	Norfolk Southern Corp. (Virginia corp.)
8/7	Inc.	Wasepi (filed 10/31; K)
9/—	Sale	Penn Central Corp. (part) to State of Michigan
9/29	Sale	Chicago, Milwaukee, St. Paul & Pacific (Mich. Lines) to Escanaba & Lake Superior
11/1	Inc.	CSX Corp.

1981

3/12	Inc.	Southern, Kent & Pacific (filed 5/13; K)
6/26	Cons.	Detroit & Toledo Shore Line into Grand Trunk Western (filed 10/1; K)
10/19	Inc.	Del-Par (filed 10/19; K)
11/23	Inc.	United RR (Delaware corp.) (filed 12/16; K)

12/7*	A-Inc.	Penn Central Corp. (undated; filing date shown; K)
12/18	Cons.	Chicago, Kalamazoo & Saginaw; Fort Wayne & Jackson; and non-Mich. companies into United RR (filed 12/21; eff. 12/31; K)
12/31	Cons.	Cleveland, Cincinnati, Chicago & St. Louis into Penn Central Corp. (filed 3/2/82; K)

1982

2/9	Sale	Chesapeake & Ohio (part) to State of Michigan
4/5	Inc.	Michigan & Western (filed 4/5; K)
6/1	Exch.	Norfolk & Western (and Southern Ry) to Norfolk Southern
8/12	Cons.	Kalamazoo, Allegan & Grand Rapids into United (filed 8/12; K)
8/10	O.Inc.	Southern Michigan Railroad Society (filed 8/10; K)
8/31	A-Inc.	Ann Arbor (filed 11/3; K)
9/—	Sale	Penn Central Corp. (part) to State of Michigan
9/—	Sale	Escanaba & Lake Superior (some lines of Chicago, Milwaukee, St. Paul & Pacific) to State of Michigan

1983

3/28	Diss.	Wyandotte Terminal (filed 3/28; K)
4/25	A-Inc.	Lake Superior & Ishpeming (filed 6/30; K)
6/8	O.Inc.	Michigan-Wisconsin Transportation (filed 6/9; K)
6/14	Cons.	Detroit, Toledo & Ironton into Grand Trunk Western (filed 12/29; K)
7/—	Sale	Escanaba & Lake Superior (some lines of Chicago, Milwaukee, St. Paul & Pacific) to State of Michigan

1984

1/31	Inc.	Coe Rail
2/15	Sale	Penn Central Corp. (part) to State of Michigan
5/31	Cons.	Detroit Terminal into Consolidated Rail
8/—	Sale	Grand Trunk Western (part) to Coe Rail
12/—	Sale	Port Huron & Detroit to Chesapeake & Ohio
12/31	Exch.	Soo Line RR to Soo Line Corp.

1985

3/25	Inc.	Huron & Eastern
3/27	O.Inc.	CNW Corp. (Delaware corp.)
4/30	Sale	Canada Southern and Detroit River Tunnel Co. (by Consolidated Rail) to Canadian National and Canadian Pacific jointly
6/21	Exch.	Chicago & Northwestern Transp. to CNW Corp. (dated 4/19)

1986

1/1	Sale	Chicago, Milwaukee, St. Paul & Pacific (non-Mich. lines) to Soo Line RR
3/27	Sale	CSX Transp. (part) to Huron & Eastern
7/1	Inc.	CSX Transportation Co.
8/18	Sale	CSX Transp. (part) to Southwestern Michigan (KLS&C line)

1987

3/13	Inc.	Wisconsin Central Ltd. (Illinois corp.)
7/15	Inc.	Central Michigan
8/6	Sale	Ann Arbor (part) to State of Michigan
9/2	Cons.	Chessie System into CSX Transportation
9/4	Sale	Grand Trunk Western (part) to Central Michigan
9/21	Sale	Soo Line RR (part) to State of Michigan
10/11	Sale	Soo Line RR (Mich. lines) to Wisconsin Central Ltd.
12/16	Inc.	Mid-Michigan
12/18	Sale	CSX Transp. (part) to Mid-Michigan

1988

12/22	Sale	CSX Transp. (part) to Huron & Eastern

1989

7/13	Inc.	Coopersville & Marne
12/14	Sale	Central Michigan (part) to Coopersville & Marne

1990

2/—	Sale	CSX Transp. (part) to Southwestern Michigan (KLS&C line)
7/31	Inc.	Alanson & Petoskey
9/27	Inc.	Michigan Shore
12/12	Sale	Central Michigan (part) to Michigan Shore

1991

1/14	Inc.	Adrian & Blissfield
2/1	Opg.Ag.	State of Michigan with Adrian & Blissfield

CORPORATE ACTIONS BY YEAR

Year	Charter	Amend	Inc	Sale	Lease
1830	1	—	—	—	—
1831	—	—	—	—	—
1832	1	—	—	—	—
1833	2	—	—	—	—
1834	2	2	—	—	—
1835	4	5	—	—	—
1836	11	1	—	—	—
1837	4	3	—	1	—
1838	4	2	—	—	—
1839	—	3	—	—	—
Decade	***29***	***16***	***0***	***1***	***0***

Year	Charter	Amend	Inc	Sale	Lease
1840	1	4	—	2	—
1841	1	—	—	—	—
1842	—	—	—	—	—
1843	—	—	—	—	—
1844	1	1	—	1	—
1845	—	2	—	—	—
1846	6	2	—	2	—
1847	6	2	—	—	—
1848	4	3	—	—	—
1849	—	2	—	—	1
Decade	***19***	***16***	***0***	***5***	***1***

Year	Charter	Amend	Inc	Sale	Lease	Cons	Forecl
1850	1	1	—	—	—	—	—
1851	—	3	—	—	—	—	—
1852	—	—	—	—	—	—	—
1853	—	—	—	—	—	—	—
1854	—	—	—	—	—	—	—
1855	2	4	12	—	—	1	—
1856	—	—	8	—	1	—	—
1857	—	2	8	—	1	3	—
1858	—	3	2	1	—	—	—
1859	—	1	—	—	1	—	1
Decade	***3***	***14***	***30***	***1***	***3***	***4***	***1***

Year	RR Inc	TrRy Inc	StRy Inc	Amend	Sale /Tf	Lease	Cons	Forecl Sale
1860	3	—	—	—	—	—	—	1
1861	—	—	—	—	—	—	—	—
1862	4	—	—	—	—	—	—	1
1863	3	2	1	3	—	—	—	—
1864	5	3	1	1	—	1	1	—
1865	8	3	—	2	—	—	—	—
1866	7	2	1	1	1	—	—	—
1867	6	2	—	1	1	—	—	1
1868	12	—	2	3	—	—	2	—
1869	29	1	2	4	—	1	3	—
Decade	***77***	***13***	***7***	***15***	***2***	***2***	***6***	***3***

Year	RR Inc	TrRy Inc	StRy Inc	Amend	Sale /Tf	Lease	Cons	Forecl Sale
1870	19	—	—	3	—	2	3	—
1871	28	—	—	10	—	2	3	—
1872	22	3	1	5	1	1	4	—
1873	8	—	6	4	1	—	2	—
1874	4	1	4	1	—	1	—	—
1875	3	2	2	3	—	—	—	4
1876	7	—	1	1	1	—	—	1
1877	6	—	2	1	—	—	—	1
1878	11	2	3	4	1		2	3
1879	20	—	—	3	—	3	—	4
Decade	***128***	***8***	***19***	***35***	***4***	***9***	***14***	***13***

Year	RR Inc	TrRy Inc	StRy Inc	Amend	Sale /Tf	Lease	Cons	Forecl Sale
1880	20	—	2	5	2	1	1	1
1881	19		2	10	2	2	1	1
1882	19	1	3	13	2	1	2	—
1883	19	3	—	9	2	3	2	1
1884	12	—	2	1	3	—	3	—
1885	10	1	3	2	—	1	—	—
1886	28	1	8	5	4	2	4	3
1887	18	2	9	13	2	1	3	—
1888	16	2	4	10	—	2	1	2
1889	23	3	5	15	3	2	—	6
Decade	***184***	***13***	***38***	***83***	***20***	***15***	***17***	***14***

Year	RR Inc	TrRy Inc	StRy Inc	Amend	Sale /Tf	Lease	Cons	Forecl Sale
1890	13	1	13	4	2	4	2	—
1891	17	2	11	9	3	2	—	—
1892	8	2	12	11	3	—	1	—
1893	13	—	5	1	5	1	—	—
1894	8	1	9	3	2	1	—	—
1895	10	4	7	3	3	3	—	—
1896	6	2	3	5	1	2	—	—
1897	9	1	8	10	2	1	2	1
1898	11	4	8	7	2	1	1	—
1899	12	2	18	8	6	1	—	—
Decade	***107***	***19***	***94***	***61***	***29***	***16***	***6***	***1***

Total	RR Inc	TrRy Inc	StRy Inc	Amend	Sale /Tf	Lease	Cons	Forecl Sale
1830-1899	***526***	***53***	***158***	***240***	***62***	***46***	***47***	***32***

Year	RR Inc	TrRy Inc	StRy Inc	Amend	Sale /Tf	Lease	Cons	Forecl Sale
1900	10	10	14	9	2	1	1	1
1901	22	5	24	18	9	1	1	1
1902	9	2	1	10	3	1	1	—
1903	11	2	10	10	5	—	—	1
1904	13	5	7	7	2	1	—	—
1905	17	6	8	7	1	3	—	2
1906	11	4	4	3	4	2	1	1
1907	5		6	8	3	4	1	3
1908	6	2	2	6	2	1	—	—
1909	4	6	2	4	3	2	—	—
Decade	***108***	***42***	***78***	***82***	***34***	***16***	***5***	***9***

Year	RR Inc	TrRy Inc	StRy Inc	Amend	Sale /Tf	Lease	Cons	Forecl Sale
1910	5	—	3	4	—	1	—	1
1911	2	2	2	2	1	1	—	—
1912	6	—	2	5	1	3	1	—
1913	4	—	3	4	2	—	—	1
1914	3	—	3	7	1	—	—	—
1915	1	1	1	3	2	—	1	1
1916	2	—	2	4	—	3	5	—
1917	5	—	1	2	2	1	—	7
1918	3	—	—	2	—	—	—	—
1919	3	—	1	1	—	2	—	—
Decade	***34***	***3***	***18***	***34***	***9***	***11***	***7***	***10***

Year	RR Inc	TrRy Inc	StRy Inc	Amend	Sale /Tf	Lease	Cons	Forecl Sale
1920	—	—	—	—	—	—	—	—
1921	3	—	2	2	—	—	—	—
1922	—	—	—	4	1	—	—	—
1923	1	—	3	10	1	1	—	—
1924	1	—	—	2	—	1	1	—
1925	3	—	—	1	1	—	—	—
1926	1	—	—	1	—	2	—	1
1927	3	—	1	4	1	—	—	—
1928	1	—	4	2	2	—	1	—
1929	—	—	4	4	—	2	—	1
Decade	***13***	***0***	***14***	***30***	***6***	***6***	***2***	***2***

Year	RR Inc	TrRy Inc	StRy Inc	Amend	Sale /Tf	Lease	Cons	Forecl Sale
1930	—	—	—	2	—	1	1	—
1931	1	—	—	2	—	—	1	—
1932	—	—	—	2	—	—	—	—
1933	1	—	—	3	—	—	—	—
1934	—	—	—	—	—	—	—	—
1935	1	—	1	1	1	—	—	—
1936	—	—	—	—	—	—	—	—
1937	—	—	—	1	—	—	—	—
1938	—	—	—	1	1	—	1	—
1939	—	—	—	1	—	—	—	—
Decade	***3***	***0***	***1***	***13***	***2***	***1***	***3***	***0***

Year	RR Inc	TrRy Inc	StRy Inc	Amend	Sale /Tf	Lease	Cons	Forecl Sale
1940	—	—	—	—	—	—	—	—
1941	1	—	—	2	—	—	—	—
1942	—	—	—	3	—	—	—	—
1943	—	—	—	1	1	—	—	—
1944	1	—	—	—	—	—	—	—
1945	—	—	—	1	—	—	—	—
1946	—	—	—	—	—	—	—	—
1947	—	—	—	—	—	—	2	—
1948	—	—	—	—	—	—	—	—
1949	1	—	—	1	1	—	1	—
Decade	***3***	***0***	***0***	***8***	***2***	***0***	***3***	***0***

Year	RR Inc	TrRy Inc	StRy Inc	Amend	Sale /Tf	Lease	Cons	Forecl Sale
1950	—	—	—	—	—	—	—	—
1951	—	—	—	—	—	—	—	—
1952	—	—	—	—	1	—	—	—
1953	—	—	—	1	—	—	2	—
1954	1	—	—	—	—	—	1	—
1955	1	—	—	1	—	1	3	—
1956	—	—	—	1	—	—	—	—
1957	—	—	—	—	—	—	—	—
1958	—	—	—	—	—	—	1	—
1959	—	—	—	1	—	—	—	—
Decade	***2***	***0***	***0***	***4***	***1***	***1***	***7***	***0***

Year	RR Inc	TrRy Inc	StRy Inc	Amend	Sale /Tf	Lease	Cons	Forecl Sale
1960	1	—	—	—	—	—	—	—
1961	—	—	—	—	—	—	1	—
1962	1	—	—	—	—	—	—	—
1963	1	—	—	—	—	—	—	—
1964	—	—	—	—	—	1	—	—
1965	—	—	—	—	—	—	—	—
1966	—	—	—	—	—	—	—	—
1967	—	—	—	—	—	—	—	—
1968	1	—	—	1	—	—	1	—
1969	—	—	—	—	—	—	2	—
Decade	***4***	***0***	***0***	***1***	***0***	***1***	***4***	***0***

Year	RR Inc	TrRy Inc	StRy Inc	Amend	Sale /Tf	Lease	Cons	Forecl Sale
1970	—	—	—	—	—	—	—	—
1971	—	—	—	—	—	—	—	—
1972	1	—	—	—	—	—	—	—
1973	1	—	—	2	—	—	—	—
1974	1	—	—	—	—	—	—	—
1975	—	—	—	1	—	—	—	—
1976	5	—	—	1	2	—	—	—
1977	3	—	—	2	—	—	—	—
1978	4	—	—	2	—	—	—	—
1979	1	—	—	2	2	—	—	—
Decade	***16***	***0***	***0***	***10***	***4***	***0***	***0***	***0***

Year	RR Inc	TrRy Inc	StRy Inc	Amend	Sale /Tf	Lease	Cons	Forecl Sale
1980	3	—	—	—	3	—	—	—
1981	3	—	—	—	1	—	3	—
1982	1	—	—	1	3	—	1	—
1983	—	—	—	1	1	—	1	—
1984	1	—	—	—	3	—	1	—
1985	1	—	—	—	1	—	—	—
1986	1	—	—	—	3	—	—	—
1987	3	—	—	—	5	—	1	—
1988	—	—	—	—	1	—	—	—
1989	1	—	—	—	1	—	—	—
Decade	***14***	***0***	***0***	***2***	***22***	***0***	***7***	***0***

Total	RR Inc	TrRy Inc	StRy Inc	Amend	Sale /Tf	Lease	Cons	Forecl Sale
1900-1989	197	0	111	184	80	36	38	21
1830-1989	723	53	269	424	142	82	85	53

COUNTY LISTINGS OF COMPANIES

This chapter lists, for each county in Michigan, those companies that operated a railroad line (shown in capital letters) and those that proposed to operate (shown in lower-case letters). The names used in this section are not the full legal names but are sufficient to locate the company in chapter 2.

The articles of incorporation of some pre-1900 companies described their purpose by naming the then-existing counties in which the company would operate. A few of these counties have been renamed or combined. Some counties, particularly in the Upper Peninsula, were organized after the company's incorporation. This listing describes the corporate intentions based on the present structure of 83 counties.

At the end of the county listings are three groups of railroad companies which did not fit into the major listing: 1. companies which did not operate a rail line and also did not specify counties of operation in the corporate articles, and companies which did operate but the county in which they operated can not now be determined; 2. reorganizing companies which were created to convey a property from one company to another and did not operate the property in its name during ownership; and 3. holding companies which owned incorporated railroad companies, but operated them in the name of the held company and not in the name of the holding company.

ALCONA COUNTY (001)

ALGER & CO.
ALGER, SMITH & CO.
Alpena & Michigan South-western
Alpena & South Western
Amboy & Traverse Bay
Amboy, Lansing & Traverse Bay
AU SABLE & NORTHWESTERN
BAY CITY & ALPENA
[J. R.] BEARD & CO.
BLACK RIVER
DETROIT & MACKINAC
DETROIT, BAY CITY & ALPENA
FLETCHER, PACK & CO.
HARRIS BROS.
Killmaster
Lake Huron & Western
MUDGETT, D. B.
NEVIN, D[AVID]
PLATT & MILLER
POTTS LOGGING RY CO.

ALGER COUNTY (002)

BURT & GAMBLE LUMBER CO.
CLEVELAND CLIFFS IRON CO.
DETROIT, MACKINAC & MARQUETTE
DULUTH, SOUTH SHORE & ATLANTIC
LAKE SUPERIOR & ISHPEMING
Mackinaw & Lake Superior
MANISTIQUE
MANISTIQUE & LAKE SUPERIOR
MANISTIQUE & NORTHERN
MANISTIQUE & NORTHWESTERN
MANISTIQUE LUMBERING CO.
MANISTIQUE, MARQUETTE & NORTHERN
MARQUETTE & SOUTHEASTERN
Marquette, Sault Ste. Marie & Mackinac
MUNISING
MUNISING, MARQUETTE & SOUTHEASTERN
NAHMA & NORTHERN
NORTHWESTERN COOPERAGE & LUMBER CO.
Ohio & Lake Superior
ONOTA CHARCOAL CO.
St. Mary's & Minneapolis
Sault Ste. Marie & Southwestern
SOO LINE
TYOGA LUMBER CO.
WILKIE,
WISCONSIN CENTRAL, LTD.
WISCONSIN LAND & LUMBER CO.
WORCESTER, C. H., CO.

ALLEGAN COUNTY (003)

Allegan & Holland
ALLEGAN & LAKE SHORE
Allegan & Marshall
ALLEGAN & SOUTH EASTERN
Benton Harbor Electric Ry & Transit
Central Michigan RR
CHESAPEAKE & OHIO
Chicago & Michigan Grand Trunk
CHICAGO & MICHIGAN LAKE SHORE
CHICAGO & WEST MICHIGAN
CINCINNATI, JACKSON & MACKINAW RR
CINCINNATI, JACKSON & MACKINAW RY
CINCINNATI NORTHERN
Columbus & Lake Michigan
Columbus, Lima & Milwaukee

CONSOLIDATED RAIL
DETROIT, TOLEDO & MILWAUKEE
DEWING, W. G. & SONS LUMBER CO.
GRAND HAVEN
Grand Rapids & Chicago RR
Grand Rapids & Chicago Ry
GRAND RAPIDS & INDIANA
Grand Rapids & Kalamazoo Electric
Grand Rapids & Kalamazoo Valley
Grand Rapids & Southern
Grand Rapids, Chicago & St. Louis
Grand Rapids Electric
GRAND RAPIDS, HOLLAND & CHICAGO
GRAND RAPIDS, HOLLAND & LAKE MICHIGAN
Grand Rapids, Kalamazoo & South Haven
KALAMAZOO, ALLEGAN & GRAND RAPIDS
Kalamazoo & Allegan
Kalamazoo & Grand Rapids
Kalamazoo & Grand River
Kalamazoo, Lake Shore & Chicago Traction
Kalamazoo River
KELLOGG AND SAWYER (LUMBER CO.)
LAKE SHORE & MICHIGAN SOUTHERN
Lake Shore RR of Western Michigan
Lansing & Lake Michigan
Mackinac & Chicago
MANSFIELD, COLDWATER & LAKE MICHIGAN
MICHIGAN & CHICAGO
Michigan & Chicago Westbound
MICHIGAN & OHIO RR
MICHIGAN CENTRAL
MICHIGAN LAKE SHORE
Michigan Light & Traction
Michigan Northern RR (1869)
MICHIGAN RR
MICHIGAN RY
Michigan Shore & Eastern
Michigan West Shore Traction
NEW YORK CENTRAL
Ohio & Grand Haven
Ohio & Michigan
Ohio, Quincy & Grand Haven
PENN CENTRAL
PENNSYLVANIA
PERE MARQUETTE
Saugatuck & South Haven
SAUGATUCK, DOUGLAS & LAKE SHORE
Southern Michigan Traction
South Haven & Lake Shore
Southwestern Michigan
Toledo & Milwaukee Ry
Trans-Michigan Street
West Michigan Traction Co.

ALPENA COUNTY (004)

ALPENA & HUBBARD LAKE
ALPENA & LONG LAKE
Alpena & Michigan South-western
ALPENA & NORTHERN
Alpena & South Western
Alpena & Western
Alpena, Gaylord & Western
ALPENA PORTLAND CEMENT CO.
Amboy & Traverse Bay
Amboy, Lansing & Traverse Bay
[JAMES] BAIRD & CO.
BAY CITY & ALPENA
BEWICKE, COMSTOCK & CO.
BOYNE CITY, GAYLORD & ALPENA
BROADWELL, HILLIARD
CAMPBELL, E. P., & CO.
CORLIES & THUNDER BAY TRAIN
DETROIT & MACKINAC
DETROIT, BAY CITY & ALPENA
FLETCHER, PACK & CO.
GILCHRIST, F. W.
Grand Rapids, Grayling & Alpena
Grand Rapids, Greenville & Alpena
HURON PORTLAND CEMENT CO.
KENNEDY, D. A.
Michigan Northern Ry (1873)
POTTER, W. H. & E. K.

ANTRIM COUNTY (005)

Alpena & Western
Alpena, Gaylord & Western
Amboy & Traverse Bay
Amboy, Lansing & Traverse Bay
BOYNE CITY & SOUTHEASTERN
BOYNE CITY, GAYLORD & ALPENA
CHESAPEAKE & OHIO
CHICAGO & NORTH MICHIGAN
CHICAGO & WEST MICHIGAN
Cincinnati & Great Northern
COLD SPRINGS
DETROIT & CHARLEVOIX
Detroit, Charlevoix & Escanaba
EAST JORDAN & SOUTHERN
EAST JORDAN LUMBER CO.
Elk Rapids, Williamsburg & Southern
Elk Short Line
GRAND RAPIDS & INDIANA
Grand Rapids & Mackinaw
Grand Rapids & Northern
Grand Rapids, Kalkaska & Southeastern
Grand Rapids, Traverse Bay & Mackinac
Grand Traverse
Grayling & Charlevoix
MANCELONA & NORTH WESTERN

MANCELONA HANDLE CO.
MICHIGAN CENTRAL
Michigan Northern RR (1869)
MICHIGAN NORTHERN RY (1976)
NEW YORK CENTRAL
Northern Michigan Central
PENN CENTRAL
PENNSYLVANIA
PERE MARQUETTE
RAPID RIVER & EASTERN
SILKMAN & HART
Toledo, Ann Arbor & Mackinaw
TUSCOLA & SAGINAW BAY

ARENAC COUNTY (006)

Amboy & Traverse Bay
Amboy, Lansing & Traverse Bay
BAY CITY & ALPENA
DETROIT & MACKINAC
DETROIT, BAY CITY & ALPENA
Erie & Michigan Ry & Navigation
JACKSON, LANSING & SAGINAW
MICHIGAN CENTRAL
NEW YORK CENTRAL
Northern Michigan RR (11/1867)
PENN CENTRAL
SAGINAW BAY & NORTHWESTERN
TAWAS & BAY COUNTY
Toledo, Saginaw & Mackinaw
TURNER, JOE

BARAGA COUNTY (007)

Baraga & Watersmeet
BARAGA LUMBER CO.
BUTTERS, MARSHALL, LUMBER CO.
CHICAGO, MILWAUKEE & ST. PAUL
CHICAGO, MILWAUKEE, ST. PAUL & PACIFIC
DEHAAS, N. N., AND CO.
DULUTH, SOUTH SHORE & ATLANTIC
FORD MOTOR CO.
HEBARD, CHARLES S. (et al)
Houghton & L'Anse
Houghton & Ontonagon
Iron Range & Huron Bay
Ishpeming, L'Anse & Ontonagon
Lake Superior Southern
L'Anse & Ontonagon
L'Anse Bay
Marquette & Ontonagon RR
Marquette & Ontonagon Ry
MARQUETTE, HOUGHTON & ONTONAGON
MILWAUKEE & NORTHERN
Mineral Range & L'Anse Bay
MINERAL RANGE RR
Ohio & Lake Superior
Peninsula
St. Mary's & Minneapolis
SOO LINE
STEARNS AND CULVER LUMBER CO.
Upper Peninsula & Green Bay
Wisconsin & Lake Superior
WISCONSIN CENTRAL, LTD.
Wisconsin, Sault Ste. Marie & Mackinac
ZENITH LUMBER CO.

BARRY COUNTY (008)

Alaska
Battle Creek & Bay City
Battle Creek & Grand Rapids
Battle Creek & Grand Rapids Inland Lakes Traction
Bay City & Battle Creek
Central Michigan RR
Chicago & Michigan Grand Trunk
CHICAGO, KALAMAZOO & SAGINAW
CINCINNATI, JACKSON & MACKINAW RR
CINCINNATI, JACKSON & MACKINAW RY
CINCINNATI NORTHERN
Columbus & Lake Michigan
Columbus, Lima & Milwaukee
Detroit, Howell, Lansing & Grand Rapids
DETROIT, TOLEDO & MILWAUKEE
Grand Haven
Grand Rapids & Kalamazoo Electric
Grand Rapids, Belding & Saginaw
Grand Rapids Electric
GRAND RIVER VALLEY
Grand Trunk RR of Michigan
Hastings, Lowell & Northern Michigan
Kalamazoo, Gull Lake & Northern
Kalamazoo, Lowell & Northern Michigan
KENT, BARRY, EATON CONNECTING
Lansing & Lake Michigan
Lowell & Hastings
Mansfield, Coldwater & Lake Michigan
MICHIGAN & CHICAGO
MICHIGAN & OHIO RR
Michigan & Ohio Ry
MICHIGAN CENTRAL
Michigan Northern RR (1919)
MICHIGAN RR
MICHIGAN RY
NEW YORK CENTRAL
Ohio & Grand Haven
Ohio & Michigan
Ohio, Quincy & Grand Haven
PENN CENTRAL
PERE MARQUETTE
Southwestern Michigan
Toledo & Milwaukee Ry

BAY COUNTY (009)

Battle Creek & Bay City
BAY CITIES CONSOLIDATED
BAY CITY & ALPENA
BAY CITY & BATTLE CREEK
Bay City & Caro
BAY CITY & EAST SAGINAW
Bay City & Midland
Bay City & Port Huron
BAY CITY & PORTSMOUTH
BAY CITY BELT LINE
Bay City, Caro & Eastern
Bay City, Caro & Port Huron
BAY CITY STREET
BAY CITY TERMINAL
BAY CITY TRACTION & ELECTRIC CO.
Bay, Tuscola & Huron
CENTRAL MICHIGAN
CHESAPEAKE & OHIO
Cincinnati & Great Northern
CINCINNATI, SAGINAW & MACKINAW
Columbus, Marshall & Northeastern
DETROIT & BAY CITY
DETROIT & MACKINAC
Detroit & Saginaw River
Detroit, Bay City & Alpena
DETROIT, BAY CITY & WESTERN
Detroit Bay City Traction
Detroit, Pontiac, Lapeer & Northern
FLINT & PERE MARQUETTE
Flint, Saginaw & Bay City
GLENCOE, PINCONNING & LAKE SHORE
Grand Rapids & Bay City
GRAND TRUNK WESTERN
HECLA BELT LINE
HURON & WESTERN
INTERURBAN RY OF SAGINAW
JACKSON, LANSING & SAGINAW
Michigan & Chicago
MICHIGAN CENTRAL
Michigan Northern RR (1919)
MICHIGAN RR
MICHIGAN RY
Midland & Northern
NEW YORK CENTRAL
Northern Michigan RR (11/1867)
Northern Michigan Ry
Ohio & Lake Superior
PENN CENTRAL
PERE MARQUETTE
PINCONNING
Port Huron & Northwestern
Port Huron, Lexington & Western
Saginaw & Bay City
Saginaw & Bay City Rapid Transit
SAGINAW BAY & NORTHWESTERN
SAGINAW-BAY CITY
Saginaw Suburban
SAGINAW VALLEY TRACTION
Southern Electric
TOLEDO, SAGINAW & MACKINAW
Toledo, Saginaw & Muskegon
Union Street
UNITED TRACTION CO.
WEST BAY CITY STREET

BENZIE COUNTY (010)

Alpena, Gaylord & Western
ANN ARBOR
CHESAPEAKE & OHIO
CHICAGO & WEST MICHIGAN
EMPIRE & SOUTH EASTERN
FRANKFORT & SOUTH EASTERN
Frankfort, Crystal Lake & Glenn Arbor
MANISTEE & NORTHEASTERN
MICHIGAN INTERSTATE
Michigan Lake Shore
Owosso & North Western
PERE MARQUETTE
Riverdale & Lake Michigan
SMITH & HULL (LUMBER CO.)
TOLEDO, ANN ARBOR & LAKE MICHIGAN
TOLEDO, ANN ARBOR & NORTH MICHIGAN
TUSCOLA & SAGINAW BAY

BERRIEN COUNTY (011)

Air Line Ry of Michigan
BENTON HARBOR & EASTMAN SPRINGS
BENTON HARBOR & ST. JOSEPH ELECTRIC
Benton Harbor Belt & Terminal
BENTON HARBOR, COLOMA & PAW PAW LAKE
Benton Harbor Electric Ry & Transit
BENTON HARBOR-ST. JOE RY & LIGHT
Benton Harbor Street
Benton Harbor Terminal
BUCHANAN & ST. JOSEPH RIVER
"Central" (of State of Michigan)
CHARLOTTEVILLE LUMBER CO.
CHESAPEAKE & OHIO
Chicago & Michigan Grand Trunk
CHICAGO & MICHIGAN LAKE SHORE
CHICAGO & WEST MICHIGAN
Chicago, Lake Michigan & Eastern
Chicago, Michigan & Indiana Electric
CINCINNATI, WABASH & MICHIGAN
CLEVELAND, CINCINNATI, CHICAGO & ST. LOUIS
CONSOLIDATED RAIL
Constantine & Niles Canal
Detroit & St. Joseph

Dowagiac
Eastern & Northwestern
East Shore & Southwestern
Elgin Terminal
Elkhart & Lake Michigan
Elkhart, Niles & Lake Michigan
Grand Rapids & Chicago RR
Grand Rapids & Chicago Ry
Grand Rapids, Chicago & St. Louis
Grand Trunk RR of Michigan
Grand Trunk Ry of Michigan
INDIANA & LAKE MICHIGAN
Indiana & Michigan
INDIANA, ILLINOIS & IOWA
Interstate
Kalamazoo & Lake Michigan Ry
KALAMAZOO, LAKE SHORE & CHICAGO RY
Kalamazoo, Lake Shore & Chicago Traction
Kalamazoo, Paw Paw & Lake Michigan
Lake Michigan & Eastern
Lake Michigan & Kalamazoo
Lake Shore RR of Western Michigan
Lake Shore Ry
Mackinac & Chicago
Maumee Branch
Michigan & Chicago
Michigan & Indiana
MICHIGAN CENTRAL
Michigan City, Lakeside & St. Joe
Michigan Electric (1901)
Michigan Light & Traction
Michigan Shore & Eastern
Michigan Terminal Transfer
Michigan West Shore Traction
MILWAUKEE, BENTON HARBOR & COLUMBUS
NATIONAL RAIL PASSENGER
New Buffalo & Lakeside
NEW YORK CENTRAL
Niles & Buchanan
Niles & South Bend
NORTHERN INDIANA
Paw Paw Valley
PENN CENTRAL
PERE MARQUETTE
PERE MARQUETTE OF INDIANA
ROGERS, BARTLETT R.
St Joe River Traction
St. Joseph
St. JOSEPH & BENTON HARBOR STREET
St. Joseph & Benton Harbor Street Train
St. Joseph & Lake Shore Street
St. Joseph River
ST. JOSEPH, SOUTH BEND & SOUTHERN
St. Joseph Terminal
St. Joseph Valley (1848)
ST. JOSEPH VALLEY (1880)
South Bend & Benton Harbor
South Bend & Southern Michigan
South Bend, Niles & St. Joseph
South-Eastern & North-Western Transcontinental
"Southern" (of State of Michigan)
SOUTHERN MICHIGAN
South Haven & Paw Paw Lake Electric
TWIN CITY (1928)
Union Electric Co.
Union Street Ry of Benton Harbor and St. Joseph
West Michigan
West Michigan Traction
WILKINSON, JOSEPH N.

BRANCH COUNTY (012)

Battle Creek & Coldwater Electric
Battle Creek & Southeastern
BATTLE CREEK & STURGIS
Battle Creek, Coldwater & Southern
Camden Southern
Central Michigan RR
Coldwater & Central Michigan
Coldwater, Marshall & Mackinaw
COLDWATER TRAIN
Columbus & Lake Michigan
Columbus, Lima & Milwaukee
CONSOLIDATED RAIL
Detroit, Hillsdale & Indiana
Eastern & Northwestern
FORT WAYNE & JACKSON
FORT WAYNE, JACKSON & SAGINAW
Grand Rapids Electric
Grand Trunk Ry of Michigan
HILLSDALE COUNTY
Jackson, Fort Wayne & Cincinnati
LAKE SHORE & MICHIGAN SOUTHERN
Mansfield, Coldwater & Lake Michigan
Marshall & Coldwater
Maumee Branch
MICHIGAN AIR LINE RR
MICHIGAN CENTRAL
Michigan Extension
Michigan-Indiana Traction
Michigan Inter-Urban
MICHIGAN SOUTHERN
MICHIGAN SOUTHERN & NORTHERN INDIANA
NEW YORK CENTRAL
Ohio & Central Michigan
Ohio & Michigan
Ohio & Southern Michigan
Ohio, Quincy & Grand Haven
PENN CENTRAL
ST. LOUIS, STURGIS & BATTLE CREEK
"Southern" (of State of Michigan)
Toledo & Michigan Electric
Tri-State Rys of Michigan

CALHOUN COUNTY (013)

Air Line Ry of Michigan
Albion, Charlotte, Northern
Allegan & Marshall
Amboy, Lansing & Traverse Bay
Battle Creek & Bay City
Battle Creek & Coldwater Electric
Battle Creek & Grand Rapids
Battle Creek & Grand Rapids Inland Lakes Traction
Battle Creek & Marshall Traction
Battle Creek & Southeastern
BATTLE CREEK & STURGIS
Battle Creek, Coldwater & Southern
BATTLE CREEK ELECTRIC
BATTLE CREEK RY
BATTLE CREEK STREET
BATTLE CREEK TRANSPORTATION
Bay City & Battle Creek
Calhoun County
"CENTRAL" (of State of Michigan)
Central Michigan RR
CHICAGO & GRAND TRUNK
CHICAGO & LAKE HURON
CINCINNATI, JACKSON & MACKINAW RR
CINCINNATI, JACKSON & MACKINAW RY
CINCINNATI NORTHERN
CITIZENS STREET RY OF BATTLE CREEK
Coldwater & Central Michigan
Coldwater, Marshall & Mackinaw
Columbus & Lake Michigan
Columbus, Lima & Milwaukee
Columbus, Marshall & Northeastern
CONSOLIDATED RAIL
Detroit & Chicago Traction
Detroit & St. Joseph
DETROIT, TOLEDO & MILWAUKEE
Erie & Kalamazoo
Grand Haven
Grand Rapids & South Michigan
Grand Rapids Electric
Grand Trunk Ry of Michigan
GRAND TRUNK WESTERN
Jackson & Albion Electric
JACKSON & BATTLE CREEK TRACTION
Jonesville, Marshall & Grand River
LAKE SHORE & MICHIGAN SOUTHERN
Lansing & Battle Creek Traction
Manchester & Homer
Mansfield, Coldwater & Lake Michigan
Marshall & Coldwater
Marshall & Northern
MICHIGAN AIR LINE RR
MICHIGAN & CHICAGO
Michigan & Indiana Traction
MICHIGAN & OHIO RR
Michigan & Ohio Ry
MICHIGAN CENTRAL
Michigan Central Traction
MICHIGAN ELECTRIC (1923)
Michigan Extension
Michigan-Indiana Traction
Michigan Inter-Urban
MICHIGAN RR
MICHIGAN RY
MICHIGAN TRACTION
Michigan Traction Extension
MICHIGAN UNITED RYS
MICHIGAN UNITED TRACTION
NEW YORK CENTRAL
NORTHERN CENTRAL MICHIGAN
Ohio & Grand Haven
Ohio & Michigan
Ohio & Southern Michigan
Ohio, Quincy & Grand Haven
PENINSULAR
Peninsular Ry Extension
PENN CENTRAL
ST. LOUIS, STURGIS & BATTLE CREEK
Toledo & Milwaukee Ry
Toledo & Northwestern
Toledo, Marshall & Northern
Toledo Michigan & Lake Huron

CASS COUNTY (014)

Air Line Ry of Michigan
Chicago & Canada Pacific
CHICAGO & GRAND TRUNK
CHICAGO & LAKE HURON
Chicago, Kalamazoo & Eastern
Chicago, Kalamazoo & Saginaw
Chicago, Lake Michigan & Eastern
CINCINNATI, WABASH & MICHIGAN
CLEVELAND, CINCINNATI, CHICAGO & ST. LOUIS
CONSOLIDATED RAIL
Constantine & Niles Canal
Dowagiac
Eastern & Northwestern
Elkhart & Lake Michigan
Elkhart, Niles & Lake Michigan
Grand Trunk Ry of Michigan
GRAND TRUNK WESTERN
Kalamazoo, Elkhart & South Bend Traction
Lake Michigan & Eastern
Maumee Branch
MICHIGAN AIR LINE RR
MICHIGAN CENTRAL
Michigan Extension
NEW YORK CENTRAL
PENINSULAR
Peninsular Ry Extension

PENN CENTRAL
St Joe River Traction
St. Joseph River
St. Joseph Valley (1848)
South-Eastern & North-Western Transcontinental
"Southern" (of State of Michigan)
West Michigan
West Michigan Traction

CHARLEVOIX COUNTY (015)

Amboy & Traverse Bay
Amboy, Lansing & Traverse Bay
Arms Lake
BAY SPRINGS & SOUTHEASTERN
BOYNE CITY
BOYNE CITY & SOUTHEASTERN
BOYNE CITY, GAYLORD & ALPENA
BOYNE FALLS & NORTHEASTERN
BOYNE VALLEY
CHESAPEAKE & OHIO
CHICAGO & NORTH MICHIGAN
CHICAGO & WEST MICHIGAN
DETROIT & CHARLEVOIX
Detroit, Charlevoix & Escanaba
EAST JORDAN & SOUTHERN
EAST JORDAN LUMBER CO.
FOX [AMOS] & CO.
GRAND RAPIDS & INDIANA
Grand Rapids & Mackinaw
Grand Rapids & Northern
Grand Rapids, Traverse Bay & Mackinac
Grand Traverse
Grayling & Charlevoix
MEDUSA PORTLAND CEMENT CO.
MICHIGAN NORTHERN RY (1976)
Northern Michigan Central
PENN CENTRAL
PENNSYLVANIA
PERE MARQUETTE
Spring Harbor & Boyne Falls
Toledo, Ann Arbor & Mackinaw
TUSCOLA & SAGINAW BAY

CHEBOYGAN COUNTY (016)

Alpena & Northern
Amboy & Traverse Bay
Amboy, Lansing & Traverse Bay
Cheboygan & East Michigan
Cheboygan Southern
Cincinnati & Great Northern
DETROIT & MACKINAC
Detroit & Petoskey
DUNCAN, J. W.
GRAND RAPIDS & INDIANA
GRAND RAPIDS, INDIANA & MACKINAW
JACKSON, LANSING & SAGINAW
MICHIGAN CENTRAL
Michigan Northern RR (1869)
MICHIGAN NORTHERN RY (1976)
NEW YORK CENTRAL
Northern Michigan Central
Northern Michigan RR (11/1867)
Ohio & Lake Superior
PENN CENTRAL
PENNSYLVANIA
Toledo, Saginaw & Mackinaw

CHIPPEWA COUNTY (017)

AMERICAN FUR CO.
BARTLETT LUMBER CO.
CADILLAC CHEMICAL CO.
CADILLAC-SOO LUMBER CO.
Canada, LaCrosse & Southwestern
CHIPPEWA LUMBER CO.
CHIPPEWA PORTAGE CO.
COOK AND WILSON
CULHANE, CON
Detour & Western
DETROIT, MACKINAC & MARQUETTE
DULUTH, SOUTH SHORE & ATLANTIC
Mackinaw & Lake Superior
MCKNIGHT BROS. & TINKER
Menominee & Sault Ste. Marie
MICHIGAN FOREST PRODUCTS CO.
MINNEAPOLIS, ST. PAUL & SAULT STE. MARIE
MINNEAPOLIS, SAULT STE. MARIE & ATLANTIC
Northern Michigan RR (11/1867)
Northern Michigan RR (1901)
Ohio & Lake Superior
St. Ignace, Sault Ste. Marie & Northern
St. Mary's & Minneapolis
Saint Mary's Falls
SAINTE MARIE UNION DEPOT CO.
Sault Ste. Marie
Sault Ste. Marie & Lake Huron
Sault Ste. Marie & Marquette
Sault Ste. Marie & Southwestern
SAULT STE. MARIE BRIDGE CO.
SAULT STE. MARIE STREET
Sault Ste. Marie Terminal
SAULT STE. MARIE TRACTION CO.
SHELDON AND CO.
Soo-Detour
SOO LINE
Soo-Snows
Soo Street
TRANS-ST. MARY'S TRACTION CO.

UNITED STATES GYPSUM CO.
UPPER MICHIGAN LOGGING CO.
WISCONSIN CENTRAL, LTD.

CLARE COUNTY (018)

Alpena & Michigan South-western
Amboy & Traverse Bay
Amboy, Lansing & Traverse Bay
ANN ARBOR
BERRY, JAMES
Central Michigan RR
CHESAPEAKE & OHIO
Cincinnati & Great Northern
Flat River & Houghton Lake
FLINT & PERE MARQUETTE
GEBHART AND ESTABROOK (LUMBER CO.)
Grand Rapids Electric
Grand Rapids, Grayling & Alpena
Grand Rapids, Greenville & Alpena
HACKLEY AND HUME
HALL, EDMUND
HOYT, JESSE
LAKE GEORGE & MUSKEGON RIVER
Lake Superior
LYNES, S. D., & CO.
MICHIGAN INTERSTATE
Michigan Northern Ry (1873)
MURPHY AND DORR
Northern Michigan Central
Owosso & North Western
PERE MARQUETTE
ROSCOMMON LUMBER CO.
SAGINAW & CLARE COUNTY
Toledo & Cadillac
Toledo, Ann Arbor & Cadillac
TOLEDO, ANN ARBOR & NORTH MICHIGAN
TUSCOLA & SAGINAW BAY

CLINTON COUNTY (019)

Alaska
Amboy & Traverse Bay
AMBOY, LANSING & TRAVERSE BAY
ANN ARBOR
Battle Creek & Bay City
CENTRAL MICHIGAN
CHESAPEAKE & OHIO
Chicago, Kalamazoo & Saginaw
Cincinnati & Great Northern
Coldwater & Central Michigan
Columbus, Marshall & Northeastern
Crystal Lake (1900)
DETROIT & MILWAUKEE
DETROIT, GRAND HAVEN & MILWAUKEE
DETROIT, GRAND RAPIDS & WESTERN
Detroit, Howell, Lansing & Grand Rapids
DETROIT, LANSING & LAKE MICHIGAN
DETROIT, LANSING & NORTHERN
GRAND TRUNK WESTERN
IONIA & LANSING
Ionia & Owosso
JACKSON, LANSING & SAGINAW
Lansing, Alma, Mt. Pleasant & Northern
Lansing & St. Johns
LANSING & SUBURBAN TRACTION
Lansing, St. Johns & Mackinac
Lansing, Saint Johns & Northern
Lansing, St. Johns & St. Louis (1897)
LANSING, ST. JOHNS & ST. LOUIS (1900)
Maple Rapids & Lansing
Maple Rapids & Southern
MICHIGAN CENTRAL
MICHIGAN ELECTRIC RY (1923)
Michigan Extension
MICHIGAN INTERSTATE
Michigan Midland
Michigan Northern RR (1919)
MICHIGAN RY
MICHIGAN SUBURBAN
MICHIGAN UNITED RYS
MICHIGAN UNITED TRACTION
NEW YORK CENTRAL
"Northern" (of State of Michigan)
Oakland & Ottawa
Ovid & Traverse Bay
Owosso & North Western
PENN CENTRAL
PERE MARQUETTE
Port Huron & Lake Michigan
Saginaw & Southwestern
Saginaw Bay South Western
Saginaw, Owosso & Lansing
TOLEDO, ANN ARBOR & NORTH MICHIGAN
TUSCOLA & SAGINAW BAY
Westphalia, Hubbardston & Northern

CRAWFORD COUNTY (020)

Amboy, Lansing & Traverse Bay
AU SABLE & NORTHWESTERN
BROWN, ARCHIE
Central Michigan RR
Cincinnati & Great Northern
DETROIT & CHARLEVOIX
DETROIT & MACKINAC
Detroit, Charlevoix & Escanaba
Grand Rapids, Grayling & Alpena
Grand Rapids, Greenville & Alpena
Grand Rapids, Kalkaska & Southeastern
GRASS LAKE & MANISTEE RIVER

Grayling & Charlevoix
GRAYLING, TWIN LAKES & NORTHEASTERN
Houghton Lake & Eastern
JACKSON, LANSING & SAGINAW
MANISTEE & NORTHEASTERN
MICHIGAN CENTRAL
Michigan Northern Ry (1873)
NEW YORK CENTRAL
Northern Michigan Central
Northern Michigan RR (11/1867)
PENN CENTRAL
PORTAGE LAKE & MANISTEE RIVER
PORTAGE LAKE & MUSKEGON RIVER
SALLING-HANSON LUMBER CO.
Toledo, Ann Arbor & Mackinaw
Toledo, Saginaw & Mackinaw
WARD, DAVID E.

DELTA COUNTY (021)

Bay De Noquet & Marquette
Canada, LaCrosse & Southwestern
CHICAGO & NORTH WESTERN
CHICAGO & NORTH WESTERN TRANSPORTATION CO.
DELTA CHEMICAL CO.
Delta Traction Co.
ESCANABA & LAKE SUPERIOR RY (1880)
ESCANABA & LAKE SUPERIOR RY (1898)
ESCANABA ELECTRIC STREET
ESCANABA, IRON MOUNTAIN & WESTERN
ESCANABA TRACTION CO.
Escanaba, Twin Cities & Western
Escanaba Western
GARDEN BAY
Gladstone Street
Iron Mountain & Wisconsin State Line
JACKSON IRON CO.
LAKE MICHIGAN & LAKE SUPERIOR
Lake Superior Ship Canal Railway & Iron Co.
Lakes Superior & Michigan Air Line
MASHEK CHEMICAL & IRON CO.
Menominee & Escanaba
Menominee & Sault Ste. Marie
MINNEAPOLIS, ST. PAUL & SAULT STE. MARIE
MINNEAPOLIS, SAULT STE. MARIE & ATLANTIC
NAHMA & NORTHERN
Northern Michigan RR (11/1867)
PENINSULA
SOO LINE
VAN HARBOR & NORTHERN
VAN HARBOR LAND & LUMBER CO.
Vieux Desert & Lake Superior
WISCONSIN CENTRAL, LTD.

DICKINSON COUNTY (022)

CHICAGO & NORTH WESTERN
CHICAGO & NORTH WESTERN TRANSPORTATION CO.
CHICAGO, MILWAUKEE & ST. PAUL
CHICAGO, MILWAUKEE, ST. PAUL & PACIFIC
Chicago, St. Paul & Fond du Lac
Deer Creek & Marble Quarry
ESCANABA & LAKE SUPERIOR RY (1880)
ESCANABA & LAKE SUPERIOR RY (1898)
ESCANABA, IRON MOUNTAIN & WESTERN
Escanaba, Twin Cities & Western
Lake Superior Ship Canal Ry & Iron Co.
Menominee Range Street
MENOMINEE RIVER
MILWAUKEE & NORTHERN
Quinnesec & Western
Republic Branch
Sault Ste. Marie & Southwestern
Upper Peninsula & Green Bay
Vieux Desert & Lake Superior
VONPLATEN LUMBER CO.
Wisconsin & Lake Superior
WISCONSIN & MICHIGAN
WISCONSIN, MICHIGAN & NORTHERN

EATON COUNTY (023)

Air Line Ry of Michigan
Alaska
Albion, Charlotte, Northern
Amboy, Lansing & Traverse Bay
Battle Creek & Bay City
BURT PORTLAND CEMENT CO.
CHESAPEAKE & OHIO
CHICAGO & GRAND TRUNK
CHICAGO & LAKE HURON
Chicago & Michigan Grand Trunk
CHICAGO, KALAMAZOO & SAGINAW
Coldwater & Central Michigan
Coldwater, Marshall & Mackinaw
Columbus, Marshall & Northeastern
DETROIT, GRAND RAPIDS & WESTERN
Detroit, Howell, Lansing & Grand Rapids
DETROIT, LANSING & LAKE MICHIGAN
DETROIT, LANSING & NORTHERN
Grand Rapids Electric
GRAND RAPIDS, LANSING & DETROIT
GRAND RIVER VALLEY
Grand Trunk RR of Michigan
GRAND TRUNK WESTERN
IONIA & LANSING
KENT, BARRY, EATON CONNECTING
LAKE SHORE & MICHIGAN SOUTHERN
Lansing & Battle Creek Traction

Lansing & Lake Michigan
Marshall & Coldwater
Marshall & Northern
Michigan & Indiana Traction
MICHIGAN CENTRAL
Michigan Central Traction
Michigan Northern RR (1919)
NEW YORK CENTRAL
NORTHERN CENTRAL MICHIGAN
Ohio & Grand Haven
Olivet
Olivet & South Eastern
PENINSULAR
PENN CENTRAL
PERE MARQUETTE
River Raisin & Grand River
Toledo & Northwestern
Toledo, Marshall & Northern
Toledo Michigan & Lake Huron

EMMET COUNTY (024)

ALANSON & PETOSKEY
Amboy & Traverse Bay
Amboy, Lansing & Traverse Bay
Bay View & Crooked Lake
BAY VIEW LITTLE TRAVERSE & MACKINAC
BOYNE FALLS & NORTHEASTERN
CADILLAC HANDLE CO.
CAREY HOOP CO.
CECIL BAY LUMBER CO.
Cheboygan & East Michigan
Cheboygan Southern
CHESAPEAKE & OHIO
CHICAGO & NORTH MICHIGAN
CHICAGO & WEST MICHIGAN
Cincinnati & Great Northern
Detroit & Petoskey
EMMET LUMBER CO.
GRAND RAPIDS & INDIANA
Grand Rapids & Mackinaw
Grand Rapids & Northern
GRAND RAPIDS, INDIANA & MACKINAW
Grand Rapids, Traverse Bay & Mackinac
HARBOR SPRINGS
JACKSON AND TINDLE, INC.
Michigan Northern RR (1869)
MICHIGAN NORTHERN RY (1976)
Northern Michigan Central
Northern Michigan RR (11/1867)
Ohio & Lake Superior
PENN CENTRAL
PENNSYLVANIA
PERE MARQUETTE
Petoskey & Harbor Springs RR
Petoskey & Harbor Springs Ry
Petoskey, Harbor Springs & Northern
Petoskey, Harbor Springs & Shore
STURGEON BAY LUMBER CO.
Toledo, Ann Arbor & Mackinaw
TUSCOLA & SAGINAW BAY

GENESEE COUNTY (025)

Canada, Michigan & Chicago
CHESAPEAKE & OHIO
CHICAGO & GRAND TRUNK
CHICAGO & LAKE HURON
CHICAGO & NORTHEASTERN
Chicago, Saginaw & Canada
CINCINNATI, SAGINAW & MACKINAW
DETROIT & FLINT
DETROIT & MILWAUKEE
Detroit, Bay City & Alpena
Detroit, Flint & Saginaw
Detroit, Flint River & Saginaw Valley
DETROIT, GRAND HAVEN & MILWAUKEE
Detroit, Lake Orion & Flint
DETROIT UNITED RY
EASTERN MICHIGAN
East Saginaw & Ann Arbor
Fenton & Grand Blanc
Fenton, Long Lake & Flint
Flint & Fentonville
Flint & Great Lakes
FLINT & HOLLY
Flint & Lansing
FLINT & PERE MARQUETTE
Flint & Saginaw Traction
FLINT BELT
Flint City
FLINT RIVER
Flint, Saginaw & Bay City
Flint Street
Flushing
Genesee & Oakland
GRAND TRUNK WESTERN
Lake Superior
Lansing & Northeastern
Macomb & Saginaw
Michigan Extension
Michigan Midland
MICHIGAN RR
MICHIGAN RY
"Northern" (of State of Michigan)
NORTH WESTERN GRAND TRUNK
Oakland & Ottawa
Ohio & Lake Superior
PERE MARQUETTE
Pontiac & Flint Electric
Pontiac & Genesee

PORT HURON & LAKE MICHIGAN
Port Huron & Milwaukee
Port Huron & Owosso
SAGINAW & FLINT
Saginaw & Genesee
Saginaw Suburban
South Lyons & Northern
Toledo, Ann Arbor & Saginaw
TOLEDO, SAGINAW & MACKINAW
Union Traction Co.

GLADWIN COUNTY (026)

Alpena & Michigan South-western
Amboy & Traverse Bay
Amboy, Lansing & Traverse Bay
BENNETT AND ROSS
Cincinnati & Great Northern
FLINT & PERE MARQUETTE
Grand Rapids Electric
MICHIGAN CENTRAL
NEW YORK CENTRAL
Northern Michigan RR (11/1867)
PENN CENTRAL
PERE MARQUETTE
PINCONNING
SAGINAW BAY & NORTHWESTERN
WRIGHT, A. W., LUMBER CO.

GOGEBIC COUNTY (027)

Baraga & Watersmeet
Bessemer & Ironwood Interurban
BONIFAS, WILLIAM, LUMBER CO.
CHICAGO & NORTH WESTERN
CHICAGO & NORTH WESTERN TRANSPORTATION CO.
Chicago, St. Paul & Fond du Lac
CHURCH QUARRY CO.
CONNOR LAND & LUMBER CO.
CONNORVILLE & LAKE SUPERIOR
DULUTH, SOUTH SHORE & ATLANTIC
Escanaba & Lake Superior Ry (1880)
FULLER, P. S., & CO.
GOGEBIC & IRON COUNTIES RY & LIGHT
GOGEBIC & MONTREAL RIVER
GOGEBIC STREET
IRON RIVER
IRONWOOD & BESSEMER RY & LIGHT
Ironwood & Hurley Street
Ironwood Electric
JENSON, L., CO. ?
LAKE SUPERIOR DISTRICT POWER CO.
LAKE SUPERIOR IRON AND COAL CO.
LIMPERT AND HOWE
MICHIGAN LOGGING CO.
MILWAUKEE, LAKE SHORE & WESTERN
Mineral Range
MINNEAPOLIS, ST. PAUL & SAULT STE. MARIE
Northern Michigan RR (1888)
Ontonagon & State Line
Ontonagon, Gogebic & Wisconsin
Ontonagon Southern
St. Mary's & Minneapolis
SCHNEIDER AND BROWN LUMBER CO.
SCOTT AND HOWE LUMBER CO.
SOO LINE
TURPENINE, H.V.
TWIN CITY (1889)
TWIN CITY GENERAL ELECTRIC CO.
UNDERWOOD VENEER CO.
UNITED LOGGING CO.
Vieux Desert & Lake Superior
Wisconsin & Lake Superior
WISCONSIN CENTRAL
WISCONSIN CENTRAL, LTD.
Wisconsin, Sault Ste. Marie & Mackinac

GRAND TRAVERSE COUNTY (028)

Alpena, Gaylord & Western
Amboy, Lansing & Traverse Bay
CHESAPEAKE & OHIO
CHICAGO & NORTH MICHIGAN
CHICAGO & WEST MICHIGAN
CHICKERING AND KYSOR
Elk Rapids, Williamsburg & Southern
GRAND RAPIDS & INDIANA
Grand Rapids & Mackinaw
Grand Rapids & Northern
Grand Rapids, Kalkaska & Southeastern
Grand Traverse
HANNAH, LAY AND CO.
MANISTEE & NORTHEASTERN
Michigan Lake Shore
Michigan Northern RR (1869)
MICHIGAN NORTHERN RY (1976)
PENN CENTRAL
PENNSYLVANIA
PERE MARQUETTE
TRAVERSE CITY
Traverse City & Leelanau
Traverse City & Peninsula
TRAVERSE CITY, LEELANAU & MANISTIQUE
Traverse City, Peninsula & Old Mission Electric
Traverse City Street
TUSCOLA & SAGINAW BAY

GRATIOT COUNTY (029)

Amboy & Traverse Bay
Amboy, Lansing & Traverse Bay
ANN ARBOR
Battle Creek & Bay City
CHESAPEAKE & OHIO
Chicago, Kalamazoo & Saginaw
CHICAGO, SAGINAW & CANADA
Cincinnati & Great Northern
Coldwater & Central Michigan
Columbus, Marshall & Northeastern
DETROIT, GRAND RAPIDS & WESTERN
Grand Rapids & Bay City
Grand Rapids & Saginaw
GRAND TRUNK WESTERN
Huron & Michigan
ITHACA & ALMA
Lansing, Alma, Mt. Pleasant & Northern
Lansing, St. Johns & Mackinac
Lansing, St. Johns & Northern
Lansing, St. Johns & St. Louis (1897)
Lansing, St. Johns & St. Louis (1900)
MICHIGAN INTERSTATE
Michigan Northern RR (1919)
MID-MICHIGAN
Northern Michigan Central
Ovid & Traverse Bay
Owosso & Big Rapids
Owosso & North Western
PERE MARQUETTE
Riverdale & Lake Michigan
SAGINAW & GRAND RAPIDS
Saginaw & Montcalm
SAGINAW & WESTERN
SAGINAW VALLEY & ST. LOUIS
TOLEDO, ANN ARBOR & MT. PLEASANT
TOLEDO, ANN ARBOR & NORTH MICHIGAN
TOLEDO, SAGINAW & MUSKEGON
TUSCOLA & SAGINAW BAY

HILLSDALE COUNTY (030)

Amboy & Traverse Bay
Amboy, Lansing & Traverse Bay
Camden Southern
Canada Southern & Chicago
Central Michigan RR
Cincinnati & Great Northern
CINCINNATI, JACKSON & MACKINAW RR
CINCINNATI, JACKSON & MACKINAW RY
CINCINNATI NORTHERN
CLEVELAND, CINCINNATI, CHICAGO & ST. LOUIS
Columbus & Lake Michigan
Columbus, Lima & Milwaukee
DETROIT, HILLSDALE & INDIANA
DETROIT, HILLSDALE & SOUTH WESTERN
DETROIT, TOLEDO & MILWAUKEE
Eastern & Northwestern
Erie & Kalamazoo
FORT WAYNE & JACKSON
FORT WAYNE, JACKSON & SAGINAW
Grand Rapids Electric
HILLSDALE COUNTY
Jackson & Ohio
Jackson, Fort Wayne & Cincinnati
Jonesville
Jonesville, Marshall & Grand River
LAKE SHORE & MICHIGAN SOUTHERN
Mansfield, Coldwater & Lake Michigan
Maumee Branch
MICHIGAN & OHIO RR
Michigan & Ohio Ry
MICHIGAN SOUTHERN
MICHIGAN SOUTHERN & NORTHERN INDIANA
NEW YORK CENTRAL
NORTHERN CENTRAL MICHIGAN
Ohio & Central Michigan
Ohio & Grand Haven
Ohio & Michigan
Ohio & Southern Michigan
PENN CENTRAL
"SOUTHERN" (of State of Michigan)
Toledo & Michigan Electric
Toledo & Milwaukee Ry
Tri-State Rys of Michigan

HOUGHTON COUNTY (031)

ANDERSON, C. L.
ATLANTIC & LAKE SUPERIOR
Baraga & Watersmeet
CALUMET AND HECLA CO.
Calumet & Lac La Belle Traction
Calumet Train (1866)
Calumet Train (1867)
CHICAGO, MILWAUKEE & ST. PAUL
CHICAGO, MILWAUKEE, ST. PAUL & PACIFIC
COPPER RANGE
DOLLAR BAY LUMBER CO.
DULUTH, SOUTH SHORE & ATLANTIC
FRANKLIN MINING CO.
FROST SHINGLE CO.
Globe Train
HANCOCK & CALUMET
HECLA & TORCH LAKE
Hecla Train
Houghton
Houghton & L'Anse
Houghton & Ontonagon
Houghton & Rockland
HOUGHTON, CHASSELL & SOUTHWESTERN

HOUGHTON COUNTY STREET
HOUGHTON COUNTY TRACTION CO.
HOUGHTON LUMBER CO.
Ishpeming, L'Anse & Ontonagon
ISLE ROYALE COPPER CO.
KEWEENAW CENTRAL
LAC LA BELLE & CALUMET
L'Anse & Ontonagon
Marquette & Ontonagon RR
Marquette & Ontonagon Ry
MARQUETTE, HOUGHTON & ONTONAGON
MILWAUKEE & NORTHERN
Mineral Range & L'Anse Bay
MINERAL RANGE RR
Mineral Range Ry
Northern Michigan RR (11/1867)
Northern Michigan RR (1888)
NORTHLAND LUMBER CO.
Ohio & Lake Superior
Ontonagon Southern
PAMPA LAND CO.
Peninsula
Portage
Portage Lake & Keweenaw
PORTAGE LAKE MINING CO.
Portage Lake Train
PRYOR, JAMES, AND SON
QUINCY & TORCH LAKE
QUINCY MINING CO.
St. Mary's & Minneapolis
SOO LINE
STRATTON, D. A.
TRAP ROCK VALLEY
Upper Peninsula & Green Bay
Wisconsin & Lake Superior
WISCONSIN CENTRAL, LTD.
Wisconsin, Sault Ste. Marie & Mackinac

HURON COUNTY (032)

Bay, Tuscola & Huron
CARO & LAKE HURON
CHESAPEAKE & OHIO
DETROIT & HURON
FLINT & PERE MARQUETTE
GRAND TRUNK WESTERN
HARBOR BEACH & PORT HOPE
HURON & EASTERN
Lapeer & Port Austin
MICHIGAN CENTRAL
NEW YORK CENTRAL
Oxford & Port Austin
PENN CENTRAL
PERE MARQUETTE
PONTIAC, OXFORD & NORTHERN
PONTIAC, OXFORD & PORT AUSTIN
PORT HURON & NORTHWESTERN
Port Huron & Port Austin Electric
SAGINAW, TUSCOLA & HURON
Thumb
TUSCOLA & SAGINAW BAY
WALLACE STONE CO.

INGHAM COUNTY (033)

Air Line Ry of Michigan
Alaska
Albion, Charlotte, Northern
Amboy & Traverse Bay
AMBOY, LANSING & TRAVERSE BAY
Canada, Michigan & Chicago
Capitol Street
CHESAPEAKE & OHIO
CHICAGO & GRAND TRUNK
CHICAGO & LAKE HURON
Chicago & Michigan Grand Trunk
CHICAGO & NORTHEASTERN
Cincinnati & Great Northern
CONSOLIDATED RAIL
Detroit & Howell
Detroit & Shiawassee
DETROIT, GRAND RAPIDS & WESTERN
Detroit, Howell & Lansing RR
Detroit, Howell & Lansing Ry
Detroit, Howell, Lansing & Grand Rapids
DETROIT, LANSING & LAKE MICHIGAN
DETROIT, LANSING & NORTHERN
Flint & Lansing
Grand Rapids Electric
GRAND RIVER VALLEY
Grand Trunk RR of Michigan
Grand Trunk Ry of Michigan
GRAND TRUNK WESTERN
Howell & Lansing
IONIA & LANSING
JACKSON, LANSING & SAGINAW
LAKE SHORE & MICHIGAN SOUTHERN
Lansing, Alma, Mt. Pleasant & Northern
Lansing & Battle Creek Traction
Lansing & Jackson RR
Lansing & Jackson Ry
Lansing & Lake Michigan
LANSING & NORTHEASTERN
Lansing & St. Johns
Lansing & Southeastern
LANSING & SUBURBAN TRACTION
LANSING CITY
LANSING CITY ELECTRIC
Lansing Connecting
Lansing, Dexter & Ann Arbor
Lansing, Dexter & Ann Arbor Electric
LANSING MANUFACTURERS
Lansing, St. Johns & Mackinac
Lansing, St. Johns & Northern

Lansing, St. Johns & St. Louis (1897)
LANSING, ST. JOHNS & ST. LOUIS (1900)
LANSING SOUTHERN
Lansing Street
Lansing Transit
LANSING TRANSIT
LANSING TRANSPORTATION CO.
Maple Rapids & Lansing
Michigan & Indiana Traction
MICHIGAN CENTRAL
Michigan Central Traction
MICHIGAN ELECTRIC (1923)
Michigan Extension
Michigan Midland
MICHIGAN RY
MICHIGAN SUBURBAN
MICHIGAN UNITED RYS
MICHIGAN UNITED TRACTION
NEW YORK CENTRAL
NORTHERN CENTRAL MICHIGAN
PENINSULAR
PENN CENTRAL
PERE MARQUETTE
Romeo & Western
Saginaw & Lansing
Saginaw, Owosso & Lansing

IONIA COUNTY (034)

Alaska
Battle Creek & Bay City
Bay City & Battle Creek
Belding Street
CENTRAL MICHIGAN
Central Michigan RR
CHESAPEAKE & OHIO
Chicago, Kalamazoo & Saginaw
Coldwater & Central Michigan
Coldwater, Marshall & Mackinaw
Columbus, Marshall & Northeastern
Crystal Lake (1900)
DETROIT & MILWAUKEE
DETROIT, GRAND HAVEN & MILWAUKEE
DETROIT, GRAND RAPIDS & WESTERN
Detroit, Howell, Lansing & Grand Rapids
DETROIT, LANSING & LAKE MICHIGAN
DETROIT, LANSING & NORTHERN
Flat River & Houghton Lake
Grand Rapids & Ionia
Grand Rapids & Saginaw
Grand Rapids, Belding & Greenville (1899)
Grand Rapids, Belding & Greenville (1905)
Grand Rapids, Belding & Ionia
GRAND RAPIDS, BELDING & SAGINAW
Grand Rapids Electric
GRAND RAPIDS, LANSING & DETROIT
GRAND TRUNK WESTERN
Hastings, Lowell & Northern Michigan
Huron & Michigan
IONIA & LANSING
Ionia & Owosso
Ionia & Stanton
Ionia, Stanton & Northern
Kalamazoo, Lowell & Northern Michigan
Marshall & Coldwater
Michigan Midland
Michigan Northern RR (1919)
MID-MICHIGAN
"Northern" (of State of Michigan)
Oakland & Ottawa
PATTERSON
PERE MARQUETTE
Port Huron & Lake Michigan
River Raisin & Grand River
Saginaw Bay South Western
Toledo, Marshall & Northern
Toledo Michigan & Lake Huron
Westphalia, Hubbardston & Northern

IOSCO COUNTY (035)

Amboy & Traverse Bay
Amboy, Lansing & Traverse Bay
AU SABLE & NORTHWESTERN
AUSABLE LUMBER CO.
BACKUS, G. AND J.
BAY CITY & ALPENA
DETROIT & MACKINAC
DETROIT, BAY CITY & ALPENA
ERIE & MICHIGAN RY & NAVIGATION
HALE, S. AND C. D.
LAKE HURON & SOUTHWESTERN
LOUD, GAY AND CO.
LOUD, H. M., AND SONS LUMBER CO.
Oscoda & AuSable Street
OSCODA SALT AND LUMBER CO.
POTTS LOGGING RY CO.
SMITH, BENJAMIN F.
TAWAS & BAY COUNTY

IRON COUNTY (036)

CHICAGO & NORTH WESTERN
CHICAGO & NORTH WESTERN TRANSPORTATION CO.
CHICAGO, MILWAUKEE & ST. PAUL
CHICAGO, MILWAUKEE, ST. PAUL & PACIFIC
Escanaba & Lake Superior (1880)
HOLMES, WILLIAM, AND SON
IRON RIVER
IRON RIVER, STAMBAUGH & CRYSTAL FALLS
Lake Superior Southern

McINTYRE AND CO.
MENOMINEE RIVER
MILWAUKEE & NORTHERN
NORTHWESTERN LAND AND LUMBER CO.
NORTHWESTERN LUMBER CO.
Ontonagon & Brule River
PAINT RIVER
PATTEN TIMBER CO.
ROSEBUSH RANCH CO.
St. Mary's & Minneapolis
Sault Ste. Marie & Southwestern
Upper Peninsula & Green Bay
Vieux Desert & Lake Superior
VONPLATEN, FOX CO.

ISABELLA COUNTY (037)

Alpena & Michigan South-western
Amboy & Traverse Bay
Amboy, Lansing & Traverse Bay
ANN ARBOR
Battle Creek & Bay City
Bay City & Battle Creek
Central Michigan RR
CHESAPEAKE & OHIO
Chippewa Valley
Cincinnati & Great Northern
Coldwater, Marshall & Mackinaw
DETROIT, GRAND RAPIDS & WESTERN
DETROIT, LANSING & NORTHERN
Flat River & Houghton Lake
FLINT & PERE MARQUETTE
Grand Rapids Electric
Grand Rapids, Grayling & Alpena
Grand Rapids, Greenville & Alpena
Ionia, Stanton & Northern
Lake Superior
Lansing, Alma, Mt. Pleasant & Northern
Lansing, St. Johns & Mackinac
MICHIGAN INTERSTATE
Michigan Northern RR (1919)
Michigan Northern Ry (1873)
Mount Pleasant & Western
Northern Michigan Central
Owosso & Big Rapids
Owosso & North Western
PERE MARQUETTE
SAGINAW & MOUNT PLEASANT
Toledo & Cadillac
Toledo & Saginaw Bay
Toledo, Ann Arbor & Cadillac
TOLEDO, ANN ARBOR & MT. PLEASANT
TOLEDO, ANN ARBOR & NORTH MICHIGAN
Toledo Michigan & Lake Huron
TUSCOLA & SAGINAW BAY
WHITNEY AND REMICK

JACKSON COUNTY (038)

Adrian & Jackson Traction
Air Line Ry of Michigan
Amboy & Traverse Bay
Amboy, Lansing & Traverse Bay
BENNET SEWER PIPE CO.
"CENTRAL" (of State of Michigan)
Cincinnati & Great Northern
CINCINNATI, JACKSON & MACKINAW RR
CINCINNATI, JACKSON & MACKINAW RY
CINCINNATI NORTHERN
CLEVELAND, CINCINNATI, CHICAGO & ST. LOUIS
CONSOLIDATED RAIL
Detroit & Chicago Traction
Detroit & St. Joseph
DETROIT, HILLSDALE & INDIANA
DETROIT, HILLSDALE & SOUTH WESTERN
DETROIT, JACKSON & CHICAGO
Detroit, Toledo & Jackson
DETROIT, TOLEDO & MILWAUKEE
DETROIT, YPSILANTI, ANN ARBOR & JACKSON
Erie & Kalamazoo
FORT WAYNE & JACKSON
FORT WAYNE, JACKSON & SAGINAW
GRAND RIVER VALLEY
Grand Trunk Ry of Michigan
GRAND TRUNK WESTERN
Hudson & Jackson
Jackson & Adrian Electric
Jackson & Albion Electric
Jackson & Ann Arbor
JACKSON & BATTLE CREEK TRACTION
JACKSON & CINCINNATI
Jackson & Eastern
JACKSON & NORTHERN
Jackson & Ohio
JACKSON & SUBURBAN TRACTION
JACKSON, ANN ARBOR & DETROIT
Jackson, Ann Arbor & Detroit Traction
JACKSON CITY
JACKSON CONSOLIDATED TRACTION
Jackson, Fort Wayne & Cincinnati
JACKSON, LANSING & SAGINAW
JACKSON RAPID TRANSPORTATION CO.
JACKSON STREET
JACKSON TRANSPORTATION CO.
Jackson Union
LAKE SHORE & MICHIGAN SOUTHERN
Lansing & Jackson RR
Lansing & Jackson Ry
Lansing & Southeastern
Main Street
Manchester & Homer
MICHIGAN AIR LINE RR
MICHIGAN AIR LINE RY

MICHIGAN & OHIO RR
MICHIGAN CENTRAL
MICHIGAN ELECTRIC (1923)
Michigan Extension
MICHIGAN RY
MICHIGAN SOUTHERN
MICHIGAN SOUTHERN & NORTHERN INDIANA
MICHIGAN UNITED RYS
MICHIGAN UNITED TRACTION
NEW YORK CENTRAL
NORTHERN CENTRAL MICHIGAN
Ohio & Southern Michigan
Palmyra & Jacksonburgh
PENN CENTRAL
River Raisin & Grand River
Romeo & Western
St. Clair River, Pontiac & Jackson
Toledo, Adrian & Jackson
Toledo & Jackson Electric
Toledo & Milwaukee Ry
Tri-State Rys of Michigan
WOLF LAKE RY AND RESORT CO.

KALAMAZOO COUNTY (039)

Allegan & Marshall
Battle Creek & Grand Rapids
Battle Creek & Grand Rapids Inland Lakes Traction
"CENTRAL" (of State of Michigan)
Chicago & Canada Pacific
CHICAGO & GRAND TRUNK
CHICAGO & KALAMAZOO TERMINAL
CHICAGO & LAKE HURON
Chicago, Kalamazoo & Eastern
CHICAGO, KALAMAZOO & SAGINAW
CINCINNATI, JACKSON & MACKINAW RR
CINCINNATI, JACKSON & MACKINAW RY
CINCINNATI NORTHERN
CITIZENS STREET
Columbus & Lake Michigan
CONSOLIDATED RAIL
Detroit & St. Joseph
DETROIT, TOLEDO & MILWAUKEE
Eastern & Northwestern
Grand Haven
GRAND RAPIDS & INDIANA
Grand Rapids & Kalamazoo Electric
Grand Rapids & Kalamazoo Valley
Grand Rapids & Southern
Grand Rapids & South Michigan
Grand Rapids Electric
Grand Rapids, Kalamazoo & South Haven
GRAND TRUNK WESTERN
KALAMAZOO, ALLEGAN & GRAND RAPIDS
Kalamazoo & Allegan
Kalamazoo & Grand Rapids
Kalamazoo & Grand River
Kalamazoo & Lake Michigan RR
Kalamazoo & Lake Michigan Ry
KALAMAZOO & SCHOOLCRAFT
KALAMAZOO & SOUTH HAVEN
KALAMAZOO & WHITE PIGEON
Kalamazoo City & County Street
Kalamazoo, Elkhart & South Bend Traction
Kalamazoo, Gull Lake & Northern
KALAMAZOO, LAKE SHORE & CHICAGO RY
Kalamazoo, Lake Shore & Chicago Traction
Kalamazoo, Lowell & Northern Michigan
Kalamazoo, Paw Paw & Lake Michigan
Kalamazoo River
KALAMAZOO STREET
KALAMAZOO TRANSPORTATION CO.
Lake Michigan & Kalamazoo
LAKE SHORE & MICHIGAN SOUTHERN
MICHIGAN & CHICAGO
Michigan & Chicago Westbound
MICHIGAN & OHIO RR
MICHIGAN CENTRAL
MICHIGAN ELECTRIC (1923)
Michigan Extension
Michigan Light & Traction
Michigan Northern RR (1869)
Michigan Northern RR (1919)
MICHIGAN RR
MICHIGAN RY
MICHIGAN TRACTION CO.
Michigan Traction Extension
MICHIGAN UNITED RYS
MICHIGAN UNITED TRACTION
NATIONAL RAIL PASSENGER
NEW YORK CENTRAL
Ohio & Grand Haven
Ohio & Michigan
Ohio & Southern Michigan
Ohio, Quincy & Grand Haven
Paw Paw Valley
PENINSULAR
Peninsular Ry Extension
PENN CENTRAL
PENNSYLVANIA
St Joe River Traction Co.
SCHOOLCRAFT & THREE RIVERS
Southern Michigan Traction
Southwestern Michigan
Sturgis, Indiana & Ohio
Toledo & Milwaukee Ry
Toledo & South Haven (St. Joseph Div.)
West Michigan
West Michigan Traction Co.
WESTERN MICHIGAN UNIVERSITY

KALKASKA COUNTY (040)

Alpena, Gaylord & Western
Amboy & Traverse Bay
Amboy, Lansing & Traverse Bay
ANTRIM IRON CO.
CHESAPEAKE & OHIO
CHICAGO & WEST MICHIGAN
Cincinnati & Great Northern
CRAWFORD & MANISTEE RIVER
DETROIT & CHARLEVOIX
Detroit, Charlevoix & Escanaba
FERRIN, M. B. (LUMBER CO.)
GRAND RAPIDS & INDIANA
Grand Rapids & Mackinaw
Grand Rapids & Northern
GRAND RAPIDS, KALKASKA & SOUTH-EASTERN
Grand Rapids, Traverse Bay & Mackinac
GRASS LAKE & MANISTEE RIVER
Grayling & Charlevoix
MANISTEE & NORTHEASTERN
Michigan Northern RR (1869)
MICHIGAN NORTHERN RY (1976)
NEW YORK CENTRAL
Northern Michigan Central
PENN CENTRAL
PENNSYLVANIA
PERE MARQUETTE
RAPID RIVER & EASTERN
SMITH LUMBER CO.
SOUTH BOARDMAN (LUMBER CO.)
STATE LUMBER CO.
Toledo, Ann Arbor & Mackinaw
Traverse City, Kalkaska & Grayling
TUSCOLA & SAGINAW BAY

KENT COUNTY (041)

Alaska
Battle Creek & Grand Rapids
Battle Creek & Grand Rapids Inland Lakes Traction
Cable Street Ry of Grand Rapids
CENTRAL MICHIGAN
Central Michigan RR
CHESAPEAKE & OHIO
CHICAGO & MICHIGAN LAKE SHORE
CHICAGO & WEST MICHIGAN
Chicago, Saginaw & Canada
City Street Ry of Grand Rapids
CONSOLIDATED RAIL
CONSOLIDATED STREET RY
DETROIT & MILWAUKEE
DETROIT, GRAND HAVEN & MILWAUKEE
DETROIT, GRAND RAPIDS & WESTERN
Detroit, Howell, Lansing & Grand Rapids
DETROIT, LANSING & LAKE MICHIGAN
DETROIT, LANSING & NORTHERN
DIVISION STREET
Division Street & Reed's Lake
Electric
Fulton Street & Reed's Lake
Grand Rapids & Bay City
Grand Rapids & Belding
Grand Rapids & Chicago RR
Grand Rapids & Chicago Ry
Grand Rapids & Holland
GRAND RAPIDS & INDIANA
Grand Rapids & Ionia
Grand Rapids & Kalamazoo Electric
Grand Rapids & Kalamazoo Valley
Grand Rapids & Lake Michigan
Grand Rapids & Lake Shore
Grand Rapids & Mackinaw
Grand Rapids & Mineral Springs
Grand Rapids & Northern
Grand Rapids & North Western
GRAND RAPIDS & REEDS LAKE STREET
Grand Rapids & Saginaw
Grand Rapids & Southern
Grand Rapids & South Michigan
Grand Rapids, Belding & Greenville (1899)
Grand Rapids, Belding & Ionia
Grand Rapids Belt Line
Grand Rapids, Chicago & St. Louis
Grand Rapids City
Grand Rapids Electric
GRAND RAPIDS, GRAND HAVEN & MUSKEGON
Grand Rapids, Grayling & Alpena
Grand Rapids, Greenville & Bay City
GRAND RAPIDS, HOLLAND & CHICAGO
GRAND RAPIDS, HOLLAND & LAKE MICHIGAN
Grand Rapids, Kalamazoo & South Haven
GRAND RAPIDS, LANSING & DETROIT
GRAND RAPIDS, NEWAYGO & LAKE SHORE
Grand Rapids RR (1855)
Grand Rapids RR (1871)
GRAND RAPIDS RR (1927)
GRAND RAPIDS RY
Grand Rapids, Rockford & Greenville
Grand Rapids, Spring Lake & Grand Haven
GRAND RAPIDS STREET
GRAND RAPIDS TERMINAL
Grand Rapids Terminal Belt
GRAND RAPIDS TRANSFER & JUNCTION
Grand Rapids, Traverse Bay & Mackinac
Grand River RR
GRAND RIVER VALLEY
GRAND TRUNK WESTERN
Hastings, Lowell & Northern Michigan
Huron & Michigan
Ionia & Lansing

KALAMAZOO, ALLEGAN & GRAND RAPIDS
Kalamazoo & Grand Rapids
Kalamazoo & Grand River
Kalamazoo, Lowell & Northern Michigan
KENT, BARRY, EATON CONNECTING
Kent County Street
LAKE SHORE & MICHIGAN SOUTHERN
LOWELL & HASTINGS
Ludington Southern
Manistee & Grand Rapids
Mason & Oceana
MICHIGAN & CHICAGO
Michigan & Chicago Westbound
Michigan & Ohio Ry
MICHIGAN CENTRAL
Michigan Light & Traction
Michigan Midland
Michigan Northern RR (1869)
Michigan Northern Ry (1873)
MICHIGAN NORTHERN RY (1976)
MICHIGAN RR
MICHIGAN RY
Michigan Terminal
Michigan West Shore Traction
MID-MICHIGAN
Muskegon & Greenville
MUSKEGON, GRAND RAPIDS & INDIANA
Muskegon Terminal
NASON, C. F.
Newaygo
NEW YORK CENTRAL
"Northern" (of State of Michigan)
North Park Bridge Co.
NORTH PARK STREET
Oakdale Park Street
Oakland & Ottawa
PENN CENTRAL
PENNSYLVANIA
PERE MARQUETTE
Port Huron & Lake Michigan
Port Sheldon & Grand Rapids
Reed's Lake Electric Ry of Grand Rapids
Reeds Lake, Grand Rapids & Soldiers Home Suburban
REEDS LAKE STREET
River Raisin & Grand River
Saginaw & Grand Rapids
Southern Michigan Traction
SOUTH GRAND RAPIDS STREET
South Park & Crystal Springs
Street Ry Construction Co.
STREET RY OF GRAND RAPIDS
TOLEDO, SAGINAW & MUSKEGON
UNITED SUBURBAN
VALLEY CITY STREET & CABLE
Valley City Street Cable Of Grand Rapids
West Michigan Interurban
WEST SIDE STREET RY OF GRAND RAPIDS
Winsor Street

KEWEENAW COUNTY (042)

ALLOUEZ MINING CO.
AMYGDALOID MINING CO.
ARNOLD & EAGLE HARBOR
CALUMET AND HECLA CO.
Calumet & Lac La Belle Traction
CONGLOMERATE MINING CO.
COPPER FALLS MINING CO.
COPPER RANGE
DULUTH, SOUTH SHORE & ATLANTIC
HANCOCK & CALUMET
HOUGHTON COUNTY STREET
HOUGHTON COUNTY TRACTION
ISLAND MINING CO.
Keweenaw & Cliff
KEWEENAW CENTRAL
LAC LA BELLE & CALUMET
MINERAL RANGE RR
Mineral Range Ry
MOHAWK MINING CO.
NORTHWEST COPPER CO.
Portage Lake & Keweenaw

LAKE COUNTY (043)

BOND, MILTON J.
CHARRON AND BOUGETTE (LUMBER CO.)
CHESAPEAKE & OHIO
CHICAGO & WEST MICHIGAN
Chippewa Valley
COPLEY, E. J.
DANAHER AND MELENDY
DUNHAM, PETERS AND CO.
FLINT & PERE MARQUETTE
FOSTER, BLACKMAN AND CO.
GRAND RAPIDS & INDIANA
Grand Rapids & Northern
Grand Rapids, Indiana & Manistee
HAAK, J. A.
HALL AND MANNING ROAD
HOBART & MANISTEE RIVER
HOVEY, S. P., AND CO.
LAKE COUNTY
Lake Superior
LAKE TRAIN
MANISTEE & GRAND RAPIDS
MANISTEE & LUTHER
MANISTEE TRAM
MARLBOROUGH
MCCOY, DANIEL
MICHIGAN EAST & WEST

Michigan Northern RR (1869)
Michigan Northern RR (1887)
Nirvana & Luther
OSCEOLA, LAKE & WEXFORD
OSTERHOUT AND FOX LUMBER CO.
Owosso & North Western
PARIS & PERE MARQUETTE RIVER
PELTON'S LOGGING
PERE MARQUETTE
Pere Marquette & Big Rapids
ROXBURGH, JAMES
SEAMAN AND WEBSTER
THOMAS, HERBERT
WARE AND TUCKER
WILSON, LUTHER AND WILSON LOGGING
WINGLETON & WOLF LAKE

LAPEER COUNTY (044)

Auburn & Lapeer
Capac & Northern
CHESAPEAKE & OHIO
CHICAGO & GRAND TRUNK
CHICAGO & LAKE HURON
Chicago, Saginaw & Canada
DETROIT, ALMONT & NORTHERN
DETROIT & BAY CITY
Detroit & Saginaw River
Detroit Bay City Traction Co.
Detroit, Lexington & Lake Huron
Detroit, Pontiac, Lapeer & Northern
DETROIT UNITED
East Saginaw & St. Clair
FLINT & PERE MARQUETTE
FLINT RIVER
GRAND TRUNK WESTERN
Lapeer & Holly
LAPEER & NORTHERN
Lapeer & Port Austin
Macomb & Saginaw
MICHIGAN CENTRAL
NEW YORK CENTRAL
"Northern" (of State of Michigan)
Northern Michigan Ry
NORTH WESTERN GRAND TRUNK
Oxford & Port Austin
PENN CENTRAL
PERE MARQUETTE
PONTIAC, OXFORD & NORTHERN
PONTIAC, OXFORD & PORT AUSTIN
PORT HURON & LAKE MICHIGAN
Port Huron & Milwaukee
PORT HURON & NORTHWESTERN
Port Huron & Owosso
Port Huron & Saginaw Valley
Port Huron & Southwestern
Port Huron, Lexington & Western
Rochester, Almont & Northern
Romeo & Almont
Saginaw & St. Clair River
Shelby & Belle River
Toledo & Saginaw Bay

LEELANAU COUNTY (045)

CHESAPEAKE & OHIO
Chicago & North Michigan
EMPIRE & SOUTH EASTERN
Frankfort, Crystal Lake & Glenn Arbor
GLEN ARBOR
LEELANAU TRANSIT CO.
MANISTEE & NORTHEASTERN
PERE MARQUETTE
Traverse City & Leelanau
TRAVERSE CITY, LEELANAU & MANISTIQUE

LENAWEE COUNTY (046)

Adrian & Ann Arbor Electric
ADRIAN & BLISSFIELD
Adrian & Detroit
Adrian & Jackson Traction
Adrian & State Line
ADRIAN CITY ELECTRIC BELT
Adrian City Train & Street
Adrian Clinton & Southern
ADRIAN STREET
Ann Arbor Interurban
BLISSFIELD
Canada Southern & Chicago
CHICAGO & CANADA SOUTHERN
CINCINNATI, JACKSON & MACKINAW RR
CINCINNATI, JACKSON & MACKINAW RY
CINCINNATI NORTHERN
Cincinnati, Saginaw & Mackinaw
CLEVELAND, CINCINNATI, CHICAGO & ST. LOUIS
Clinton & Adrian
Detroit, Adrian, Logansport & St. Louis
Detroit & Adrian Traction
DETROIT & CHICAGO
Detroit & Cincinnati
DETROIT & LIMA NORTHERN
Detroit Ann Arbor & Adrian
DETROIT, BUTLER & ST. LOUIS
Detroit, Eel River & Illinois
DETROIT SOUTHERN
DETROIT, TOLEDO & IRONTON
Detroit, Toledo & Jackson
DETROIT, TOLEDO & MILWAUKEE
Eastern & Northwestern

ERIE & KALAMAZOO
Gibralter & Clinton
Hudson & Jackson
Jackson & Adrian Electric
JACKSON & CINCINNATI
Jackson & Ohio
LAKE SHORE & MICHIGAN SOUTHERN
LENAWEE COUNTY
LIMA NORTHERN
Maumee Branch
Medina & Canandaigua
MICHIGAN & OHIO RR
MICHIGAN SOUTHERN
MICHIGAN SOUTHERN & NORTHERN INDIANA
NEW YORK CENTRAL
NORFOLK & WESTERN
OHIO & MORENCI
PALMYRA & JACKSONBURGH
PENN CENTRAL
River Raisin & Grand River
River Raisin & Lake Erie
South Eastern Michigan
"SOUTHERN" (of State of Michigan)
SOUTHERN MICHIGAN RR SOCIETY
Toledo, Adrian & Jackson
Toledo & Jackson Electric
Toledo & Michigan Electric
Toledo & Milwaukee Ry
TOLEDO & WESTERN RR
TOLEDO & WESTERN RY
Tri-State Rys of Michigan
WABASH
WABASH, ST. LOUIS & PACIFIC
WABASH WESTERN
Ypsilanti & Tecumseh

LIVINGSTON COUNTY (047)

Air Line Ry of Michigan
ANN ARBOR
CHESAPEAKE & OHIO
Chicago & Michigan Grand Trunk
Cincinnati, Saginaw & Mackinaw
Detroit & Howell
Detroit & Shiawassee
DETROIT, GRAND RAPIDS & WESTERN
Detroit, Howell & Lansing RR
Detroit, Howell & Lansing Ry
Detroit, Howell, Lansing & Grand Rapids
DETROIT, LANSING & LAKE MICHIGAN
DETROIT, LANSING & NORTHERN
East Saginaw & Ann Arbor
Grand Trunk RR of Michigan
Grand Trunk Ry of Michigan
GRAND TRUNK WESTERN
Howell & Lansing
Jackson & Eastern
Lansing, Dexter & Ann Arbor
Lansing, Dexter & Ann Arbor Electric
MICHIGAN AIR LINE RY
Michigan Extension
MICHIGAN INTERSTATE
Michigan Midland
Northern Michigan Central
Ohio & Lake Superior
OHIO AND MICHIGAN SAND AND GRAVEL CO.
PERE MARQUETTE
Romeo & Western
ST. CLAIR & CHICAGO AIR LINE
ST. CLAIR RIVER, PONTIAC & JACKSON
South Lyons & Northern
Toledo, Ann Arbor & Grand Trunk
Toledo, Ann Arbor & Northern
TOLEDO, ANN ARBOR & NORTH MICHIGAN
Toledo, Ann Arbor & Saginaw
TUSCOLA & SAGINAW BAY

LUCE COUNTY (048)

BARNETT LUMBER CO.
Canada, LaCrosse & Southwestern
CHARCOAL IRON CO. OF AMERICA
CULHANE, CON
DANAHER AND MELENDY
DETROIT, MACKINAC & MARQUETTE
DOLLAR [ROBERT] LUMBER CO.
DULUTH, SOUTH SHORE & ATLANTIC
LAKE SUPERIOR IRON & CHEMICAL CO.
Mackinaw & Lake Superior
MANISTIQUE
Marquette, Sault Ste. Marie & Mackinac
NEWBERRY LUMBER & COAL CO.
St. Mary's & Minneapolis
Sault Ste. Marie & Southwestern
SOO LINE
TAHQUAMENON BOAT SERVICE, INC.
WISCONSIN CENTRAL, LTD.
WISCONSIN LAND AND LUMBER CO.

MACKINAC COUNTY (049)

Canada, LaCrosse & Southwestern
DETROIT, MACKINAC & MARQUETTE
DULUTH, SOUTH SHORE & ATLANTIC
ESCANABA LUMBER CO.
LAKE MICHIGAN & NORTHERN
Mackinaw & Lake Superior
MANISTIQUE
Marquette, Sault Ste. Marie & Mackinac
MCCOY, D. M., LUMBER CO.
Menominee & Sault Ste. Marie

MINNEAPOLIS, ST. PAUL & SAULT STE. MARIE
MINNEAPOLIS, SAULT STE. MARIE & ATLANTIC
NAUBINWAY LOGGING CO.
Northern Michigan RR (11/1867)
Northern Michigan RR (1901)
Ohio & Lake Superior
QUAY, D., AND SON
St. Ignace, Sault Ste. Marie & Northern
Sault Ste. Marie & Lake Huron
SOO LINE
Soo-Snows
STAFFORD, E. H., MFG. CO.
UNITED STATES STEEL CO.
WISCONSIN CENTRAL, LTD.

MACOMB COUNTY (050)

Air Line Ry of Michigan
Canada, Michigan & Chicago
Canada Southern & Chicago
Chicago & Michigan Grand Trunk
CHICAGO, DETROIT & CANADA GRAND TRUNK JUNCTION
Chicago, Saginaw & Canada
DETROIT, ALMONT & NORTHERN
DETROIT & BAY CITY
DETROIT & FLINT
Detroit & Lake Orion
DETROIT & LAKE ST. CLAIR
Detroit & Northern
Detroit & Port Huron
DETROIT & PORT HURON SHORE LINE
DETROIT & RIVER ST. CLAIR
Detroit & Saginaw River
Detroit & St. Clair River
Detroit, Armada & Northern
DETROIT, LAKE SHORE & MT. CLEMENS
Detroit, Lexington & Lake Huron
DETROIT, MT. CLEMENS & MARINE CITY
Detroit, Mt. Clemens, Romeo & Armada
Detroit, Port Huron & Sarnia
Detroit, Romeo & Port Huron
DETROIT, UTICA & ROMEO
EASTERN MICHIGAN
Grand Trunk RR of Michigan
Grand Trunk Ry of Michigan
GRAND TRUNK WESTERN
Lexington & Utica
Macomb & Saginaw
Michigan Air Line Extension
MICHIGAN AIR LINE RR
MICHIGAN AIR LINE RY
MICHIGAN CENTRAL
Michigan Midland
MICHIGAN, MIDLAND & CANADA
MOUNT CLEMENS & LAKESIDE ELECTRIC STREET
MOUNT CLEMENS & LAKESIDE TRACTION
MOUNT CLEMENS STREET
NEW YORK CENTRAL
Northern Michigan RR (2/1867)
Northern Michigan Ry
PENN CENTRAL
Port Huron & Northwestern
RAPID RR
RAPID RY
Rochester, Almont & Northern
Rochester & Romeo
Rochester & St. Clair
Romeo & Almont
Romeo & Mt. Clemens
Romeo & Western
ST. CLAIR & CHICAGO AIR LINE
St. Clair & Romeo
ST. CLAIR & WESTERN
ST. CLAIR RIVER, PONTIAC & JACKSON
Shelby & Belle River
SHELBY & DETROIT
Thumb
Utica & Lexington

MANISTEE COUNTY (051)

ADDIS, WILLIAM
ANN ARBOR
ARCADIA & BETSEY RIVER
ARCADIA & BETSEY RIVER TRAIN
BEAR LAKE & EASTERN
BEAR LAKE TRAIN
BUCKLEY AND DOUGLAS
CHESAPEAKE & OHIO
Chicago & Michigan Lake Shore
Chippewa Valley
FLINT & PERE MARQUETTE
FRANKFORT & SOUTH EASTERN
Grand Rapids & Lake Shore
Grand Rapids, Indiana & Manistee
Grand Rapids, Newaygo & Lake Shore
MANISTEE & GRAND RAPIDS
MANISTEE & LUTHER
MANISTEE & NORTHEASTERN
MANISTEE, FILER CITY & EAST LAKE
MANISTEE LIGHT & TRACTION CO.
MANISTEE RR
MANISTEE RY
Manistee Street
MANISTEE TRAM
MICHIGAN EAST & WEST
MICHIGAN INTERSTATE
Michigan Lake Shore
Montague, Pentwater & Manistee

Muskegon, Ludington & Manistee
NORTHERN MICHIGAN TRACTION
Owosso & North Western
PERE MARQUETTE
PETERS MANISTEE TRAIN
PETERS TRAIN
RUDDOCK, NUTTAL AND CO.
SANDS, LOUIS
TOLEDO, ANN ARBOR & LAKE MICHIGAN
TOLEDO, ANN ARBOR & NORTH MICHIGAN
TUSCOLA & SAGINAW BAY

MARQUETTE COUNTY (052)

ALLEN, WILLIAM
BAY DE NOQUET & MARQUETTE
BOURKE, HENRY P., CO.
CHICAGO & NORTH WESTERN
CHICAGO & NORTH WESTERN TRANSPORTATION CO.
CHICAGO, MILWAUKEE & ST. PAUL
CHICAGO, MILWAUKEE, ST. PAUL & PACIFIC
Chicago, St. Paul & Fond du Lac
CLEVELAND CLIFFS IRON CO.
Dead River
DETROIT, MACKINAC & MARQUETTE
DULUTH, SOUTH SHORE & ATLANTIC
Escanaba & Lake Superior Ry (1880)
ESCANABA & LAKE SUPERIOR RY (1898)
FORD MOTOR CO.
Houghton & Ontonagon
Iron Bay
Iron Mountain & Wisconsin State Line
IRON MOUNTAIN RR
Iron Mountain Ry
IRON RANGE
Iron Range & Huron Bay
Ishpeming & Negaunee
Ishpeming, L'Anse & Ontonagon
LAKE INDEPENDENCE LUMBER CO.
LAKE MICHIGAN & LAKE SUPERIOR
LAKE SUPERIOR & ISHPEMING
Lake Superior Iron Mountain
Lake Superior Southern
Lakes Superior & Michigan Air Line
Mackinaw & Lake Superior
Manistique & Northwestern
Marquette & Chicago
MARQUETTE & HURON MOUNTAIN
Marquette & Iron Range
MARQUETTE & ONTONAGON RR
Marquette & Ontonagon Ry
Marquette & Peninsula
MARQUETTE & SOUTHEASTERN
Marquette & State Line
MARQUETTE & WESTERN
Marquette, Champion & Chicago
MARQUETTE CITY
MARQUETTE CITY & PRESQUE ISLE
MARQUETTE COUNTY ELECTRIC
MARQUETTE COUNTY GAS AND ELECTRIC CO.
MARQUETTE COUNTY GAS LIGHT AND TRACTION CO.
MARQUETTE, HOUGHTON & ONTONAGON
Marquette Iron Range Cable Transit
Marquette, Negaunee & Ishpeming Interurban
Marquette, Sault Ste. Marie & Mackinac
MILWAUKEE & NORTHERN
MUNISING
MUNISING, MARQUETTE & SOUTHEASTERN
Negaunee & Ishpeming Street (1891)
NEGAUNEE & ISHPEMING STREET (1892)
NEGAUNEE & PALMER
Northern Iron
NORTHERN LUMBER CO.
Northern Michigan RR (11/1867)
Ohio & Lake Superior
PENINSULA
Peninsula Branch RR of Michigan
PIQUA HANDLE AND MANUFACTURING CO.
Pittsburgh & Lake Superior
Republic Branch
St. Mary's & Minneapolis
Sault Ste. Marie & Southwestern
SOO LINE
Superior Terminal
Upper Peninsula & Green Bay
Wisconsin & Lake Superior
WISCONSIN CENTRAL, LTD.
Wisconsin, Sault Ste. Marie & Mackinac

MASON COUNTY (053)

BUTTERS AND PETERS
CHARRON AND BOUGETTE (LUMBER CO.)
CHESAPEAKE & OHIO
Chicago & Michigan Lake Shore
Chippewa Valley
CROSS AND MORRISON
EPWORTH LEAGUE
FLINT & PERE MARQUETTE
Grand Rapids & Lake Shore
Grand Rapids & North Western
Grand Rapids, Indiana & Manistee
Grand Rapids, Newaygo & Lake Shore
Lake County
Lake Superior
LUDINGTON & NORTHERN
Ludington Southern
MANISTEE & GRAND RAPIDS
MANISTEE RR
MASON & OCEANA

MICHIGAN EAST & WEST
Michigan Lake Shore
Montague, Pentwater & Manistee
Muskegon, Ludington & Manistee
NORTH BRANCH & SAUBLE RIVER
PERE MARQUETTE
Pere Marquette & Big Rapids
PETERS MANISTEE TRAIN
Street Ry of Ludington

MECOSTA COUNTY (054)

Alpena & Michigan South-western
BIG RAPIDS & WESTERN
Central Michigan RR
CHESAPEAKE & OHIO
CHIPPEWA LAKE LOGGING
Chippewa Valley
COLFAX & BIG RAPIDS
DETROIT, GRAND RAPIDS & WESTERN
DETROIT, LANSING & NORTHERN
Flat River & Houghton Lake
GRAND RAPIDS & INDIANA
Grand Rapids & Mackinaw
Grand Rapids & Northern
Grand Rapids Electric
Grand Rapids, Grayling & Alpena
Grand Rapids, Greenville & Alpena
Grand Rapids, Traverse Bay & Mackinac
Ionia, Stanton & Northern
JEROME AND WILLIAMS
LONG, A. B., AND SONS
MECOSTA
Michigan Northern RR (1869)
MICHIGAN NORTHERN RY (1976)
MIDLAND GRAVEL CO.
Mount Pleasant & Western
Muskegon & Big Rapids
Owosso & Big Rapids
Owosso & North Western
PARIS & PERE MARQUETTE RIVER
PENN CENTRAL
PENNSYLVANIA
PERE MARQUETTE
Pere Marquette & Big Rapids
WENTWORTH, J. AND G.

MENOMINEE COUNTY (055)

BIRD AND HOLCOMB
Canada, LaCrosse & Southwestern
CHICAGO & NORTH WESTERN
CHICAGO & NORTH WESTERN TRANSPORTATION CO.
CHICAGO, MILWAUKEE & ST. PAUL
CHICAGO, MILWAUKEE, ST. PAUL & PACIFIC
Deer Creek & Marble Quarry
ESCANABA & LAKE SUPERIOR RY (1898)
ESCANABA & LAKE SUPERIOR RY (1880)
ESCANABA, IRON MOUNTAIN & WESTERN
Escanaba, Twin Cities & Western
HERMANSVILLE & WESTERN
INDIANTOWN & SOUTHERN
INGALLS, WHITE RAPIDS & NORTHERN
Iron Mountain & Wisconsin State Line
Lake Superior Ship Canal Ry
Marquette & State Line
Menominee & Escanaba
MENOMINEE & MARINETTE LIGHT AND TRACTION
Menominee & Northern
MENOMINEE & ST. PAUL
Menominee & Sault Ste. Marie
MENOMINEE BRANCH
MENOMINEE ELECTRIC LIGHT RY AND POWER
MENOMINEE ELECTRIC RY AND POWER
MENOMINEE RIVER
Menominee Street
MILWAUKEE & NORTHERN
MINNEAPOLIS, ST. PAUL & SAULT STE. MARIE
MINNEAPOLIS, SAULT STE. MARIE & ATLANTIC
Peninsula
QUINNESEC & WESTERN
SOO LINE
Vieux Desert & Lake Superior
WELLS LUMBER CO.
Wisconsin & Lake Superior
WISCONSIN & MICHIGAN
WISCONSIN CENTRAL, LTD.
WISCONSIN, MICHIGAN & NORTHERN

MIDLAND COUNTY (056)

Amboy & Traverse Bay
Amboy, Lansing & Travere Bay
Battle Creek & Bay City
BAY CITY & BATTLE CREEK
Bay City & Midland
CENTRAL MICHIGAN
CHESAPEAKE & OHIO
Cincinnati & Great Northern
Columbus, Marshall & Northeastern
DOW CHEMICAL CO.
FLINT & PERE MARQUETTE
Grand Rapids & Bay City
Lake Superior
MICHIGAN CENTRAL
Michigan Northern RR (1919)
MIDLAND & HUBBARD

Midland & Northern
MIDLAND TRAIN
NEW YORK CENTRAL
Northern Michigan RR (11/1867)
PENN CENTRAL
PERE MARQUETTE
SAGINAW & MOUNT PLEASANT
Tittabawassee
TITTABAWASSEE & HOPE
WRIGHT AND KETCHUM

MISSAUKEE COUNTY (057)

Amboy & Traverse Bay
Amboy, Lansing & Traverse Bay
ANN ARBOR
Cadillac & Evart
CADILLAC & LAKE CITY
CADILLAC & NORTHEASTERN
Cincinnati & Great Northern
CLAM RIVER
COBBS AND MITCHELL
GRAND RAPIDS & INDIANA
Grand Rapids, Grayling & Alpena
GRAND RAPIDS, KALKASKA & SOUTH-EASTERN
Grand Rapids, Traverse Bay & Mackinac
HARING & LAKE CITY
JENNINGS & NORTHEASTERN
MICHIGAN INTERSTATE
Missaukee
MITCHELL BROTHERS
MUSKRAT LAKE & CLAM RIVER
Northern Michigan Central
PENNSYLVANIA
PERE MARQUETTE
THAYER LUMBER CO.
Toledo & Cadillac
Toledo, Ann Arbor & Cadillac
Toledo, Ann Arbor & Mackinaw
TOLEDO, ANN ARBOR & NORTH MICHIGAN
TUSCOLA & SAGINAW BAY
WEST BRANCH & MOORESTOWN

MONROE COUNTY (058)

ANN ARBOR
Ann Arbor Interurban
Canada Southern & Chicago
CHESAPEAKE & OHIO
CHICAGO & CANADA SOUTHERN
Chicago, Detroit & Toledo
CINCINNATI, JACKSON & MACKINAW RR
CINCINNATI, JACKSON & MACKINAW RY
CINCINNATI NORTHERN
CONSOLIDATED RAIL
Detroit, Adrian, Logansport & St. Louis
DETROIT & CHICAGO
Detroit & Cincinnati
DETROIT & LIMA NORTHERN
Detroit & Maumee
Detroit & Monroe
Detroit & State Line
Detroit & Toledo
DETROIT & TOLEDO SHORE LINE
DETROIT, BUTLER & ST. LOUIS
DETROIT EDISON CO.
Detroit, Lincoln & Denver
DETROIT, MONROE & TOLEDO
Detroit, Monroe & Toledo Shore Line
DETROIT, MONROE & TOLEDO SHORT LINE
DETROIT SOUTHERN
DETROIT, TOLEDO & IRONTON
Detroit, Toledo & Jackson
DETROIT, TOLEDO & MILWAUKEE
DETROIT UNITED
Eastern & Northwestern
EASTERN MICHIGAN TOLEDO
ERIE & KALAMAZOO
FLINT & PERE MARQUETTE
Gibralter & Clinton
Havre Branch
HOLLY, WAYNE & MONROE
LAKE SHORE & MICHIGAN SOUTHERN
LA PLAISANCE BAY HARBOR CO.
Maumee Branch
Michigan & Ohio Electric
MICHIGAN & OHIO RR
MICHIGAN CENTRAL
MICHIGAN INTERSTATE
Michigan, Ohio & Indiana
MICHIGAN SOUTHERN
MICHIGAN SOUTHERN & NORTHERN INDIANA
Monroe & Ann Arbor
MONROE & TOLEDO
Monroe & Ypsilanti
Monroe Connecting
Monroe, Dundee & Lake Erie
Monroe Traction Co.
NEW YORK CENTRAL
NORFOLK & WESTERN
Ohio & Lake Superior
Ohio & Michigan Interurban
Ohio & Michigan Traction Co.
Ohio Northern & Michigan
Ottawa Beach & Southern
PENN CENTRAL
PENNSYLVANIA
PENNSYLVANIA-DETROIT
PENNSYLVANIA, OHIO & DETROIT
PERE MARQUETTE

Pleasant Bay
Raisin River
River Raisin & Grand River
RIVER RAISIN & LAKE ERIE
South Eastern Michigan
"SOUTHERN" (of State of Michigan)
Toledo, Adrian & Jackson
TOLEDO & ANN ARBOR
Toledo & Jackson Electric
Toledo & Michigan Terminal
Toledo & Milwaukee Ry
TOLEDO & MONROE
Toledo & Northern of Michigan
Toledo, Ann Arbor & Detroit
TOLEDO, ANN ARBOR & GRAND TRUNK
TOLEDO, ANN ARBOR & JACKSON
Toledo, Ann Arbor & Northern
TOLEDO, ANN ARBOR & NORTH MICHIGAN
Toledo, Ann Arbor & Saginaw
TOLEDO, CANADA SOUTHERN & DETROIT
TOLEDO-DETROIT
Toledo, Monroe & Detroit Electric
TOLEDO, OTTAWA BEACH & NORTHERN
Toledo, Ypsilanti & Saginaw Air Line
WABASH
WABASH, ST. LOUIS & PACIFIC
WABASH WESTERN

MONTCALM COUNTY (059)

Alpena & Michigan South-western
Battle Creek & Bay City
Bay City & Battle Creek
BELLOWS [W. D.]
BOND, MILTON J.
Carson City & Palo
Central Michigan RR
Central Michigan Ry
CHESAPEAKE & OHIO
CHICAGO, SAGINAW & CANADA
CLARK, SNYDER AND CO.
Coldwater & Central Michigan
Coldwater, Marshall & Mackinaw
Columbus, Marshall & Northeastern
Crystal Lake (1900)
Crystal Lake RR (1891)
CUTLER AND SAVIDGE LUMBER CO.
DETROIT, GRAND RAPIDS & WESTERN
DETROIT, LANSING & LAKE MICHIGAN
DETROIT, LANSING & NORTHERN
Flat River & Houghton Lake
FROST, S., AND CO.
GIBBS, J. H.
GRAND HAVEN LUMBER CO.
Grand Rapids & Bay City
Grand Rapids & Belding
GRAND RAPIDS & INDIANA
Grand Rapids & Mackinaw
Grand Rapids, Belding & Greenville (1899)
Grand Rapids, Belding & Greenville (1905)
GRAND RAPIDS, BELDING & SAGINAW
Grand Rapids Electric
Grand Rapids, Grayling & Alpena
Grand Rapids, Greenville & Alpena
Grand Rapids, Greenville & Bay City
Grand Rapids, Rockford & Greenville
Grand Rapids, Traverse Bay & Mackinac
GRAND TRUNK WESTERN
Greenville, Stanton & St. Louis
HAYNES AND SESSIONS
Huron & Michigan
Ionia & Lansing
Ionia & Stanton
Ionia, Stanton & Northern
JUST, W. J., AND BROS.
LONG, A. B., AND SONS
LOUDEN, ANDERSON & CO.
Marshall & Coldwater
Michigan Northern RR (1869)
Michigan Northern Ry (1873)
MICHIGAN NORTHERN RY (1976)
MID-MICHIGAN
Muskegon & Greenville
Owosso & Big Rapids
PENN CENTRAL
PENNSYLVANIA
PERE MARQUETTE
SAGINAW & GRAND RAPIDS
Saginaw & Montcalm
SAGINAW & WESTERN
SLAGHT, N.
SMITH, H.
STEELE, WILLIAM
THOMAS LOG & LUMBER CO.
Toledo, Marshall & Northern
Toledo Michigan & Lake Huron
TOLEDO, SAGINAW & MUSKEGON
TOWLE, JAMES
WHITE AND FRIANT
WHITNEY AND STINCHFIELD
WOOD LAKE LOGGING
WRIGHT, F. N., & CO.
WYMAN, BUSWELL AND CO.

MONTMORENCY COUNTY (060)

ALPENA & NORTHERN
Alpena & South Western
Alpena & Western
Alpena, Gaylord & Western
Amboy & Traverse Bay
Amboy, Lansing & Traverse Bay

AU SABLE & NORTHWESTERN
BOYNE CITY, GAYLORD & ALPENA
Central Michigan RR
Cincinnati & Great Northern
DETROIT & MACKINAC
Grand Rapids, Grayling & Alpena
Grand Rapids, Greenville & Alpena
GRAYLING, TWIN LAKES & NORTHEASTERN
LEWISTON & SOUTHEASTERN
MICHIGAN CENTRAL
Michigan Northern Ry (1873)
MINOR, JOHN S.
NEW YORK CENTRAL
Northern Michigan RR (11/1867)
Ohio & Lake Superior
POTTS, J. E.
POTTS LOGGING RY CO.
Toledo, Saginaw & Mackinaw

MUSKEGON COUNTY (061)

CENTRAL MICHIGAN
CHESAPEAKE & OHIO
CHICAGO & MICHIGAN LAKE SHORE
Chicago, Saginaw & Canada
Fruitport & Lake Shore
GRAND HAVEN
GRAND RAPIDS & INDIANA
Grand Rapids & Lake Shore
Grand Rapids & North Western
GRAND RAPIDS, GRAND HAVEN & MUSKEGON
Grand Rapids, Holland & Lake Michigan
GRAND RAPIDS, NEWAYGO & LAKE SHORE
Grand River & Muskegon
GRAND TRUNK WESTERN
Lake Harbor
Lake Shore RR of Western Michigan
Lakewood Street
Ludington Southern
Manistee & Grand Rapids
MICHIGAN LAKE SHORE
MICHIGAN SHORE
Michigan Terminal
Montague, Pentwater & Manistee
Muskegon & Big Rapids
Muskegon & Ferrysburg
Muskegon & Greenville
MUSKEGON, GRAND RAPIDS & INDIANA
MUSKEGON LAKE
Muskegon, Ludington & Manistee
MUSKEGON RY
MUSKEGON RY & NAVIGATION
Muskegon Street (1880)
MUSKEGON STREET (1897)
Muskegon Terminal
MUSKEGON TRACTION & LIGHTING CO.
MUSKEGON TRACTION CO.
PENN CENTRAL
PENNSYLVANIA
PERE MARQUETTE
Ravenna & Spring Lake Narrow Gauge
SHAW BOX, CRANE AND HOIST CO.
STAPLES AND COVELL
STIMSON, THOMAS D.
TOLEDO, SAGINAW & MUSKEGON
West Michigan Interurban

NEWAYGO COUNTY (062)

ALLEYTON & BIG LAKE
AYERS, A. D.
BIG RAPIDS & WESTERN
BLAKE LOGGING CO.
BURGESS AND LADNER
CHAMPION AND HEYWARD LUMBER CO.
CHESAPEAKE & OHIO
CHICAGO & MICHIGAN LAKE SHORE
Chicago, Saginaw & Canada
Chippewa Valley
CODY AND ADDIS LUMBER CO.
COMSTOCK, C. C.
CONSUMERS POWER CO.
CONVERSE LUMBER CO.
Grand Rapids & Lake Shore
Grand Rapids & Northern
Grand Rapids & North Western
GRAND RAPIDS, NEWAYGO & LAKE SHORE
HARROUN, H. M.
HART AND HORNING
HUNGERFORD LAKE
Ionia & Lansing
JEANNOTT, P., & CO.
Ludington Southern
Manistee & Grand Rapids
Mason & Oceana
Michigan Northern RR (1869)
Michigan Northern RR (1887)
MOON, ROBERT A.
NEIL, ROBERT
Newaygo
PARIS & PERE MARQUETTE RIVER
PERE MARQUETTE
Pere Marquette & Big Rapids
PICKEREL LAKE & MUSKEGON RIVER
RUMSEY LUMBER CO.
RYERSON, HILLS AND CO.
WEST MICHIGAN LUMBER CO.
WESTON, ISAAC M.
WETZELL BROTHERS
WHITE RIVER
WYMAN, BUSWELL AND CO.

OAKLAND COUNTY (063)

Air Line Ry of Michigan
Auburn & Lapeer
Bloomfield & Orchard Lake
Canada, Michigan & Chicago
CHESAPEAKE & OHIO
Chicago & Michigan Grand Trunk
COE RAIL
DETROIT, ALMONT & NORTHERN
DETROIT & BAY CITY
DETROIT & FLINT
Detroit & Lake Orion
DETROIT & MILWAUKEE
DETROIT & NORTHWESTERN
DETROIT & PONTIAC RR
Detroit & Pontiac Ry
Detroit & Shiawassee
Detroit & South Lyon
Detroit, Bay City & Alpena
Detroit Bay City Traction
DETROIT, GRAND HAVEN & MILWAUKEE
DETROIT, GRAND RAPIDS & WESTERN
Detroit, Howell & Lansing RR
Detroit, Howell & Lansing Ry
Detroit, Howell, Lansing & Grand Rapids
Detroit, Lake Orion & Flint
DETROIT, LANSING & LAKE MICHIGAN
DETROIT, LANSING & NORTHERN
Detroit, Pontiac & Northern
Detroit, Pontiac, Lapeer & Northern
DETROIT, ROCHESTER, ROMEO & LAKE ORION
DETROIT UNITED
DETROIT, UTICA & ROMEO
EASTERN MICHIGAN
FLINT & HOLLY
FLINT & PERE MARQUETTE
Genesee & Oakland
Grand Trunk RR of Michigan
Grand Trunk Ry of Michigan
GRAND TRUNK WESTERN
Highland Park & Royal Oak
HOLLY, WAYNE & MONROE
Jackson & Eastern
Lake Superior
Lapeer & Holly
Macomb & Saginaw
Michigan Air Line RR
MICHIGAN AIR LINE RY
MICHIGAN CENTRAL
Michigan Extension
NEW YORK CENTRAL
Northern Michigan Central
OAKLAND
Oakland & Ottawa
Ohio & Lake Superior
Oxford & Port Austin
PENN CENTRAL
PERE MARQUETTE
Pontiac & Detroit
Pontiac & Flint Electric
Pontiac & Genesee
Pontiac & Orchard Lake Street
Pontiac & Oxford
Pontiac & Southern
PONTIAC & SYLVAN LAKE
Pontiac Belt
Pontiac, Orion & Detroit
PONTIAC, OXFORD & NORTHERN
PONTIAC, OXFORD & PORT AUSTIN
Rochester, Almont & Northern
Rochester & Romeo
Rochester & St. Clair
Romeo & Western
ST. CLAIR & CHICAGO AIR LINE
St. Clair River, Pontiac & Jackson
South Lyons & Northern
STANDARD GRAVEL CO.
Toledo & Port Austin
Toledo & Saginaw Bay
TOLEDO, ANN ARBOR & GRAND TRUNK
Toledo, Ann Arbor & North Eastern
Toledo, Ypsilanti & Saginaw Air Line
Troy & Rochester

OCEANA COUNTY (064)

BIGELOW LUMBER CO.
BUTTERS AND PETERS
CHESAPEAKE & OHIO
CHICAGO & MICHIGAN LAKE SHORE
COOK, CHARLES H.
COVELL BROTHERS
Grand Rapids & Lake Shore
Grand Rapids & North Western
Grand Rapids, Newaygo & Lake Shore
Ionia & Lansing
Ludington Southern
Manistee & Grand Rapids
MASON & OCEANA
Michigan Lake Shore
Michigan Northern RR (1887)
Montague Pentwater & Manistee
Muskegon & Big Rapids
Muskegon, Ludington & Manistee
PERE MARQUETTE
STAPLES AND COVELL
West Michigan Interurban

OGEMAW COUNTY (065)

Alpena & Michigan South-western
Alpena & South Western
Amboy & Traverse Bay
Amboy, Lansing & Traverse Bay
AMBROSE, GEORGE, & SON
AU SABLE & NORTHWESTERN
Cincinnati & Great Northern
DETROIT & MACKINAC
DETROIT, BAY CITY & ALPENA
HORR, R. G.
JACKSON, LANSING & SAGINAW
LAKE HURON & SOUTHWESTERN
MICHIGAN CENTRAL
NEW YORK CENTRAL
Northern Michigan RR (11/1867)
OGEMAW SPRINGS
Ohio & Lake Superior
PENN CENTRAL
PLUMMER, C. H.
POTTS LOGGING RY CO.
TAWAS & BAY COUNTY
Toledo, Saginaw & Mackinaw

ONTONAGON COUNTY (066)

ADVENTURE MINING CO
ALEXANDER, TRUEMAN.
ANDERSON, R. E.
Baraga & Watersmeet
BELT COPPER MINES
BENNETT AND BROWN LUMBER CO.
BERGLAND LUMBER CO.
BRUNSWICK-EWEN LUMBER CO.
CALDERWOOD LUMBER CO.
CHICAGO & NORTH WESTERN
CHICAGO & NORTH WESTERN TRANSPORTATION
CHICAGO, MILWAUKEE & ST. PAUL
CHICAGO, MILWAUKEE, ST. PAUL & PACIFIC
Chicago, St. Paul & Fond du Lac
COPPER RANGE
DELATRIE AND ANDERSON LUMBER CO.
DIAMOND LUMBER CO.
DULUTH, SOUTH SHORE & ATLANTIC
GREENWOOD LUMBER CO.
HOLT LUMBER CO.
Houghton & Ontonagon
Houghton & Rockland
HOUGHTON, CHASSELL & SOUTHWESTERN
Ishpeming, L'Anse & Ontonagon
LAKE MINING CO.
LAKE SUPERIOR LUMBER CO.
L'Anse & Ontonagon
Marquette & Ontonagon RR
Marquette & Ontonagon Ry
Marquette, Houghton & Ontonagon
McMILLAN, C. V., LUMBER CO.
MENASHA WOODENWARE CO.
MERCER, DELATRIE LUMBER CO.
MILWAUKEE & NORTHERN
MILWAUKEE, LAKE SHORE & WESTERN
MINERAL RANGE RR
Mineral Range Ry
Northern Michigan RR (11/1867)
Northern Michigan RR (1888)
NORWICH MINING CO.
Ohio & Lake Superior
ONTONAGON
ONTONAGON & BRULE RIVER
Ontonagon & Flintsteel
Ontonagon & Montreal River
Ontonagon & Southwestern
Ontonagon & State Line
ONTONOGAN FIBRE CO.
Ontonagon, Gogebic & Wisconsin
Ontonagon Southern
Peninsula
ROCKLAND MINING CO.
St. Mary's & Minneapolis
SAWYER, GOODMAN CO.
SOO LINE
SPIES-THOMPSON LUMBER CO.
THOMPSON & WELLS CO.
TROUT CREEK LUMBER CO.
UNION BAY & NONESUCH
Upper Peninsula & Green Bay
Vieux Desert & Lake Superior
WEIDMAN & SON LUMBER CO.
Wisconsin & Lake Superior
WISCONSIN CENTRAL, LTD.
Wisconsin, Sault Ste. Marie & Mackinac

OSCEOLA COUNTY (067)

ANN ARBOR
Cadillac & Evart
CHESAPEAKE & OHIO
COMSTOCK, C. C.
DENNIS BROTHERS SALT AND LUMBER CO.
DEWING AND SON (LUMBER CO.)
EVART & OSCEOLA
FLINT & PERE MARQUETTE
GRAND RAPIDS & INDIANA
Grand Rapids & Mackinaw
Grand Rapids & Northern
Grand Rapids, Indiana & Manistee
Grand Rapids, Traverse Bay & Mackinac
HERSEY GRAVEL CO.
Hobart & Manistee River
Ionia, Stanton & Northern

KELLOGG AND SAWYER (LUMBER CO.)
Lake Superior
MANISTEE & GRAND RAPIDS
MICHIGAN EAST & WEST
MICHIGAN INTERSTATE
Michigan Northern RR (1869)
MICHIGAN NORTHERN RY (1976)
MUSKEGON RIVER & CAT CREEK
MUSKEGON RIVER & ROSE LAKE
Owosso & North Western
PENN CENTRAL
PENNSYLVANIA
PERE MARQUETTE
Riverdale & Lake Michigan
Toledo & Cadillac
Toledo, Ann Arbor & Cadillac
Toledo, Ann Arbor & Mackinaw
TOLEDO, ANN ARBOR & NORTH MICHIGAN
TUSCOLA & SAGINAW BAY
WHITE, FRIANT AND LETELLIER

OSCODA COUNTY (068)

Alpena & Michigan South-western
Alpena & South Western
Amboy & Traverse Bay
Amboy, Lansing & Traverse Bay
AU SABLE & NORTHWESTERN
Central Michigan RR
Cincinnati & Great Northern
DETROIT & MACKINAC
Grand Rapids, Grayling & Alpena
Grand Rapids, Greenville & Alpena
GRAYLING, TWIN LAKES & NORTHEASTERN
LEWISTON & SOUTHEASTERN
Michigan Northern Ry (1873)
Northern Michigan RR (11/1867)
Ohio & Lake Superior
POTTS, J. E.
POTTS, J. E., SALT AND LUMBER CO.
POTTS LOGGING RY CO.
ROBINSON LUMBER CO.
Toledo, Saginaw & Mackinaw

OTSEGO COUNTY (069)

Alpena & Western
Alpena, Gaylord & Western
Amboy, Lansing & Traverse Bay
AU SABLE & NORTHWESTERN
BOYNE CITY & SOUTHEASTERN
BOYNE CITY, GAYLORD & ALPENA
Cincinnati & Great Northern
CRAPO LAKE & NORTHWESTERN
DETROIT & CHARLEVOIX
DETROIT & MACKINAC
GRAND RAPIDS & INDIANA
Grayling & Charlevoix
GRAYLING, TWIN LAKES & NORTHEASTERN
JACKSON, LANSING & SAGINAW
KNEELAND-BIGELOW CO.
MICHIGAN CENTRAL
MICHIGAN NORTHERN RY (1976)
NEW YORK CENTRAL
Northern Michigan Central
Northern Michigan RR (11/1867)
PENN CENTRAL
PENNSYLVANIA
Toledo, Ann Arbor & Mackinaw
Toledo, Saginaw & Mackinaw
TUSCOLA & SAGINAW BAY

OTTAWA COUNTY (070)

Allegan & Holland
BLENDON LUMBER CO.
CENTRAL MICHIGAN
Central Michigan RR
CHESAPEAKE & OHIO
CHICAGO & MICHIGAN LAKE SHORE
Chicago, Saginaw & Canada
COOPERSVILLE & MARNE
DETROIT & MILWAUKEE
DETROIT, GRAND HAVEN & MILWAUKEE
FERRY AND SONS
Fruitport & Lake Shore
GILBERT TRAMWAY
GRAND HAVEN
Grand Haven & Southeastern
GRAND HAVEN STREET
Grand Rapids & Chicago Ry
Grand Rapids & Holland
GRAND RAPIDS & INDIANA
Grand Rapids & Lake Michigan
Grand Rapids & North Western
Grand Rapids, Chicago & St. Louis
Grand Rapids Electric
GRAND RAPIDS, GRAND HAVEN & MUSKEGON
GRAND RAPIDS, HOLLAND & CHICAGO
GRAND RAPIDS, HOLLAND & LAKE MICHIGAN
Grand Rapids, Spring Lake & Grand Haven
Grand River & Muskegon
Grand River RR
GRAND TRUNK WESTERN
HOLLAND & LAKE MICHIGAN
Holland South Shore
Lake Shore RR of Western Michigan
Lansing & Lake Michigan
Ludington Southern
Michigan & Ohio Ry
MICHIGAN LAKE SHORE

Michigan Midland
MICHIGAN RR
MICHIGAN RY
Michigan Shore & Eastern
Muskegon & Ferrysburg
MUSKEGON, GRAND RAPIDS & INDIANA
"Northern" (of State of Michigan)
Oakland & Ottawa
Ohio & Grand Haven
OHIO DOCK HORSE
Ohio, Quincy & Grand Haven
PAINTER, PARKS AND THOMPSON
PENN CENTRAL
PENNSYLVANIA
PERE MARQUETTE
Port Huron & Lake Michigan
Port Sheldon & Grand Rapids
TOLEDO, SAGINAW & MUSKEGON
WEATHERWAX LUMBER CO.
WILLARD, W. F.

PRESQUE ISLE COUNTY (071)

ALPENA & NORTHERN
Amboy & Traverse Bay
Amboy, Lansing & Traverse Bay
Central Michigan RR
Cheboygan & East Michigan
DETROIT & MACKINAC
HURON HANDLE AND MFG. CO.
LOBDELL AND BAILEY
MICHIGAN LIMESTONE & CHEMICAL CO.
ONAWAY & NORTH MICHIGAN

ROSCOMMON COUNTY (072)

Alpena & Michigan South-western
Alpena & South Western
Amboy, Lansing & Traverse Bay
Central Michigan RR
Cincinnati & Great Northern
DARRAGH AND SELLINGER
DENTON AND ROWE
DETROIT & MACKINAC
Flat River & Houghton Lake
GRAND RAPIDS & INDIANA
Grand Rapids, Grayling & Alpena
Grand Rapids, Greenville & Alpena
Houghton Lake & Eastern
JACKSON, LANSING & SAGINAW
MICHIGAN CENTRAL
Michigan Northern Ry (1873)
NEW YORK CENTRAL
Northern Michigan RR (11/1867)
PENN CENTRAL
PENNSYLVANIA
ROSCOMMON LUMBER CO.
ST. HELEN'S LAKE & SOUTHERN
STEPHENS, HENRY, AND CO.
WRIGHT, A. W., LUMBER CO.

SAGINAW COUNTY (073)

Amboy & Traverse Bay
Amboy, Lansing & Traverse Bay
BAY CITY & EAST SAGINAW
Cass River
CENTRAL MICHIGAN
CHESAPEAKE & OHIO
Chicago, Kalamazoo & Saginaw
Chicago, Saginaw & Canada
Cincinnati & Great Northern
CINCINNATI, SAGINAW & MACKINAW
DETROIT & BAY CITY
Detroit & Saginaw River
Detroit, Bay City & Alpena
DETROIT, FLINT & SAGINAW
Detroit, Flint River & Saginaw Valley
DETROIT, GRAND RAPIDS & WESTERN
East Saginaw
East Saginaw & Ann Arbor
EAST SAGINAW & ST. CLAIR
EAST SAGINAW CITY
East Saginaw Street
FLINT & PERE MARQUETTE
Flint & Saginaw Traction
Flint, Saginaw & Bay City
GRAND TRUNK WESTERN
HURON & EASTERN
Huron & Michigan
INTERURBAN RY OF SAGINAW
JACKSON, LANSING & SAGINAW
Lake Superior
Lansing & Northeastern
Macomb & Saginaw
Michigan & Chicago
MICHIGAN CENTRAL
MICHIGAN RR
MICHIGAN RY
MID-MICHIGAN
NEW YORK CENTRAL
Northern Michigan Central
Northern Michigan RR (11/1867)
Northern Michigan Ry
Ohio & Lake Superior
PENN CENTRAL
PERE MARQUETTE
Port Huron & Lexington
PORT HURON & NORTHWESTERN
Port Huron & Saginaw Valley
Port Huron, Lexington & Western

Riverside Park Ry of Saginaw
Saginaw & Bay City
Saginaw & Bay City Rapid Transit
SAGINAW & FLINT
Saginaw & Frankenmuth
Saginaw & Genesee
Saginaw & Lansing
Saginaw & Montcalm
Saginaw & St. Clair River
Saginaw & Southwestern
SAGINAW-BAY CITY
Saginaw Bay South Western
SAGINAW CONSOLIDATED STREET
Saginaw, Owosso & Lansing
Saginaw Southern
Saginaw Street RR
SAGINAW STREET RY (1864)
SAGINAW STREET RY (1886)
Saginaw Suburban
SAGINAW TRANSIT CO.
SAGINAW, TUSCOLA & HURON
SAGINAW UNION STREET
SAGINAW VALLEY & ST. LOUIS
SAGINAW VALLEY TRACTION CO.
Salina Street
Southern Electric
Street RR of East Saginaw
Toledo, Ann Arbor & Saginaw
TOLEDO, SAGINAW & MACKINAW
Toledo, Saginaw & Muskegon
TUSCOLA & SAGINAW BAY
UNION STREET RY OF SAGINAW
Union Traction Co.
UNITED TRACTION CO.

ST. CLAIR COUNTY (074)

Air Line Ry of Michigan
ALGONAC TRANSIT CO.
Bay City & Port Huron
Bay City, Caro & Port Huron
Canada, Michigan & Chicago
CANADIAN NATIONAL
Capac & Northern
CHESAPEAKE & OHIO
CHICAGO & GRAND TRUNK
CHICAGO & LAKE HURON
Chicago & Michigan Grand Trunk
CHICAGO, DETROIT & CANADA GRAND TRUNK JUNCTION
Chicago, Saginaw & Canada
CITY ELECTRIC OF PORT HURON (1892)
City Electric of Port Huron (1923)
City RR
Detroit & Northern
Detroit & Port Huron
DETROIT & PORT HURON SHORE LINE
Detroit & River St. Clair
Detroit & St. Clair River
DETROIT, BAY CITY & WESTERN
Detroit, Lexington & Lake Huron
Detroit, Mt. Clemens & Marine City
Detroit, Port Huron & Sarnia
Detroit, Romeo & Port Huron
East Saginaw & St. Clair
FAIR HAVEN WOODEN
FLINT & PERE MARQUETTE
Fort Gratiot & Lexington
Grand Trunk Ry of Michigan
GRAND TRUNK WESTERN
GRATIOT ELECTRIC
Lexington & Utica
Michigan Air Line Extension
MICHIGAN CENTRAL
Michigan Extension
Michigan Midland
MICHIGAN, MIDLAND & CANADA
NEW YORK CENTRAL
"Northern" (of State of Michigan)
NORTH WESTERN GRAND TRUNK
PERE MARQUETTE
PORT HURON & DETROIT
PORT HURON & GRATIOT STREET
PORT HURON & LAKE MICHIGAN
Port Huron & Lexington
Port Huron & Milwaukee
Port Huron & Northern
PORT HURON & NORTHWESTERN
Port Huron & Owosso
Port Huron & Port Austin Electric
Port Huron & Saginaw Valley
Port Huron & St. Clair River
Port Huron & Southwestern
PORT HURON ELECTRIC
Port Huron, Lexington & Western
Port Huron RR Tunnel Co.
PORT HURON RY
PORT HURON, ST. CLAIR & MARINE CITY
PORT HURON SOUTHERN
RAPID RR
RAPID RY
Saginaw & St. Clair River
St. Clair & Romeo
ST. CLAIR & WESTERN
St. Clair City
ST. CLAIR RIVER, PONTIAC & JACKSON
ST. CLAIR TUNNEL CO.
Thumb
Toledo & Port Austin
Utica & Lexington

ST. JOSEPH COUNTY (075)

Air Line Ry of Michigan
BATTLE CREEK & STURGIS
CANADA & ST. LOUIS
Chicago & Canada Pacific
CHICAGO & GRAND TRUNK
CHICAGO & LAKE HURON
CONSOLIDATED RAIL
Constantine & Niles
Eastern & Northwestern
GRAND RAPIDS & INDIANA
Grand Rapids & Southern
Grand Trunk Ry of Michigan
GRAND TRUNK WESTERN
KALAMAZOO & WHITE PIGEON
Kalamazoo, Elkhart & South Bend
LAKE SHORE & MICHIGAN SOUTHERN
Maumee Branch
MICHIGAN AIR LINE RR
MICHIGAN CENTRAL
Michigan Extension
Michigan, Indiana & St. Louis
Michigan Northern RR (1869)
MICHIGAN SOUTHERN
MICHIGAN SOUTHERN & NORTHERN INDIANA
Mottville & White Pigeon
NEW YORK CENTRAL
Ohio & Southern Michigan
PENN CENTRAL
PENNSYLVANIA
ST. JOSEPH VALLEY RR (1848)
ST. LOUIS, STURGIS & BATTLE CREEK
SCHOOLCRAFT & THREE RIVERS
"Southern" (of State of Michigan)
Sturgis & Indiana
Sturgis & Mansfield
Sturgis & State Line
STURGIS, GOSHEN & ST. LOUIS
Sturgis, Indiana & Ohio
Toledo & South Haven (St. Joseph Co. Div.)
Toledo & South Haven (St. Joseph Div.)
Tri-State Rys of Michigan
White Pigeon & State Line

SANILAC COUNTY (076)

Bay City & Port Huron
Bay City, Caro & Port Huron
Capac & Northern
CHESAPEAKE & OHIO
Croswell & Peck
DETROIT, BAY CITY & WESTERN
DETROIT, CARO & SANDUSKY
Detroit, Lexington & Lake Huron
FLINT & PERE MARQUETTE
Fort Gratiot & Lexington
HURON & EASTERN
Lapeer & Port Austin
Lexington & Utica
PERE MARQUETTE
Port Huron & Lexington
PORT HURON & NORTHWESTERN
Port Huron & Port Austin Electric
SANILAC
Thumb
Utica & Lexington

SCHOOLCRAFT COUNTY (077)

BLANEY & SOUTHERN
Canada, LaCrosse & Southwestern
DELTA LUMBER CO.
DETROIT, MACKINAC & MARQUETTE
DULUTH, SOUTH SHORE & ATLANTIC
GARDEN BAY
INLAND LIME AND STONE CO.
LAKE MICHIGAN & SUPERIOR
LAKE SUPERIOR & ISHPEMING
Mackinaw & Lake Superior
MANISTIQUE
MANISTIQUE & LAKE SUPERIOR
MANISTIQUE & NORTHERN
MANISTIQUE & NORTHWESTERN
MANISTIQUE LUMBERING CO.
MANISTIQUE, MARQUETTE & NORTHERN
MANISTIQUE PULP AND PAPER CO.
MARQUETTE & SOUTHEASTERN
Marquette, Sault Ste. Marie & Mackinac
Menominee & Sault Ste. Marie
MINNEAPOLIS, ST. PAUL & SAULT STE. MARIE
MINNEAPOLIS, SAULT STE. MARIE & ATLANTIC
MUNISING
MUNISING, MARQUETTE & SOUTHEASTERN
Northern Michigan RR (11/1867)
St. Mary's & Minneapolis
Sault Ste. Marie & Southwestern
SOO LINE
WISCONSIN CENTRAL, LTD.
WISCONSIN LAND AND LUMBER CO.

SHIAWASSEE COUNTY (078)

Amboy & Traverse Bay
AMBOY, LANSING & TRAVERSE BAY
ANN ARBOR
Canada, Michigan & Chicago
CENTRAL MICHIGAN
CHICAGO & GRAND TRUNK
CHICAGO & LAKE HURON

CHICAGO & NORTHEASTERN
Cincinnati & Great Northern
CINCINNATI, SAGINAW & MACKINAW
DETROIT & MILWAUKEE
Detroit & Shiawassee
DETROIT, GRAND HAVEN & MILWAUKEE
Flint & Lansing
GRAND TRUNK WESTERN
Ionia & Owosso
JACKSON, LANSING & SAGINAW
LANSING & NORTHEASTERN
Long Lake, Durand & Corunna Electric
Michigan & Chicago
MICHIGAN CENTRAL
MICHIGAN ELECTRIC (1923)
Michigan Extension
MICHIGAN INTERSTATE
Michigan Midland
MICHIGAN RY
Michigan Ry & Light
MICHIGAN UNITED TRACTION
NEW YORK CENTRAL
"Northern" (of State of Michigan)
Northern Michigan Central
Oakland & Ottawa
Owosso & Big Rapids
OWOSSO & CORUNNA ELECTRIC CO.
Owosso & Corunna Electric Street
Owosso & Corunna Street
OWOSSO & CORUNNA TRACTION CO.
Owosso & North Western
Owosso City Electric
PENN CENTRAL
Port Huron & Lake Michigan
Port Huron & Milwaukee
Port Huron & Owosso
Saginaw & Lansing
Saginaw & Southwestern
Saginaw Bay South Western
Saginaw, Owosso & Lansing
Shiawassee & Vernon
Toledo, Ann Arbor & Grand Trunk
Toledo, Ann Arbor & Northern
TOLEDO, ANN ARBOR & NORTH MICHIGAN
TOLEDO, SAGINAW & MACKINAW
TUSCOLA & SAGINAW BAY
Union Depot Co. of Durand

TUSCOLA COUNTY (079)

Bay City & Caro
Bay City & Port Huron
Bay City, Caro & Eastern
Bay City, Caro & Port Huron
Bay, Tuscola & Huron
CARO & LAKE HURON
Cass River
CHESAPEAKE & OHIO
DETROIT & BAY CITY
Detroit & Saginaw River
DETROIT, BAY CITY & WESTERN
Detroit Bay City Traction
DETROIT, CARO & SANDUSKY
Detroit, Flint & Saginaw
Detroit, Pontiac, Lapeer & Northern
East Saginaw & St. Clair
FLINT & PERE MARQUETTE
GRAND TRUNK WESTERN
HURON & EASTERN
Lapeer & Port Austin
MICHIGAN CENTRAL
NEW YORK CENTRAL
Northern Michigan Ry
Oxford & Port Austin
PENN CENTRAL
PERE MARQUETTE
PONTIAC, OXFORD & NORTHERN
PONTIAC, OXFORD & PORT AUSTIN
Port Huron & Lexington
PORT HURON & NORTHWESTERN
Port Huron & Saginaw Valley
Port Huron, Lexington & Western
Saginaw & St. Clair River
SAGINAW, TUSCOLA & HURON
Toledo & Saginaw Bay
TUSCOLA & SAGINAW BAY

VAN BUREN COUNTY (080)

Benton Harbor Electric Ry & Transit
"Central" (of State of Michigan)
CHESAPEAKE & OHIO
CHICAGO & MICHIGAN LAKE SHORE
Chicago, Kalamazoo & Eastern
Detroit & St. Joseph
Eastern & Northwestern
East Shore & Southwestern
Grand Rapids & Chicago RR
Grand Rapids, Chicago & St. Louis
Grand Rapids, Kalamazoo & South Haven
Grand Trunk RR of Michigan
Kalamazoo & Lake Michigan RR
Kalamazoo & Lake Michigan Ry
KALAMAZOO & SOUTH HAVEN
KALAMAZOO, LAKE SHORE & CHICAGO RY
Kalamazoo, Lake Shore & Chicago Traction
Kalamazoo, Paw Paw & Lake Michigan
Lake Michigan & Kalamazoo
Lake Shore RR of Western Michigan
Lawton, Paw Paw & South Haven
Mackinac & Chicago
Michigan & Chicago

MICHIGAN CENTRAL
Michigan Light & Traction
Michigan Shore & Eastern
Michigan West Shore Traction
MILLS AND LEIGHTON
NATIONAL RAIL PASSENGER
NEW YORK CENTRAL
PACKARD, ALFRED H., JR.
PAW PAW
Paw Paw Valley
PENN CENTRAL
PERE MARQUETTE
St Joe River Traction Co.
Saugatuck & South Haven
SOUTH HAVEN & EASTERN
South Haven & Lake Shore
South Haven & Paw Paw Lake Electric
South Haven Traction Co.
SOUTHWESTERN MICHIGAN
Sturgis, Indiana & Ohio
TOLEDO & SOUTH HAVEN
Trans-Michigan Street
West Michigan
West Michigan Traction Co.
WILLIARD, W. F.

WASHTENAW COUNTY (081)

Adrian & Ann Arbor Electric
Adrian & Detroit
Air Line Ry of Michigan
ANN ARBOR
ANN ARBOR & YPSILANTI ELECTRIC
ANN ARBOR & YPSILANTI STREET
Ann Arbor Interurban
Ann Arbor Street (1866)
ANN ARBOR STREET (1888)
Ann Arbor, Ypsilanti & Detroit Street
CADILLAC SAND AND GRAVEL CO.
"CENTRAL" (of State of Michigan)
CHESAPEAKE & OHIO
Cincinnati, Saginaw & Mackinaw
CONSOLIDATED RAIL
Detroit, Adrian, Logansport & St. Louis
Detroit & Ann Arbor
Detroit & Chicago Traction
Detroit & Howell
Detroit & St. Joseph
Detroit Ann Arbor & Adrian
DETROIT, BUTLER & ST. LOUIS
DETROIT, GRAND RAPIDS & WESTERN
DETROIT, HILLSDALE & INDIANA
DETROIT, HILLSDALE & SOUTH WESTERN
Detroit, Howell & Lansing RR
Detroit, Howell & Lansing Ry
Detroit, Howell, Lansing & Grand Rapids
DETROIT, JACKSON & CHICAGO RY
DETROIT, LANSING & LAKE MICHIGAN
DETROIT, LANSING & NORTHERN
Detroit, Plymouth & Northville
DETROIT UNITED
DETROIT, YPSILANTI & ANN ARBOR
DETROIT, YPSILANTI, ANN ARBOR & JACKSON
East Saginaw & Ann Arbor
Grand Trunk Ry of Michigan
Jackson & Ann Arbor
Jackson & Eastern
JACKSON, ANN ARBOR & DETROIT
Jackson, Ann Arbor & Detroit Traction
LAKE SHORE & MICHIGAN SOUTHERN
Lansing & Southeastern
Lansing, Dexter & Ann Arbor
Lansing, Dexter & Ann Arbor Electric
Manchester & Homer
Michigan Air Line RR
Michigan Air Line Ry
MICHIGAN CENTRAL
MICHIGAN INTERSTATE
MICHIGAN SOUTHERN
MICHIGAN SOUTHERN & NORTHERN INDIANA
Monroe & Ann Arbor
Monroe & Ypsilanti
NEW YORK CENTRAL
NORFOLK & WESTERN
Ohio & Lake Superior
Ohio & Michigan Interurban
Ohio & Michigan Traction Co.
Ohio Northern & Michigan
Palmyra & Jacksonburgh
PENN CENTRAL
PERE MARQUETTE
Romeo & Western
South Lyons & Northern
TOLEDO & ANN ARBOR
TOLEDO, ANN ARBOR & GRAND TRUNK
Toledo, Ann Arbor & Jackson
Toledo, Ann Arbor & North Eastern
Toledo, Ann Arbor & Northern
TOLEDO, ANN ARBOR & NORTH MICHIGAN
Toledo, Ann Arbor & Saginaw
TUSCOLA & SAGINAW BAY
UNIVERSITY OF MICHIGAN
YPSILANTI & SALINE ELECTRIC
Ypsilanti & Tecumseh

WAYNE COUNTY (082)

AMERICAN SHIPBUILDING CO.
ANN ARBOR & YPSILANTI ELECTRIC
Ann Arbor, Ypsilanti & Detroit Street
BELLE ISLE SCENIC
Canada Southern & Chicago

CANADA SOUTHERN BRIDGE CO.
CANADIAN NATIONAL RYS
CASS AVENUE
"CENTRAL" (of State of Michigan)
CENTRAL MARKET, CASS AVENUE & THIRD STREET
CHESAPEAKE & OHIO
CHICAGO & CANADA SOUTHERN
CHICAGO, DETROIT & CANADA GRAND TRUNK JUNCTION
Chicago, Detroit & Toledo
City & Suburban Traction Co.
City Contract Co.
CONGRESS & BAKER STREET
CONSOLIDATED RAIL
DELRAY CONNECTING
DELRAY TERMINAL
DEPARTMENT OF STREET RAILWAYS, CITY OF DETROIT
Detroit, Adrian, Logansport & St. Louis
DETROIT, ALMONT & NORTHERN
Detroit & Adrian Traction
Detroit & Ann Arbor
DETROIT & BAY CITY
DETROIT & CHICAGO
Detroit & Chicago Traction
Detroit & Cincinnati
Detroit & Dearborn Street
DETROIT & FLINT
DETROIT & GRAND TRUNK JUNCTION
Detroit & Highland Park
Detroit & Howell
DETROIT & IRONTON
Detroit & Lake Orion
DETROIT & LAKE ST. CLAIR
DETROIT & LIMA NORTHERN
Detroit & Maumee
DETROIT & MILWAUKEE
Detroit & Monroe
DETROIT & NORTHWESTERN
DETROIT & PONTIAC RR
Detroit & Pontiac Ry
Detroit & Port Huron
DETROIT & PORT HURON SHORE LINE
Detroit & Saginaw River
Detroit & St. Clair River
Detroit & St. Joseph
Detroit & Shiawassee
Detroit & South Lyon
Detroit & State Line
Detroit & Toledo
DETROIT & TOLEDO SHORE LINE
DETROIT & WESTERN
Detroit Ann Arbor & Adrian
Detroit, Armada & Northern
Detroit, Bay City & Alpena
Detroit Bay City Traction Co.
Detroit Belt RR (1892)
DETROIT BELT LINE RR (1909)
Detroit Belt Ry & Depot Co.
DETROIT, BUTLER & ST. LOUIS
DETROIT CITIZENS' STREET
DETROIT CITY
DETROIT CONNECTING
DETROIT, DELRAY & DEARBORN
DETROIT ELECTRIC (1886)
DETROIT ELECTRIC (1896)
DETROIT, FORT WAYNE & BELLE ISLE
DETROIT, GRAND HAVEN & MILWAUKEE
DETROIT, GRAND RAPIDS & WESTERN
Detroit, Howell & Lansing RR
Detroit, Howell & Lansing Ry
Detroit, Howell, Lansing & Grand Rapids
DETROIT, JACKSON & CHICAGO
DETROIT, LAKE SHORE & MT. CLEMENS
DETROIT, LANSING & LAKE MICHIGAN
DETROIT, LANSING & NORTHERN
Detroit, Lexington & Lake Huron
Detroit, Lincoln & Denver
DETROIT MANUFACTURERS
Detroit Metropolitan Street
DETROIT, MONROE & TOLEDO
DETROIT, MONROE & TOLEDO SHORT LINE
Detroit Municipal
DETROIT, PLYMOUTH & NORTHVILLE
Detroit, Pontiac & Northern
Detroit, Pontiac, Lapeer & Northern
Detroit, Port Huron & Sarnia
Detroit River & Lake Erie Terminal
Detroit River Bridge Co.
Detroit River Marine
Detroit River RR & Bridge Co.
Detroit River RR Tunnel Co.
Detroit River Section Floating Dock
Detroit River Street
Detroit River Subways Co.
Detroit River Terminal
DETROIT RIVER TUNNEL CO.
DETROIT, ROCHESTER, ROMEO & LAKE ORION
Detroit, Romeo & Port Huron
Detroit, Rouge River & Dearborn
Detroit, Rouge River & Dearborn Street
Detroit RR & Tunnel Co.
DETROIT RY
Detroit Service-at-Cost
DETROIT SHIPBUILDING CO.
DETROIT SOUTHERN
Detroit, Springwells & Dearborn
DETROIT STREET
Detroit Suburban Street
DETROIT TERMINAL RR
DETROIT TERMINAL RY
DETROIT, TOLEDO & IRONTON
Detroit Transit RR

DETROIT TRANSIT RY
DETROIT TRANSPORTATION CORP.
Detroit Union Bridge Co.
DETROIT UNION RR DEPOT & STATION
DETROIT UNITED
DETROIT, UTICA & ROMEO
Detroit Western Transit
DETROIT, WESTERN TRANSIT & JUNCTION
DETROIT, YPSILANTI & ANN ARBOR
DETROIT, YPSILANTI, ANN ARBOR & JACKSON
EAST DETROIT & GROSSE POINTE
EASTERN MICHIGAN
EASTERN MICHIGAN TOLEDO
Electric Depot Co.
FLINT & PERE MARQUETTE
FORD TRANSPORTATION CO.
FORT STREET & ELMWOOD
FORT STREET UNION DEPOT CO.
FORT WAYNE & BELLE ISLE
FORT WAYNE & ELMWOOD
Gibralter & Clinton
GRAND RIVER ELECTRIC
GRAND RIVER RY
GRAND RIVER STREET
GRAND TRUNK WESTERN
Gratiot Avenue
Grosse Ile
HAMTRAMCK & GROSS POINTE
HAMTRAMCK STREET
HIGHLAND PARK
Highland Park & Royal Oak
HOLLY, WAYNE & MONROE
HUDSON MOTOR CAR CO.
Jackson & Eastern
JACKSON, ANN ARBOR & DETROIT
Jackson, Ann Arbor & Detroit Traction
JEFFERSON AVENUE
LAKE SHORE & MICHIGAN SOUTHERN
Metropolitan
Metropolitan Electric
Michigan & Canada Bridge & Tunnel Co.
Michigan & Ohio Electric
MICHIGAN CENTRAL
Michigan Central Bridge Co.
MICHIGAN SOUTHERN & NORTHERN INDIANA
NEW YORK CENTRAL
NORFOLK & WESTERN
NORTH DETROIT ELECTRIC
Northern Michigan RR (2/1867)
Northern Michigan Ry
OAKLAND
Ohio & Lake Superior
PENN CENTRAL
PENNSALT
PENNSYLVANIA
PENNSYLVANIA-DETROIT
PENNSYLVANIA, OHIO & DETROIT
Peoples Ry of Detroit
PERE MARQUETTE
Pere Marquette International Bridge Co.
Pontiac & Detroit
Pontiac & Southern
Port Huron & Northwestern
Rapid RR
RAPID RY
River Rouge
RUSSELL STREET, ST. AUBIN AVENUE & DETROIT
St. Aubin Avenue Street
SHELBY & DETROIT
SIBLEY QUARRY CO.
SOLVAY PROCESS CO.
South Eastern Michigan
Springwells, Ecorse & Wyandotte
TOLEDO, CANADA SOUTHERN & DETROIT
Toledo, Monroe & Detroit Electric
Toledo, Ypsilanti & Saginaw Air Line
WABASH
WABASH, ST. LOUIS & PACIFIC
WABASH WESTERN
WYANDOTTE & DETROIT RIVER
WYANDOTTE SOUTHERN
WYANDOTTE TERMINAL

WEXFORD COUNTY (083)

ANDERSON, A. F.
ANN ARBOR
BOND, MILTON J.
Cadillac & Evart
CADILLAC & LAKE CITY
CADILLAC & NORTHEASTERN
CADILLAC CHEMICAL CO.
Cadillac, Manistee Valley & Lake Michigan
Cadillac Traction
CHITTENDON LUMBER CO.
COBBS AND MITCHELL
CUMMER [JACOB] AND DIGGINS
CUMMER [JACOB] AND SON
CUMMER [JACOB] LUMBER CO.
Frankfort & South Eastern
GRAND RAPIDS & INDIANA
Grand Rapids & Mackinaw
Grand Rapids & Northern
Grand Rapids, Traverse Bay & Mackinac
HARING & LAKE CITY
Hobart & Manistee River
MANISTEE & LUTHER
MANISTEE & NORTHEASTERN
MICHIGAN INTERSTATE
Michigan Northern RR (1869)
MICHIGAN NORTHERN RY (1976)
Missaukee
OSCEOLA, LAKE & WEXFORD

Owosso & North Western
PENN CENTRAL
PENNSYLVANIA
Riverdale & Lake Michigan
Toledo & Cadillac
Toledo, Ann Arbor & Cadillac
TOLEDO, ANN ARBOR & LAKE MICHIGAN
Toledo, Ann Arbor & Mackinaw
TOLEDO, ANN ARBOR & NORTH MICHIGAN
TUSCOLA & SAGINAW BAY

COUNTY NOT DETERMINED OR NOT GIVEN IN ARTICLES

ADDIS, [WILLIAM] AND CREIGHTON
ALABASTER
ASH BROTHERS
BARNARD [N. and A.]
BRADLEY AND KELLY
BRIGGS & COOPER
BROWN, JOHN C.
CURTIS, W. A., LUMBER CO.
Del-Par
Detroit, Lansing & Grand Rapids
Detroit, Pontiac & Owosso
Fenn Valley
FREDERIC[K] & CHARLEVOIX
Jefferson Avenue
Lansing & Northern
MATHINSON AND WHITE
MERRILL AND RING LOGGING CO.
MICHIGAN ALKALI CO.
Michigan & Western
Michigan Traction Extension Co. (1906)
NESTER LOGGING
NICHOLAS, CHURCH AND CO.
Northern Michigan Power Co.
PORTAGE LAKE
SAGINAW LUMBER AND SALT CO.
Southern, Kent & Pacific
Wasepi
WILHELM AND BROTHERS

HOLDING COMPANIES

CANADA SOUTHERN
CHESSIE SYSTEM INC.
CHICAGO MILWAUKEE CORP.
CNW CORP.
COMMONWEALTH POWER RAILWAY & LIGHT
CONNECTING RY
CSX CORP.
DETROIT & PORT HURON SHORE LINE
DETROIT SUBURBAN
GRAND TRUNK CORP.
GRAND TRUNK INDUSTRIES
GRAND TRUNK RY OF CANADA
NORFOLK SOUTHERN CORP.
PENN CENTRAL CORP.
PENNDEL CO.
PENNSYLVANIA CO.
RAIL-TEX CORP.
SAGINAW-BAY CITY RY & LIGHT
SOO LINE CORP.
TOLEDO RY & LIGHT CO.
UNITED RR CORP.
WISCONSIN CENTRAL TRANSPORTATION CORP.

REORGANIZING COMPANIES

Allegan & State Line
CINCINNATI & MICHIGAN
DETROIT & STATE LINE WABASH
ESCANABA, FRANKFORT & SOUTHEASTERN
MACKINAW & MARQUETTE
MICHIGAN & MACKINAW
MICHIGAN RY (1880)
PENNSYLVANIA NEW YORK CENTRAL TRANSPORTATION
PENTWATER & MANISTEE
PORT HURON & INDIANA
TOLEDO & MILWAUKEE RR

Grand Trunk Western #19, Detroit, March 1960

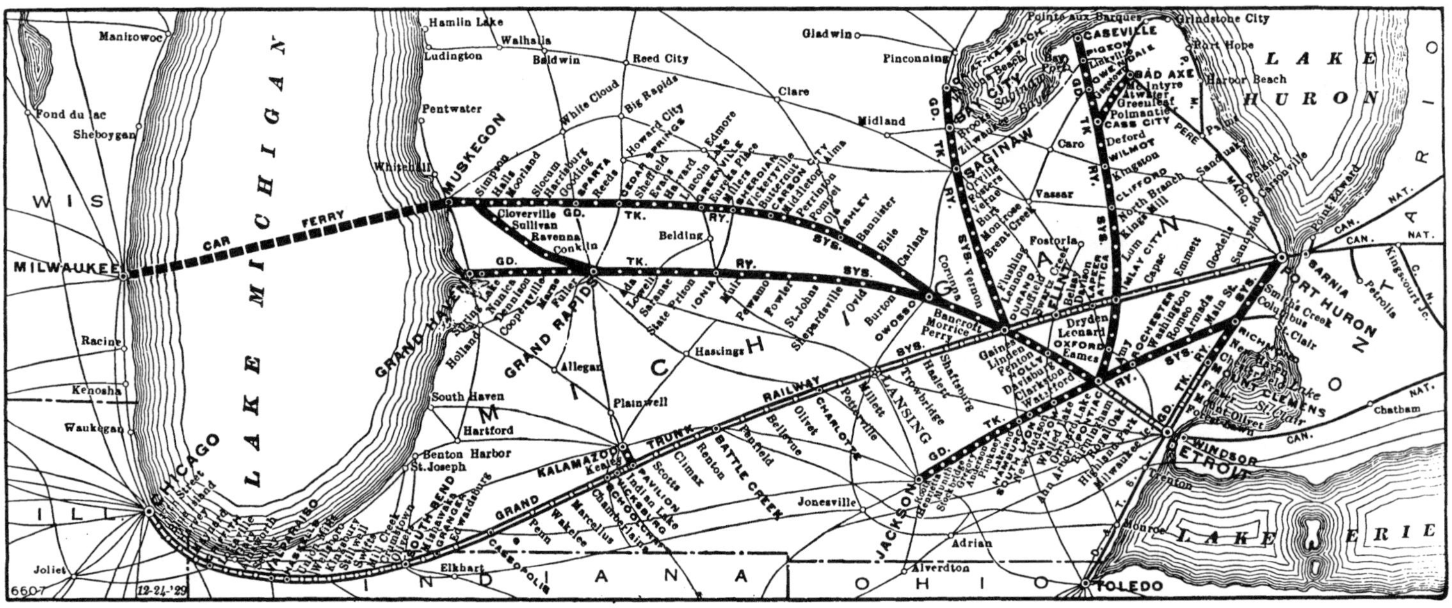

Map of Grand Trunk Railway System Lines west of Detroit and St. Clair Rivers, June 30, 1938

BIBLIOGRAPHY

The material in this work is from two principal sources. The originals of many of the documents of incorporation, filed over the years with the Michigan Secretary of State, Department of Commerce, Corporation and Securities Division, are held in the State Records Center in Lansing. Chapter 4, the Chronology section of this work, gives the Lot Number used to access these records. The documents are filed alphabetically and are reasonably easy to use. Lot 756 is a set of folio volumes into which clerks painstakingly transcribed the written articles. The entries are in sequence by date of filing with the state. Few documents of events other than incorporations are to be found in these records.

The second major source of data is the publication *Aids, Gifts, Grants and Donations to Railroads including Outline of Development and Successions in Titles to Railroads in Michigan.* Published in 1919 by the Michigan Railroad Commission, it takes the companies existing at the time of publication forward from their inception to that time. It details consolidations, leases, purchases, and sales, and also outlines the construction and abandonments of lines. It has two weaknesses: that it covers only companies that were active at the time of publication, and that it has not been brought forward to current times. It remains, however, a valuable resource, generally found only in photocopy form, and is unusually reliable.

In addition to these two principal sources, some data have been obtained from the following:

—The annual *Acts of the Legislature* and the compiled *Laws of the Territory of Michigan*, both of which contain the charters of companies created by legislative act (which was necessary before the passage of the General Incorporation Act in 1855) and consolidations of chartered companies.

—*Valuation Documents* of the Interstate Commerce Commission, issued after World War I, which duplicate to some extent the material in *Aids* but include non-Michigan work.

—*Finance Documents* of the Interstate Commerce Commission which record post-1920 consolidations.

—Microfiche records of the Michigan Department of Transportation which deal with more recent incorporations and consolidations.

—Poor's *Manual of Railroads* and Moody's *Railroads*, various years, both of which contain material about electric lines as well as steam railroads.

—Railroad company records, some of which are available at the Michigan Historical Collections at the Bentley Library, Ann Arbor; some of which are available in reference documents prepared by the companies themselves; and some by direct correspondence.

—The research of Graham Hardy, Forrest Meek, and Carl Jay Bajema for their work on Michigan logging and lumbering roads.

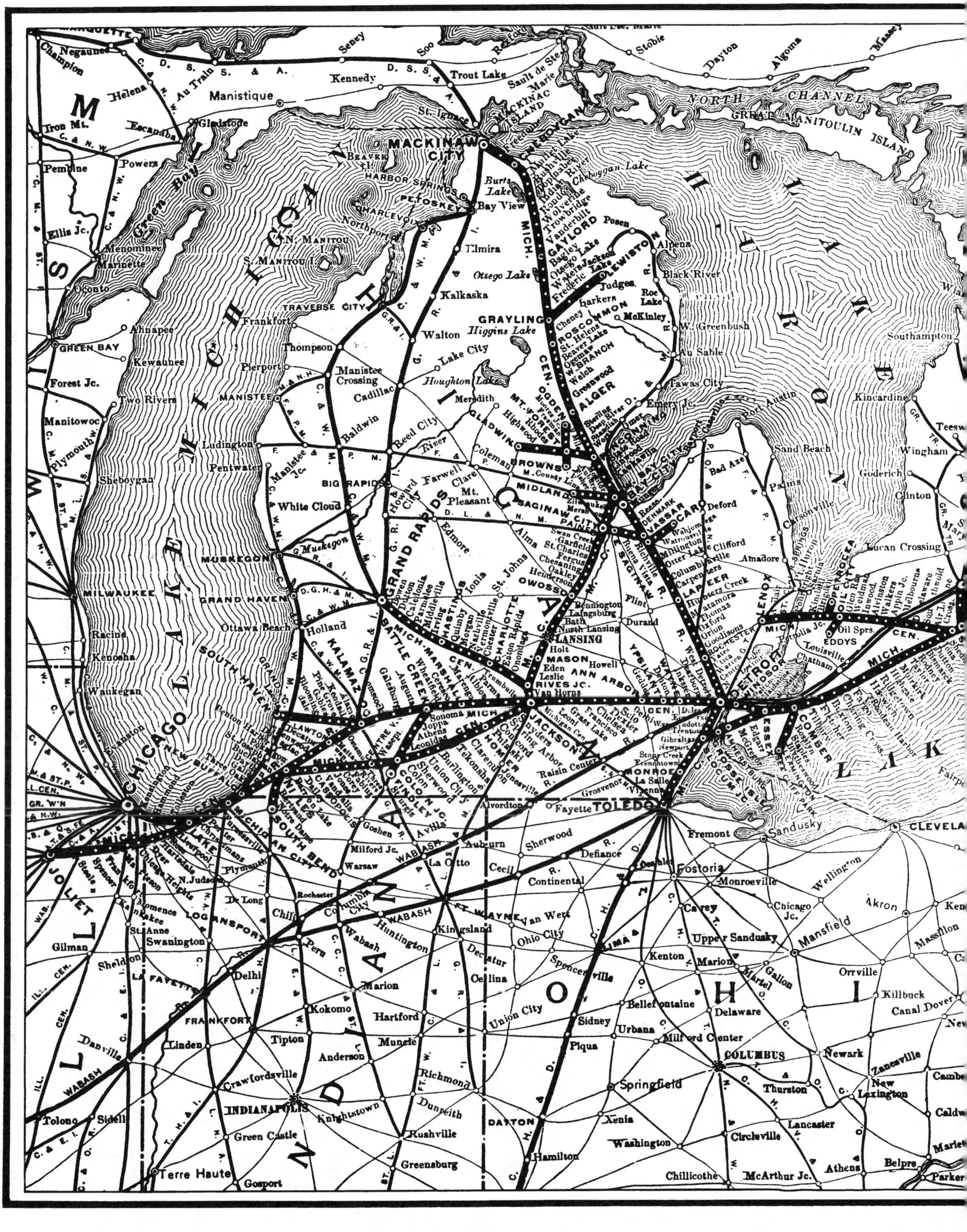

MARQUETTE
Negaunee
Champion
Seney
Soo
Trout Lake
Kennedy
Manistique
Helena
Au Train
Gladstone
Escanaba
Iron Mt.
Pembine
Powers
Ellis Jc.
Menominee
Marinette
Oconto
GREEN BAY
Ahnapee
Kewaunee
Forest Jc.
Two Rivers
Manitowoc
Plymouth
Sheboygan
MILWAUKEE
Racine
Kenosha
Waukegan
Evanston
CHICAGO
Sault de Ste. Marie
Stobie
Dayton
Algoma
NORTH CHANNEL
GREAT MANITOULIN ISLAND
St. Ignace
MACKINAC ISLAND
MACKINAW CITY
CHEBOYGAN
BEAVER I.
HARBOR SPRINGS
PETOSKEY
Bay View
CHARLEVOIX
Northport
N. MANITOU I.
S. MANITOU I.
TRAVERSE CITY
Frankfort
Thompson
Pierport
MANISTEE
Manistee Crossing
Ludington
Pentwater
White Cloud
MUSKEGON
GRAND HAVEN
Ottawa Beach
Holland
SOUTH HAVEN
Elmira
Kalkaska
Otsego Lake
GAYLORD
Posen
Alpena
LEWISTON
Black River
GRAYLING
Higgins Lake
Walton
Lake City
Houghton Lake
Cadillac
Baldwin
Reed City
BIG RAPIDS
Farwell
Clare
Mt. Pleasant
Meredith
GLADWIN
ROSCOMMON
McKinley
W. Greenbush
Au Sable
Tawas City
Emery Jc.
Port Austin
Bad Axe
Sand Beach
MIDLAND
SAGINAW
BAY CITY
VASSAR
CARO
Deford
Edmore
Alma
GRAND RAPIDS
Ionia
St. Johns
OWOSSO
Flint
Durand
LANSING
HASTINGS
CHARLOTTE
BATTLE CREEK
MARSHALL
KALAMAZOO
JACKSON
ANN ARBOR
YPSILANTI
DETROIT
WINDSOR
LAPEER
LENOX
Oil Sprs.
EDDYS
Chatham
Louisville
Kincardine
Southampton
Wingham
Goderich
Clinton
Lucan Crossing
Teeswater
Mason
Howell
MONROE
TOLEDO
Fayette
Alvordton
Sandusky
Fremont
CLEVELAND
Fostoria
Monroeville
Wellington
Akron
Chicago Jc.
Mansfield
Carey
Upper Sandusky
Kenton
Marion
Galion
Orrville
Massillon
Killbuck
Canal Dover
Bellefontaine
Delaware
Sidney
Urbana
Milford Center
COLUMBUS
Newark
Zanesville
New Lexington
Thurston
Piqua
Springfield
Xenia
DAYTON
Hamilton
Washington
Circleville
Lancaster
Chillicothe
McArthur Jc.
Athens
Belpre
Parkersburg
Defiance
Continental
Van Wert
Ohio City
Spencerville
LIMA
Celina
Union City
Kingsland
Huntington
FT. WAYNE
Decatur
Auburn
Sherwood
Cecil
La Otto
Avilla
Goshen
Milford Jc.
Warsaw
SOUTH BEND
NILES
CASSOPOLIS
ELKHART
MICHIGAN CITY
Plymouth
Rochester
Columbia City
Wabash
Peru
LOGANSPORT
LA FAYETTE
Delphi
FRANKFORT
Kokomo
Marion
Hartford
Tipton
Muncie
Anderson
Richmond
INDIANAPOLIS
Knightstown
Dunreith
Rushville
Greensburg
Crawfordsville
Green Castle
Gosport
Terre Haute
Linden
Danville
Tolono
Sidell
Gilman
Sheldon
Swanington
St. Anne
Kankakee
Momence
De Long
N. Judson
JOLIET
WABASH
MICHIGAN CENTRAL
LAKE MICHIGAN
LAKE HURON
WISCONSIN
ILLINOIS
INDIANA
OHIO

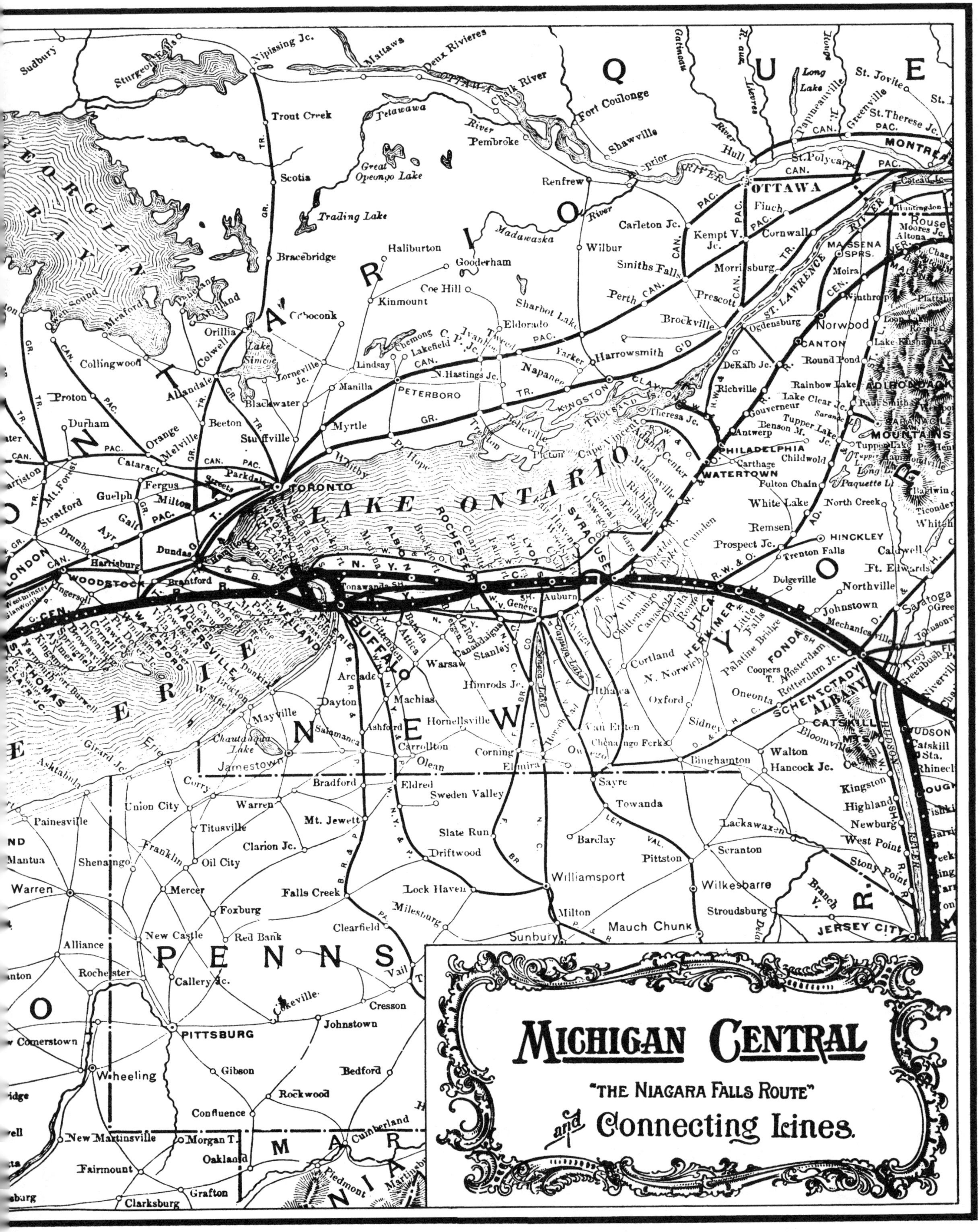
MICHIGAN CENTRAL
"THE NIAGARA FALLS ROUTE"
and Connecting Lines.
LAKE ONTARIO
TORONTO
BUFFALO
OTTAWA
SYRACUSE
PITTSBURG
ALBANY
Williamsport
Binghamton
Wheeling